COMPUTER BASED NUMERICAL AND STATISTICAL TECHNIQUES

COMPUTER BASED NUMERICAL AND STATISTICAL TECHNIQUES

(According to the latest revised syllabus of II year B. Tech. and I year MCA of U.P. Technical University, Lucknow)

By

DR. MANISH GOYAL

M.Sc. (Mathematics), Ph.D., CSIR-NET
Associate Professor
Department of Mathematics
Institute of Applied Sciences and Humanities
G.L.A. University, Mathura
U.P.

(An Imprint of Laxmi Publications Pvt. Ltd.)
An ISO 9001:2015 Company

BENGALURU • CHENNAI • GUWAHATI • HYDERABAD
KOCHI • KOLKATA • LUCKNOW • RANCHI
NEW DELHI

Printed and bound in India
First Edition: 2003; *Second Edition*: 2005; *Third Edition:* 2006
Reprint: 2007, 2008, 2009, 2011, 2012; *Fourth Edition*: 2015; *Fifth Edition:* 2015, *Edition :* 2017 *Edition* : 2025
ISBN : 978-93-81159-27-9

Branches

✆	Bengaluru	080-26 75 69 30
✆	Chennai	044-24 34 47 26
✆	Guwahati	0361-254 36 69
✆	Hyderabad	040-27 55 53 83
✆	Kochi	0484-405 13 03
✆	Kolkata	033-40 04 77 79
✆	Lucknow	0522-430 36 13
✆	Ranchi	0651-224 24 64

Published in India by

(An Imprint of Laxmi Publications Pvt. Ltd.)

An ISO 9001:2015 Company
113, GOLDEN HOUSE, GURUDWARA ROAD, DARYAGANJ,
NEW DELHI - 110002, INDIA

Corporate Office : B-33, Sector-5, Noida,
Gautambuddha Nagar (U.P.) - 201 301, INDIA
Telephone : +91-120-44 46 900
www.laxmipublications.com
info@laxmipublications.com

DEDICATED

TO

MY PARENTS

CONTENTS

UNIT-II

UNIT-III

UNIT-IV

PREFACE TO THE FIFTH EDITION

"मय्येव मन आधत्स्व मयि बुद्धिं निवेशय ।
निवसिष्यसि मय्येव अत ऊर्ध्वं न संशयः ॥"

This fifth edition has grown multifold in its utilitarian value for the readers of not only B.Tech. and M.Tech. but also for those of B.C.A and M.C.A.

This recent revision in the syllabi (NCS 303 and NMCA 212) of Computer Based Numerical and Statistical Techniques (C.B.N.S.T) by U.P. Technical University, Lucknow has triggered the needful additions also incorporating the suggestions of learned readers over a period of time. However, the basic outline of the book and its underlying object remain unaltered.

The units have again been reshuffled according to the new prescribed syllabus NCS-303 of B.Tech. II year students of CSE and IT branches. However, the full syllabus NMCA-212 of MCA I year students have also been covered. I have put in a lot of efforts to make the readers easily grasp the newly written topics by presenting them in the simplest possible way.

This fifth edition is successfully authored in a very short period of time but inspite of it, no stone has been left unturned. Misprints/mistakes have been removed and number of solved examples have been increased a lot.

I am highly thankful to all my readers all over India and abroad who encourage me by continuously providing their thoughts, suggestions and also sending a number of sweet letters of appreciation and constructive criticism through e-mail or phone.

My heart is indebted to my parents for all their blessings, guidelines and sincere support throughout my illustrious academic career and also in the making of this textbook.

Author

PREFACE TO THE FIRST EDITION

It gives me great pleasure to present before dear students and learned fellow faculty members the maiden edition of this book for *II year of B. Tech.* of all U.P. Engineering Colleges, conducted by *U.P. Technical University, Lucknow.*

The book comprehensively explains *Errors; Algebraic and Transcendental Equations: Interpolation ; Curve Fitting, Cubic Spline and Approximation; Numerical Integration and Differentiation* and finally *Statistical Computation.*

Neat, accurate, attractive figures and *statistical graphs* add to the beauty of the book. It is a text of *unique style* only meant for the welfare of the students. If this book serves the purpose of those for whom it is written and published, I will feel my labour amply rewarded.

A *unique feature* of this book is to provide with an *algorithm* and *flow-chart prior to the computer program in C-language* to understand the steps and methodology used in writing the program.

A model paper for the present session has been appended in the last to let the students know about the most important questions that may be asked in the ensuing examination.

All *questions of previous year's paper* of U.P.T.U., Lucknow have been marked and included at proper places.

All *questions of Question Bank* supplied by the university have been incorporated in the body of the text.

A large number of examples have been provided to let the readers understand the various skills necessary to solve the problems.

We have tried to bring the book free from errors. However, it is not unusual that certain flaws might have crept into the body of the text. I take personal responsibility for the same and request the readers to let me know of those misprints or mistakes. I assure the readers to remove them in the next edition of this book.

I am highly thankful to *Mr. Manoj Kumar Chaubey,* Lecturer in Computer Science and Engg. G.L.A.I.T.M., Mathura who has designed the computer base of this text. He has enormously helped me in preparing the manuscript for the first unit on Introduction to C-language. The *programmes* of various methods in *C-language* have been *successfully run on the computer* by him along with *Mr. Harvinder Singh,* M.C.A. and *Mr. Tapesh Dutt Bhardwaj,* programmer, G.L.A.I.T.M., Mathura and are ultimately thoroughly checked by senior professors and experienced faculty members of Computer Science and Engg. Department.

My students *Pragyanshu Kumar Shukla* and *Vakul Agrawal;* as well as my friend *Dr. Vivek Sharma* need special mention as all of them have always uplifted me morally.

In the last, but not the least, *I am obliged to my sister Mrs. Sangeeta Agrawal* and *brother-in-law Dr. Alok Agrawal for their kind blessings.*

Author

Syllabus

B.Tech. II year, IV Semester

(IT&CS Branches)

NCS-303: Computer Based Numerical and Statistical Techniques

Unit-I

Computer Arithmetic and Errors: Floating point arithmetic, Machine epsilon, Round off error, Chopping error, Truncation error, Associative and Distributive law in floating point arithmatic, Inherent error, Error propagation, Numerical instability

Roots of Equation: Secant method, Newton Raphson method and fixed point iteration methods for simple roots and derivation of their rate of convergence, Aitken acceleration of convergence, Modified Newton Raphson method for multiple roots, Birge-Vieta Method for polynomials, Bairstrow method for quadratic factors, Computer Algorithms of these methods.

Unit-II

Interpolation: Algorithms and error analysis of Lagrange and Newton divided difference interpolations, Relationship in various difference operators, Piecewise linear interpolation, Cubic spline interpolation, Natural Spline, Chebyshev polynomial Approximation, Lanczos Economization of power series.

Curve Fitting: Linear and Non-linear least squares Approximation, ill conditioning in least squares methods, Gram-Schmidt process of orthogonailzation. Computer algorithms of least square curve fitting.

Unit-III

Differentiation: Methods based on interpolation and finite differences, Richardson Extrapolation.

Integration: Error analysis of Trepezoidal and Simpson methods, Newton cotes integration methods, Gaussian integration methods, Gauss Legendre method, Lobatto integration method and Radau integration method, Error terms in integration methods.

Unit-IV

Solution of Simultaneous Linear Algebraic Equations: Gauss Elimination method, ill conditioned systems, Condition number, Successive over relaxation method, Rate of convergence.

Solution of Ordinary Differential Equations: Single step methods-Runge-Kutta Second order, Third order and Fourth order methods, Multi step Method-Predictor-Corrector Method.

Statistical Techniques: Statistical Hypotheses, Test to Hypotheses, Type-I and Type-II Errors, Level of significance, Test involving normal distribution.

Syllabus
MCA I year, II Semester
NMCA-212
Computer Based Numerical and Statistical Techniques

Unit-I

Floating Point Arithmetic: Representation of floating point numbers, Operations, Normalization, Pitfalls of floating point representation, Errors in numerical computation.

Iterative Methods: Zeros of a single transcendental equation and zeros of polynomial using Bisection method, Iteration method, Regula-Falsi method, Newton Raphson method, Secant method, Rate of convergence of iterative methods.

Unit-II

Simultaneous Linear Equations: Solutions of systems of linear equations, Gauss elimination direct method and pivoting, III Conditioned system of equations, Refinement of solution. Gauss Seidel iterative method, Rate of convergence.

Interpolation and approximation: Finite Differences, Difference tables

Polynomial Interpolation: Newton's forward and backward formula

Central Difference Formulae: Gauss forward and backward formula, Stirling's Neverett's formula.

Interpolation with Unequal Intervals: Langrange's Interpolation, Newton Divided difference formula, Hermite's interpolation.

Approximation of function by Taylor's series and Chebyshev polynomial.

Unit-III

Numerical Differentiation and Integration: Introduction, Numerical Differentiation, Numerical Integration, Trapezoidal rule, Simpson's rules, Boole's Rule, Weddle's Rule Euler-Maclaurin Formula **Solution of differential equation:** Picard's Method, Euler's Method, Taylor's Method, Runge-Kutta methods, Predictor-corrector method, Automatic error monitoring, stability of solution.

Unit-IV

Curve fitting, Cubic Spline and Approximation: Method of least squares, fitting of straight lines, polynomials, exponential curves etc.

Frequency Chart: Different frequency chart like Histogram, Frequency curve, Pi-chart.

Regression analysis: Linear and Non-linear regression, Multiple regression.

Unit-V

Time Series and Forcasting: Moving averages, smoothening of curves, forecasting models and methods. Statistical quality controls methods.

Testing of Hypothesis: Test of significance, Chi-square test, *t*-test, ANOVA, F-test

Application to medicine, agriculture etc.

NCS-353: Numerical Techniques LAB

Write Programs in 'C' Language:

1. To deduce error involved in polynomial equation.
2. To find out the root of the Algebraic and Transcendental equations using Bisection, Regula-Falsi, Newton Raphson and Iterative Methods. Also give the rate of convergence of roots in tabular form for each of these methods.
3. To implement Newton's Forward and Backward Interpolation formula.
4. To implement Gauss Forward and Backward, Bessel's, Sterling's and Everett's Interpolation formula.
5. To implement Newton's Divided Difference and Langranges Interpolation formula.
6. To implement numerical differentiations.
7. To implement numerical integration using Trapezoidal, Simpson 1/3 and 0 Simpson 3/8 rule.
8. To implement Least Square method for curve fitting.
9. To draw frequency chart like histogram, frequency curve and pie-chart etc.
10. To estimate regression equation from sampled data and evaluate values of standard deviation, t-statistics, regression coefficient, value of χ^2 for at least two independent variables.

Note: The instructor may add/delete/modify/tune experiments, wherever he/she feels in a justified manner.

NMCA-252
Computer Based Numerical and Statistical Techniques LAB

Write a Program in C:

1. To demonstrate the errors produced during numerical computations with floating point numbers.
2. To find roots of algebraic/transcendental equations using Bisection, Newton-Raphson, Regula-Falsi methods.
3. To determine interpolating polynomial using Langrange method, Newton's divided difference method of interpolation.
4. To implement method of least square curve fitting.
5. To determine numerical differentiation.
6. To implement numerical integration using Trapezoidal rule and Simpson's 3/8 rules.
7. To implement Runge-Kutta second order and fourth order method for solving differential equations.
8. To implement Predictor-Corrector method for solving differential equations.
9. To display various types of frequency chart.

Note: The instructor may add/delete/modify/tune experiments, wherever he/she feels in a justified manner.

NUMERICAL TECHNIQUES LAB

(NCS-353) & (NMCA-252)

B.TECH. II YEAR & MCA I YEAR

Following Practicals **should be** performed in the computer lab by the students.

1. **Algebraic and Transcendental Equations**

   (*i*) Write a program in 'C' for finding the root of an equation of the form $f(x) = 0$ using **Bisection method.**

   (*ii*) Write a program in 'C' for finding the root of an equation of the form $f(x) = 0$ using **iteration method.**

   (*iii*) Write a program in 'C' for finding the root of an equation of the form $f(x) = 0$ using **method of false position.**

   (*iv*) Write a program in 'C' for finding the root of an equation of the form $f(x) = 0$ using **Newton-Raphson method.**

2. **Interpolation with equal and unequal intervals**

   (*i*) Write a program in 'C' to find out the unknown values with the help of given set of observations using **Newton's forward difference interpolation formula.**

   (*ii*) Write a program in 'C' to find out the unknown values with the help of given set of observations using **Newton's backward difference interpolation formula.**

   (*iii*) Write a program in 'C' to find out the unknown values with the help of given set of observations using **Stirling's formula.**

   (*iv*) Write a program in 'C' to find out the unknown values with the help of given set of observations using **Gauss's forward difference interpolation formula.**

   (*v*) Write a program in 'C' to find out the unknown values with the help of given set of observations using **Lagrange's interpolation formula.**

   (*vi*) Write a program in 'C' to find out the unknown values with the help of given set of observations using **Bessel's formula.**

   (*vii*) Write a program in 'C' to find out the unknown values with the help of given set of observations using **Gauss' backward formula.**

   (*vii*) Write a program in 'C' to find out the unknown values with the help of given set of observations using **Laplace-Everett's formula.**

3. **Numerical Integration**

   (*i*) Write a program in 'C' to find out a numerical integration using **Trapezoidal rule.**

   (*ii*) Write a program in 'C' to find out a numerical integration using **Simpson's** $\left(\frac{3}{8}\right)^{\text{th}}$ **rule.**

   (*iii*) Write a program in 'C' to find out a numerical integration using **Simpson's** $\left(\frac{1}{3}\right)^{\text{rd}}$ **rule.**

4. **Curve Fitting**

   (*i*) Write a program in 'C' to fit a straight line of the form **y = a + bx** for a given set of data points.

(*ii*) Write a program in 'C' to fit a second degree parabola of the form $\mathbf{y = a + bx + cx^2}$ for a given set of data points.

(*iii*) Write a program in 'C' to fit a curve of the form $\mathbf{y = ax^b}$.

(*iv*) Write a program in 'C' to fit a curve of the form $\mathbf{y = ab^x}$.

(*v*) Write a program in 'C' to fit a curve of the form $\mathbf{y = ae^{bx}}$.

5. Statistical Computation

(*i*) Write a program in 'C' to find **regression line of y on x** from the given set of points.

(*ii*) Write a program in 'C' to find **regression line of x on y** from the given set of points.

B.Tech. Computer Science and Engineering

Study and Evaluation Scheme

(Effective from session 2014-15)

2nd Year **Semester-III**

Sl. No.	*Course Code*	*Subject*	*Periods*			*Evaluations Scheme*				*Subject Total*	*Credit*
						Sessional Exam					
			L	*T*	*P*	*CT*	*TA*	*Total*	*ESE*		
Theory Subject											
1.	NAS-301/ NOE-031 to NOE-039	Mathematics III/Science Based open Elective	3	1	0	30	20	50	100	150	4
2.	NEC 309	Digital Logic Design	3	1	0	30	20	50	100	150	4
3.	NCS 301	Data Structures Using C	3	1	0	30	20	50	100	150	4
4.	NCS 302	Discrete Structure and Graph Theory	3	1	0	30	20	50	100	150	4
5.	NHU 301/ NHU 302	Industrial Psychology/ Industrial Sociology	2	0	0	15	10	25	50	75	2
6.	NCS 303	Computer Based Numerical and Statistical Techniques	2	1	0	15	10	25	50	75	3
	AUC-001/ AUC-002	Human Values and Professional Ethics/ Cyber Security	2	0	0	15	10	25	50	75*	
Practical/Design/Drawing											
7.	NEC 359	Digital Logic Design Lab	0	0	3	10	10	20	30	50	1
8.	NCS 351	Data Structure Using C Lab	0	0	3	10	10	20	30	50	1
9.	NCS 353	Numerical Techniques Lab	0	0	2	10	10	20	30	50	1
10.	NCS 355	Advance Programming Lab	0	0	2	10	10	20	30	50	1
11.	NGP 301	GP						50		50	
		Total	18	5	10					1000	25

Science Based Open Elective:

NOE 031 Introduction to Soft Computing (Neural Network, Fuzzy Logic and Genetic Algorithm)
NOE 032 Nano Sciences
NOE 033 Laser Systems and Applications
NOE 034 Space Sciences
NOE 035 Polymer Science and Technology
NOE 036 Nuclear Science
NOE 037 Material Science
NOE 038 Discrete Mathematics
NOE 039 Applied Linear Algebra

* Human values and Professional Ethics/Cyber Security will be offered as a compulsory audit course for which passing marks are 30% in End Semester Examination and 40% in aggregate.

UP TECHNICAL UNIVERSITY, LUCKNOW

STUDY AND EVALUATION SCHEME

MCA (Master of Computer Applications)

(Effective from session 2013-14)

Year-I Semester-I

Sl. No.	Course Code	Subject	Periods			Evaluations scheme				
						Sessional Exam			ESE	Subject Total
			L	T	P	CT	TA	Total		
1.	NAS-104	Professional Communication	3	1	0	30	20	50	100	150
2.	NMCA-112	Accounting and Financial Management	3	1	0	30	20	50	100	150
3.	NMCA-113	Computer Concepts and Programming	3	1	0	30	20	50	100	150
4.	NMCA-114	Discrete Mathematics	3	1	0	30	20	50	100	150
5.	NMCA-115	Digital Logic Design	3	1	0	30	20	50	100	150
Practicals										
6.	NMCA-151	Programming Lab	0	0	3	30	20	50	50	100
7.	NAS-154	Professional Communication Lab	0	0	3	30	20	50	50	100
8.	GP-101	General Proficiency	0	0	0	–	–	50	–	50
		Total	15	5	6					1000

Year-I Semester-II

Sl. No.	Course Code	Subject	Periods			Evaluations Scheme				
						Sessional Exam			ESE	Subject Total
			L	T	P	CT	TA	Total		
1.	NAS-105/ NAS-205	Environmental and Ecology	3	1	0	30	20	50	100	150
2.	NMCA-212	Computer Based Numerical and Statistical Techniques	3	1	0	30	20	50	100	150
3.	NMCA-213	Data Structure Using 'C'	3	1	0	30	20	50	100	150
4.	NMCA-214	Introduction to Automata Theory and Languages	3	1	0	30	20	50	100	150
5.	NMCA-215	Computer Organization	3	1	0	30	20	50	100	150
Practicals										
6.	NMCA-251	Data Structures Lab	0	0	3	30	20	50	50	100
7.	NMCA-252	Computer Based Numerical and Statistical Techniques Lab	0	0	3	30	20	50	50	100
8.	GP-201	General Proficiency	0	0	0	–	–	50	–	50
		Total	15	5	6					1000

SALIENT FEATURES

- The book covers the syllabus of II year of B. Tech. and I year of MCA of all U.P. Engineering Colleges.
- The book is presented with an approach to explain the concepts in lucid style and communicable language.
- The subject matter is exposed systematically and the students are better prepared to solve the problems.
- All fundamentals of the included topics have been explained with a micro-analysis.
- Sufficient number of illustrative examples have been given to let the readers understand the various skills necessary to solve the problems. These examples are well-graded.
- Unsolved exercises of multi-varieties have been given in a well-graded style. To attempt these will enable a student to create confidence and independence in him/her regarding the understanding of the subject.
- Daily life problems and practical problems have been incorporated in the body of text.
- A large number of attractive and accurate figures and graphs have been drawn which enable a student to grasp the subject in an easier way.
- The programmes of various methods in C-language have been successfully run on the computer and checked by experienced faculty members of Computer Engg. and Applications Department.
- A unique feature of the book is to provide with an algorithm and flow chart prior to the program to understand the steps used in writing the program.
- First chapter supplies the basic information regarding C-Language to be used for writing a program.
- The programmes which should be performed by all the students are listed while giving the syllabus of Numerical Techniques Lab (NCS-353). This lab runs alongside the theory course.
- All questions of previous year's papers of U.P. Technical University, Lucknow have been marked and included at proper places.
- All questions of Question Bank supplied by the university have been incorporated in the body of the text.

FOREWORD

I feel privileged to go through the text of the book. What I feel is that the book has been written merely with a view-point of welfare of the concerned students. It reflects upon the labour to which the author has been put to in the preparation of the book. The author has left no stone unturned in giving the most comprehensive shape to the matter included there in staying true to the title. The statistical graphs and numerous programmes attract the readers. It appears that there was really a need of a book of this type. It also hints the capability of the author and confirms that he must have been a successful teacher. The mathematical formulations are self-explanatory and are anticipated with perfection. The inclusion of U.P.T.U. Question Bank makes this work remarkable. In the last, I can say without any partiality and bias that the author has become successful in achieving his goal.

I wish him all success in life.

Dr. Hari Kishan
Senior Reader in Mathematics
K.R. (P.G.) College
Mathura (U.P.)

UNIT-I

Computer Arithmetic and Errors: Floating point arithmetic, Machine epsilon, Round-off error, Chopping error, Truncation error, Associative and Distributive law in Floating point arithmetic, Inherent error, Error propagation, Numerical instability.

Roots of Equation: Secant method, Newton-Raphson method and Fixed point iteration methods for simple roots and derivation of their rate of convergence, Aitken acceleration of convergence, Modified Newton-Raphson method for multiple roots, Birge-Vieta method for polynomials, Bairstow method for quadratic factors, Computer algorithms of these methods.

UNIT-I

1

Introduction

The limitations of analytical methods in practical applications have led mathematicians to evolve numerical methods.

We know that exact methods often fail in drawing plausible inferences from a given set of tabulated data or in finding roots of transcendental equations or in solving non-linear differential equations.

Even if analytical solutions are available, they are not amenable to direct numerical interpretation.

The aim of numerical analysis is therefore to provide constructive methods for obtaining answers to such problems in a numerical form. With the advent of high speed computers and increasing demand for numerical solution to various problems, numerical techniques have become indispensible tools in the hands of engineers and scientists.

e.g., we can solve equations $x^2 - 5x + 6 = 0$, $ax^2 + bx + c = 0$, $y'' + 3y' + 2y = 0$ by analytical methods, but transcendental equations such as $a \cos^2 x + be^x = 0$ cannot be solved by analytical methods. Such equations are solved by numerical analysis.

Methods of numerical analysis are used to approximate the problem satisfactorily so that an approximate solution, amenable to precise analysis, within a desired degree of accuracy is obtained.

To attain desired degree of accuracy, an insight into the process and resulting error is essential.

Consequently, numerical analysis may be regarded as a process to develop and evaluate the methods for computing required mathematical numerical results from the given numerical data.

It incorporates three broad steps in process

(*i*) Given data called input information

(*ii*) Algorithm

(*iii*) The results obtained, called output information.

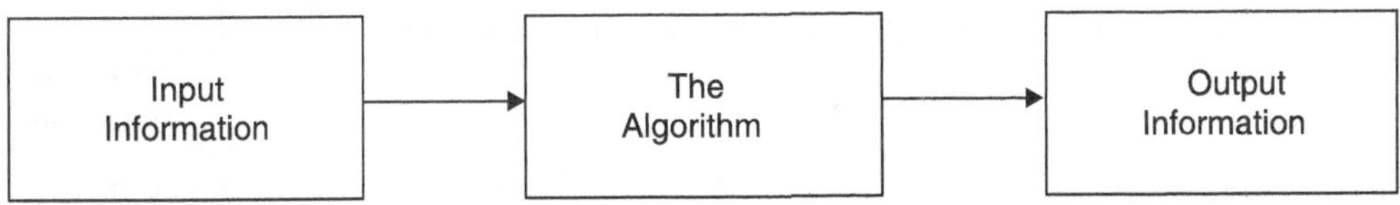

Computers have changed, almost revolutionized, numerical methods the field as a whole as well as many individual methods and that development is continuing.

Much research work is going on in creating new methods, adapting existing methods to new computer generations, improving methods in large scale work even small improvements bring large savings in time or storage space and investigating stability and accuracy of methods.

1.1. INTRODUCTION TO COMPUTERS

Computer is an information-processing and information-accessing tool. It accepts some information or data from the outside world and processes it to produce a new information or it can retrieve the stored information efficiency.

Hence, "Computer is an electronic device capable of accepting information, applying prescribed processes to the information and supplying the results of these processes."

It usually consists of input and output devices, storage arithmetic and logical units and a control unit.

1.2. DEFINITIONS

Cursor. A position indicator or say blinking character employed in a display on video terminal to indicate a character to be corrected or a position in which data is to be entered.

Algorithm. A finite step by step procedure made up of mathematical and/or logical operations designed to solve a problem is called an algorithm.

Flow-chart. A pictorial or graphical representation of a specific sequence of steps to be used by a computer is called a flow-chart. It is essentially a convenient way of planning the order of operations involved in an algorithm and helps in writing a program.

A flow-chart contains certain symbols to represent the various operations . These symbols are connected by arrows to indicate the flow of information. The commonly used symbols with meanings are given below :

1. This oval shaped symbol is used to indicate **'Start'** or **'Stop/End'** of a program. It is also used to mark end of a sub-program by writing **'Return'.**

(Terminal point)

2. This parallelogram shaped symbol is used to indicate an input or output of data.

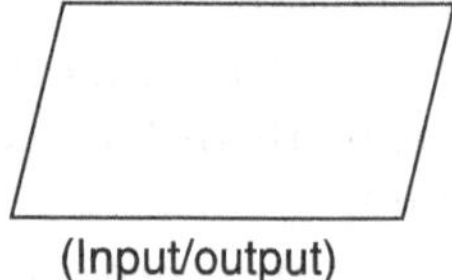

(Input/output)

3. This rectangle shaped symbol is a processing symbol *e.g.,* addition, subtraction and movement of data to computer memory.

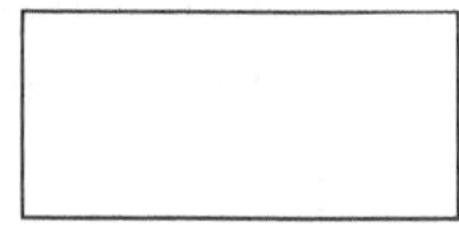

(Processing operation box)

4. This diamond shaped symbol is a decision-making symbol. A particular path is chosen depending on 'Yes' or 'No' answer.

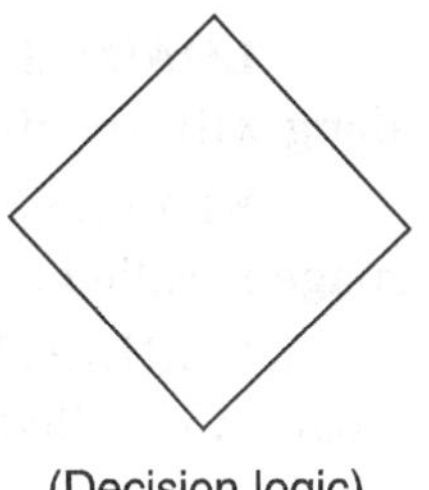

(Decision logic)

5. A small circle with any number or letter in it is used as a connector symbol. It connects various parts of flow-chart which are far apart or spread over pages.

(Connector point)

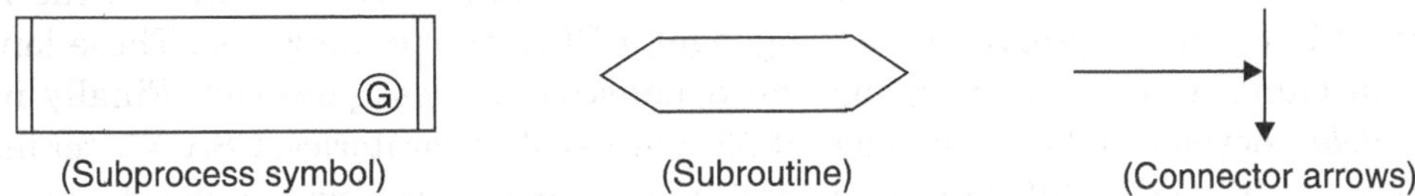

(Subprocess symbol) (Subroutine) (Connector arrows)

A rectangle with double vertical sides is used to denote a subprocess which is given elsewhere as indicated by connector symbol.

When this box is encountered, the flow goes to the subroutine and it continues till a 'Return' statement is encountered. Then it goes back to main flow-chart and flow resumes onward processing.

The flow-chart can be translated into any computer language and also can be executed on the computer.

PROGRAM. A computer does not have the capability of reading and understanding instructions written in a natural language like English. Thus it is necessary to express the algorithm in a language understood by the computer. An algorithm coded in a computer language is called a program and the language used for coding is called a programming language.

INSTRUCTION. A single operation to be executed by the computer is called an instruction.

LOGIC. The science that deals with the canons and criteria of validity in thought and demonstration. or the science of the formal principles of reasoning is called logic.

LOOP. A series of instructions or one instruction in a program that is repeated for prescribed number of times, followed by a branch instruction that exits the program form the loop.

COMPILER. A program designed to translate high level language (source program into machine language object program) is called a compiler.

ASSEMBLER. It converts all instructions into the binary format. This would be a machine language program.

LOADER. A program required on practically all systems that loads the user's program along with required system routines into the central processor for execution.

SYNTAX. The set of grammatical rules defining the structure of a programming language is called syntax.

GARBAGE. An accumulation of unwanted, meaningless data after processing of any program is called Garbage.

1.3. INTRODUCTION TO "C" LANGUAGE

In 1960, a number of computer languages had come into existence, among them were *COBOL* and *FORTRAN*. Drawback of these languages was that, they were suitable for specific purposes. So, there was a need for a single computer language which could cater to the needs of different applications uniformly and efficiently.

This led to the formation of an International Committee to develop such a language. The result came out with a language called *ALGOL 60*. It could not become popular as it was too abstract and too general. Successive refinements on *ALGOL 60* results in the birth of language CPL (combined programming language), BCPL, and 'B' language. These languages were again found to be either very big and exhaustive or less powerful. Finally in 1972, '*Dennis Ritchie*' developed the 'C' language at AT and T Bell Laboratories, USA. Writer inherited the features of 'B' and BCPL languages and added some of his own in development of 'C' language.

Languages can be classified into two categories:

(*i*) **High level languages** (Problem Oriented Languages). *e.g.,*—FORTRAN, BASIC, PASCAL, etc.

(*ii*) **Low level languages** (Machine Oriented Languages). *e.g.,*—Assembly and machine language.

'C' language was designed to give both a relatively good programming efficiency and a relatively good machine efficiency. Hence 'C' is said to be a Middle level language as it stands between the above two categories.

1.4. ADVANTAGES/FEATURES OF 'C' LANGUAGE

(*i*) Portability.

(*ii*) Suitable for low level programming.

(*iii*) Less key words.

(*iv*) 'C' is a structured language.

(*v*) 'C' is a programmers language.

1.5. 'C' CHARACTER SET

Character denotes any alphabet, digit or special symbol used to represent information. Following table shows the valid alphabets, digits and special symbols allowed in 'C' ;

Alphabets : A, B, C, ..., Y, Z.
a, b, c, ..., y, z.

Digits : 0, 1, 2, ..., 8, 9.

Special symbols: '–', '–', + , = , /, \, { }, [ ], < >, ?.

The alphabets, digits and special symbol when properly combined form constants, variables and keywords.

1.6. 'C' CONSTANTS

A constant is a quantity that doesn't change. 'C' constants can be divided into two major categories.

(*i*) Primary constants (also called primary data types).

(*ii*) Secondary constants (also called secondary data types).

Primary constants can be of 3 types :

(*a*) Integer constant

(*b*) Real constant

(*c*) Character constant.

Secondary data types or constants are :

(*a*) Array (*b*) Pointer (*c*) Structure (*d*) Union (*e*) Enum.

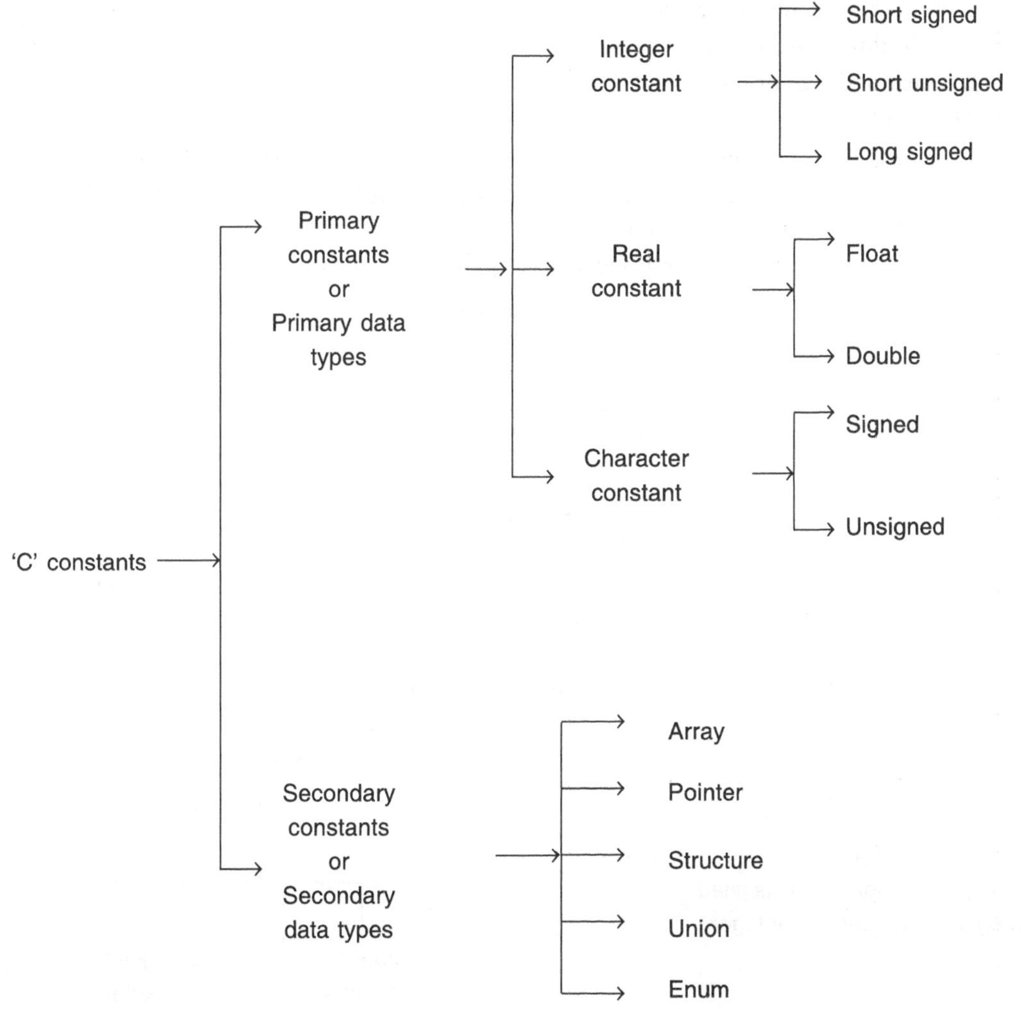

1.6.1. Primary Data Types

Data types	*Byte occupied*	*Range*	*Format*
(*i*) Signed character	One	– 128 to + 127	% C
(*ii*) Unsigned character	One	0 to 255	% C
(*iii*) Short signed integer	Two	– 32768 to + 32767	% *d*
(*iv*) Short unsigned integer	Two	0 to 65535	% *u*
(*v*) Long signed integer	Four	– 2147483648 to + 214748 3647	% *l*
(*vi*) Float	Four	± 3.4 *e* – 38 to ± 3.4 *e* + 38	% *f*
(*vii*) Double	Eight	± 1.7 *e* – 308 to ± 1.7 *e* + 308	% *lf*

1.7. "C" VARIABLES

Suppose we want to find the average of three numbers. The three numbers are the input and the average is the output.

Following are the works to be done by the computer.

1. Read the three numbers.
2. Calculate the average.
3. Output the average.

The computer actually works as follows :

* Reads the three numbers and stores them in three locations of memory.
* Adds the contents of the three locations and divides the result by 3. The result is stored in a fourth location.
* The content of the fourth location is printed as output.

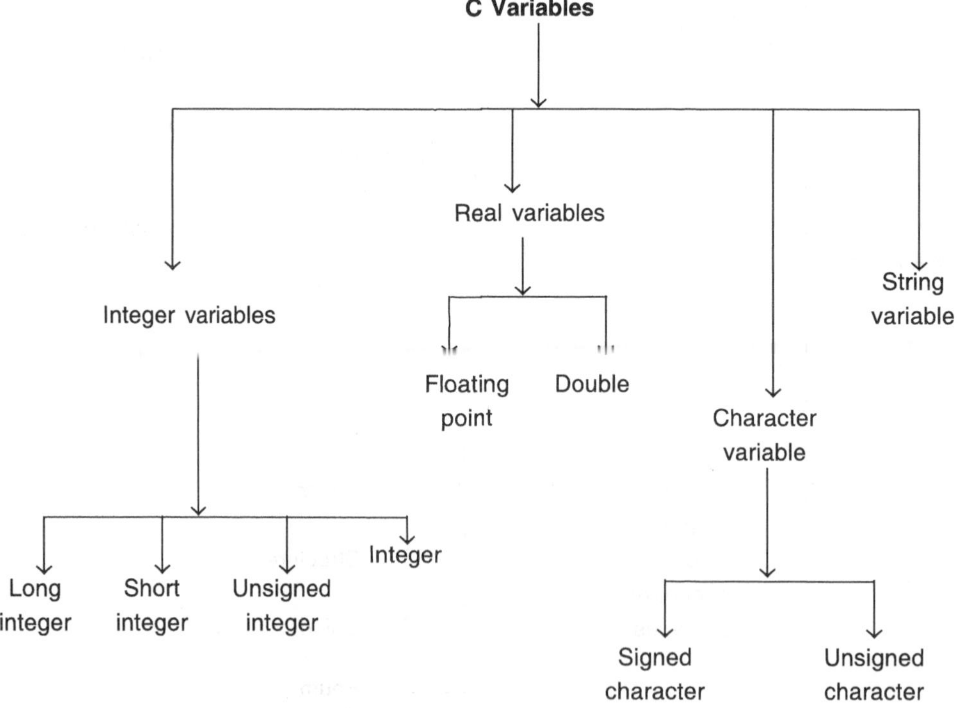

When numbers are stored in various locations of memory, it becomes necessary to name each of the memory location. The name of the memory location is called **variable.**

Memory locations may contain integer, real or character constants. Depending upon the data contained in the memory location, the variables are classified as integer, real, character and string variables.

Secondary variables can be

(*a*) Array variables (*b*) Pointer variables (*c*) Structure variables (*d*) Union variables (*e*) Enum variables.

1.8. 'C' KEY WORDS

Key words (also called reserved words) are an integral part of a language. Their meanings are predefined and hence these words cannot be used as variable names. There are 32 key words in C language.

1.9. "C INSTRUCTIONS"

The constants, variables and key words are combined to form instructions. Basically there on 4 type of instructions in 'C' :

(*a*) *Type declaration Instruction :*

e.g. : int bas_sal ;
float tot_sal ;
char name ;

(*b*) *Arithmetic Instruction :*

e.g. : int a ;
float b, C ;
C = a ∗ b ;
└→ assignment operator.

(*c*) *Input/Output Instruction :*

e.g. : print f ("<format string>", <list of variables>) ;
<format string> could be
% f — for real values
% d — for integer values
% C — for character values
% S — for printing a string (sequence of character).

(*d*) *Control Instructions :*

Control Instructions specify the order in which the various instructions in a program are to be executed by the computer. They define the flow of control in a program.

There are four types of Control Instructions in 'C'

(*i*) Sequence Control Instruction.

(*ii*) Selection or Decision Control Instruction.

(*iii*) Repetition or Loop Control Instruction.

(*iv*) Case Control Instruction.

1.10. HIERARCHY OF OPERATIONS

The order or priority in which the arithmetic operations are performed in an arithmetic statement is called as the hierarchy of operations. Hierarchy of operations are given below :

Priority	*Operators*
1.	Parantheses—All parantheses are evaluated first
2.	Multiplication and division
3.	Addition and Subtraction.

1.11. ESCAPE SEQUENCES

In 'C' the backslash symbol (\) is called an escape character.

\ t — (also called tab)

\ n — new line character takes control to the next line.

\ b — Backspace. It moves the cursor one position to the left of its current position.

\ r — Carriage return. It takes cursor to the beginning of the line in which it is currently placed.

\ a — Alert, it alerts the user by sounding the speaker inside the computer.

1.12. BASIC STRUCTURE OF "C" PROGRAM

A program is defined as a valid set of instructions which perform a given task. Each instruction in C program is written as a separate statement. However big a problem or program is, following rules are applicable to all 'C' Statements :

(*a*) Blank spaces may be inserted between two words to improve readability of the statement.

(*b*) Usually all the statements are entered in small case letters.

(*c*) C is free from language *i.e.,* there is no restriction on position of statements within the program.

(*d*) A 'C' statement always ends with a semicolon (;).

Any 'C' program is combination of functions. main( ) is one such function. Empty parantheses after main is must. The set of statements belonging to a function are enclosed within a pair of braces. *e.g.,*

```
main( )
{
        Statement 1 ;
        Statement 2 ;
        Statement 3 ;
}
```

Functions can be of two types :

(*i*) Library functions or Built-in functions or intrinsic functions

(*ii*) User defined functions.

Library functions are those which are available as a part of 'C' language (C Compiler). These can be used by the programmers (user) directly to do a specific task. *For example* the input/output operations are performed by a group as functions which belong to a particular set. These sets are called as a header files in 'C'. The header file is denoted by file extension . *h*.

The following table shows some popular library functions.

S. No.	Functions	Meaning	Argument	Value
1.	sqrt (x)	$\sqrt{x}$	float	float
2.	log (x)	$\log_e x$	float	float
3.	abs (x)	$\| x \|$	integer	integer
4.	fabs (x)	$\| x \|$	float	float
5.	exp (x)	e^x	float	float
6.	pow (x, y)	x^y	float	float
7.	ceil (x)	Rounding x to next integer value	float	float
8.	f mod (x, y)	returns the remainder of x/y	float	float
9.	rand ( )	generates a (+) ve random integer	—	integer
10.	srand (v)	to initialize the random no. generator	Unsigned	—
11.	sin (x)	sin x	float in radian measure	float
12.	cos (x)	cos x	"	"
13.	tan (x)	tan x	float in radian measure	float
14.	toascii (x)	returns integer value to particular character	character integer	integer
15.	tolower (x)	To convert character to lower case	"	character
16.	toupper (x)	To convert character to upper case	character	"

1.12.1. Simple 'C' Program

```
#include<stdio.h>
/*program for average of three numbers*/
main( )
    {
        int a, b, c, d ;
        a = 2 ;
        b = 3 ;
        c = 6 ;
        d = (a + b + c)/3 ;
        Print f("% d", d) ;
    }
```

In the above C-program, the first line contains a reference to a *header file*. Since any standard program will have some i/o functions, the above statement appears as the first line in every C program.

Library functions of stdio.*h* are scan *f* , print *f*, getchr, putchr, putc, puts.

If we want to use certain mathematical functions then the header file **math.h** is included using statement

#include <math.h>

Library functions of math. *h* are cos, cosh, sin, sinh, tan, log, *a* cos, *a* sin, exp.

The second line of the above program is a *comment line.* It can be any where in the program and any number of comment lines are allowed. This comment line improves the readability and helps the programmer to understand the program.

Then the function name main( ) is written. Function name is always followed by a set of parenthesis. Argument, if any, are placed within the parenthesis. The opening brace and the closing brace indicate the beginning and end of the function.

Then the variables are declared as integers. The declaration part must be written as the first part of the function.

Then a, b, c values are assigned and d is calculated.

In the next line, d is printed using print f function.

The basic rules for a program can be stated as follows :

1. Proper header file must be referred.
2. There should be one and only one main function.
3. Contents of the function should be enclosed by an opening and closing braces.
4. Variables must be declared first in the function.
5. Every C statement except the comment line headlines and function names in a function must end with a semicolon.

1.13. DECISION MAKING INSTRUCTIONS IN "C"–

Ability to take decision regarding execution of the instructions in a "C" program is accomplished using decision control instruction. C has three major decision making instructions :

(*i*) The if statement

(*ii*) The if-else statement and

(*iii*) The switch statement.

(*i*) **The if statement.** The general form (syntax) of this statement is as follows :

```
if (this condition is true)
   execute this statement;
```

e.g. :
```
if (exp > 5)
  {
        bonus = 3000;
        print f ("% d", bonus);
  }
```

(*ii*) **The if-else statement.** The if statement executes a single statement or a group of statements if the condition following if is true. The ability to execute a group of statements if the condition is true and to execute another group of statements if the condition is false, is provided by if-else statement.

The general syntax of if-else is as follows :

```
if (condition)
        statement 1 ;
else
        statement 2 ;
```

or

```
if (condition)
        {
                statement 1 ;
                statement 2 ;
        }
else
        {
                statement 1 ;
                statement 2 ;
        }
```

The group of statements after the if upto and not including the else is called as if block. Similarly, the statements after the else forms the else block.

(iii) **Decision using switch.** The control structure which allows to make a decision from the number of choices is called as switch or switch-case-default. Since these 3 keywords together make up the control structure.

Syntax is as follows :

```
Switch (integer expression)
        {
                case constant 1 ;
                        do this ;
                        break ;
                case constant 2 :
                        do this ;
                        break ;
                default :
                        do this ;
        }
```

The integer expression following keyword switch in any C expression that will yield an integer value. The keyword case is followed by an integer or a character constant.

Each constant in each case must be different from all others. The break statement helps in getting out of the control structure.

Note. There is no need for break statement after the default, since the control automatically comes out of the control structure as it is at the last.

e.g. :

```
main( )
        {
                int i = 6 ;
                switch (i)
                {
                case 1 :
                        printf ("This is case 1") ;
                        break ;
```

```
        case 2 :
                printf ("This is case 2") ;
                break ;
                default :
                printf ("This is default") ;
        }
}
```

Points to Remember. (*i*) The cases need not be arranged in any specific order.

(*ii*) It is allowed to use char values in case and switch.

(*iii*) Some times there may be no statements in some of the cases in switch, but still they can be useful.

(*iv*) The switch statement is very useful while writing menu driven programs.

1.14. LOOP CONTROL STRUCTURE

The process of repeating some portion of the program either a specified number of times or until a particular condition is satisfied is called *looping.*

Three methods of implementing a loop in "C" are :

(*a*) using a *for* statement

(*b*) using a *while* statement

(*c*) using a *do-while* statement.

(*a*) **The for statement.** It is the most popular loop control structure.

General form is as below :

for (initialise counter ; test counter ; increment counter).

This control structure allows us to specify 3 things about a loop in a single line.

(*i*) Setting a loop counter to an initial value.

(*ii*) Testing the loop counter to determine whether its value has reached the number of repetitions desired.

(*iii*) Increasing the value of loop counter each time the program segment within the loop has been executed.

e.g. :

```
for (i = 1 ; i < = 10 ; i = i + 1)          | i = i + 1 may be written as i++
  print f ("% d", i) ;
o/p = prints values from 1 to 10.
```

(*b*) **The while loop.** General form is ;

```
initialise the loop counter ;
while (test of loop counter using a condition)
{
        do this ;                  ⎤
        :                          ⎥  Body of while loop
        increment loop counter ;   ⎦
}
```

Note. (*i*) The statement within the loop keep on getting executed as long as the condition being tested remains true. As soon as it becomes false, the control passes to the first statement that follows the body of the while loop.

(*ii*) The condition being tested may use relational or logical operators.

(*iii*) Instead of incrementing the loop counter, it can be decremented also.

e.g. :
```
int i = 4 ;
while (i > = 1)
{
        print f ("% d", i) ;
        i = i – 1 ;
}
```

(*iv*) The loop counter need not be of int type, it can be of float type also.

(*c*) **The do-while loop.** General form (syntax)

```
do
    {
            this ;
            and this ;
            and this ;
    }       while (this condition is true) ;
```

The difference between while and do-while is that the do-while executes its statements atleast once even if the condition fails for the first time itself. The while loop however does not execute the statements even once if the condition is false.

The break and continue keywords are usually associated with all the three loops *i.e.,* for, while and do-while. A break keyword inside the loop takes the control out of the loop bypassing the conditional test. A continue keyword on the other hand takes the control to the conditional test.

1.15. ARRAYS AND STRING

Arrays. Array is a collection of similar elements. These elements could all be ints, or all floats or all charcs. etc. However there are situations in which it is required to store more than one value at a time in a single variable.

e.g. : if it is required to arrange the marks obtained by 100 students in a particular subject then the two following methods can be used.

(*a*) Construct 100 variable to store marks obtained by 100 students in a particular subject

or

(*b*) Construct a single variable (called as a subscripted variable) capable of holding all the 100 values of the students, of a particular subject.

A subscripted variable is a collective name given to a group of similar quantities.

e.g. : marks = {20, 50, 60, 80}

Array declaration. In order to use array in the program, we need to declare it in order to tell the 'C' Compiler what type and size of array, we want.

e.g. : int marks [100] ;

An array can be of more than one dimension. The two dimensional array is also called as *Matrix.*

e.g. : Marks [i] [J] ;

String. The character arrays are called strings. Character arrays or strings are the data types used by programming languages to manipulate text such as words or sentences. *e.g.* :

Static character name [ ] = {'A', 'S', 'H', 'I', '\o'};

Static character name [ ] = "ASHISH";

Note. (*i*) The length of the string entered while using scanf, should not exceed the size of the character array.

(*ii*) Scanf is not capable of receiving multiword strings. Hence names such as *"Mansi Choubey"* would be unacceptable. In order to get around this limitation of scanf function, gets ( ) and puts ( ) functions are used.

Syntex : gets (Name);

puts (" Hello ! ");

1.16. POINTERS

When a variable is declared in a program, the compiler does three things

(*i*) Reserves space in memory for this variable.

(*ii*) Associate the name of the variable with the memory location.

(*iii*) If some value is assigned of the variable then, this value is stored at this location.

If it is required to find the memory address of a variable then it is possible using an "address of " (&) operator. *e.g.* : if the integer variable i is stored in memory as follows :

Memory location (address)	*Value*	*Location name*
1000	2	i

then its memory address can be printed using a *printf* statement as shown below :

printf ("Address of i = % d", and i) ;

Similarly there is another operator called 'value at address' (*) operator which returns the value stored at a particular address. *e.g.* :

printf ("value of i = % d", * (& i)) ;

1.17. STRUCTURE AND UNIONS

Structures. A structure is a data type which facilitates storage of similar or dissimilar type of information about a particular entity.

e.g. : all information regarding an employee.

```
struct employee
{
        char name [10] ;
        int code ;
        char address [20] ;
        char sex ;
} ;
```

The keyword *struct* is used to declare a structure data type.

Union. In 'C', a union is a memory location that is shared by two or more different variables, generally of different types, at different times.

Defining a union is similar to defining a structure.

```
Its general form is ;
union union_name
{
  type variable_name ;
  type variable_name ;
          :
} union_variables ;
```

Example :

```
union item
{
  int i ;
  char ch ;
} ;
```

Unions are useful when :

(*i*) It is required to produce portable (machine independent) code. It is so, because the compiler keeps track of actual sizes of the variables that make up the union, no machine dependecies are produced.

(*ii*) When type conversion are needed because we can refer to the data held in the union in different ways.

1.18. STORAGE CLASSES IN 'C'

In order to fully define a variable, two things are required :

(*i*) The type of the variable

(*ii*) The storage class of a variable.

There are 4 storage classes provided in 'C'

(*a*) Automatic storage classes

(*b*) Register storage classes

(*c*) Static storage classes

(*d*) Extern storage classes

EXAMPLES

Example 1. *Draw a flow-chart to find real roots of the equation* $ax^2 + bx + c = 0$. (U.P.T.U. 2002)

Sol. We know that the roots of quadratic equation $ax^2 + bx + c = 0$ are given by

$$x_1 = \frac{-b + \sqrt{b^2 - 4ac}}{2a} \quad \text{and} \quad x_2 = \frac{-b - \sqrt{b^2 - 4ac}}{2a}$$

or

$$x_1 = \frac{-b + \sqrt{d}}{2}, x_2 = \frac{-b - \sqrt{d}}{2}, \text{ where } d = b^2 - 4ac.$$

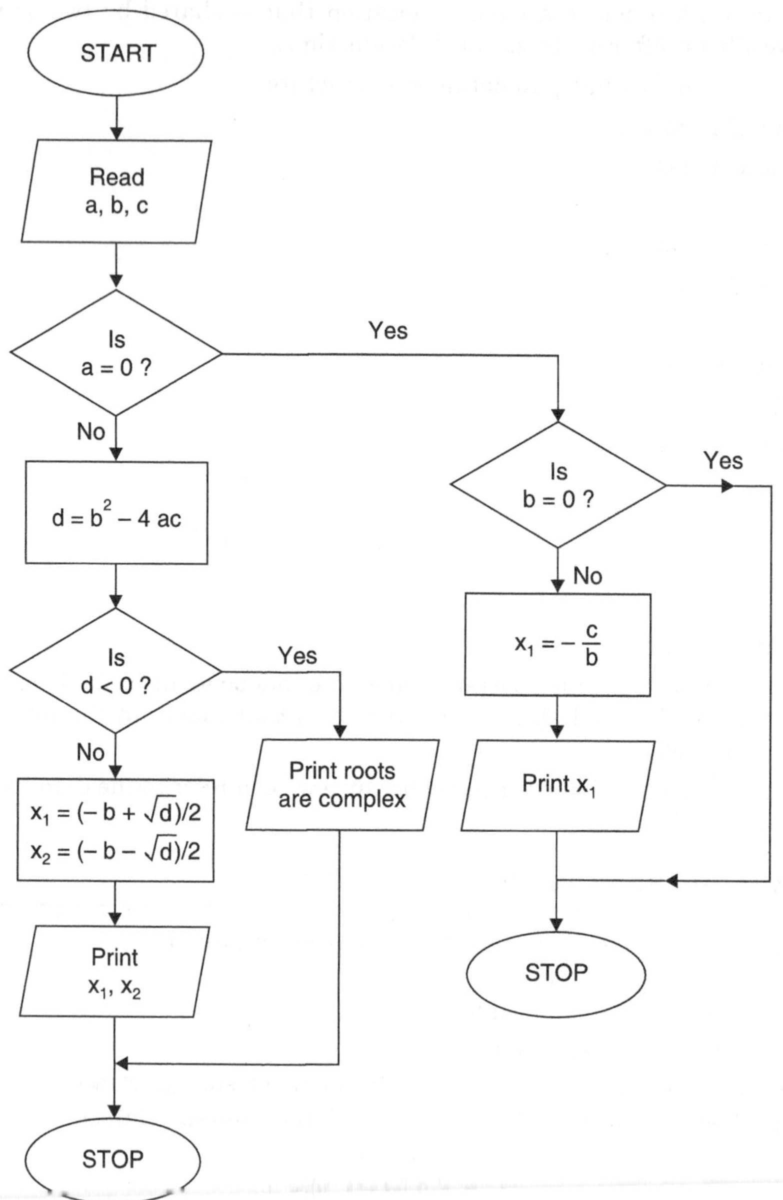

Flow-chart

Example 2. *Develop a flow-chart to select the largest number of a given set of 100 numbers.*

Sol.

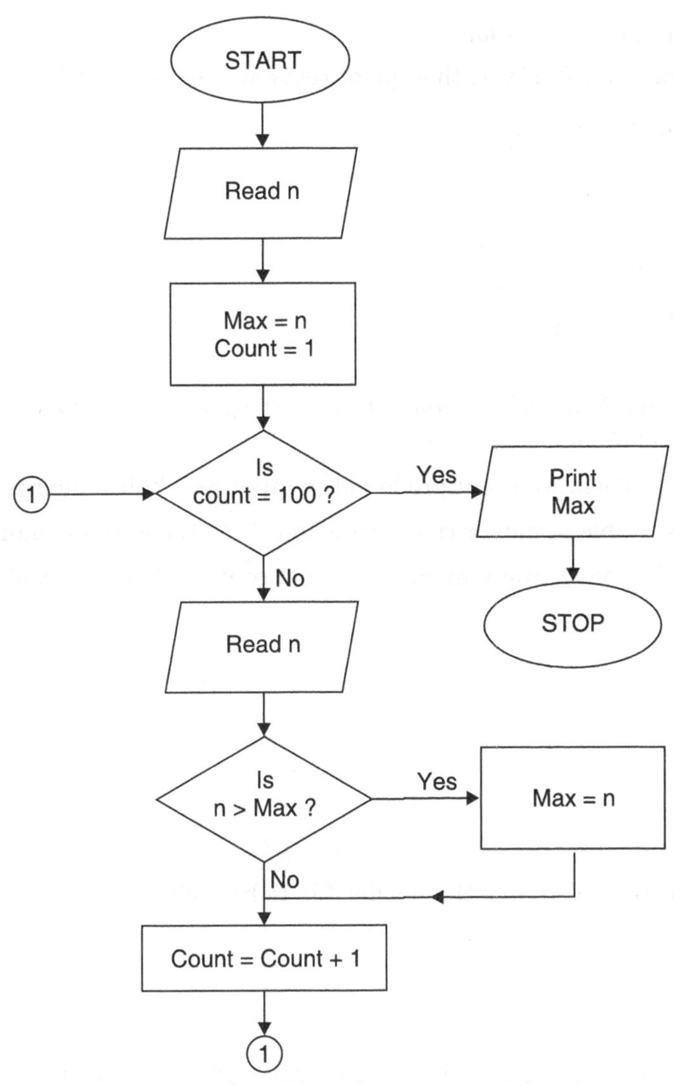

Example 3. *Write down an algorithm to find the real roots of the equation $ax^2 + bx + c = 0$; a, b, c are real and $a, b \neq 0$.*

Sol. We know that the roots of the equation

$$ax^2 + bx + c = 0$$

are $$x_1 = \frac{-b+e}{2}, \quad x_2 = \frac{-b-e}{2} \quad \text{where } e = \sqrt{b^2 - 4ac} = \sqrt{d}$$

Algorithm is

Step 1. Input a, b, c.

Step 2. Calculate $d = b^2 - 4ac$.

Step 3. Check if $d < 0$. If yes, then print roots are complex, go to step 8.

Step 4. Calculate $e = \sqrt{d}$.

Step 5. Calculate $x_1 = \dfrac{-b+e}{2a}$.

Step 6. Calculate $x_2 = \dfrac{-b-e}{2a}$.

Step 7. Print x_1 and x_2.

Step 8. Stop.

Example 4. *Write an algorithm for converting a temperature from centigrade to Fahrenheit. Also write its program in ' C'.*

Sol. For this problem, the centigrade is the input and Fahrenheit is the output.

Let c be the variable name for centigrade and f be the variable name for Fahrenheit.

The formula for converting temperature from centigrade to Fahrenheit is

f = (9/5) * c + 32

So, the algorithm is

1. read c
2. f = (9/5) * c + 32
3. printf
4. end

In the first section, we name the header file to be included.

```
1. # include<stdio.h>
```

Then the function name is written as

```
main( )
```

In the second section, the variables c and f are declared as floating point variables

```
2. float c, f ;
```

In the third section, reading the values for c, calculating f and printing the value of f takes place.

```
3. scanf ("% f ", & c);
   f = (9.0 /5.0) * c + 32.0 ;
   printf ("Fahrenheit = % f", f) ;
```

The complete program is given below :

```
# include<stdio.h>
```

```
main( )
{
        float c, f ;
        scanf ("% f", & c) ;
        f = (9.0/5.0) * c + 32.0 ;
printf ("Fahrenheit = % f", f) ;
}
```

The sample output is shown below :

40.0

Fahrenheit = 104.00.

Example 5. *Write a C program to determine the area of a triangle using the formula* $area = \sqrt{s(s-a)(s-b)(s-c)}$, *where* $s = \dfrac{a+b+c}{2}$.

Sol. The algorithm is

1. read a, b, c
2. $s = \dfrac{a+b+c}{2}$
3. area = sqrt (s * ($s - a$) * ($s - b$) * ($s - c$))
4. print area
5. end.

The program is given below

```
# include<stdio.h>
# include<math.h>
main( )
{
        float a, b, c, s, area ;
        printf ("Type the sides a, b, c") ;
        scanf ("%f  %f  %f", & a, & b, & c ) ;
        s = (a + b + c) /2.0 ;
        area  = sqrt (s * (s – a) * (s – b) * (s – c)) ;
        printf ("Area = % f ", area) ;
}
```

Following is a sample output

Type the sides a, b, c

2.0 3.0 4.0

Area = 2.905.

Example 6. *Write a flow-chart to evaluate the sum of the series* $1 + x + x^2 + x^3 + ... + x^n$.

Sol.

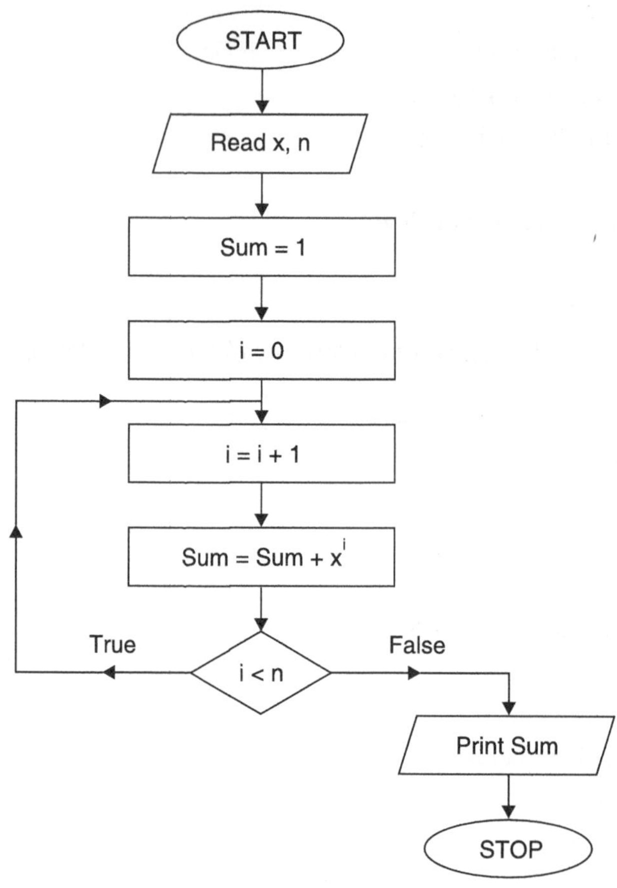

Example 7. *Write a C-program to print all the Fibonacci numbers less than 50.*

Sol. The following are the Fibonacci numbers.

0, 1, 1, 2, 3, 5, 8, 13, ...

The first Fibonacci number is 0. The second Fibonacci number is 1.

Any k^{th} Fibonacci number = $(k - 1)^{th}$ Fibonacci number + $(k - 2)^{th}$ Fibonacci number

The algorithm is

1. $n_0 = 0$
2. $n_1 = 1$
3. print n_0 , n_1
4. $n = n_0 + n_1$
5. if n > = 50 stop
6. print n
7. $n_0 = n_1$
8. $n_1 = n$
9. goto step 4 .

For this problem, there is no input.

The C–program is given below :

```
/* Program for Fibonacci Numbers */
# include<stdio.h>
main( )
{
int n, no, n1 ;
no = 0 ;
n1 = 1 ;
printf (“% d \t %d”, no, n1) ;
step 1 : n = n1 + n0 ;
        if (n > = 50)
        goto end ;
else
        { print f (“\ t % d”, n) ;
        no = n1 ;
        n1 = n ;
                goto step 1 ;}
end : printf (“  ”) ;
  }
```

The sample output is

0 1 1 2 3 5 8 13 21 34

Example 8. *Write a C-program to*

(*i*) *print integers from 1 to 10* (*ii*) *print odd numbers from 1 to 10.*

Sol. (*i*)

```
# include<stdio.h>
main( )
{
        int i ;
        for (i = 1; i < = 10 ; i + +)
        print f (“% d\t” , i) ;
}
```

The output will be

1 2 3 4 5 6 7 8 9 10

(*ii*)

```
# include<stdio.h>
main( )
{
        int i ;
        for (i = 1 ; i < = 10 ; i + = 2)
        print f (“%d\t”, i) ;
}
```

The output will be

1 3 5 7 9

ASSIGNMENT

1. Write a C-program to find the magnitude of a vector $\bar{a} = a_1 i + a_2 j + a_3 k$.

2. State whether the following statements are correct or not :

(*i*) scanf ("Enter the value of A% d", a) ; (*ii*) scanf ("%d ; %d, %d", & a, & b, & c) ;

3. Write a C-program to solve a set of linear equations with two variables

$$a_1 x + b_1 y = c_1$$
$$a_2 x + b_2 y = c_2$$

$$\left[\textbf{Hint : } \text{Solution is } x = \frac{b_2 c_1 - b_1 c_2}{a_1 b_2 - a_2 b_1}, y = \frac{a_1 c_2 - a_2 c_1}{a_1 b_2 - a_2 b_1} \right].$$

4. Write a C-program to read the principal, rate of interest, and the number of years and find the simple interest using the formula

$$\text{Simple interest} = \frac{\text{PNR}}{100}$$

5. Write a C-program to find the volume of a cone $V = \frac{1}{3}\pi r^2 h$.

6. Give algorithm and write the program in C to check whether a given number is prime or not.

7. What will be the value of x and the sum after the execution of the following program :

```
        x = 1 ;
        sum = 0 ;
step 1 : if (x < 10)
{
        sum + = 1.0/x ;
        x + = 1 ;
        go to step 1
}
```

8. Write a program in C language to determine whether a number is odd or even. Also give its flow-chart.

9. Given a circle $x^2 + y^2 = c$,

Write a C-program to determine whether a point (x, y) lies inside the circle, on the circle or outside the circle.

10. Give a flow-chart for adding marks of 5 subjects for a student and print the total.

11. Write a C-program to print the message CRICKET WORLD CUP-2015 six times.

12. Write a flow-chart for finding the average of 10 numbers. Also give its program in "C".

13. Write a program in C to print the following triangle of numbers

```
1
1   2
1   2   3
1   2   3   4
1   2   3   4   5
1   2   3   4   5   6
```

14. Write an algorithm for addition of two matrices of same order.

15. Write a C-program to find the multiplication of two square matrices each of order 2.

16. Write a C-program to find factorial of a given number.

17. Give a flow-chart for finding the determinant of a square non-singular matrix.

18. Write an algorithm for finding inverse of a square non-singular matrix.

19. The PH value of a solution is given by the formula

$$PH = -\log_{10}(H^+)$$

where H^+ is the hydrogen ion concentration of the solution.

Write a C-program to read H^+ and determine PH. [check your program with the data $H^+ = 10^{-7}$, PH = 7].

20. Write a C-program to find whether a year is leap year.

21. Develop a flow-chart to select the largest number of a given set of 500 numbers.

22. Write a program in 'C' to evaluate eigen value of A^{-1} if eigen value of A is λ.

Answers

2. (*i*) Incorrect (*ii*) Correct

7. $x = 10.0$

$$\text{Sum} = 1 + \frac{1}{2} + \frac{1}{3} + \frac{1}{4} + \frac{1}{5} + \frac{1}{6} + \frac{1}{7} + \frac{1}{8} + \frac{1}{9}.$$

❑❑❑

2

Computer Arithmetic and Errors

2.1. ERRORS AND THEIR ANALYSIS

2.1.1. Sources of Errors

Following are the broad sources of errors in numerical analysis:

(1) Input errors: The input information is rarely exact since it comes from the experiments and any experiment can give results of only limited accuracy. Moreover, the quantity used can be represented in a computer for only a limited number of digits.

(2) Algorithmic errors: If direct algorithms based on a finite sequence of operations are used, errors due to limited steps don't amplify the existing errors but if infinite algos are used, ideally exact results are expected only after an infinite number of steps. As this cannot be done in practice, the algorithm has to be stopped after a finite number of steps and as a consequence thereof the results are not exact.

(3) Computational errors: Even when elementary operations, such as multiplication and division are used, the number of digits increases greatly so that the results cannot be held fully in a register available in a given computer. In such cases, a certain number of digits must be discarded. Furthermore, the errors here accumulate one after another from operation to operation, changing during the process and producing new errors.

Following diagram gives a schematic sequence for solving a problem using a digital computer pointing out the sources of errors.

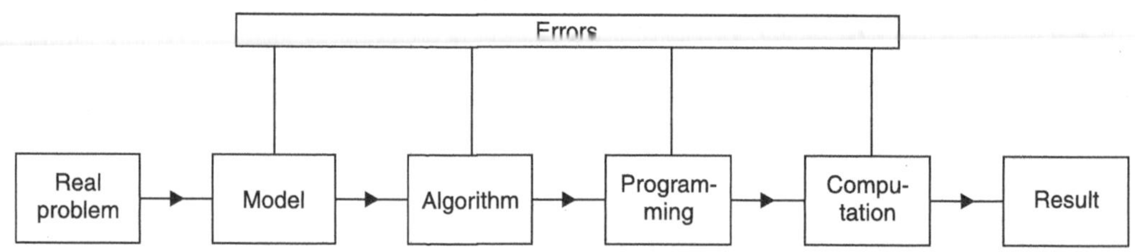

Our effort will be to minimize these errors so as to get best possible results.

We, therefore, begin by explaining various kinds of errors and approximations which may occur in a problem and derive some results on error propagation in numerical calculations.

2.2. ACCURACY OF NUMBERS

(1) Approximate numbers: There are two types of numbers: exact and approximate. Exact numbers are 2, 4, 9, $\frac{7}{2}$, 6.45, ... etc. but there are numbers such that

$\frac{4}{3}$ (= 1.333 ......), $\sqrt{2}$ (= 1.414213 ...) and π (= 3.141592......) which cannot be expressed by a finite number of digits. These may be approximated by numbers 1.3333, 1.4141 and 3.1416 respectively.

Such numbers which represent the given numbers to a certain degree of accuracy are called approximate numbers.

(2) Significant digits: The digits used to express a number are called significant digits.

The digits 1, 2, 3, 4, 5, 6, 7, 8, 9 are significant digits. '0' is also a significant digit except when it is used to fix the decimal point or to fill the places of unknown or discarded digits.

For example, Each of numbers 7845, 3.589, 0.4758 contains 4 significant figures while the numbers 0.00386, 0.000587, 0.0000296 contain only three significant figures since zeros only help to fix the position of the decimal point.

Similarly, in the number 0.0003090, the first four '0' s' are not significant digits since they serve only to fix the position of the decimal point and indicate the place values of the other digits. The other two '0' s' are significant.

To be more clear, the number 3.0686 contains five significant digits.

A. The significant figure in a number **in positional notation** consists of

(*i*) All non-zero digits

(*ii*) Zero digits which

(*a*) lie between significant digits.

(*b*) lie to the right of decimal point and at the same time, to the right of a non-zero digit.

(*c*) are specifically indicated to be significant.

B. The significant figure in a number written **in scientific notation** (*e.g.* $M \times 10^k$) consists of all the digits explicitly in M.

Note. Significant digits are counted from left to right starting with the left most non-zero digit.

A list is being provided to make the students clearly understand how to calculate significant digits in a given number:

Number	*Significant digits*	*No. of significant digits*
3969	3, 9, 6, 9	04
3060	3, 0, 6	03
3900	3, 9	02
39.69	3, 9, 6, 9	04
0.3969	3, 9, 6, 9	04
39.00	3, 9, 0, 0	04
0.00039	3, 9	02
0.00390	3, 9, 0	03
3.0069	3, 0, 0, 6, 9	05
3.9×10^6	3, 9	02
3.909×10^5	3, 9, 0, 9	04
6×10^{-2}	6	01

(3) Rounding off: There are numbers with large no. of digits *e.g.* $\frac{22}{7} = 3.142857143$. In practice, it is desirable to limit such numbers to a manageable no. of digits such as 3.14 or 3.143. This process of dropping unwanted digits is called rounding-off.

Numbers are rounded-off according to following rule:

To round-off a number to n significant digits, discard all digits to the right of nth digit and if this discarded number is

(*i*) less than 5 in $(n + 1)^{th}$ place, leave the nth digit unaltered. *e.g.* 7.893 to 7.89.

(*ii*) greater than 5 in $(n + 1)^{th}$ place, increase the nth digit by unity *e.g.* 6.3456 to 6.346.

(*iii*) exactly 5 in $(n + 1)^{th}$ place, increase the nth digit by unity if it is odd otherwise leave it unchanged.

For example : $12.675 \simeq 12.68$

$12.685 \simeq 12.68$

The number thus rounded-off is said to be correct to n significant figures.

A list is being provided to grasp it easily:

Number	*Rounded-off to*		
	Three digits	*Four digits*	*Five digits*
00.543241	00.543	00.5432	00.54324
39.5255	39.5	39.52	39.526
69.4155	69.4	69.42	69.416
00.667676	00.668	00.6677	00.66768

2.3. ERRORS

Machine epsilon

We know that a computer has a finite word length so only a fixed number of digits are stored and used during computation. Hence even in storing an exact decimal number in its converted form in the computer memory, an error is introduced. This error is machine dependant and is called machine epsilon.

Error = True value – Approximate value

In any numerical computation, we come across following types of errors:

(1) Inherent errors: Errors which are already present in the statement of a problem before its solution are called inherent errors. Such errors arise either due to the given data being approximate or due to limitations of mathematical tables, calculators or the digital computer.

Inherent errors can be minimized by taking better data or by using high precision* computing aids. Accuracy refers to the number of significant digits in a value *e.g.,* 53.965 is accurate to 5 significant digits.

Precision refers to the number of decimal position or order of magnitude of the last digit in the value. *e.g.* in 53.965, precision is 10^{-3}.

Example. *Which of the following numbers have greatest precision?*

4.3201, 4.32, 4.320106.

*Concept of accuracy and precision are closely related to significant digits.

Sol. In 4.3201, precision is 10^{-4}

In 4.32, precision is 10^{-2}

In 4.320106, precision is 10^{-6}.

Hence the number 4.320106 has the greatest precision.

(2) Rounding errors: They arise from the process of rounding off the numbers during the computation. It is also called procedual error or numerical error. Such errors are unavoidable in most of the calculations due to limitations of computing aids.

These errors can be reduced however by

(*i*) changing the calculation procedure so as to avoid subtraction of nearly equal numbers or division by a small number.

(*ii*) retaining at least one more significant digit at each step and rounding off at last step. Rounding off may be executed in two ways:

(*a*) **Chopping:** In it, extra digits are dropped by trucation of number. Suppose we are using a computer with a fixed word length of four digits then a number like 12.92364 will be stored as 12.92.

We can express the number 12.92364 in the floating point form as

$$\begin{aligned}
\text{True} \quad x &= 12.92364 \\
&= 0.1292364 \times 10^2 = (0.1292 + 0.0000364) \times 10^2 \\
&= 0.1292 \times 10^2 + 0.364 \times 10^{-4+2} = f_x \cdot 10^{\text{E}} + g_x \cdot 10^{\text{E}-d} \\
&= \text{Approximate } x + \text{Error}
\end{aligned}$$

$$\therefore \quad \text{Error} = g_x \cdot 10^{\text{E}-d},\ 0 \le g_x \le d$$

Here, g_x is the maintessa, d is the length of mantissa and E is exponent

Since $\quad 0 \le g_x < 1$

$\therefore$ Absolute error $\le 10^{\text{E}-d}$

Case I. If $g_x < 0.5$ then approximate $x = f_x \cdot 10^{\text{E}}$

Case II. If $g_x \ge .5$ then approximate $x = f_x \cdot 10^{\text{E}} + 10^{\text{E}-d}$

$$\begin{aligned}
\text{Error} &= \text{True value} - \text{Approximate value} \\
&= f_x \cdot 10^{\text{E}} + g_x \cdot 10^{\text{E}-d} - f_x \cdot 10^{\text{E}} - 10^{\text{E}-d} = (g_x - 1) \cdot 10^{\text{E}-d}
\end{aligned}$$

absolute error $\le 0.5 \cdot (10)^{\text{E}-d}$.

(*b*) **Symmetric round off:** In it, the last retained significant digit is rounded up by unity if the first discarded digit is ≥ 5 otherwise the last retained digit is unchanged.

(3) Truncation errors

They are caused by using approximate results or on replacing an infinite process by a finite one.

If we are using a decimal computer having a fixed word length of 4 digits; rounding off of 13.658 gives 13.66 whereas truncation gives 13.65.

e.g., If $\text{S} = \sum_{i=1}^{\infty} a_i x_i$ is replaced by or truncated to $\text{S} = \sum_{i=1}^{n} a_i x_i$ then error developed is called truncation error.

Truncation error is a type of algorithm error. Also,

If $e^x = 1 + x + \frac{x^2}{2!} + \frac{x^3}{3!} + \frac{x^4}{4!} + \cdots\cdots \infty = \text{X (say)}$ is truncated to $1 + x + \frac{x^2}{2!} + \frac{x^3}{3!} = \text{X}'$ (say)

then truncation error = X – X′

Example. *Find the truncation error for e^x at $x = \frac{1}{5}$ if first three terms are retained in expansion.*

Sol. Error = True value – Approximate value

$$= \left(1 + x + \frac{x^2}{2!} + \frac{x^3}{3!} + \ldots\ldots\right) - \left(1 + x + \frac{x^2}{2!}\right) = \frac{x^3}{3!} + \frac{x^4}{4!} + \frac{x^5}{5!} + \ldots\ldots$$

Put $x = \frac{1}{5}$

$$\text{error} = \frac{0.008}{6} + \frac{0.0016}{24} + \frac{0.00032}{120} + \ldots\ldots$$

$$= 0.0013333 + 0.0000666 + 0.0000026 + \ldots = 0.0014025$$

(4) Absolute error

Absolute error is the numerical difference between the true value of a quantity and its approximate value.

Thus if X is the true value of a quantity and X′ is its approximate value then | X – X′ | is called the absolute error e_a.

$$e_a = |\, \text{X} - \text{X}' \,| = |\, \text{Error} \,|$$

(5) Relative error

The relative error e_r is defined by

$$e_r = \frac{|\,\text{Error}\,|}{\text{True value}} = \left| \frac{\text{X} - \text{X}'}{\text{X}} \right|$$

where X is true value and X – X′ is error.

(6) Percentage error

Percentage error e_p is defined as

$$e_p = 100\, e_r = 100 \left| \frac{\text{X} - \text{X}'}{\text{X}} \right|.$$

Remark 1. The relative and percentage errors are independent of units used while absolute error is expressed in terms of these units.

Remark 2. If a number is correct to n decimal places, then error = $\frac{1}{2}(10^{-n})$.

e.g. if the no. 3.1416 is correct to 4 decimal places, then error = $\frac{1}{2}(10^{-4}) = 0.00005$.

Remark 3. If the first significant digit of a number is k and the number is correct to n significant digits then, relative error $< \frac{1}{(k \times 10^{n-1})}$.

EXAMPLES

Example 1. *Suppose 1.414 is used as an approximation to $\sqrt{2}$. Find the absolute and relative errors.*

Sol. True value $= \sqrt{2} = 1.41421356$

Approximate value $= 1.414$

$$\text{Error} = \text{True value} - \text{Approximate value}$$

$$= \sqrt{2} - 1.414 = 1.41421356 - 1.414 = 0.00021356$$

Absolute error $e_a = |\text{ Error }| = |\ 0.00021356\ | = 0.21356 \times 10^{-3}$

Relative error $e_r = \dfrac{e_a}{\text{True value}} = \dfrac{0.21356 \times 10^{-3}}{\sqrt{2}} = 0.151 \times 10^{-3}.$

Example 2. *If 0.333 is the approximate value of $\frac{1}{3}$, find absolute, relative and percentage errors.*

Sol. True value $(X) = \dfrac{1}{3}$

Approximate value $(X') = 0.333$

$\therefore$ Absolute error $e_a = |\ X - X'\ |$

$$= \left|\frac{1}{3} - 0.333\right| = |0.333333 - 0.333| = 0.000333$$

Relative error $e_r = \dfrac{e_a}{X} = \dfrac{0.000333}{0.333333} = 0.000999$

Percentage error $e_p = e_r \times 100 = 0.000999 \times 100 = 0.099\%.$

Example 3. *An approximate value of π is given by 3.1428571 and its true value is 3.1415926. Find absolute and relative errors.*

Sol. True value $= 3.1415926$

Approximate value $= 3.1428571$

$$\text{Error} = \text{True value} - \text{Approximate value}$$

$$= 3.1415926 - 3.1428571 = -\ 0.0012645$$

Absolute error $e_a = |\text{ Error }| = 0.0012645$

Relative error $e_r = \dfrac{e_a}{\text{True value}} = \dfrac{0.0012645}{3.1415926} = 0.000402502.$

Example 4. *Three approximate values of number $\frac{1}{3}$ are given as 0.30, 0.33 and 0.34. Which of these three is the best approximation?*

Sol. The best approximation will be the one which has the least absolute error.

True value $= \dfrac{1}{3} = 0.33333.$

Case I. Approximate value = 0.30

Absolute error = | True value – Approximate value |

= | 0.33333 – 0.30 | = 0.03333

Case II. Approximate value = 0.33

Absolute error = | True value – Approximate value |

= | 0.33333 – 0.33 | = 0.00333.

Case III. Approximate value = 0.34

Absolute error = | True value – Approximate value |

= | 0.33333 – 0.34 | = | – 0.00667 | = 0.00667

Since absolute error is **least** in case II. Hence 0.33 is the best approximation.

Example 5. *Find the relative error of the number 8.6 if both of its digits are correct.*

Sol. Here, $e_a = 0.05$ $\left(\because \; e_a = \frac{1}{2} \times 10^{-1}\right)$

$$\therefore \qquad e_r = \frac{0.05}{8.6} = 0.0058.$$

Example 6. *Find the relative error, absolute error and percentage error if $\frac{2}{3}$ is approximated to 0.667.*

Sol. True value $= \frac{2}{3} = 0.666666$

Approximate value = 0.667

Absolute error e_a = | True value – approximate value |

= | 0.666666 – 0.667 | = 0.000334

Relative error $e_r = \frac{0.000334}{0.666666} = 0.0005$

Percentage error $e_p = 0.0005 \times 100 = 0.05\%$.

Example 7. *Find the percentage error if 625.483 is approximated to three significant figures.*

Sol. $e_a = |\, 625.483 - 625 \,| = 0.483$

$$e_r = \frac{e_a}{625.483} = \frac{0.483}{625.483} = 0.000772$$

$$\therefore \qquad e_p = e_r \times 100 = .077\%.$$

Example 8. *Round off the numbers 865250 and 37.46235 to four significant figures and compute e_a, e_r, e_p in each case.*

Sol. (*i*) Number rounded off to four significant digits = 865200

X = 865250

X′ = 865200

Error = X – X′ = 865250 – 865200 = 50

Absolute error e_a = | error | = 50

Relative error $e_r = \frac{e_a}{X} = \frac{50}{865250} = 5.77 \times 10^{-5}$

Percentage error $e_p = e_r \times 100 = 5.77 \times 10^{-3}$

(*ii*) Number rounded off to four significant digits = 37.46

$$X = 37.46235$$

$$X' = 37.46$$

$$\text{Error} = X - X' = 0.00235$$

Absolute error $e_a = |\text{ error }| = 0.00235$

Relative error $e_r = \frac{e_a}{X} = \frac{0.00235}{37.46235} = 6.2729 \times 10^{-5}$

Percentage error $e_p = e_r \times 100 = 6.2729 \times 10^{-3}$.

Example 9. *Round off the number 75462 to four significant digits and then calculate the absolute error and percentage error.*

Sol. Number rounded off to four significant digits = 75460

Absolute error $e_a = |\ 75462 - 75460\ | = 2$

Relative error $e_r = \frac{e_a}{75462} = \frac{2}{75462} = 0.0000265$

Percentage error $e_p = e_r \times 100 = 0.00265$.

Example 10. *Find the absolute, relative and percentage errors if x is rounded-off to three decimal digits. Given x = 0.005998.*

Sol. Number rounded off to three decimal digits = 0.006

$$\text{Error} = 0.005998 - 0.006 = -0.000002$$

Absolute error $e_a = |\text{ error }| = 0.000002$

Relative error $e_r = \frac{e_a}{0.005998} = \frac{0.000002}{0.005998} = 0.0033344$

Percentage error $e_p = e_r \times 100 = 0.33344$.

Example 11. *Evaluate the sum $S = \sqrt{3} + \sqrt{5} + \sqrt{7}$ to 4 significant digits and find its absolute and relative errors.*

Sol $\sqrt{3} = 1.732, \quad \sqrt{5} = 2.236, \quad \sqrt{7} = 2.646$

Hence, $S = 6.614$

and $e_a = 0.0005 + 0.0005 + 0.0005 = 0.0015$.

The total absolute error shows that the sum is correct to 3 significant figures only.

∴ We take, $S = 6.61$

then, $e_r = \frac{0.0015}{6.61} = 0.0002$.

Example 12. *It is required to obtain the roots of $X^2 - 2X + \log_{10} 2 = 0$ to four decimal places. To what accuracy should $\log_{10} 2$ be given?*

Sol. Roots of $X^2 - 2X + \log_{10} 2 = 0$ are given by

$$X = \frac{2 \pm \sqrt{4 - 4\log_{10} 2}}{2} = 1 \pm \sqrt{1 - \log_{10} 2}$$

$$\therefore \qquad |\Delta X| = \frac{1}{2}\frac{\Delta(\log 2)}{\sqrt{1-\log 2}} < 0.5 \times 10^{-4}$$

or $$\Delta(\log 2) < 2 \times 0.5 \times 10^{-4}\,(1 - \log 2)^{1/2} < 0.83604 \times 10^{-4} \approx 8.3604 \times 10^{-5}.$$

ASSIGNMENT

1. Round-off the following numbers correct to four significant digits:

3.26425, 35.46735, 4985561, 0.70035, 0.00032217, 1.6583, 30.0567, 0.859378, 3.14159.

2. The height of an observation tower was estimated to be 47 m whereas its actual height was 45 m. Calculate the percentage relative error in the measurement.

3. If the number p is correct to three decimal places, what will be the error?

4. If true value $= \frac{10}{3}$, approximate value = 3.33 then find the absolute and relative errors.

5. Round-off the following numbers to two decimal places.

48.21416, 2.3742, 52.275, 2.375, 2.385, 81.255.

6. Discuss the significant digits with suitable example.

7. If X = 2.536, find the absolute error and relative error when

(*i*) X is rounded-off (*ii*) X is truncated to two decimal digits.

8. If $\pi = \frac{22}{7}$ is approximated as 3.14, find the absolute error, relative error and percentage relative error.

9. Given the solution of a problem as X′ = 35.25 with the relative error in the solution at most 2%. Find, to four decimal digits, the range of values within which the exact value of the solution must lie.

$$\left[\textbf{Hint: } \left|1 - \frac{X'}{X}\right| < 0.02\right]$$

10. (*i*) Define absolute, relative and percentage errors.

(*ii*) What do you mean by truncation error? Explain with examples.

11. What do you understand by machine epsilon of a computer? Explain.

12. Differentiate between accuracy and precision.

Answers

1. 3.264, 35.47, 4986000, 0.7004, 0.0003222, 1.658, 30.06, 0.8594, 3.142.

2. 4.44% **3.** 0.0005 **4.** $e_a = 0.003333, e_r = 0.000999$

5. 48.21, 2.37, 52.28, 2.38, 2.38, 81.26

7. (*i*) 0.004, 0.0015772 (*ii*) 0.006, 0.0023659

8. 0.002857, 0.0009, 0.09% **9.** (34.5588, 35.9694)

2.4. A GENERAL ERROR FORMULA

Let $y = f(x_1, x_2)$ be a function of two variables x_1, x_2.

Let $\delta x_1, \delta x_2$ be the errors in x_1, x_2, then the error δy in y is given by

$$y + \delta y = f(x_1 + \delta x_1, x_2 + \delta x_2)$$

Expanding RHS by Taylor's series, we get

$$y + \delta y = f(x_1, x_2) + \left(\frac{\partial f}{\partial x_1} \delta x_1 + \frac{\partial f}{\partial x_2} \delta x_2 \right) + \text{terms involving higher powers of } \delta x_1 \text{ and } \delta x_2 \quad \ldots(1)$$

If the errors δx_1, δx_2 be so small that their squares and higher powers can be neglected then (1) gives

$$\delta y = \frac{\partial f}{\partial x_1} \delta x_1 + \frac{\partial f}{\partial x_2} \delta x_2 \text{ approximately}$$

Hence,
$$\delta y = \frac{\partial y}{\partial x_1} \delta x_1 + \frac{\partial y}{\partial x_2} \delta x_2$$

In general, the error δy in the function $y = f(x_1, x_2, \ldots\ldots, x_n)$ corresponding to the errors δx_i in x_i $(i = 1, 2, \ldots\ldots, n)$ is given by

$$\delta y \approx \frac{\partial y}{\partial x_1} \delta x_1 + \frac{\partial y}{\partial x_2} \delta x_2 + \ldots\ldots + \frac{\partial y}{\partial x_n} \delta x_n$$

and relative error in y is

$$e_r = \frac{\delta y}{y} = \frac{\partial y}{\partial x_1} \cdot \frac{\delta x_1}{y} + \frac{\partial y}{\partial x_2} \cdot \frac{\delta x_2}{y} + \ldots\ldots + \frac{\partial y}{\partial x_n} \cdot \frac{\delta x_n}{y}.$$

2.5. ERRORS IN NUMERICAL COMPUTATIONS

(1) Error in addition of numbers

Let
$$X = x_1 + x_2 + \cdots\cdots + x_n$$

$$\therefore \quad X + \Delta X = (x_1 + \Delta x_1) + (x_2 + \Delta x_2) + \cdots\cdots + (x_n + \Delta x_n)$$

Absolute error is

$$\therefore \quad \Delta X = \Delta x_1 + \Delta x_2 + \cdots\cdots + \Delta x_n$$

$$\Rightarrow \quad \frac{\Delta X}{X} = \frac{\Delta x_1}{X} + \frac{\Delta x_2}{X} + \ldots\ldots + \frac{\Delta x_n}{X}$$

which is relative error.

Max. relative error is

$$\left| \frac{\Delta X}{X} \right| \le \left| \frac{\Delta x_1}{X} \right| + \left| \frac{\Delta x_2}{X} \right| + \ldots\ldots + \left| \frac{\Delta x_n}{X} \right|.$$

It is clear that if two numbers are added then the magnitude of absolute error in the result is the sum of the magnitudes of the absolute errors in the two numbers.

Note. While adding up several numbers of different absolute accuracies, the following procedure is adopted.

(*i*) Isolate the number with the greatest absolute error.

(*ii*) Round-off all other numbers retaining in them one digit more than in the isolated number.

(*iii*) Add up.

(*iv*) Round-off the sum by discarding one digit.

(2) Error in subtraction of numbers

Let $X = x_1 - x_2$

$\therefore \quad X + \Delta X = (x_1 + \Delta x_1) - (x_2 + \Delta x_2) = (x_1 - x_2) + (\Delta x_1 - \Delta x_2)$

$\therefore \quad \Delta X = \Delta x_1 - \Delta x_2$ is absolute error

and $\dfrac{\Delta X}{X} = \dfrac{\Delta x_1}{X} - \dfrac{\Delta x_2}{X}$ is relative error.

$$\text{Max. relative error } = \left|\frac{\Delta X}{X}\right| \le \left|\frac{\Delta x_1}{X}\right| + \left|\frac{\Delta x_2}{X}\right|$$

and $\quad$ Max. absolute error $= |\ \Delta X\ | \le |\ \Delta x_1\ | + |\ \Delta x_2\ |$.

(3) Error in product of numbers

Let $X = x_1\, x_2 \,......\, .\, x_n$

We know that if X is a function of $x_1, x_2, ..., x_n$

then,
$$\Delta X = \frac{\partial X}{\partial x_1}\Delta x_1 + \frac{\partial X}{\partial x_2}\Delta x_2 + ... + \frac{\partial X}{\partial x_n}\Delta x_n$$

Now,
$$\frac{\Delta X}{X} = \frac{1}{X}\frac{\partial X}{\partial x_1}\Delta x_1 + \frac{1}{X}\frac{\partial X}{\partial x_2}\Delta x_2 + ... + \frac{1}{X}\frac{\partial X}{\partial x_n}\Delta x_n$$

Now,
$$\frac{1}{X}\frac{\partial X}{\partial x_1} = \frac{x_2 \cdot x_3 \,......\, x_n}{x_1 x_2 x_3 \,......\, x_n} = \frac{1}{x_1}$$

$$\frac{1}{X}\frac{\partial X}{\partial x_2} = \frac{x_1 x_3 \,......\, x_n}{x_1 x_2 x_3 \,......\, x_n} = \frac{1}{x_2}$$

$$\vdots \qquad\qquad\qquad \vdots$$

$$\frac{1}{X}\frac{\partial X}{\partial x_n} = \frac{1}{x_n}$$

$$\therefore \quad \frac{\Delta X}{X} = \frac{\Delta x_1}{x_1} + \frac{\Delta x_2}{x_2} + ... + \frac{\Delta x_n}{x_n}.$$

$\therefore$ Relative and absolute errors are given by,

$$\text{Max. relative error } = \left|\frac{\Delta X}{X}\right| \le \left|\frac{\Delta x_1}{x_1}\right| + \left|\frac{\Delta x_2}{x_2}\right| + ... + \left|\frac{\Delta x_n}{x_n}\right|$$

$$\text{Max. absolute error } = \left|\frac{\Delta X}{X}\right| X = \left|\frac{\Delta X}{X}\right| . (x_1 x_2 x_3 \,......\, x_n)$$

(4) Error in division of numbers

Let, $X = \dfrac{x_1}{x_2}$

$$\therefore \quad \frac{\Delta X}{X} = \frac{1}{X}\frac{\partial X}{\partial x_1}\Delta x_1 + \frac{1}{X} \cdot \frac{\partial X}{\partial x_2} . \Delta x_2$$

$$= \frac{\Delta x_1}{\left(\dfrac{x_1}{x_2}\right)} \cdot \frac{1}{x_2} + \frac{\Delta x_2}{\left(\dfrac{x_1}{x_2}\right)} \left(\frac{-x_1}{x_2^2}\right) = \frac{\Delta x_1}{x_1} - \frac{\Delta x_2}{x_2}$$

$\therefore$ $$\left|\frac{\Delta X}{X}\right| \le \left|\frac{\Delta x_1}{x_1}\right| + \left|\frac{\Delta x_2}{x_2}\right| \text{ which is relative error.}$$

$$\text{Absolute error } = |\Delta X| \le \left|\frac{\Delta X}{X}\right| \cdot X.$$

(5) **Error is evaluating x^k**

$$X = x^k, \quad \text{where } k \text{ is an integer or fraction}$$

$$\Delta X = \frac{dX}{dx} \Delta x = kx^{k-1} \cdot \Delta x$$

$$\frac{\Delta X}{X} = k \cdot \frac{\Delta x}{x}$$

$\therefore$ $$\left|\frac{\Delta X}{X}\right| \le k \cdot \frac{\Delta x}{x}$$

Relative error in evaluating $x^k = k \cdot \left|\dfrac{\Delta x}{x}\right|$.

EXAMPLES

Example 1. *If* $u = \dfrac{4x^2y^3}{z^4}$ *and errors in x, y, z be 0.001, compute the relative max. error in u when* $x = y = z = 1$.

Sol. $$\delta u = \frac{\partial u}{\partial x}\delta x + \frac{\partial u}{\partial y}\delta y + \frac{\partial u}{\partial z}\delta z$$

$$= \frac{8x\,y^3}{z^4}\delta x + \frac{12x^2y^2}{z^4}\delta y - \frac{16x^2y^3}{z^5}\delta z$$

Since the errors δx, δy, δz may be (+) ve or (–) ve, we take the absolute values of terms on RHS giving,

$$(\delta u)_{\text{max.}} = \left|\frac{8xy^3}{z^4}\delta x\right| + \left|\frac{12x^2y^2}{z^4}\delta y\right| + \left|\frac{16x^2y^3}{z^5}\delta z\right|$$

$$= 8(0.001) + 12(0.001) + 16(0.001) = 0.036$$

$\therefore$ $$\text{Max. relative error } = \frac{0.036}{4} = 0.009.$$

Example 2. *Find the relative error in the function* $y = ax_1^{m_1}x_2^{m_2} \ldots\ldots x_n^{m_n}$.

Sol. We have $$\log y = \log a + m_1 \log x_1 + m_2 \log x_2 + \cdots\cdots + m_n \log x_n$$

$\therefore$ $$\frac{1}{y}\left(\frac{\partial y}{\partial x_1}\right) = \frac{m_1}{x_1}, \frac{1}{y}\frac{\partial y}{\partial x_2} = \frac{m_2}{x_2}, \ldots\ldots \text{ etc.}$$

$$\therefore \qquad e_r = \frac{\partial y}{\partial x_1}\cdot\frac{\delta x_1}{y} + \frac{\partial y}{\partial x_2}\cdot\frac{\delta x_2}{y} + \ldots\ldots + \frac{\partial y}{\partial x_n}\cdot\frac{\delta x_n}{y}$$

$$= m_1 \frac{\delta x_1}{x_1} + \frac{m_2}{x_2}\delta x_2 + \ldots\ldots + m_n \cdot \frac{\delta x_n}{x_n}$$

Since errors δx_1, δx_2 may be (+) ve or (–), ve we take absolute values of terms on RHS This gives,

$$(e_r)_{\max.} \le m_1 \left|\frac{\delta x_1}{x_1}\right| + m_2 \left|\frac{\delta x_2}{x_2}\right| + \ldots\ldots + m_n \left|\frac{\delta x_n}{x_n}\right|.$$

Corollary. If $\qquad y = x_1\, x_2 \ldots\ldots, x_n$

$$e_r \approx \frac{\delta x_1}{x_1} + \frac{\delta x_2}{x_2} + \ldots\ldots + \frac{\delta x_n}{x_n}$$

$\therefore$ Relative error of a product of n numbers is approximately equal to the algebraic sum of their relative errors.

Example 3. *Compute the percentage error in the time period* $T = 2\pi\sqrt{\frac{l}{g}}$ *for* $l = 1$ *m if the error in the measurement of* l *is 0.01.*

Sol. $$T = 2\pi\sqrt{\frac{l}{g}}$$

Taking log

$$\log T = \log 2\pi + \frac{1}{2}\log l - \frac{1}{2}\log g$$

$$\Rightarrow \qquad \frac{1}{T}\delta T = \frac{1}{2}\frac{\delta l}{l}$$

$$\frac{\delta T}{T}\times 100 = \frac{\delta l}{2l}\times 100 = \frac{0.01}{2\times 1}\times 100 = 0.5\%\,.$$

Example 4. *If* $u = 2V^6 - 5V$, *find the percentage error in* u *at* $V = 1$ *if error in* V *is 0.05.*

Sol. $$u = 2V^6 - 5V$$

$$\delta u = \frac{\partial u}{\partial V}\delta V = (12\,V^5 - 5)\,\delta V$$

$$\frac{\delta u}{u}\times 100 = \left(\frac{12V^5 - 5}{2V^6 - 5V}\right)\cdot \delta V \times 100$$

$$= \frac{(12-5)}{(2-5)}\times(0.05)\times 100 = -\frac{7}{3}\times 5 = -\,11.667\%$$

Max. percentage error = 11.667%.

Example 5. *If* $r = 3h(h^6 - 2)$, *find the percentage error in* r *at* $h = 1$, *if the percentage error in* h *is 5.*

Sol. $$\delta r = \frac{\partial r}{\partial h}\delta h = (21h^6 - 6)\,\delta h$$

$$\frac{\delta r}{r}\times 100 = \left(\frac{21h^6 - 6}{3h^7 - 6h}\right)\delta h \times 100$$

$$= \left(\frac{21-6}{3-6}\right)\left(\frac{\delta h}{h} \times 100\right) = \frac{15}{(-3)} \cdot 5\% \ = -25\%$$

Percentage error $= \left|\frac{\delta r}{r} \times 100\right| = 25\%$.

Example 6. *The discharge Q over a notch for head H is calculated by the formula $Q = kH^{5/2}$, where k is a given constant. If the head is 75 cm and an error of 0.15 cm is possible in its measurement, estimate the percentage error in computing the discharge.*

Sol. $Q = kH^{5/2}$

$$\log Q = \log k + \frac{5}{2} \log H$$

Differentiating, $\frac{\delta Q}{Q} = \frac{5}{2} \cdot \frac{\delta H}{H}$

$$\frac{\delta Q}{Q} \times 100 = \frac{5}{2} \times \frac{0.15}{75} \times 100 = \frac{1}{2} = 0.5.$$

Example 7. *The error in the measurement of the area of a circle is not allowed to exceed 0.1%. How accurately should the diameter be measured?*

Sol. $A = \pi \frac{d^2}{4}$

$$\log A = \log \pi + 2 \log d - \log 4$$

$$\frac{\delta A}{A} \times 100 = \frac{2}{d} (\delta d \times 100)$$

$$\frac{\delta d}{d} \times 100 = \frac{0.1}{2} = 0.05.$$

Example 8. (*i*) *Prove that the absolute error in the common logarithm of a number is less than half the relative error of the given number.*

(*ii*) *Prove that error in antilogarithm is many times the error in logarithm.*

Sol. (*i*) $N = \log_{10} x = 0.43429 \log_e x$

Hence, $\Delta N = 0.43429 \frac{\Delta x}{x} < \frac{1}{2}\left(\frac{\Delta x}{x}\right).$

(*ii*) From (*i*), $\Delta x = \frac{x \Delta N}{0.43429} = 2.3026\, x(\Delta N).$

Example 9. *Find the smaller root of the equation $x^2 - 32x + 1 = 0$ correct to four significant figures.*

Sol. Roots of the equation $x^2 - 32x + 1 = 0$ are $\frac{32 - \sqrt{(32)^2 - 4}}{2}$ and $\frac{32 + \sqrt{(32)^2 - 4}}{2}$

The smaller root is $\frac{32 - \sqrt{1020}}{2} = 16 - \sqrt{255}$

I Algorithm. Smaller root $= 16 - \sqrt{255} = 16 - 15.97 = 0.03$

II Algorithm. Smaller root $= (16 - \sqrt{255}) \cdot \frac{16 + \sqrt{255}}{16 + \sqrt{255}} = \frac{1}{16 + 15.97} = \frac{1}{31.97} = 0.0313$

Second algorithm is evidently a better one as this gives the result correct to 4 figures.

Example 10. *If* $X = x + e$ *prove that* $\sqrt{X} - \sqrt{x} \approx \dfrac{e}{2\sqrt{X}}$.

Sol. $$\sqrt{X} - \sqrt{x} = \sqrt{X} - \sqrt{X - e} = \sqrt{X} - \sqrt{X}\left(1 - \frac{e}{X}\right)^{1/2} = \sqrt{X} - \sqrt{X}\left(1 - \frac{e}{2X}\right)$$

$$= \sqrt{X} - \sqrt{X} + \frac{e}{2\sqrt{X}} \approx \frac{e}{2\sqrt{X}}.$$

Example 11. *In a* ΔABC, $a = 6$ *cm,* $c = 15$ *cm,* $\angle B = 90°$. *Find the possible error in computed value of A if errors in measurements of a and c are 1 mm and 2 mm respectively.*

Sol. Here, $\tan A = \dfrac{a}{c}$

$\therefore$ $$A = \tan^{-1}\left(\frac{a}{c}\right)$$

$$\delta A = \frac{\partial A}{\partial a}\delta a + \frac{\partial A}{\partial c}\delta c$$

$$= \frac{c}{a^2 + c^2}\delta a - \frac{a}{a^2 + c^2}\delta c$$

C

6 cm

90°

A 15 cm B

or $$|\delta A| \le \left|\frac{c}{a^2 + c^2}\cdot \delta a\right| + \left|\frac{a}{a^2 + c^2}\cdot \delta c\right|$$

$$= \frac{15}{261}\cdot(0.1) + \frac{6}{261}\cdot(0.2) = 0.0103 \text{ radians}$$

$\therefore$ $\delta A \le 0.0103$ radians.

Example 12. *In a* ΔABC, $a = 30$ *cm,* $b = 80$ *cm,* $\angle B = 90°$, *find the maximum error in computed value of A if possible errors in a and b are* $\frac{1}{3}\%$ *and* $\frac{1}{4}\%$ *respectively.*

Sol. $$\sin A = \frac{a}{b} \Rightarrow A = \sin^{-1}\left(\frac{a}{b}\right)$$

$$|\delta A| < \left|\frac{\partial A}{\partial a}\delta a\right| + \left|\frac{\partial A}{\partial b}\delta b\right| \quad \ldots(1)$$

Here, $\dfrac{\delta a}{a} \times 100 = \dfrac{1}{3}$ $\therefore$ $\delta a = 0.1$

$\dfrac{\delta b}{b} \times 100 = \dfrac{1}{4}$ $\therefore$ $\delta b = 0.2$

$\therefore$ $$\frac{\partial A}{\partial a} = \frac{1}{\sqrt{b^2 - a^2}}, \quad \frac{\partial A}{\partial b} = \frac{-a}{b\sqrt{b^2 - a^2}}$$

Substituting in (1), we get $\delta A < 0.00135 + 0.00100 < 0.00235$.

Example 13. *Approximate values of* $\frac{1}{7}$ *and* $\frac{1}{11}$ *correct to 4 decimal places are 0.1429 and 0.0909 respectively. Find the possible relative error and absolute error in the sum of 0.1429 and 0.0909.*

Sol. Numbers 0.1429 and 0.0909 are correct to four places of decimal. Max. error in each case is $\dfrac{1}{2} \times 0.0001 = 0.00005$.

(*i*) **Relative error**

$$\frac{|\Delta X|}{|X|} < \frac{|\Delta x_1|}{|X|} + \frac{|\Delta x_2|}{|X|} < \frac{0.00005}{0.2338} + \frac{0.00005}{0.2338} \qquad (\because \; X = x_1 + x_2)$$

$$\left|\frac{\Delta X}{X}\right| < \frac{0.0001}{0.2338} = 0.00043.$$

(*ii*) **Absolute error**

$$\Delta X = \Delta x_1 + \Delta x_2 = 0.00005 + 0.00005 = 0.0001.$$

Example 14. *Approximate values of* $\frac{1}{7}$ *and* $\frac{1}{15}$ *correct to four decimal places are 0.1429 and 0.0667 respectively. Find the relative error for the sum of 0.1429 and 0.0667.*

Sol. $$\left|\frac{\Delta X}{X}\right| < \frac{0.0001}{0.2096} = 0.000477.$$

Example 15. $\sqrt{29}$ *= 5.385 and* $\sqrt{11}$ *= 3.317 correct to four significant figures. Find the relative error in their sum and difference?*

Sol. Numbers 5.385 and 3.317 are correct to four significant figures

$\therefore$ Maximum error in each case is $\frac{1}{2} \times 10^{-3} = 0.0005$

$\therefore$ $\Delta x_1 = \Delta x_2 = 0.0005$

Relative error in their sum

$$\left|\frac{\Delta X}{X}\right| \le \left|\frac{\Delta x_1}{X}\right| + \left|\frac{\Delta x_2}{X}\right| \qquad \Big| \because \; X = x_1 + x_2 = 8.702$$

$$\le \left|\frac{0.0005}{8.702}\right| + \left|\frac{0.0005}{8.702}\right| < 1.149 \times 10^{-4}$$

Relative error in their difference

$$\left|\frac{\Delta X}{X}\right| \le \left|\frac{\Delta x_1}{X}\right| + \left|\frac{\Delta x_2}{X}\right|, \text{ where } X = x_1 - x_2 = 2.068$$

$$\le \left|\frac{0.0005}{2.068}\right| + \left|\frac{0.0005}{2.068}\right| < 4.835 \times 10^{-4}.$$

Example 16. *Sum the following numbers: 0.1532, 15.45, 0.000354, 305.1, 8.12, 143.3, 0.0212, 0.643 and 0.1734, where digits are correct.*

Sol. 305.1 and 143.3 have the greatest absolute error in each of which error is 0.05.

Rounding off all other numbers to two decimal digits, we have 0.15, 15.45, 0.00, 8.12, 0.02, 0.64 and 0.17.

The sum S is given by

$$S = 305.1 + 143.3 + 0.15 + 15.45 + 0.00 + 8.12 + 0.02 + 0.64 + 0.17$$
$$= 472.59 = 472.6$$

To determine absolute error, we note that first two numbers have each an absolute error of 0.05 and remaining seven numbers have an absolute error of 0.005 each.

∴ Absolute error in all 9 numbers

$$= 2(0.05) + 7(0.005) = 0.1 + 0.035 = 0.135 \approx 0.14$$

In addition to the above absolute error, we have to take into account rounding error which is 0.01. Hence the total absolute error in S = 0.14 + 0.01 = 0.15

Thus, $S = 472.6 \pm 0.15.$

Example 17. $\sqrt{5.5} = 2.345$ *and* $\sqrt{6.1} = 2.470$ *correct to four significant figures. Find the relative error in taking the difference of these numbers.*

Sol. Max. error in each case $= \frac{1}{2} \times 0.001 = 0.0005$

$$\therefore \quad \text{Relative error} < \left|\frac{\Delta x_1}{X}\right| + \left|\frac{\Delta x_2}{X}\right| = 2\left|\frac{\Delta x_1}{X}\right| = 2\left(\frac{0.0005}{0.125}\right) = 0.008.$$

Example 18. $\sqrt{10} = 3.162$ *and* $e \simeq 2.718$ *correct to three decimal places. Find the percentage error in their difference.*

Sol. Relative error $= 2 \times \frac{0.0005}{(3.162 - 2.718)} = \frac{0.001}{0.444}$

∴ Percentage error $= \frac{0.001}{0.444} \times 100 \simeq 0.23$.

Example 19. *Find the product of 346.1 and 865.2. State how many figures of the result are trustworthy? Given that the numbers are correct to four significant figures.*

Sol. $\Delta x_1 = 0.05, \Delta x_2 = 0.05$

$X = 346.1 \times 865.2 = 299446$ (correct to 6 digits)

$$\text{Max. relative error } (e_r) \le \left|\frac{\Delta x_1}{x_1}\right| + \left|\frac{\Delta x_2}{x_2}\right|$$

$$= \left|\frac{0.05}{346.1}\right| + \left|\frac{0.05}{865.2}\right| = 0.000144 + 0.000058 = 0.000202$$

∴ Absolute error $= e_r \cdot X = 0.000202 \times 299446 \simeq 60$

∴ True value of the product of the numbers given lies between 299446 – 60 = 299386 and 299446 + 60 = 299506.

Mean of these values is $\frac{299386 + 299506}{2} = 299446$

which is 299.4×10^3 correct to four significant digits. There is some uncertainty about last digit.

Example 20. *Two numbers are given as 2.5 and 48.289 both of which being correct to the significant figures given. Find their product.*

Sol. 2.5 is the number with greatest absolute error. Rounding off the other number to three significant digits, we get 48.3.

Their product is given by,

$$P = 48.3 \times 2.5 = 120.75 = 1.2 \times 10^2$$

where, we have retained only two significant digits.

Example 21. *Find the relative error in calculation of* $\frac{7.342}{0.241}$. *Numbers are correct to three decimal places. Determine the smallest interval in which true result lies.*

Sol. $\Delta x_1 = \Delta x_2 = 0.0005$

Relative error $\leq \left|\frac{0.0005}{7.342}\right| + \left|\frac{0.0005}{0.241}\right| \leq 0.0005\left(\frac{1}{7.342}+\frac{1}{0.241}\right) = 0.0021$

Absolute error $= 0.0021 \times \frac{x_1}{x_2} = 0.0021 \times \frac{7.342}{0.241} = 0.0639$

Now, $\frac{x_1}{x_2} = \frac{7.342}{0.241} = 30.4647$

$\therefore$ True value of x_1/x_2 lies between $30.4647 - 0.0639 = 30.4008$ and 30.5286.

Example 22. *Find the number of trustworthy figure in* $(0.491)^3$ *assuming that the number 0.491 is correct to last figure.*

Sol. Relative error $e_r = k\frac{\Delta x}{x} = 3 \cdot \frac{0.0005}{0.491} = 0.003054989$

Absolute error $< e_r \cdot X$

$= (0.003054989) \cdot (0.491)^3 = 0.000361621$

The error effects the fourth decimal place therefore X is correct to three decimal places.

Example 23. *Given that:*

$a = 10.00 \pm 0.05,\qquad b = 0.0356 \pm 0.0002$

$c = 15300 \pm 100,\qquad d = 62000 \pm 500$

Find the maximum value of the absolute error in

(i) $a + b + c + d$ *(ii)* $a + 5c - d$ *(iii)* d^3

Sol. (*i*) Max. absolute error $= \Delta a + \Delta b + \Delta c + \Delta d$

$= 0.05 + 0.0002 + 100 + 500$

$= 600.0502$

(*ii*) Max. absolute error $= \Delta a + 5\,\Delta c + \Delta d = 0.05 + 500 + 500 = 1000.05$

(*iii*) Max. absolute error $= \Delta d^2\,\Delta d = 3(62000)^2\,(500) = 5.766 \times 10^{12}$.

2.6. ERROR IN A SERIES APPROXIMATION

The error committed in a series approximation can be evaluated by using the remainder after n terms.

Taylor's series for $f(x)$ at $x = a$ is given by

$$f(x) = f(a) + (x-a)f'(a) + \frac{(x-a)^2}{2!}f''(a) + \cdots\cdots + \frac{(x-a)^{n-1}}{(n-1)!}f^{(n-1)}(a) + R_n(x)$$

where $R_n(x) = \frac{(x-a)^n}{n!}f^{(n)}(\xi);\ a < \xi < x.$

For a convergent series, $R_n(x) \to 0$ as $n \to \infty$. If we approximate $f(x)$ by first n terms of series then max. error committed is given by $R_n(x)$.

If the accuracy required is specified in advance, it would be possible to find n, the number of terms such that the finite series yields the required accuracy.

EXAMPLES

Example 1. *Find the number of terms of the exponential series such that their sum gives the value of e^x correct to six decimal places at $x = 1$.*

Sol.
$$e^x = 1 + x + \frac{x^2}{2!} + \frac{x^3}{3!} + \ldots\ldots + \frac{x^{n-1}}{(n-1)!} + R_n(x) \quad \ldots(1)$$

where
$$R_n(x) = \frac{x^n}{n!} e^{\theta},\ 0 < \theta < x$$

Max. absolute error (at $\theta = x$) $= \dfrac{x^n}{n!} e^x$

and Max. relative error $= \dfrac{x^n}{n!}$

Hence, $(e_r)_{\text{max.}}$ at $x = 1$ is $= \dfrac{1}{n!}$

For a six decimal accuracy at $x = 1$, we have

$$\frac{1}{n!} < \frac{1}{2} \times 10^{-6} \quad \textit{i.e.,} \quad n! > 2 \times 10^6$$

which gives $n = 10$.

Hence we need 10 terms of series (1) in order that its sum is correct to 6 decimal places.

Example 2. *Use the series* $\log_e \left(\dfrac{1+x}{1-x}\right) = 2\left(x + \dfrac{x^3}{3} + \dfrac{x^5}{5} + \ldots\ldots\right)$ *to compute the value of log (1.2) correct to seven decimal places and find the number of terms retained.*

Sol.
$$\log_e \left(\frac{1+x}{1-x}\right) = 2\left(x + \frac{x^3}{3} + \frac{x^5}{5} + \ldots + \frac{x^{2n-1}}{2n-1}\right) + R_n(x)$$

If we retain n terms then,

$$(n+1)^{\text{th}} \text{ term} = \frac{2}{2n+1} x^{2n+1}$$

Let
$$\frac{1+x}{1-x} = 1.2 \Rightarrow x = \frac{1}{11}$$

Hence
$$(e_r)_{\text{max.}} \text{ at } x = \frac{1}{11} \text{ is } = \frac{2}{2n+1}\left(\frac{1}{11}\right)^{2n+1}.$$

For seven decimal accuracy, $\dfrac{2}{2n+1}\cdot\left(\dfrac{1}{11}\right)^{2n+1} < \dfrac{1}{2}\times 10^{-7}$

$$(2n + 1)\,(11)^{2n+1} > 4 \times 10^7$$

which gives $n \geq 3$.

Hence retaining the first three terms of the given series, we get

$$\log_e (1.2) = 2\left(x + \frac{x^3}{3} + \frac{x^5}{5}\right) \text{ at } \left(x = \frac{1}{11}\right) = 0.1823215.$$

Example 3. *The function f(x) = $tan^{-1}x$ can be expanded as*

$$tan^{-1}x = x - \frac{x^3}{3} + \frac{x^5}{5} - \ldots\ldots + (-1)^{n-1}\cdot\frac{x^{2n-1}}{2n-1} + \ldots\ldots$$

Find n such that series determines $tan^{-1}(1)$ correct to eight significant digits.

Sol. If we retain n terms then $(n + 1)^{\text{th}}$ term $= (-1)^n \cdot \dfrac{x^{2n+1}}{2n+1}$

For $x = 1$, $(n + 1)^{\text{th}}$ term $= \dfrac{(-1)^n}{2n+1}$

For the determination of $\tan^{-1}(1)$ correct up to eight significant digit accuracy,

$$\left|\frac{(-1)^n}{2n+1}\right| < \frac{1}{2}\times 10^{-8}$$

$$\Rightarrow \qquad 2n + 1 > 2 \times 10^8$$

which $n = 10^8 + 1$ satisfies.

Example 4. *The function f(x) = cos x can be expanded as*

$$\cos x = 1 - \frac{x^2}{2!} + \frac{x^4}{4!} - \frac{x^6}{6!} + \cdots$$

Compute the number of terms required to estimate $\cos\left(\dfrac{\pi}{4}\right)$ *so that the result is correct to at least two significant digits.*

Sol.
$$\cos x = 1 - \frac{x^2}{2!} + \frac{x^4}{4!} - \frac{x^6}{6!} + \cdots + R_n(x)$$

where
$$R_n(x) = (-1)^n \frac{x^{2n}}{2n!} \cos \xi;\ 0 < \xi < x$$

Max. absolute error (at $\xi = x$) $= \left|(-1)^n \dfrac{x^{2n}}{(2n)!}\cos x\right| = \dfrac{x^{2n}}{(2n)!}\cos x$

Max. relative error $= \dfrac{x^{2n}}{(2n)!}$

At $x = \dfrac{\pi}{4}$, $(e_r)_{\text{max.}} = \dfrac{(\pi/4)^{2n}}{(2n)!}$

For two significant digit accuracy,

$$\frac{(\pi/4)^{2n}}{(2n)!} \le \frac{1}{2} \times 10^{-2}$$

i.e.,

$$\frac{(2n)!}{(\pi/4)^{2n}} \ge 200$$

$n = 3$ satisfies it.

ASSIGNMENT

1. If $R = 4xy^2z^{-3}$ and errors in x, y, z be 0.001, show that maximum relative error at $x = y = z = 1$ is 0.006.
2. If $R = 10x^3y^2z^2$ and errors in x, y, z are 0.03, 0.01, 0.02 respectively at $x = 3, y = 1, z = 2$. Calculate absolute error and percentage relative error in evaluating R.
3. If $R = 4x^2y^3z^{-4}$, find the maximum absolute error and maximum relative error in R when errors in $x = 1, y = 2, z = 3$ respectively are equal to 0.001, 0.002, 0.003.
4. If $u = \frac{5xy^2}{z^3}$ and error in x, y, z are 0.001 at $x = 1, y = 1, z = 1$; calculate maximum relative error in evaluating u.
5. Find the number of terms of the exponential series such that their sum yields the value of e^x correct to 8 decimal places at $x = 1$.
6. Find the product of the numbers 56.54 and 12.4 which are both correct to the significant digits given.
7. Find the quotient $q = \frac{x}{y}$, where $x = 4.536$ and $y = 1.32$; both x and y being correct to the digits given. Find also the relative error in the result.
8. Write a short note on Errors in numerical computation.
9. What are different types of error that may arise in numerical computations. Describe.
10. Find smaller root of the equation $x^2 - 30x + 1 = 0$ correct to three places of decimal. State different algorithms. Which algorithm is better and why?

Answers

2. 75.6, 7% **3.** 0.00355, 0.0089 **4.** 0.006

5. 12 **6.** 701 **7.** $q = 3.43636, e_r = 0.020857$

10. 0.0333704.

2.7. MATHEMATICAL PRELIMINARIES

Following are certain mathematical results which would be useful in the sequel.

Theorem 1. If $f(x)$ is continuous in $a \le x \le b$ and if $f(a)$ and $f(b)$ are of opposite signs then $f(c) = 0$ for at least one number c such that $a < c < b$.

Theorem 2. Rolle's theorem:

If (*i*) $f(x)$ in continuous in $[a, b]$ (*ii*) $f'(x)$ exists in (a, b) (*iii*) $f(a) = f(b) = 0$.

then $\exists$ at least one value of x, say c, such that

$$f'(c) = 0, a < c < b.$$

Theorem 3. Mean value theorem for derivatives:

If (*i*) $f(x)$ is continuous in $[a, b]$ (*ii*) $f'(x)$ exists in (a, b)

then, $\exists$ at least one value of x, say c, between a and b s.t. $f'(c) = \dfrac{f(b) - f(a)}{b - a}$, $a < c < b$.

Theorem 4. Taylor's series for a function of one variable: If $f(x)$ is continuous and possesses continuous derivatives of order n in an interval that includes $x = a$ then in that interval

$$f(x) = f(a) + (x - a) f'(a) + \frac{(x - a)^2}{2!} f''(a) + \dots\dots + \frac{(x - a)^{n-1}}{(n-1)!} f^{(n-1)}(a) + R_n(x)$$

where $R_n(x)$ is remainder term, can be expressed in the form

$$R_n(x) = \frac{(x - a)^n}{n!} f^n(c), \; a < c < x.$$

Theorem 5. Maclaurin's expansion:

$$f(x) = f(0) + x f'(0) + \frac{x^2}{2!} f''(0) + \dots\dots + \frac{x^n}{n!} f^{(n)}(0) + \dots\dots$$

Theorem 6. Taylor's series for a function of two variables:

$f(x_1 + \Delta x_1, x_2 + \Delta x_2)$

$$= f(x_1, x_2) + \frac{\partial f}{\partial x_1} \Delta x_1 + \frac{\partial f}{\partial x_2} \Delta x_2 + \frac{1}{2}\left[\frac{\partial^2 f}{\partial {x_1}^2}(\Delta x_1)^2 + 2\frac{\partial^2 f}{\partial x_1 \partial x_2} \Delta x_1 \cdot \Delta x_2 + \frac{\partial^2 f}{\partial {x_2}^2}(\Delta x_2)^2\right] + \dots\dots$$

2.8. FLOATING POINT ARITHMETIC

There are two types of arithmetic operations available in a computer.

They are:

(*i*) Integer arithmetic (*ii*) Real or floating point arithmetic.

Integer arithmetic deals with integer operands and used mainly in counting and as subscripts. Real arithmetic uses numbers with fractional parts as operands and is used in most computations. Computers are usually designed such that each location, called **word,** in memory stores only a finite number of digits. Consequently, all operands in arithmetic operations have only a finite number of digits.

Let us assume a hypothetical computer having memory in which each location can store 6 digits and having provision to store one or more signs. One method of representing real numbers in that computer would be to assume a fixed position for the decimal point and store all numbers after appropriate shifting if necessary with an assumed decimal point.

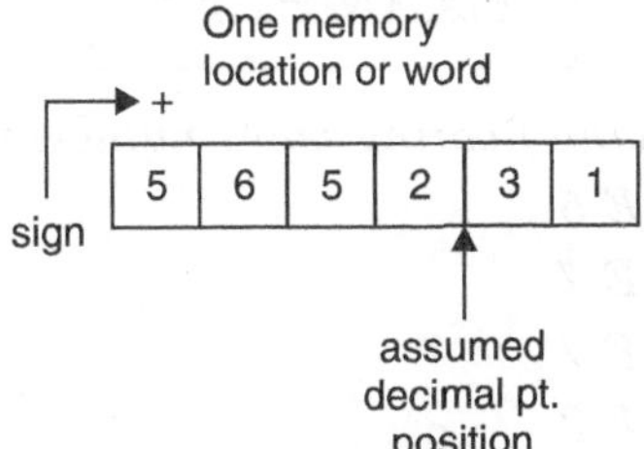

A memory location storing number 5652.31

In such convention, the max. and min. possible numbers to be stored are 9999.99 and 0000.01 respectively in magnitude. This range is quite inadequate in practice.

For this, a new convention is adopted which aims to preserve the max. number of significant digits in a real number and also increase the range of values of real numbers stored. This representation is called the **normalized floating point** mode of representing and storing real numbers.

In this mode, a real number is expressed as a combination of a **mantissa** and an **exponent.** The mantissa is made less than 1 or ≥ .1 and the exponent is the power of 10 which multiplies the mantissa.

e.g.: The number 43.76×10^6 is represented in this notation as .4376 E 8, where E 8 is used to represent 10^8. The mantissa is .4376 and the exponent is 8.

The number is stored in memory location as:

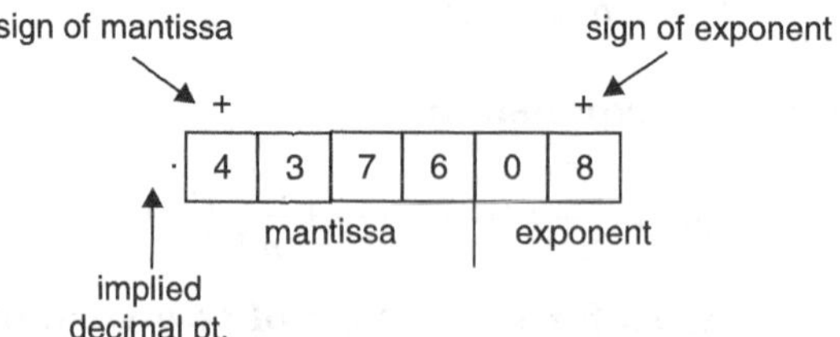

Moreover, the shifting of the mantissa to the left till its most significant digit is non-zero is called **normalization.**

e.g. : The number .006831 may be stored as .6831 E–2 because the leading zeros serve only to locate the decimal point.

By doing so, the range of numbers that may be stored are $.9999 \times 10^{99}$ to $.1000 \times 10^{-99}$ in magnitude which is obviously much larger than that used earlier in fixed decimal point notation.

This increment in range has been obtained by reducing the number of significant digits in a number by 2.

2.9. ARITHMETIC OPERATIONS WITH NORMALIZED FLOATING POINT NUMBERS

2.9.1. Addition and Subtraction

If two numbers represented in normalized floating point notation are to be added, the exponents of the two numbers must be made equal and the Mantissa shifted appropriately. The operation of subtraction is nothing but adding a negative number. Thus the principles are the same.

EXAMPLES

Example 1. *Add the following floating point numbers:*

(*i*) *.4546 E 5 and .5433 E 5*

(*ii*) *.4546 E 5 and .5433 E 7*

(*iii*) *.4546 E 3 and .5433 E 7*

(*iv*) *.6434 E 3 and .4845 E 3*

(*v*) *.6434 E 99 and .4845 E 99.*

Sol. (*i*) Here exponents are equal ∴ Mantissas are added

∴ Sum = .9979 E 5

(*ii*) Here exponents are not equal. The operand with the larger exponent is kept as it is

.5433 E 7
+ .0045 E 7 | .4546 E 5 = .0045 E 7

.5478 E 7

(*iii*) The addition will be as follows :

.5433 E 7
+ .0000 E 7 | ∵ .4546 E 3 = .0000 E 7

.5433 E 7

(*iv*) The exponents are equal but when mantissas are added, the sum is 1.1279 E 3. As the mantissa has 5 digits and is > 1, it is shifted right one place before it is stored.

Hence Sum = .1127 E 4

(*v*) Here, again sum of mantissas exceeds 1. Mantissa is shifted right and exponent increased by 1 resulting in a value of 100 for the exponent. Exponent part cannot store more than two digits. This condition is called an **overflow** condition and the arithmetic unit will intimate an error condition.

Example 2. *Subtract the following floating point numbers:*

(*i*) *.9432 E – 4 from .5452 E – 3* (*ii*) *.5424 E 3 from .5452 E 3*

(*iii*) *.5424 E – 99 from .5452 E – 99.*

Sol. (*i*)
.5452 E – 3
– .0943 E – 3

.4509 E – 3

(*ii*)
.5452 E 3
– .5424 E 3

.0028 E 3

In normalized floating point, the mantissa is ≥ .1

Hence result is .28 E 1

(*iii*)
.5452 E – 99
– .5424 E – 99

.0028 E – 99

For normalization, the mantissa is shifted left and exponent is reduced by 1 the exponent would thus become – 100 with the first left shift which can not be accommodated in the exponent part of the number.

This condition is called an **underflow** condition and the arithmetic unit will signal an error condition.

Note. If the result of an arithmetic operation gives a number smaller than .1000 E – 99 then it is called an **underflow** condition. Similarly, any result greater than .9999 E 99 leads to an **overflow** condition.

Example 3. *In normalized floating point mode, carry out the following mathematical operations:*

(*i*) *(.4546 E 3) + (.5454 E 8)*

(*ii*) *(.9432 E – 4) – (.6353 E – 5).*

Sol. (*i*)

$$\begin{array}{r} .5454 \text{ E } 8 \\ + .0000 \text{ E } 8 \\ \hline .5454 \text{ E } 8 \\ \hline \end{array} \qquad | \because \; .4546 \text{ E } 3 = .0000 \text{ E } 8$$

(*ii*)

$$\begin{array}{r} .9432 \text{ E} - 4 \\ - .0635 \text{ E} - 4 \\ \hline .8797 \text{ E} - 4 \\ \hline \end{array} \qquad | \because \; .6353 \text{ E} - 5 = .0635 \text{ E} - 4$$

2.9.2. Multiplication

Two numbers are multiplied in the normalized floating point mode by multiplying the mantissas and adding the exponents. After the multiplication of the mantissas, the result mantissa is normalized as in addition or subtraction operation and the exponent appropriately adjusted.

EXAMPLES

Example 1. *Multiply the following floating point numbers:*

(*i*) *.5543 E 12 and .4111 E – 15* (*ii*) *.1111 E 10 and .1234 E 15*

(*iii*) *.1111 E 51 and .4444 E 50* (*iv*) *.1234 E – 49 and .1111 E – 54.*

Sol. (*i*) .5543 E 12 × .4111 E – 15 = .2278 E – 3

(*ii*) .1111 E 10 × .1234 E 15 = .1370 E 24

(*iii*) .1111 E 51 × .4444 E 50 = .4937 E 100

The result overflows.

(*iv*) .1234 E – 49 × .1111 E – 54 = .1370 E – 104

The result underflows.

Example 2. *Apply the procedure for the following multiplications:*

$$(.5334 \times 10^{9}) * (.1132 \times 10^{-25})$$

$$(.1111 \times 10^{74}) * (.2000 \times 10^{80})$$

Indicate if the result is overflow or underflow.

Sol. (*i*) .5334 E 9 × .1132 E – 25 = .6038 E – 17

(*ii*) .1111 E 74 × .2000 E 80 = .2222 E 153

Hence the above result overflows.

2.9.3. Division

In division, the mantissa of the numerator is divided by that of the denominator. The denominator exponent is subtracted from the numerator exponent. The quotient mantissa is normalized to make the most significant digit non-zero and the exponent appropriately adjusted. The mantissa of the result is chopped down to occupy 4 digits.

EXAMPLES

Example 1. *Perform the following operations:*

(i) .9998 E 1 ÷ .1000 E – 99 *(ii) .9998 E – 5 ÷ .1000 E 98*

(iii) .1000 E 5 ÷ .9999 E 3.

Sol. *(i)* .9998 E 1 ÷ .1000 E – 99 = .9998 E 101

Hence the result overflows.

(ii) .9998 E – 5 ÷ .1000 E 98 = .9998 E – 102

Hence the result underflows.

(iii) .1000 E 5 ÷ .9999 E 3 = .1000 E 2.

Example 2. *Evaluate, applying normalized floating point arithmetic for the following:*

1 – cos x at x = .1396 radian

Assume cos (.1396) = .9903

Compare it when evaluated $2\sin^2 \frac{x}{2}$. *Assume sin .0698 = .6974 E – 1.*

Sol.
$$1 - \cos(.1396) = .1000 \text{ E } 1 - .9903 \text{ E } 0$$
$$= .1000 \text{ E } 1 - .0990 \text{ E } 1 = .1000 \text{ E } -1$$

Now,
$$\sin \frac{x}{2} = \sin(.0698) = .6974 \text{ E } -1$$
$$2\sin^2 \frac{x}{2} = (.2000 \text{ E } 1) \times (.6974 \text{ E } -1) \times (.6974 \text{ E } -1) = .9727 \text{ E } -2$$

The value obtained by alternate formula is closer to the true value .9728 E – 2.

Example 3. *For x = .4845 and y = .4800, calculate the value of* $\frac{x^2 - y^2}{x + y}$ *using normalized floating point arithmetic. Compare with the value of (x – y). Indicate the error in the former.*

Sol.
$$x + y = .4845 \text{ E } 0 + .4800 \text{ E } 0 = .9645 \text{ E } 0$$
$$x^2 = (.4845 \text{ E } 0) \times (.4845 \text{ E } 0) = .2347 \text{ E } 0$$
$$y^2 = (.4800 \text{ E } 0) \times (.4800 \text{ E } 0) = .2304 \text{ E } 0$$
$$x^2 - y^2 = .2347 \text{ E } 0 - .2304 \text{ E } 0 = .0043 \text{ E } 0$$

Now,
$$\frac{x^2 - y^2}{x + y} = .0043 \text{ E } 0 \div .9645 \text{ E } 0 = .4458 \text{ E } -2$$

Also,
$$x - y = .4845 \text{ E } 0 - .4800 \text{ E } 0 = .0045 \text{ E } 0 = .4500 \text{ E } -2$$

Relative error
$$= \frac{.4500 - 0.4458}{.4500} = .93\%.$$

Example 4. *For e = 2.7183, calculate the value of* e^x *when x = .5250 E 1. The expression for* e^x *is*

$$e^x = 1 + x + \frac{x^2}{2!} + \frac{x^3}{3!}.$$

Sol. $$e^{.5250 \text{ E } 1} = e^5 * e^{.25} \qquad ...(1)$$

$$e^5 = (.2718 \text{ E } 1) \times (.2718 \text{ E } 1) \times (.2718 \text{ E } 1) \times (.2718 \text{ E } 1) \times (.2718 \text{ E } 1)$$
$$= .1484 \text{ E } 3$$

Also, $$e^{.25} = 1 + (.25) + \frac{(.25)^2}{2!} + \frac{(.25)^3}{3!}$$
$$= 1.25 + .03125 + .002604 = .1284 \text{ E } 1$$

Now, $$e^{.5250 \text{ E } 1} = (.1484 \text{ E } 3) \times (.1284 \text{ E } 1) = .1905 \text{ E } 3.$$

Example 5. *Find the solution of the following equation using floating point arithmetic with 4 digit mantissa*

$$x^2 - 1000x + 25 = 0$$

Give comments or the result so obtained.

Sol. $$x^2 - 1000\,x + 25 = 0$$

$$\Rightarrow \qquad x = \frac{1000 \pm \sqrt{10^6 - 10^2}}{2}$$

Now, $10^6 = .1000 \text{ E } 7$ and $10^2 = .1000 \text{ E } 3$

$$\therefore \quad 10^6 - 10^2 = .1000 \text{ E } 7$$

$$\therefore \quad \sqrt{10^6 - 10^2} = .1000 \text{ E } 4$$

$$\therefore \quad \text{Roots are } \left(\frac{.1000 \text{ E } 4 + .1000 \text{ E } 4}{2}\right) \text{ and } \left(\frac{.1000 \text{ E } 4 - .1000 \text{ E } 4}{2}\right)$$

which are .1000 E 4 and .0000 E 4 respectively. One of the roots becomes zero due to the limited precision allowed in calculation. Let us reformulate the problem and remembering that in quadratic equation $ax^2 + bx + c = 0$, the product of roots is given by $\frac{c}{a}$, the smaller root may be obtained by dividing (c/a) by the larger root.

So, First root $= .1000 \text{ E } 4$

and Second root $$= \frac{25}{.1000 \text{ E } 4} = \frac{.2500 \text{ E } 2}{.1000 \text{ E } 4} = .2500 \text{ E} - 1$$

Such a situation may be recognised in an algorithm by checking to see if $b^2 >> |\, 4\,ac \,|$.

Example 6. *Find the smaller root of the equation $x^2 - 400\,x + 1 = 0$ using four digit arithmetic.*

Sol. Here $b^2 >> |\, 4ac \,|$ | See Example 5

Roots of equation $ax^2 - bx + c = 0$ are $\frac{b + \sqrt{b^2 - 4ac}}{2a}$ and $\frac{b - \sqrt{b^2 - 4ac}}{2a}$

Product of roots are $\frac{c}{a}$.

$$\therefore \quad \text{Smaller root is } \frac{c/a}{\left(\frac{b + \sqrt{b^2 - 4ac}}{2a}\right)} \text{ i.e., } \frac{2c}{b + \sqrt{b^2 - 4ac}}$$

Here $\quad a = 1 = .1000\text{ E }1,\ b = 400 = .4000\text{ E }3,\quad c = 1 = .1000\text{ E }1$

$$b^2 - 4ac = .1600\text{ E }6 - .4000\text{ E }1 = .1600\text{ E }6 \text{ (to four digit accuracy)}$$

$$\therefore \quad \sqrt{b^2 - 4ac} = .4000\text{ E }3$$

$$\therefore \quad \text{Smaller root} = \frac{2 \times (.1000\text{ E }1)}{.4000\text{ E }3 + .4000\text{ E }3} = \frac{.2000\text{ E }1}{.8000\text{ E }3} = .25\text{ E} - 2 = .0025.$$

Example 7. *Compute the middle value of numbers* $a = 4.568$ *and* $b = 6.762$ *using the four digit arithmetic and compare the result by taking* $c = a + \left(\frac{b-a}{2}\right)$.

Sol. $\quad a = .4568\text{ E }1,\ b = .6762\text{ E }1$

Let c be the middle value of numbers then,

$$c = \frac{a+b}{2} = \frac{.4568\text{ E }1 + .6762\text{ E }1}{.2000\text{ E }1} = \frac{.1133\text{ E }2}{.2000\text{ E }1} = .5665\text{ E }1$$

However if we use the formula

$$c = a + \left(\frac{b-a}{2}\right) = .4568\text{ E }1 + \left(\frac{.6762\text{ E }1 - .4568\text{ E }1}{.2000\text{ E }1}\right)$$

$$= .4568\text{ E }1 + .1097\text{ E }1 = .5665\text{ E }1$$

The results are the same.

Example 8. *Obtain a second degree polynomial approximation to* $f(x) = (1+x)^{1/2}$, $x \in [0, 0.1]$ *using Taylor's series expansion about* $x = 0$. *Use the expansion to approximate* $f(0.05)$ *and bound the truncation error.*

Sol. $\quad f(x) = (1+x)^{1/2}, \qquad f(0) = 1$

$$f'(x) = \frac{1}{2}(1+x)^{-1/2}, \qquad f'(0) = \frac{1}{2}$$

$$f''(x) = -\frac{1}{4}(1+x)^{-3/2}, \qquad f''(0) = -\frac{1}{4}$$

$$f'''(x) = \frac{3}{8}(1+x)^{-5/2}$$

Taylor's series expansion with remainder term may be written as

$$(1+x)^{1/2} = 1 + \frac{x}{2} - \frac{x^2}{8} + \frac{1}{16}\frac{x^3}{[(1+\xi)^{1/2}]^5}\ ;\ 0 < \xi < 0.1$$

The truncation term is given by

$$T = (1+x)^{1/2} - \left(1 + \frac{x}{2} - \frac{x^2}{8}\right) = \frac{1}{16} \cdot \frac{x^3}{[(1+\xi)^{1/2}]^5}$$

We have, $\quad f(0.05) = 1 + \dfrac{0.05}{2} - \dfrac{(0.05)^2}{8} = 0.10246875 \times 10^1$

Bound of the truncation error, for $x \in [0, 0.1]$ is

$$| \text{T} | \leq \frac{(0.1)^3}{16\,[(1+\xi)^{1/2}]^5} \leq \frac{(0.1)^3}{16} = 0.625 \times 10^{-4}.$$

Example 9. *In case of normalized floating point representation, associative and distributive laws are not always valid. Give examples to prove this statement.*

Or

If the normalization on floating point is carried out at each stage, prove the following:

(i) $a\,(b - c) \neq ab - ac$

where $a = .5555\text{ E }1$, $b = .4545\text{ E }1$, $c = .4535\text{ E }1$

(ii) $(a + b) - c \neq (a - c) + b$

where $a = .5665\text{ E }1$, $b = .5556\text{ E} - 1$, $c = .5644\text{ E }1$.

Sol. This is a **consequence** of the normalized floating point representation that the associative and the distributive laws of arithmetic are not always valid.

The following examples are chosen intentionally to illustrate the inaccuracies that may build up due to shifting and truncation of numbers in arithmetic operations.

Non-distributivity of arithmetic

Let
$$a = .5555\text{ E }1$$
$$b = .4545\text{ E }1$$
$$c = .4535\text{ E }1$$
$$(b - c) = .0010\text{ E }1 = .1000\text{ E} - 1$$
$$a(b - c) = (.5555\text{ E }1) \times (.1000\text{ E} - 1)$$
$$= (.0555\text{ E }0) = .5550\text{ E} - 1$$

Also,
$$ab = (.5555\text{ E }1) \times (.4545\text{ E }1) = .2524\text{ E }2$$
$$ac = (.5555\text{ E }1) \times (.4535\text{ E }1) = .2519\text{ E }2$$

$\therefore$
$$ab - ac = .0005\text{ E }2 = .5000\text{ E} - 1$$

Thus,
$$a(b - c) \neq ab - ac$$

which shows the non-distributivity of arithmetic.

Non-associativity of arithmetic

Let
$$a = .5665\text{ E }1$$
$$b = .5556\text{ E} - 1$$
$$c = .5644\text{ E }1$$

$\therefore$
$$(a + b) = .5665\text{ E }1 + .5556\text{ E} - 1$$
$$= .5665\text{ E }1 + .0055\text{ E }1 = .5720\text{ E }1$$
$$(a + b) - c = .5720\text{ E }1 - .5644\text{ E }1 = .0076\text{ E }1 = .7600\text{ E} - 1$$
$$a - c = .5665\text{ E }1 - .5644\text{ E }1 = .0021\text{ E }1 = .2100\text{ E} - 1$$
$$(a - c) + b = .2100\text{ E} - 1 + .5556\text{ E} - 1 = .7656\text{ E} - 1$$

Thus,
$$(a + b) - c \neq (a - c) + b$$

which proves the non-associativity of arithmetic.

2.10. NUMERICAL INSTABILITY

While performing arithmetic operations in normalized floating point representation, we avoid taking the difference of two nearly equal numbers and division of a number by a very small number as they cause a considerable loss of significant digits and magnification of errors in the result.

It is observed that every arithmetic operation, performed during computation, gives rise to some error which once generated may decay or grow in subsequent calculations. In some cases, errors may grow so large as to make the computed result totally redundant and such a procedure is called numerically unstable.

For example, consider $F(x) = \dfrac{1}{1-x^2}$

The exact value of $F(x)$ for $x = 0.9$ is

$$F(x) = 0.526316 \times 10^1 \text{ correct to 6 decimal places.}$$

But if $x' = 0.900005$ (error is in 6th decimal place)

then $$F(x') = 0.526341 \times 10^1$$

Therefore, an error in the sixth place in x has caused an error in the fifth place in $F(x)$. While finding numerical solution of problems, we often encounter problems with two types of numerical instability:

(*i*) **Inherent instability:** It may arise due to ill-conditionedness of the problem. We can avoid this instability by suitable reformulation of the problem.

(*ii*) **Induced instability:** It may arise due to the wrong choice of the method of solution. We can avoid it by a suitable modification of the method of solution.

2.11. ILL-POSED PROBLEM

Take the function $f(x) = \dfrac{1}{x-1}$.

The data is x and the output is $f(x)$.

Note that $f(1.1) = 10$ and $f(1.001) = 1000$

So a change in x of less than 0.1 turns into a change in $f(x)$ of nearly 1000.

Evaluation of $f(x)$ near $x = 1$ is an ill-posed problem.

2.12. MACHINE COMPUTATION

To obtain meaningful results for a given problem using computers, there are five distinct phases:

(*i*) Choice of a method
(*ii*) Designing the algorithm
(*iii*) Flow charting
(*iv*) Programming
(*v*) Computer execution

A method is defined to be a mathematical formula for finding the solution of a given problem. There may be more than one method available to solve the same problem. We should choose the method which suits the given problem best. The inherent assumptions and limitations of the method must be studied carefully.

Once the method has been decided, we must describe a complete and unambiguous set of computational steps to be followed in a particular sequence to obtain the solution. This description is called an **algorithm.** It may be emphasized that the computer is concerned with the algorithm and not with the method. The algorithm tells the computer where to start, what information to use, what operations to be carried out and in which order, what information to be printed and when to stop.

An algorithm has five important features:

(1) finiteness: an algorithm must terminate after a finite number of steps.

(2) definiteness: each step of an algorithm must be clearly defined or the action to be taken must be unambiguously specified.

(3) inputs: an algorithm must specify the quantities which must be read before the algorithm can begin.

(4) outputs: an algorithm must specify the quantities which are to be outputted and their proper place.

(5) effectiveness: an algorithm must be effective which means that all operations are executable.

A **flow chart** is a graphical representation of a specific sequence of steps (algorithm) to be followed by the computer to produce the solution of a given problem. It makes use of the flow chart symbols to represent the basic operations to be carried out. The various symbols are connected by arrows to indicate the flow of information and processing. While drawing a flow chart any logical error in the formulation of the problem or applying the algorithm can be easily seen and corrected.

ASSIGNMENT

1. Represent 44.85×10^6 in normalized floating point mode.
2. Subtract the following two floating point numbers as

   (*i*) .36143448 E 7 – .36132346 E 7

   (*ii*) (.9682 E – 7) – (.3862 E – 9).
3. Explain underflow and overflow conditions of error in floating point's addition and subtraction.
4. Find the solution of the following equation using floating point arithmetic with 4-digit mantissa.

   $$x^2 - 7x + 4 = 0$$

   Give comments on the results so obtained.
5. Explain how floating point numbers are stored in computers. What factors affect their accuracy and range?
6. Calculate the value of $x^2 + 2x - 2$ and $(2x - 2) + x^2$ where $x = .7320$ E 0

   using normalized floating point arithmetic and prove that they are not the same. Compare with value of $(x^2 - 2) + 2x$.
7. Find the value of $(1 + x)^2$ and $(x^2 + 2x) + 1$ when $x = .5999$ E – 2.
8. Find the value of $\sin x \simeq x - \frac{x^3}{3!} + \frac{x^5}{5!}$

   with an absolute error smaller than .005 for $x = .2000$ E 0 using normalized floating point arithmetic with 4 digit mantissa.

9. Define normalized floating point representation of numbers and round off errors in representation. Find the sum of 0.123×10^3 and 0.456×10^2 and write the result in three digit mantissa form.

10. Prove the following consequence of the normalized floating point representation of numbers by taking $x = .6667$

$$6x \neq x + x + x + x + x + x.$$

11. Using floating point arithmetic with 4 digit mantissa, solve the following system of linear equations

$$ax + by = c$$

$$px + qy = r$$

where $a = 2.500$, $b = 5.200$, $c = 6.200$

$p = 1.251$, $q = 2.605$, $r = 3.152$

However, if the value of q is changed to 2.606, will there be any change in the result ? Compare.

12. (*i*) Calculate the value of the polynomial

$$p_3(x) = 2.75x^3 - 2.95x^2 + 3.16x - 4.67$$

for $x = 1.07$ using both chopping and rounding off to three digits, proceeding through the polynomial term by term from left to right. [*U.P.T.U. MCA (C.O.) 2005*]

(*ii*) Explain how floating point numbers are stored in computers. What factors affect their accuracy and range? [*U.P.T.U. (MCA) 2005*]

Answers

1. .4485 E 8

2. (*i*) .1110 E 4 (*ii*) .9644 E – 7

4. .6370 E 1, .6280 E 0

6. – .1000 E – 2, – .2000 E – 3

7. .1010 E 1, .1012 E 1; correct value = .1012034 E 1

8. .1987 E 0

9. $.168 \times 10^3$.

11. (*i*) $x = -$ .3217 E 2, $y =$ .1666 E 2 ; yes

(*ii*) $x = -$ .2352 E 2, $y =$ .1250 E 2.

❑❑❑

3

Roots of Equation

Consider the equation of the form $f(x) = 0$

If $f(x)$ is a quadratic, cubic or biquadratic expression then algebraic formulae are available for expressing the roots. But when $f(x)$ is a polynomial of higher degree or an expression involving transcendental functions *e.g.* $1 + \cos x - 5x$, $x \tan x - \cosh x$, $e^{-x} - \sin x$ etc. algebraic methods are not available.

Here, we shall describe some numerical methods for the solution of $f(x) = 0$, where $f(x)$ is algebraic or transcendental or both.

3.1. BISECTION (OR BOLZANO) METHOD [*U.P.T.U. (MCA) 2004*]

This method is based on the repeated application of intermediate value property.

Let the function $f(x)$ be continuous between a and b. For definiteness, let $f(a)$ be (–)ve and $f(b)$ be (+)ve. Then the first approximation to the root is $x_1 = \frac{1}{2}(a + b)$.

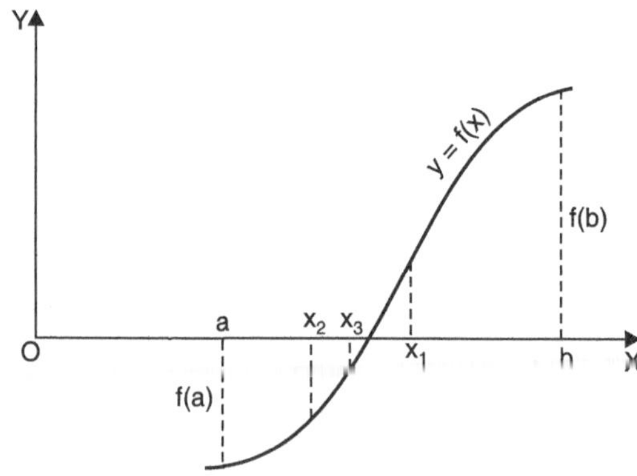

If $f(x_1) = 0$, then x_1 is a root of $f(x) = 0$ otherwise, the root lies between a and x_1 or x_1 and b according as $f(x_1)$ is (+)ve or (–)ve. Then we bisect the interval as before and continue the process until the root is found to desired accuracy.

In the above figure, $f(x_1)$ is (+)ve so that the root lies between a and x_1. Then second approximation to the root is $x_2 = \frac{1}{2}(a + x_1)$. If $f(x_2)$ is (–)ve; the root lies between x_1 and x_2. Then the third approximation to the root is $x_3 = \frac{1}{2}(x_1 + x_2)$ and so on.

We observe that this method uses only the end points of the interval $[a_n, b_n]$ for which $f(a_n) \cdot f(b_n) < 0$ and not the values of $f(x)$ at these end points to obtain the next approximation to the root.

The number of iterations required may be determined from the relation

$$\frac{|b-a|}{2^n} \leq \varepsilon$$

or,
$$n \geq \frac{\ln|b-a| - \ln \varepsilon}{\ln 2}$$

where ε is the permissible error.

This method requires a large number of iterations to achieve a reasonable degree of accuracy for the root. It requires one function evaluation for each iteration. This method is also called as *Bolzano method* or *Interval halving method.*

Once the method of calculation has been decided. We must describe clearly the computational steps to be followed in a particular sequence. These steps constitute the algorithm of method.

3.2. ALGORITHM

[U.P.T.U. (MCA) 2004]

Step 01. Start of the program

Step 02. Input the variables x1, x2 for the task

Step 03. Check f(x1) *f(x2) < 0

Step 04. If yes proceed

Step 05. If no exit and print error message

Step 06. Repeat 7-11 if condition not satisfied

Step 07. x0 = (x1 + x2)/2

Step 08. If f(x0) *f(x1) < 0

Step 09. x2 = x0.

Step 10. ELSE

Step 11. x1 = x0

Step 12. Condition :

Step 13. | (x1–x2)/x1 | < maximum possible error or f(x0) = 0

Step 14. Print output

Step 15. End of program.

3.3. FLOW-CHART

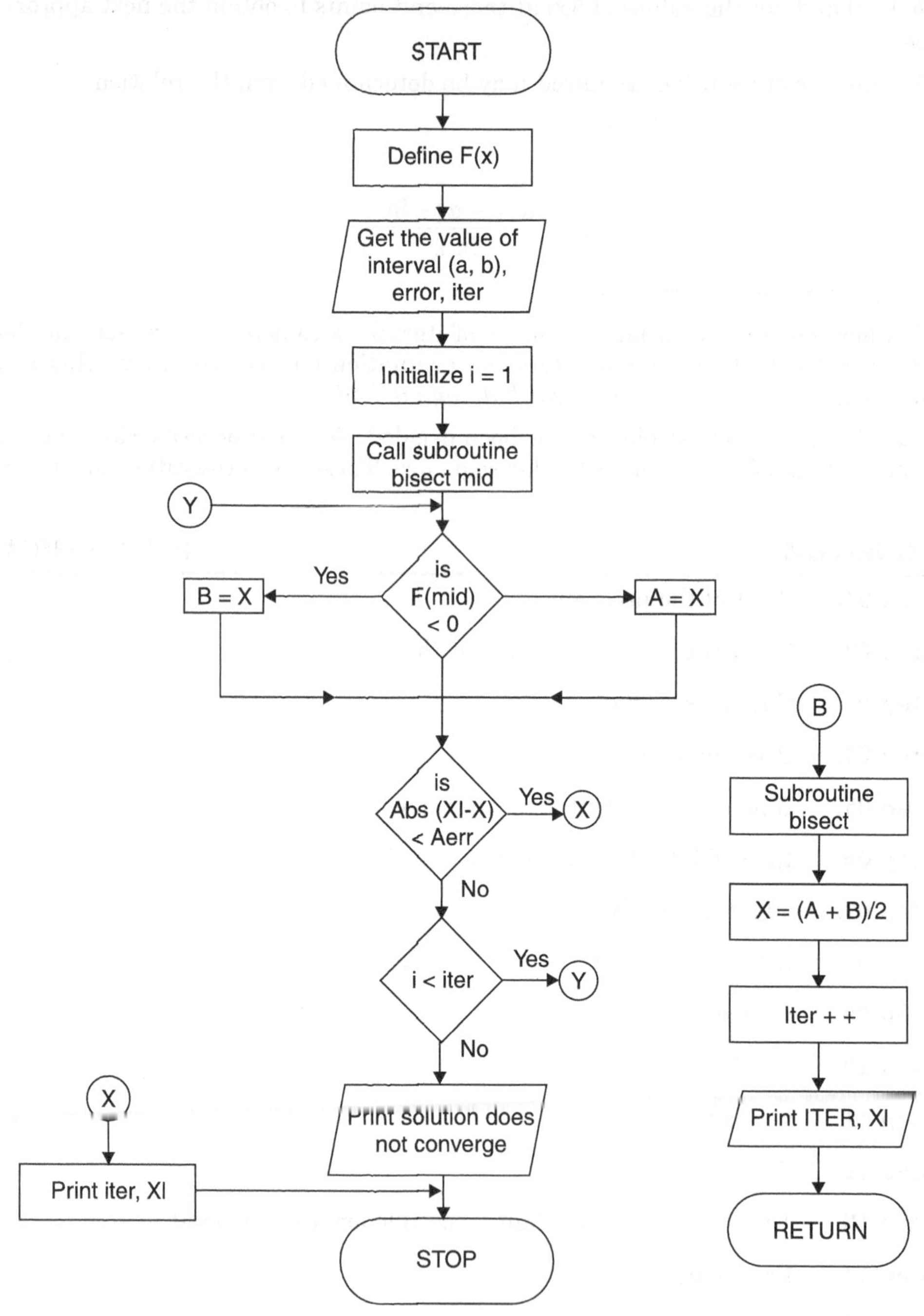

3.4. PROGRAM WRITING

Based on the flow chart, we write the instructions in a code which the computer can understand. A series of such instructions is called a **program.**

If there are any errors in the program, they will be pointed by the computer during compilation. After correcting compilation errors, program is executed with input data to check for logical errors which may be due to misinterpretation of the algorithm. The process of finding the errors and correcting them is called **debugging.**

3.5. ORDER OF CONVERGENCE OF ITERATIVE METHODS

Convergence of an iterative method is judged by the order at which the error between successive approximations to the root decreases.

An iterative method is said to be k^{th} order convergent if k is the largest positive real number such that

$$\lim_{i\to\infty}\left|\frac{e_{i+1}}{e_i^{\,k}}\right| \le \text{A}$$

where A is a non-zero finite number called asymptotic error constant and it depends on derivative of $f(x)$ at an approximate root x.

e_i and e_{i+1} are the errors in successive approximations. k^{th} order convergence gives us idea that in each iteration, the no. of significant digits in each approximation increases k times.

The error in any step is proportional to the kth power of the error in the previous step.

3.6. ORDER OF CONVERGENCE OF BISECTION METHOD

In Bisection method, the original interval is divided into half interval in each iteration. If we take mid-points of successive intervals to be the approximations of the root, one half of the current interval is the upper bound to the error.

In Bisection method,

$$e_{i+1} = 0.5\, e_i \quad \text{or} \quad \frac{e_{i+1}}{e_i} = 0.5 \qquad \ldots(1)$$

where e_i and e_{i+1} are the errors in the ith and $(i + 1)^{\text{th}}$ iterations respectively.

Comparing (1) with

$$\lim_{i\to\infty}\left|\frac{e_{i+1}}{e_i^{\,k}}\right| \le \text{A}$$

we get $k = 1$ and $\text{A} = 0.5$

Thus the *Bisection method is I order convergent or linearly convergent.*

In this method, the error decreases linearly with each step by a factor of 0.5. The convergence is slow. To achieve desired accuracy, a large number of iterations are required.

3.7. CONVERGENCE OF A SEQUENCE

A sequence $< x_n >$ of successive approximations of a root $x = \alpha$ of the equation $f(x) = 0$ is said to converge to $x = \alpha$ with order $p \ge 1$ iff

$$| x_{n+1} - \alpha | \le c \, | x_n - \alpha |^p, n \ge 0$$

c being some constant greater than zero.

Particularly, if $| x_{n+1} - \alpha | = c \, | x_n - \alpha |$, $n \ge 0$, $0 < c < 1$ then convergence is called **geometric.** Also, If $p = 1$ and $0 < c < 1$ then convergence is called **linear** or of first order. Constant c is called the **rate of linear convergence.** Convergence is rapid or slow according as c is near 0 or 1.

Using induction, condition for linear convergence can be simplified to the form

$$| x_n - \alpha | \le c^n \, | x_0 - \alpha |, n \ge 0, 0 < c < 1.$$

3.8. PROVE THAT BISECTION METHOD ALWAYS CONVERGES

Let $[p_n, q_n]$ be the interval at n^{th} step of bisection, having a root of the equation $f(x) = 0$. Let x_n be the nth approximation for the root. Then initially $p_1 = a$ and $q_1 = b$.

$$\Rightarrow \quad x_1 = \text{first approximation} = \left(\frac{p_1 + q_1}{2}\right)$$

$$\Rightarrow \quad p_1 < x_1 < q_1$$

Now either the root lies in $[a, x_1]$ or in $[x_1, b]$.

$\therefore$ either $[p_2, q_2] = [p_1, x_1]$ or $[p_2, q_2] = [x_1, q_1]$

$\Rightarrow$ either $p_2 = p_1, q_2 = x_1$ or $p_2 = x_1, q_2 = q_1$

$$\Rightarrow \quad p_1 \le p_2, q_2 \le q_1$$

Also, $x_2 = \dfrac{p_2 + q_2}{2}$ so that $p_2 < x_2 < q_2$

Continuing this way, we obtain that at n^{th} step,

$$x_n = \frac{p_n + q_n}{2}, \; p_n < x_n < q_n$$

and $\quad p_1 \le p_2 \le \ldots\ldots \le p_n$ and $q_1 \ge q_2 \ge \ldots\ldots \ge q_n$

$\therefore$ $< p_1, p_2, \ldots\ldots, p_n, \ldots\ldots >$ is bounded non-decreasing sequence bounded by b and $< q_1, q_2, \ldots\ldots, q_n, \ldots\ldots >$ is a bounded non-increasing sequence of numbers bounded by a.

Hence both these sequences converge.

Let, $\lim\limits_{n \to \infty} p_n = p$ and $\lim\limits_{n \to \infty} q_n = q$.

Now since length of the interval is decreasing at every step, we get that

$$\lim_{n \to \infty} (q_n - p_n) = 0 \;\Rightarrow\; q = p$$

Also, $\quad p_n < x_n < q_n$

$$\Rightarrow \quad \lim p_n \le \lim x_n \le \lim q_n$$

$$\Rightarrow \quad p \le \lim x_n \le q$$

$$\Rightarrow \quad \lim x_n = p = q \qquad \ldots(1)$$

Further since a root lies in $[p_n, q_n]$, we shall have

$$f(p_n) \,.\, f(q_n) < 0$$

$$\Rightarrow \quad 0 \ge \lim_{n \to \infty} [f(p_n) \,.\, f(q_n)]$$

$$\Rightarrow \quad 0 \ge f(p) \,.\, f(q)$$

$$\Rightarrow \quad 0 \ge [f(p)]^2$$

But $[f(p)]^2 \geq 0$ being a square

$\therefore$ we get $f(p) = 0$

$\therefore$ p is a root of $f(x) = 0$ ...(2)

From (1) and (2), we see that $<x_n>$ converges *necessarily* to a root of equation $f(x) = 0$

The method is not rapidly converging but it is useful in the sense that it converges surely.

EXAMPLES

Example 1. *Find the real root of the equation $x \log_{10} x = 1.2$ by Bisection method correct to four decimal places. Also write its program in C-language.*

Sol. $f(x) = x \log_{10} x - 1.2$ ...(1)

Since, $f(2.74) = -.000563$ *i.e.,* (–)ve

and $f(2.75) = .0081649$ *i.e.,* (+)ve

Hence, a root lies between 2.74 and 2.75.

$\therefore$ First approximation to the root is

$$x_1 = \frac{2.74 + 2.75}{2} = 2.745$$

Now, $f(x_1) = f(2.745) = .003798$ *i.e.,* (+)ve

Hence, root lies between 2.74 and 2.745.

$\therefore$ Second approximation to the root is

$$x_2 = \frac{2.74 + 2.745}{2} = 2.7425$$

Now, $f(x_2) = f(2.7425) = .001617$ *i.e.,* (+)ve

Hence, root lies between 2.74 and 2.7425.

$\therefore$ Third approximation to the root is

$$x_3 = \frac{2.74 + 2.7425}{2} = 2.74125$$

Now, $f(x_3) = f(2.74125) = .0005267$ *i.e.,* (+)ve

Hence, root lies between 2.74 and 2.74125.

$\therefore$ Fourth approximation to the root is

$$x_4 = \frac{2.74 + 2.74125}{2} = 2.740625$$

Now, $f(x_4) = f(2.740625) = -.00001839$ *i.e.,* (–)ve.

Hence, root lies between 2.740625 and 2.74125.

$\therefore$ Fifth approximation to the root is

$$x_5 = \frac{2.740625 + 2.74125}{2} = 2.7409375$$

Now, $f(x_5) = f(2.7409375) = .000254$ *i.e.,* (+)ve

Hence, root lies between 2.740625 and 2.7409375.

$\therefore$ Sixth approximation to the root is

$$x_6 = \frac{2.740625 + 2.7409375}{2} = 2.74078125$$

Now, $f(x_6) = f(2.74078125) = .0001178$ *i.e.,* (+)ve

Hence, root lies between 2.740625 and 2.74078125.

∴ Seventh approximation to the root is

$$x_7 = \frac{2.740625 + 2.74078125}{2} = 2.740703125$$

Now, $f(x_7) = f(2.740703125) = .00004973$ *i.e.,* (+)ve

Hence, root lies between 2.740625 and 2.740703125.

∴ Eighth approximation to the root is

$$x_8 = \frac{2.740625 + 2.740703125}{2} = 2.740664063$$

Now, $f(x_8) = f(2.740664063) = .00001567$ *i.e.,* (+)ve

Hence, root lies between 2.740625 and 2.740664063.

∴ Ninth approximation to the root is

$$x_9 = \frac{2.740625 + 2.740664063}{2} = 2.740644532$$

Since, x_8 and x_9 are same upto four decimal places hence the approximate real root is **2.7406.** C-program for above problem is being given below:

3.9. PROGRAM TO IMPLEMENT BISECTION METHOD (*U.P.T.U. 2009*)

```
//...Included Header Files
#include<stdio.h>
#include<math.h>
#include<conio.h>
#include<process.h>
#include<string.h>
#define EPS          0.00000005
#define F(x)         (x)*log10(x)-1.2
//...Function Prototype Declaration
void Bisect();
//...Global Variable Declaration field
int count=1,n;
float root=1;
//... Main Function Implementation
void main()
           {
           clrscr();
           printf("\n Solution by BISECTION method \n");
           printf("\n Equation is ");
```

```
    printf("\n\t\t\t x*log x) - 1.2 = 0\n\n");
    printf("Enter the number of iterations:");
    scanf("%d",&n);
    Bisect();
    getch();
    }
//... Function Declaration
void Bisect()
    {
    float x0,x1,x2;
    float f0,f1,f2;
    int i=0;
    /*Finding an Approximate ROOT of Given Equation, Having +ve Value*/
    for(x2=1; ;x2++)
        {
        f2=F(x2);
        if (f2>0)
            {
            break;
            }
        }
    /*Finding an Approximate ROOT of Given Equation, Having -ve Value*/
    for(x1=x2-1;;x2--)
        {
        f1=F(x1);
        if(f1<0)
            {
            break;
            }
   }
    //...Printing Result
printf("\t\t-----------------------------------------------");
printf("\n\t\t ITERATIONS\t\t       ROOTS\n");
printf("\t\t-----------------------------------------------");
for(;count<=n;count++)
    {
    x0=(x1+x2)/2.0;
    f0=F(x0);
    if(f0==0)
```

```
                {
                root=x0;
                }
        if(f0*f1<0)
                {
                x2=x0;
                }
        else
                {
                x1=x0;
                f1=f0;
                }
        printf("\n\t\t ITERATION %d", count);
        printf("\t   :\t   %f",x0);
        if(fabs((x1-x2)/x1) < EPS)
          {
         printf("\n\t\t-----------------------------------------");
         printf("\n\t\t        Root = %f",x0);
         printf("\n\t\t  Iterations = %d\n", count);
         printf("\t\t-----------------------------------------");
         getch();
         exit(0);
         }
    }
printf("\n\t\t-----------------------------------------");
printf("\n\t\t\t Root = %7.4f",x0);
printf("\n\t\t\t Iterations = %d\n", count-1);
printf("\t\t-----------------------------------------");
getch();
}
```

OUTPUT

```
 Solution by BISECTION method
 Equation is
                         x* log(x) - 1.2=0
Enter the number of iterations: 15
            -----------------------------------------
              ITERATIONS                      ROOTS
              -----------------------------------------
              ITERATION 1       :            2.500000
```

```
ITERATION 2      :      2.750000
ITERATION 3      :      2.625000
ITERATION 4      :      2.687500
ITERATION 5      :      2.718750
ITERATION 6      :      2.734375
ITERATION 7      :      2.742187
ITERATION 8      :      2.738281
ITERATION 9      :      2.740234
ITERATION 10     :      2.741211
ITERATION 11     :      2.740723
ITERATION 12     :      2.740479
ITERATION 13     :      2.740601
ITERATION 14     :      2.740662
ITERATION 15     :      2.740631

-----------------------------------------
          Root = 2.7406
    Iterations = 15
-----------------------------------------
C:\tc\exe>
```

Example 2. *Find a root of the equation $x^3 - 4x - 9 = 0$ using Bisection method in four stages.*

Sol. Let $f(x) \equiv x^3 - 4x - 9$

Since, $f(2.706) = -.009488$ *i.e.,* (–)ve

and $f(2.707) = .008487$ *i.e.,* (+)ve

Hence, a root lies between 2.706 and 2.707.

$\therefore$ First approximation to the root is

$$x_1 = \frac{2.706 + 2.707}{2} = 2.7065$$

Now, $f(x_1) = -.0005025$ *i.e.,* (–)ve

Hence, root lies between 2.7065 and 2.707.

$\therefore$ Second approximation to the root is

$$x_2 = \frac{2.7065 + 2.707}{2} = 2.70675$$

Now, $f(x_2) = .003992$ *i.e.,* (+)ve

Hence, root lies between 2.7065 and 2.70675.

$\therefore$ Third approximation to the root is

$$x_3 = \frac{2.7065 + 2.70675}{2} = 2.706625$$

Now, $f(x_3) = 0.001744$ *i.e.,* (+)ve

Hence, root lies between 2.7065 and 2.706625.

∴ Fourth approximation to the root is

$$x_4 = \frac{2.7065 + 2.706625}{2} = 2.7065625$$

Hence, the root is **2.706** correct to three decimal places.

Example 3. *Find a positive real root of $x - \cos x = 0$ by bisection method, correct upto 4 decimal places between 0 and 1.*

Sol. Let $f(x) = x - \cos x$

$$f(0.73) = (-)\text{ve} \quad \text{and} \quad f(0.74) = (+)\text{ve}$$

Hence, the root lies between 0.73 and 0.74.

First approximation to the root is

$$x_1 = \frac{0.73 + 0.74}{2} = 0.735$$

Now, $f(0.735) = (-)$ve

Hence, the root lies between 0.735 and 0.74.

Second approximation to the root is

$$x_2 = \frac{0.73 + 0.74}{2} = 0.7375$$

Now, $f(0.7375) = (-)$ve

Hence, the root lies between 0.7375 and 0.74.

Third approximation to the root is

$$x_3 = \frac{0.7375 + 0.74}{2} = 0.73875$$

Now, $f(0.73875) = (-)$ve

Hence, the root lies between 0.73875 and 0.74.

Fourth approximation to the root is

$$x_4 = \frac{1}{2}(0.73875 + 0.74) = 0.739375$$

Now, $f(x_4) = f(0.739375) = (+)$ve

Hence, the root lies between 0.73875 and 0.739375

Fifth approximation to the root is

$$x_5 = \frac{1}{2}(0.73875 + 0.739375) = 0.7390625$$

Now, $f(0.7390625) = (-)$ve

Hence, the root lies between 0.7390625 and 0.739375

Sixth approximation to the root is

$$x_6 = \frac{1}{2}(0.7390625 + 0.739375) = 0.73921875$$

Now, $f(0.73921875) = (+)\text{ve}$

Hence, the root lies between 0.7390625 and 0.73921875

Seventh approximation to the root is

$$x_7 = \frac{1}{2}(0.7390625 + 0.73921875) = 0.73914$$

Now, $f(0.73914) = (+)\text{ve}$

Hence, the root lies between 0.7390625 and 0.73914

Eighth approximate to the root is

$$x_8 = \frac{1}{2}(0.7390625 + 0.73914) = 0.73910$$

Hence, the approximate real root is 0.7391.

Example 4. *Perform five iterations of bisection method to obtain the smallest positive root of equation*

$$f(x) \equiv x^3 - 5x + 1 = 0. \qquad \text{(G.B.T.U. 2011)}$$

Sol. $$f(x) = x^3 - 5x + 1 \qquad \text{...(1)}$$

Since, $f(0.2016) = 0.0001935$ *i.e.,* (+)ve

and $f(0.2017) = -0.0002943$ *i.e.,* (–)ve

Hence, root lies between 0.2016 and 0.2017.

First approximation to the root is

$$x_1 = \frac{0.2016 + 0.2017}{2} = 0.20165$$

Now, $f(x_1) = -0.00005036$ *i.e.,* (–)ve

Hence, root lies between .2016 and .20165.

Second approximation to the root is

$$x_2 = \frac{0.2016 + 0.20165}{2} = 0.201625$$

Now, $f(x_2) = 0.00007159$ *i.e.,* (+)ve

Hence, root lies between .201625 and .20165.

Third approximation to the root is

$$x_3 = \frac{0.201625 + 0.20165}{2} = 0.2016375$$

Now, $f(x_3) = 0.00001061$ *i.e.,* (+)ve

Hence, root lies between 0.2016375 and 0.20165.

Fourth approximation to the root is

$$x_4 = \frac{0.2016375 + 0.20165}{2} = 0.20164375$$

Now, $f(x_4) = -0.00001987$ *i.e.,* (–)ve

Hence, root lies between 0.2016375 and 0.20164375.

∴ Fifth approximation to the root is

$$x_5 = \frac{0.2016375 + 0.20164375}{2} = 0.201640625$$

Hence, after performing five iterations, the **smallest positive root** of the given equation is **.20164** correct to **five decimal places.**

Example 5. *Find a real root of $x^3 - x = 1$ between 1 and 2 by bisection method. Compute five iterations.*

Sol. Here, $f(x) = x^3 - x - 1$ ...(1)

Since, $f(1.324) = -\ .00306$ *i.e.,* (–)ve

and $f(1.325) = .00120$ *i.e.,* (+)ve

Hence, root lies between 1.324 and 1.325.

∴ First approximation to the root is

$$x_1 = \frac{1.324 + 1.325}{2} = 1.3245$$

Now, $f(x_1) = -\ .000929$ *i.e.,* (–)ve

Hence, root lies between 1.3245 and 1.325

∴ Second approximation to the root is

$$x_2 = \frac{1.3245 + 1.325}{2} = 1.32475$$

Now, $f(x_2) = .000136$ *i.e.,* (+)ve

Hence, root lies between 1.3245 and 1.32475.

Third approximation to the root is

$$x_3 = \frac{1.3245 + 1.32475}{2} = 1.324625$$

Now, $f(x_3) = -\ .000396$ *i.e.,* (–)ve

Hence, root lies between 1.324625 and 1.32475.

∴ Fourth approximation to the root is

$$x_4 = \frac{1.324625 + 1.32475}{2} = 1.3246875$$

Now, $f(x_4) = -\ .0001298$ *i.e.,* (–)ve

Hence, root lies between 1.3246875 and 1.32475

∴ Fifth approximation to the root is

$$x_5 = \frac{1.3246875 + 1.32475}{2} = 1.32471875$$

Hence, the real root of the given equation is **1.324** correct to three decimal places after computing five iterations.

Example 6. *Use bisection method to find out the positive square root of 30 correct to 4 decimal places.*

Sol. Let $f(x) = x^2 - 30$ ...(1)

Since, $f(5.477) = -\ 0.00247$ *i.e.,* (–)ve

and $f(5.478) = 0.00848$ *i.e.,* (+)ve

Hence, root lies between 5.477 and 5.478

∴ First approximation to the root is

$$x_1 = \frac{5.477 + 5.478}{2} = 5.4775$$

Now, $f(x_1) = 0.003$ *i.e.,* (+)ve

Hence, root lies between 5.477 and 5.4775

∴ Second approximation to the root is

$$x_2 = \frac{5.477 + 5.4775}{2} = 5.47725$$

Now, $f(x_2) = 0.00026$ *i.e.,* (+)ve

Hence, root lies between 5.477 and 5.47725

∴ Third approximation to the root is

$$x_3 = \frac{5.477 + 5.47725}{2} = 5.477125$$

Now, $f(x_3) = -\ 0.0011$ *i.e.,* (–)ve

Hence, root lies between 5.477125 and 5.47725

∴ Fourth approximation to the root is

$$x_4 = \frac{5.477125 + 5.47725}{2} = 5.4771875$$

Since, x_3 and x_4 are same upto four decimal places hence the positive square root of 30 correct to 4 decimal places is **5.4771.**

ASSIGNMENT

1. (*i*) Transcendental equation is given as

$$f(x) = 2^x - x - 3$$

Calculate $f(x)$ for $x = -4, -3, -2, -1, 0, 1, 2, 3, 4$ and compute, between which integers values roots are lying.

(*ii*) The equation $x^2 - 2x - 3\cos x = 0$ is given. Locate the smallest root in magnitude in an interval of length one unit.

2. Find a real root of $e^x = 3x$ by Bisection method.

3. The smallest positive root of the equation

$$f(x) = x^4 - 3x^2 + x - 10 = 0 \text{ is to be obtained.}$$

(*i*) Find an interval of unit length which contains this root.

(*ii*) Perform two iterations of the bisection method.

4. Find real root lying in interval (1, 2) upto four decimal places for the equation $x^6 - x^4 - x^3 - 1 = 0$ by bisection method.

5. Find a real root of $\cos x = xe^x$ upto three decimal places using Bisection method.(*U.P.T.U. 2008*)

6. The negative root of the smallest magnitude of the equation $f(x) = 3x^3 + 10x^2 + 10x + 7 = 0$ is to be obtained.

(*i*) Find an interval of unit length which contains this root.

(*ii*) Perform two iterations of the bisection method.

7. Compute the root of $f(x) = \sin 10x + \cos 3x$ by computer using Bisection method. The initial approximations are 4 and 5.

8. Find the real root correct to three decimal places for the following equations:

(*i*) $x^3 - x - 4 = 0$ (*ii*) $x^3 - x^2 - 1 = 0$

(*iii*) $x^3 + x^2 - 1 = 0$ (*iv*) $x^3 - 3x - 5 = 0$.

9. Solve $x^3 - 9x + 1 = 0$ for the root between $x = 2$ and $x = 4$ by the method of Bisection. Also find the smallest positive root.

10. (*i*) Find a real root of the equation $x^3 - 2x - 5 = 0$ using Bisection method.

(*ii*) Find a positive root of the equation $xe^x = 1$ which lies between 0 and 1.

11. If a root of $f(x) = 0$ lies in the interval (a, b), then find the minimum number of iterations required when the permissible error is E.

12. Apply Bisection method to find a root of the equation $x^4 + 2x^3 - x - 1 = 0$ in the interval [0, 1].

13. Find the approximate value of the root of the equation $3x = \sqrt{1 + \sin x}$ by bisection method. (five iterations) [*U.P.T.U. (MCA) 2008*]

14. Find a real root of $x^3 - 2x - 1 = 0$ which lies between 1 and 2 by using Bisection method correct to 2 places of decimals.

15. Find a positive root of the equation $x^3 + 3x - 1 = 0$ by bisection method.

Answers

1. (*i*)

x	– 4	– 3	– 2	– 1	0	1	2	3	4
$f(x)$	1.0625	.125	– .75	– 1.5	– 2	– 2	– 1	2	9

Roots lie in (– 3, – 2) and (2, 3).

(*ii*) 1.7281 in interval (1, 2).

2. 1.5121375 **3.** (*i*) (2, 3) (*ii*) Root lies in the interval (2, 2.25).

4. 1.4036 **5.** 0.517

6. (*i*) (– 3, – 2) (*ii*) Root lies in the interval (– 2.5, – 2.25)

7. 4.712389 **8.** (*i*) 1.796 (*ii*) 1.466 (*iii*) 0.755 (*iv*) 2.279

9. 2.94282, 0.111 **10.** (*i*) 2.094551482 (*ii*) 0.56714333 **11.** $n \geq \dfrac{\log_e\left(\dfrac{|b-a|}{E}\right)}{\log_e 2}$

12. 0.8667605 **13.** 0.39188 **14.** 1.618 **15.** 0.322

3.10. FIXED POINT ITERATION METHOD—(Successive Approximation Method)

To find the roots of the equation $f(x) = 0$ by successive approximations, we write it in the form $x = \phi(x)$

The roots of $f(x) = 0$ are the same as the points of intersection of the straight line $y = x$ and the curve representing $y = \phi(x)$.

Let $x = x_0$ be an initial approximation of the desired root α then first approximation x_1 is given by

$$x_1 = \phi(x_0)$$

Now, treating x_1 as the initial value, the second approximation is

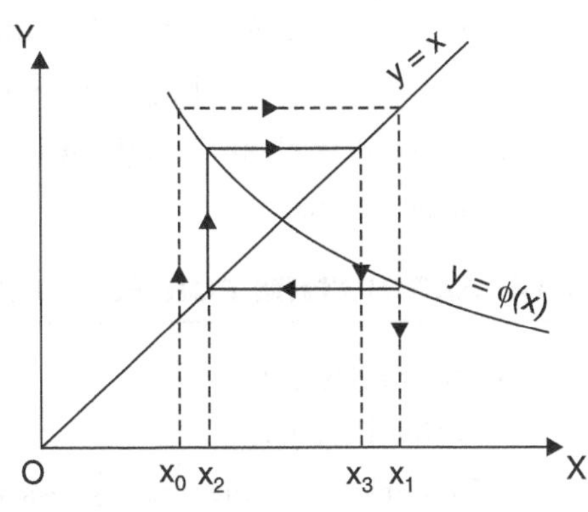

(Working of Iteration method)

$$x_2 = \phi(x_1)$$

Proceeding in this way, the nth approximation is given by

$$x_n = \phi(x_{n-1}).$$

3.11. SUFFICIENT CONDITION FOR CONVERGENCE OF ITERATIONS

Now it is not sure whether the sequence of approximations $x_1, x_2, ..., x_n$ always converges to the same number which is a root of $f(x) = 0$ or not.

As such, we have to choose the initial approximation x_0 suitably so that the successive approximations $x_1, x_2, ..., x_n$ converge to the root α. The following theorem helps in making the right choice of x_0.

3.12. THEOREM

If (*i*) α be a root of $f(x) = 0$ which is equivalent to $x = \phi(x)$*.

(*ii*) I be any interval containing $x = \alpha$.

(*iii*) $|\ \phi'(x)\ | < 1$ for all x in I, then the sequence of approximations $x_0, x_1, x_2, ..., x_n$ will converge to the root α provided the initial approximation x_0 is chosen in I.

Note. This method of iteration is particularly useful for finding the real roots of an equation given in the form of an infinite series.

3.13. CONVERGENCE OF FIXED POINT ITERATION METHOD

Since, α is a root of $x = \phi(x)$, we have $\alpha = \phi(\alpha)$

If x_{n-1} and x_n be two successive approximations to α, we have

$$x_n = \phi(x_{n-1}), \quad x_n - \alpha = \phi(x_{n-1}) - \phi(\alpha) \qquad ...(1)$$

By mean value theorem,

$$\frac{\phi(x_{n-1}) - \phi(\alpha)}{x_{n-1} - \alpha} = \phi'(\xi), \text{ where } x_{n-1} < \xi < \alpha$$

*x is obtained in terms of $\phi(x)$ such that $|\ \phi'(x)\ | < 1$.

Hence (1) becomes, $x_n - \alpha = (x_{n-1} - \alpha)\, \phi'(\xi)$

If $|\phi'(x_i)| \le k < 1$ for all i, then

$$|x_n - \alpha| \le k\,|x_{n-1} - \alpha|, k < 1$$

Hence it is clear that iteration method is linearly convergent.

Note. Smaller the value of $\phi'(x)$, more rapid will be the convergence.

3.14. ALGORITHM FOR FIXED POINT ITERATION METHOD

3.14.1. Algorithm 1

1. Read x_0, e, n

Remarks. x_0 is the initial guess, e is allowed error in root, n is total iterations to be allowed for convergence.

2. $x_1 \leftarrow g(x_0)$

Remarks. Steps 4 to 6 are repeated until the procedure converges to a root or iterations reach n.

3. For $i = 1$ to n in steps of 1 do

4. $x_0 \leftarrow x_1$

5. $x_1 \leftarrow g(x_0)$

6. If $\left|\dfrac{x_1 - x_0}{x_1}\right| \le e$ then, GO TO 9

   end for.

7. Write 'Does not converge to a root', x_0, x_1

8. Stop

9. Write 'converges to a root', i, x_1

10. Stop.

3.14.2. Algorithm 2. (Aliter)

1. Define function $f(x)$
2. Define function $df(x)$
3. Get the value of a, max_err.
4. Initialize j
5. If $df(a) < 1$ then $b = 1$, $a = f(a)$
6. Print root after j, iteration is $f(a)$
7. If $fabs(b - a) >$ max_err then
8. j++, goto (5)

   End if

   Else print root doesn't exist

9. End.

3.15. FLOW-CHART FOR ITERATION METHOD

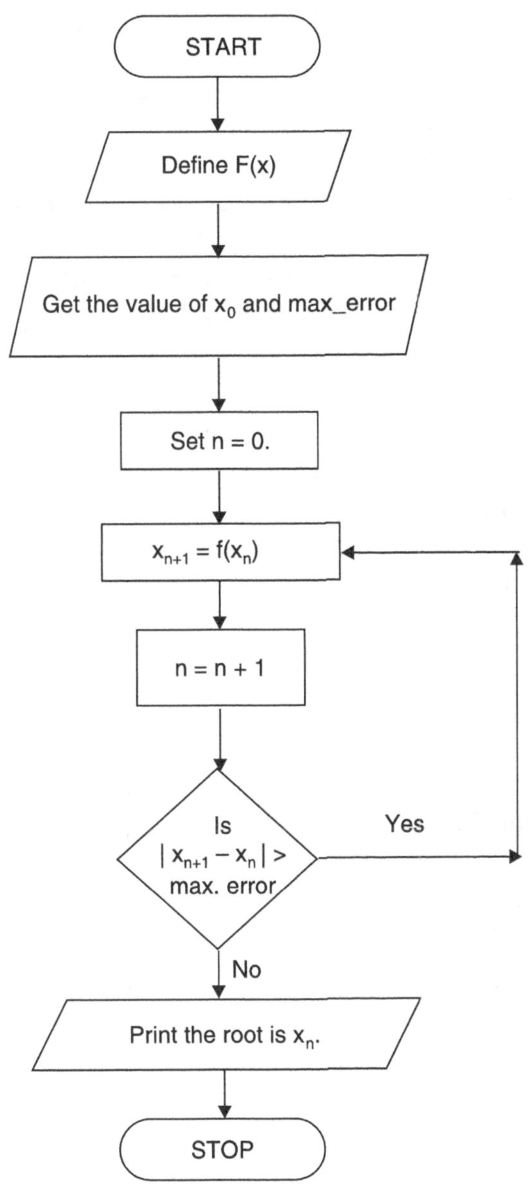

3.16. COMPUTER PROGRAM

```
//Program for Solution by ITERATION method
#include<stdio.h>
#include<math.h>
#include<conio.h>
#define EPS 0.00005
```

```
#define F(x)        (x*x*x + 1)/2
#define f(x)        x*x*x - 2*x + 1
void ITER();
void main ()
{
     clrscr();
     printf("\n\t Solution by ITERATION method \n");
     printf("\n\t Equation is ");
     printf("\n\t\t\t\t X*X*X - 2*X + 1 = 0\n\n");
     ITER();
     getch();
}
void ITER()
{
     float x1,x2,x0,f0,f1,f2,error;
     int i=0,n;
     for(x1=1; ;x1++)
     {
           f1=F(x1);
           if (f1>0)
                 break;
     }
     for(x0=x1-1;;x0--)
    {
     f0=f(x0);
     if(f0<0)
           break;
    }
    x2=(x0+x1)/2;
     printf("Enter the number of iterations:");
     scanf("%d",&n);
     printf("\n\n\t\t The 1 approximation to the root is : %f",x2);
     for(;i<n-1;i++)
     {
     f2=F(x2);
     printf("\n\n\t\t The %d approximation to the root is : %f",i+2,f2);
                 x2=F(x2);
                 error=fabs(f2-f1);
```

```
                if(error<EPS)
                    break;
                f1=f2;
    }
            if(error>EPS)
                printf("\n\n\t NOTE :- The number of iterations are not
sufficient.");
            printf("\n\n\n\t\t\t-----------------------------------");
            printf("\n\t\t\t  The root is %.4f",f2);
            printf("\n\t\t\t---------------------------------------");
    }
```

3.16.1. Output

```
 Solution by ITERATION method
 Equation is
                        x*x*x-2*x+1=0
Enter the number of iterations: 15
               The 1 approximation to the root is :0.000000
               The 2 approximation to the root is :0.500000
               The 3 approximation to the root is :0.562500
               The 4 approximation to the root is :0.588989
               The 5 approximation to the root is :0.602163
               The 6 approximation to the root is :0.609172
               The 7 approximation to the root is :0.613029
               The 8 approximation to the root is :0.615190
               The 9 approximation to the root is :0.616412
               The 10 approximation to the root is :0.617107
               The 11 approximation to the root is :0.617504
               The 12 approximation to the root is :0.617730
               The 13 approximation to the root is :0.617860
               The 14 approximation to the root is :0.617934
               The 15 approximation to the root is :0.617977
            -----------------------------------------------------
               The Root is 0.6179 (Correct to four decimal places)
             ----------------------------------------------------
```

3.16.2. Insufficient Output

```
    Solution by ITERATION method
    Equation is
               x*x*x-2*x+1=0
Enter the no. of Iterations:5
               The 1 approximation to the root is : 0.000000
               The 2 approximation to the root is : 0.500000
```

```
        The 3 approximation to the root is : 0.562500
        The 4 approximation to the root is : 0.588989
        The 5 approximation to the root is : 0.602163
Note. The number of Iterations are not sufficient.
 -----------------------------------------------------
                 The Root is 0.6022
```

EXAMPLES

Example 1. *Find a real root of the equation cos x = 3x – 1 correct to 3 decimal places using iteration method.*

Sol. We have $f(x) = \cos x - 3x + 1 = 0$

Now, $f(0) = 2$ and $f(\pi/2) = -\frac{3\pi}{2} + 1 = (-)\text{ve}$

$\therefore$ A root lies between 0 and $\pi/2$.

Rewriting the given equation as,

$$x = \frac{1}{3}(\cos x + 1) = \phi(x)$$

We have $\phi'(x) = -\frac{\sin x}{3}$ and $|\phi'(x)| = \frac{1}{3}|\sin x| < 1$ in $(0, \pi/2)$

Hence iteration method can be applied and we start with $x_0 = 0$. Then the successive approximations are

$$x_1 = \phi(x_0) = \frac{1}{3}(\cos 0 + 1) = 0.6667$$

$$x_2 = \phi(x_1) = \frac{1}{3}[\cos(0.6667) + 1] = 0.5953$$

$$x_3 = \phi(x_2) = \frac{1}{3}[\cos(0.5953) + 1] = 0.6093$$

$$x_4 = \phi(x_3) = 0.6067$$

$$x_5 = \phi(x_4) = 0.6072$$

$$x_6 = \phi(x_5) = 0.6071.$$

Since, x_5 and x_6 are almost same, the root is 0.607 correct to three decimal places.

Example 2. *Find a real root of* $2x - \log_{10} x = 7$ *correct to four decimal places using iteration method.*

Sol. We have
$$f(x) = 2x - \log_{10} x - 7$$
$$f(3) = 6 - \log 3 - 7 = 6 - 0.4771 - 7 = -1.4471$$
$$f(4) = 0.398$$

$\therefore$ A root lies between 3 and 4.

Rewriting the given equation as

$$x = \frac{1}{2}(\log_{10} x + 7) = \phi(x)$$

We have $\phi'(x) = \frac{1}{2}\left(\frac{1}{x}\log_{10} e\right)$

$\therefore$ $|\phi'(x)| < 1$ when $3 < x < 4$ ($\because$ $\log_{10} e = 0.4343$)

Since, $|f(4)| < |f(3)|$, the root is near 4.

Hence iteration method can be applied.

Take $x_0 = 3.6$, the successive approximations are

$$x_1 = \phi(x_0) = \frac{1}{2}(\log_{10} 3.6 + 7) = 3.77815$$

$$x_2 = \phi(x_1) = \frac{1}{2}(\log_{10} 3.77815 + 7) = 3.78863$$

$$x_3 = \phi(x_2) = 3.78924$$

$$x_4 = \phi(x_3) = 3.78927$$

Since, x_3 and x_4 almost being equal, the root is 3.7892 correct to four decimal places.

Example 3. *Find the smallest root of the equation*

$$1 - x + \frac{x^2}{(2!)^2} - \frac{x^3}{(3!)^2} + \frac{x^4}{(4!)^2} - \frac{x^5}{(5!)^2} + \ldots\ldots = 0.$$

Sol. Writing the given equation as

$$x = 1 + \frac{x^2}{(2!)^2} - \frac{x^3}{(3!)^2} + \frac{x^4}{(4!)^2} - \frac{x^5}{(5!)^2} + \ldots\ldots = \phi(x)$$

Omitting x^2 and higher powers of x, we get $x = 1$ approximately.

Taking $x_0 = 1$, we obtain,

$$x_1 = \phi(x_0) = 1 + \frac{1}{(2!)^2} - \frac{1}{(3!)^2} + \frac{1}{(4!)^2} - \frac{1}{(5!)^2} + \ldots\ldots = 1.2239$$

$$x_2 = \phi(x_1) = 1 + \frac{(1.2239)^2}{(2!)^2} - \frac{(1.2239)^3}{(3!)^2} + \frac{(1.2239)^4}{(4!)^2} - \frac{(1.2239)^5}{(5!)^2} + \ldots\ldots$$

$$= 1.3263$$

Similarly, $x_3 = \phi(x_2) = 1.38$

$$x_4 = 1.409, \quad x_5 = 1.425, \quad x_6 = 1.434, \quad x_7 = 1.439$$

Values of x_6 and x_7 indicate that the root is 1.43 correct to two decimal places.

Example 4. *If* α, β *are the roots of* $x^2 + ax + b = 0$, *show that the iteration* $x_{n+1} = -\left(\frac{ax_n + b}{x_n}\right)$ *will converge near* $x = \alpha$ *if* $|\alpha| > |\beta|$ *and the iteration* $x_{n+1} = \frac{-b}{x_n + a}$ *will converge near* $x = \alpha$ *if* $|\alpha| < |\beta|$.

Sol. Since, α, β are the roots of $x^2 + ax + b = 0$

We have $\alpha + \beta = -a$ and $\alpha\beta = b$

The formula $x_{n+1} = -\left(\dfrac{ax_n + b}{x_n}\right)$ which is of the form $x_{n+1} = f(x_n)$ will converge to $x = \alpha$ if

$$\left|\left[\frac{d}{dx}\left\{\frac{-(ax+b)}{x}\right\}\right]_{x = x_n}\right| < 1$$ | Using condition of iteration method

$$\Rightarrow \quad \left|\frac{b}{{x_n}^2}\right| < 1$$

$$\Rightarrow \quad |{x_n}^2| > |b| \quad \text{or} \quad {x_n}^2 > |b|$$

or $$|\alpha|^2 > |b| \quad \text{as} \quad x_n \to \alpha$$

or $$|\alpha|^2 > |\alpha|\,|\beta| \qquad (\because \alpha\beta = b)$$

or $$|\alpha| > |\beta|$$

Similarly, $x_{n+1} = \dfrac{-b}{x_n + a}$ will converge to $x = \alpha$ if

$$\left|\left[\frac{d}{dx}\left(\frac{-b}{x+a}\right)\right]_{x = x_n}\right| < 1$$

or $$\left|\frac{b}{(x_n + a)^2}\right| < 1$$

or $$(x_n + a)^2 > |b| \quad \text{or} \quad (\alpha + a)^2 > |b| \quad \text{as } x_n \to \alpha$$

or $$\beta^2 > |b| \qquad (\because \alpha + a = -\beta)$$

or $$|\beta|^2 > |\alpha|\,|\beta|$$

or $$|\beta| > |\alpha| \quad \text{or} \quad |\alpha| < |\beta|.$$

Example 5. *The equation $x^4 + x = e$ where e is a small number has a root close to e. Computation of this root is done by the expression $\alpha = e - e^4 + 4e^7$.*

(i) Find an iterative formula $x_{n+1} = F(x_n)$, $x_0 = 0$ for the computation. Show that, we get the above expression after three iterations when neglecting terms of higher order.

(ii) Give a good estimate (of the form Ne^k, where N and k are integers) of the maximum error when the root is estimated by the above expression.

Sol. $x^4 + x = e$ may be written as

$$x = \frac{e}{x^3 + 1}$$

Consider the formula

$$x_{n+1} = \frac{e}{x_n^3 + 1}$$

Starting with $x_0 = 0$, we get

$$x_1 = e$$

$$x_2 = \frac{e}{1 + e^3} = e(1 + e^3)^{-1} = e\,(1 - e^3 + e^6 - \ldots\ldots)$$

$$= e - e^4 + e^7 \qquad \text{(neglecting higher powers of } e)$$

$$x_3 = \frac{e}{1+(e-e^4+e^7)^3}$$

$$= e - e^4 + 4e^7 \qquad \text{(neglecting higher powers of } e)$$

Taking $\alpha = e - e^4 + 4e^7$, we find that

$$\text{error} = \alpha^4 + \alpha - e$$

$$= (e - e^4 + 4e^7)^4 + (e - e^4 + 4e^7) - e$$

$$= 22e^{10} + \text{higher powers of } e.$$

Example 6. *Show that the following rearrangement of equation $x^3 + 6x^2 + 10x - 20 = 0$ does not yield a convergent sequence of successive approximations by iteration method near $x = 1$,*

$$x = (20 - 6x^2 - x^3)/10.$$

Sol. Here,
$$x = \frac{20 - 6x^2 - x^3}{10} = \phi(x)$$

Hence,
$$\phi'(x) = \frac{-12x - 3x^2}{10}$$

Clearly, $\phi'(x) < -1$ in nbd. of $x = 1$. Hence $|\phi'(x)| > 1$ and therefore the method and hence the sequence $< x_n >$ does not converge.

Example 7. *Suggest a value of constant k so that the iteration formula $x = x + k(x^2 - 3)$ may converge at a good rate, given that $x = \sqrt{3}$ is a root.*

Sol. Formula is, $x = \phi(x)$ where $\phi(x) = x + k(x^2 - 3)$

It will converge if

$$|\phi'(x)| < 1 \quad \text{or} \quad -1 < \phi'(x) < 1$$

i.e., if
$$-1 < 1 + 2kx < 1$$

Moreover the convergence will be rapid if $\phi'(a) \simeq 0$

i.e., if
$$1 + 2ka \simeq 0$$

i.e.,
$$1 + 2k\sqrt{3} \simeq 0 \Rightarrow k = -\frac{1}{2\sqrt{3}}$$

We may take $k = -\frac{1}{4}$ to insure a rapid convergence by this formula.

Example 8. *If $F(x)$ is sufficiently differentiable and the iteration $x_{n+1} = F(x_n)$ converges, prove that the order of convergence is a positive integer.*

Sol. Let $x = a$ be a root of the equation $x = F(x)$ then, $a = F(a)$

Let for some p(positive integer)

$$F'(a) = 0, \quad F''(a) = 0, \ \ldots\ldots, F^{(p-1)}(a) = 0 \text{ and } F^{(p)}(a) \neq 0$$

then expanding $F(x_n)$ about a, we get

$$x_{n+1} = F(x_n) = F(a + x_n - a)$$

$$= F(a) + (x_n - a)\,F'(a) + \ldots\ldots + \frac{(x_n - a)^{p-1}}{(p-1)!}F^{(p-1)}(a) + \frac{(x_n - a)^p}{p!}F^{(p)}(\xi)$$

where ξ is some point between $x = x_n$ and $x = a$.

$$\Rightarrow \qquad x_{n+1} = a + \frac{(x_n - a)^p}{p!}F^{(p)}(\xi)$$

$$\Rightarrow \qquad x_{n+1} - a = (x_n - a)^p \,.\, \frac{F^{(p)}(\xi)}{p!}$$

$\therefore$ The order of convergence is p, a positive integer.

Example 9. *The equation $\sin x = 5x - 2$ can be put as $x = \sin^{-1}(5x - 2)$ and also as $x = \frac{1}{5}(\sin x + 2)$ suggesting two iterating procedures for its solution. Which of these, if any, would succeed and which would fall to give root in the neighbourhood of 0.5.*

Sol. In First case, $\phi(x) = \sin^{-1}(5x - 2)$

$$\therefore \qquad \phi'(x) = \frac{5}{\sqrt{1-(5x-2)^2}}$$

Hence, $|\phi'(x)| > 1$ for all x for which $(5x - 2)^2 < 1$ or $x < 3/5$ or $x < 0.6$ in nbd of 0.5. Thus the method would not give a convergent sequence.

In Second case, $\phi(x) = \frac{1}{5}(\sin x + 2)$

$$\therefore \qquad \phi'(x) = \frac{1}{5}\cos x$$

Hence, $|\phi'(x)| \le \frac{1}{5}$ for all x because $|\cos x| \le 1$

$\therefore$ $\phi(x)$ will succeed.

Hence, taking $x = \phi(x) = \frac{1}{5}(\sin x + 2)$ and initial value $x_0 = 0.5$, we have the first approximation x_1 given by

$$x_1 = \frac{1}{5}(\sin 0.5 + 2) = 0.4017$$

$$x_2 = \frac{1}{5}[\sin(0.4017) + 2] = 0.4014$$

$$x_3 = \frac{1}{5}[\sin(0.4014) + 2] = 0.4014$$

Hence, up to four places of decimals, the value of required root is 0.4014.

Example 10. *Starting with $x = 0.12$, solve $x = 0.21\sin(0.5 + x)$ by using iteration method.*

Sol. Here, $x = 0.21 \sin (0.5 + x)$

$\therefore$ First approximation of x is given by

$$x^{(1)} = 0.21 \sin (0.5 + 0.12) = 0.122$$

$$x^{(2)} = 0.21 \sin (0.5 + 0.122) = 0.1224$$

Similarly, $x^{(3)} = 0.12242,\ x^{(4)} = 0.12242$

Obviously, $x^{(3)} = x^{(4)}$

Hence, required root is 0.12242.

Example 11. *Find a real root of the equation $x^3 + x^2 - 1 = 0$ on the interval [0, 1] with an accuracy of 10^{-4} by the iteration method.*

Sol. Here, $f(0) = -1$ and $f(1) = 1$ so a root lies between 0 and 1. Now, $x = \dfrac{1}{\sqrt{1+x}}$ so that,

$$\phi(x) = \frac{1}{\sqrt{1+x}}$$

$$\therefore \qquad \phi'(x) = -\frac{1}{2(1+x)^{3/2}}$$

We have, $|\ \phi'(x)\ | < 1$ for $x < 1$

Hence, iterative method can be applied.

Take, $x_0 = 0.5$, we get

$$x_1 = \phi(x_0) = \frac{1}{\sqrt{1.5}} = 0.81649$$

$$x_2 = \phi(x_1) = \frac{1}{\sqrt{1.81649}} = 0.74196$$

$$x_3 = \phi(x_2) = 0.75767$$

$$x_4 = \phi(x_3) = 0.75427$$

$$x_5 = \phi(x_4) = 0.75500$$

$$x_6 = \phi(x_5) = 0.75485$$

$$x_7 = \phi(x_6) = 0.75488$$

Since, x_6 and x_7 agree up to four decimal places hence the required root is 0.7548.

Example 12. *Find the cube root of 15 correct to four significant figures by iterative method.*

Sol. Let $x = (15)^{1/3} \quad \therefore \quad x^3 - 15 = 0$

Real root of above equation lies in (2, 3). The equation may be written as

$$x = \frac{15 + 20x - x^3}{20} = \phi(x)$$

Now, $\phi'(x) = 1 - \dfrac{3x^2}{20} \quad \therefore \quad |\ \phi'(x)\ | < 1$ (for $x \approx 2.5$)

Iterative formula is $x_{i+1} = \dfrac{15 + 20x_i - x_i^3}{20}$ ...(1)

Put $i = 0, x_0 = 2.5$, we get $x_1 = 2.47$

Put $i = 1$ in (1), $x_2 = 2.466$ (where $x_1 = 2.47$)

Similarly, $x_3 = 2.4661$

$\therefore$ $\sqrt[3]{20}$ correct to 3 decimal places is 2.466.

ASSIGNMENT

1. Apply fixed point iteration method to solve $e^{-x} = 10x$.

   $\left[\textbf{Hint. } |\phi'(x)| = \frac{1}{10}\left|\frac{1}{e^x}\right| < 1 \text{ if } x \geq 0. \right]$

2. Find by iterative method, the real root of the equation $3x - \log_{10} x = 6$ correct to four significant figures.

3. Solve by fixed point iteration method:

   (*i*) $1 + \log x = \frac{x}{2}$ (*ii*) $\sin x = \frac{x+1}{x-1}$ (*iii*) $x^3 = x^2 + x + 1$

   (*iv*) $x^3 + x + 1 = 0$ (*v*) $x^3 - 2x^2 - 5 = 0$ (*vi*) $x^3 - 2x^2 - 4 = 0$.

4. Use the iterative method to find correct to four significant figures, a real root of each of the following equations:

   (*i*) $x = \frac{1}{(x+1)^2}$ (*ii*) $x = (5 - x)^{1/3}$ (*iii*) $\sin x = 10(x - 1)$

   (*iv*) $x \sin x = 1$ (*v*) $e^x = \cot x$ (*vi*) $1 + x^2 - x^3 = 0$

   (*vii*) $x^2 - 1 = \sin^2 x$ (*viii*) $5x^3 - 20x + 3 = 0$.

5. By fixed point iteration method, find $\sqrt{30}$.

6. The root of the equation $x = \frac{1}{2} + \sin x$ by using the iteration method

   $$x_{n+1} = \frac{1}{2} + \sin x_n,\ x_0 = 1$$

   correct to 6 decimal places is $x = 1.497300$. Determine the number of iteration steps required to reach the root by the linear iteration.

7. The equation $f(x) = 0$, where

   $$f(x) = 0.1 - x + \frac{x^2}{(2!)^2} - \frac{x^3}{(3!)^2} + \frac{x^4}{(4!)^2} - \ldots$$

   has one root in the interval (0, 1). Calculate this root correct to 5 decimal places.

8. Find a catenary $y = c \cosh \left(\frac{x-a}{c}\right)$ passing through the points (1, 1) and (2, 3).

9. The equation $x^2 + ax + b = 0$ has two real roots α and β. Show that the iteration method

   $$x_{n+1} = -\left(\frac{{x_n}^2 + b}{a}\right)$$

   is convergent near $x = \alpha$ if $2|\alpha| < |\alpha + \beta|$.

10. Use the method of fixed point iteration to find a positive root, between 0 and 1, of the equation $xe^x = 1$.

11. The equation $x^3 - 5x^2 + 4x - 3 = 0$ has one root near $x = 4$ which is to be computed by the iteration

$$x_{n+1} = \frac{3 + (k-4)\, x_n + 5x_n^2 - x_n^3}{k}, \; k \text{ integer; } x_0 = 4$$

(*i*) Determine which value of k will give the fastest convergence.

(*ii*) Using this value of k, iterate three times and estimate the error in x_3.

[**Hint:** Put $x_n = \alpha + e_n$, $\alpha = 4 + \delta$ where α is exact root. Find the error equation

$$ke_{n+1} = (k - 12)e_n + O(\delta e_n)]$$

Answers

1. 0.0912 **2.** 2.108 **3.** (*i*) 2.9353 (*ii*) – .420365 (*iii*) 1.83928 (*iv*) – .682327803 (*v*) 2.690647448 (*vi*) 2.594313016

4. (*i*) 0.4656 (*ii*) 1.5159 (*iii*) 1.088 (*iv*) 1.114 (*v*) 0.5314 (*vi*) 1.466 (*vii*) 1.404 (*viii*) 0.1508, 1.920

5. 5.4772 **6.** $n = 6$ **7.** 0.10260

8. $c = 0.777305$, $a = 0.424822$ (Take $c_0 = 0.5$) **10.** 0.5671.

11. (*i*) $k = 12$; $x_1 = 4.25$, $x_2 = 4.2122$, $x_3 = 4.2230$, $x_4 = 4.2201$;
Since root is correct to two decimal places, max. error is 0.005.

3.17. THE METHOD OF ITERATION FOR SYSTEM OF NON-LINEAR EQUATIONS

Let the equation be $f(x, y) = 0$, $g(x, y) = 0$ whose real roots are required within a specified accuracy.

We assume, $x = F(x, y)$ and $y = G(x, y)$
where functions F and G satisfy conditions

$$\left|\frac{\partial F}{\partial x}\right| + \left|\frac{\partial F}{\partial y}\right| < 1 \quad \text{and} \quad \left|\frac{\partial G}{\partial x}\right| + \left|\frac{\partial G}{\partial y}\right| < 1 \text{ in nbd. of root.}$$

Let (x_0, y_0) be the initial approximation to a root (α, β) of the system. We construct then successive approximations as

$$x_1 = F(x_0, y_0), \qquad y_1 = G(x_0, y_0)$$
$$x_2 = F(x_1, y_1), \qquad y_2 = G(x_1, y_1)$$
$$x_3 = F(x_2, y_2), \qquad y_3 = G(x_2, y_2)$$
$$\dots\dots\dots\dots\dots\dots\dots\dots\dots$$
$$x_{n+1} = F(x_n, y_n), \qquad y_{n+1} = G(x_n, y_n)$$

If iteration process converges, then we get

$$\alpha = F(\alpha, \beta)$$
$$\beta = G(\alpha, \beta) \text{ in the limit.}$$

Thus α, β are the roots of the system.

Example. *Find a real root of the equations by iteration method*

$$x = 0.2x^2 + 0.8, \quad y = 0.3xy^2 + 0.7.$$

Sol. We have $F(x, y) = 0.2x^2 + 0.8$

$$G(x, y) = 0.3xy^2 + 0.7$$

$$\frac{\partial F}{\partial x} = 0.4x \qquad \frac{\partial G}{\partial x} = 0.3y^2$$

$$\frac{\partial F}{\partial y} = 0 \qquad \frac{\partial G}{\partial y} = 0.6xy$$

It is easy to see that $x = 1$ and $y = 1$ are the roots of the system.

Choosing $x_0 = \frac{1}{2}, y_0 = \frac{1}{2}$, we find that

$$\left|\frac{\partial F}{\partial x}\right|_{(x_0, y_0)} + \left|\frac{\partial F}{\partial y}\right|_{(x_0, y_0)} = 0.2 < 1$$

and $$\left|\frac{\partial G}{\partial x}\right|_{(x_0, y_0)} + \left|\frac{\partial G}{\partial y}\right|_{(x_0, y_0)} = 0.225 < 1$$

∴ Conditions are satisfied. Hence,

$$x_1 = F(x_0, y_0) = \frac{0.2}{4} + 0.8 = 0.85$$

and $$y_1 = G(x_0, y_0) = \frac{0.3}{8} + 0.7 = 0.7375$$

For II approximation, we obtain

$$x_2 = F(x_1, y_1) = 0.2\,(0.85)^2 + 0.8 = 0.9445$$

$$y_2 = G(x_1, y_1) = 0.3\,(0.85)\,(0.7375)^2 + 0.7 = 0.8386$$

Convergence to the root (1, 1) is obvious.

3.18. METHOD OF FALSE POSITION *Or* REGULA-FALSI METHOD

The bisection method guarantees that the iterative process will converge. It is however slow. Thus attempts have been made to speed up* bisection method retaining its guaranteed convergence. A method of doing this is called the **method of false position.**

It is sometimes known as **method of linear interpolation.**

This is the oldest method for finding the real roots of a numerical equation and closely resembles the bisection method.

In this method, we choose two points x_0 and x_1 such that $f(x_0)$ and $f(x_1)$ are of opposite signs. Since the graph of $y = f(x)$ crosses the X-axis between these two points, a root must lie in between these points.

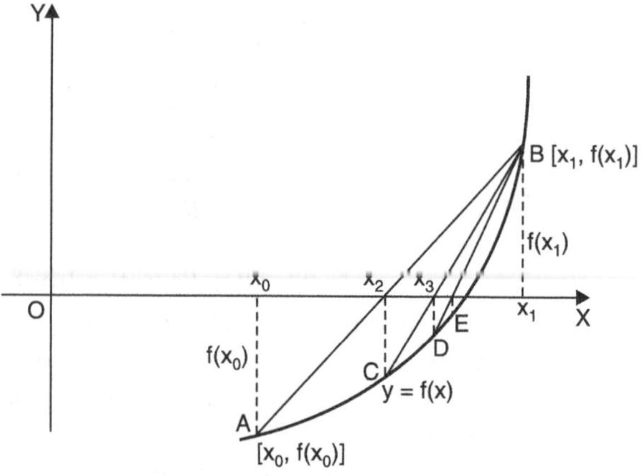

Consequently, $f(x_0)\, f(x_1) < 0$

Equation of the chord joining points $[x_0, f(x_0)]$ and $[x_1, f(x_1)]$ is

$$y - f(x_0) = \frac{f(x_1) - f(x_0)}{x_1 - x_0}(x - x_0)$$

The method consists in replacing the curve AB by means of the chord AB and taking the point of intersection of the chord with X-axis as an approximation to the root.

*Order of convergence greater than 1.

So the abscissa of the point where chord cuts $y = 0$ is given by

$$x_2 = x_0 - \left[\frac{x_1 - x_0}{f(x_1) - f(x_0)}\right] f(x_0) \qquad \ldots(1)$$

which is an approximation to the root.

If now $f(x_0)$ and $f(x_2)$ are of opposite signs, then the root lies between x_0 and x_2. So replacing x_1 by x_2 in (1), we obtain the next approximation x_3. However the root could as well lie between x_1 and x_2 then we find x_3 accordingly.

This procedure is repeated till the root is found to the desired accuracy.

3.19. ALGORITHM

Step 01. Start of the program.
Step 02. Input the variables x0, x1, e, n for the task.
Step 03. f0 = f(x0)
Step 04. f1 = f(x1)
Step 05. for i = 1 and repeat if i < = n
Step 06. x2 = (x0 f1-x1 f0)/(f1-f0)
Step 07. f2 = x2
Step 08. if | f2 | < = e
Step 09. Print "convergent", x2, f2
Step 10. If sign (f2) ! = sign (f0)
Step 11. x1 = x2 & f1 = f2
Step 12. else
Step 13. x0 = x2 & f0 = f2
Step 14. End loop
Step 15. Print output
Step 16. End of program.

3.19.1. Aliter Algorithm: Method of False Position

1. Read x_0, x_1, e, n

Remarks. x_0 and x_1 are two initial guesses to the root s.t. sign $f(x_0) \neq$ sign $f(x_1)$. The prescribed precision is e and n is maximum number of iterations. Steps 2 and 3 are initialization steps.

2. $f_0 \leftarrow f(x_0)$
3. $f_1 \leftarrow f(x_1)$
4. For $i = 1$ to n in steps of 1 do
5. $x_2 \leftarrow (x_0 f_1 - x_1 f_0)/(f_1 - f_0)$
6. $f_2 \leftarrow f(x_2)$
7. If $| f_2 | \leq e$ then
8. Begin write 'convergent solution', x_2, f_2
9. Stop end
10. If sign $(f_2) \neq$ sign (f_0)
11. Then begin $x_1 \leftarrow x_2$
12. $f_1 \leftarrow f_2$ end
13. Else begin $x_0 \leftarrow x_2$
14. $f_0 \leftarrow f_2$ end

end for

15. Write 'Does not converge in n iterations'
16. Write x_2, f_2
17. Stop.

3.20. FLOW-CHART

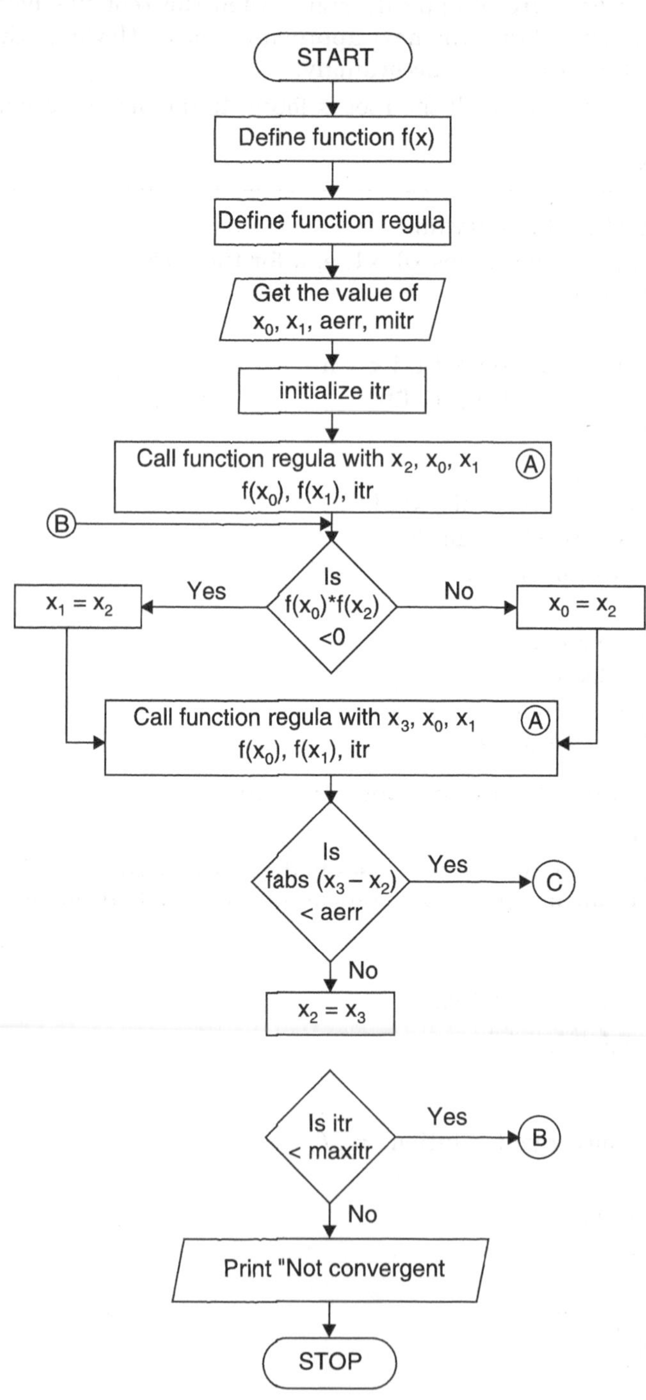

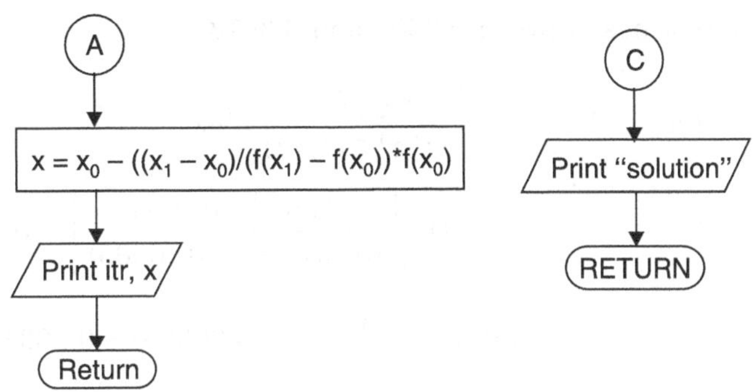

EXAMPLES

Example 1. *Find a real root of the equation $3x + \sin x - e^x = 0$ by the method of false position correct to four decimal places. Choose suitable initial approximations. Also write its program in 'C' language.* (U.P.T.U. 2010)

Sol. Let $f(x) \equiv 3x + \sin x - e^x = 0$

$f(0.3) = -0.154$ *i.e.,* (–)ve

and $f(0.4) = 0.0975$ *i.e.,* (+)ve

∴ The root lies between 0.3 and 0.4.

Using Regula-Falsi method,

$$x_2 = x_0 - \frac{x_1 - x_0}{f(x_1) - f(x_0)} f(x_0)$$

$$= (0.3) - \frac{(0.4) - (0.3)}{(0.0975) - (-0.154)} (-0.154)$$

| ∵ $x_0 = 0.3$ and $x_1 = 0.4$ (let)

$$= (0.3) + \left(\frac{0.1 \times 0.154}{0.2515}\right) = 0.3612$$

Now, $f(x_2) = f(0.3612) = 0.0019 =$ (+)ve

Hence, the root lies between 0.3 and 0.3612.

Now, again, $x_3 = x_0 - \frac{(x_2 - x_0)}{f(x_2) - f(x_0)} f(x_0)$ | Replacing x_1 by x_2

$$= (0.3) - \left\{\frac{(0.3612) - (0.3)}{(0.0019) - (-0.154)}\right\} (-0.154)$$

$$= (0.3) + \left(\frac{0.0612}{0.1559}\right)(0.154) = 0.3604$$

Now, $f(x_3) = f(0.3604) = -0.00005 =$ (–)ve

∴ The root lies between 0.3604 and 0.3612.

Now, again, $$x_4 = x_3 - \left\{\frac{x_2 - x_3}{f(x_2) - f(x_3)}\right\} f(x_3)$$ | Replacing x_0 by x_3

$$= (0.3604) - \left[\frac{(0.3612 - 0.3604)}{(0.0019) - (-0.00005)}\right](-0.00005)$$

$$= 0.3604 + \left(\frac{0.0008}{0.00195}\right)(0.00005) = 0.36042$$

Since, x_3 and x_4 are approximately the same hence the required real root is **0.3604** correct to four decimal places.

```
/* ******************************************************************
Program to Implement the Method of Regula-Falsi (False Position)
****************************************************************** */
// ... Included Header files
#include<stdio.h>
#include<math.h>
#include<conio.h>
#include<string.h>
#include<process.h>

//...Formulae declaration
#define EPS                     0.00005
#define f(x)                    3*x+sin(x)-exp(x)

//...Function Declaration Prototype
void FAL_POS();

//...Main Execution Thread
void main()
     {
     clrscr();
     printf("\n Solution by FALSE POSITION method\n");
     printf("\n Equation is ");
     printf("\n\t\t\t 3*x + sin(x)-exp(x)=0\n\n");
     FAL_POS();
     }
//...Function Definition
void FAL_POS()
```

```
{
float f0,f1,f2;
float x0,x1,x2;
int itr;
int i;
printf("Enter the number of iteration:");
scanf("%d",&itr);
for(x1=0.0;;)
        {
        f1=f(x1);
        if(f1>0)
                {
                break;
                }
        else
                {
                x1=x1+0.1;
                }
}
x0=x1-0.1;
f0=f(x0);
printf("\n\t\t-----------------------------------------------------");
printf("\n\t\t     ITERATION\t x2\t\t F(x)\n");
printf("\t\t-----------------------------------------------------");
for(i=0;i<itr;i++)
        {
        x2=x0-((x1-x0)/(f1-f0))*f0;
        f2=f(x2);
        if(f0*f2>0)
                {
                x1=x2;
                f1=f2;
                }
        else
                {
                x0=x2;
                f0=f2;
                }
        if(fabs(f(2))>EPS)
                {
```

```
                printf("\n\t\t                  %d\t%f\t%f\n",i+1,x2,f2);
                }

         }
    printf("\t\t---------------------------------------------------");
    printf("\n\t\t\t\tRoot=%f\n",x2);
    printf("\t\t---------------------------------------------------");
    getch();
}
```

OUTPUT

```
Solution by FALSE POSITION method
Equation is
                 3*x+sin(x)-exp(x)=0
Enter the number of iteration: 6

    -------------------------------------------------------
    ITERATION              X2                    F(x)
    -------------------------------------------------------
        1               0.361262              0.002101
        2               0.360409             -0.000031
        3               0.360422              0.000000
        4               0.360422             -0.000000
        5               0.360422              0.000000
        6               0.360422              0.000000
    -------------------------------------------------------
                        Root=0.360422
    -------------------------------------------------------
```

Example 2. *Find the root of the equation $xe^x = \cos x$ in the interval (0, 1) using Regula-Falsi method correct to four decimal places. Write its computer programme in 'C' language.*

[U.P.T.U. (MCA) 2006]

Sol. Let $f(x) = \cos x - xe^x = 0$ so that

$$f(0) = 1, f(1) = \cos 1 - e = -2.17798$$

i.e., the root lies between 0 and 1.

By Regula-Falsi method,

$$x_2 = x_0 - \frac{(x_1 - x_0)}{f(x_1) - f(x_0)} f(x_0) = 0 - \frac{1-0}{-3.17798}(1) = 0.31467$$

Now, $f(x_2) = f(0.31467) = 0.51987$

i.e., the root lies between 0.31487 and 1.

Again, $$x_3 = 0.31487 - \frac{(1-0.31487)}{(-2.17798 - 0.51987)}(0.51987) = 0.44673$$

Now, $f(x_3) = 0.20356$

∴ The root lies between 0.44673 and 1. Repeating this process, $x_{10} = 0.51775$ corrected as 0.5177 upto 4 decimal places.

COMPUTER PROGRAMME

```
\\METHOD OF FALSE POSITION
#include<stdio.h>
#include<conio.h>
#include<math.h>
float f(float x)
{
return cos(x)-x*exp(x);
}
void regula (float *x, float x0,float x1, float fx0, float fx1,int*itr)
{
*x=x0-((x1-x0)/(fx1-fx0))*fx0;
++(*itr);
printf("Iteration no.%3d x=%7.5f\n",*itr,*x);
}
main()
{
     int itr=0,maxitr;
     float x0,x1,x2,x3,aerr;
     printf("Enter the values for x0,x1, allowed error, max.iteration\n");
     scanf("%f%f%f%d",&x0,&x1,&aerr,&maxitr);
     regula(&x2,x0,x1,f(x0),f(x1),&itr);
     do
     {           if(f(x0)*f(x2)<0)
                       x1=x2;
                 else
                       x0=x2;
                 regula(&x3,x0,x1,f(x0),f(x1),&itr);
                 if(fabs(x3-x2)<aerr)
           {
                 printf("After %d iterations, root=%6.4f\n",itr,x3);
                 getch();
                 return (0);
           }
```

```
            x2=x3;
}while (itr<maxitr);
printf("Solution does not converge, iterations not sufficient\n");
getch();
return(1);
```

OUTPUT

```
Enter the values for x0,x1, allowed error, max.iteration
0
1
.00005
20
Iteration no.   1 x = 0.31467
Iteration no.   2 x = 0.44673
Iteration no.   3 x = 0.49402
Iteration no.   4 x = 0.50995
Iteration no.   5 x = 0.51520
Iteration no.   6 x = 0.51692
Iteration no.   7 x = 0.51748
Iteration no.   8 x = 0.51767
Iteration no.   9 x = 0.51773
Iteration no.  10 x = 0.51775
After 10 iterations, root = 0.5177
```

Example 3. *Solve $x^3 - 5x + 3 = 0$ by using Regula-Falsi method.*

Sol. Let $f(x) = x^3 - 5x + 3$

Since, $f(0.65) = 0.024625$ and $f(0.66) = -0.012504$

Hence, root lies between 0.65 and 0.66.

Let $x_0 = 0.65$ and $x_1 = 0.66$

Using method of false position,

$$x_2 = x_0 - \left\{\frac{x_1 - x_0}{f(x_1) - f(x_0)}\right\} f(x_0)$$

$$= 0.65 - \left(\frac{0.66 - 0.65}{-0.012504 - 0.024625}\right)(0.024625)$$

$$= 0.656632282$$

Now, $f(x_2) = -0.00004392$

Hence, root lies between 0.65 and 0.656632282.

Using method of false position,

$$x_3 = x_0 - \left\{\frac{x_2 - x_0}{f(x_2) - f(x_0)}\right\} f(x_0)$$ | Replacing x_1 by x_2

$$= 0.65 - \left(\frac{0.656632282 - 0.65}{-0.00004392 - 0.024625}\right)(0.024625)$$

$$= 0.656620474.$$

Since, x_2 and x_3 agree upto 4 decimal places hence the required root is **0.6566** correct up to four decimal places. Similarly the other roots of this equation are 1.8342 and – 2.4909.

Example 4. *Find the root of the equation tan x + tanh x = 0 which lies in the interval (1.6, 3.0) correct to four significant digits using method of false position.* (G.B.T.U. 2013)

Sol. Let $f(x) \equiv \tan x + \tanh x = 0$

Since, $f(2.35) = -0.03$ and $f(2.37) = 0.009$

Hence, the root lies between 2.35 and 2.37.

Using Regula-Falsi method,

$$x_2 = x_0 - \left\{\frac{x_1 - x_0}{f(x_1) - f(x_0)}\right\} f(x_0)$$

$$= 2.35 - \left(\frac{2.37 - 2.35}{0.009 + 0.03}\right)(-0.03)$$ | Let $x_0 = 2.35$ and $x_1 = 2.37$

$$= 2.35 + \left(\frac{0.02}{0.039}\right)(0.03) = 2.365$$

Now, $f(x_2) = -0.00004$ (–)ve

Hence, the root lies between 2.365 and 2.37.

Using Regula-Falsi method,

$$x_3 = x_2 - \left\{\frac{x_1 - x_2}{f(x_1) - f(x_2)}\right\} f(x_2)$$ | Replacing x_0 by x_2

$$= 2.365 - \left(\frac{2.37 - 2.365}{0.009 + 0.00004}\right)(-0.00004)$$

$$= 2.365 + \left(\frac{0.005}{0.00904}\right)(0.00004) = 2.365$$

Hence, the required root is **2.365** correct to four significant digits.

Example 5. *Using the method of false position, find the root of equation* $x^6 - x^4 - x^3 - 1 = 0$ *up to four decimal places.*

Sol. Let $f(x) = x^6 - x^4 - x^3 - 1$

$f(1.4) = -0.056, \quad f(1.41) = 0.102$

Hence, the root lies between 1.4 and 1.41.

Using method of false position,

$$x_2 = x_0 - \left\{\frac{x_1 - x_0}{f(x_1) - f(x_0)}\right\} f(x_0)$$

$$= 1.4 - \left(\frac{1.41 - 1.4}{0.102 + 0.056}\right)(-0.056)$$ | Let, $x_0 = 1.4$ and $x_1 = 1.41$

$$= 1.4 + \left(\frac{0.01}{0.158}\right)(0.056) = 1.4035$$

Now, $f(x_2) = -0.0016$ (–)ve

Hence, the root lies between 1.4035 and 1.41.

Using the method of false position,

$$x_3 = x_2 - \left\{\frac{x_1 - x_2}{f(x_1) - f(x_2)}\right\} f(x_2)$$ | Replacing x_0 by x_2

$$= 1.4035 - \left(\frac{1.41 - 1.4035}{0.102 + 0.0016}\right)(-0.0016) = 1.4036$$

Now, $f(x_3) = -0.00003$ (–)ve

Hence, the root lies between 1.4036 and 1.41.

Using the method of false position,

$$x_4 = x_3 - \left\{\frac{x_1 - x_3}{f(x_1) - f(x_3)}\right\} f(x_3)$$

$$= 1.4036 + \left(\frac{1.41 - 1.4036}{0.102 + 0.00003}\right)(0.00003) = 1.4036$$

Since, x_3 and x_4 are approximately the same upto four places of decimal, hence the required root of the given equation is **1.4036.**

Example 6. *Find a real root of the equation $x \log_{10} x = 1.2$ by Regula-Falsi method correct to four decimal places.*

Sol. Let $f(x) = x \log_{10} x - 1.2$ ...(1)

Since, $f(2.74) = -0.0005634$ and $f(2.741) = 0.0003087$

Hence, the root lies between 2.74 and 2.741.

Using method of False position,

$$x_2 = x_0 - \left\{\frac{x_1 - x_0}{f(x_1) - f(x_0)}\right\} f(x_0)$$ | Let $x_0 = 2.74$ and $x_1 = 2.741$

$$= 2.74 - \left\{\frac{2.741 - 2.74}{0.0003087 - (-0.0005634)}\right\}(-0.0005634)$$

$$= 2.74 + \left(\frac{0.001}{0.0008721}\right)(0.0005634)$$

$$= 2.740646027$$

Now, $\quad f(x_2) = -\ 0.00000006016 \quad$ *i.e.,* (–)ve

Hence, the root lies between 2.740646027 and 2.741.

Using method of false position,

$$x_3 = x_2 - \left\{\frac{x_1 - x_2}{f(x_1) - f(x_2)}\right\} f(x_2) \qquad \text{| Replacing } x_0 \text{ by } x_2$$

$$= 2.740646027 - \left(\frac{2.741 - 2.740646027}{0.0003087 + 0.00000006016}\right)(-\ 0.00000006016)$$

$$= 2.740646096$$

Since, x_2 and x_3 agree upto seven decimal places, the required root correct to four decimal places is **2.7406.**

Example 7. (*i*) *Apply False position method to find smallest positive root of the equation* $x - e^{-x} = 0$ *correct to three decimal places.*

(*ii*) *Using Regula-Falsi method, compute the smallest positive root of the equation* $xe^x - 2 = 0$, *correct up to four decimal places.* (U.P.T.U. 2006)

Sol. (*i*) Let $\quad f(x) = x - e^{-x}$

Since $\quad f(0.56) = -\ 0.01121 \quad$ and $\quad f(0.58) = 0.0201$

Hence, root lies between 0.56 and 0.58.

Let $\quad x_0 = 0.56 \quad$ and $\quad x_1 = 0.58$

Using method of false position,

$$x_2 = x_0 - \left\{\frac{x_1 - x_0}{f(x_1) - f(x_0)}\right\} f(x_0)$$

$$= 0.56 - \left(\frac{0.58 - 0.56}{0.0201 + 0.01121}\right)(-\ 0.01121) = 0.56716$$

Now, $\quad f(x_2) = 0.00002619 \quad$ *i.e.,* (+)ve

Hence the root lies between 0.56 and 0.56716.

Using method of false position,

$$x_3 = x_0 - \left\{\frac{x_2 - x_0}{f(x_2) - f(x_0)}\right\} f(x_0) \qquad \text{| Replacing } x_1 \text{ by } x_2$$

$$= 0.56 - \left(\frac{0.56716 - 0.56}{0.00002619 + 0.01121}\right)(-0.01121)$$

$$= 0.567143$$

Since, x_2 and x_3 agree up to four decimal places, the required root correct to three decimal places is **0.567.**

(*ii*) Let $f(x) = xe^x - 2$

Since, $f(0.852) = -0.00263$ and $f(0.853) = 0.001715$

Hence, root lies between 0.852 and 0.853.

Let $x_0 = 0.852$ and $x_1 = 0.853$

Using method of false position,

$$x_2 = x_0 - \left\{\frac{x_1 - x_0}{f(x_1) - f(x_0)}\right\} f(x_0)$$

$$= 0.852 - \left\{\frac{0.853 - 0.852}{0.001715 - (-0.00263)}\right\}(-0.00263) = 0.852605293$$

Now $f(x_2) = -0.00000090833$

Hence, root lies between 0.852605293 and 0.853

Using method of false position,

$$x_3 = x_2 - \left\{\frac{x_1 - x_2}{f(x_1) - f(x_2)}\right\} f(x_2) \qquad | \text{ Replacing } x_0 \text{ by } x_2$$

$$= (0.852605293) - \left\{\frac{0.853 - 0.852605293}{0.001715 - (-0.00000090833)}\right\}(-0.00000090833)$$

$$= 0.852605501$$

Since, x_2 and x_3 agree up to 6 decimal places, hence the required root correct to 4 decimal places is **0.8526.**

3.21. CONVERGENCE OF REGULA-FALSI METHOD *(M.T.U. 2013)*

If $< x_n >$ be the sequence of approximations obtained from

$$x_{n+1} = x_n - \frac{(x_n - x_{n-1})}{f(x_n) - f(x_{n-1})} f(x_n) \qquad \text{...(1)}$$

and α be the exact value of the root of equation $f(x) = 0$, then

Let $x_n = \alpha + e_n,\ x_{n+1} = \alpha + e_{n+1}$

where e_n, e_{n+1} being errors involved in n^{th} and $(n + 1)^{\text{th}}$ approximations respectively.

Clearly, $f(\alpha) = 0$. Hence (1) gives,

$$\alpha + e_{n+1} = \alpha + e_n - \frac{(e_n - e_{n-1})}{f(\alpha + e_n) - f(\alpha + e_{n-1})} . f(\alpha + e_n)$$

or
$$e_{n+1} = \frac{e_{n-1} f(\alpha + e_n) - e_n f(\alpha + e_{n-1})}{f(\alpha + e_n) - f(\alpha + e_{n-1})}$$

$$= \frac{e_{n-1}\left[f(\alpha) + e_n f'(\alpha) + \frac{e_n^2}{2!} f''(\alpha) + \ldots\ldots\right] - e_n\left[f(\alpha) + e_{n-1} f'(\alpha) + \frac{e_{n-1}^2}{2!} f''(\alpha) + \ldots\ldots\right]}{\left[f(\alpha) + e_n f'(\alpha) + \frac{e_n^2}{2!} f''(\alpha) + \ldots\ldots\right] - \left[f(\alpha) + e_{n-1} f'(\alpha) + \frac{e_{n-1}^2}{2!} f''(\alpha) + \ldots\ldots\right]}$$

$$= \frac{(e_{n-1} - e_n) f(\alpha) + \frac{e_{n-1} e_n}{2!} (e_n - e_{n-1}) f''(\alpha) + \ldots\ldots}{(e_n - e_{n-1}) f'(\alpha) + \frac{(e_n - e_{n-1})(e_n + e_{n-1})}{2!} f''(\alpha) + \ldots\ldots}$$

$$= \frac{\frac{e_{n-1} e_n}{2} f''(\alpha) + \ldots\ldots}{f'(\alpha) + \left(\frac{e_n + e_{n-1}}{2}\right) f''(\alpha) + \ldots\ldots} \qquad | \because \; f(\alpha) = 0$$

or
$$e_{n+1} \approx \frac{e_n e_{n-1}}{2!} \frac{f''(\alpha)}{f'(\alpha)} \qquad \ldots(2) \qquad \text{(neglecting high powers of } e_n, e_{n-1})$$

or
$$e_{n+1} = c\, e_n\, e_{n-1} \qquad \ldots(3)$$

where $c = \frac{1}{2}\frac{f''(\alpha)}{f'(\alpha)}$. Relation of the form (3) is called the error equation.

If the function $f(x)$ in the equation $f(x) = 0$ is convex in the interval (x_0, x_1) that contains the root, then one of the points x_0 or x_1 is always fixed and the other point varies with n. If the point x_0 is fixed then the function $f(x)$ is approximated by the straight line passing through the points (x_0, f_0) and (x_n, f_n), $k = 1, 2, \ldots$. The error equation (3) becomes

$$e_{n+1} = c\, e_0\, e_n$$

where $e_0 = x_0 - \alpha$ is independent of n. Therefore, we can write

$$e_{n+1} = c^* e_n$$

where $c^* = c\, e_0$ is the asymptotic error constant. Hence **the Regula-Falsi method has linear rate of convergence.**

ASSIGNMENT

1. Solve $x^3 - 9x + 1 = 0$ for the root lying between 2 and 4 by the method of false position.
2. Find real cube root of 18 by Regula-Falsi method.
3. Find the smallest positive root correct to three decimal places of the equation $\cosh x \cos x = -1$.
4. Find all the roots of $\cos x - x^2 - x = 0$ to 5 decimal places.
5. A root of the equation $f(x) = x - \phi(x) = 0$ can often be determined by combining the iteration method with Regula-Falsi.

   (*i*) With a given approximate value x_0, we compute

   $$x_1 = \phi(x_0),\ x_2 = \phi(x_1)$$

   (*ii*) Observing that $f(x_0) = x_0 - x_1$ and $f(x_1) = x_1 - x_2$, we find a better approximation x' using Regula-Falsi on the points $(x_0, x_0 - x_1)$ and $(x_1, x_1 - x_2)$.

   (*iii*) This last x' is taken as a new x_0 and we start from (*i*) all over again.

   Compute the smallest root of the equation $x - 5 \log_e x = 0$ with an error less than 0.5×10^{-4} starting with $x_0 = 1.3$.
6. Solve the following equations by Regula-Falsi method.

   (*i*) $(5 - x) e^x = 5$ near $x = 5$ (*ii*) $x^3 + x - 1 = 0$ near $x = 1$

   (*iii*) $2x - \log_{10} x = 7$ lying between 3.5 and 4 (*iv*) $x^3 + x^2 - 3x - 3 = 0$ lying between 1 and 2

   (*v*) $x^3 - 3x + 4 = 0$ between -2 and -3 (*vi*) $x^4 + x^3 - 7x^2 - x + 5 = 0$ lying between 2 and 3.
7. Find the real root of the equations

   (*i*) $x^3 - 4x + 1 = 0$ (*ii*) $x^3 - x^2 - 2 = 0$

   (*iii*) $x^3 + x - 3 = 0$ (*iv*) $x^3 - 5x - 7 = 0$

   by using method of false position.
8. Find the real root of the equations

   (*i*) $x^4 - x^3 - 2x^2 - 6x - 4 = 0$ (*ii*) $x^6 - x^4 - x^3 - 3 = 0$

   (*iii*) $xe^x = 3$ (*iv*) $x^2 - \log_e x - 12 = 0$

   by using method of false position.
9. (*i*) Explain Regula-Falsi method by stating at least one advantage over bisection method.

   (*ii*) Discuss method of false position. (*G.B.T.U. 2011, U.P.T.U. 2009*)

   (*iii*) State Regula-Falsi method. Explain with example.
10. (*i*) Find the rate of convergence for Regula-Falsi method. (*M.T.U. 2013*)

    (*ii*) Determine the order of convergence of the iterative method

    $$x_{k+1} = \frac{x_0\, f(x_k) - x_k\, f(x_0)}{f(x_k) - f(x_0)}$$

    for finding a simple root of the equation $f(x) = 0$
11. Find a real root of the following equations by Regula-Falsi method

    (*i*) $\cos x = 3x - 1$ (*G.B.T.U. 2011*) (*ii*) $2x(1 - x^2 + x) \ln x = x^2 - 1$ (*U.P.T.U. 2014*)

    (*iii*) $x^3 - 5x + 1 = 0$ (*M.T.U. 2012*) (*iv*) $x^4 - x - 10 = 0$ (*G.B.T.U. 2012*)

Answers

1. 2.942821 **2.** 2.620741394 **3.** 1.875 **4.** – 1.25115 and 0.55000

5. 1.2959

6. (*i*) 4.9651142 (*ii*) .682327803 (*iii*) 3.7892782 (*iv*) 1.73205
(*v*) – 2.195823345 (*vi*) 2.0608526

7. (*i*) 1.860, .2541 (*ii*) 1.69562 (*iii*) 1.2134 (*iv*) 2.7473

8. (*i*) 2.7320506 (*ii*) 1.501844 (*iii*) 1.04991 (*iv*) 3.5425

10. (*ii*) linear : $e_{k+1} = ce_0e_k$

11. (*i*) 0.607 (*ii*) 1, 0.3279 (*iii*) 0.2016 (*iv*) 1.855

3.22. SECANT METHOD

This method is quite similar to that of Regula-Falsi method except for the condition $f(x_1) . f(x_2) < 0$. Here the graph of the function $y = f(x)$ in the neighbourhood of the root is approximated by a secant line or chords. Further the interval at each iteration may not contain the root. This method is also called as **chord method.**

Let initially the limits of interval be x_0 and x_1.

Then the first approximation is given by

$$x_2 = x_1 - \left[\frac{x_1 - x_0}{f(x_1) - f(x_0)}\right] f(x_1)$$

Again, the formula for successive approximation in general form is

$$x_{n+1} = x_n - \left[\frac{x_n - x_{n-1}}{f(x_n) - f(x_{n-1})}\right] f(x_n)$$

In case at any stage $f(x_n) = f(x_{n-1})$, this method will fail.

Hence, this method does not converge always while Regula-Falsi method will always converge. The only advantage in this method lies in the fact that if it converges, then it will converge more rapidly than the Regula-Falsi method.

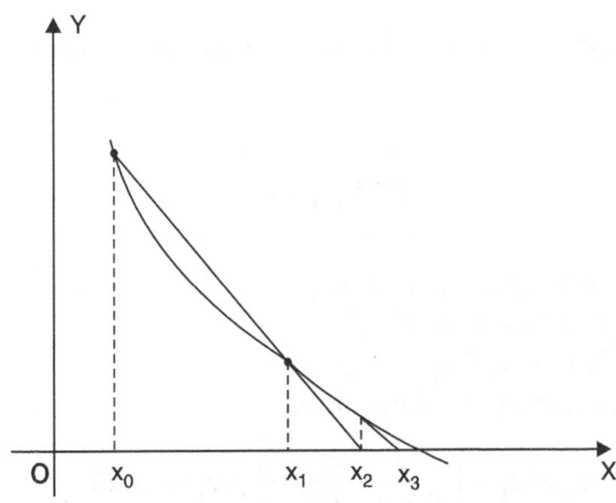

Secant Method

3.23. CONVERGENCE OF SECANT METHOD

From the article 3.21, we have

$$e_{n+1} \approx \frac{e_n\, e_{n-1}}{2!} \frac{f''(\alpha)}{f'(\alpha)} \qquad \ldots(2)$$

where the terms have their usual meanings.

Let $e_{n+1} = c\, e_n^{\,k}$ where c is a constant and $k > 0$

$$\therefore \qquad e_n = c\, e_{n-1}^{\,k} \quad \text{or} \quad e_{n-1} = c^{-1/k}\, e_n^{\,1/k}$$

$$\therefore \text{ From (2),} \qquad c\, e_n^{\,k} = \frac{e_n\, c^{-1/k}}{2!}\, e_n^{\,1/k} \frac{f''(\alpha)}{f'(\alpha)}$$

$$= \frac{c^{-1/k}}{2!}\, e_n^{\,1+1/k} \frac{f''(\alpha)}{f'(\alpha)}$$

Comparing two sides, we get

$$k = 1 + \frac{1}{k} \quad \text{and} \quad c = \frac{c^{-1/k}}{2!} \frac{f''(\alpha)}{f'(\alpha)}$$

Now,
$$k = 1 + \frac{1}{k} \;\Rightarrow\; k^2 - k - 1 = 0 \;\Rightarrow\; k = 1.618$$

Also,
$$c = c^{-1/k} \cdot \frac{1}{2} \frac{f''(\alpha)}{f'(\alpha)}$$

$$\Rightarrow \qquad c^{1+1/k} = c^{1.618} = \frac{1}{2} \frac{f''(\alpha)}{f'(\alpha)}$$

$$\Rightarrow \qquad c = \left[\frac{1}{2} \frac{f''(\alpha)}{f'(\alpha)}\right]^{0.618}$$

This gives rate of convergence and $k = 1.618$ gives the order of convergence of secant method.

EXAMPLES

Example 1. *A real root of the equation $f(x) = x^3 - 5x + 1 = 0$ lies in the interval (0, 1). Perform four iterations of the secant method.*

Sol. We have, $x_0 = 0$, $x_1 = 1$, $f(x_0) = 1$, $f(x_1) = -3$

By Secant Method, First approximation is

$$x_2 = x_1 - \left[\frac{x_1 - x_0}{f(x_1) - f(x_0)}\right] f(x_1) = 0.25$$

$$f(x_2) = -0.234375.$$

Second approximation is

$$x_3 = x_2 - \left[\frac{x_2 - x_1}{f(x_2) - f(x_1)}\right] f(x_2) = 0.186441$$

$$f(x_3) = 0.074276$$

Third approximation is

$$x_4 = x_3 - \left[\frac{x_3 - x_2}{f(x_3) - f(x_2)}\right] f(x_3) = 0.201736$$

$$f(x_4) = -\ 0.000470$$

Fourth approximation is

$$x_5 = x_4 - \left[\frac{x_4 - x_3}{f(x_4) - f(x_3)}\right] f(x_4) = 0.201640.$$

Example 2. *Compute root of the equation $x^2e^{-x/2} = 1$ in the interval [0, 2] using secant method. The root should be correct to three decimal places.*

Sol. We have,

$$x_0 = 1.42, \quad x_1 = 1.43, \quad f(x_0) = -\ 0.0086, \quad f(x_1) = 0.00034.$$

By secant method, first approximation is

$$x_2 = x_1 - \left[\frac{x_1 - x_0}{f(x_1) - f(x_0)}\right] f(x_1)$$

$$= 1.43 - \left(\frac{1.43 - 1.42}{0.00034 + 0.0086}\right) (0.00034) = 1.4296$$

$$f(x_2) = -\ 0.000011$$

Second approximation is

$$x_3 = x_2 - \left[\frac{x_2 - x_1}{f(x_2) - f(x_1)}\right] f(x_2)$$

$$= 1.4296 - \left(\frac{1.4296 - 1.42}{-\ 0.000011 - 0.00034}\right) (-\ 0.000011) = 1.4292$$

Since x_2 and x_3 agree up to three decimal places hence the required root is **1.429.**

ASSIGNMENT

1. Write the procedure of secant method to find a root of a polynomial equation to implement it in 'C'.
2. The equation $x^2 - 2x - 3 \cos x = 0$ is given
   (*i*) Locate the smallest root in magnitude in an interval of length one unit.
   (*ii*) Hence, find this root correct to 3 decimals using the secant method.
3. Use secant method to determine the root of the equation $\cos x - xe^x = 0$. Choose suitable initial approximation.

Answers

2. (*ii*) 1.728 **3.** 0.5177573637.

3.24. POLYNOMIAL EQUATIONS

Consider a real polynomial equation of degree n

$$P_n(x) = a_0x^n + a_1x^{n-1} + ... + a_{n-1}\, x + a_n = 0;\ a_0 \neq 0$$

where $a_0, a_1, ..., a_n$ are real numbers.

If all the roots (real and complex) of a polynomial equation are to be determined, it is always useful to know the following facts about the roots :

(*i*) Exact number of real and complex roots along with their multiplicity.

(*ii*) The interval in which each real root lies.

3.25. DESCARTES' RULE OF SIGNS

The number of positive real roots of $P_n(x) = 0$ cannot exceed the number of sign changes in $P_n(x)$ and the number of negative real roots of $P_n(x) = 0$ cannot exceed the number of sign changes in $P_n(-x)$.

3.26. STURM SEQUENCE

Let $f(x)$ be a given polynomial of degree n and let $f_1(x)$ be its first order derivative. Denote by $f_2(x)$, the remainder of $f(x)$ divided by $f_1(x)$ taken with the reverse sign and $f_3(x)$ for the remainder of $f_1(x)$ divided by $f_2(x)$ with the reverse sign and so on until a constant is arrived at. We thus obtain a sequence of functions $f(x), f_1(x), f_2(x), ..., f_n(x)$ which are called the Sturm sequence or the Sturm functions. We can multiply or divide the elements of sturm sequence by any non-zero positive constant to avoid rational coefficients.

EXAMPLE

Example. *Find the number of real and complex roots of the polynomial equations*

(*i*) $4x^4 + 2x^2 - 1 = 0$

(*ii*) $x^4 - 4x^3 + 3x^2 + 4x - 4 = 0$ *using Sturm sequences.*

Sol. (*i*) We have

$$f(x) = 4x^4 + 2x^2 - 1$$

$$f_1(x) = 16x^3 + 4x \text{ or as } f_1(x) = 4x^3 + x$$

Now,
$$\frac{f(x)}{f_1(x)} = x + \frac{x^2 - 1}{4x^3 + x}$$

$\therefore$
$$f_2(x) = -\left[\text{Remainder of } \frac{f(x)}{f_1(x)}\right] = 1 - x^2$$

Now,
$$\frac{f_1(x)}{f_2(x)} = \frac{4x^3 + x}{1 - x^2} = -4x + \frac{5x}{1 - x^2}$$

$\therefore \qquad f_3(x) = -5x$ or as $f_3(x) = -x$

Now, $\qquad \dfrac{f_2(x)}{f_3(x)} = \dfrac{1-x^2}{-x} = x + \dfrac{1}{-x}$

$\therefore \qquad f_4(x) = -1$

Let V(a) denote the number of sign changes is Sturm's sequence at $x = a$. We construct the following table of sign changes in the Sturm sequence:

x	$f(x)$	$f_1(x)$	$f_2(x)$	$f_3(x)$	$f_4(x)$	V(x)
$-\infty$	+	–	–	+	–	3
– 1	+	–	0 (–)	+	–	3
0	–	0 (–)	+	0 (+)	–	2
1	+	+	0 (+)	–	–	1
∞	+	+	–	–	–	1

We note that if any element in Sturm sequence becomes 0 for some value of x, we give to it the sign of the immediate preceding element.

We observe that the polynomial has two real roots in the interval (– 1, 0) and one in the interval (0, 1). Therefore the polynomial has a pair of complex roots.

(*ii*) We have

$$f(x) = x^4 - 4x^3 + 3x^2 + 4x - 4$$
$$f_1(x) = 2x^3 - 6x^2 + 3x + 2$$
$$f_2(x) = x^2 - 3x + 2$$
$$f_3(x) = x - 2$$

When we divide $f_2(x)$ by $f_3(x)$, we get zero as the remainder. Hence $f_3(x)$ is the last element of the Sturm sequence. Hence $x = 2$ is a double root of the polynomial. Now we divide each element of the Sturm sequence by $x - 2$ and obtain the new sequence as

$$f^*(x) = x^3 - 2x^2 - x + 2$$
$$f_1^*(x) = 2x^2 - 2x - 1$$
$$f_2^*(x) = x - 1$$
$$f_3^*(x) = 1$$

Table of sign changes :

x	$f^*(x)$	$f_1^*(x)$	$f_2^*(x)$	$f_3^*(x)$	V(x)
$-\infty$	–	+	–	+	3
– 1.5	–	+	–	+	3
0	+	–	–	+	2
1.5	–	+	+	+	1
2.5	+	+	+	+	0
∞	+	+	+	+	0

The polynomial has two simple roots in the intervals (– 1.5, 0) and (0, 1.5) and a double root in the interval (1.5, 2.5).

Now we proceed to discuss some methods also useful for obtaining **complex roots** of polynomial equations $f(x) = 0$.

3.27. LIN-BAIRSTOW'S METHOD FOR QUADRATIC FACTORS

This method is applied to obtain complex roots of an algebraic equation with real coefficients. The complex roots of such an equation occur in pairs $a \pm ib$. Each such pair corresponds to a quadratic factor

$$\{x - (a + ib)\}\{x - (a - ib)\} = x^2 - 2ax + a^2 + b^2 = x^2 + px + q$$

where coefficients p and q are real.

Let, $f(x) = x^n + a_1 x^{n-1} + \ldots\ldots + a_{n-1} x + a_n$

If we divide $f(x)$ by $x^2 + px + q$, we obtain a quotient

$$Q_{n-2} = x^{n-2} + b_1 x^{n-3} + \ldots\ldots + b_{n-2}$$

and a remainder $R_n = Rx + S$

Thus, $$f(x) = (x^2 + px + q)(x^{n-2} + b_1 x^{n-3} + \ldots\ldots + b_{n-2}) + Rx + S \quad \ldots(1)$$

If $x^2 + px + q$ divides $f(x)$ completely, the remainder $Rx + S = 0$ *i.e.*, $R = 0, S = 0$. Obviously R and S both depend upon p and q.

So, our problem is to find p and q such that

$$R(p, q) = 0, \quad S(p, q) = 0 \quad \ldots(2)$$

Let $p + \Delta p$, $q + \Delta q$ be the actual values of p and q which satisfy (2) then,

$$R(p + \Delta p, q + \Delta q) = 0 \; ; \quad S(p + \Delta p, q + \Delta q) = 0$$

To find the corrections $\Delta p, \Delta q$, we have the following equations

$$c_{n-2}\,\Delta p + c_{n-3}\,\Delta q = b_{n-1}$$

$$(c_{n-1} - b_{n-1})\,\Delta p + c_{n-2}\,\Delta q = b_n$$

After finding the values of b_i' s and c_i' s by synthetic division scheme, we obtain approximate values of Δp and Δq say Δp_0 and Δq_0.

If p_0, q_0 be the initial approximations then their improved values are

$$p_1 = p_0 + \Delta p_0, \; q_1 = q_0 + \Delta q_0.$$

Now taking p_1 and q_1 as the initial values and repeating the process, we can get better values of p and q.

Remark 1. Synthetic division scheme is as follows

$a_0\ (= 1)$	a_1	a_2	$a_3 \ldots\ldots a_{n-2}$	a_{n-1}	a_n	
	$-pb_0$	$-pb_1$	$-pb_2 \ldots\ldots -pb_{n-3}$	$-pb_{n-2}$	$-pb_{n-1}$	$-p$
		$-qb_0$	$-qb_1 \ldots\ldots -qb_{n-4}$	$-qb_{n-3}$	$-qb_{n-2}$	$-q$
$b_0\ (= 1)$	b_1	b_2	$b_3 \ldots\ldots b_{n-2}$	b_{n-1}	b_n	
	$-pc_0$	$-pc_1$	$-pc_2 \ldots\ldots -pc_{n-3}$	$-pc_{n-2}$		$-p$
		$-qc_0$	$-qc_1 \ldots\ldots -qc_{n-4}$	$-qc_{n-3}$		$-q$
$c_0\ (= 1)$	c_1	c_2	$c_3 \ldots\ldots c_{n-2}$	c_{n-1}		

Remark 2. Values of p_0 and q_0 should be given, otherwise we pick values of p and q which make R and S both zero. But one is usually not so lucky.

Remark 3. Bairstow's method works well only if the starting trial values of p and q are close to the correct values. In this case the convergence is quite rapid. If the starting values are arbitrarily chosen then the method does not converge but very often diverges.

Note. Δp, Δq provide new guesses. Process is repeated until approximate error falls below prespectified tolerance.

$$|\varepsilon_p| = \left|\frac{\Delta p_i}{p_{i+1}}\right| \times 100\% \quad \text{and} \quad |\varepsilon_q| = \left|\frac{\Delta q_i}{q_{i+1}}\right| \times 100\%.$$

EXAMPLES

Example 1. *Solve $x^4 - 5x^3 + 20x^2 - 40x + 60 = 0$ given that all the roots of $f(x) = 0$ are complex, by using Lin-Bairstow method. Take the values as $p_0 = -4$, $q_0 = 8$.*

Sol. Starting with the values $p_0 = -4$, $q_0 = 8$, we have

1	−5	20	−40	60	
–	4	−4	32	0	4
		−8	8	−64	−8
1	−1	8	$0(= b_{n-1})$	$-4(= b_n)$	
	4	12	48		4
		−8	−24		−8
1	$3(= c_{n-3})$	$12(= c_{n-2})$	$24(= c_{n-1})$		

$$\therefore \quad c_{n-1} - b_{n-1} = 24 - 0 = 24 \quad \text{...(1)}$$

Corrections Δp_0 and Δq_0 are given by,

$$c_{n-2}\,\Delta p_0 + c_{n-3}\,\Delta q_0 = b_{n-1} \Rightarrow 12\,\Delta p_0 + 3\,\Delta q_0 = 0 \quad \text{...(2)}$$

and $$(c_{n-1} - b_{n-1})\,\Delta p_0 + c_{n-2}\,\Delta q_0 = b_n \Rightarrow 24\,\Delta p_0 + 12\,\Delta q_0 = -4 \quad \text{...(3)}$$

Solving (2) and (3), we get

$$\Delta p_0 = 0.1667, \quad \Delta q_0 = -0.6667$$

$$\therefore \quad p_1 = p_0 + \Delta p_0 = -3.8333$$

$$q_1 = q_0 + \Delta q_0 = 7.3333$$

Also, $$|\varepsilon_p| = \left|\frac{\Delta p_0}{p_1}\right| \times 100\% = \left|\frac{0.1667}{-3.8333}\right| \times 100\% = 4.3487\%$$

and $$|\varepsilon_q| = \left|\frac{\Delta q_0}{q_1}\right| \times 100\% = \left|\frac{-0.6667}{7.3333}\right| \times 100\% = 9.0914\%$$

Now, repeating same process *i.e.*, dividing $f(x)$ by $x^2 - 3.8333x + 7.3333$, we get

1	– 5	20	– 40	60	
	3.8333	– 4.4723	31.4116	– 0.125	3.8333
		– 7.3333	8.5558	– 60.092	– 7.3333
1	– 1.1667	8.1944	– 0.0326	– 0.217	
			$\begin{pmatrix} \parallel \\ b_{n-1} \end{pmatrix}$	$\begin{pmatrix} \parallel \\ b_n \end{pmatrix}$	
	3.8333	10.2219	42.4845		3.8333
		– 7.3333	– 19.555		– 7.3333
1	2.6666	11.083	22.8969		
	$(= c_{n-3})$	$(= c_{n-2})$	$(= c_{n-1})$		

$$\therefore \qquad c_{n-1} - b_{n-1} = 22.8969 - (-0.0326) = 22.9295$$

Corrections Δp_1 and Δq_1 are given by,

$$11.083\ \Delta p_1 + 2.6666\ \Delta q_1 = -0.0326$$
$$22.9295\ \Delta p_1 + 11.083\ \Delta q_1 = -0.217$$

Solving, we get $\quad \Delta p_1 = 0.0033 \quad$ and $\quad \Delta q_1 = -0.0269$

$$\therefore \qquad p_2 = p_1 + \Delta p_1 = -3.83$$
$$q_2 = q_1 + \Delta q_1 = 7.3064$$

Also,
$$|\varepsilon_p| = \left|\frac{\Delta p_1}{p_2}\right| \times 100\% = \left|\frac{0.0033}{-3.83}\right| \times 100\% = 0.08616\%$$

and
$$|\varepsilon_q| = \left|\frac{\Delta q_1}{q_2}\right| \times 100\% = \left|\frac{-0.0269}{7.3064}\right| \times 100\% = 0.3682\%$$

So, one of the quadratic factors of $f(x)$ is

$$x^2 - 3.83x + 7.3064 \qquad \ldots(4)$$

If $\alpha \pm i\beta$ be its roots, then, $\quad 2\alpha = 3.83, \quad \alpha^2 + \beta^2 = 7.3064$

giving, $\quad \alpha = 1.9149, \quad \beta = 1.9077$

Hence, a pair of roots is $1.9149 \pm 1.9077i$

To find the remaining two roots of $f(x) = 0$, we divide $f(x)$ by (4) as follows

1	– 5	20	– 40	60	
	3.83	– 4.4811	31.4539		3.83
		– 7.3064	8.5485	– 60.0038	– 7.3064
1	– 1.17	8.2125	0.0024	– 0.0038	
			≈ 0	≈ 0	

The other quadratic factor is $x^2 - 1.17x + 8.2125$

If $\gamma \pm i\delta$ be its roots then, $\quad 2\gamma = 1.17, \quad \gamma^2 + \delta^2 = 8.2125$

giving, $\quad \gamma = 0.585, \quad \delta = 2.8054$

Hence, the pair of roots is $0.585 \pm 2.8054\ i$.

Example 2. *Find a quadratic factor of the polynomial*

$$x^4 + 5x^3 + 3x^2 - 5x - 9 = 0$$

starting with $p_0 = 3$, $q_0 = -5$ *by using Bairstow's method.*

Sol. We have

1	5	3	– 5	– 9	
	– 3	– 6	– 6	3	– 3
		5	10	10	5
1	2	2	$-1(=b_{n-1})$	$4(=b_n)$	
	– 3	3	– 30		– 3
		5	– 5		5
1	– 1	10	– 36		
	↓	↓	↓		
	c_{n-3}	c_{n-2}	c_{n-1}		

$$\therefore \qquad c_{n-1} - b_{n-1} = -36 + 1 = -35$$

Corrections Δp_0 and Δq_0 are given by

$$c_{n-2}\,\Delta p_0 + c_{n-3}\,\Delta q_0 = b_{n-1} \quad \Rightarrow \quad 10\,\Delta p_0 - \Delta q_0 = -1 \qquad \text{...(1)}$$

and $$(c_{n-1} - b_{n-1})\,\Delta p_0 + c_{n-2}\,\Delta q_0 = b_n \quad \Rightarrow \quad -35\,\Delta p_0 + 10\,\Delta q_0 = 4 \qquad \text{...(2)}$$

Solving (1) and (2), we get

$$\Delta p_0 = -0.09, \quad \Delta q_0 = 0.08$$

Thus p_1, q_1, the first approximations of p and q are given by

$$p_1 = p_0 + \Delta p_0 = 2.91$$

$$q_1 = q_0 + \Delta q_0 = -4.92$$

$$|\,\varepsilon_p\,| = \left|\frac{\Delta p_0}{p_1}\right| \times 100\% = \left|\frac{-0.09}{2.91}\right| \times 100\% = 3.0927\%$$

$$|\,\varepsilon_q\,| = \left|\frac{\Delta q_0}{q_1}\right| \times 100\% = \left|\frac{0.08}{-4.92}\right| \times 100\% = 1.6260\%.$$

Repeating same process *i.e.,* dividing $f(x)$ by $x^2 + 2.91x - 4.92$, we get

1	5	3	– 5	– 9	
	– 2.91	– 6.08	– 5.35	0.20	– 2.91
		4.92	10.28	9.05	4.92
1	2.09	1.84	– 0.07	0.25	
	– 2.91	2.37	– 26.57		– 2.91
		4.92	– 4.03		4.92
1	– 0.82	9.13	– 30.67		

At this step, the corrections Δp_1 and Δq_1 are given by,

$$9.13\,\Delta p_1 - 0.82\,\Delta q_1 = -0.07$$

$$-30.60\,\Delta p_1 + 9.13\,\Delta q_1 = 0.25$$

$$\Rightarrow \qquad \Delta p_1 = -0.00745, \; \Delta q_1 = 0.00241$$

Hence, second approximation of p and q are given by,

$$p_2 = p_1 + \Delta p_1 = 2.91 - 0.00745 = 2.90255$$

$$q_2 = q_1 + \Delta q_1 = -4.92 + 0.00241 = -4.91759$$

$$|\varepsilon_p| = \left|\frac{\Delta p_1}{p_2}\right| \times 100\% = \left|\frac{-0.00745}{2.90255}\right| \times 100\% = 0.2566\%$$

$$|\varepsilon_q| = \left|\frac{\Delta q_1}{q_2}\right| \times 100\% = \left|\frac{0.00241}{-4.91759}\right| \times 100\% = 0.04901\%.$$

Thus a quadratic factor is

$$x^2 + 2.90255\,x - 4.91759$$

Dividing the given equation by this factor, we can obtain the other quadratic factor.

ASSIGNMENT

1. Find the quadratic factor of $x^3 - 3.7x^2 + 6.25x - 4.069$ after two iterations. Use $p_0 = -2.5$, $q_0 = 0$.
2. Solve the equation $x^4 - 8x^3 + 39x^2 - 62x + 50 = 0$ starting with $p = q = 0$.
3. Find the quadratic factor of $x^4 - 3x^3 + 20x^2 + 44x + 54 = 0$ close to $x^2 + 2x + 2$.
   [**Hint.** Take $p_0 = 2$, $q_0 = 2$]
4. Perform one iteration of the Bairstow method to extract a quadratic factor $x^2 + px + q$ from the polynomial $x^4 + x^3 + 2x^2 + x + 1 = 0$ using the initial approximation $p_0 = 0.5$ and $q_0 = 0.5$.

Answers

1. $x^2 - 2.40402\,x + 3.0927$ **2.** $1 \pm i,\ 3 \pm 4i$

3. $x^2 + 1.94184\,x + 1.95685$ **4.** $x^2 + 0.6666\,x + 1$.

3.28. NEWTON-RAPHSON METHOD

(*M.T.U. 2013, U.P.T.U. 2009*]

This method is generally used to improve the result obtained by one of the previous methods. Let x_0 be an approximate root of $f(x) = 0$ and let $x_1 = x_0 + h$ be the correct root so that $f(x_1) = 0$.

Expanding $f(x_0 + h)$ by Taylor's series, we get

$$f(x_0) + hf'(x_0) + \frac{h^2}{2!} f''(x_0) + \ldots\ldots = 0$$

Since, h is small, neglecting h^2 and higher powers of h, we get

$$f(x_0) + hf'(x_0) = 0 \quad \text{or} \quad h = -\frac{f(x_0)}{f'(x_0)} \qquad \ldots(1)$$

A better approximation than x_0 is therefore given by x_1, where

$$x_1 = x_0 - \frac{f(x_0)}{f'(x_0)}$$

Successive approximations are given by $x_2, x_3, \ldots\ldots, x_{n+1}$, where

$$\boxed{x_{n+1} = x_n - \frac{f(x_n)}{f'(x_n)}} \qquad \ldots(2) \quad (n = 0, 1, \ldots\ldots)$$

which is the Newton-Raphson formula.

Remarks. (1) This method is useful in cases of large values of $f'(x)$ *i.e.,* when the graph of $f(x)$ while crossing the x-axis is nearly vertical.

(2) If $f'(x)$ is zero or nearly 0, the method fails.

(3) Newton's formula converges provided the initial approximation x_0 is chosen sufficiently close to the root. This method is also called the method of tangents.

(4) This method is also used to obtain complex roots.

3.29. CONVERGENCE

Comparing (2) with $x_{n+1} = \phi(x_n)$ of the iteration method, we get

$$\phi(x_n) = x_{n+1} = x_n - \frac{f(x_n)}{f'(x_n)}$$

In general, $$\phi(x) = x - \frac{f(x)}{f'(x)}$$

which gives $$\phi'(x) = \frac{f(x)\, f''(x)}{[f'(x)]^2}$$

Since, iteration method converges if $|\phi'(x)| < 1$

$\therefore$ Newton's method converges if

$$|f(x)\, f''(x)| < [f'(x)]^2$$

in the interval considered.

Assuming $f(x)$, $f'(x)$ and $f''(x)$ to be continuous, we can select a small interval in the vicinity of the root α in which above condition is satisfied.

The rate at which the iteration method converges if the initial approximation to the root is sufficiently close to the desired root is called the **rate of convergence.**

[G.B.T.U. 2011, 2012, 2013]

3.30. ORDER OF CONVERGENCE

[M.T.U. 2012, G.B.T.U. (MCA) 2011; G.B.T.U. 2010; G.B.T.U. (M.Tech.) 2011]

Suppose x_n differs from the root α by a small quantity e_n so that

$$x_n = \alpha + e_n \quad \text{and} \quad x_{n+1} = \alpha + e_{n+1}$$

Then equation (2) becomes,

$$e_{n+1} = e_n - \frac{f(\alpha + e_n)}{f'(\alpha + e_n)}$$

$$= e_n - \frac{f(\alpha) + e_n f'(\alpha) + \dfrac{e_n^{\,2}}{2!} f''(\alpha) + \ldots\ldots}{f'(\alpha) + e_n f''(\alpha) + \ldots\ldots} \qquad \text{(By Taylor's expansion)}$$

$$= e_n - \frac{e_n\, f'(\alpha) + \dfrac{e_n^{\,2}}{2} f''(\alpha) + \ldots\ldots.}{f'(\alpha) + e_n\, f''(\alpha) + \ldots\ldots} \qquad \mid \because\ f(\alpha) = 0$$

$$= \frac{e_n^{\,2}\, f''(\alpha)}{2[f'(\alpha) + e_n\, f''(\alpha)]} \qquad \mid \text{Neglect higher powers of } e_n$$

$$= \frac{e_n^2}{2} \frac{f''(\alpha)}{f'(\alpha)\left\{1 + e_n \dfrac{f''(\alpha)}{f'(\alpha)}\right\}}$$

$$= \frac{e_n^2}{2} \cdot \frac{f''(\alpha)}{f'(\alpha)} \left\{1 + e_n \frac{f''(\alpha)}{f'(\alpha)}\right\}^{-1}$$

$$= \frac{e_n^2}{2} \frac{f''(\alpha)}{f'(\alpha)} \left\{1 - e_n \frac{f''(\alpha)}{f'(\alpha)} + \ldots\ldots.\right\}$$

or
$$\frac{e_{n+1}}{e_n^{\,2}} = \frac{1}{2} \frac{f''(\alpha)}{f'(\alpha)} - \frac{e_n}{2} \left\{\frac{f''(\alpha)}{f'(\alpha)}\right\}^2 + \ldots\ldots.$$

$$\approx \frac{f''(\alpha)}{2f'(\alpha)} \qquad \text{(Neglecting terms containing powers of } e_n)$$

Hence, by definition, the order of convergence of Newton-Raphson method is 2 *i.e.*, Newton-Raphson method is **quadratic convergent**.

This also shows that subsequent error at each step is proportional to the square of the previous error and as such the *convergence is quadratic.*

Hence, if at the first iteration, we have an answer correct to one decimal place then it should be correct to two places at the II iteration, to four places at III iteration.

It means that the number of correct decimal places at each iteration is almost doubled.

∴ Method converges very rapidly.

Due to its quadratic convergence, the formula (2) is also termed as **second order formula.**

3.31. GEOMETRICAL INTERPRETATION

Let x_0 be a point near the root α of equation $f(x) = 0$, then tangent at A $\{x_0, f(x_0)\}$ is

$$y - f(x_0) = f'(x_0)(x - x_0)$$

It cuts x-axis at $x_1 = x_0 - \frac{f(x_0)}{f'(x_0)}$

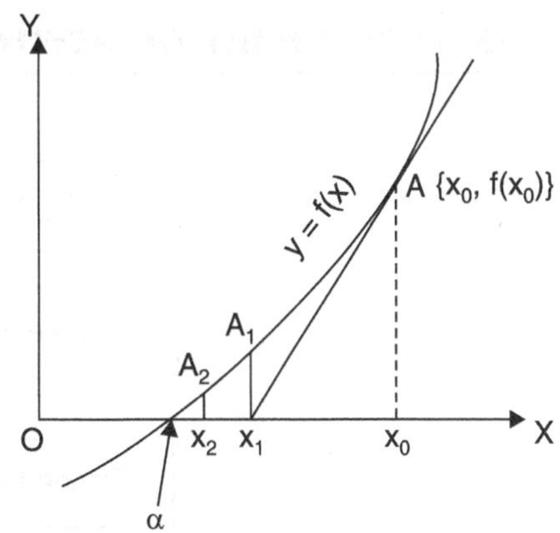

which is I approximation to root α. If A_1 corresponds to x_1 on the curve, then tangent at A_1 will cut x-axis at x_2, nearer to α and is therefore II approximation to root α.

Repeating this process, we approach the root α quite rapidly. Hence, the method consists in replacing the part of the curve between A and x-axis by the means of the tangent to the curve at A_0.

3.32. ALGORITHM OF NEWTON-RAPHSON METHOD

Step 01. Start of the program

Step 02. Input the variables x0, n for the task

Step 03. Input Epsilon & delta

Step 04. for i = 1 and repeat if i <= n

Step 05. f0 = f(x0)

Step 06. df0 = df(x1)

Step 07. if |df0| <= delta

a. Print Slope too small

b. Print x0, f0, df0, i

c. End of Program

Step 08. x1 = x0-(f0/df0)

Step 09. if |(x1-x0)/x1| <epsilon

a. Print convergent

b. Print x1, f(x1), i

c. End of Program

Step 10. x0 = x1

Step 11. End Loop

3.33. FLOW-CHART OF NEWTON–RAPHSON METHOD

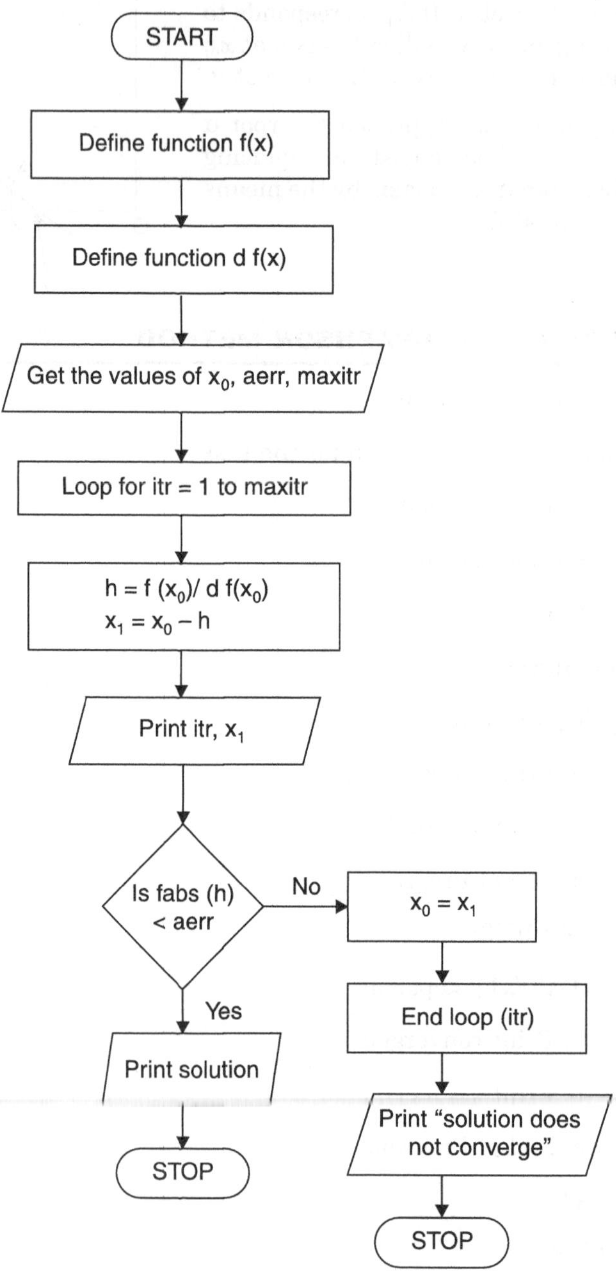

3.34. NEWTON'S ITERATIVE FORMULAE FOR FINDING INVERSE, SQUARE ROOT ETC.

1. Inverse. The reciprocal or inverse of a number 'a' can be considered as a root of the equation $\frac{1}{x} - a = 0$ which can be solved by Newton's method.

Since, $$f(x) = \frac{1}{x} - a,\ f'(x) = -\frac{1}{x^2}$$

$\therefore$ Newton's formula gives,

$$x_{n+1} = x_n + \frac{\left(\frac{1}{x_n} - a\right)}{\left(\frac{1}{x_n^2}\right)}$$

$$\boxed{x_{n+1} = x_n (2 - ax_n)}$$

2. Square root. The square root of 'a' can be considered as a root of equation $x^2 - a = 0$ solvable by Newton's method.

Since, $$f(x) = x^2 - a, \quad f'(x) = 2x$$

$$x_{n+1} = x_n - \frac{x_n^2 - a}{2x_n}$$

$$\boxed{x_{n+1} = \frac{1}{2}\left(x_n + \frac{a}{x_n}\right)}$$

3. Inverse square root. Equation is $\frac{1}{x^2} - a = 0$

Iterative formula is

$$\boxed{x_{n+1} = \frac{1}{2} x_n (3 - ax_n^2)}$$

4. General formula for p^th^ root. The pth root of a can be considered as a root of the equation $x^p - a = 0$. To solve this by Newton's method, we have

$$f(x) = x^p - a \quad \text{and hence,} \quad f'(x) = px^{p-1}$$

$\therefore$ Iterative formula is, $$x_{n+1} = x_n - \frac{(x_n^p - a)}{px_n^{p-1}}$$

$$\boxed{x_{n+1} = \frac{(p-1)\, x_n^p + a}{px_n^{p-1}}}$$ [*U.P.T.U. MCA (SUM) 2008*]

Also the general formula for reciprocal of pth root of a is

$$x_{n+1} = x_n \left(\frac{p + 1 - ax_n^p}{p}\right).$$

3.35. ORDER OF CONVERGENCE OF NEWTON'S SQUARE ROOT FORMULA

Let $\sqrt{a} = \alpha$ so that $a = \alpha^2$. If we write

$$x_n = \alpha\left(\frac{1+e_n}{1-e_n}\right)$$

then,
$$x_{n+1} = \alpha\left(\frac{1+e_{n+1}}{1-e_{n+1}}\right) \quad ...(1)$$

Also, by formula, $x_{n+1} = \frac{1}{2}\left(x_n + \frac{a}{x_n}\right)$, we get

$$x_{n+1} = \frac{1}{2}\left[\alpha\left(\frac{1+e_n}{1-e_n}\right) + \frac{a}{\alpha}\left(\frac{1-e_n}{1+e_n}\right)\right]$$

$$= \alpha\left(\frac{1+e_n^2}{1-e_n^2}\right) \quad ...(2) \quad (\because \; a = \alpha^2)$$

Comparing (1) and (2), we get $e_{n+1} = e_n^2$ confirming quadratic convergence of Newton's method.

3.36. ORDER OF CONVERGENCE OF NEWTON'S INVERSE FORMULA

Let $\alpha = \frac{1}{a}$ *i.e.,* $a = \frac{1}{\alpha}$. If we write $x_n = \alpha(1 - e_n)$

then, $x_{n+1} = \alpha(1 - e_{n+1})$

By formula, $x_{n+1} = x_n(2 - ax_n)$, we get

$$x_{n+1} = \alpha(1 - e_n)[2 - a\alpha(1 - e_n)] = \alpha(1 - e_n^2) \quad | \because \; a\alpha = 1$$

Comparing, we get $e_{n+1} = e_n^2$, hence, convergence is quadratic.

EXAMPLES

Example 1. *Using Newton-Raphson method, find the real root of the equation $3x = \cos x + 1$ correct to four decimal places. Give computer programme using 'C' language.*

[G.B.T.U. (M. Tech.) 2010, 2011]

Sol. Let $f(x) = 3x - \cos x - 1$

Since, $f(0) = -2 = (-)\text{ve}$;

$f(1) = 1.4597 = (+)\text{ve}$

$\therefore$ A root of $f(x) = 0$ lies between 0 and 1. It is nearer to 1. Let us take $x_0 = 0.6$.

Also, $f'(x) = 3 + \sin x$

Newton's iteration formula gives,

$$x_{n+1} = x_n - \frac{f(x_n)}{f'(x_n)}$$

$$= x_n - \frac{3x_n - \cos x_n - 1}{3 + \sin x_n} = \frac{x_n \sin x_n + \cos x_n + 1}{3 + \sin x_n} \quad ...(1)$$

Put $n = 0$, the first approximation x_1 is given by,

$$x_1 = \frac{x_0 \sin x_0 + \cos x_0 + 1}{3 + \sin x_0} = \frac{0.6 \sin 0.6 + \cos 0.6 + 1}{3 + \sin 0.6} = 0.6071$$

Put $n = 1$ then second approximation is

$$x_2 = \frac{x_1 \sin x_1 + \cos x_1 + 1}{3 + \sin x_1}$$

$$= \frac{0.6071 \sin (0.6071) + \cos(0.6071) + 1}{3 + \sin (0.6071)} = 0.6071$$

Clearly, $x_1 = x_2$. Hence, desired root is **0.6071** correct to 4 decimal places.

```
/*  ************************************************************************
           Program made for NEWTON RAPHSON to solve the equation
**********************************************************************  *\
```

[*U.P.T.U. (SUM) 2004*]

```
//....including source header files

# include <stdio.h>
# include <conio.h>
# include <math.h>
# include <process.h>
# include <string.h>

//....defining formulae

# define f(x)          3*x -cos(x)-1
# define df(x)   3+sin(x)

//...Function Declaration prototype

void NEW_RAP();

//... Main Execution Thread
void main()
     {
     clrscr();
     printf ("\n Solution by NEWTON RAPHSON method \n");
     printf ("\n Equation is: ");
     printf ("\n\t\t\t 3*X - COS X - 1=0 \n\n ");
     NEW_RAP();
     getch();
     }

//...Function Declaration

void NEW_RAP()
     {
```

```
//...Internal Declaration Field

long float x1,x0;
long float f0,f1;
long float df0;

int i=1;
int itr;

float EPS;
float error;

/*Finding an Approximate ROOT of Given Equation, Having +ve Value*/

for(x1=0; ;x1 +=0.01)
      {
      f1=f(x1);
      if (f1 > 0)
            {
            break;
            }
      }
/*Finding an Approximate ROOT of Given Equation, Having -ve value*/
x0=x1-0.01;
f0=f(x0);

printf(" Enter the number of iterations: ");
scanf(" %d",&itr);

printf(" Enter the maximum possible error: ");
scanf("%f",&EPS);

if (fabs(f0) > f1)

      {
      printf("\n\t\t The root is near to %.4f\n",x1);
      }

If (f1 > fabs(f(x0)))
      {
      printf("\n\t\t The root is near to %.4f\n",x0);
      }

x0=(x0+x1)/2;

for(;i<=itr;i++)
      {
      f0=f(x0);
      df0=df(x0);
```

```
        x1=x0 - (f0/df0);
        printf("\n\t\t The %d approximation to the root is :%f",i,x1);

        error=fabs(x1-x0);

        if(error<EPS)
              {
              break;
              }

        x0 = x1;
  }
  if(error>EPS)
        {
        prinf("\n\n\t NOTE :- ");
        printf("The number of iterations are not sufficient.");
        }

  printf("\n\n\n\t\t\t -----------------------------");
  printf("\n\t\t\t        The root is %.4f ",x1);
  printf("\n\t\t\t -----------------------------");
  }
```

OUTPUT

```
Solution by NEWTON RAPHSON method
Equation is:
                3*X - cos X - 1=0
Enter the number of iterations : 10
Enter the maximum possible error: .0000001
 The root is near to 0.6100
 The 1 approximation to the root is :0.607102
 The 2 approximation to the root is :0.607102
 The 3 approximation to the root is :0.607102
       -------------------------------
                The root is 0.6071
       -------------------------------
```

Example 2. *Using Newton's iterative method, find the real root of* $x \log_{10} x = 1.2$ *correct to six decimal places.*

Sol. $f(x) = x \log_{10} x - 1.2$

$\because$ $f(2.7) = -0.0353 = (-)\text{ve}$

$f(2.8) = 0.05204 = (+)\text{ve}$

Hence, a root of $f(x) = 0$ lies between 2.7 and 2.8.

Since $|f(2.7)| < |f(2.8)|$

Hence, root is nearer to 2.7.

Let us take $x_0 = 2.71$

Also, $f'(x) = \log_{10} x + \log_{10} e = \log_{10} x + 0.43429$

Newton's iteration formula gives,

$$x_{n+1} = x_n - \frac{f(x_n)}{f'(x_n)}$$

$$= x_n - \left(\frac{x_n \log_{10} x_n - 1.2}{\log_{10} x_n + 0.43429}\right) = \frac{0.43429x_n + 1.2}{\log_{10} x_n + 0.43429} \qquad ...(1)$$

Put $n = 0$, the first approximation is

$$x_1 = \frac{0.43429\, x_0 + 1.2}{\log_{10} x_0 + 0.43429} = 2.74073 \qquad | \text{ Taking } x_0 = 2.71$$

Similarly, Putting $n = 1, 2$, in (1), we get

$$x_2 = 2.740646$$
$$x_3 = 2.740646$$

Since x_2 and x_3 are same up to 6 decimal places, hence the required root is **2.740646.**

Example 3. *Evaluate $\sqrt{12}$ to five decimal places by Newton's iterative method.*

Sol. Let $x = \sqrt{12}$ so that $x^2 - 12 = 0$ ...(1)

Take $f(x) = x^2 - 12$, Newton's iteration formula gives,

$$x_{n+1} = x_n - \frac{f(x_n)}{f'(x_n)} = x_n - \frac{x_n^2 - 12}{2x_n} = \frac{1}{2}\left(x_n + \frac{12}{x_n}\right) \qquad ...(2)$$

Now since, $f(3) = -3$ (–)ve

$f(4) = 4$ (+)ve

∴ The root of (1) lies between 3 and 4.

Since $|f(3)| < |f(4)|$, hence, root is nearer to 3.

Take $x_0 = 3.4$, equation (2) gives,

$$x_1 = \frac{1}{2}\left(x_0 + \frac{12}{x_0}\right) = \frac{1}{2}\left(3.4 + \frac{12}{3.5}\right) = 3.464706$$

$$x_2 = \frac{1}{2}\left(x_1 + \frac{12}{x_1}\right) = 3.464102$$

$$x_3 = \frac{1}{2}\left(x_2 + \frac{12}{x_2}\right) = 3.4641016$$

Since, x_2 and x_3 are same up to 5 decimal places,

$$x = \sqrt{12} = \mathbf{3.46410.}$$

Example 4. *Using Newton's iterative method, find the real root of $x \sin x + \cos x = 0$ which is near $x = \pi$ correct to 3 decimal places.* [G.B.T.U. (C.O.) 2010]

Sol. We have $f(x) = x \sin x + \cos x$ and $f'(x) = x \cos x$

The iteration formula is,

$$x_{n+1} = x_n - \frac{x_n \sin x_n + \cos x_n}{x_n \cos x_n}$$

with $x_0 = \pi$, $$x_1 = x_0 - \frac{x_0 \sin x_0 + \cos x_0}{x_0 \cos x_0} = \pi - \frac{\pi \sin \pi + \cos \pi}{\pi \cos \pi} = 2.8233$$

Successive iteratives are,

$$x_2 = 2.7986, \quad x_3 = 2.7984$$

Since, x_2 and x_3 are same up to three decimal places hence required root is **2.798.**

Example 5. *Find a real root of the equation $x = e^{-x}$ using the Newton-Raphson method.* [U.P.T.U. (MCA) 2008]

Sol. We have $f(x) = x - e^{-x}$

$\therefore$ $f'(x) = 1 + e^{-x}$

Since, $f(.5) = -0.1065$ (–)ve

$f(.6) = 0.05118$ (+)ve

Hence, the root lies between .5 and .6.

Since, $|f(.6)| < |f(.5)|$

$\therefore$ Root is nearer to 0.6.

Let us take $x_0 = 0.58$.

Newton's iterative formula is

$$x_{n+1} = x_n - \frac{f(x_n)}{f'(x_n)} = x_n - \left(\frac{x_n - e^{-x_n}}{1 + e^{-x_n}}\right)$$

Putting $n = 0$, we get

$$x_1 = x_0 - \frac{(x_0 - e^{-x_0})}{(1 + e^{-x_0})} = 0.567113$$

Putting $n = 1, 2$, we get successively

$$x_2 = 0.567143$$
$$x_3 = 0.56714329$$

Since x_2 and x_3 are same up to 6 decimal places, hence, the required real root is **0.567143.**

Example 6. *Find a positive value of $(17)^{1/3}$ correct to six decimal places by Newton-Raphson method.* (M.T.U. 2013, U.P.T.U. 2007)

Sol. Let $x = (17)^{1/3}$ so that $x^3 - 17 = 0$ ...(1)

Let $f(x) = x^3 - 17 \quad \therefore \quad f'(x) = 3x^2$

Since $f(2.5) = -1.375$ (–)ve

and $f(2.6) = 0.576$ (+)ve

$\therefore$ The root lies between 2.5 and 2.6.

Since, $|f(2.6)| < |f(2.5)|$

Therefore, root is nearer to 2.6. Let us take $x_0 = 2.58$.

Newton-Raphson formula is

$$x_{n+1} = x_n - \frac{f(x_n)}{f'(x_n)} = x_n - \left(\frac{x_n^3 - 17}{3x_n^2}\right)$$

Putting $n = 0, 1, 2, \ldots$, successively, we get

$$x_1 = x_0 - \left(\frac{x_0^3 - 17}{3x_0^2}\right) = 2.571311 \qquad | \because \; x_0 = 2.58$$

$$x_2 = 2.571281$$
$$x_3 = 2.5712815$$

Since x_2 and x_3 are same up to 6 decimal places, hence, the required positive root is **2.571281.**

Example 7. *Show that the following two sequences, both have convergence of the second order with the same limit* $\sqrt{a}$.

$$x_{n+1} = \frac{1}{2}x_n\left(1 + \frac{a}{x_n^2}\right) \text{ and, } x_{n+1} = \frac{1}{2}x_n\left(3 - \frac{x_n^2}{a}\right).$$

(U.P.T.U. 2006, 2009)

Sol. Since, $\quad x_{n+1} = \frac{1}{2}x_n\left(1 + \frac{a}{x_n^2}\right)$, we have

$$x_{n+1} - \sqrt{a} = \frac{1}{2}x_n\left(1 + \frac{a}{x_n^2}\right) - \sqrt{a} = \frac{1}{2}\left(x_n + \frac{a}{x_n} - 2\sqrt{a}\right)$$

$$= \frac{1}{2}\left(\sqrt{x_n} - \frac{\sqrt{a}}{\sqrt{x_n}}\right)^2 = \frac{1}{2x_n}(x_n - \sqrt{a})^2$$

Thus, $$e_{n+1} = \frac{1}{2x_n}e_n^2 \qquad \ldots(1)$$

which shows the quadratic convergence. Similarly for the second,

$$x_{n+1} - \sqrt{a} = \frac{1}{2}x_n\left(3 - \frac{x_n^2}{a}\right) - \sqrt{a} = \frac{1}{2}x_n\left(1 - \frac{x_n^2}{a}\right) + (x_n - \sqrt{a})$$

$$= \frac{x_n}{2a}(a - x_n^2) + (x_n - \sqrt{a}) = (x_n - \sqrt{a})\left[1 - \frac{x_n}{2a}(x_n + \sqrt{a})\right]$$

$$e_{n+1} = \frac{x_n - \sqrt{a}}{2a}[2a - x_n^2 - x_n\sqrt{a}] = \frac{x_n - \sqrt{a}}{2a}[(a - x_n^2) + (a - x_n\sqrt{a})]$$

$$= -\left(\frac{x_n - \sqrt{a}}{2a}\right)(x_n - \sqrt{a})(x_n + 2\sqrt{a})$$

$$e_{n+1} = -\frac{(x_n - \sqrt{a})^2}{2a}(x_n + 2\sqrt{a}) = -\frac{(x_n + 2\sqrt{a})}{2a}.e_n^2 \qquad \ldots(2)$$

which shows the quadratic convergence.

Example 8. *If x_n is suitable close approximation to $\sqrt{a}$, show that error in the formula* $x_{n+1} = \frac{1}{2} x_n \left(1 + \frac{a}{x_n^2}\right)$ *is about $\frac{1}{3}$rd that in the formula, $x_{n+1} = \frac{1}{2} x_n \left(3 - \frac{x_n^2}{a}\right)$ and deduce that the formula $x_{n+1} = \frac{x_n}{8}\left(6 + \frac{3a}{x_n^2} - \frac{x_n^2}{a}\right)$ gives a sequence with third order convergence.*

Sol. Since x_n is very close to $\sqrt{a}$

$$e_{n+1} \simeq -\left(\frac{x_n + 2x_n}{2x_n^2}\right) e_n^2 \qquad | \text{ From (2)}$$

$$= 3 \cdot \frac{1}{2x_n} e_n^2 \qquad \text{...(3)}$$

A simple observation shows that from (1) (see example 7) and (3), error in first formula for e_{n+1} is about $\frac{1}{3}$rd of that in second formula.

To find the rate of convergence of given formula, we have

$$x_{n+1} - \sqrt{a} = \frac{x_n}{8}\left(6 + \frac{3a}{x_n^2} - \frac{x_n^2}{a}\right) - \sqrt{a} = \frac{x_n(6x_n^2 a + 3a^2 - x_n^4)}{8\,ax_n^2} - \sqrt{a}$$

$$= \frac{6\,x_n^2 a + 3a^2 - x_n^4 - 8\,x_n\,a\sqrt{a}}{8\,x_n a} = \frac{-(x_n + 3\sqrt{a})(x_n - \sqrt{a})^3}{8x_n a}$$

$$\therefore \qquad e_{n+1} = -\left(\frac{x_n + 3\sqrt{a}}{8x_n a}\right) e_n^3$$

It shows that above formula has a convergence of third order.

Example 9. *Show that the square root of $N = AB$ is given by*

$$\sqrt{N} \simeq \frac{S}{4} + \frac{N}{S}, \text{ where } S = A + B.$$

Sol. Let $\qquad x = \sqrt{N} \Rightarrow x^2 - N = 0$

Now, let $\qquad f(x) = x^2 - N$

$\therefore \qquad f'(x) = 2x$

By Newton-Raphson formula,

$$x_{n+1} = x_n - \frac{f(x_n)}{f'(x_n)} = x_n - \frac{x_n^2 - N}{2x_n} = \frac{x_n}{2} + \frac{N}{2x_n}$$

Let $\qquad x_n = \frac{A + B}{2}$

then, $\qquad x_{n+1} = \frac{A+B}{4} + \frac{N}{A+B} \simeq \frac{S}{4} + \frac{N}{S} \qquad | \text{ Since } S = A + B$

Example 10. *Using the starting value 2(1 + i), solve $x^4 - 5x^3 + 20x^2 - 40x + 60 = 0$ by Newton-Raphson method given that all the roots of the given equation are complex.*

Sol. Let $\qquad f(x) = x^4 - 5x^3 + 20x^2 - 40x + 60$

so that, $\qquad f'(x) = 4x^3 - 15x^2 + 40x - 40$

∴ Newton-Raphson method gives,

$$x_{n+1} = x_n - \frac{f(x_n)}{f'(x_n)} = x_n - \frac{x_n^4 - 5x_n^3 + 20x_n^2 - 40x_n + 60}{4x_n^3 - 15x_n^2 + 40x_n - 40}$$

$$= \frac{3x_n^4 - 10x_n^3 + 20x_n^2 - 60}{4x_n^3 - 15x_n^2 + 40x_n - 40}$$

Put $n = 0$, take $x_0 = 2(1 + i)$ by trial, we get

$$x_1 = 1.92\ (1 + i)$$

Again, $x_2 = 1.915 + 1.908\ i$

Since, imaginary roots occur in conjugate pairs, roots are $1.915 \pm 1.908\ i$ up to three places of decimal. Assuming other pair of roots to be $\alpha \pm i\beta$, then

$$\text{Sum} = \begin{pmatrix} \alpha + i\beta + \alpha - i\beta \\ + 1.915 + 1.908\ i \\ + 1.915 - 1.908\ i \end{pmatrix} = 2\alpha + 3.83 = 5$$

⇒ $\alpha = 0.585$

Also, product of roots $= (\alpha^2 + \beta^2)\ [(1.915)^2 + (1.908)^2] = 60$

⇒ $\beta = 2.805$

Hence, other two roots are $0.585 \pm 2.805\ i$.

Example 11. *Determine the value of p and q so that rate of convergence of the iterative method* $x_{n+1} = px_n + q\dfrac{N}{x_n^2}$ *for computing* $N^{1/3}$ *becomes as high as possible.*

Sol. We have $x^3 = N$

$$\therefore \quad f(x) = x^3 - N \qquad \text{...(1)}$$

Let α be the exact root, we have

$$\alpha^3 = N \qquad \text{...(2)}$$

Substituting $x_n = \alpha + e_n$, $x_{n+1} = \alpha + e_{n+1}$, $N = \alpha^3$ in

$$x_{n+1} = px_n + q\frac{N}{x_n^2}, \text{ we get}$$

$$\alpha + e_{n+1} = p(\alpha + e_n) + q\,\frac{\alpha^3}{(\alpha + e_n)^2}$$

$$= p(\alpha + e_n) + q\frac{\alpha^3}{\alpha^2\left(1 + \frac{e_n}{\alpha}\right)^2} = p(\alpha + e_n) + q\alpha\left(1 + \frac{e_n}{\alpha}\right)^{-2}$$

$$= p(\alpha + e_n) + q\alpha\left\{1 - 2\frac{e_n}{\alpha} + 3\left(\frac{e_n}{\alpha}\right)^2 - \ldots\ldots\right\}$$

$$= p(\alpha + e_n) + q\alpha - 2qe_n + 3q\frac{e_n^2}{\alpha} - \ldots\ldots$$

$$\Rightarrow \qquad e_{n+1} = (p+q-1)\alpha + (p-2q)e_n + O(e_n^2) + \ldots\ldots$$

Now, for the method to become of order as high as possible *i.e.*, of order 2, we must have

$$p + q = 1 \quad \text{and} \quad p - 2q = 0$$

so that, $$p = \frac{2}{3} \quad \text{and} \quad q = \frac{1}{3}.$$

Example 12. *The graph of $y = 2 \sin x$ and $y = \log x + c$ touch each other in the nbd. of point $x = 8$. Find c and the coordinates of point of contact.*

Sol. The graphs will touch each other if values of dy/dx at their point of contact is same.

For $\quad y = 2 \sin x, \quad \dfrac{dy}{dx} = 2 \cos x$

For $\quad y = \log x + c \quad \dfrac{dy}{dx} = \dfrac{1}{x}$

$\therefore \quad 2 \cos x = \dfrac{1}{x} \quad \Rightarrow \quad x \cos x - 0.5 = 0$

Let $\quad f(x) = x \cos x - 0.5$

$\therefore \quad f'(x) = \cos x - x \sin x$

$\therefore$ Newton's iterative formula is $x_{n+1} = x_n - \dfrac{x_n \cos x_n - 0.5}{\cos x_n - x_n \sin x_n}$

For $n = 0$, $x_0 = 8$, first app. $x_1 = 7.793$

Second approximation, $\quad x_2 = 7.789 \approx 7.79$

Now, $\quad y = 2 \sin 7.79 = 1.9960$

$\therefore$ Point of contact $\rightarrow (7.79, 1.996)$

Now, $\quad y = \log x + c$

$\Rightarrow \quad 1.996 = \log 7.79 + c \quad \Rightarrow \quad c = -0.054.$

Example 13. *How should the constant α be chosen to ensure the fastest possible convergence with the iteration formula $x_{n+1} = \dfrac{\alpha x_n + x_n^{-2} + 1}{\alpha + 1}$?*

Sol. Since, $\quad \lim\limits_{n \to \infty} x_n = \lim\limits_{n \to \infty} x_{n+1} = \xi$, we have

$$\xi = \left(\frac{\alpha\xi + \dfrac{1}{\xi^2} + 1}{\alpha + 1} \right)$$

$$\Rightarrow \qquad (\alpha + 1)\xi^3 = \alpha\xi^3 + \xi^2 + 1$$

$$\Rightarrow \qquad \xi^3 - \xi^2 - 1 = 0$$

ξ can be obtained by finding a root of the equation $x^3 - x^2 - 1 = 0$.

We have $f(x) = x^3 - x^2 - 1$

$f'(x) = 3x^2 - 2x$

Since, $f(1.45) = (-)$ve and $f(1.47) = (+)$ve

$\therefore$ Root lies between 1.45 and 1.47. Let $x_0 = 1.46$.

By Newton-Raphson method,

First approximation is

$$x_1 = x_0 - \frac{f(x_0)}{f'(x_0)} = x_0 - \left(\frac{{x_0}^3 - {x_0}^2 - 1}{3{x_0}^2 - 2x_0}\right) = 1.465601.$$

Second approximation is

$$x_2 = x_1 - \frac{f(x_1)}{f'(x_1)} = x_1 - \left(\frac{{x_1}^3 - {x_1}^2 - 1}{3{x_1}^2 - 2x_1}\right) = 1.46557$$

Hence, $\xi = 1.465$ correct to three decimal places.

Now, we have

$$x_{n+1} = \frac{\alpha x_n + {x_n}^{-2} + 1}{\alpha + 1} \quad ...(1)$$

Putting $x_n = \xi + e_n$ and $x_{n+1} = \xi + e_{n+1}$ in (1), we get

$$(\alpha + 1)(\xi + e_{n+1}) = \alpha(\xi + e_n) + \frac{1}{(\xi + e_n)^2} + 1 = \alpha(\xi + e_n) + \frac{1}{\xi^2}\left(1 + \frac{e_n}{\xi}\right)^{-2} + 1$$

which gives,

$$(1 + \alpha)e_{n+1} = \left(\alpha - \frac{2}{\xi^3}\right) e_n + O({e_n}^2)$$

For fastest convergence, we must have $\alpha = \frac{2}{\xi^3} = \frac{2}{(1.465)^3} = 0.636.$

Example 14. *Use the Newton-Raphson method to find a solution accurate to within 10^{-5} for the problem, $e^{6x} + 1.441\, e^{2x} - 2.079\, e^{4x} - 0.3330 = 0$; $-1 \le x \le 0$. Use the initial point as $x_0 = -0.5$.* [U.P.T.U. MCA (SUM) 2008]

Sol. $f(x) = e^{6x} + 1.441\, e^{2x} - 2.079\, e^{4x} - 0.3330$

$x_0 = -0.5$ | Given

Also $f'(x) = 6e^{6x} + 2.882e^{2x} - 8.316e^{4x}$

By Newton-Raphson formula,

$$x_{n+1} = x_n - \frac{f(x_n)}{f'(x_n)}$$

$$= x_n - \left[\frac{e^{6x_n} + 1.441e^{2x_n} - 2.079e^{4x_n} - 0.3330}{6e^{6x_n} + 2.882e^{2x_n} - 8.316e^{4x_n}}\right] \quad ...(1)$$

Putting $n = 0$, the first approximation is, $x_1 = -0.35241839$

Putting $n = 1$, the second approximation is, $x_2 = -0.284980263$

Putting $n = 2$, the third approximation is, $x_3 = -0.246813527$

Putting $n = 3$, the fourth approximation is, $x_4 = -0.223232852$

Putting $n = 4$, the fifth approximation is, $x_5 = -0.207509457$

Putting $n = 5$, the sixth approximation is, $x_6 = -0.195400823$

Similarly, putting $n = 6, 7, 8, 9, ...$ in (1), we get at last,

$$x_{12} = -0.169602323 \text{ and } x_{13} = -0.16960655$$

Since x_{12} and x_{13} are same up to five decimal places, hence, the root of the given equation is -0.16960 correct up to five decimal places.

ASSIGNMENT

1. (*i*) By using Newton-Raphson method, find the root of $x^4 - x - 10 = 0$ which is near to $x = 2$ correct to three places of decimal. (*U.P.T.U. 2014, G.B.T.U. 2012*)

   (*ii*) Find the root of $2 \sin x - 2x + 1 = 0$ correct to five significant digits with initial approximation $x_0 = 1.0$. (*M.T.U. 2012*)

2. (*i*) Compute one positive root of $2x - \log_{10} x = 7$ by Newton-Raphson method correct to four decimal places. [*G.B.T.U. (C.O.) 2011*]

   (*ii*) Find the real root of the equation $\log_{10} x - x + 3 = 0$ correct to four demical places using Newton-Raphson method. (*G.B.T.U. 2011*)

   (*iii*) Use Newton-Raphson method to find the root of $3x - \log_{10} x = 6$ correct to four decimal places. (*G.B.T.U. 2012*)

3. (*i*) Use the Newton-Raphson method to find a root of the equation $x^3 - 2x - 5 = 0$.

   (*ii*) Use Newton-Raphson method to find a root of the equation $x^3 - 3x - 5 = 0$.

4. Find the real root of the equations:

   (*i*) $\log x = \cos x$ (*ii*) $x^2 + 4 \sin x = 0$ (*iii*) $x^3 - 4x + 1 = 0$ (*M.T.U. 2012*)

   by Newton-Raphson method correct to three decimal places.

5. Use Newton-Raphson method to obtain a root, correct to three decimal places of following equations:

   (*i*) $\sin x = 1 - x$ (*ii*) $x^3 - 5x + 3 = 0$ (*iii*) $x^4 + x^2 - 80 = 0$

   (*iv*) $x^3 + 3x^2 - 3 = 0$ (*v*) $4(x - \sin x) = 1$ (*vi*) $x - \cos x = 0$

   (*vii*) $\sin x = \frac{x}{2}$ (*viii*) $x \log_{10} x = 4.77$ (*G.*B.T.U. 2011*)

6. (*i*) Explain the method of Newton-Raphson for computing roots. [*U.P.T.U. 2009, U.P.T.U. MCA (SUM) 2009, G.B.T.U. (MCA) 2010*]

   (*ii*) Explain the limitations of Newton-Raphson method for finding out the root of an equation. (*U.P.T.U. 2009*)

   (*iii*) Explain the order of convergence and prove that Newton-Raphson method is second order convergent. (*M.T.U. 2012, G.B.T.U. 2010, 2011*)

   (*iv*) Compute the rate of convergence of Newton-Raphson method. (*G.B.T.U. 2012, 2013*)

7. Determine p, q and r so that the order of the iterative method

$$x_{n+1} = px_n + \frac{qa}{x_n^2} + \frac{ra^2}{x_n^5}$$

   for $a^{1/3}$ becomes as high as possible. [*U.P.T.U. (MCA) 2007*]

   [**Hint:** $p + q + r = 1, p - 2q - 5r = 0, 3q + 15r = 0$.]

8. Find all the roots of $\cos x - x^2 - x = 0$ to five decimal places by Newton-Raphson method. (*U.P.T.U. 2006*)

9. Find all positive roots of the equation $10 \int_0^x e^{-x^2}\, dt - 1 = 0$ with six correct decimals. Use Newton-Raphson method. *(U.P.T.U. 2008)*

10. Use Newton-Raphson method to find the smallest positive root of the equation $\tan x = x$.

$\left[\textbf{Hint: } x \text{ lies in } \left(\pi, \frac{3\pi}{2}\right)\right]$ *(G.B.T.U. 2011, U.P.T.U. 2007)*

11. Find the positive root of the equation $e^x = 1 + x + \frac{x^2}{2} + \frac{x^3}{6} e^{0.3x}$ correct to 6 decimal places.

12. Show that the equation $f(x) = \cos\left\{\frac{\pi(x+1)}{8}\right\} + 0.148x - 0.9062 = 0$ has one root in the interval $(-1, 0)$ and one in $(0, 1)$. Calculate the negative root correct to 4 decimals. *(U.P.T.U. 2009)*

13. (*i*) Use Newton's formula to prove that square root of N can be obtained by the recursion formula,

$$x_{i+1} = x_i\left(1 - \frac{x_i^2 - N}{2N}\right)$$

Hence, find the square root of

(*a*) 13 *(U.P.T.U. 2008)* (*b*) 21 *[U.P.T.U. (MCA) 2009]* (*c*) 35.

correct to 4 decimal places.

(*ii*) Find the positive value of $\left(\frac{1}{17}\right)^{1/3}$ correct up to 4 decimal places using Newton-Raphson method. *(U.P.T.U. 2009)*

14. Find the iterative method based on Newton-Raphson method to find cube root of N where N is a positive real number. Apply the method for N = 18 and obtain result correct to two decimal places. *[G.B.T.U. MCA (SUM) 2010]*

15. (*i*) The equation $2e^{-x} = \frac{1}{x+2} + \frac{1}{x+1}$ has two roots greater than -1. Calculate these roots correct to five decimal places. *(M.T.U. 2012, G.B.T.U. 2013)*

(*ii*) Use Newton-Raphson method to find a root of non-linear equation $f(x) = x^3 + 2x^2 + 10x - 20 = 0$ up to 10 iterations. *(U.P.T.U. 2009)*

Answers

1. (*i*) 1.855 (*ii*) 1.4973

2. (*i*) 3.7892 (*ii*) 3.5502 (*iii*) 2.1079

3. (*i*) 2.094568 (*ii*) 2.279

4. (*i*) 1.303 (*ii*) – 1.934 (*iii*) 1.860, 0.2541, – 2.1147

5. (*i*) 0.511 (*ii*) 0.657 (*iii*) 2.908 (*iv*) – 2.533
(*v*) 1.171 (*vi*) .739 (*vii*) 1.896 (*viii*) 6.083

7. $p = \frac{5}{9}, q = \frac{5}{9}, r = -\frac{1}{9}$; Third order **8.** 0.55000 ; – 1.25115

9. Roots lie in (0, 1) and (1, 2) ; 0.100336, 1.679631 **10.** 4.4934 **11.** 2.363376

12. – 0.5081. **13.** (*i*) (*a*) 3.6055 (*b*) 4.5825 (*c*) 5.9160 (*ii*) 0.3889

14. 2.62 **15.** (*i*) Roots lie in (– 0.8, 0) and (0, 1) ; – 0.689752, 0.770091 (*ii*) 1.3688.

3.37. DEFINITIONS

1. A number α is a solution of $f(x) = 0$ if $f(\alpha) = 0$. Such a solution α is a root or a zero of $f(x) = 0$. Geometrically, a root of the eqn. $f(x) = 0$ is the value of x at which the graph of $y = f(x)$ intersects x-axis.

2. If we can write $f(x) = 0$ as

$$f(x) = (x - \alpha)^m g(x) = 0$$

where $g(x)$ is bounded and $g(\alpha) \neq 0$ then α is called a **multiple root** of multiplicity m. In this case,

$$\mathbf{f(\alpha) = f'(\alpha) = \ldots\ldots\ldots = f^{(m-1)}(\alpha) = 0, f^{(m)}(\alpha) \neq 0}$$

For $m = 1$, the number α is said to be a simple root.

3.38. MODIFIED NEWTON-RAPHSON METHOD FOR MULTIPLE ROOTS

If α is a multiple root of multiplicity m of the eqn. $f(x) = 0$ then, we have

$$f(\alpha) = f'(\alpha) = \ldots\ldots = f^{(m-1)}(\alpha) = 0 \quad \text{and} \quad f^{(m)}(\alpha) \neq 0$$

It can easily be verified that all the iteration methods discussed so far have only linear rate of convergence when $m > 1$.

For example, in Newton-Raphson method, we have

$$f(x_k) = f(\alpha + e_k) = \frac{e_k^m}{m!} f^{(m)}(\alpha) + \frac{e_k^{m+1}}{(m+1)!} f^{(m+1)}(\alpha) + \frac{e_k^{m+2}}{(m+2)!} f^{(m+2)}(\alpha) + \ldots\ldots$$

$$f'(x_k) = f'(\alpha + e_k) = \frac{e_k^{m-1}}{(m-1)!} f^{(m)}(\alpha) + \frac{e_k^m}{m!} f^{(m+1)}(\alpha) + \ldots\ldots$$

The error equation for N–R method becomes,

$$e_{k+1} = \left(1 - \frac{1}{m}\right) e_k + \frac{1}{m^2(m+1)} \frac{f^{(m+1)}(\alpha)}{f^{(m)}(\alpha)} e_k^2 + O(e_k^3)$$

If $m \neq 1$, we obtain,

$$e_{k+1} = \left(1 - \frac{1}{m}\right) e_k + O(e_k^2) \qquad \ldots(1)$$

which shows that the method has **only linear rate of convergence.**

However, if the multiplicity of the root is known in advance, we can modify the methods by introducing parameters dependent on the multiplicity of the root to increase their order of convergence.

For example, consider Newton-Raphson method in the form

$$x_{k+1} = x_k - \beta \frac{f_k}{f_k'} \qquad \ldots(2)$$

where β is an arbitrary parameter to be determined.

If α is a multiple root of multiplicity m, we obtain from (2), the error equation

$$e_{k+1} = \left(1 - \frac{\beta}{m}\right) e_k + \frac{\beta}{m^2(m+1)} \frac{f^{(m+1)}(\alpha)}{f^{(m)}(\alpha)} e_k^2 + O(e_k^3)$$

If the method (2) is to have the quadratic rate of convergence then the coefficient of e_k must vanish which gives

$$1-\frac{\beta}{m}=0 \quad \text{or} \quad \beta = m$$

Thus, the method

$$\boxed{x_{k+1} = x_k - m\frac{f_k}{f_k'}}$$

has quadratic rate of convergence for determining a multiple root of multiplicity m.

If the multiplicity of the root is not known in advance, then we use the following procedure.

It is known that if $f(x) = 0$ has a root α of multiplicity m, then $f'(x) = 0$ has the same root α of multiplicity $m - 1$.

Hence, $g(x) = \dfrac{f(x)}{f'(x)}$ has a simple root α, we can now use Newton-Raphson method

$$x_{k+1} = x_k - \frac{g(x_k)}{g'(x_k)}$$

to find the approximate value of the multiple root α.

Simplifying, we have

$$x_{k+1} = x_k - \frac{f_k f_k'}{f_k'^2 - f_k f_k''}$$

which has quadratic rate of convergence for multiple roots.

Note. If initial approximation x_0 is sufficiently close to the root, then the expressions,

$$x_0 - m\frac{f(x_0)}{f'(x_0)},\ x_0 - (m-1)\frac{f'(x_0)}{f''(x_0)},\ x_0 - (m-2)\frac{f''(x_0)}{f'''(x_0)} \text{ will have same value.}$$

EXAMPLES

Example 1. *Show that the modified Newton-Raphson method* $x_{n+1} = x_n - \dfrac{2f(x_n)}{f'(x_n)}$ *gives a quadratic convergence when* $f(x) = 0$*, has a pair of double roots in neighbourhood of* $x = x_n$.

Sol. $e_{n+1} = e_n - \dfrac{2f(a+e_n)}{f'(a+e_n)}$, where a, e_n and e_{n+1} have their usual meanings. Expanding in powers of e_n and using $f(a) = 0$, $f'(a) = 0$ since, $x = a$ is a double root near $x = x_n$, we get

$$e_{n+1} = e_n - \frac{2\left[\frac{e_n^2}{2!}f''(a) + \ldots\ldots.\right]}{\left[e_n f''(a) + \frac{e_n^2}{2!}f'''(a) + \ldots\ldots.\right]}$$

$$= e_n - \frac{2e_n^2\left[\frac{1}{2!}f''(a) + \frac{1}{3!}f'''(a) + \ldots\ldots.\right]}{e_n\left[f''(a) + \frac{e_n}{2!}f'''(a) + \ldots\ldots\right]}$$

$$\simeq e_n - \frac{2e_n\left[\frac{1}{2!}f''(a) + \frac{1}{3!}f'''(a)\right]}{f''(a) + \frac{e_n}{2!}f'''(a)}$$

$$e_{n+1} \simeq \frac{1}{6}e_n^2 \cdot \frac{f'''(a)}{\left[f''(a) + \frac{e_n}{2!}f'''(a)\right]}$$

$$\therefore \qquad e_{n+1} \approx \frac{1}{6}e_n^2 \frac{f'''(a)}{f''(a)}$$

$$\Rightarrow \qquad e_{n+1} \propto e_n^2$$

and hence convergence is quadratic.

Example 2. *Find the double root of the equation $x^3 - x^2 - x + 1 = 0$.*

Sol. Let $\qquad f(x) = x^3 - x^2 - x + 1$

so that $\qquad f'(x) = 3x^2 - 2x - 1, f''(x) = 6x - 2$

Starting with $x_0 = 0.9$, we have

$$x_0 - 2\frac{f(x_0)}{f'(x_0)} = 0.9 - \frac{2 \times 0.019}{(-0.37)} = 1.003$$

and $$x_0 - (2-1)\frac{f'(x_0)}{f''(x_0)} = 0.9 - \frac{(-0.37)}{3.4} = 1.009$$

The closeness of these values implies that there is a double root near $x = 1$.

Choosing $x_1 = 1.01$ for next approximation, we get

$$x_1 - 2\frac{f(x_1)}{f'(x_1)} = 1.01 - 2 \times \frac{0.0002}{0.0403} = 1.0001$$

and $$x_1 - (2-1)\frac{f'(x_1)}{f''(x_1)} = 1.01 - \frac{0.0403}{4.06} = 1.0001$$

This shows that there is a double root at $x = 1.0001$ which is quite near the actual root $x = 1$.

ASSIGNMENT

1. The equation $f(x) \equiv x^3 - 7x^2 + 16x - 12 = 0$ has a double root at $x = 2$. Starting with the initial approximation $x_0 = 1$, find the root correct to 3 decimal places using the modified Newton-Raphson method with $m = 2$.
2. Show that the equation $f(x) \equiv 1 - xe^{1-x} = 0$
has a double root at $x = 1$. The root is obtained by using the modified Newton-Raphson method with $m = 2$ starting with $x_0 = 0$.

3.39. NEARLY EQUAL ROOTS

So far, Newton's method is applicable when $f'(x) \neq 0$ in the neighbourhood of actual root $x = a$, *i.e.*, in the interval $(a - h, a + h)$.

If the quantity h is very very small, it will not satisfy the above restriction. The application of Newton's method will not be practical in that case. This condition arrives when roots are very close to each other.

We know that in case of double root $x = a$, $f(x)$ and $f'(x)$ both vanish at $x = a$. Thus, while applying Newton's method, if x_i is simultaneously near zeros of $f(x)$ and $f'(x)$ *i.e.*, $f(x_i)$ and $f'(x_i)$ both are very small, then it is usually practical to depart from the standard sequence and proceed to obtain two new starting values for the two nearly equal roots.

To obtain these values, we first apply Newton's method to the equation $f'(x) = 0$ *i.e.*, we use the iteration formula

$$x_{i+1} = x_i - \frac{f'(x_i)}{f''(x_i)} \qquad \text{...(1)}$$

with last available iterate as the initial value x_0 for (1).

Suppose $x = c$ is the solution obtained by (1).

Now by Taylor's series, we have

$$f(x) = f(c) + (x - c) f'(c) + \frac{1}{2}(x - c)^2 f''(c) + \text{.......}$$

$$= f(c) + \frac{1}{2}(x - c)^2 f''(c) + \text{R} \qquad | \because \; f'(c) = 0$$

Assuming R to be small, we conclude that the zeros of $f(x)$ near $x = c$ are approximately given by

$$f(c) + \frac{1}{2}(x - c)^2 f''(c) = 0 \;\Rightarrow\; x = c \pm \sqrt{\frac{-2f(c)}{f''(c)}} \qquad \text{...(2)}$$

Using these values as starting values, we can use the original iteration formula to get two close roots of $f(x) = 0$.

Example. *Use synthetic division to solve* $f(x) \equiv x^3 - x^2 - 1.0001\, x + 0.9999 = 0$ *in the neighbourhood of* $x = 1$.

Sol. To find $f(1)$ and $f'(1)$,

1	–1	–1.0001	0.9999	1
	1	0	– 1.0001	
1	0	– 1.0001	– 0.0002 = $f(1)$	
	1	1		
1	1	– .0001 = $f'(1)$		
	1			
1	$2 = \frac{1}{2} f''(1)$			

From the above synthetic division, we observe that $f(1)$ and $f'(1)$ are small. Hence, there exists two nearly equal roots. Taking $x_0 = 1$, we will use $x_{i+1} = x_i - \dfrac{f'(x_i)}{f''(x_i)}$ to modify the root. For this, we require $f''(1)$.

From the above synthetic division, we have

$$\frac{1}{2} f''(1) = 2 \Rightarrow f''(1) = 4$$

$\therefore$ First approximation $x_1 = 1 - \dfrac{f'(1)}{f''(1)} = 1 - \dfrac{(-0.0001)}{4} = 1.000025$

Now, we again calculate $f(x_1)$ and $f''(x_1)$ by synthetic division.

1	–1	– 1.000100	0.999900	1.000025
	1.000025	0.000025	– 1.000075	
1	0.000025	– 1.000075	$-0.000175 = f(x_1)$	
	1.000025	1.000050		
1	1.000050	$-0.000025 = f'(x_1)$		
	1.000025			
1	$2.000075 = \frac{1}{2} f''(x_1)$			

$\therefore$ $f(1.000025) = -0.000175$ and $f''(1.000025) = 4.000150$

Now, for nearly equal roots,

$$x = c \pm \sqrt{\frac{-2f(c)}{f''(c)}}, \quad \text{where } c = 1.000025$$

$$= 1.000025 \pm \sqrt{\frac{-2(-.000175)}{4.000150}} = 1.009378, 0.990671$$

ASSIGNMENT

1. The equation $f(x) = (x-1)^2 (x-3)^2$ has roots at $x = 1$ and $x = 3$. Which of the following methods can be applied to find all the roots?

   (*i*) Bisection method (*ii*) False position method (*iii*) Newton-Raphson method

   Justify your answer. *(G.B.T.U. 2010)*

2. A sphere of wood, 2 m in diameter, floating in water sinks to a depth d given by

   $$d^3 - 3d^2 + 2.5 = 0$$

   Find d correct to two decimal places.

Answers

1. (*iii*) Newton-Raphson method since it deals with multiple roots as well.
2. 1.16

3.40. CHEBYSHEV METHOD

Consider $f(x)$ as a polynomial of degree two.

$$f(x) = a_0x^2 + a_1x + a_2 = 0 \; ; a_0 \neq 0 \qquad ...(1)$$

where a_0, a_1, a_2 are arbitrary parameters to be determined by prescribing three appropriate conditions on $f(x)$ or its derivatives.

We determine a_0, a_1, a_2 in (1) using the conditions

$$\left.\begin{aligned} f_k &= a_0{x_k}^2 + a_1x_k + a_2 \\ f_k' &= 2a_0x_k + a_1 \\ f_k'' &= 2a_0 \end{aligned}\right\} \qquad ...(2)$$

Eliminating a_0, a_1 and a_2 from (1) and (2), we get

$$f_k + (x - x_k) f_k' + \frac{1}{2}(x - x_k)^2 f_k'' = 0 \qquad ...(3)$$

which is the Taylor series expansion of $f(x)$ about $x = x_k$ such that terms of order $(x - x_k)^3$ and higher powers are neglected.

In order to get the next approximation to the correct root, we write (3) as

$$x_{k+1} - x_k = -\frac{f_k}{f_k'} - \frac{1}{2}(x_{k+1} - x_k)^2 \frac{f_k''}{f_k'} \qquad ...(4)$$

By Newton-Raphson formula

$$x_{k+1} = x_k - \frac{f_k}{f_k'} \qquad ...(5)$$

Using (5) in (4), we get

$$\boxed{x_{k+1} = x_k - \frac{f_k}{f_k'} - \frac{1}{2}\frac{{f_k}^2}{{f_k'}^3} f_k''}$$

which is called the Chebyshev method. Rate of convergence of this method is 3.

Example. *Perform two iterations of Chebyshev method to find the smallest positive root of $x^3 - 5x + 1 = 0$. Take the initial approximation as $x_0 = 0.5$.*

Sol.

$$f(x) = x^3 - 5x + 1, \qquad f(0.5) = -1.375$$

$$f'(x) = 3x^2 - 5, \qquad f'(0.5) = -4.25$$

$$f''(x) = 6x, \qquad f''(0.5) = 3$$

First approximation is

$$x_1 = x_0 - \frac{f_0}{f_0'} - \frac{1}{2}\frac{{f_0}^2}{{f_0'}^3} f_0'' = 0.213414$$

Again, $f(x_1) = -0.05735, f'(x_1) = -4.863363, f''(x_1) = 1.280484$

Second approximation is

$$x_2 = x_1 - \frac{f_1}{f_1'} - \frac{1}{2}\frac{f_1^{\,2}}{f_1'^{\,3}} f_1'' = 0.20164.$$

3.41. AITKEN'S Δ^2 METHOD

The linear convergence of an iterative method of the form $x_{n+1} = \phi(x_n)$ can be improved with the help of the Aitken's Δ^2 method.

The error in two successive approximations may be written as

$$\left.\begin{aligned} e_{n+1} &= c\, e_n \\ \text{and} \quad e_{n+2} &= c\, e_{n+1} \end{aligned}\right\} \qquad ...(1)$$

Eliminating c, we get

$$e_{n+2}\, e_n = e_{n+1}^{\ 2}$$

or

$$(\alpha - x_{n+2})(\alpha - x_n) = (\alpha - x_{n+1})^2$$

Solving for α, we get

$$\alpha = \frac{x_n\, x_{n+2} - x_{n+1}^{\ 2}}{x_{n+2} - 2x_{n+1} + x_n} = x_n - \frac{(x_{n+1} - x_n)^2}{(x_{n+2} - 2x_{n+1} + x_n)}$$

$$\alpha = x_n - \frac{(\Delta x_n)^2}{\Delta^2 x_n}$$

where α gives an improved value of the approximation x_{n+2}.

Example. *Perform two iterations of the linear iteration method followed by one iteration of the Aitken's Δ^2 method to find the root of the equation $f(x) = x^3 - 5x + 1 = 0$; $x_0 = 0.5$.*

Sol. $f(0) = 1, \qquad f(1) = -3$

Hence, the root lies in the interval (0, 1).

Rewriting the given equation as

$$x = \frac{1}{5}(1 + x^3) = \phi(x) \qquad | \text{ say}$$

$$\phi'(x) = \frac{3}{5}x^2 \quad \text{and} \quad |\,\phi'(x)\,| < 1 \ \forall\ x \in (0, 1).$$

Hence, iteration method can be applied.

$$x_1 = \phi(x_0) = 0.225$$

$$x_2 = \phi(x_1) = 0.202278$$

$$x_0^* = x_0 - \frac{(x_1 - x_0)^2}{(x_2 - 2x_1 + x_0)} = 0.200232.$$

3.42. BIRGE-VIETA METHOD FOR POLYNOMIALS

Consider a real polynomial equation of degree n

$$P_n(x) \equiv a_0x^n + a_1x^{n-1} + a_2x^{n-2} + \ldots + a_{n-1}x + a_n = 0, \; a_0 \neq 0$$

where $a_0, a_1, a_2, \ldots, a_{n-1}$ and a_n are real numbers.

Let $\quad P_n(x) = (x - p)\, Q_{n-1}(x) + R \qquad \ldots(1)$

where $Q_{n-1}(x)$ is a quotient of degree $(n - 1)$ and R is remainder.

The value of remainder R depends on real number p. We start with an initial approximation p_0 to p and use some iterative method *e.g.*, Newton-Raphson method to improve the value of p in such a way that

$$P_n(p) = R(p) = 0 \qquad \ldots(2)$$

Newton-Raphson method for eqn. (2) becomes

$$p_{k+1} = p_k - \frac{P_n(p_k)}{P_n'(p_k)}, \; k = 0, 1, 2, 3, \ldots \qquad \ldots(3)$$

For polynomial equations, $P_n(p_0)$ and $P_n'(p_0)$ can be computed using synthetic division as follows:

p	a_0	a_1	a_2	...	a_{n-2}	a_{n-1}	a_n
		pb_0	pb_1	...	pb_{n-3}	pb_{n-2}	pb_{n-1}
	b_0	b_1	b_2	...	b_{n-2}	b_{n-1}	$b_n = R$

We get a relation (by introducing b_n),

$$b_k = a_k + pb_{k-1}, \; k = 1, 2, \ldots, n; \; b_0 = a_0 \qquad \ldots(4)$$

From (1), we have $\quad P_n(p) = R = b_n \qquad \ldots(5)$

Now, from (4) $\quad \dfrac{db_k}{dp} = b_{k-1} + p\dfrac{db_{k-1}}{dp}$

$$c_{k-1} = b_{k-1} + pc_{k-2} \qquad \ldots(6) \; \left(\text{if } \frac{db_k}{dp} = c_{k-1}\right)$$

or $\quad c_k = b_k + pc_{k-1}; \; k = 1, 2, \ldots, n - 1$

and $\quad c_0 = \dfrac{db_1}{dp} = \dfrac{d}{dp}(a_1 + pb_0) = b_0$

$\therefore \quad P_n'(p) = \dfrac{dR}{dp} = \dfrac{db_n}{dp} = c_{n-1} \qquad$ | Using (5) and (6)

The Newton-Raphson method in above notation becomes

$$p_{k+1} = p_k - \frac{b_n}{c_{n-1}}, \; k = 0, 1, 2, \ldots$$

This method is often called the *Birge-Vieta method.* Synthetic division for a complete polynomial can completely be written as,

p	a_0	a_1	a_2	...	a_{n-2}	a_{n-1}	a_n
		pb_0	pb_1	...	pb_{n-3}	pb_{n-2}	pb_{n-1}
p	b_0	b_1	b_2	...	b_{n-2}	b_{n-1}	$b_n = R = P_n(p)$
		pc_0	pc_1	...	pc_{n-3}	pc_{n-2}	
	c_0	c_1	c_2	...	c_{n-2}	$c_{n-1} = \dfrac{dR}{dp} = P_n'(p)$	

Q_{n-1} [of degree $(n - 1)$] is called the deflated polynomial. We repeat the first step of Birge-Vieta method using the last value of p to obtain the deflated polynomial. The next real root is obtained using the deflated polynomial.

EXAMPLES

Example 1. *Find the smallest positive root of the polynomial equation $P_3(x) \equiv 2x^3 - 5x + 1 = 0$ using synthetic division and performing two iterations of the Birge-Vieta method. Also find the deflated polynomial. Use the initial approximation $p_0 = 0.5$.*

Sol.

0.5	2	0	– 5	1
		1	0.5	–2.25
0.5	2	1	– 4.5	– 1.25 = b_3
		1	1	
	2	2	– 3.5 = c_2	

$$p_1 = p_0 - \frac{b_3}{c_2} = 0.5 - \left[\frac{-1.25}{-3.5}\right] = 0.142857$$

Again,

0.142857	2	0	– 5	1
		0.285714	0.040816	– 0.708454
	2	0.285714	– 4.959184	0.291546 = b_3
		0.285714	0.081632	
	2	0.571428	– 4.877552 = c_2	

$$p_2 = p_1 - \frac{b_3}{c_2} = 0.202630$$

To obtain the deflated polynomial, we repeat the first part of the Birge-Vieta method, we get

0.202630	2	0	– 5	1
		0.405260	0.082118	– 0.996510
	2	0.405260	– 4.917882	0.003490

Since $b_3 = 0.00349$, this gives the remaining error in satisfying $P_3(x) = 0$. The deflated, polynomial is

$$Q_2(x) = b_0x^2 + b_1x + b_2 = 2x^2 + 0.405260\,x - 4.917882$$

Example 2. *Use Birge-Vieta method to find a real root correct to three decimal places of the equation*

$$x^6 - x^4 - x^3 - 1 = 0, \quad p = 1.5. \text{ Perform three iterations.}$$

Sol.

1.5	1	0	– 1	– 1	0	0	– 1
		1.5	2.25	1.875	1.3125	1.96875	2.953125
1.5	1	1.5	1.25	0.875	1.3125	1.96875	1.953125 = b_6
		1.5	4.5	8.625	14.25	23.34375	
	1	3	5.75	9.5	15.5625	25.3125 = c_5	

$$p_1 = p_0 - \frac{b_6}{c_5} = 1.4228$$

Again

1.4228	1	0	– 1	– 1	0	0	– 1
		1.4228	2.0243	1.4573	0.6506	0.9256	1.3169
1.4228	1	1.4228	1.0243	0.4573	0.6506	0.9256	$0.3169 = b_6$
		1.4228	4.0487	7.2178	10.9201	16.4627	
	1	2.8456	5.073	7.6751	11.5707	$17.3883 = c_5$	

$$p_2 = p_1 - \frac{b_6}{c_5} = 1.4045$$

Again,

1.4045	1	0	– 1	– 1	0	0	– 1
		1.4045	1.9726	1.3660	0.5140	0.7219	1.0139
1.4045	1	1.4045	0.9726	0.3660	0.5140	0.7219	$0.0193 = b_6$
		1.4045	3.9452	6.9070	10.2149	15.0687	
	1	2.8090	4.9178	7.273	10.7289	$15.7906 = c_5$	

$$p_3 = p_2 - \frac{b_6}{c_5} = 1.4036$$

After three iterations, the approximate real root is 1.4036.

ASSIGNMENT

1. Use synthetic division and perform two iterations of the Birge-Vieta method to find the smallest positive root of the equation

$$x^4 - 3x^3 + 3x^2 - 3x + 2 = 0$$

use the initial approximation $p_0 = 0.5$.

2. Use Birge-Vieta method to find a real root correct to three decimals of the following equations:

(*i*) $x^5 - x + 1 = 0, p_0 = -1.5$ (*ii*) $x^3 - 11x^2 + 32x - 22 = 0, p_0 = 0.5$

Answers

1. 1.0

2. (*i*) – 1.167, (*ii*) 1.0

❑❑❑

UNIT-II

Interpolation: Algorithms and Error Analysis of Lagrange and Newton divided difference interpolations, Relationship in various difference operators, Piecewise Linear Interpolation, Cubic Spline Interpolation, Natural Spline, Chebshev Polynomial Approximations, Lanczos Economization of Power Series.

Curve Fitting: Linear and Non Linear Least Squares Approximation, ill Conditioning in Least Squares Methods, Gram-Schmidt Process of Orthogonalization. Computer Algorithms of Least Square Curve fitting.

UNIT-II

Interpolation: Algorithms and Error Analysis of Lagrange and Newton divided difference interpolation, Relationship between various difference operators, Piecewise Linear Interpolation, Cubic Spline Interpolation, Natural Spline, Chebyshev Polynomial Approximations, Lanczos Economization of Power Series.

Curve Fitting: Linear and Non Linear Least Square Approximation, Ill Conditioning in Least Squares Methods, Gram-Schmidt Process of Orthogonalization, Computer Algorithms of Least Squares Curve Fitting.

4

Interpolation

4.1. INTRODUCTION [G.B.T.U. (MCA) 2010, G.B.T.U. MCA (SUM) 2010]

According to Theile, *'Interpolation is the art of reading between the lines of the table'.*

It also means insertion or filling up intermediate terms of the series.

Suppose, we are given the following values of $y = f(x)$ for a set of values of x:

x :	x_0	x_1	x_2	......	x_n
y :	y_0	y_1	y_2	......	y_n

Thus, the process of finding the value of y corresponding to any value of $x = x_i$ between x_0 and x_n is called **interpolation.**

Hence, interpolation is the technique of estimating the value of a function for any intermediate value of the independent variable while the process of computing the value of the function outside the given range is called **extrapolation.**

4.2. ASSUMPTIONS FOR INTERPOLATION

1. There are no sudden jumps or falls in the values during the period under consideration.

2. The rise and fall in the values should be uniform.

e.g., if we are given data regarding deaths in various years in a particular town and some of the observations are for the years in which epidemic or war overtook the town then interpolation methods are not applicable in such cases.

3. When we apply calculus of finite differences, we assume that the given set of observations are capable of being expressed in a polynomial form.

If the function $f(x)$ is known explicitly, the value of y corresponding to any value of x can easily be found.

If the function $f(x)$ is not known, it is required to find a simpler function, say $\phi(x)$ such that $f(x)$ and $\phi(x)$ agree at the set of tabulated points. Such a process is called interpolation. If $\phi(x)$ is a polynomial, then the process is called polynomial interpolation and $\phi(x)$ is called the interpolating polynomial.

4.3. ERRORS IN POLYNOMIAL INTERPOLATION

Let the function $y(x)$ defined by $(n + 1)$ points (x_i, y_i) $i = 0, 1, 2, ..., n$ be continuous and differentiable $(n + 1)$ times and let $y(x)$ be approximated by a polynomial $\phi_n(x)$ of degree not exceeding n such that

$$\phi_n(x_i) = y_i \; ; \; i = 0, 1, 2, ..., n \qquad ...(1)$$

Now problem lies in finding the accuracy of this approximation if we use $\phi_n(x)$ to obtain approximate values of $y(x)$ at some points other than those defined above.

Since the expression $y(x) - \phi_n(x)$ vanishes for $x = x_0, x_1, \ldots\ldots, x_n$, we put

$$y(x) - \phi_n(x) = L\,\Pi_{n+1}(x) \qquad \ldots(2)$$

where $$\Pi_{n+1}(x) = (x - x_0)(x - x_1) \ldots\ldots (x - x_n) \qquad \ldots(3)$$

and L is to be determined such that equation (2) holds for any intermediate value of x say x' where $x_0 < x' < x_n$.

Clearly, $$L = \frac{y(x') - \phi_n(x')}{\Pi_{n+1}(x')} \qquad \ldots(4)$$

Construct a function, $$F(x) = y(x) - \phi_n(x) - L\,\Pi_{n+1}(x) \qquad \ldots(5)$$

where L is given by (4).

It is clear that, $$F(x_0) = F(x_1) = \ldots\ldots = F(x_n) = F(x') = 0$$

i.e., $F(x)$ vanishes $(n + 2)$ times in interval $[x_0, x_n]$ consequently, by repeated application of Rolle's theorem, $F'(x)$ must vanish $(n + 1)$ times, $F''(x)$ must vanish n times in the interval $[x_0, x_n]$.

Particularly, $F^{(n+1)}(x)$ must vanish once in $[x_0, x_n]$.

Let this point be $x = \xi\,;\, x_0 < \xi < x_n$.

Differentiating (5) $(n + 1)$ times w.r.t. x and put $x = \xi$, we get

$$0 = (y)^{(n+1)}(\xi) - L\,(n+1)! \qquad \left|\ \frac{d^{n+1}}{dx^{n+1}}(x^{n+1}) = (n+1)!\right.$$

so that, $$L = \frac{y^{(n+1)}(\xi)}{(n+1)!} \qquad \ldots(6)$$

Comparison of (4) and (6) gives

$$y(x') - \phi_n(x') = \frac{y^{(n+1)}(\xi)}{(n+1)!}\,\Pi_{n+1}(x')$$

Hence, required expression for error is

$$y(x) - \phi_n(x) = \frac{\Pi_{n+1}(x)}{(n+1)!}\,y^{n+1}(\xi),\ x_0 < \xi < x_n \qquad \ldots(7)$$

Since $y(x)$ is generally unknown, hence we do not have any information concerning $y^{(n+1)}(x)$, equation (7) is useless in practical computations.

Particularly, we will use it to determine errors in Newton's interpolating formulae.

The various methods of interpolation are as follows:

(1) The method of graph (2) The method of curve fitting

(3) Use of calculus of finite difference formulae.

The merits of last method over others are

(*i*) It does not assume the form of function to be known.

(*ii*) It is less approximate than method of graphs.

(*iii*) Calculations remain simple even if some additional observations are included in the given data.

The demerit is that there is no definite way to verify whether the assumptions for the application of finite difference calculus are valid for the given set of observations.

4.4. FINITE DIFFERENCES

The calculus of finite differences deals with the changes that take place in the value of the function (dependent variable) due to finite changes in the independent variable.

Suppose, we are given a set of values (x_i, y_i) ; $i = 1, 2, 3, \ldots\ldots, n$ of any function $y = f(x)$. A value of independent variable x is called **argument** and the corresponding value of dependent variable y is called **entry.**

Suppose that the function $y = f(x)$ is tabulated for the equally spaced values $x = x_0$, $x_0 + h, x_0 + 2h, \ldots\ldots, x_0 + nh$ giving $y = y_0, y_1, y_2, \ldots\ldots, y_n$. To determine the values of $f(x)$ or $f'(x)$ for some intermediate values of x, given three types of differences are useful:

1. Forward differences. The differences $y_1 - y_0, y_2 - y_1, y_3 - y_2, \ldots\ldots, y_n - y_{n-1}$ when denoted by $\Delta y_0, \Delta y_1, \Delta y_2, \ldots\ldots, \Delta y_{n-1}$ respectively, are called the first forward differences where Δ is the forward difference operator. *(U.P.T.U. 2009)*

Thus, the first forward differences are

$$\Delta y_r = y_{r+1} - y_r$$

Similarly, the second forward differences are defined by

$$\Delta^2 y_r = \Delta y_{r+1} - \Delta y_r$$

Particularly, $\Delta^2 y_0 = \Delta y_1 - \Delta y_0 = y_2 - y_1 - (y_1 - y_0) = y_2 - 2y_1 + y_0$

Similarly, $\Delta^3 y_0 = y_3 - 3y_2 + 3y_1 - y_0$

$$\Delta^4 y_0 = y_4 - 4y_3 + 6y_2 - 4y_1 + y_0.$$

Clearly, any higher order difference can easily be expressed in terms of ordinates since the coefficients occurring on RHS are the binomial coefficients*. In general, $\Delta^p y_r = \Delta^{p-1} y_{r+1} - \Delta^{p-1} y_r$ defines the pth forward differences.

Following table shows how the forward differences of all orders can be formed.

Forward difference table

x	y	Δy	$\Delta^2 y$	$\Delta^3 y$	$\Delta^4 y$	$\Delta^5 y$
x_0	y_0					
		Δy_0				
x_1	y_1		$\Delta^2 y_0$			
$(= x_0 + h)$		Δy_1		$\Delta^3 y_0$		
x_2	y_2		$\Delta^2 y_1$		$\Delta^4 y_0$	
$(= x_0 + 2h)$		Δy_2		$\Delta^3 y_1$		$\Delta^5 y_0$
x_3	y_3		$\Delta^2 y_2$		$\Delta^4 y_1$	
$= (x_0 + 3h)$		Δy_3		$\Delta^3 y_2$		
x_4	y_4		$\Delta^2 y_3$			
$= (x_0 + 4h)$		Δy_4				
x_5	y_5					
$= (x_0 + 5h)$						

Here, the first entry y_0 is called leading term and Δy_0, $\Delta^2 y_0$, ... are called leading differences.

* $\Delta^n(y_0) = y_n - {}^nC_1\, y_{n-1} + {}^nC_2 y_{n-2} + \cdots\cdots + (-1)^n\, y_0$

Remark. Δ obeys distributive, commutative and index laws:

1. $\Delta [f(x) \pm \phi(x)] = \Delta f(x) \pm \Delta\phi (x)$ 2. $\Delta [c\, f(x)] = c\, \Delta\, f(x)$; c is constant
3. $\Delta^m \Delta^n f(x) = \Delta^{m+n} f(x)$, m, n being (+)ve integers.

But, $\Delta[f(x) \,.\, \phi(x)] \neq f(x) \,.\, \Delta\, \phi(x)$.

2. Backward differences. The differences $y_1 - y_0, y_2 - y_1, ..., y_n - y_{n-1}$ when denoted by $\nabla y_1, \nabla y_2, ..., \nabla y_n$ respectively are called first backward differences where ∇ is the backward difference operator. *(U.P.T.U. 2009)*

Similarly, we define higher order backward differences as,

$$\nabla y_r = y_r - y_{r-1}$$
$$\nabla^2 y_r = \nabla y_r - \nabla y_{r-1}$$
$$\nabla^3 y_r = \nabla^2 y_r - \nabla^2 y_{r-1} \text{ etc.}$$

Particularly,
$$\nabla^2 y_2 = \nabla y_2 - \nabla y_1 = y_2 - y_1 - (y_1 - y_0) = y_2 - 2y_1 + y_0$$
$$\nabla^3 y_3 = \nabla^2 y_3 - \nabla^2 y_2 = y_3 - 3y_2 + 3y_1 - y_0 \text{ etc.}$$

Backward difference table

x	y	∇y	$\nabla^2 y$	$\nabla^3 y$	$\nabla^4 y$	$\nabla^5 y$
x_0	y_0					
		∇y_1				
x_1 $(= x_0 + h)$	y_1		$\nabla^2 y_2$			
		∇y_2		$\nabla^3 y_3$		
x_2 $(= x_0 + 2h)$	y_2		$\nabla^2 y_3$		$\nabla^4 y_4$	
		∇y_3		$\nabla^3 y_4$		$\nabla^5 y_5$
x_3 $(= x_0 + 3h)$	y_3		$\nabla^2 y_4$		$\nabla^4 y_5$	
		∇y_4		$\nabla^3 y_5$		
x_4 $(= x_0 + 4h)$	y_4		$\nabla^2 y_5$			
		∇y_5				
x_5 $(= x_0 + 5h)$	y_5					

3. Central differences. The central difference operator δ is defined by the relations

$$y_1 - y_0 = \delta y_{1/2}, y_2 - y_1 = \delta y_{3/2}, ..., y_n - y_{n-1} = \delta y_{n-\frac{1}{2}}.$$

[G.B.T.U. 2012, U.P.T.U. 2009]

Similarly, high order central differences are defined as

$$\delta y_{3/2} - \delta y_{1/2} = \delta^2 y_1, \quad \delta y_{5/2} - \delta y_{3/2} = \delta^2 y_2 \text{ and so on.}$$

These differences are shown as follows:

Central difference table

x	y	δy	$\delta^2 y$	$\delta^3 y$	$\delta^4 y$	$\delta^5 y$
x_0	y_0					
		$\delta y_{1/2}$				
x_1	y_1		$\delta^2 y_1$			
		$\delta y_{3/2}$		$\delta^3 y_{3/2}$		
x_2	y_2		$\delta^2 y_2$		$\delta^4 y_2$	
		$\delta y_{5/2}$		$\delta^3 y_{5/2}$		$\delta^5 y_{5/2}$
x_3	y_3		$\delta^2 y_3$		$\delta^4 y_3$	
		$\delta y_{7/2}$		$\delta^3 y_{7/2}$		
x_4	y_4		$\delta^2 y_4$			
		$\delta y_{9/2}$				
x_5	y_5					

Note: 1. The central differences on the same horizontal line have same suffix.

2. It is only the notation which changes, not the differences *e.g.*,

$$y_1 - y_0 = \Delta y_0 = \nabla y_1 = \delta y_{1/2}.$$

4.5. OTHER DIFFERENCE OPERATORS

1. Shift operator E. [*G.B.T.U. 2012, U.P.T.U. 2009*]

It is the operation of increasing the argument x by h so that

$$\text{E}f(x) = f(x + h)$$

$$\text{E}^2 f(x) = f(x + 2h) \text{ and so on.}$$

The inverse operator E^{-1} is defined by

$$\text{E}^{-1} f(x) = f(x - h).$$

Also $\quad \text{E}^n y_x = y_{x+nh}.$

2. Averaging operator μ. [*G.B.T.U. 2012, U.P.T.U. 2009*]

It is defined by

$$\mu y_x = \frac{1}{2}\left[y_{x+\frac{1}{2}h} + y_{x-\frac{1}{2}h} \right]$$

In difference calculus, E is fundamental operator and ∇, Δ, δ, μ can be expressed in terms of E.

4.6. RELATION BETWEEN OPERATORS

1. $\boxed{\Delta = \text{E} - 1 \quad \text{or} \quad \text{E} = 1 + \Delta.}$

[*M.T.U. (MCA) 2012, U.P.T.U. (MCA) 2009*]

Proof. We know that,

$$\Delta y_x = y_{x+h} - y_x = \text{E}y_x - y_x = (\text{E} - 1)y_x$$

$\Rightarrow \quad \Delta = \text{E} - 1$

or $\quad \text{E} = 1 + \Delta$

2. $\boxed{\nabla = 1 - \text{E}^{-1}}$

Proof. $\quad \nabla y_x = y_x - y_{x-h} = y_x - \text{E}^{-1} y_x$

$\therefore \quad \nabla = 1 - \text{E}^{-1}$

3. $\boxed{\delta = \text{E}^{1/2} - \text{E}^{-1/2}}$

Proof. $\quad \delta y_x = y_{x+\frac{h}{2}} - y_{x-\frac{h}{2}} = \text{E}^{1/2} y_x - \text{E}^{-1/2} y_x = (\text{E}^{1/2} - \text{E}^{-1/2})\, y_x$

$\therefore \quad \delta = \text{E}^{1/2} - \text{E}^{-1/2}$

4. $\boxed{\mu = \frac{1}{2}(\text{E}^{1/2} + \text{E}^{-1/2})}$

Proof. $\quad \mu y_x = \frac{1}{2}(y_{x+\frac{h}{2}} + y_{x-\frac{h}{2}}) = \frac{1}{2}(\text{E}^{1/2} + \text{E}^{-1/2})\, y_x$

$\Rightarrow \quad \mu = \frac{1}{2}(\text{E}^{1/2} + \text{E}^{-1/2})$

5. $$\boxed{\Delta = E\nabla = \nabla E = \delta E^{1/2}}$$

[*G.B.T.U. 2011, U.P.T.U. (MCA) 2009, M.T.U. 2012*]

Proof.
$$E(\nabla y_x) = E(y_x - y_{x-h}) = y_{x+h} - y_x = \Delta y_x$$
$$\Rightarrow \quad E\nabla = \Delta$$
$$\nabla(E\, y_x) = \nabla\, y_{x+h} = y_{x+h} - y_x = \Delta y_x$$
$$\Rightarrow \quad \nabla E = \Delta$$
$$\delta E^{1/2}\, y_x = \delta y_{x+\frac{h}{2}} = y_{x+h} - y_x = \Delta y_x$$
$$\Rightarrow \quad \delta E^{1/2} = \Delta$$

6. $$\boxed{E = e^{hD}}$$

[*U.P.T.U. (MCA) 2009*]

Proof.
$$Ef(x) = f(x + h)$$
$$= f(x) + h\, f'(x) + \frac{h^2}{2!} f''(x) + \cdots\cdots \qquad \text{(By Taylor series)}$$
$$= f(x) + hDf(x) + \frac{h^2}{2!} D^2 f(x) + \cdots\cdots$$
$$= \left[1 + hD + \frac{(h\,D)^2}{2!} + \cdots\cdots\right] f(x) = e^{hD} f(x)$$
$$\therefore \quad E = e^{hD} \quad \text{or} \quad \Delta = e^{hD} - 1.$$

4.7. DIFFERENCES OF A POLYNOMIAL

The nth differences of a polynomial of nth degree are constant and all higher order differences are zero when the values of the independent variable are at equal interval.

Let
$$f(x) = ax^n + bx^{n-1} + cx^{n-2} + \ldots\ldots + kx + l$$
$$\therefore \quad \Delta f(x) = f(x + h) - f(x)$$
$$= a[(x + h)^n - x^n] + b\,[(x + h)^{n-1} - x^{n-1}] + \ldots\ldots + kh$$
$$= anhx^{n-1} + b'x^{n-2} + c'x^{n-3} + \ldots\ldots + k'x + l' \qquad \ldots(1)$$

where b', c', ..., l' are new constant coefficients.

$\therefore$ First differences of a polynomial of nth degree is a polynomial of degree $(n - 1)$.

Similarly,
$$\Delta^2 f(x) = \Delta f(x + h) - \Delta f(x)$$
$$= anh\,[(x + h)^{n-1} - x^{n-1}] + b'[(x + h)^{n-2} - x^{n-2}] + \ldots\ldots + k'h$$
$$= an(n - 1)\, h^2 x^{n-2} + b''x^{n-3} + \ldots\ldots + k'' \qquad \ldots(2)$$

$\therefore$ Second differences represent a polynomial of degree $(n - 2)$.

Continuing this process, for n^{th} differences, we get a polynomial of degree zero *i.e.*,
$$\Delta^n f(x) = an(n - 1)\,(n - 2) \ldots\ldots 1\, h^n = a\, n!\, h^n$$

which is a constant. Hence, the $(n + 1)^{th}$ and higher differences of a polynomial of nth degree will be zero. Converse of this theorem is also true.

EXAMPLES

Example 1. *Construct the forward difference table, given that*

x:	5	10	15	20	25	30
y:	9962	9848	9659	9397	9063	8660

and point out the values of $\Delta^2 y_{10}$, $\Delta^4 y_5$.

Sol. Forward difference table is as follows:

x	y	Δy	$\Delta^2 y$	$\Delta^3 y$	$\Delta^4 y$
5	9962				
		– 114			
10	9848		– 75		
		– 189		2	
15	9659		– 73		– 1
		– 262		1	
20	9397		– 72		2
		– 334		3	
25	9063		– 69		
		– 403			
30	8660				

From the table, $\Delta^2 y_{10} = -73$ and $\Delta^4 y_5 = -1$.

Example 2. *Construct a backward difference table for* $y = \log x$ *given that*

x:	10	20	30	40	50
y:	1	1.3010	1.4771	1.6021	1.6990

and find values of $\nabla^3 \log 40$ *and* $\nabla^4 \log 50$.

Sol. Backward difference table is:

x	y	∇y	$\nabla^2 y$	$\nabla^3 y$	$\nabla^4 y$
10	1				
		0.3010			
20	1.3010		– 0.1249		
		0.1761		0.0738	
30	1.4771		– 0.0511		– 0.0508
		0.1250		0.0230	
40	1.6021		– 0.0281		
		0.0969			
50	1.6990				

From the table, $\nabla^3 \log 40 = 0.0738$ and $\nabla^4 \log 50 = -0.0508$.

Example 3. (*i*) *Find* $f(6)$ *given* $f(0) = -3$, $f(1) = 6$, $f(2) = 8$, $f(3) = 12$; *third difference being constant.*

(*ii*) *Find* $\Delta^{10}(1 - ax)(1 - bx^2)(1 - cx^3)(1 - dx^4)$.

Sol. (*i*) The difference table is:

x	$f(x)$	$\Delta f(x)$	$\Delta^2 f(x)$	$\Delta^3 f(x)$
0	– 3			
		9		
1	6		– 7	
		2		9
2	8		2	
		4		
3	12			

$$f(0 + 6) = E^6 f(0) = (1 + \Delta)^6 f(0) = (1 + 6\Delta + 15\Delta^2 + 20\Delta^3)\, f(0)$$
$$= -3 + 6\,(9) + 15\,(-7) + 20\,(9) = 126.$$

(*ii*) Maximum power of x in polynomial will be 10 and co-efficient of x^{10} will be $abcd$.

Here, $k = abcd,\ h = 1,\ n = 10$

$\therefore$ Expression $= kh^n n\,! = abcd\ 10\,!$

Example 4. *Evaluate:*

(*i*) $\Delta\ tan^{-1} x$ (*ii*) $\Delta^2\ cos\ 2x$

where h is the interval of differencing.

Sol. (*i*) $\Delta \tan^{-1} x = \tan^{-1}(x + h) - \tan^{-1} x$

$$= \tan^{-1}\left\{\frac{x + h - x}{1 + x\,(x + h)}\right\} = \tan^{-1}\left(\frac{h}{1 + hx + x^2}\right)$$

(*ii*) $\Delta^2 \cos 2x = \Delta[\cos 2(x + h) - \cos 2x]$

$$= [\cos 2(x + 2h) - \cos 2(x + h)] - [\cos 2(x + h) - \cos 2x]$$
$$= -2 \sin(2x + 3h) \sin h + 2 \sin(2x + h) \sin h$$
$$= -2 \sin h\, [2 \cos(2x + 2h) \sin h] = -4 \sin^2 h \cos 2(x + h).$$

Example 5. *If* $f(x) = exp(ax)$, *evaluate* $\Delta^n f(x)$.

Sol. $\Delta e^{ax} = e^{a(x+h)} - e^{ax} = (e^{ah} - 1)e^{ax}$

$$\Delta^2 e^{ax} = \Delta(\Delta e^{ax}) = \Delta[(e^{ah} - 1)e^{ax}] = (e^{ah} - 1)(e^{ah} - 1)e^{ax} = (e^{ah} - 1)^2 e^{ax}$$

Similarly, $\Delta^3 e^{ax} = (e^{ah} - 1)^3 e^{ax}$

$\vdots \quad \vdots \quad \vdots$

$$\Delta^n e^{ax} = (e^{ah} - 1)^n e^{ax}.$$

Example 6. *With usual notations, prove that,*

$$\Delta^n\left(\frac{1}{x}\right) = (-1)^n \cdot \frac{n!\,h^n}{x\,(x + h)\,......\,(x + nh)}.$$

Sol.
$$\Delta^n\left(\frac{1}{x}\right) = \Delta^{n-1}\,\Delta\left(\frac{1}{x}\right) = \Delta^{n-1}\left[\frac{1}{x + h} - \frac{1}{x}\right] = (-1)\,\Delta^{n-2}\left[\Delta\left(\frac{1}{x} - \frac{1}{x + h}\right)\right]$$

$$= (-1)\,\Delta^{n-2}\left[\left(\frac{1}{x + h} - \frac{1}{x}\right) - \left(\frac{1}{x + 2h} - \frac{1}{x + h}\right)\right]$$

$$= (-1)\,\Delta^{n-2}\left[\frac{2}{x+h}-\frac{1}{x}-\frac{1}{x+2h}\right] = (-1)\,\Delta^{n-2}\left[\frac{-2h^2}{x(x+h)(x+2h)}\right]$$

$$= (-1)^2\,\Delta^{n-2}\left[\frac{2!\,h^2}{x(x+h)(x+2h)}\right] = (-1)^3\,\Delta^{n-3}\left[\frac{3!\,h^3}{x(x+h)(x+2h)(x+3h)}\right]$$

$$\vdots$$

$$= (-1)^n\,\frac{n!\,h^n}{x(x+h)\,......\,(x+nh)}.$$

Example 7. *Evaluate:* (*i*) Δ^n [*sin* $(ax + b)$] (*ii*) Δ^n [*cos* $(ax + b)$].

Sol. (*i*) $\Delta \sin(ax + b) = \sin[a(x + h) + b] - \sin(ax + b)$

$$= 2\sin\frac{ah}{2}\cos\left[a\left(x+\frac{h}{2}\right)+b\right] = 2\sin\frac{ah}{2}\sin\left(ax+b+\frac{ah+\pi}{2}\right)$$

$$\therefore \quad \Delta^2 \sin(ax+b) = \Delta\left[2\sin\frac{ah}{2}\sin\left(ax+b+\frac{ah+\pi}{2}\right)\right]$$

$$= \left(2\sin\frac{ah}{2}\right)\left(2\sin\frac{ah}{2}\right)\sin\left[ax+b+\frac{ah+\pi}{2}+\frac{ah+\pi}{2}\right]$$

$$= \left(2\sin\frac{ah}{2}\right)^2\sin\left[ax+b+2\left(\frac{ah+\pi}{2}\right)\right]$$

Proceeding in the same manner, we get

$$\Delta^3 \sin(ax+b) = \left(2\sin\frac{ah}{2}\right)^3\sin\left[ax+b+\frac{3(ah+\pi)}{2}\right]$$

$$\vdots \qquad\qquad \vdots$$

$$\Delta^n \sin(ax+b) = \left(2\sin\frac{ah}{2}\right)^n\sin\left[ax+b+\frac{n(ah+\pi)}{2}\right]$$

Similarly,

$$(ii) \quad \Delta^n \cos(ax+b) = \left(2\sin\frac{ah}{2}\right)^n\cos\left[ax+b+n\left(\frac{ah+\pi}{2}\right)\right].$$

Example 8. *Prove that*

(*i*) $\Delta \log f(x) = \log\left[1+\frac{\Delta f(x)}{f(x)}\right]$ (*ii*) $\mu = \sqrt{\left(1+\frac{\delta^2}{4}\right)}$.

[G.B.T.U. 2013, U.P.T.U. 2009]

Sol. (*i*)

$$\text{LHS} = \log f(x+h) - \log f(x)$$

$$= \log[f(x) + \Delta f(x)] - \log f(x) \qquad | \because \Delta f(x) = f(x+h) - f(x)$$

$$= \log\left[\frac{f(x)+\Delta f(x)}{f(x)}\right] = \log\left[1+\frac{\Delta f(x)}{f(x)}\right] = \text{RHS}$$

(*ii*)
$$\text{RHS} = \sqrt{1+\frac{\delta^2}{4}}$$
$$= \sqrt{1+\frac{1}{4}(E^{1/2}-E^{-1/2})^2} \qquad | \because \quad \delta = E^{1/2} - E^{-1/2}$$
$$= \frac{1}{2}\sqrt{4+(E^{1/2}-E^{-1/2})^2}$$
$$= \frac{1}{2}\sqrt{(E^{1/2}+E^{-1/2})^2} = \frac{E^{1/2}+E^{-1/2}}{2} = \mu = \text{LHS}$$

Example 9. *Prove that* $e^x = \left(\frac{\Delta^2}{E}\right) e^x \cdot \frac{Ee^x}{\Delta^2 e^x}$. (M.T.U. 2013)

Sol.
$$\left(\frac{\Delta^2}{E}\right) e^x = \Delta^2 E^{-1} e^x = \Delta^2 e^{x-h} = e^{-h} \Delta^2 e^x$$
$$\text{RHS} = e^{-h} \cdot \Delta^2 e^x \cdot \frac{E\, e^x}{\Delta^2 e^x} = e^{-h} \cdot E\, e^x = e^{-h} e^{x+h} = e^x.$$

Example 10. *Prove that,*

(*i*) $(E^{1/2} + E^{-1/2})(1 + \Delta)^{1/2} = 2 + \Delta$ (U.P.T.U. 2009)

(*ii*) $\Delta = \frac{1}{2}\delta^2 + \delta\sqrt{1+(\delta^2/4)}$ [G.B.T.U. 2013, U.P.T.U. 2009, G.B.T.U. (C.O.) 2011]

(*iii*) $\Delta^3 y_2 = \nabla^3 y_5$.

(*iv*) $hD = -\log(1-\nabla) = \sin h^{-1}(\mu\delta)$. (M.T.U. 2013, U.P.T.U. 2006)

Sol. (*i*) $(E^{1/2} + E^{-1/2})\, E^{1/2} = E + 1 = 1 + \Delta + 1 = \Delta + 2$

(*ii*)
$$\frac{1}{2}\delta^2 + \delta\sqrt{1+\frac{\delta^2}{4}} = \frac{1}{2}(E^{1/2}-E^{-1/2})^2 + (E^{1/2}-E^{-1/2})\sqrt{1+\frac{1}{4}(E^{1/2}-E^{-1/2})^2}$$
$$= \frac{1}{2}(E + E^{-1} - 2) + (E^{1/2}-E^{-1/2})\left(\frac{E^{1/2}+E^{-1/2}}{2}\right)$$
$$= \frac{1}{2}(2E - 2) = E - 1 = \Delta$$

(*iii*)
$$\Delta^3 y_2 = (E-1)^3 y_2$$
$$= (E^3 - 3E^2 + 3E - 1)\, y_2 = y_5 - 3y_4 + 3y_3 - y_2$$
$$\nabla^3 y_5 = (1 - E^{-1})\, y_5$$
$$= (1 - 3E^{-1} + 3E^{-2} - E^{-3})\, y_5 = y_5 - 3y_4 + 3y_3 - y_2$$

(*iv*)
$$hD = \log E = -\log(E^{-1}) = -\log(1-\nabla) \qquad | \because \quad E^{-1} = 1 - \nabla$$

Also,
$$\mu = \frac{1}{2}(E^{1/2} + E^{-1/2}) \quad \text{and} \quad \delta = E^{1/2} - E^{-1/2}$$

$\therefore$
$$\mu\delta = \frac{1}{2}(E - E^{-1}) = \frac{1}{2}(e^{hD} - e^{-hD}) = \sinh(hD)$$

or
$$hD = \sinh^{-1}(\mu\delta).$$

Example 11. *Prove that*

(i) $\Delta + \nabla = \frac{\Delta}{\nabla} - \frac{\nabla}{\Delta}$, *where* Δ *and* ∇ *are forward difference and backward difference operators respectively.* [G.B.T.U. 2012, G.B.T.U. (MCA) 2010, 2011; U.P.T.U. 2008, 2009]

(ii) $\sum_{r=0}^{n-1} \Delta^2 y_r = \Delta y_n - \Delta y_0$ *(iii)* $\Delta^r y_k = \nabla^r y_{k+r}$.

Sol. *(i)*

$$\frac{\Delta}{\nabla} - \frac{\nabla}{\Delta} = \frac{E-1}{1-E^{-1}} - \frac{1-E^{-1}}{E-1} = \frac{E-1}{\left(\frac{E-1}{E}\right)} - \frac{\left(\frac{E-1}{E}\right)}{E-1} = E - \frac{1}{E} = E - E^{-1}$$

$$= (E-1) + (1-E^{-1}) = \Delta + \nabla$$

(ii)

$$\sum_{r=0}^{n-1} \Delta^2 y_r = \sum_{r=0}^{n-1} (\Delta y_{r+1} - \Delta y_r) = \Delta y_1 - \Delta y_0 + \Delta y_2 - \Delta y_1 + \cdots\cdots + \Delta y_n - \Delta y_{n-1}$$

$$= \Delta y_n - \Delta y_0.$$

(iii)

$$\nabla^r y_{k+r} = (1-E^{-1})^r y_{k+r} = \left(\frac{E-1}{E}\right)^r y_{k+r} = (E-1)^r E^{-r} y_{k+r} = \Delta^r y_k.$$

Example 12. *Prove that*

(i) $\mu\delta = \frac{1}{2}(\Delta + \nabla) = \frac{\Delta E^{-1}}{2} + \frac{\Delta}{2}$ [G.B.T.U. 2011]

(ii) $1 + \left(\frac{\delta^2}{2}\right) = \sqrt{1 + \delta^2\mu^2}$ [G.B.T.U. 2013, U.P.T.U. 2014]

(iii) $\nabla^2 = h^2D^2 - h^3D^3 + \frac{7}{12} h^4D^4 \ldots\ldots$ *(iv)* $\nabla - \Delta = -\nabla\Delta$

[G.B.T.U. (C.O.) 2010; G.B.T.U. (MCA) 2010, 2011]

Sol. *(i)*

$$\mu\delta = \frac{1}{2}(E^{1/2} + E^{-1/2})(E^{1/2} - E^{-1/2})$$

$$= \frac{1}{2}(E - E^{-1}) = \frac{1}{2}[(E-1) + (1-E^{-1})] \qquad \ldots(1)$$

$$\Rightarrow \qquad \mu\delta = \frac{1}{2}(\Delta + \nabla)$$

Also from (1),

$$\mu\delta = \frac{1}{2}[\Delta + (E-1)E^{-1}] = \frac{1}{2}(\Delta + \Delta E^{-1}) = \frac{\Delta E^{-1}}{2} + \frac{\Delta}{2}$$

Hence, the results.

(ii) $$\text{LHS} = 1+\left(\frac{\delta^2}{2}\right) = 1+\frac{(E^{1/2}-E^{-1/2})^2}{2}$$

$$= 1+\left(\frac{E+E^{-1}-2}{2}\right) = \frac{1}{2}(E+E^{-1})$$

$$\text{RHS} = \sqrt{1+\delta^2\mu^2}$$

$$= \left[1+\left\{(E^{1/2}-E^{-1/2})^2 \cdot \frac{1}{4}(E^{1/2}+E^{-1/2})^2\right\}\right]^{1/2}$$

$$= \left\{1+\left(\frac{(E-E^{-1})^2}{4}\right)\right\}^{1/2} = \left(\frac{E^2+E^{-2}+2}{4}\right)^{1/2} = \left(\frac{E+E^{-1}}{2}\right)$$

Hence, LHS = RHS

(iii) $E = e^{hD}$ and $\nabla = 1 - E^{-1}$

$\therefore$ $\nabla^2 = (1-e^{-hD})^2$

$$= \left[1-\left\{1-hD+\frac{(hD)^2}{2!}-\frac{(hD)^3}{3!}+\frac{(hD)^4}{4!}-\ldots\right\}\right]^2$$

$$= \left\{hD-\frac{(hD)^2}{2!}+\frac{(hD)^3}{3!}-\frac{(hD)^4}{4!}+\ldots\right\}^2$$

$$= h^2D^2\left[1-\left\{\frac{hD}{2}-\frac{(hD)^2}{6}+\ldots\right\}\right]^2$$

$$= h^2D^2\left[1+\left\{\frac{hD}{2}-\frac{(hD)^2}{6}+\ldots\right\}^2-2\left\{\frac{hD}{2}-\frac{(hD)^2}{6}+\ldots\right\}\right]$$

$$= h^2D^2\left[1-hD+\left(\frac{1}{4}+\frac{1}{3}\right)(hD)^2-\ldots\right]$$

$$= h^2D^2\left(1-hD+\frac{7}{12}h^2D^2-\ldots\right) = h^2D^2-h^3D^3+\frac{7}{12}h^4D^4-\ldots$$

(iv) $$\nabla-\Delta = (1-E^{-1})-(E-1) = \left(\frac{E-1}{E}\right)-(E-1) = (E-1)(E^{-1}-1)$$

$$= -(E-1)(1-E^{-1}) = -\nabla\Delta$$

Example 13. *Prove that if m is a (+)ve integer then*

$$\frac{(x+1)^{(m)}}{m!} = \frac{x^{(m)}}{m!}+\frac{x^{(m-1)}}{(m-1)!}$$

Sol. RHS $= \dfrac{x(x-1)......(x-m+1)}{m!} + \dfrac{x(x-1)......(x-m+2)}{(m-1)!}$

$= \dfrac{x(x-1)(x-2)......(x-m+2)}{m!}[(x-m+1)+m]$

$= \dfrac{(x+1)\,x(x-1)(x-2)......(x-m+2)}{m!} = \dfrac{(x+1)^{(m)}}{m!} = \text{LHS}$

Example 14. *Given* $u_0 + u_8 = 1.9243$, $u_1 + u_7 = 1.9590$
$u_2 + u_6 = 1.9823$, $u_3 + u_5 = 1.9956$. *Find* u_4.

Sol. Taking $\Delta^8 u_0 = 0$

$\Rightarrow$ $(E-1)^8 u_0 = 0$

$\Rightarrow$ $u_8 - 8c_1u_7 + 8c_2u_6 - 8c_3u_5 + 8c_4u_4 - 8c_5u_3 + 8c_6u_2 - 8c_7u_1 + 8c_8u_0 = 0$

$\Rightarrow$ $(u_0 + u_8) - 8(u_1 + u_7) + 28(u_2 + u_6) - 56(u_3 + u_5) + 70\,u_4 = 0$

$\Rightarrow$ $u_4 = 0.99996.$ (After putting the values)

ASSIGNMENT

1. (*i*) Form a table of differences for the function:
$f(x) = x^3 + 5x - 7$ for $x = -1, 0, 1, 2, 3, 4, 5$. Continue the table to obtain $f(6)$ and $f(7)$.
(*ii*) If $y = x^3 + x^2 - 2x + 1$, calculate values of y for $x = 0, 1, 2, 3, 4, 5$ and form the difference table. Find the value of y at $x = 6$ by extending the table and verify that the same value is obtained by substitution.

2. Prove that: $D \sin^{-1} x = \sin^{-1}[(x+1)\sqrt{1-x^2} - x\sqrt{1-(x+1)^2}]$.

3. (*i*) Write forward difference table for

x:	10	20	30	40
y:	1.1	2.0	4.4	7.9.

(*ii*) Assuming that the following values of y belong to a polynomial of degree 4, compute the next three values:

x :	0	1	2	3	4	5	6	7
y :	1	– 1	1	– 1	1	—	—	—

4. Construct the table of differences for the data below.

x :	0	1	2	3	4
$f(x)$:	1.0	1.5	2.2	3.1	4.6

Evaluate $\Delta^3 f(2)$.

5. Prove that:

(*i*) $\nabla = \Delta E^{-1} = E^{-1}\Delta = 1 - E^{-1}$ (*ii*) $E^{1/2} = \mu + \frac{1}{2}\delta$

(*iii*) $\delta = \Delta E^{-1/2} = \nabla E^{1/2}$ (*iv*) $E = (1-\nabla)^{-1}$

(*v*) $\Delta\nabla = \nabla\Delta = \delta^2$ (*G.B.T.U. 2011*) (*vi*) $\delta = \Delta(1+\Delta)^{-1/2} = \nabla(1-\nabla)^{-1/2}$ (*U.P.T.U. 2009*)

(*vii*) $\delta^2 E = \Delta^2$ (*G.B.T.U. 2012*) (*viii*) $\mu\delta = \frac{1}{2}(E - E^{-1})$ (*G.B.T.U. 2012*)

(*ix*) $\Delta \equiv \nabla(1-\nabla)^{-1}$ [*M.T.U. (MCA) 2012*]

6. u_x is a function of x for which fifth differences are constant and
$u_1 + u_7 = -786$, $u_2 + u_6 = 686$, $u_3 + u_5 = 1088$. Find u_4.

7. Prove that:

(*i*) $u_4 = u_3 + \Delta u_2 + \Delta^2 u_1 + \Delta^3 u_1$ (*ii*) $u_4 = u_0 + 4\Delta u_0 + 6\Delta^2 u_{-1} + 10\Delta^3 u_{-1}$.

8. Evaluate:

(*i*) $\Delta(e^{ax} \log bx)$ (*ii*) $\Delta\left(\dfrac{2^x}{(x+1)!}\right)$; $h = 1$.

Answers

1. (*i*) 239, 371 (*ii*) 1, 1, 9, 31, 73, 141; 241
3. (*ii*) 31, 129, 351 4. 0.4
6. 570.9.
8. (*i*) $e^{ax}\left[e^{ah} \log\left(1 + \dfrac{h}{x}\right) + (e^{ah} - 1) \log bx\right]$ (*ii*) $-\dfrac{x}{(x+2)!}\ 2^x$.

4.8. FACTORIAL NOTATION

A product of the form $x(x-1)(x-2)$ ...... $(x - r + 1)$ is denoted by $[x]^r$ and is called a factorial.

Particularly, $[x] = x$; $[x]^2 = x(x-1)$; $[x]^3 = x(x-1)(x-2)$ etc.

In case the interval of differencing is h then

$$[x]^n = x(x-h)(x-2h) \ldots\ldots (x - \overline{n-1}\, h)$$

Factorial notation helps in finding the successive differences of a polynomial directly by simple rule of differentiation.

4.9. TO SHOW THAT (i) $\Delta^n[x]^n = n!$ (ii) $\Delta^{n+1}[x]^n = 0$

$$\Delta[x]^n = [(x+h)]^n - [x]^n$$

$$= (x+h)(x+h-h)(x+h-2h) \ldots\ldots (x + h - \overline{n-1}\, h)$$

$$- x(x-h)(x-2h) \ldots\ldots (x - \overline{n-1}\, h)$$

$$= x(x-h) \ldots\ldots (x - \overline{n-2}\, h)\,[x + h - (x - nh + h)] = nh\,[x]^{n-1}$$

Similarly, $\Delta^2[x]^n = \Delta[nh\,[x]^{n-1}] = nh\,\Delta[x]^{n-1} = n(n-1)\,h^2\,[x]^{n-2}$

$$\vdots$$

$$\Delta^n[x]^n = n(n-1) \ldots.. 2\,.\,1\,.\,h^{n-1}(x + h - x) = n!\,h^n$$

Also, $\Delta^{n+1}[x]^n = n!\,h^n - n!\,h^n = 0$

when $h = 1$, $\Delta[x]^n = n[x]^{n-1}$ and $\Delta^n[x]^n = n!$

Hence, the result of differencing $[x]^r$ is analogous to that of differencing x^r when $h = 1$.

4.10. TO SHOW THAT $x^{(-n)} = \dfrac{1}{(x+n)^{(n)}}$, THE INTERVAL OF DIFFERENCING BEING UNITY

By definition of $x^{(n)}$, we have

$$x^{(n)} = (x - \overline{n-1}\, h)\, x^{(n-1)} \quad \ldots(1)$$

when interval of differencing is h.

$\therefore$ When $n = 0$, we have $\quad x^{(0)} = (x + h)\, x^{(-1)}$ ...(2)

Since, $\quad \Delta x^{(n)} = nhx^{(n-1)}$ ...(3)

when $n = 1$, $\Delta x^{(1)} = hx^{(0)}$.

$$\Rightarrow \quad \Delta x = h\, x^{(0)} \;\Rightarrow\; h = hx^{(0)} \;\Rightarrow\; x^{(0)} = 1$$

From (2), $\quad x^{(-1)} = \dfrac{1}{(x+h)}$ ...(4)

when $n = -1$, from (1),

$$x^{(-1)} = (x + 2h)\, x^{(-2)}$$

$$\Rightarrow \quad \frac{1}{x+h} = (x + 2h)\, x^{(-2)} \quad \Rightarrow \quad x^{(-2)} = \frac{1}{(x+h)(x+2h)}$$

In general, $\quad x^{(-n)} = \dfrac{1}{(x+h)(x+2h)\ldots\ldots(x+nh)}$ ...(5)

$$x^{(-n)} = \frac{1}{(x+nh)^{(n)}}$$

Here $x^{(-n)}$ is called reciprocal factorial where n is a (+)ve integer.

Particular case. When $h = 1$, $\quad x^{(-n)} = \dfrac{1}{(x+n)^{(n)}}$.

4.11. MISSING TERM TECHNIQUE

Suppose n values out of $(n + 1)$ values of $y = f(x)$ are given, the values of x being equidistant.

Let the unknown value be N. We construct the difference table.

Since only n values of y are known, we can assume $y = f(x)$ to be a polynomial of degree $(n - 1)$ in x.

Equating to zero the nth difference, we can get the value of N.

EXAMPLES

Example 1. *Express $f(x) = x^4 - 12x^3 + 24x^2 - 30x + 9$ and its successive differences in factorial notation. Hence show that $\Delta^5 f(x) = 0$.*

Sol. Let $\quad f(x) = \text{A}[x]^4 + \text{B}[x]^3 + \text{C}[x]^2 + \text{D}[x] + \text{E}$

Using method of synthetic division, we divide by x, $x - 1$, $x - 2$, $x - 3$ etc. successively, then

1	1	− 12	24	− 30	9 = E
		1	− 11	13	
2	1	− 11	13	− 17 = D	
		2	− 18		
3	1	− 9	− 5 = C		
		3			
4	1	− 6 = B			
	1 = A				

Hence, $f(x) = [x]^4 - 6[x]^3 - 5[x]^2 - 17[x] + 9$

$$\therefore \quad \Delta f(x) = 4[x]^3 - 18[x]^2 - 10[x] - 17$$

$$\Delta^2 f(x) = 12[x]^2 - 36[x] - 10$$

$$\Delta^3 f(x) = 24[x] - 36$$

$$\Delta^4 f(x) = 24 \quad \text{and} \quad \Delta^5 f(x) = 0.$$

Example 2. *Obtain the function whose first difference is* $9x^2 + 11x + 5$.

Sol. Let $f(x)$ be the required function so that $\Delta f(x) = 9x^2 + 11x + 5$

Let $9x^2 + 11x + 5 = 9[x]^2 + A[x] + B = 9x(x - 1) + Ax + B$

Putting $x = 0,\ B = 5$ and $x = 1,\ A = 20$

$$\therefore \quad \Delta f(x) = 9[x]^2 + 20[x] + 5$$

Integrating, we get

$$f(x) = 9\,\frac{[x]^3}{3} + 20\,\frac{[x]^2}{2} + 5[x] + c$$

$$= 3x(x - 1)(x - 2) + 10x(x - 1) + 5x + c = 3x^3 + x^2 + x + c$$

where c is the constant of integration.

Example 3. *Find the missing values in the table:*

x:	45	50	55	60	65
y:	3	—	2	—	− 2.4.

Sol. Difference table is as follows:

x	y	Δy	$\Delta^2 y$	$\Delta^3 y$
45	3			
		$y_1 - 3$		
50	y_1		$5 - 2y_1$	
		$2 - y_1$		$3y_1 + y_3 - 9$
55	2		$y_1 + y_3 - 4$	
		$y_3 - 2$		$3.6 - y_1 - 3y_3$
60	y_3		$-0.4 - 2y_3$	
		$-2.4 - y_3$		
65	-2.4			

As only three entries y_0, y_2, y_4 are given, the function y can be represented by a second degree polynomial.

$$\therefore \quad \Delta^3 y_0 = 0 \quad \text{and} \quad \Delta^3 y_1 = 0$$

$$\Rightarrow \quad 3y_1 + y_3 = 9 \quad \text{and} \quad y_1 + 3y_3 = 3.6$$

Solving these, we get

$$y_1 = 2.925, \quad y_2 = 0.225.$$

Example 4. *Find the relation between* α, β *and* γ *in order that* $\alpha + \beta x + \gamma x^2$ *may be expressible in one term in the factorial notation.*

Sol. Let $$f(x) = \alpha + \beta x + \gamma x^2 = (a + bx)^{(2)}$$

where a and b are certain unknown constants.

Now,
$$(a + bx)^{(2)} = (a + bx)\,[a + b(x - 1)]$$
$$= (a + bx)(a - b + bx) = (a + bx)^2 - ab - b^2x$$
$$= (a^2 - ab) + (2ab - b^2)x + b^2x^2 = \alpha + \beta x + \gamma x^2$$

Comparing the co-efficients of various powers of x, we get
$$\alpha = a^2 - ab,\ \beta = 2ab - b^2,\ \gamma = b^2$$

Eliminating a and b from the above equations, we get $\gamma^2 + 4\alpha\gamma = \beta^2$

Example 5. (*i*) *Estimate the missing term in the following table:*

x:	*0*	*1*	*2*	*3*	*4*
y = f(x):	*1*	*3*	*9*	*?*	*81.*

[G.B.T.U. (C.O.) 2010]

(*ii*) *Find the missing term in the table:*

x:	*2*	*3*	*4*	*5*	*6*
f(x):	*45*	*49.2*	*54.1*	*?*	*67.4*

[M.T.U. 2013, U.P.T.U. 2008]

Sol. (*i*) We are given Four values

$\therefore$ $$\Delta^4 f(x) = 0 \quad \forall\, x$$
$\Rightarrow$ $$(\mathrm{E} - 1)^4 f(x) = 0 \quad \forall\, x$$
$\Rightarrow$ $$(\mathrm{E}^4 - 4\mathrm{E}^3 + 6\mathrm{E}^2 - 4\mathrm{E} + 1) f(x) = 0 \quad \forall\, x$$
$\Rightarrow$ $$f(x + 4) - 4f(x + 3) + 6f(x + 2) - 4f(x + 1) + f(x) = 0 \quad \forall\, x$$

where interval of differencing is 1.

Now putting $x = 0$, we obtain,

$$f(4) - 4f(3) + 6f(2) - 4f(1) + f(0) = 0 \qquad ...(1)$$
$\Rightarrow$ $$81 - 4f(3) + 54 - 12 + 1 = 0 \qquad \text{(From table)}$$
$\Rightarrow$ $$4f(3) = 124 \Rightarrow f(3) = 31.$$

(*ii*) We are given four values.

$\therefore$ $$\Delta^4 f(x) = 0 \quad \forall\, x$$
$\Rightarrow$ $$(\mathrm{E} - 1)^4 f(x) = 0 \quad \forall\, x$$
$\Rightarrow$ $$(\mathrm{E}^4 - 4\mathrm{E}^3 + 6\mathrm{E}^2 - 4\mathrm{E} + 1) f(x) = 0 \quad \forall x$$
$\Rightarrow$ $$f(x + 4) - 4f(x + 3) + 6f(x + 2) - 4f(x + 1) + f(x) = 0 \quad \forall\, x$$

where interval of differencing is 1.

Now, putting $x = 2$, we obtain,

$$f(6) - 4f(5) + 6f(4) - 4f(3) + f(2) = 0$$
$\Rightarrow$ $$67.4 - 4f(5) + (6 \times 54.1) - (4 \times 49.2) + 45 = 0$$
$\Rightarrow$ $$4f(5) = 240.2$$
$\Rightarrow$ $$f(5) = 60.05$$

Example 6. *Estimate the production for 1964 and 1966 from the following data:*

Year:	*1961*	*1962*	*1963*	*1964*	*1965*	*1966*	*1967*
Production:	*200*	*220*	*260*	—	*350*	—	*430*

Sol. Since five figures are known, assume all the fifth order differences as zero. Since two figures are unknown, we need two equations to determine them.

Hence, $\Delta^5 y_0 = 0$ and $\Delta^5 y_1 = 0$

$\Rightarrow$ $(E - 1)^5 y_0 = 0$ and $(E - 1)^5 y_1 = 0$

$\Rightarrow$ $y_5 - 5y_4 + 10y_3 - 10y_2 + 5y_1 - y_0 = 0$

and $y_6 - 5y_5 + 10y_4 - 10y_3 + 5y_2 - y_1 = 0$

Substituting the known values, we get

$$y_5 - 1750 + 10y_3 - 2600 + 1100 - 200 = 0$$

and $430 - 5y_5 + 3500 - 10y_3 + 1300 - 220 = 0$

$\Rightarrow$ $y_5 + 10y_3 = 3450$ ...(1)

and $-5y_5 - 10y_3 = -5010$ ...(2)

Adding (1) and (2), we get

$$-4y_5 = -1560 \quad \Rightarrow \quad y_5 = 390$$

From (1), $390 + 10y_3 = 3450$

$\Rightarrow$ $10y_3 = 3060 \quad \Rightarrow \quad y_3 = 306$

Hence production for year 1964 = 306

and production for year 1966 = 390.

ASSIGNMENT

1. (*i*) Estimate the missing term in the following:

x :	1	2	3	4	5	6	7
y :	2	4	8	—	32	64	128

Explain why the result differs from 16?

(*ii*) Find the missing value of the following data:

x :	1	2	3	4	5
$f(x)$:	7	☒	13	21	37

2. (*i*) From the following data, find the value of U_{47}:

$$U_{46} = 0.2884, \quad U_{48} = 0.5356, \quad U_{49} = 0.6513, \quad U_{50} = 0.7620.$$

[**Hint.** $\Delta^4 U_x = 0 \Rightarrow (E - 1)^4 U_x = 0$.]

(*ii*) Given: log 100 = 2, log 101 = 2.0043, log 103 = 2.0128, log 104 = 2.0170. Find log 102.

3. (*i*) Determine the missing values in the following table:

x :	0	5	10	15	20	25
y :	6	10	—	17	—	31

(*G.B.T.U. 2011*)

(*ii*)

x :	1	1.5	2	2.5	3	3.5	4
$f(x)$:	6	?	10	20	?	15	5

[*G.B.T.U. 2010; G.B.T.U. (C.O.) 2011*]

(*iii*)

x :	1	2	3	4	5	6	7	8
$f(x)$:	1	8	?	64	?	216	343	512

(*iv*)

x :	2	2.1	2.2	2.3	2.4	2.5	2.6
y :	0.135	—	0.111	0.100	—	0.082	0.074

(*v*)

x :	10	15	20	25	30	35
$f(x)$:	43	—	29	32	—	77

[*M.T.U. 2012, G.B.T.U. 2011*]

(*vi*) x :	1	2	3	4	5	6	7	8
$f(x)$:	2	4	8	—	32	—	128	256

Explain why the results differ from 16 and 64. [*G.B.T.U. 2013*]

4. Express $f(x) = \dfrac{x-1}{(x+1)(x+3)}$ in terms of negative factorial polynomials.

Answers

1. (*i*) 16.1, 2^x is not a polynomial (*ii*) 9.5
2. (*i*) 0.4147 (*ii*) 2.0086
3. (*i*) 13.25, 22.5 (*ii*) 0.222, 22.022
   (*iii*) 27, 125 (*iv*) 0.123, 0.0904
   (*v*) 33.933, 46.733 (*vi*) 16.257, 63.476; 2^x is not a polynomial
4. $x^{(-1)} - 4x^{(-2)} + 4x^{(-3)}$

4.12. METHOD OF SEPARATION OF SYMBOLS

The relationship E = 1 + Δ can be used to prove a number of useful identities. The method is known as separation of symbols.

4.13. DETECTION OF ERRORS BY USE OF DIFFERENCE TABLES

Difference tables can be used to check errors in tabular values. Let $f(x_1), f(x_2), \ldots\ldots, f(x_n)$ be the true values of $f(x)$ at $x = x_1, x_2, \ldots\ldots, x_n$. If $f(x)$ at $x = x_i$ is incorrect, we have to determine error in such case and correct the functional value.

In particular, let the functional value at $x = x_5$ be $f(x_5) + e$ and let other true functional values $f(x_1), f(x_2), \ldots\ldots, f(x_4), f(x_6), \ldots\ldots, f(x_9)$ be known.

x	$f(x)$	$\Delta f(x)$	$\Delta^2 f(x)$	$\Delta^3 f(x)$	$\Delta^4 f(x)$
x_1	$f(x_1)$				
		$\Delta f(x_1)$			
x_2	$f(x_2)$		$\Delta^2 f(x_1)$		
		$\Delta f(x_2)$		$\Delta^3 f(x_1)$	
x_3	$f(x_3)$		$\Delta^2 f(x_2)$		$\Delta^4 f(x_1) + e$
		$\Delta f(x_3)$		$\Delta^3 f(x_2) + e$	
x_4	$f(x_4)$		$\Delta^2 f(x_3) + e$		$\Delta^4 f(x_2) - 4e$
		$\Delta f(x_4) + e$		$\Delta^3 f(x_3) - 3e$	
$\overline{x_5}$	$\overline{f(x_5)}$		$\Delta^2 f(x_4) - 2e$		$\Delta^4 f(x_3) + 6e$
		$\Delta f(x_5) - e$		$\Delta^3 f(x_4) + 3e$	
x_6	$f(x_6)$		$\Delta^2 f(x_5) + e$		$\Delta^4 f(x_4) - 4e$
		$\Delta f(x_6)$		$\Delta^3 f(x_5) - e$	
x_7	$f(x_7)$		$\Delta^2 f(x_6)$		$\Delta^4 f(x_5) + e$
		$\Delta f(x_7)$		$\Delta^3 f(x_6)$	
x_8	$f(x_8)$		$\Delta^2 f(x_7)$		
		$\Delta f(x_8)$			
x_9	$f(x_9)$				

From table, we observe that,

(*i*) Error spreads in triangular form.

(*ii*) Coefficient of e's are binomial coeff. with alternate signs + , –, ...

(*iii*) Algebraic sum of errors in each column is 0.

(*iv*) In even differences columns, the max. error occurs in a horizontal line in which incorrect y lies.

(*v*) In odd differences columns, the incorrect value of y lies b/w two middle terms.

(*vi*) If n^{th} differences are constant, $(n + 1)^{th}$ differences vanish. Sum of all the values in $(n + 1)^{th}$ differences column is zero Or the sum is very small as compared to the functional values

These observations help us in finding out the error and hence required correct value of y can be found.

EXAMPLES

Example 1. *Find the error and correct the wrong figure in the following functional values :*

$$2, 5, 10, 18, 26, 37, 50.$$

Sol.

x	y	Δy	$\Delta^2 y$	$\Delta^3 y$
1	2			
		3		
2	5		2	
		5		1
3	10		3	
		8		– 3
4	18 ←		0	
		8		3
5	26		3	
		11		– 1
6	37		2	
		13		
7	50			

Sum of all the third differences is zero.

Adjacent values – 3, 3 are equal in magnitude. Horizontal line between – 3 and 3 points out the incorrect functional value 18.

Coefficient of first middle term on expansion of $(1-p)^3 = -3$

$$\Rightarrow \qquad -3e = -3 \Rightarrow e = 1$$

$\therefore$ Correct functional value $= 18 - 1 = 17$.

Example 2. *Locate the error in following entries and correct it :*

1.203, 1.424, 1.681, 1.992, 2.379, 2.848, 3.429 and 4.136.

Sol. Difference table is as follows:

10^3y	$10^3\Delta y$	$10^3\Delta^2 y$	$10^3\Delta^3 y$	$10^3\Delta^4 y$
1203				
	221			
1424		36		
	257		18	
1681		54		4
	311		22	
1992		76		– 16
	387		6	
2379 ←		82		24
	469		30	
2848		112		– 16
	581		14	
3429		126		
	707			
4136				

Sum of all values in column of fourth difference is – 0.004 which is very small as compared to sum of values in other columns

$\therefore \qquad \Delta^4 y = 0$

Error in this column are e, $-4e$, $6e$, $-4e$ and e.

Term of Max. value = 24 $\Rightarrow$ $6e = 24$ $\Rightarrow$ $e = 4$

Error lies in 2379.

Hence required correct entry = 2379 – 4 = 2375

Hence correct value = 2.375.

Example 3. *Using the method of separation of symbols, show that*

$$u_0 - u_1 + u_2 - u_3 + \ldots = \frac{1}{2}u_0 - \frac{1}{4}\Delta u_0 + \frac{1}{8}\Delta^2 u_0 - \ldots\ldots .$$

Sol. RHS $= \frac{1}{2}\left[1 - \frac{1}{2}\Delta + \left(\frac{1}{2}\Delta\right)^2 - \left(\frac{1}{2}\Delta\right)^3 + \ldots\ldots\right] u_0$

$$= \frac{1}{2}\cdot\frac{1}{\left(1+\frac{1}{2}\Delta\right)} u_0 = \frac{1}{2}\left(1+\frac{1}{2}\Delta\right)^{-1} u_0 = (2+\Delta)^{-1} u_0 = (1+E)^{-1} u_0$$

$$= (1 - E + E^2 - E^3 + \ldots) u_0 = u_0 - u_1 + u_2 - u_3 + \ldots\ldots = \text{LHS}$$

Example 4. *Using method of separation of symbols, show that:*

$$\Delta^n u_{x-n} = u_x - n u_{x-1} + \frac{n(n-1)}{2} u_{x-2} + \cdots\cdots + (-1)^n u_{x-n}.$$

Sol. $$\text{RHS} = u_x - n\text{E}^{-1} u_x + \frac{n(n-1)}{2} \text{E}^{-2} u_x + \cdots\cdots + (-1)^n \text{E}^{-n} u_x$$

$$= \left[1 - n\text{E}^{-1} + \frac{n(n-1)}{2} \text{E}^{-2} + \cdots\cdots + (-1)^n \text{E}^{-n}\right] u_x = (1 - \text{E}^{-1})^n u_x$$

$$= \left(1 - \frac{1}{\text{E}}\right)^n u_x = \left(\frac{\text{E}-1}{\text{E}}\right)^n u_x = \frac{\Delta^n}{\text{E}^n} u_x = \Delta^n \text{E}^{-n} u_x = \Delta^n u_{x-n} = \text{LHS}$$

Example 5. *Show that :*

$$e^x \left(u_0 + x \Delta u_0 + \frac{x^2}{2!} \Delta^2 u_0 + \cdots\cdots\right) = u_0 + u_1 x + u_2 \frac{x^2}{2!} + \cdots\cdots.$$

Sol. $$\text{LHS} = e^x \left(1 + x\Delta + \frac{x^2\Delta^2}{2!} + \cdots\cdots\right) u_0 = e^x \,.\, e^{x\Delta} u_0 = e^{x(1+\Delta)} u_0 = e^{x\text{E}} u_0$$

$$= \left(1 + x\text{E} + \frac{x^2\text{E}^2}{2!} + \cdots\cdots\right) u_0 = \left(u_0 + x u_1 + \frac{x^2}{2!} u_2 + \cdots\cdots\right) = \text{RHS}$$

Example 6. *Prove the following identity:*

$$u_1 x + u_2 x^2 + u_3 x^3 + \cdots\cdots = \frac{x}{1-x} u_1 + \frac{x^2}{(1-x)^2} \Delta u_1 + \cdots\cdots$$

Sol. $$\text{LHS} = x u_1 + x^2 \text{E} u_1 + x^3 \text{E}^2 u_1 + \cdots\cdots = x(1 + x\text{E} + x^2\text{E}^2 + \cdots\cdots) u_1$$

$$= x \,.\, \frac{1}{(1 - x\text{E})} u_1 = x \,.\, \frac{1}{[1 - x(1+\Delta)]} u_1$$

$$= x \left[\frac{1}{1 - x - x\Delta}\right] u_1 = \frac{x}{1-x} \left[\frac{1}{1 - \dfrac{x\Delta}{1-x}}\right] u_1$$

$$= \frac{x}{1-x} \left[1 - \frac{x\Delta}{1-x}\right]^{-1} (u_1) = \frac{x}{1-x} \left[1 + \frac{x\Delta}{1-x} + \frac{x^2\Delta^2}{(1-x)^2} + \cdots\cdots\right] u_1$$

$$= \frac{x}{1-x} u_1 + \frac{x^2}{(1-x)^2} \Delta u_1 + \frac{x^3}{(1-x)^3} \Delta^2 u_1 + \cdots\cdots = \text{RHS}$$

Example 7. *Prove that:* $u_x = u_{x-1} + \Delta u_{x-2} + \Delta^2 u_{x-3} + \cdots\cdots + \Delta^{n-1} u_{x-n} + \Delta^n u_{x-n}$

Hence or otherwise prove that: $u_3 = u_2 + \Delta u_1 + \Delta^2 u_0 + \Delta^3 u_0$.

Sol. $u_x - \Delta^n u_{x-n} = (1 - \Delta^n \text{E}^{-n}) u_x$

$$= \left[1 - \left(\frac{\Delta}{\text{E}}\right)^n\right] u_x = \frac{1}{\text{E}^n} (\text{E}^n - \Delta^n) u_x = \frac{1}{\text{E}^n} \left(\frac{\text{E}^n - \Delta^n}{\text{E} - \Delta}\right) u_x \qquad | \because \; 1 + \Delta = \text{E}$$

$$= \frac{1}{\text{E}^n} [\text{E}^{n-1} + \Delta\text{E}^{n-2} + \Delta^2\text{E}^{n-3} + \cdots\cdots + \Delta^{n-1}] u_x$$

$$= (E^{-1} + \Delta E^{-2} + \Delta^2 E^{-3} + \ldots\ldots + \Delta^{n-1} E^{-n})\, u_x$$

$$= u_{x-1} + \Delta u_{x-2} + \Delta^2 u_{x-3} + \ldots\ldots + \Delta^{n-1} u_{x-n}$$

To prove the second result put $x = 3$ and $n = 3$.

Example 8. *Prove that :*

$$\Delta x^n - \frac{1}{2}\Delta^2 x^n + \frac{1\cdot 3}{2\cdot 4}\Delta^3 x^n - \frac{1\cdot 3\cdot 5}{2\cdot 4\cdot 6}\Delta^4 x^n + \ldots\ldots \ n \ terms = \left(x + \frac{1}{2}\right)^n - \left(x - \frac{1}{2}\right)^n$$

Sol.

$$\text{LHS} = \Delta\left[1 - \frac{1}{2}\Delta + \frac{\left(-\frac{1}{2}\right)\left(-\frac{3}{2}\right)}{1\cdot 2}.\Delta^2 + \ldots\ldots\infty\right] x^n$$

$$= \Delta\,(1 + \Delta)^{-1/2}\, x^n = \Delta\, E^{-1/2}\, x^n = \Delta\left(x - \frac{1}{2}\right)^n$$

$$= \left(x + \frac{1}{2}\right)^n - \left(x - \frac{1}{2}\right)^n = \text{RHS}$$

Example 9. *Sum the following series $1^3 + 2^3 + 3^3 + \ldots\ldots + n^3$ using the calculus of finite differences.*

Sol. Let us denote $1^3, 2^3, 3^3, \ldots\ldots$ by $u_0, u_1, u_2, \ldots\ldots$, respectively, we get

$$S = u_0 + u_1 + u_2 + \ldots\ldots + u_{n-1} = (1 + E + E^2 + \ldots\ldots + E^{n-1})\, u_0$$

$$= \left(\frac{E^n - 1}{E - 1}\right) u_0 = \left[\frac{(1+\Delta)^n - 1}{\Delta}\right] u_0$$

$$= \frac{1}{\Delta}\left[1 + n\Delta + \frac{n(n-1)}{2!}\Delta^2 + \frac{n\,(n-1)(n-2)}{3!}\Delta^3 + \ldots\ldots + \Delta^n - 1\right] u_0$$

$$= n + \frac{n(n-1)}{2!}\Delta u_0 + \frac{n\,(n-1)\,(n-2)}{3!}\Delta^2 u_0 + \ldots\ldots$$

Now, $\Delta u_0 = u_1 - u_0 = 2^3 - 1^3 = 7$

and $\Delta^2 u_0 = u_2 - 2u_1 + u_0 = 3^3 - 2(2)^3 + (1)^3 = 12$

Similarly, $\Delta^3 u_0 = u_3 - 3u_2 + 3u_1 - u_0 = (4)^3 - 3(3)^3 + 3(2)^3 - (1)^3 = 6$

and $\Delta^4 u_0$, $\Delta^5 u_0$, ...are all zero as $u_r = r^3$ is a polynomial of third degree.

$$\therefore \qquad S = n + \frac{n(n-1)}{2!}(7) + \frac{n\,(n-1)\,(n-2)}{6}(12) + \frac{n\,(n-1)\,(n-2)\,(n-3)}{24}(6)$$

$$= \frac{n^2}{4}(n^2 + 2n + 1) = \left[\frac{n\,(n+1)}{2}\right]^2.$$

ASSIGNMENT

1. The values of a polynomial of degree 5 are tabulated below :

If $f(3)$ is known to be in error, find its correct value.

x :	0	1	2	3	4	5	6
$f(x)$:	1	2	33	254	1025	3126	7777.

2. If $y = f(x)$ is a polynomial of degree 3 and the following table gives the values of x and y. Locate and correct wrong values of y

x :	0	1	2	3	4	5	6
y :	4	10	30	75	160	294	490.

3. Prove the identities :

(*i*) $u_x - \Delta^2 u_x + \Delta^3 u_x - \Delta^5 u_x + \Delta^6 u_x - \Delta^8 u_x + \ldots\ldots = u_x - \Delta^2 u_{x-1} + \Delta^4 u_{x-2} - \Delta^6 u_{x-3} + \Delta^8 u_{x-4} - \ldots\ldots$

(*ii*) $\sum_{x=0}^{\infty} u_{2x} = \frac{1}{2} \sum_{x=0}^{\infty} u_x + \frac{1}{4}\left(1 - \frac{\Delta}{2} + \frac{\Delta^2}{4} - \ldots\ldots\right) u_0.$

4. Prove that : $x^2 + \frac{1}{2}(1+x)^2 + \frac{1}{2^2}(2+x)^2 + \frac{1}{2^3}(3+x)^2 + \cdots\cdots = 2(x^2 + 2x + 3)$ using calculus of finite differences and taking the interval of differencing unity.

[**Hint.** $(1+x)^2 = Ex^2$, $(2+x)^2 = E^2x^2$, $(3+x)^2 = E^3x^3$, ...]

5. If $f(E)$ is a polynomial in E s.t. $f(E) = a_0 E^n + a_1 E^{n-1} + a_2 E^{n-2} + \ldots\ldots + a_n$

Prove that, $f(E)\, e^x = e^x f(e)$ taking the interval of differencing unity.

Answers

1. 244 **2.** Correct value of $y(3) = 74$.

We now proceed to study the use of finite difference calculus for the purpose of interpolation. This we shall do in three cases which are as follows :

(*i*) The value of argument in given data varies by an equal interval. The technique is called an **interpolation with equal intervals.**

(*ii*) The values of argument are not at equal intervals. This is known as **interpolation with unequal intervals.**

(*iii*) The technique of **central differences.**

4.14. NEWTON'S FORMULAE FOR INTERPOLATION

Newton's formula is used for constructing the interpolation polynomial. It makes use of divided differences. This result was first discovered by the Scottish mathematician James Gregory (1638–1675) a contemporary of Newton.

Gregory and Newton did extensive work on methods of interpolation but now the formula is referred to as Newton's interpolation formula. Newton has derived general forward and backward difference interpolation formulae.

4.15. NEWTON'S GREGORY FORWARD INTERPOLATION FORMULA

(M.T.U. 2013)

Let $y = f(x)$ be a function of x which assumes the values $f(a)$, $f(a + h)$, $f(a + 2h)$, ..., $f(a + nh)$ for $(n + 1)$ equidistant values $a, a + h, a + 2h$, ..., $a + nh$ of the independent variable x. Let $f(x)$ be a polynomial of nth degree.

Let $f(x) = A_0 + A_1 (x - a) + A_2 (x - a)(x - a - h) + A_3 (x - a)(x - a - h)(x - a - 2h) +$ .... $+ A_n (x - a) ...... (x - a - \overline{n-1}h)$ ...(1)

where A_0, A_1, A_2, ..., A_n are to be determined.

Put $x = a, a + h, a + 2h$, ..., $a + nh$ in (1) successively.

For $x = a$, $\quad f(a) = A_0$ ...(2)

For $x = a + h$, $\quad f(a + h) = A_0 + A_1 h$

$\Rightarrow \quad f(a + h) = f(a) + A_1 h$ | By (2)

$$\Rightarrow \quad A_1 = \frac{\Delta f(a)}{h} \qquad \text{...(3)}$$

For $x = a + 2h$,

$$f(a + 2h) = A_0 + A_1 (2h) + A_2 (2h) h$$

$$= f(a) + 2h \left\{\frac{\Delta f(a)}{h}\right\} + 2h^2 A_2$$

$$\Rightarrow \quad 2h^2 A_2 = f(a + 2h) - 2f(a + h) + f(a) = \Delta^2 f(a)$$

$$\Rightarrow \quad A_2 = \frac{\Delta^2 f(a)}{2!\,h^2}$$

Similarly, $\quad A_3 = \dfrac{\Delta^3 f(a)}{3!\,h^3}$ and so on.

Thus, $\quad A_n = \dfrac{\Delta^n f(a)}{n!\,h^n}$.

From (1),

$$f(x) = f(a) + (x - a)\frac{\Delta f(a)}{h} + (x - a)(x - a - h)\frac{\Delta^2 f(a)}{2!\,h^2} + ...$$

$$+ (x - a) ...... (x - a - \overline{n-1}\,h)\frac{\Delta^n f(a)}{n!\,h^n}$$

Put $x = a + hu \Rightarrow u = \dfrac{x - a}{h}$, we have

$$f(a + hu) = f(a) + hu\frac{\Delta f(a)}{h} + \frac{(hu)(hu - h)}{2!\,h^2}\Delta^2 f(a) + ...$$

$$+ \frac{(hu)(hu - h)(hu - 2h) .... (hu - \overline{n-1}\,h)}{n!\,h^n}\Delta^n f(a)$$

$$\Rightarrow \quad f(a + hu) = f(a) + u\Delta f(a) + \frac{u(u-1)}{2!} \Delta^2 f(a) + \ldots + \frac{u(u-1)(u-2)\ldots(u-n+1)}{n!} \Delta^n f(a)$$

This formula is particularly useful for interpolating the values of $f(x)$ near the beginning of the set of values given. h is called interval of differencing while Δ is forward difference operator.

4.15.1. Algorithm for Newton's Forward difference formula

Step 01. Start of the program

Step 02. Input no. of terms n

Step 03. Input the array ax

Step 04. Input the array ay

Step 05. h=ax[1] – ax[0]

Step 06. for i=0 ; i<n-1 ; i++

Step 07. diff[i] [1]=ay[i + 1] – ay[i]

Step 08. End Loop i

Step 09. for j=2 ; j<=4 ; j++

Step 10. for i = 0 ; i <n – j ; i++

Step 11. diff[i][j]=diff [i + 1] [j – 1]-diff [i][j – 1]

Step 12. End Loop i

Step 13. End Loop j

Step 14. i=0

Step 15. Repeat Step 16 until ax[i]<x

Step 16. i=i + 1

Step 17. i=i – 1 ;

Step 18. p=(x – ax [i])/h

Step 19. y1=p*diff[i – 1][1]

Step 20. y2=p*(p+1)*diff [i – 1][2]/2

Step 21. y3=(p+1)*p*(p-1)*diff[i –2][3]/6

Step 22. y4=(p+2)*(p+1)*p*(p – 1)*diff[i – 3][4]/24

Step 23. y=ay[i]+y1+y2+y3+y4

Step 24. Print output x, y

Step 25. End of program.

4.15.2. Flow-chart

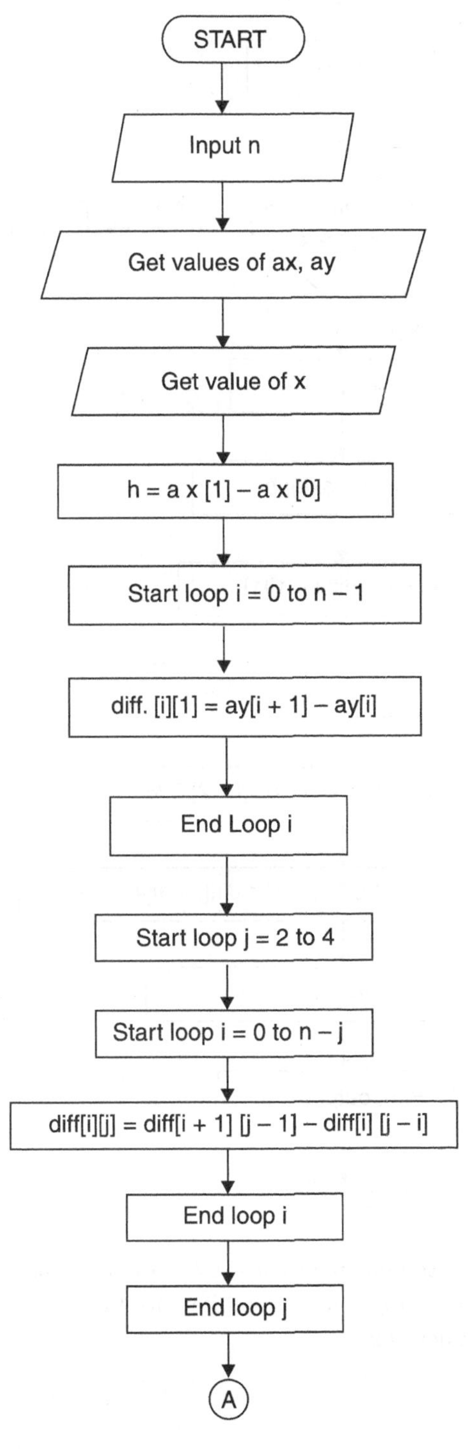

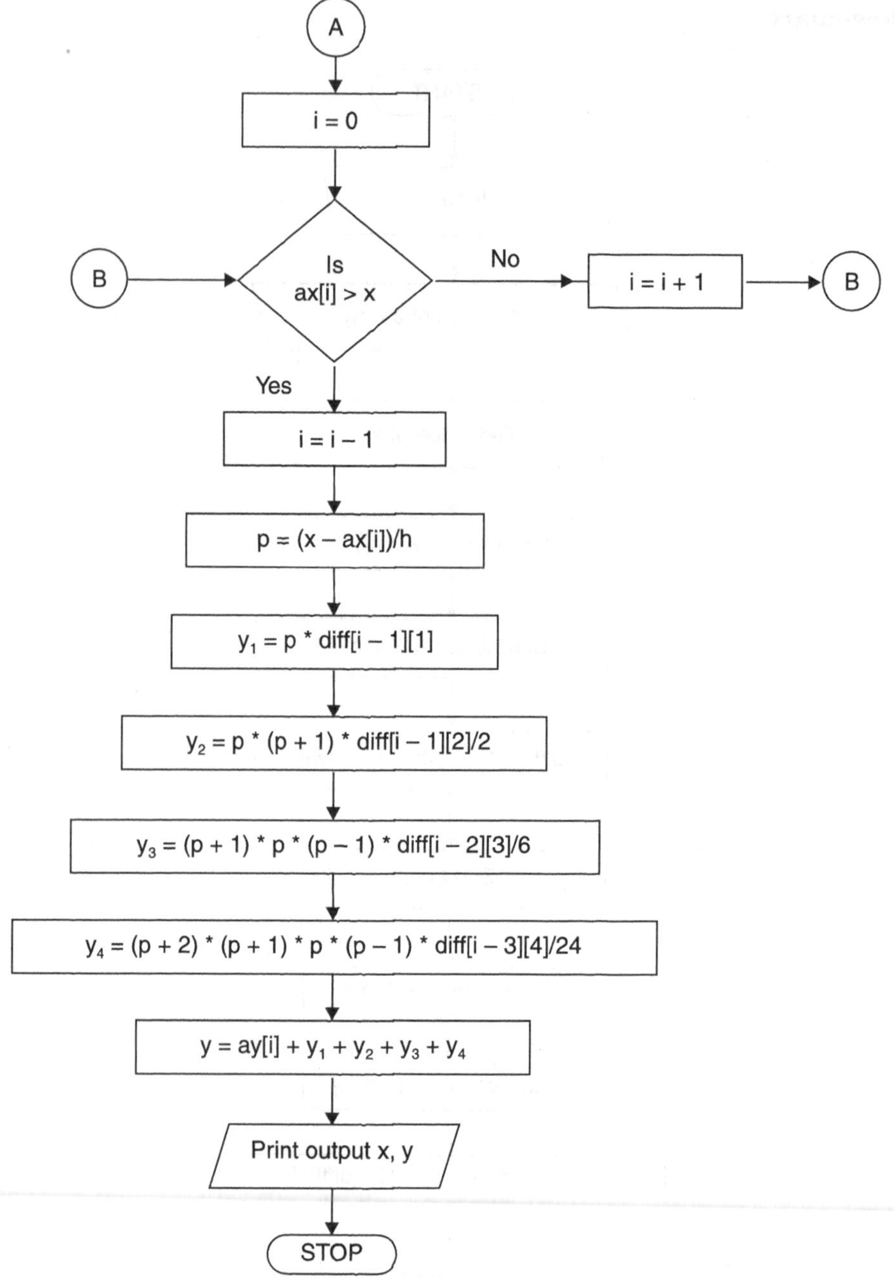

Note. ax is an array containing values of x, ay is an array containing values of y, Diff. is a two dimensional array containing difference table,
h is spacing between values of x

* ***

4.15.3. Program to Implement Newton's Forward Method of Interpolation

*** */

```
//... HEADER FILES DECLARATION
# include <stdio.h>
# include <conio.h>
# include <math.h>
# include <process.h>
# include <string.h>

//... MAIN EXECUTION THREAD

void main()
     {
     //... Variable declaration Field

     //... Integer Type

     int n;                                //... No. of terms
     int i,j;                              //... Loop Variables

     //...Floating Type
     float ax[10];                         //... array limit 9
     float ay[10];                         //... array limit 9
     float x;                              //... User Querry
     float y = 0;                          //... Initial value 0
     float h;                              //... Calc. section
     float p;                              //... Calc. section
     float diff[20][20];                   //... array limit 19,19
     float y1,y2,y3,y4;                    //... Formulae variables

     //... Invoke Function Clear Screen

     clrscr();

     //... Input Section

     printf("\n Enter the number of terms - ");
     scanf("%d",&n);

     //... Input Sequel for array X

     Printf ("\n\n Enter the value in the form of x - ");

     //... Input Loop for X

     for (i=0;i<n;i++)
```

```
                {
                printf("\n\n Enter the value of x%d - ",i+1);

                scanf("%f",&ax[i]);

                }

//... Input Sequel for array Y

printf("\n\n Enter the value in the form of y - ");
//... Input Loop for Y

for (i=0;i<n;i++)

        {

        printf ("\n\n Enter the value of y%d - ", i+1);

        scanf ("%f",&ay [i]);

        }

//... Inputting the required value quarry

printf("\nEnter the value of x for");
printf("\nwhich you want the value of y - ");

scanf("%f",&x);

//... Calculation and Processing Section

h=ax[1]-ax[0];

for(i=0;i<n-1;i++)
        {
        diff[i][1]=ay[i+1]-ay[i];
        }
for(j=2;j<=4;j++)
        {
        for(i=0;i<n-j;i++)
                        {
                        diff[i][j]=diff[i+1][j-1]-diff[i][j-1];
                        }

        }

i=0;

do      {
```

```
        i++;
        }while(ax[i]<x);
    i--;
    p=(x-ax[i])/h;
    y1=p*diff[i-1][1];
    y2=p*(p+1)*diff[i-1][2]/2;
    y3=(p+1)*p*(p-1)*diff[i-2][3]/6;
    y4=(p+2)*(p+1)*p*(p-1)*diff[i-3][4]/24;

    //... Taking Sum

    y=ay[i]+y1+y2+y3+y4;

    //... Output Section

    printf("\nwhen x=%6.4f, y=%6.8f ",x,y);

    //... Invoke User Watch Halt Function

    Printf("\n\n\n Press Enter to Exit");

    getch();

    }
//... Termination of Main Execution Thread
```

4.15.4. Output

```
Enter the number of terms - 7
Enter the value in the form of x -
Enter the value of x1 - 100
Enter the value of x2 - 150
Enter the value of x3 - 200
Enter the value of x4 - 250
Enter the value of x5 - 300
Enter the value of x6 - 350
Enter the value of x7 - 400
Enter the value in the form of y -
Enter the value of y1 - 10.63
Enter the value of y2 - 13.03
Enter the value of y3 - 15.04
Enter the value of y4 - 16.81
Enter the value of y5 - 18.42
Enter the value of y6 - 19.9
Enter the value of y7 - 21.27
Enter the value of x for which you want the value of y-218
When X=218.0000, Y=15.69701481
Press Enter to Exit
```

EXAMPLES

Example 1. *The population of a town in the decennial census was as given below. Estimate the population for the year 1895.* (G.B.T.U. 2011)

Year x:	*1891*	*1901*	*1911*	*1921*	*1931*
Population y: *(in thousands)*	*46*	*66*	*81*	*93*	*101*

Sol. Here $a = 1891, h = 10,$

$$a + hu = 1895 \Rightarrow 1891 + 10\,u = 1895 \Rightarrow u = 0.4$$

The difference table is as under:

x	y	Δy	$\Delta^2 y$	$\Delta^3 y$	$\Delta^4 y$
1891	46				
		20			
1901	66		– 5		
		15		2	
1911	81		– 3		– 3
		12		– 1	
1921	93		– 4		
		8			
1931	101				

Applying Newton's forward difference formula,

$$y(1895) = y(1891) + u\,\Delta y(1891) + \frac{u(u-1)}{2!}\Delta^2 y(1891) + \frac{u(u-1)(u-2)}{3!}\Delta^3 y(1891) + \frac{u(u-1)(u-2)(u-3)}{4!}\Delta^4 y(1891)$$

$$\Rightarrow \quad y(1895) = 46 + (0.4)(20) + \frac{(0.4)(0.4-1)}{2}(-5) + \frac{(0.4)(0.4-1)(0.4-2)}{6}(2) + \frac{(0.4)(0.4-1)(0.4-2)(0.4-3)}{24}(-3)$$

$$\Rightarrow \quad y(1895) = 54.8528 \text{ thousands} = 54852.8 \approx 54853$$

Hence the population for the year 1895 is **54853** approximately.

Example 2. *From the following table of half-yearly premium for policies maturing at different ages, estimate the premium for policies maturing at age of 46.*

Age	*45*	*50*	*55*	*60*	*65*
Premium *(in rupees)*	*114.84*	*96.16*	*83.32*	*74.48*	*68.48*

(G.B.T.U. 2010)

Sol. Here $h = 5, a = 45, a + hu = 46$

$\therefore \quad 45 + 5u = 46 \Rightarrow u = 0.2$

The difference table is:

Age *(x)*	*Premium* *(in rupees)* *(y)*	Δy	$\Delta^2 y$	$\Delta^3 y$	$\Delta^4 y$
45	114.84				
		– 18.68			
50	96.16		5.84		
		– 12.84		– 1.84	
55	83.32		4		0.68
		– 8.84		– 1.16	
60	74.48		2.84		
		– 6			
65	68.48				

By Newton's forward difference formula,

$$y_{46} = y_{45} + u\,\Delta y_{45} + \frac{u(u-1)}{2!}\Delta^2 y_{45} + \frac{u(u-1)(u-2)}{3!}\Delta^3 y_{45} + \frac{u(u-1)(u-2)(u-3)}{4!}\Delta^4 y_{45}$$

$$= 114.84 + (0.2)(-18.68) + \frac{(0.2)(0.2-1)}{2!}(5.84)$$

$$+ \frac{(0.2)(0.2-1)(0.2-2)}{3!}(-1.84) + \frac{(0.2)(0.2-1)(0.2-2)(0.2-3)}{4!}(0.68)$$

$$= 110.525632$$

Hence the premium for policies maturing at the age of 46 is **₹ 110.52.**

Example 3. *From the following table, find the value of* $e^{0.24}$:

x:	0.1	0.2	0.3	0.4	0.5
e^x:	1.10517	1.22140	1.34986	1.49182	1.64872.

Sol. The difference table is:

x	$10^5 y$	$10^5 \Delta y$	$10^5 \Delta^2 y$	$10^5\, \Delta^3 y$	$10^4 \Delta^4 y$
0.1	110517				
		11623			
0.2	122140		1223		
		12846		127	
0.3	134986		1350		17
		14196		144	
0.4	149182		1494		
		15690			
0.5	164872				

Here $h = 0.1$. $\therefore$ $0.24 = 0.1 + (0.1)\,u$ or $u = 1.4$

Newton-Gregory forward difference formula is

$$y(0.24) = y(0.1) + u\,\Delta\,y(0.1) + \frac{u(u-1)}{2!}\Delta^2\,y(0.1) + \frac{u(u-1)(u-2)}{3!}\Delta^3 y(0.1) + \frac{u(u-1)(u-2)(u-3)}{4!}\Delta^4\,y(0.1)$$

$$\Rightarrow \quad 10^5\,y(0.24) = 10^5\,y(0.1) + u\,10^5\,\Delta y(0.1) + \frac{u(u-1)}{2!}10^5\,\Delta^2 y(0.1) + \frac{u(u-1)(u-2)}{3!}10^5\,\Delta^3 y(0.1) + \frac{u(u-1)(u-2)(u-3)}{4!}10^5\,\Delta^4 y(0.1)$$

$$\Rightarrow \quad 10^5\,y(0.24) = 110517 + (1.4)(11623) + \frac{(1.4)(1.4-1)}{2}(1223) + \frac{(1.4)(1.4-1)(1.4-2)}{3!}(127) + \frac{(1.4)(1.4-1)(1.4-2)(1.4-3)}{4!}(17)$$

$$= 127124.9088$$

$$\therefore \quad y(0.24) = e^{.24} = 1.271249088$$

Example 4. *The following table gives the population of a town during the last six censuses. Estimate the population in 1913 by Newton's forward difference formula*

Year	*1911*	*1921*	*1931*	*1941*	*1951*	*1961*
Population (in thousands)	*12*	*15*	*20*	*27*	*39*	*52*

[U.P.T.U. (MCA) 2009]

Sol. Here, $a = 1911,\ h = 10,\ x = 1913$

$$\therefore \quad u = \frac{x-a}{h} = \frac{1913-1911}{10} = 0.2$$

Forward difference table is

x	$f(x)$	$\Delta f(x)$	$\Delta^2 f(x)$	$\Delta^3 f(x)$	$\Delta^4 f(x)$	$\Delta^5 f(x)$
1911	12					
		3				
1921	15		2			
		5		0		
1931	20		2		3	
		7		3		− 10
1941	27		5		− 7	
		12		− 4		
1951	39		1			
		13				
1961	52					

Newton's forward difference formula is

$$f(1913) = f(1911) + u\Delta f(1911) + \frac{u(u-1)}{2!}\Delta^2 f(1911) + \frac{u(u-1)(u-2)}{3!}\Delta^3 f(1911)$$

$$+ \frac{u(u-1)(u-2)(u-3)}{4!}\Delta^4 f(1911) + \frac{u(u-1)(u-2)(u-3)(u-4)}{5!}\Delta^5 f(1911)$$

$$= 12 + (0.2)(3) + \frac{(0.2)(-0.8)}{2}(2) + \frac{(0.2)(-0.8)(-1.8)(-2.8)}{4!}(3)$$

$$+ \frac{(0.2)(-0.8)(-1.8)(-2.8)(-3.8)}{5!}(-10)$$

$f(1913) = 12.08384$ thousands

Hence the population of the town in the year 1913 $\simeq$ 12083.84 = 12084 (approximately).

Example 5. *From the table, estimate the number of students who obtained marks between 40 and 45.* (M.T.U. 2013)

Marks:	*30–40*	*40–50*	*50–60*	*60–70*	*70–80*
No. of students:	*31*	*42*	*51*	*35*	*31.*

Sol. Difference table is:

Marks less than (*x*)	y	Δy	$\Delta^2 y$	$\Delta^3 y$	$\Delta^4 y$
40	31				
		42			
50	73		9		
		51		– 25	
60	124		– 16		37
		35		12	
70	159		– 4		
		31			
80	190				

We shall find y_{45}, number of students with marks less than 45.

$$a = 40,\ h = 10,\ a + hu = 45.$$

$\therefore \quad 40 + 10u = 45 \Rightarrow u = 0.5$

By Newton's forward difference formula,

$$y(45) = y(40) + u\,\Delta y(40) + \frac{u(u-1)}{2!}\Delta^2 y(40)$$

$$+ \frac{u(u-1)(u-2)}{3!}\Delta^3 y(40) + \frac{u(u-1)(u-2)(u-3)}{4!}\Delta^4 y(40)$$

$$= 31 + (0.5)(42) + \frac{(0.5)(0.5-1)}{2}(9) + \frac{(0.5)(0.5-1)(0.5-2)}{6}(-25)$$
$$+ \frac{(0.5)(0.5-1)(0.5-2)(0.5-3)}{24}(37)$$
$$= 47.8672 \approx 48$$

Hence number of students getting marks less than 45 = 48

By number of students getting marks less than 40 = 31

Hence number of students getting marks between 40 and 45 = 48 – 31 = 17.

Example 6. *Find the cubic polynomial which takes the following values:*

x:	*0*	*1*	*2*	*3*
f(x):	*1*	*2*	*1*	*10.*

Sol. Let us form the difference table:

x	y	Δy	$\Delta^2 y$	$\Delta^3 y$
0	1			
		1		
1	2		– 2	
		– 1		12
2	1		10	
		9		
3	10			

Here, $h = 1$. Hence using the formula, $x = a + hu$

and choosing $a = 0$, we get $x = u$

∴ By Newton's forward difference formula,

$$y = y_0 + x\,\Delta y_0 + \frac{x(x-1)}{2!}\Delta^2 y_0 + \frac{x(x-1)(x-2)}{3!}\Delta^3 y_0$$

$$= 1 + x(1) + \frac{x(x-1)}{2!}(-2) + \frac{x(x-1)(x-2)}{3!}(12)$$

$$= 2x^3 - 7x^2 + 6x + 1$$

Hence the required cubic polynomial is

$$y = f(x) = 2x^3 - 7x^2 + 6x + 1.$$

Example 7. *The following table gives the marks secured by100 students in the Numerical Analysis subject:*

Range of marks:	*30–40*	*40–50*	*50–60*	*60–70*	*70–80*
No. of students:	*25*	*35*	*22*	*11*	*7*

Use Newton's forward difference interpolation formula to find.

(i) the number of students who got more than 55 marks.

(ii) the number of students who secured marks in the range from 36 to 45.

Sol. The given table is re-arranged as follows:

Marks obtained	*No. of students*
Less than 40	25
Less than 50	60
Less than 60	82
Less than 70	93
Less than 80	100

(*i*) Here, $a = 40$, $h = 10$, $a + hu = 55$

$\therefore$ $40 + 10u = 55$ $\Rightarrow$ $u = 1.5$

First, we find the number of students who got less than 55 marks.

The difference table is as under:

Marks obtained less than	*No. of students = y*	Δy	$\Delta^2 y$	$\Delta^3 y$	$\Delta^4 y$
40	25				
		35			
50	60		– 13		
		22		2	
60	82		– 11		5
		11		7	
70	93		– 4		
		7			
80	100				

Applying Newton's forward difference formula,

$$y_{55} = y_{40} + u\,\Delta y_{40} + \frac{u(u-1)}{2!}\Delta^2 y_{40} + \frac{u(u-1)(u-2)}{3!}\Delta^3 y_{40} + \frac{u(u-1)(u-2)(u-3)}{4!}\Delta^4 y_{40}$$

$$= 25 + (1.5)(35) + \frac{(1.5)(0.5)}{2!}(-13) + \frac{(1.5)(0.5)(-0.5)}{3!}(2) + \frac{(1.5)(0.5)(-0.5)(-1.5)}{4!}(5)$$

$$= 71.6171875 \approx 72$$

There are 72 students who got less than 55 marks.

$\therefore$ No. of students who got more than 55 marks = 100 – 72 = 28

(*ii*) To calculate the number of students securing marks between 36 and 45, take the difference of y_{45} and y_{36}.

$$u = \frac{x-a}{h} = \frac{36-40}{10} = -0.4$$

Also, $$u = \frac{45-40}{10} = 0.5$$

By Newton's forward difference formula.

$$y_{36} = y_{40} + u\,\Delta y_{40} + \frac{u(u-1)}{2!}\Delta^2 y_{40} + \frac{u(u-1)(u-2)}{3!}\Delta^3 y_{40} + \frac{u(u-1)(u-2)(u-3)}{4!}\Delta^4 y_{40}$$

$$= 25 + (-0.4)(35) + \frac{(-0.4)(-1.4)}{2!}(-13) + \frac{(-0.4)(-1.4)(-2.4)}{3!}(2)$$

$$+ \frac{(-0.4)(-1.4)(-2.4)(-3.4)}{4!}(5) = 7.864 \approx 8$$

Also,
$$y_{45} = y_{40} + u\,\Delta y_{40} + \frac{u(u-1)}{2!}\Delta^2 y_{40} + \frac{u(u-1)(u-2)}{3!}\Delta^3 y_{40}$$

$$+ \frac{u(u-1)(u-2)(u-3)}{4!}\Delta^4 y_{40}$$

$$= 25 + (0.5)(35) + \frac{(0.5)(-0.5)}{2}(-13) + \frac{(0.5)(-0.5)(-1.5)}{6}(2)$$

$$+ \frac{(0.5)(-0.5)(-1.5)(-2.5)}{24}(5)$$

$$= 44.0546 \approx 44.$$

Hence, the number of students who secured marks in the range from 36 to 45 is $= y_{45} - y_{36} = 44 - 8 = 36$.

Example 8. *The following are the numbers of deaths in four successive ten year age groups. Find the number of deaths at 45–50 and 50–55.*

Age group:	*25–35*	*35–45*	*45–55*	*55–65*
Deaths:	*13229*	*18139*	*24225*	*31496.*

Sol. Difference table of cumulative frequencies:

Age up to x	*No. of deaths* $f(x)$	$\Delta f(x)$	$\Delta^2 f(x)$	$\Delta^3 f(x)$
35	13229			
		18139		
45	31368		6086	
		24225		1185
55	55593		7271	
		31496		
65	87089			

Here, $h = 10, a = 35, a + hu = 50$

$\therefore$ $35 + 10u = 50 \Rightarrow u = 1.5$

By Newton's forward difference formula,

$$y_{50} = y_{35} + u\,\Delta y_{35} + \frac{u(u-1)}{2!}\Delta^2 y_{35} + \frac{u(u-1)(u-2)}{3!}\Delta^3 y_{35}$$

$$= 13229 + (1.5)(18139) + \frac{(1.5)(0.5)}{2}(6086) + \frac{(1.5)(0.5)(-0.5)}{6}(1185)$$

$$= 42645.6875 \approx 42646$$

$\therefore$ Deaths at the age between 45 – 50 is 42646 – 31368 = 11278

and Deaths at the age between 50 – 55 is 55593 – 42646 = 12947.

ASSIGNMENT

1. Estimate the value of $f(22)$ from the following available data:

x:	20	25	30	35	40	45
$f(x)$:	354	332	291	260	231	204

2. Given that:

x:	1	2	3	4	5	6
$y(x)$:	0	1	8	27	64	125

Find the value of $f(2.5)$. [*U.P.T.U. (MCA) 2008*]

3. (*i*) The table below gives value of tan x for $0.10 \le x \le 0.30$.

x:	0.10	0.15	0.20	0.25	0.30
tan x:	0.1003	0.1511	0.2027	0.2553	0.3093

Evaluate tan 0.12 using Newton's forward difference formula.

(*ii*) Find the value of sin 52° from the following table using Newton's forward difference formula:

θ:	45°	50°	55°	60°
sin θ:	0.7071	0.7660	0.8192	0.8660

4. (*i*) Fit a polynomial of degree 3 and hence determine $y(3.5)$ for the following data:

x:	3	4	5	6
y:	6	24	60	120

[*M.T.U. 2013, G.B.T.U. 2011, 2012*]

(*ii*) Find the interpolating polynomial to the following data and hence find the value of y for $x = 5$:

x:	4	6	8	10
$f(x)$:	1	3	8	16

(*G.B.T.U. 2013*)

(*iii*) Express the value of θ in terms of x using the following data:

x:	40	50	60	70	80	90
θ:	184	204	226	250	276	304

Also find θ at $x = 43$. (*M.T.U. 2012*)

5. (*i*) Obtain the value of $f(3.5)$ from the following data:

x:	3	4	5	6	7
$f(x)$:	3	6.6	15	22	35

(*G.B.T.U. 2010*)

(*ii*) Use Newton-Gregory formula to compute y at $x = 24$ from the following data:

x:	21	25	29	33	37
y:	18.4	17.8	17.1	16.3	15.5

[*G.B.T.U. (C.O.) 2011*]

6. (*i*) Find the cubic polynomial which takes the following values:

$$y(0) = 1, \quad y(1) = 0, \quad y(2) = 1 \text{ and } y(3) = 10$$

Hence or otherwise obtain $y(4)$.

(*ii*) Find the polynomial interpolating the data:

x:	0	1	2
y:	0	5	2

(*U.P.T.U. 2008*)

7. Ordinates $f(x)$ of a normal curve in terms of standard deviation x are given as

x:	1.00	1.02	1.04	1.06	1.08
$f(x)$:	0.2420	0.2371	0.2323	0.2275	0.2227

Find the ordinate for standard deviation $x = 1.025$.

8. Find the number of men getting wages between ₹ 10 and ₹ 15 from following table:

Wages (in ₹):	0–10	10–20	20–30	30–40
Frequency:	9	30	35	42

(G.B.T.U. 2011)

9. Following are the marks obtained by 492 candidates in a certain examination

Marks:	0–40	40–45	45–50	50–55	55–60	60–65
No. of candidates:	210	43	54	74	32	79

Find out the number of candidates who secured

(*a*) more than 48 but not more than 50 marks

(*b*) less than 48 but not less than 45 marks.

10. Find the number of students from the following data who secured marks not more than 45

Marks range:	30–40	40–50	50–60	60–70	70–80
No. of students:	35	48	70	40	22

11. Use Newton's forward difference formula to obtain the interpolating polynomial $f(x)$ satisfying the following data:

x:	1	2	3	4
$f(x)$:	26	18	4	1

If another point $x = 5$, $f(x) = 26$ is added to the above data, will the interpolating polynomial be the same as before or different. Explain why?

12. Find the polynomial of degree four which takes the following values:

x:	2	4	6	8	10
y:	0	0	1	0	0

(U.P.T.U. 2007)

13. Use Newton's method to find a polynomial $p(x)$ of lowest possible degree such that $p(n) = 2^n$ for $n = 0, 1, 2, 3, 4$.

14. Find the order of the polynomial which might be suitable for the following function:

x:	2	2.1	2.2	2.3	2.4	2.5	2.6	2.7
$f(x)$:	0.577	0.568	0.556	0.540	0.520	0.497	0.471	0.442

Also find the value of $f(2.15)$ using difference formulae. *[G.B.T.U. (MCA) 2010]*

Answers

1. 352.22304 **2.** 3.375

3. (*i*) 0.1205 (*ii*) 0.7880

4. (*i*) $x^3 - 3x^2 + 2x$, 13.125 (*ii*) $\frac{3}{8}x^2 - \frac{11}{4}x + 6$, 1.625 (*iii*) $\frac{1}{100}x^2 + \frac{11}{10}x + 124$, 189.79

5. (*i*) 3.28125 (*ii*) 17.9571

6. (*i*) $x^3 - 2x^2 + 1$; 33 (*ii*) $9x - 4x^2$

7. 0.23589625 **8.** 15

9. (*a*) 27 (*b*) 27 **10.** 51

11. $\frac{17}{6}x^3 - 20x^2 + \frac{193}{6}x + 11$; no change since third differences are constant.

12. $\frac{1}{64}(x^4 - 24x^3 + 196x^2 - 624x + 640)$ **13.** $\frac{x^4}{24} - \frac{x^3}{12} + \frac{11}{12}x^2 + \frac{7x}{12} + 1$

14. 7th, 0.562425293.

4.16. NEWTON'S GREGORY BACKWARD INTERPOLATION FORMULA

[*U.P.T.U. MCA (SUM) 2008*]

Let $y = f(x)$ be a function of x which assumes the values $f(a), f(a + h), f(a + 2h), ..., f(a + nh)$ for $(n + 1)$ equidistant values $a, a + h, a + 2h, ..., a + nh$ of the independent variable x.

Let $f(x)$ be a polynomial of nth degree.

Let, $f(x) = A_0 + A_1(x - a - nh) + A_2 (x - a - nh)(x - a - \overline{n-1}\, h) + ...$
$$+ A_n (x - a - nh)(x - a - \overline{n-1}\, h) ...... (x - a - h)$$
where $A_0, A_1, A_2, A_3, ..., A_n$ are to be determined. ...(1)

Put $x = a + nh, a + \overline{n-1}\, h, ..., a$ in (1) respectively.

Put $x = a + nh$, then $f(a + nh) = A_0$ ...(2)

Put $x = a + (n - 1)h$, then
$$f(a + \overline{n-1}\, h) = A_0 - h A_1 = f(a + nh) - h A_1 \qquad | \text{ By } (2)$$
$$\Rightarrow \qquad A_1 = \frac{\nabla f(a+nh)}{h} \qquad ...(3)$$
Put $x = a + (n - 2)h$, then
$$f(a + \overline{n-2}\, h) = A_0 - 2hA_1 + (-2h)(-h) A_2$$
$$\Rightarrow \qquad 2!\, h^2 A_2 = f(a + \overline{n-2}\, h) - f(a + nh) + 2\nabla f(a + nh) = \nabla^2 f(a + nh)$$
$$A_2 = \frac{\nabla^2 f(a+nh)}{2!\, h^2} \qquad ...(4)$$
Proceeding, we get $A_n = \dfrac{\nabla^n f(a+nh)}{n!\, h^n}$ ...(5)

Substituting the values in (1), we get
$$f(x) = f(a + nh) + (x - a - nh)\frac{\nabla f(a+nh)}{h} + ... + (x - a - nh)(x - a - \overline{n-1}\, h)$$
$$...... (x - a - h)\frac{\nabla^n f(a+nh)}{n!\, h^n} \qquad ...(6)$$
Put $x = a + nh + uh$, then
$$x - a - nh = uh$$
and
$$x - a - (n - 1)h = (u + 1)h$$
$$\vdots$$
$$x - a - h = (u + \overline{n-1})\, h$$
$\therefore$ (6) becomes,
$$f(x) = f(a + nh) + u\, \nabla f(a + nh) + \frac{u(u+1)}{2!}\nabla^2 f(a + nh)$$
$$+ ...... + uh\, .\, (u + 1)h ...... (u + \overline{n-1})(h)\frac{\nabla^n f(a+nh)}{n!\, h^n}$$
or
$$\boxed{f(a + nh + uh) = f(a + nh) + u\, \nabla f(a + nh) + \frac{u(u+1)}{2!}\nabla^2 f(a + nh) + ... + \frac{u(u+1)......(u+\overline{n-1})}{n!}\nabla^n f(a + nh)}$$
This formula is useful when the value of $f(x)$ is required near the end of the table.

4.16.1. Algorithm for Newton's Backward Difference formula

Step. 01. Start of the program.

Step. 02. Input no. of terms n

Step. 03. Input the array ax

Step. 04. Input the array ay

Step. 05. *h*=*ax*[1]-ax[0]

Step. 06. for i=0 ; i<n–1 ; i++

Step. 07. diff[i][1]=ay[i+1]–ay[i]

Step. 08. End Loop i

Step. 09. for j = 2 ; j < = 4 ; j + +

Step. 10. for i=0 ; i<n–j ; i++

Step. 11. diff[i][j]=diff[i+1][j–1]–diff [i][j–1]

Step. 12. End Loop i

Step. 13. End Loop j

Step. 14. i=0

Step. 15. Repeat Step 16 until (!ax[i]<x)

Step. 16. i=i+1

Step. 17. x0=mx[i]

Step. 18. sum=0

Step. 19. y0=my[i]

Step. 20. fun=1

Step. 21. p=(x–x0)/h

Step. 22. sum=y0

Step. 23. for k=1 ; k<=4 ; k++

Step. 24. fun=(fun*(p–(k–1)))/k

Step. 25. sum=sum+fun*diff[i][k]

Step. 26. End loop k

Step. 27. Print Output x,sum

Step. 28. End of Program

4.16.2. Flow-chart

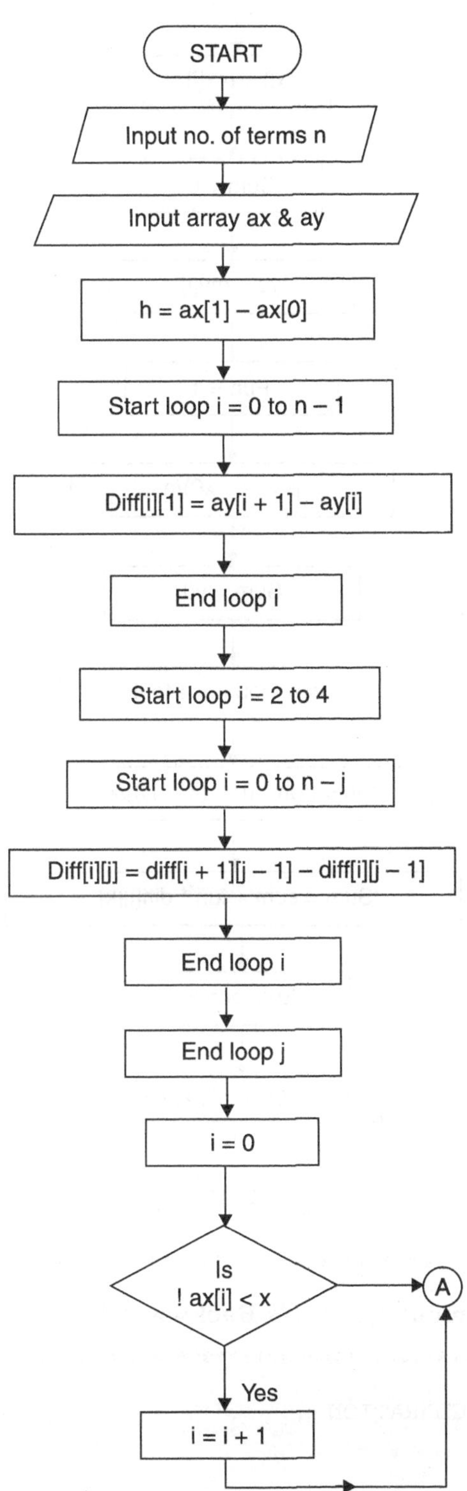

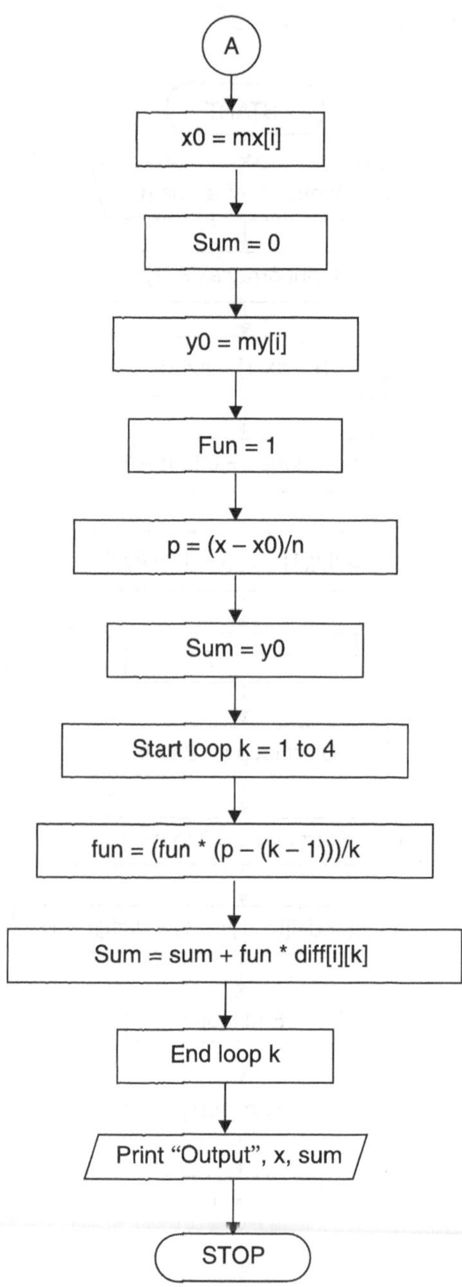

* **

4.16.3. Program to Implement Newton's Backward Method of Interpolation

* ** */

```
//...HEADER FILES DECLARATION
# include <stdio.h>
# include <conio.h>
```

```
# include <math.h>
# include <process.h>
# include <string.h>

//... MAIN EXECUTION THREAD

void main()
     {
     //...Variable declaration Field

     //...Integer Type

     int n;                                    //...No. of terms
     int i,j,k;                                //...Loop Variables

     //...Floating Type
     float mx[10];                             //... array limit 9
     float my[10];                             //... array limit 9
     float x;                                  //... User Querry
     float x0 = 0;                             //... Initial value 0
     float y0;                                 //... Calc. Section
     float sum;                                //... Calc. Section
     float h;                                  //... Calc. Section
     float fun;                                //... Calc. Section
     float p;                                  //... Calc. Section
     float diff[20][20] ;                      //... array limit 19,19
     float y1, y2, y3, y4 ;                    //... Formulae variables

     //...Invoke Function Clear Screen

     clrscr();

     //...Input Section

     printf("\n Enter the number of terms - ");
     scanf("%d",&n);

     //...Input Sequel for array X

     printf("\n\n Enter the value in the form of x - ");

     //...Input Loop for X

     for (i=0;i<n;i++)
           {
```

```
        printf("\n\n Enter the value of x%d - ",i+1);
        scanf ("%f",&mx[i]) ;

        }

//...Input Sequel for array Y

printf ("\n\n Enter the value in the form of y -");

//...Input Loop for Y

for (i=0;i<n;i++)

        {

        printf ("\n\n Enter the value of y%d - ",i+1);

        scanf ("%f",&my[i]);

        }

//...Inputting the required value querry

printf ("\nEnter the value of x for");
printf("\nwhich you want the value of y - ");

scanf("%f",&x);

//...Calculation and Processing Section

h=mx[1]-mx[0];

for(i=0;i<n-1;i++)
        {
        diff[i][1]=my[i+1]-my[i];
        }
for (j=2;j<=4;j++)

        {

        for (i=0;i<n-j;i++)

                {

                diff[i][j]=diff[i+1][j-1]-diff[i][j-1];

                }

        }

i=0;

while(!mx[i]>x)
        {
```

```
        i++;

        }

    x0=mx[i];
    sum=0;

    y0=my[i];
    fun=1;

    p=(x-x0)/h;
    sum=y0;

    for  (k=1;k<=4;k++)
        {

        fun=(fun*(p-(k-1)))/k;
        sum=sum+fun*diff[i][k]  ;

        }

    //...Output Section

    printf ("\nwhen x=%6.4f,y=%6.8f",x,sum);

    //...Invoke User Watch Halt Function

    printf("\n\n\n Press Enter to Exit");

    getch( );

    }

//...Termination of Main Execution Thread
```

4.16.4. Output

```
Enter the number of terms-7
Enter the value in the form of x-
Enter the value of x1 - 100
Enter the value of x2 - 150
Enter the value of x3 - 200
Enter the value of x4 - 250
Enter the value of x5 - 300
Enter the value of x6 - 350
Enter the value of x7 - 400
Enter the value in the form of y -
Enter the value of y1 - 10.63
Enter the value of y2 - 13.03
Enter the value of y3 - 15.04
```

```
Enter the value of y4 - 16.81
Enter the value of y5 - 18.42
Enter the value of y6 - 19.90
Enter the value of y7 - 21.27
Enter the value of x for which you want the value of y - 410
When x = 410.0000, y = 21.34462738
Press Enter to Exit
```

EXAMPLES

Example 1. *The population of a town was as given. Estimate the population for the year 1925.*

Years (x) :	*1891*	*1901*	*1911*	*1921*	*1931*
Population (y) : *(in thousands)*	*46*	*66*	*81*	*93*	*101*

Sol. Here, $a + nh = 1931, h = 10, \quad a + nh + uh = 1925$

$$\therefore \quad u = \frac{1925 - 1931}{10} = -0.6$$

Difference table is :

x	y	∇y	$\nabla^2 y$	$\nabla^3 y$	$\nabla^4 y$
1891	46				
		20			
1901	66		– 5		
		15		2	
1911	81		– 3		– 3
		12		– 1	
1921	93		– 4		
		8			
1931	101				

Applying Newton's Backward difference formula, we get

$$y_{1925} = y_{1931} + u\nabla y_{1931} + \frac{u(u+1)}{2!} \nabla^2 y_{1931} + \frac{u(u+1)(u+2)}{3!} \nabla^3 y_{1931} + \frac{u(u+1)(u+2)(u+3)}{4!} \nabla^4 y_{1931}$$

$$= 101 + (-.6)(8) + \frac{(-.6)(.4)}{2!}(-4) + \frac{(-.6)(.4)(1.4)}{3!}(-1) + \frac{(-.6)(.4)(1.4)(2.4)}{4!}(-3)$$

$$= 96.8368 \text{ thousands.}$$

Hence the population for the year 1925 = 96836.8 ≈ 96837.

Example 2. *The population of a town is as follows:*

Year:	*1921*	*1931*	*1941*	*1951*	*1961*	*1971*
Population: (in Lakhs)	*20*	*24*	*29*	*36*	*46*	*51*

Estimate the increase in population during the period 1955 to 1961.

Sol. Here, $a + nh = 1971,\ h = 10,\ a + nh + uh = 1955$

$\therefore \quad 1971 + 10u = 1955 \Rightarrow u = -1.6$

Difference table is:

x	y	∇y	$\nabla^2 y$	$\nabla^3 y$	$\nabla^4 y$	$\nabla^5 y$
1921	20					
		4				
1931	24		1			
		5		1		
1941	29		2		0	
		7		1		−9
1951	36		3		−9	
		10		−8		
1961	46		−5			
		5				
1971	51					

Applying Newton's backward difference formula, we get

$$y_{1955} = y_{1971} + u\nabla y_{1971} + \frac{u(u+1)}{2!}\nabla^2 y_{1971} + \frac{u(u+1)(u+2)}{3!}\nabla^3 y_{1971}$$

$$+ \frac{u(u+1)(u+2)(u+3)}{4!}\nabla^4 y_{1971} + \frac{u(u+1)(u+2)(u+3)(u+4)}{5!}\nabla^5 y_{1971}$$

$$= 51 + (-1.6)(5) + \frac{(-1.6)(-0.6)}{2!}(-5) + \frac{(-1.6)(-0.6)(0.4)}{6}(-8)$$

$$+ \frac{(-1.6)(-0.6)(.4)(1.4)}{24}(-9) + \frac{(-1.6)(-0.6)(0.4)(1.4)(2.4)}{120}(-9)$$

$$= 39.789632$$

$\therefore$ Increase in population during period 1955 to 1961 is

$$= 46 - 39.789632 = 6.210368 \text{ Lakhs} = 621036.8 \approx 621037.$$

Example 3. *Evaluate from following table f(3.8) to three significant figures using Gregory-Newton backward interpolation formula*

x:	*0*	*1*	*2*	*3*	*4*
f(x):	*1*	*1.5*	*2.2*	*3.1*	*4.6*

(U.P.T.U. 2009)

Sol. Here, $a + nh = 4,\ h = 1,\ a + nh + uh = 3.8$

$$\therefore \quad u = \frac{3.8 - 4}{1} = -0.2$$

Backward difference table is

x	$f(x)$	$\nabla f(x)$	$\nabla^2 f(x)$	$\nabla^3 f(x)$	$\nabla^4 f(x)$
0	1				
		0.5			
1	1.5		0.2		
		0.7		0	
2	2.2		0.2		0.4
		0.9		0.4	
3	3.1		0.6		
		1.5			
4	4.6				

By Newton's backward difference formula,

$$f(3.8) = f(4) + u\,\nabla f(4) + \frac{u(u+1)}{2}\nabla^2 f(4) + \frac{u(u+1)(u+2)}{3!}\nabla^3 f(4)$$

$$+ \frac{u(u+1)(u+2)(u+3)}{4!}\nabla^4 f(4)$$

$$= 4.6 + (-0.2)(1.5) + \frac{(-0.2)(0.8)}{2}(0.6) + \frac{(-0.2)(0.8)(1.8)}{3!}(0.4)$$

$$+ \frac{(-0.2)(0.8)(1.8)(2.8)}{4!}(0.4) = 4.21936.$$

Example 4. *Given log x for x = 40, 45, 50, 55, 60 and 65 according to the following table:*

x:	*40*	*45*	*50*	*55*	*60*	*65*
log x:	*1.60206*	*1.65321*	*1.69897*	*1.74036*	*1.77815*	*1.81291*

Find the value of log 5875. [M.T.U. (MCA) 2012]

Sol. The difference table is:

x	$10^5 \log x = 10^5 y_x$	$10^5 \nabla y_x$	$10^5 \nabla^2 y_x$	$10^5 \nabla^3 y_x$	$10^5 \nabla^4 y_x$	$10^5 \nabla^5 y_x$
40	160206					
		5115				
45	165321		– 539			
		4576		102		
50	169897		– 437		– 25	
		4139		77		5
55	174036		– 360		– 20	
		3779		57		
60	177815		– 303			
		3476				
65	181291					

Newton's Backward difference formula is

$$f(a + nh + uh) = f(a + nh) + u\nabla f(a + nh) + \frac{u(u+1)}{2!}\nabla^2 f(a + nh)$$

$$+ \frac{u(u+1)(u+2)}{3!}\nabla^3 f(a + nh) + \frac{u(u+1)(u+2)(u+3)}{4!}\nabla^4 f(a + nh)$$

$$+ \frac{u(u+1)(u+2)(u+3)(u+4)}{5!}\nabla^5 f(a + nh) \qquad ...(1)$$

First we shall find the value of log(58.75).

Here, $a + nh = 65,\ h = 5,\ a + nh + uh = 58.75$

$\therefore$ $65 + 5u = 58.75 \Rightarrow u = -1.25$

From (1),

$$10^5 f(58.75) = 181291 + (-1.25)(3476) + \frac{(-1.25)(-0.25)}{2!}(-303)$$

$$+ \frac{(-1.25)(-0.25)(0.75)}{3!}(57) + \frac{(-1.25)(-0.25)(0.75)(1.75)}{4!}(-20)$$

$$+ \frac{(-1.25)(-0.25)(0.75)(1.75)(2.75)}{5!}(5)$$

$\Rightarrow$ $10^5 f(58.75) = 176900.588$

$\therefore$ $f(58.75) = \log 58.75 = 176900.588 \times 10^{-5} = 1.76900588$

Hence, $\log 5875 = 3.76900588$ | $\because$ Mantissa remain the same

Example 5. *From the following table of half-yearly premium for policies maturing at different ages, estimate the premium for policy maturing at the age of 63:*

Age:	*45*	*50*	*55*	*60*	*65*
Premium: (in rupees)	*114.84*	*96.16*	*83.32*	*74.48*	*68.48*

Sol. The difference table is:

Age (*x*)	*Premium (in rupees)* (*y*)	∇y	$\nabla^2 y$	$\nabla^3 y$	$\nabla^4 y$
45	114.84				
		– 18.68			
50	96.16		5.84		
		– 12.84		– 1.84	
55	83.32		4		0.68
		– 8.84		– 1.16	
60	74.48		2.84		
		– 6			
65	68.48				

Here $a + nh = 65,\ \ h = 5,\ a + nh + uh = 63$

$\therefore$ $65 + 5u = 63 \Rightarrow u = -0.4$

By Newton's backward difference formula,

$$y(63) = y(65) + u\nabla y(65) + \frac{u(u+1)}{2!}\nabla^2 y(65) + \frac{u(u+1)(u+2)}{3!}\nabla^3 y(65) + \frac{u(u+1)(u+2)(u+3)}{4!}\nabla^4 y(65)$$

$$= 68.48 + (-0.4)(-6) + \frac{(-0.4)(0.6)}{2}(2.84) + \frac{(-0.4)(0.6)(1.6)}{6}(-1.16) + \frac{(-0.4)(0.6)(1.6)(2.6)}{24}(.68)$$

$$= 70.585152$$

ASSIGNMENT

1. Find a polynomial of degree three using Newton-Gregory backward difference formula which takes the following values. Hence find $y(7)$:

x:	3	4	5	6
y:	6	24	60	120

(*G.B.T.U. 2012*)

2. The population of a town in decennial census is as under. Estimate the population for the year 1955:

Year:	1921	1931	1941	1951	1961
Population (in lacs):	46	66	81	93	101

(*M.T.U. 2012*)

3. Estimate the value of $f(42)$ from the following available data:

x:	20	25	30	35	40	45
$f(x)$:	354	332	291	260	231	204

4. The table below gives the value of tan x for $0.10 \le x \le 0.30$:

x:	0.10	0.15	0.20	0.25	0.30
$y = \tan x$:	0.1003	0.1511	0.2027	0.2553	0.3093

Find: (*i*) tan 0.50 (*ii*) tan 0.26 (*iii*) tan 0.40.

5. (*i*) Given:

x:	1	2	3	4	5	6	7	8
$f(x)$:	1	8	27	64	125	216	343	512

Find $f(7.5)$ using Newton's Backward difference formula.

(*ii*) Compute $f(8)$ from the following data:

x:	1	3	5	7	9
$f(x)$:	9	21	81	237	537

(*G.B.T.U. 2013*)

6. Using Newton's backward difference formula, find the value of $e^{-1.9}$ from the following table of values of e^{-x}:

x:	1	1.25	1.50	1.75	2.00
e^{-x}:	0.3679	0.2865	0.2231	0.1738	0.1353

7. If $y(10) = 35.3$, $y(15) = 32.4$, $y(20) = 29.2$, $y(25) = 26.1$, $y(30) = 23.2$ and $y(35) = 20.5$, find $y(12)$ using Newton's forward as well as backward interpolation formula. Also explain why the difference (if any) in the result occur. (*U.P.T.U. 2007*)

8. From the following table of values of x and $f(x)$, determine (*i*) $f(0.23)$ (*ii*) $f(0.29)$:

x:	0.20	0.22	0.24	0.26	0.28	0.30
$f(x)$:	1.6596	1.6698	1.6804	1.6912	1.7024	1.7139

9. From the following table, find the value of tan 17°

$\theta°$:	0	4	8	12	16	20	24
tan $\theta°$:	0	0.0699	0.1405	0.2126	0.2867	0.3640	0.4402

10. From the following table:

x:	10°	20°	30°	40°	50°	60°	70°	80°
cos x:	0.9848	0.9397	0.8660	0.7660	0.6428	0.5000	0.3420	0.1737

Calculate cos 25° and cos 73° using Gregory Newton formula. *(U.P.T.U. 2006)*

Answers

1. $x^3 - 3x^2 + 2x$, 210 **2.** 9683680 **3.** 219

4. (*i*) 0.5543 (*ii*) 0.2662 (*iii*) 0.4241

5. (*i*) 421.875 (*ii*) 366 **6.** 0.1496

7. 34.22007, 34.30866 **8.** (*i*) 1.6751 (*ii*) 1.7081

9. 0.3057 **10.** 0.9063, 0.2923

4.17. CENTRAL DIFFERENCE INTERPOLATION FORMULAE

We shall study now the central difference formulae most suited for interpolation near the middle of a tabulated set.

4.18. GAUSS' FORWARD DIFFERENCE FORMULA

Newton's Gregory forward difference formula is

$$f(a + hu) = f(a) + u\Delta f(a) + \frac{u(u-1)}{2!}\Delta^2 f(a) + \frac{u(u-1)(u-2)}{3!}\Delta^3 f(a) + \frac{u(u-1)(u-2)(u-3)}{4!}\Delta^4 f(a) + \ldots\ldots \quad (1)$$

Put $a = 0$, $h = 1$, we get

$$f(u) = f(0) + u\Delta f(0) + \frac{u(u-1)}{2!}\Delta^2 f(0) + \frac{u(u-1)(u-2)}{3!}\Delta^3 f(0) + \frac{u(u-1)(u-2)(u-3)}{4!}\Delta^4 f(0) + \ldots\ldots \quad \ldots(2)$$

Now, $\Delta^3 f(-1) = \Delta^2 f(0) - \Delta^2 f(-1) \Rightarrow \Delta^2 f(0) = \Delta^3 f(-1) + \Delta^2 f(-1)$

Also, $\Delta^4 f(-1) = \Delta^3 f(0) - \Delta^3 f(-1) \Rightarrow \Delta^3 f(0) = \Delta^4 f(-1) + \Delta^3 f(-1)$

and $\Delta^5 f(-1) = \Delta^4 f(0) - \Delta^4 f(-1) \Rightarrow \Delta^4 f(0) = \Delta^5 f(-1) + \Delta^4 f(-1)$ and so on.

$\therefore$ From (2),

$$f(u) = f(0) + u\Delta f(0) + \frac{u(u-1)}{2!}\{\Delta^2 f(-1) + \Delta^3 f(-1)\} + \frac{u(u-1)(u-2)}{3!}\{\Delta^3 f(-1) + \Delta^4 f(-1)\} + \frac{u(u-1)(u-2)(u-3)}{4!}\{\Delta^4 f(-1) + \Delta^5 f(-1)\} + \ldots\ldots$$

$$= f(0) + u\Delta f(0) + \frac{u(u-1)}{2!}\Delta^2 f(-1) + \frac{u(u-1)}{2}\left\{1 + \frac{u-2}{3}\right\}\Delta^3 f(-1) + \frac{u(u-1)(u-2)}{6}\left\{1 + \frac{u-3}{4}\right\}\Delta^4 f(-1) + \frac{u(u-1)(u-2)(u-3)}{4!}\Delta^5 f(-1) + \ldots\ldots$$

$$= f(0) + u\Delta f(0) + \frac{u(u-1)}{2!}\Delta^2 f(-1) + \frac{(u+1)u(u-1)}{3!}\Delta^3 f(-1)$$

$$+ \frac{(u+1)u(u-1)(u-2)}{4!}\Delta^4 f(-1) + \frac{u(u-1)(u-2)(u-3)}{4!}\Delta^5 f(-1) + \ldots\ldots \qquad \ldots(3)$$

But, $\quad \Delta^5 f(-2) = \Delta^4 f(-1) - \Delta^4 f(-2)$

$\therefore \quad \Delta^4 f(-1) = \Delta^4 f(-2) + \Delta^5 f(-2)$

then (3) becomes,

$$f(u) = f(0) + u\Delta f(0) + \frac{u(u-1)}{2!}\Delta^2 f(-1) + \frac{(u+1)u(u-1)}{3!}\Delta^3 f(-1)$$

$$+ \frac{(u+1)u(u-1)(u-2)}{4!}\{\Delta^4 f(-2) + \Delta^5 f(-2)\} + \frac{u(u-1)(u-2)(u-3)}{4!}\Delta^5 f(-1) + \ldots\ldots$$

$$\boxed{f(u) = f(0) + u\Delta f(0) + \frac{u(u-1)}{2!}\Delta^2 f(-1) + \frac{(u+1)u(u-1)}{3!}\Delta^3 f(-1) + \frac{(u+1)u(u-1)(u-2)}{4!}\Delta^4 f(-2) + \ldots\ldots}$$

This is called **Gauss' forward difference formula.**

Remark. This formula is useful when u lies between 0 and $\frac{1}{2}$.

4.18.1. Algorithm

Step. 01. Start of the program.
Step. 02. Input no. of terms n
Step. 03. Input the array ax
Step. 04. Input the array ay
Step. 05. h=ax[1]-ax[0]
Step. 06. for i=0;i<n–1;i++
Step. 07. diff[i][1]=ay[i+1]-ay[i]
Step. 08. End Loop i
Step. 09. for j=2;j<=4;j++
Step. 10. for i=0;i<n–j;i++
Step. 11. diff[i][j]=diff[i+1][j–1]–diff[i][j–1]
Step. 12. End Loop i
Step. 13. End Loop j
Step. 14. i=0
Step. 15. Repeat Step 16 until ax[i]<x
Step. 16. i=i+1
Step. 17. i=i–1;
Step. 18. p=(x–ax[i])/h
Step. 19. y1=p*diff[i][1]
Step. 20. y2=p*(p–1)*diff[i–1][2]/2
Step. 21. y3=(p+1)*p*(p-1)*diff[i–2][3]/6

Step. 22. y4=(p+1)*p*(p–1)*(p–2)*diff[i–3][4]/24

Step. 23. y=ay[i]+y1+y2+y3+y4

Step. 24. Print Output x,y

Step. 25. End of Program

4.18.2. Flow-chart

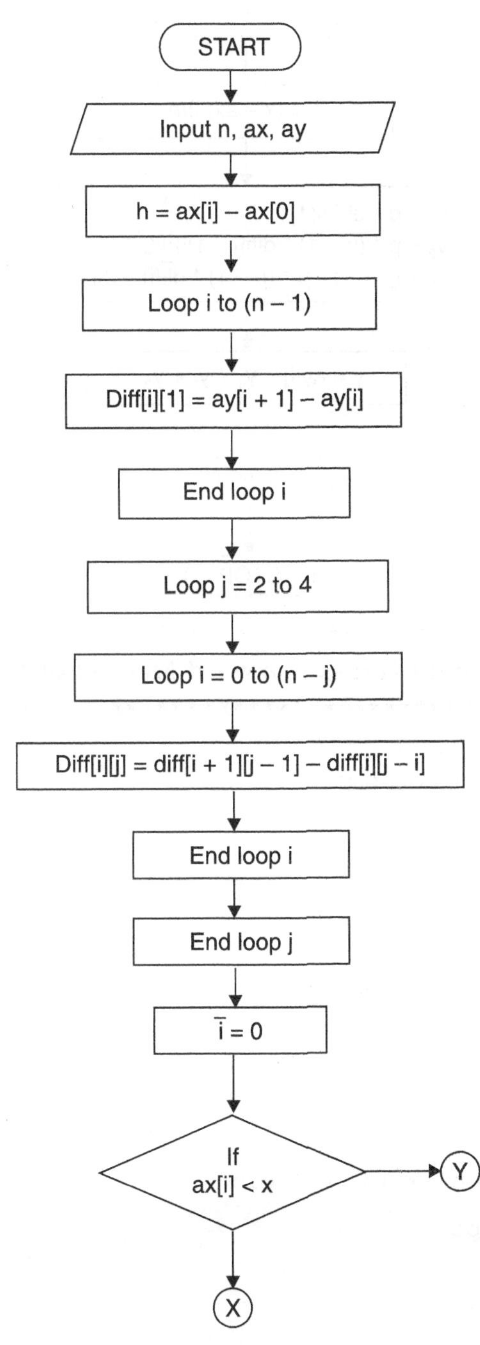

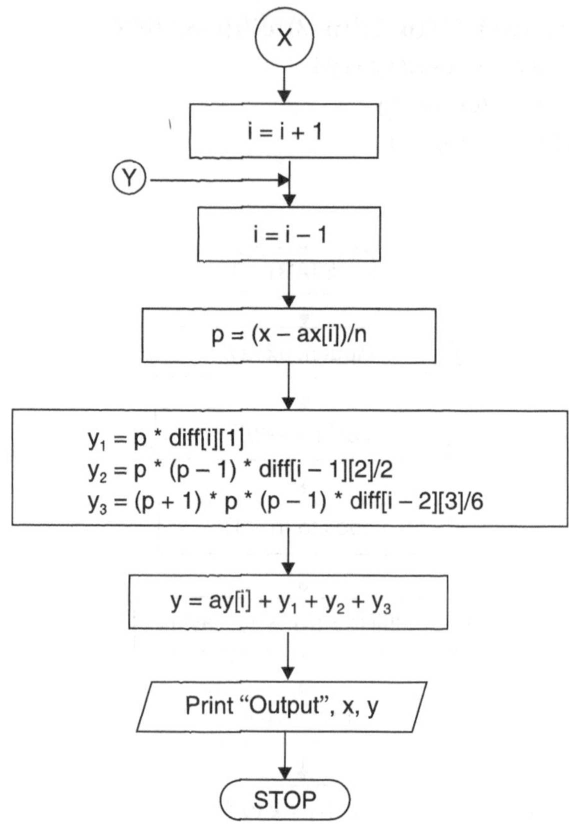

/* **

4.18.3. Program to Implement Gauss' Forward Method of Interpolation

** */

```
//...HEADER FILES DECLARATION

# include <stdio.h>
# include <conio.h>
# include <math.h>
# include <process.h>
# include <string.h>

//...MAIN EXECUTION THREAD

void main()
     {
     //...Variable declaration Field

     //...Integer Type

     int n;
     int i,j;
```

```
//...Floating Type
float ax[10];                              //...array limit 9
float ay[10];                              //...array limit 9
float x;
float nr,dr;
float y=0;                                 //...Initial value 0
float h;
float p;
float diff[20][20];                        //...array limit 19,19
float y1,y2,y3,y4 ;

//...Invoke Function Clear Screen
clrscr();

//...Input Section
printf("\n Enter the number of terms - ");
scanf("%d",&n);
//...Input Sequel for array X
printf("\n\n Enter the value in the form of x - ");
//...Input loop for Array X
for (i=0;i<n;i++)
     {
     printf("\n\n Enter the value of x%d - ",i+i);
     scanf("%f",&ax[i]);
     }
printf("\n\n Enter the value in the form of y - ");
//...Input Loop for Array Y
for(i=0;i<n;i++)
     {
     printf("\n\n Enter the value of y%d-",i+1);
     scanf("%f",&ay[i]);
     }

//...Inputting the required value querry
printf("\nEnter the value of x for");
printf("\nwhich you want the value of y-");
```

```
     scanf ("%f",&x);

     //... Calculation and Processing Section

     h=ax[1]-ax[0];

     for(i=0;i<n-1;i++)
            {
            diff[i][1]=ay[i+1]-ay[i];
            }
     for(j=2;j<=4;j++)
            {
            for(i=0;i<n-j;i++)
                   {
                   diff[i][j]=diff[i+1][j-1]-diff[i][j-1];
                   }
            }
     i=0;
     do     {
            i++;
            }while(ax[i]<x);
     i--;

     p=(x-ax[i])/h;

     y1=p*diff[i][1];
     y2=p*(p-1)*diff[i-1][2]/2;
     y3=(p+1)*p*(p-1)*diff[i-2][3]/6;
     y4=(p+1)*p*(p-1)*(p-2)*diff[i-3][4]/24;
     //...Taking Sum
     y=ay[i]+y1+y2+y3+y4;
     //...Output Section
     printf("\nwhen x=%6.4f,y=%6.8f ",x,y);
     //... Invoke User Watch Halt Function
     printf("\n\n\n Press Enter to Exit");
     getch();
     }
//...Termination of Main Execution Thread
```

4.18.4. Output

```
Enter the number of terms - 7
Enter the value in the form of x -
Enter the value of x1 - 1.00
Enter the value of x2 - 1.05
Enter the value of x3 - 1.10
Enter the value of x4 - 1.15
Enter the value of x5 - 1.20
Enter the value of x6 - 1.25
Enter the value of x7 - 1.30
Enter the value in the form of y -
Enter the value of y1 - 2.7183
Enter the value of y2 - 2.8577
Enter the value of y3 - 3.0042
Enter the value of y4 - 3.1582
Enter the value of y5 - 3.3201
Enter the value of y6 - 3.4903
Enter the value of y7 - 3.6693
Enter the value of x for
which you want the value of y - 1.17
When x = 1.17, y = 3.2221
Press Enter to Exit
```

EXAMPLES

Example 1. *Apply a central difference formula to obtain f(32) given that :*

$$f(25) = 0.2707,\ f(35) = 0.3386,\quad f(30) = 0.3027\quad f(40) = 0.3794.$$

Sol. Here $a + hu = 32$ and $h = 5$

Take origin at 30 $\therefore$ $a = 30$ then $u = 0.4$

Forward difference table is

u	x	$f(x)$	$\Delta f(x)$	$\Delta^2 f(x)$	$\Delta^3 f(x)$
– 1	25	0.2707			
			0.032		
0	30	0.3027		0.0039	
			0.0359		0.0010
1	35	0.3386		0.0049	
			0.0408		
2	40	0.3794			

Applying Gauss' forward difference formula, we have

$$f(u) = f(0) + u\Delta f(0) + \frac{u(u-1)}{2!}\Delta^2 f(-1) + \frac{(u+1)u(u-1)}{3!}\Delta^3 f(-1)$$

$$\therefore \quad f(0.4) = 0.3027 + (0.4)(0.0359) + \frac{(0.4)(0.4-1)}{2!}(0.0039) + \frac{(1.4)(0.4)(0.4-1)}{3!}(0.0010)$$

$$= 0.316536.$$

Example 2. *Use Gauss' forward formula to find a polynomial of degree four which takes the following values of the function f(x):*

x:	*1*	*2*	*3*	*4*	*5*
f(x):	*1*	*– 1*	*1*	*– 1*	*1*

Sol. Taking origin at 3 and $h = 1$

$$a + hu = x$$

$$\Rightarrow \quad 3 + u = x \quad \Rightarrow \quad u = x - 3$$

Difference table is

u	x	$f(x)$	$\Delta f(x)$	$\Delta^2 f(x)$	$\Delta^3 f(x)$	$\Delta^4 f(x)$
– 2	1	1				
			– 2			
– 1	2	– 1		4		
			2		– 8	
0	3	1		– 4		16
			– 2		8	
1	4	– 1		4		
			2			
2	5	1				

Gauss' forward difference formula is

$$f(u) = f(0) + u\Delta f(0) + \frac{u(u-1)}{2!}\Delta^2 f(-1) + \frac{(u+1)u(u-1)}{3!}\Delta^3 f(-1)$$

$$+ \frac{(u+1)u(u-1)(u-2)}{4!}\Delta^4 f(-2)$$

$$= 1 + (x-3)(-2) + \frac{(x-3)(x-4)}{2}(-4) + \frac{(x-2)(x-3)(x-4)}{6}(8)$$

$$+ \frac{(x-2)(x-3)(x-4)(x-5)}{24}(16)$$

$$\therefore \quad \boxed{F(x) = \frac{2}{3}x^4 - 8x^3 + \frac{100}{3}x^2 - 56x + 31}$$

Example 3. *The values of e^{-x} at $x = 1.72$ to $x = 1.76$ are given in the following table:*

x :	1.72	1.73	1.74	1.75	1.76
e^{-x} :	0.17907	0.17728	0.17552	0.17377	0.17204

Find the value of $e^{-1.7425}$ using Gauss' forward difference formula.

Sol. Here taking the origin at 1.74 and $h = 0.01$.

$$\therefore \quad x = a + uh$$

$$\Rightarrow \quad u = \frac{x-a}{h} = \frac{1.7425 - 1.7400}{0.01} = 0.25$$

The difference table is as follows:

u	x	$10^5 f(x)$	$10^5 \Delta f(x)$	$10^5 \Delta^2 f(x)$	$10^5 \Delta^3 f(x)$	$10^5 \Delta^4 f(x)$
− 2	1.72	17907				
			− 179			
− 1	1.73	17728		3		
			− 176		− 2	
0	1.74	17552		1		3
			− 175			
1	1.75	17377		2	1	
			− 173			
2	1.76	17204				

Gauss's forward formula is

$$f(u) = f(0) + u\Delta f(0) + \frac{u(u-1)}{2!}\Delta^2 f(-1) + \frac{(u+1)u(u-1)}{3!}\Delta^3 f(-1) + \frac{(u+1)u(u-1)(u-2)}{4!}\Delta^4 f(-2)$$

$$\therefore \quad 10^5 f(0.25) = 17552 + (0.25)(-175) + \frac{(0.25)(-0.75)}{2}(1) + \frac{(1.25)(0.25)(-0.75)}{6}(1) + \frac{(1.25)(0.25)(-0.75)(-1.75)}{24}(3)$$

$$= 17508.16846$$

$$\therefore \quad f(0.25) = e^{-1.7425} = 0.1750816846.$$

Example 4. *Apply Gauss' forward formula to find the value of u_9, if $u_0 = 14$, $u_4 = 24$, $u_8 = 32$, $u_{12} = 35$, $u_{16} = 40$.*

Sol. The difference table is (taking origin at 8)

u	x	$f(x)$	$\Delta f(x)$	$\Delta^2 f(x)$	$\Delta^3 f(u)$	$\Delta^4 f(x)$
− 2	0	14				
			10			
− 1	4	24		− 2		
			8		− 3	
0	8	32		− 5		10
			3		7	
1	12	35		2		
			5			
2	16	40				

Here $\quad a = 8, h = 4, \quad a + hu = 9$

$\therefore \quad 8 + 4u = 9 \Rightarrow u = .25$

Gauss' forward difference formula is

$$f(.25) = f(0) + u\Delta f(0) + \frac{u(u-1)}{2!}\Delta^2 f(-1) + \frac{(u+1)\,u(u-1)}{3!}\Delta^3 f(-1) + \frac{(u+1)\,u(u-1)(u-2)}{4!}\Delta^4 f(-2)$$

$$= 32 + (0.25)(3) + \frac{(0.25)(-0.75)}{2}(-5) + \frac{(1.25)(0.25)(-0.75)}{6}(7) + \frac{(1.25)(0.25)(-0.75)(-1.75)}{24}(10)$$

$\Rightarrow \quad u_9 = 33.11621094.$

ASSIGNMENT

1. Apply Gauss' forward formula to find the value of $f(x)$ at $x = 3.75$ from the table :

x :	2.5	3.0	3.5	4.0	4.5	5.0
$f(x)$:	24.145	22.043	20.225	18.644	17.262	16.047.

[M.T.U. (MCA) 2012]

2. Given that

x :	25	30	35	40	45
$\log x$:	1.39794	1.47712	1.54407	1.60206	1.65321

Find the value of log 3.7, using Gauss' forward formula.

3. Find the value of $f(41)$ by applying Gauss' forward formula from the following data :

x :	30	35	40	45	50
$f(x)$:	3678.2	2995.1	2400.1	1876.2	1416.3

4. From the following table, find the value of $e^{1.17}$ using Gauss forward formula :

x :	1	1.05	1.10	1.15	1.20	1.25	1.30
e^x :	2.7183	2.8577	3.0042	3.1582	3.3201	3.4903	3.6693

5. From the following table find y when $x = 1.45$

x :	1.0	1.2	1.4	1.6	1.8	2.0
y :	0.0	– .112	– .016	.336	.992	2.0

6. Use Gauss' forward interpolation formula to find $y(30)$, given that :

x :	21	25	29	33	37
$f(x)$:	18.470	17.814	17.107	16.343	15.515

Answers

1. 19.407426 **2.** 0.56849 **3.** 2290.0017 **4.** 3.22199

5. .046 **6.** 16.9216.

4.19. GAUSS' BACKWARD DIFFERENCE FORMULA

Newton's Gregory forward difference formula is

$$f(a + hu) = f(a) + u\Delta f(a) + \frac{u(u-1)}{2!}\Delta^2 f(a) + \frac{u(u-1)(u-2)}{3!}\Delta^3 f(a) + \ldots\ldots \quad \ldots(1)$$

Put $a = 0,\ h = 1$, we get

$$f(u) = f(0) + u\Delta f(0) + \frac{u(u-1)}{2!}\Delta^2 f(0) + \frac{u(u-1)(u-2)}{3!}\Delta^3 f(0) + \frac{u(u-1)(u-2)(u-3)}{4!}\Delta^4 f(0) + \ldots\ldots \quad \ldots(2)$$

Now, $\Delta f(0) = \Delta f(-1) + \Delta^2 f(-1),\ \Delta^2 f(0) = \Delta^2 f(-1) + \Delta^3 f(-1)$

$\Delta^3 f(0) = \Delta^3 f(-1) + \Delta^4 f(-1),\ \Delta^4 f(0) = \Delta^4 f(-1) + \Delta^5 f(-1)$ and so on.

$\therefore$ From (2),

$$f(u) = f(0) + u[\Delta f(-1) + \Delta^2 f(-1)] + \frac{u(u-1)}{2!}[\Delta^2 f(-1) + \Delta^3 f(-1)] + \frac{u(u-1)(u-2)}{3!}[\Delta^3 f(-1) + \Delta^4 f(-1)] + \frac{u(u-1)(u-2)(u-3)}{4!}[\Delta^4 f(-1) + \Delta^5 f(-1)] + \ldots\ldots \quad \ldots(3)$$

$$= f(0) + u\Delta f(-1) + u\left(1 + \frac{u-1}{2}\right)\Delta^2 f(-1) + \frac{u(u-1)}{2}\left(1 + \frac{u-2}{3}\right)\Delta^3 f(-1) + \frac{u(u-1)(u-2)}{6}\left\{1 + \frac{u-3}{4}\right\}\Delta^4 f(-1) + \frac{u(u-1)(u-2)(u-3)}{4!}\Delta^5 f(-1) + \ldots\ldots$$

$$= f(0) + u\Delta f(-1) + \frac{(u+1)u}{2!}\Delta^2 f(-1) + \frac{(u+1)u(u-1)}{3!}\Delta^3 f(-1) + \frac{(u+1)u(u-1)(u-2)}{4!}\Delta^4 f(-1) + \ldots\ldots \quad \ldots(4)$$

Again, $\Delta^3 f(-1) = \Delta^3 f(-2) + \Delta^4 f(-2)$

and $\Delta^4 f(-1) = \Delta^4 f(-2) + \Delta^5 f(-2)$ and so on

$\therefore$ (4) gives

$$f(u) = f(0) + u\Delta f(-1) + \frac{(u+1)u}{2!}\Delta^2 f(-1) + \frac{(u+1)u(u-1)}{3!}\{\Delta^3 f(-2) + \Delta^4 f(-2)\} + \frac{(u+1)u(u-1)(u-2)}{4!}\{\Delta^4 f(-2) + \Delta^5 f(-2)\} + \ldots\ldots$$

$$f(u) = f(0) + u\Delta f(-1) + \frac{(u+1)u}{2!}\Delta^2 f(-1) + \frac{(u+1)\,u(u-1)}{3!}\Delta^3 f(-2) + \frac{(u+2)(u+1)u(u-1)}{4!}\Delta^4 f(-2) + \ldots\ldots \quad \ldots(5)$$

This is known as **Gauss' backward difference formula.**

This formula is useful when u lies between $-\frac{1}{2}$ and 0.

4.19.1. Algorithm of Gauss' Backward Formula

Step 01. Start of the program.

Step 02. Input no. of terms n

Step 03. Input the array ax

Step 04. Input the array ay

Step 05. h=ax[1]-ax[0]

Step 06. for i=0;i<n-l;i++

Step. 07. diff[i][1]=ay[i+1]-ay[i]

Step. 08. End Loop i

Step. 09. for j=2;j<=4;j++

Step. 10. for i=0;i<n–j;i++

Step. 11. diff[i][j]=diff[i+1][j–1]–diff[i][j–1]

Step. 12. End Loop i

Step. 13. End Loop j

Step. 14. i=0

Step. 15. Repeat Step 16 until ax[i]<x

Step. 16. i=i+1

Step. 17. i=i–1;

Step. 18. p=(x–ax[i])/h

Step. 19. y1=p*diff[i-1][1]

Step. 20. y2=p*(p+1)*diff[i–1][2]/2

Step. 21. y3=(p+1)*p*(p-1)*diff[i–2][3]/6

Step. 22. y4=(p+2)*(p+1)*p*(p–1)*diff[i–3][4]/24

Step. 23. y=ay[i]+y1+y2+y3+y4

Step. 24. Print Output x,y

Step. 25. End of Program

4.19.2. Flow-chart

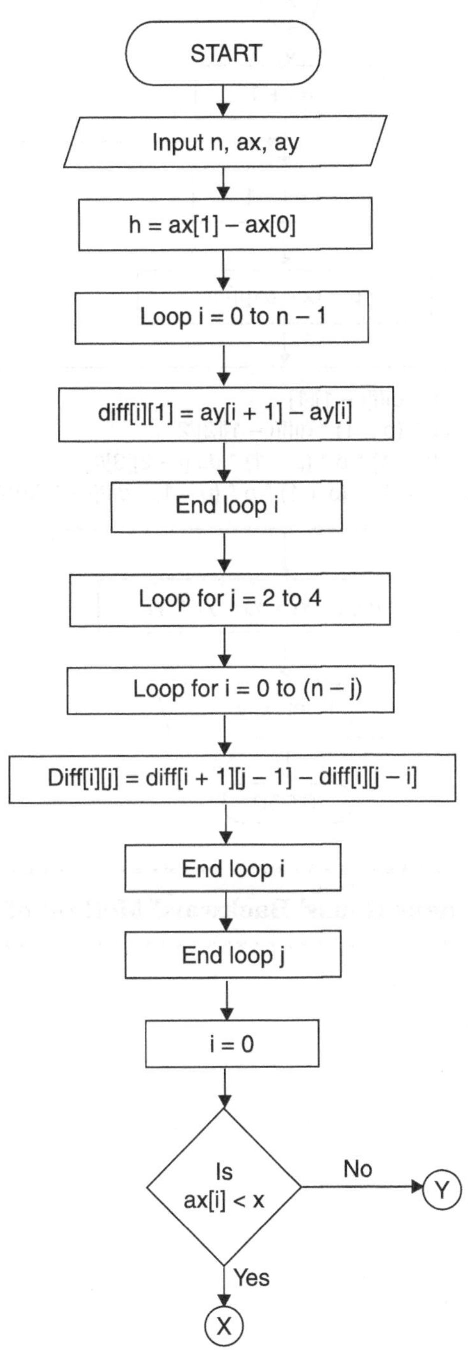

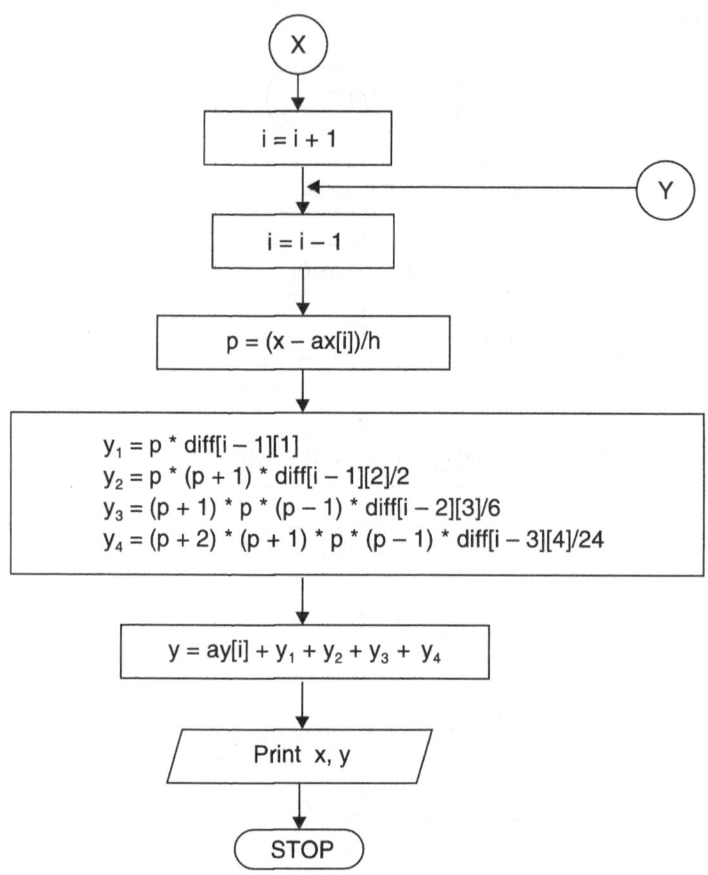

/* ***

4.19.3. Program to Implement Gauss' Backward Method of Interpolation

**/*

```
//...HEADER FILES DECLARATION

# include <stdio.h>
# include <conio.h>
# include <math.h>
# include <process.h>
# include <string.h>

//...MAIN EXECUTION THREAD

void main()
     {
     //...Variable declaration Field
```

```
//...Integer Type

int n;                                  //... No. of terms
int i,j;                                //... Loop Variables

//...Floating Type
float ax[10];                           //... array limit 9
float ay[10];                           //... array limit 9
float x;                                //... User Querry
float y=0;                              //... Initial value 0
float h;                                //... Calc. section
float p;                                //... Calc. section
float diff[20][20];                     //... array limit 19, 19
float y1,y2,y3,y4;                      //... Formulae variables

//... Invoke Function Clear Screen

clrscr();

//... Input Section

printf("\n Enter the number of terms - ");
scanf("%d",&n);

//... Input Sequel for array X

printf("\n\n Enter the value in the form of x - ");

//... Input loop for X

for  (i=0;i<n;i++)
      {
      printf("\n\n Enter the value of x%d-",i+1);
      scanf("%f",&ax[i]);
      }
//...Input Sequel for array Y

printf("\n\n Enter the value in the form of y-");

//...Input Loop for Y

for(i=0;i<n;i++)
      {
      printf("\n\n Enter the value of y%d-",i+1);
      scanf("%f",&ay[i]);
      }
```

```
//... Inputting the required value querry

printf("\nEnter the value of x for");
printf("\nwhich you want the value of y - ");

scanf("%f",&x);

//... Calculation and Processing Section

h=ax[1]-ax[0];

for(i=0;i<n-1;i++)
       {
       diff[i][1]=ay[i+1]-ay[i];
       }

for(j=2;j<=4;j++)
       {
       for(i=0;i<n-j;i++)
              {
              diff[i][j]=diff[i+1][j-1]-diff[i][j-1];
              }
       }

i=0;

do            {
              i++;
              }while (ax[i]<x);

i--;
p=(x-ax[i])/h;
y1=p*diff[i-1][1];
y2=p*(p+1)*diff[i-1][2]/2;
y3=(p+1)*p*(p-1)*diff[i-2][3]/6;
y4=(p+2)*(p+1)*p*(p-1)*diff[i-3][4]/24;

//... Taking Sum

y=ay[i]+y1+y2+y3+y4;
```

```
    //... Output Section
    printf("\nwhen x=%6.1f,y=%6.4f ",x,y);
    //... Invoke User Watch Halt Function
    printf("\n\n\n Press Enter to Exit");
    getch();
    }
//... Termination of Main Execution Thread
```

4.19.4. Output

```
Enter the number of terms - 7
Enter the value in the form of x -
Enter the value of x1 - 1.00
Enter the value of x2 - 1.05
Enter the value of x3 - 1.10
Enter the value of x4 - 1.15
Enter the value of x5 - 1.20
Enter the value of x6 - 1.25
Enter the value of x7 - 1.30
Enter the value in the form of y -
Enter the value of y1 - 2.1783
Enter the value of y2 - 2.8577
Enter the value of y3 - 3.0042
Enter the value of y4 - 3.1582
Enter the value of y5 - 3.3201
Enter the value of y6 - 3.4903
Enter the value of y7 - 3.6693
Enter the value of x for
which you want the value of y - 1.35
When x = 1.35, y=3.8483
Press Enter to Exit
```

EXAMPLES

Example 1. *Given that*

$$\sqrt{12500} = 111.803399, \ \sqrt{12510} = 111.848111$$

$$\sqrt{12520} = 111.892806, \ \sqrt{12530} = 111.937483$$

Show by Gauss' backward formula that $\sqrt{12516} = 111.8749301$.

Sol. Taking the origin at 12520

$$\therefore \qquad u = \frac{x-a}{h} = \frac{12516 - 12520}{10} = -\frac{4}{10} = -0.4$$

Gauss' backward formula is

$$f(u) = f(0) + u\Delta f(-1) + \frac{(u+1)\,u}{2!}\,\Delta^2 f(-1) + \frac{(u+1)\,u(u-1)}{3!}\,\Delta^3 f(-2) + \ldots\ldots \quad \ldots(1)$$

The difference table is :

u	x	$10^6 f(x)$	$10^6 \Delta f(x)$	$10^6 \Delta^2 f(x)$	$10^6 \Delta^3 f(x)$
-2	12500	111803399			
			44712		
-1	12510	111848111		-17	
			44695		-1
0	12520	111892806		-18	
			44677		
1	12530	111937483			

From (1),

$$10^6 f(-0.4) = 111892806 + (-0.4)(44695) + \frac{(0.6)(-0.4)}{2!}(-18) + \frac{(0.6)(-0.4)(-1.4)}{3!}(-1)$$

$$= 111874930.1$$

$\therefore \quad f(-0.4) = 111.8749301$

Hence, $\sqrt{12516} = 111.8749301.$

Example 2. *Using Gauss backward interpolation formula, find the population for the year 1936 given that*

Year :	*1901*	*1911*	*1921*	*1931*	*1941*	*1951*
Population :	*12*	*15*	*20*	*27*	*39*	*52*

(in thousands)

Sol. Taking the origin at 1941 and $h = 10$,

$$x = a + uh \quad \therefore \quad u = \frac{x-a}{h} = \frac{1936-1941}{10} = -0.5$$

Gauss's backward formula is

$$f(u) = f(0) + u\Delta f(-1) + \frac{(u+1)u}{2!}\Delta^2 f(-1) + \frac{(u+1)u(u-1)}{3!}\Delta^3 f(-2)$$

$$+ \frac{(u+2)(u+1)u(u-1)}{4!}\Delta^4 f(-2) + \frac{(u+2)(u+1)u(u-1)(u-2)}{5!}\Delta^5 f(-3) \quad \ldots(1)$$

The difference table is

u	$f(u)$	$\Delta f(u)$	$\Delta^2 f(u)$	$\Delta^3 f(u)$	$\Delta^4 f(u)$	$\Delta^5 f(u)$
– 4	12					
		3				
– 3	15		2			
		5		0		
– 2	20		2		3	
		7		3		– 10
– 1	27		5		– 7	
		12		– 4		
0	39		1			
		13				
1	52					

From (1),

$$f(-0.5) = 39 + (-0.5)(12) + \frac{(0.5)(-0.5)}{2}(1) + \frac{(0.5)(-0.5)(-1.5)}{6}(-4)$$

$$= 32.625 \text{ thousands}$$

Hence, the population for the year 1936 = 32625

Example 3. *$f(x)$ is a polynomial of degree four and given that*

$$f(4) = 270,\ f(5) = 648,\ \Delta f(5) = 682,\ \Delta^3 f(4) = 132.$$

Find the value of $f(5.8)$ using Gauss' backward formula.

Sol. $\Delta f(5) = f(6) - f(5)$

$\therefore$ $f(6) = f(5) + \Delta f(5) = 648 + 682 = 1330$

$\Delta^3 f(4) = (E - 1)^3 f(4) = f(7) - 3 f(6) + 3 f(5) - f(4) = 132$

$\therefore$ $f(7) = 3f(6) - 3f(5) + f(4) + 132 = 2448.$

The difference table is (Taking origin at 6):

u	x	$f(x)$	$\Delta f(x)$	$\Delta^2 f(x)$	$\Delta^3 f(x)$
– 2	4	270			
			378		
– 1	5	648		304	
			682		132
0	6	1330		436	
			1118		
1	7	2448			

Here, $a = 6, \quad h = 1, \quad a + hu = 5.8$

$\therefore$ $6 + u = 5.8 \Rightarrow u = -0.2$

Gauss's backward formula is

$$f(-0.2) = f(0) + u\Delta f(-1) + \frac{(u+1)u}{2!}\Delta^2 f(-1) + \frac{(u+1)u(u-1)}{3!}\Delta^3 f(-2)$$

$$= 1330 + (-0.2)(682) + \frac{(0.8)(-0.2)}{2}(436) + \frac{(0.8)(-0.2)(-1.2)}{6}(132)$$

$$= 1162.944$$

$\therefore$ $f(5.8) = 1162.944.$

ASSIGNMENT

1. The population of a town in the years 1931, ..., 1971 are as follows :

Year	:	1931	1941	1951	1961	1971
Population (in thousands)	:	15	20	27	39	52

Find the population of the town in 1946 by applying Gauss' backward formula.

2. Apply Gauss' backward formula to find the value of $(1.06)^{19}$ if $(1.06)^{10} = 1.79085$, $(1.06)^{15} = 2.39656$, $(1.06)^{20} = 3.20714$, $(1.06)^{25} = 4.29187$ and $(1.06)^{30} = 5.74349$.

3. Given that

x	:	50	51	52	53	54
$\tan x$	:	1.1918	1.2349	1.2799	1.3270	1.3764

Using Gauss' backward formula, find the value of tan 51° 42′.

4. Interpolate by means of Gauss' backward formula, the population of a town KOSIKALAN for the year 1974 given that :

Year	:	1939	1949	1959	1969	1979	1989
Population (in thousands)	:	12	15	20	27	39	52

5. Apply Gauss' backward formula to find sin 45° from the following table :

θ°	:	20	30	40	50	60	70	80
$\sin \theta$	:	0.34202	0.502	0.64279	0.76604	0.86603	0.93969	0.98481

6. Using Gauss' backward formula, estimate the no. of persons earning wages between ₹ 60 and ₹ 70 from the following data:

Wages (₹)	:	Below 40	40—60	60—80	80—100	100—120
No. of persons (in thousands)	:	250	120	100	70	50

Answers

1. 22898 **2.** 3.025646784 **3.** 1.2662

4. 32.345 thousands (approx.) **5.** 0.70711 **6.** 54000.

4.20. STIRLING'S FORMULA

Gauss' forward formula is

$$f(u) = f(0) + u\Delta f(0) + \frac{u(u-1)}{2!}\Delta^2 f(-1) + \frac{(u+1)\,u(u-1)}{3!}\Delta^3 f(-1) + \frac{(u+1)\,u(u-1)(u-2)}{4!}\Delta^4 f(-2) + \ldots\ldots \quad \ldots(1)$$

Gauss' backward formula is

$$f(u) = f(0) + u\Delta f(-1) + \frac{(u+1)u}{2!}\Delta^2 f(-1) + \frac{(u+1)u(u-1)}{3!}\Delta^3 f(-2)$$

$$+ \frac{(u+2)(u+1)u(u-1)}{4!}\Delta^4 f(-2) + \ldots\ldots \quad \ldots(2)$$

Take mean of (1) and (2),

$$f(u) = f(0) + u\left\{\frac{\Delta f(0) + \Delta f(-1)}{2}\right\} + \frac{u^2}{2!}\Delta^2 f(-1) + \frac{(u+1)u(u-1)}{3!}\left\{\frac{\Delta^3 f(-1) + \Delta^3 f(-2)}{2}\right\}$$

$$+ \frac{u^2(u^2-1)}{4!}\Delta^4 f(-2) + \ldots\ldots \quad \ldots(3)$$

This is called Stirling's formula. It is useful when $|u| < \frac{1}{2}$ or $-\frac{1}{2} < u < \frac{1}{2}$. It gives best estimate when $-\frac{1}{4} < u < \frac{1}{4}$.

4.20.1. Algorithm of Stirling's formula

Step 01. Start of the program.
Step 02. Input no. of terms n
Step 03. Input the array ax
Step 04. Input the array ay
Step 05. h = ax[1]-ax[0]
Step 06. for i = 1;i < n-1 ; i++
Step 07. diff [i][1] = ay[i + 1]-ay[i]
Step 08. End loop i
Step 09. for j = 2 ; j < = 4 ; j++
Step 10. for i = 0 ; i < n-j ; i++
Step 11. diff[i][j] = diff[i + 1][j-1]-diff[i][j-1]
Step 12. End loop i
Step 13. End loop j
Step 14. i = 0
Step 15. Repeat step 16 until ax[i] < x
Step 16. i = i + 1
Step 17. i = i-1 ;
Step 18. p = (x-ax[i])/h
Step 19. y1= p*(diff[i][1] + diff[i-1][1])/2
Step 20. y2 = p*p*diff[i-1][2]/2
Step 21. y3 = p*(p*p-1)*(diff[i-1][3]+diff[i-2][3])/6
Step 22. y4 = p*p*(p*p-1)*diff[i-2][4]/24

Step 23. y = ay[i]+y1 + y2 + y3 + y4

Step 24. Print output

Step 25. End of program

4.20.2. Flow-chart

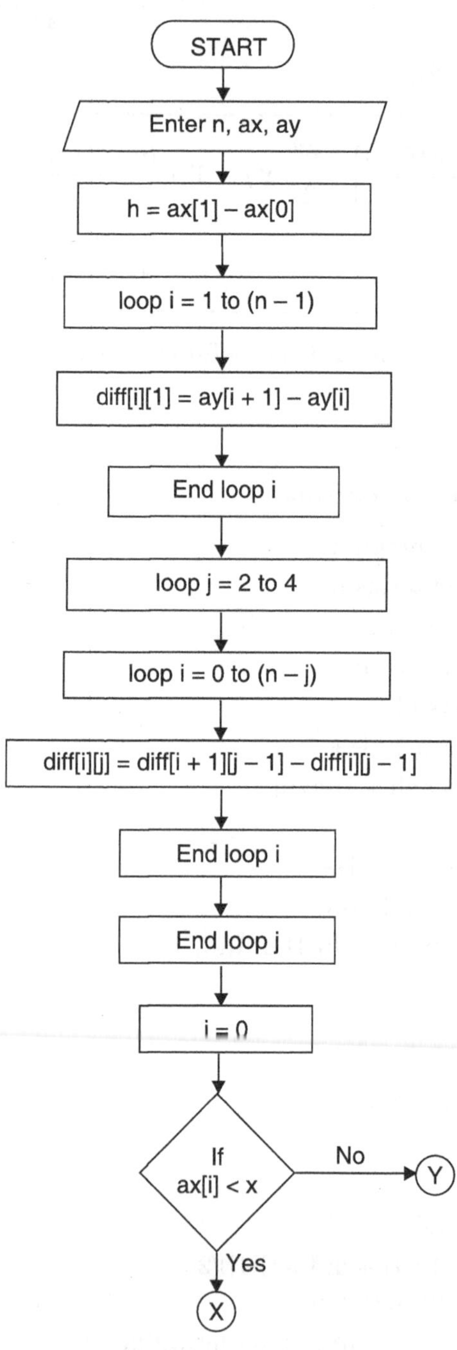

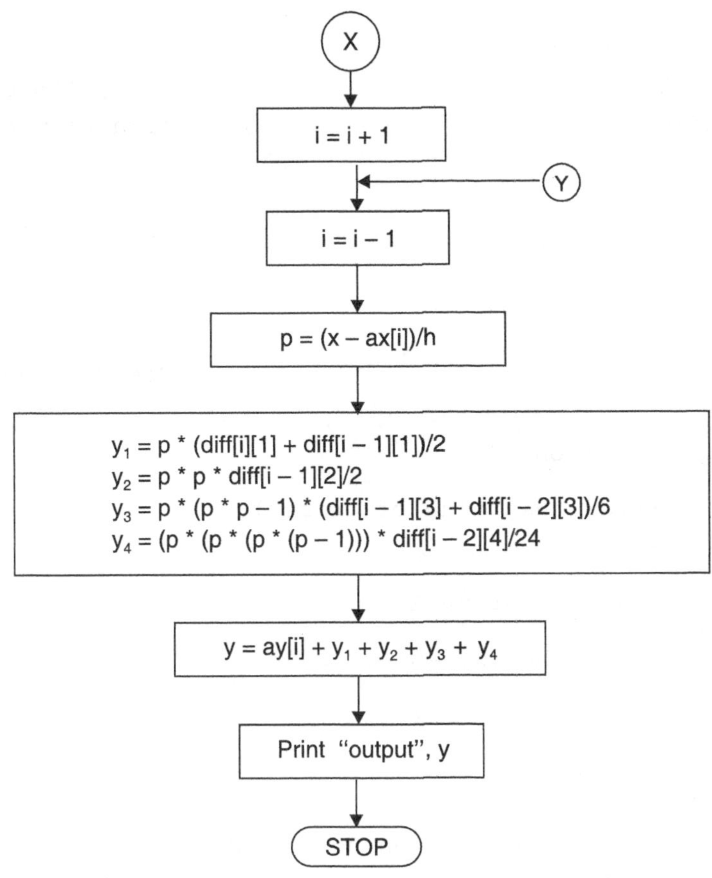

*/ **

4.20.3. Program to Implement Stirling Method of Interpolation

** /*

```
//... HEADER FILES DECLARATION

#include<stdio.h>
#include<conio.h>
#include<math.h>
#include<process.h>

//...MAIN EXECUTION THREAD

void main()
     {
     //...Variable declaration Field

     //...Integer Type
     int n;
```

```
int i,j;
//...Floating Type
float ax[10];                          //... array-limit 9
float ax[10];                          //... array-limit 9
float h;
float p;
float diff[20][20];                    //...array 2d-limit 19,19
float x,y;
float y1,y2,y3,y4;

clrscr();                              //... Clear Screen

//... Input Section

printf("\n Enter the value of terms");
scanf("%d",&n);

//... Input Section Array X

printf("\n Enter the values for x \n");

//...Input Section Loop for X

for(i=0;i<n;i++)
     {
     printf("\n Enter the value for x%d-",i+1);
     scanf("%f",&ax[i]);
     }
//... Input Section for Y
printf("\n Enter the values for y \n");
//... Input Section Loop for Y
for(i=0;i<n;i++)
     {
     printf("\n Enter the value for y%d-",i+1);
     scanf("%f",&ay[i]);
     }

//... Input Section Loop for Value of X for Y

printf("\n Enter the value of x for");
printf("\n which you want the value of y");
scanf("%f",&x);

//...Calculation and Processing Section

h=ax[1]-ax[0];
```

```
for(i=0;i<n-1;i++)
        {
        diff[i][1]=ay[i+1]-ay[i];
        }
for(j=2;j<=4;j++)
        {
        for(i=0;i<n-j;i++)
                {
                diff[i][j]=diff[i+1][j-1]-diff[i][j-1];
                }

        }

i=0;

do      {
        i++;
        }while(ax[i]<x);
i--;
p=(x-ax[i])/h;

y1=p*(diff[i][1]+diff[i-1][1])/2;
y2=p*p*diff[i-1][2]/2;
y3=p*(p*p-1)*(diff[i-1][3]+diff[i-2][3])/6;
y4=p*p*(p*p-1)*diff[i-2][4]/24;

y=ay[i]+y1+y2+y3+y4;

//...Output Section

printf("\n\n When x=%6.2f, y=%6.8f",x,y);

//... Producing User Watch Halt Function

getch();

}
```

4.20.4. Output

```
Enter the value of terms-7
Enter the values for x
Enter the value for x1 - .61
Enter the value for x2 - .62
Enter the value for x3 - .63
Enter the value for x4 - .64
Enter the value for x5 - .65
Enter the value for x6 - .66
```

```
Enter the value for x7 - .67

Enter the values for y
Enter the value for y1 - 1.840431
Enter the value for y2 - 1.858928
Enter the value for y3 - 1.877610
Enter the value for y4 - 1.896481
Enter the value for y5 - 1.915541
Enter the value for y6 - 1.934792
Enter the value for y7 - 1.954237

Enter the value of x for
which you want the value of y - 0.6440
When x=0.6440,y=1.90408230
Press Enter to Continue
```

EXAMPLES

Example 1. *Given :*

θ :	0°	5°	10°	15°	20°	25°	30°
$\tan\theta$:	0	0.0875	0.1763	0.2679	0.364	0.4663	0.5774

Find the value of tan 16° using Stirling formula.

Sol. Take origin at 15°

$$\therefore \qquad a = 15°,\ h = 5$$

$$a + hu = 16$$

$$\Rightarrow \qquad 15 + 5u = 16 \ \Rightarrow\ u = .2$$

Difference table is

u	θ	$10^4 f(\theta)$	$10^4 \Delta f(\theta)$	$10^4 \Delta^2 f(\theta)$	$10^4 \Delta^3 f(\theta)$	$10^4 \Delta^4 f(\theta)$	$10^4 \Delta^5 f(\theta)$	$10^4 \Delta^6 f(\theta)$
– 3	0	0						
			875					
– 2	5	875		13				
			888		15			
– 1	10	1763		28		2		
			916		17		– 2	
0	15	2679		45		0		11
			961		17		9	
1	20	3640		62		9		
			1023		26			
2	25	4663		88				
			1111					
3	30	5774						

Using Stirling's formula,

$$10^4 f(.2) = 2679 + (.2)\left(\frac{961+916}{2}\right) + \frac{(.2)^2}{2!}(45) + \frac{(1.2)(.2)(-.8)}{3!}\left(\frac{17+17}{2}\right)$$

$$+ \frac{(.2)^2\{(.2)^2-1\}}{4!}(0) + \frac{(2.2)(1.2)(.2)(-.8)(-1.8)}{5!}\left\{\frac{9+(-2)}{2}\right\} + \frac{(.2)^2\{(.2)^2-1\}\{(.2)^2-4\}}{6!}(11)$$

$$= 2866.980499$$

$\therefore \qquad f(.2) = .2866980499$

Hence $\qquad \tan 16° = 0.2866980499.$

Example 2. *Apply Stirling's formula to find the value of f(1.22) from the following table which gives the values of* $f(x) = \frac{1}{\sqrt{2\pi}}\int_0^x e^{-\frac{x^2}{2}}\, dx$, *at intervals of x = 0.5 from x = 0 to 2.*

x :	0	0.5	1.0	1.5	2.0
$f(x)$:	0	0.191	0.341	0.433	0.477.

Sol. Let the origin be at 1 and $h = 0.5$

$$\therefore \qquad x = a + hu,\ u = \frac{x-a}{h} = \frac{1.22 - 1.00}{0.5} = 0.44$$

Applying Stirling's formula

$$f(u) = f(0) + u \,.\, \frac{1}{2}[\Delta f(0) + \Delta f(-1)] + \frac{u^2}{2!}\Delta^2 f(-1)$$

$$+ \frac{u(u^2-1)}{3!}\cdot\frac{1}{2}[\Delta^3 f(-1) + \Delta^3 f(-2)] + \frac{u^2(u^2-1)}{4!}\,.\,\Delta^4 f(-2) + \ldots\ldots$$

$$\therefore \qquad f(0.44) = f(0) + (0.44)\,\frac{1}{2}[\Delta f(0) + \Delta f(-1)] + \frac{(0.44)^2}{2}\Delta^2 f(-1)$$

$$+ \frac{(0.44)[(0.44)^2 - 1]}{6}\cdot\frac{1}{2}[\Delta^3 f(-1) + \Delta^3 f(-2)] + \frac{(0.44)^2[(0.44)^2-1]}{24}\Delta^4 f(-2) \quad \ldots(1)$$

The difference table is as follows :

u	x	$10^3 f(x)$	$10^3\, \Delta f(x)$	$10^3 \Delta^2 f(x)$	$10^3 \Delta^3 f(x)$	$10^3 \Delta^4 f(x)$
− 2	0	0				
			191			
− 1	.5	191		− 41		
			150		− 17	
0	1	341	...	− 58		27
			92		10	
1	1.5	433				
			44	− 48		
2	2	477				

$f(0)$ and the differences are being multiplied by 10^3

$$\therefore \qquad 10^3 f(0.44) \simeq 341 + 0.22 \times (150 + 92) + 0.0968 \times (-58)$$
$$- 0.029568 \times [-17 + 10] - 0.006505 \times 27$$

$$= 388.66$$

$\therefore \qquad f(0.44) = 0.389$

Hence the required value of $f(x)$ at $x = 1.22$ is 0.389.

Example 3. *Use Stirling's formula to find y_{28}, given*

$$y_{20} = 49225, \quad y_{25} = 48316, \quad y_{30} = 47236, \quad y_{35} = 45926, \quad y_{40} = 44306.$$

Sol. Let the origin be at 30 and $h = 5$

$$a + hu = 28$$

$\Rightarrow$ $30 + 5u = 28 \Rightarrow u = -0.4$

The difference table is as follows :

u	x	y	Δy	$\Delta^2 y$	$\Delta^3 y$	$\Delta^4 y$
– 2	20	49225				
			– 909			
– 1	25	48316		– 171		
			– 1080		– 59	
0	30	47236		– 230		– 21
			– 1310		– 80	
1	35	45926		– 310		
			– 1620			
2	40	44306				

By Stirling's formula,

$$f(-0.4) = 47236 + (-0.4)\left(\frac{-1080 - 1310}{2}\right) + \frac{(-.4)^2}{2!}(-230)$$

$$+ \frac{(0.6)(-0.4)(-1.4)}{3!}\left(\frac{-59-80}{2}\right) + \frac{(-0.4)^2\{(-0.4)^2 - 1\}}{4!}(-21)$$

$$= 47691.8256$$

Hence $y_{28} = 47691.8256.$

Example 4. *Use Stirling's formula to find y_{35}, given $y_{20} = 512$, $y_{30} = 439$, $y_{40} = 346$ and $y_{50} = 243$.*

Sol. Let the origin be at 30 and $h = 10$

$$a + hu = 35$$

$$30 + 10u = 35 \Rightarrow u = 0.5$$

The difference table is as follows :

u	x	y	Δy	$\Delta^2 y$	$\Delta^3 y$
– 1	20	512			
			– 73		
0	30	439		– 20	
			– 93		10
1	40	346		– 10	
			– 103		
2	50	243			

By Stirling's formula,

$$f(0.5) = 439 + (0.5)\left(\frac{-93-73}{2}\right) + \frac{(0.5)^2}{2!}(-20) + \frac{(1.5)(0.5)(-0.5)}{3!}\left(\frac{10}{2}\right) = 394.6875$$

Hence, $y_{35} = 394.6875.$

ASSIGNMENT

1. Use Stirling's formula to find the value of $f(1.22)$ from the table.

x	$f(x)$
1.0	0.84147
1.1	0.89121
1.2	0.93204
1.3	0.96356
1.4	0.98545
1.5	0.99749
1.6	0.99957
1.7	0.99385
1.8	0.97385

2. Find $f(0.41)$ using Stirling's formula, if

$f(0.30) = 0.1179$, $f(0.35) = 0.1368$, $f(0.40) = 0.1554$, $f(0.45) = 0.1736$, $f(0.50) = 0.1915$.

3. Evaluate sin (0.197) from the data given below :

x :	0.15	0.17	0.19	0.21	0.23
sin x :	0.14944	0.16918	0.18886	0.20846	0.22798

4. Use Stirling's formula to find u_{32} from the following table :

$u_{20} = 14.035$ $u_{30} = 13.257$

$u_{40} = 12.089$ $u_{25} = 13.674$

$u_{35} = 12.734$ $u_{45} = 11.309.$

5. Employ Stirling's formula to evaluate $y_{12.2}$ from the following table ($y_x = 1 + \log_{10} \sin x$) :

$x°$:	10	11	12	13	14
$10^5 y_x$:	23967	28060	31788	35209	38368.

6. Following table gives the values of e^x for certain equidistant values of x. Find the value of e^x when $x = 0.644$ using Stirling's method.

x :	0.61	0.62	0.63	0.64	0.65	0.66	0.67
$y = e^x$:	1.840431	1.858928	1.877610	1.896481	1.915541	1.934792	1.954237

Answers

1. 0.9391002 **2.** 0.15907168 **3.** 0.19573 **4.** 13.062

5. 0.32495 **6.** 1.904082.

4.21. BESSEL'S INTERPOLATION FORMULA

Gauss' forward formula is

$$f(u) = f(0) + u\Delta f(0) + \frac{u(u-1)}{2!}\Delta^2 f(-1) + \frac{(u+1)u(u-1)}{3!}\Delta^3 f(-1)$$

$$+ \frac{(u+1)u(u-1)(u-2)}{4!}\Delta^4 f(-2) \ldots\ldots \qquad \ldots(1)$$

Gauss' backward formula is

$$f(u) = f(0) + u\Delta f(-1) + \frac{(u+1)u}{2!}\Delta^2 f(-1) + \frac{(u+1)u(u-1)}{3!}\Delta^3 f(-2)$$

$$+ \frac{(u+2)(u+1)u(u-1)}{4!}\Delta^4 f(-2) + \ldots\ldots \qquad \ldots(2)$$

In eqn. (2), shift the origin to 1 by replacing u by $u - 1$ and adding 1 to each argument 0, – 1, – 2, ..., we get

$$f(u) = f(1) + (u-1)\Delta f(0) + \frac{u(u-1)}{2!}\Delta^2 f(0) + \frac{u(u-1)(u-2)}{3!}\Delta^3 f(-1)$$

$$+ \frac{(u+1)u(u-1)(u-2)}{4!}\Delta^4 f(-1) + \ldots\ldots \qquad \ldots(3)$$

Taking mean of (1) and (3), we get

$$f(u) = \left\{\frac{f(0)+f(1)}{2}\right\} + \left\{\frac{u+(u-1)}{2}\right\}\Delta f(0) + \frac{u(u-1)}{2!}\left\{\frac{\Delta^2 f(-1)+\Delta^2 f(0)}{2}\right\}$$

$$+ \frac{u(u-1)}{3!}(u+1+u-2)\frac{\Delta^3 f(-1)}{2}$$

$$+ \frac{(u+1)u(u-1)(u-2)}{4!}\left\{\frac{\Delta^4 f(-2)+\Delta^4 f(-1)}{2}\right\} + \ldots\ldots$$

Finally, we get

$$f(u) = \left\{\frac{f(0)+f(1)}{2}\right\} + \left(u-\frac{1}{2}\right)\Delta f(0) + \frac{u(u-1)}{2!}\left\{\frac{\Delta^2 f(-1)+\Delta^2 f(0)}{2}\right\}$$

$$+ \frac{(u-1)\left(u-\frac{1}{2}\right)u}{3!}\Delta^3 f(-1) + \frac{(u+1)u(u-1)(u-2)}{4!}\left\{\frac{\Delta^4 f(-2)+\Delta^4 f(-1)}{2}\right\} + \ldots\ldots$$

...(4)

This is called **Bessel's formula.**

It is very useful when $u = \frac{1}{2}$. It gives better estimate when $\frac{1}{4} < \mathbf{u} < \frac{3}{4}$.

It is used mainly to compute entry against any argument between 0 and 1.

4.21.1. Algorithm of Bessel's Formula

Step 01. Start of the program.

Step 02. Input no. of terms n

Step 03. Input the array ax

Step 04. Input the array ay

Step 05. h=ax[1]-ax[0]

Step 06. for i=1;i<n-1;i++

Step 07. diff[i][1]=ay[i+1]-ay[i]

Step 08. End Loop i

Step 09. for j=2;j<=4;j++

Step 10. for i=0;i<n–j;i++

Step 11. diff[i][j]=diff[i+1][j–1]–diff[i][j–1]

Step 12. End Loop i

Step 13. End Loop j

Step 14. i=0

Step 15. Repeat Step 16 until ax[i]<x

Step 16. i=i+1

Step 17. i=i–1;

Step 18. p=(x–ax[i])/h

Step 19. y1=p*(diff[i][1])

Step 20. y2=p*(p-1)*(diff[i][2]+diff[i–1][2])/4

Step 21. y3=p*(p-1)*(p-0.5)*(diff[i–1][3])/6

Step 22. y4=(p+1)*p*(p–1)*(p–2)*(diff[i–2][4]+diff[i–1][4])/48

Step 23. y=ay[i]+y1+y2+y3+y4

Step 24. Print Output

Step 25. End of Program

4.21.2. Flow-chart

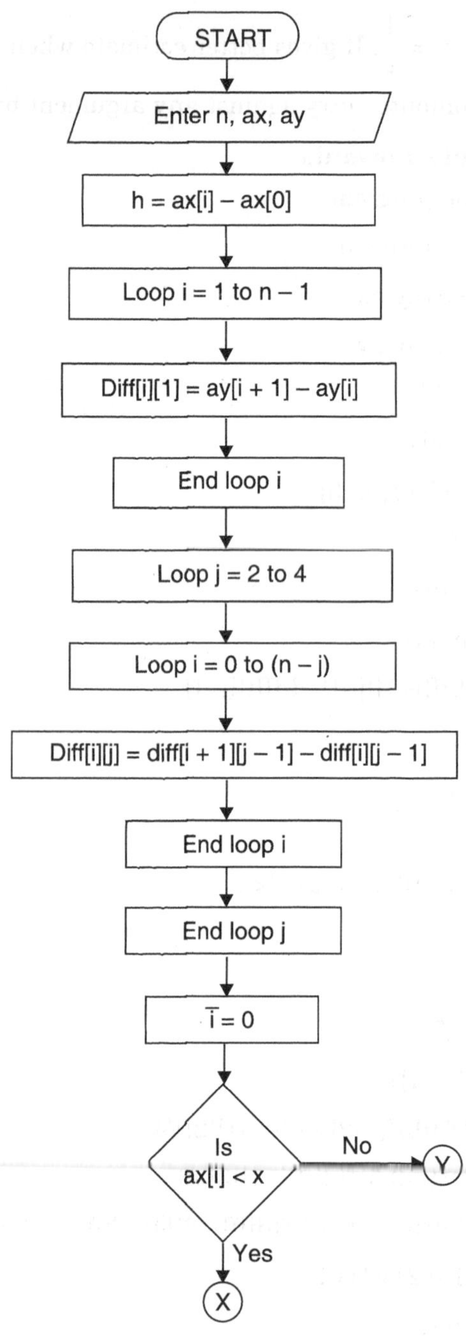

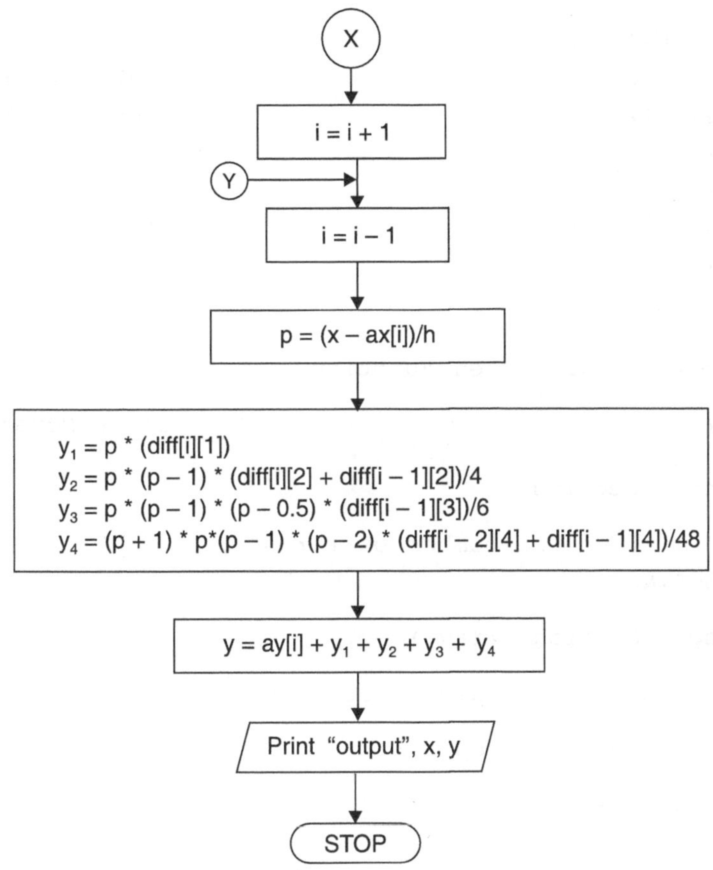

/* ***

4.21.3. Program to Implement Bessel's Method of Interpolation

*** */

```
//...HEADER FILES DECLARATION

#include<stdio.h>
#include<conio.h>
#include<math.h>
#include<process.h>

//... MAIN EXECUTION THREAD

void main()
    {
    //...Variable declaration Field

    //...Integer Type
    int n;
    int i,j;
```

```
//...Floating Type
float ax[10];                        //...array - limit 9
float ay[10];                        //...array - limit 9
float h;
float p;
float diff[20][20];                  //... array 2d - limit 19, 19
float x,y;
float y1,y2,y3,y4,

//...Invoke Clear Screen Function

clrscr();                            //... Clear Screen

//... Input Section

printf("\n Enter the number of terms");
scanf("%d",&n);

//... Input Section Array X

printf("\n Enter the values for x \n");

//... Input Section Loop for X

for(i=0;i<n;i++)
     {
     printf("\n Enter the value for x%d-",i+1);
     scanf("%f",&ax[i]);
     }

//... Input Section for Array Y

printf("\n Enter the values for y\n");

//...Input Section Loop for Y

for(i=0;i<n;i++)
{
     printf("\n Enter the value for y%d-",i+1);
     scanf("%f",&ay[i]);
     }

//...Input Section Loop for Value Of X for Y

printf("\n Enter the value of x for   ");
printf("\n which you want the value of y ");

scanf ("%f",&x);                          //...Input X
```

```
//...Calculation and Processing Section

h=ax[1]-ax[0];

for(i=0;i<n-1;i++)
      {
      diff[i][1]=ay[i+1]-ay[i];
      }

for(j=2;j<=4;j++)
      {
      for(i=0;i<n-j;i++)
            {
            diff[i][j]=diff[i+1][j-1]-diff[i][j-1];
            }

      }
i=0;
do    {
      i++;
      }while (ax[i]<x);
i--;

//... Bessel formulae Calculation

p=(x-ax[i])/h;

y1=p*(diff[i][1]);
y2=p*(p-1)*diff[i][2]+diff[i-1][2])/4;
y3=p*(p-1)*(p-0.5)*(diff[i-1][3])/6;
y4=(p+1)*p*(p-1)*(p-2)*(diff[i-2][4]+diff[i-1][4])/48;
//...Taking Sum

y=ay[i]+y1+y2+y3+y4;

//...Output Section

printf("\nwhen x=%6.2f,y=%6.8f ",x,y);

//...Invoke User Watch Halt Function

printf("\n\n Press Enter to Exit \t");
getch();
}

*End of Main Execution Thread */
```

4.21.4. Output

```
Enter the number of terms - 7
Enter the values of x
Enter the value of x1 - .61
Enter the value of x2 - .62
Enter the value of x3 - .63
Enter the value of x4 - .64
Enter the value of x5 - .65
Enter the value of x6 - .66
Enter the value of x7 - .67
Enter the values of y
Enter the value of y1 - 1.840431
Enter the value of y2 - 1.858928
Enter the value of y3 - 1.877610
Enter the value of y4 - 1.896481
Enter the value of y5 - 1.915541
Enter the value of y6 - 1.934792
Enter the value of y7 - 1.954237
Enter the value of x for
which you want the value of y - .644
When x = 0.644, y=1.90408230
Press Enter to Exit
```

EXAMPLES

Example 1. *Given $y_{20} = 24$, $y_{24} = 32$, $y_{28} = 35$ and $y_{32} = 40$ find y_{25} by Bessel's interpolation formula.*

Sol. Take origin at 24.

Here, $a = 24, \quad h = 4, \quad a + hu = 25$

$\therefore \quad 24 + 4u = 25 \Rightarrow u = 0.25$

Difference table is

u	x	y	Δy	$\Delta^2 y$	$\Delta^3 y$
−1	20	24			
			8		
0	24	32		−5	
			3		7
1	28	35		2	
			5		
2	32	40			

Using Bessel's formula,

$$f(u) = \left\{\frac{f(0)+f(1)}{2}\right\} + \left(u - \frac{1}{2}\right)\Delta f(0) + \frac{u(u-1)}{2}\left\{\frac{\Delta^2 f(-1) + \Delta^2 f(0)}{2}\right\} + \frac{(u-1)\left(u-\frac{1}{2}\right)u}{3!}\Delta^3 f(-1)$$

$$\Rightarrow \quad f(0.25) = \left(\frac{32+35}{2}\right) + (0.25 - 0.5)(3) + \frac{(0.25)(0.25-1)}{2}\left\{\frac{-5+2}{2}\right\} + \frac{(0.25-1)(0.25-0.5)(0.25)}{3!}(7)$$

$$= 32.9453125$$

Hence $\quad y_{25} = 32.9453125.$

Example 2. *Apply Bessel's formula to find the value of f(27.4) from the table*

x :	25	26	27	28	29	30
$f(x)$:	4.000	3.846	3.704	3.571	3.448	3.333.

Sol. Taking origin at 27 and $h = 1$

$$x = a + uh \quad \Rightarrow 27.4 = 27 + u\,(1)$$

$$\therefore \quad u = 0.4$$

The difference table is as follows :

u	$10^3 f(u)$	$10^3\,\Delta f(u)$	$10^3\,\Delta^2 f(u)$	$10^3\,\Delta^3 f(u)$	$10^3\,\Delta^4 f(u)$	$10^3\,\Delta^5 f(u)$
– 2	4000					
		– 154				
– 1	3847		12			
		– 142		– 3		
0	3704		9		4	
		– 133		1		– 7
1	3571		10		– 3	
		– 123		– 2		
2	3448		8			
		– 115				
3	3333					

Bessel's formula is

$$f(u) = \left\{\frac{f(0)+f(1)}{2}\right\} + \left(u - \frac{1}{2}\right)\Delta f(0) + \frac{u(u-1)}{2!}\left\{\frac{\Delta^2 f(0) + \Delta^2 f(-1)}{2}\right\}$$

$$+ \frac{(u-1)\left(u-\frac{1}{2}\right)u}{3!}\Delta^3 f(-1) + \frac{(u+1)u(u-1)(u-2)}{4!}\left\{\frac{\Delta^4 f(-1) + \Delta^4 f(-2)}{2}\right\}$$

$$+ \frac{(u-2)(u-1)\left(u-\frac{1}{2}\right)u(u+1)}{5!}\Delta^5 f(-2)$$

$$\therefore \quad 10^3 f(0.4) = \left\{\frac{3704 + 3571}{2}\right\} + (0.4 - 0.5)(-133) + \frac{(0.4)(0.4-1)}{2!}\left(\frac{10+9}{2}\right)$$

$$+ \frac{(0.4-1)(0.4-0.5)(0.4)}{3!}(1) + \frac{(0.4+1)(0.4)(0.4-1)(0.4-2)}{4!}\left(\frac{-3+4}{2}\right)$$

$$+ \frac{(0.4-2)(0.4-1)(0.4-0.5)(0.4)(0.4+1)}{5!}(-7)$$

$$= 3649.678336$$

$$\Rightarrow \quad f(.4) = 3.649678336$$

Hence $f(27.4) = 3.649678336$.

Example 3. *Given that*

x :	*4*	*6*	*8*	*10*	*12*	*14*
$f(x)$:	*3.5460*	*5.0753*	*6.4632*	*7.7217*	*8.8633*	*9.8986*

Apply Bessel's formula to find the value of f(9).

Sol. Taking the origin at 8, $h = 2$,

$$9 = 8 + 2u \quad \text{or} \quad u = \frac{1}{2}$$

The difference table is

u	$10^4 y_u$	$10^4 \Delta^2 y_u$	$10^4 \Delta^2 y_u$	$10^4 \Delta^3 y_u$	$10^4 \Delta^4 y_u$	$10^5 \Delta^5 y_u$
– 2	35460					
		15293				
– 1	50753		– 1414			
		13879		120		
0	64632		– 1294		5	
		1258		125		– 24
1	77217		– 1169		– 19	
		11416		106		
2	88633		– 1063			
		10353				
3	98986					

Bessel's formula is

$$y_u = \frac{1}{2}(y_1 + y_0) + \left(u - \frac{1}{2}\right)\Delta y_0 + \frac{u(u-1)}{2!}\,\frac{1}{2}(\Delta^2 y_0 + \Delta^2 y_{-1})$$

$$+ \frac{\left(u - \frac{1}{2}\right)u(u-1)}{3!}\Delta^3 y_{-1} + \frac{(u+1)\,u(u-1)(u-2)}{4!} \times \frac{1}{2}(\Delta^4 y_{-3} + \Delta^4 y_{-2})$$

$$+ \frac{(u-2)(u-1)\left(u - \frac{1}{2}\right)u\,(u+1)}{5!}\Delta^5 y_{-2}$$

$$10^4 y_{1/2} = \frac{1}{2}(77217 + 64632) + 0 + \frac{\frac{1}{2}\left(-\frac{1}{2}\right)}{2} \cdot \frac{1}{2}(-1169 - 1294)$$

$$+ 0 + \frac{\frac{3}{2}\cdot\frac{1}{2}\cdot\left(-\frac{1}{2}\right)\left(-\frac{3}{2}\right)}{24} \cdot \frac{1}{2}(-19 + 5) + 0$$

$\Rightarrow \quad 10^4 y_{1/2} = 71078.27344$

$\therefore \quad y_{1/2} = 7.107827344$

Hence, $\quad f(9) = 7.107827344.$

Example 4. *Given $y_0, y_1, y_2, y_3, y_4, y_5$ (fifth differences constant), prove that*

$$y_{2\frac{1}{2}} = \frac{1}{2}c + \frac{25(c-b) + 3(a-c)}{256}$$

where $a = y_0 + y_5,\ b = y_1 + y_4,\ c = y_2 + y_3.$

Sol. Put $\quad u = \frac{1}{2}$ in Bessel's formula, we get

$$y_{1/2} = \frac{1}{2}(y_0 + y_1) - \frac{1}{16}(\Delta^2 y_0 + \Delta^2 y_{-1}) + \frac{3}{256}(\Delta^4 y_{-1} + \Delta^4 y_{-2})$$

Shifting origin to 2, we have

$$y_{2\frac{1}{2}} = \frac{1}{2}(y_2 + y_3) - \frac{1}{16}(\Delta^2 y_2 + \Delta^2 y_1) + \frac{3}{256}(\Delta^4 y_1 + \Delta^4 y_0)$$

$$= \frac{c}{2} - \frac{1}{16}(y_3 - 2y_2 + y_1 + y_4 - 2y_3 + y_2) + \frac{3}{256}(y_5 - 3y_4 + 2y_3 + 2y_2 - 3y_1 + y_0)$$

$$y_{2\frac{1}{2}} = \frac{c}{2} - \frac{1}{16}(y_4 - y_3 - y_2 + y_1) + \frac{3}{256}(a - 3b + 2c)$$

$$= \frac{c}{2} - \frac{1}{16}(b - c) + \frac{3}{256}(a - 3b + 2c)$$

$$y_{2\frac{1}{2}} = \frac{c}{2} + \frac{1}{256}[25(c - b) + 3(a - c)].$$

Example 5. *Find the value of y_{15}, using Bessel's formula, if*

$$y_{10} = 2854, \quad y_{14} = 3162, \quad y_{18} = 3544, \quad y_{22} = 3992.$$

Sol. Taking the origin at 14, $h = 4$

$\therefore \quad 15 = 14 + 4 \cdot u \quad \therefore \quad u = \frac{1}{4}$

Difference table is

u	x	$f(x)$	$\Delta f(x)$	$\Delta^2 f(x)$	$\Delta^3 f(x)$
−1	10	2854			
				308	
0	14	3162		74	
			382		−8
1	18	3544		66	
			448		
2	22	3992			

Bessel's formula is

$$f(u) = \left\{\frac{f(0)+f(1)}{2}\right\} + \left(u-\frac{1}{2}\right)\Delta f(0) + \frac{u(u-1)}{2!}\left\{\frac{\Delta^2 f(-1)+\Delta^2 f(0)}{2}\right\} + \frac{(u-1)\left(u-\frac{1}{2}\right)u}{3!}\Delta^3 f(-1)$$

$$\therefore \quad f(.25) = \left(\frac{3162+3544}{2}\right) + (.25-.5)(382) + \frac{(.25)(.25-1)}{2}\left(\frac{74+66}{2}\right) + \frac{(.25-1)(.25-.5)(.25)}{6}(-8)$$

$$= 3250.875$$

Hence $y_{15} = 3250.875$.

ASSIGNMENT

1. Apply Bessel's formula to find the value of $y_{2.73}$ given that

$y_{2.5} = 0.4938,\ y_{2.6} = 0.4953,\ y_{2.7} = 0.4965,\ y_{2.8} = 0.4974,\ y_{2.9} = 0.4981,\ y_{3.0} = 0.4987.$

2. Find the value of y if $x = 3.75$, given that

x :	2.5	3.0	3.5	4.0	4.5	5.0
y :	24.145	22.043	20.225	18.644	17.262	16.047.

Use Bessel's formula.

3. Apply Bessel's formula to find $u_{62.5}$ from the following data:

x :	60	61	62	63	64	65
u_x :	7782	7853	7924	7993	8062	8129.

4. Apply Bessel's formula to find the value of $f(12.2)$ from the following table:

x :	0	5	10	15	20	25	30
$f(x)$:	0	0.19146	0.34634	0.43319	0.47725	0.49379	0.49865

5. Following table gives the values of e^x for certain equidistant values of x. Find the value of e^x when $x = 0.644$ using Bessel's formula:

x :	0.61	0.62	0.63	0.64	0.65	0.66	0.67
e^x :	1.840431	1.858928	1.877610	1.896481	1.915541	1.934792	1.954237

6. Using Bessel's formula, compute the value of $f(1.95)$ from the following data:

x	:	1.7	1.8	1.9	2.0	2.1	2.2	2.3
$f(x)$	:	2.979	3.144	3.283	3.391	3.463	3.997	4.491

7. Apply Bessel's formula to obtain y_{25} given $y_{20} = 2854, y_{24} = 3162, y_{28} = 3544, y_{32} = 3992$.

8. The pressure p of wind corresponding to velocity v is given by following data.

Estimate p when $v = 25$.

v	:	10	20	30	40
p	:	1.1	2	4.4	7.9

Answers

1. 0.496798 **2.** 19.40745 **3.** 7957.1407 **4.** 0.39199981
5. 1.904082 **6.** 3.347 **7.** 3250.875 **8.** 3.0375

4.22. LAPLACE-EVERETT'S FORMULA

Gauss' forward formula is

$$f(u) = f(0) + u\Delta f(0) + \frac{u(u-1)}{2!}\Delta^2 f(-1) + \frac{(u+1)u(u-1)}{3!}\Delta^3 f(-1)$$
$$+ \frac{(u+1)u(u-1)(u-2)}{4!}\Delta^4 f(-2) + \frac{(u+2)(u+1)u(u-1)(u-2)}{5!}\Delta^5 f(-2) + ... \quad ...(1)$$

We have,

$$\Delta f(0) = f(1) - f(0)$$
$$\Delta^3 f(-1) = \Delta^2 f(0) - \Delta^2 f(-1)$$
$$\Delta^5 f(-2) = \Delta^4 f(-1) - \Delta^4 f(-2)$$

$\therefore$ From (1),

$$f(u) = f(0) + u\{f(1) - f(0)\} + \frac{u(u-1)}{2!}\Delta^2 f(-1) + \frac{(u+1)u(u-1)}{3!}\{\Delta^2 f(0) - \Delta^2 f(-1)\}$$
$$+ \frac{(u+1)u(u-1)(u-2)}{4!}\Delta^4 f(-2)$$
$$+ \frac{(u+2)(u+1)u(u-1)(u-2)}{5!}\{\Delta^4 f(-1) - \Delta^4 f(-2)\} + ...$$
$$= (1-u) f(0) + uf(1) + \frac{(u+1)u(u-1)}{3!}\Delta^2 f(0) - \frac{u(u-1)(u-2)}{3!}\Delta^2 f(-1)$$
$$+ \frac{(u+2)(u+1)u(u-1)(u-2)}{5!}\Delta^4 f(-1)$$
$$- \frac{(u+1)u(u-1)(u-2)(u-3)}{5!}\Delta^4 f(-2) + ...$$

$$= \left\{u\, f(1) + \frac{(u+1)\,u\,(u-1)}{3!}\,\Delta^2 f(0) + \frac{(u+2)(u+1)\,u\,(u-1)(u-2)}{5!}\,\Delta^4 f(-1) + \ldots..\right\}$$

$$+ \left\{(1-u)f(0) + \frac{(1-u+1)(1-u)(1-u-1)}{3!}\,\Delta^2 f(-1) + \frac{(1-u+2)(1-u+1)(1-u)(1-u-1)(1-u-2)}{5!}\,\Delta^4 f(-2) + \ldots..\right\}$$

$$\boxed{\begin{aligned} f(u) = &\left\{uf(1) + \frac{(u+1)\,u\,(u-1)}{3!}\,\Delta^2 f(0) + \frac{(u+2)(u+1)\,u\,(u-1)(u-2)}{5!}\,\Delta^4 f(-1) + \ldots..\right\} \\ &+ \left\{wf(0) + \frac{(w+1)\,w\,(w-1)}{3!}\,\Delta^2 f(-1) + \frac{(w+2)(w+1)\,w\,(w-1)(w-2)}{5!}\,\Delta^4 f(-2) + \ldots..\right\} \end{aligned}} \quad \ldots(2)$$

where $w = 1 - u$

This is called **Laplace–Everett's formula.** It gives best estimate when $u > \frac{1}{2}$. It is used to compute any entry against any argument between 0 and 1. It is useful when intervening values in successive intervals are required.

4.22.1. Algorithm of Laplace' Everett Formula

Step 01. Start of the program
Step 02. Input no. of terms n
Step 03. Input the array ax
Step 04. Input the array ay
Step 05. h=ax[1]-ax[0]
Step 06. for i=0 ; i<n-l ; i++
Step 07. diff[i][1]=ay[i+1]-ay[i]
Step 08. End Loop i
Step 09. for j=2 ; j<=4 ; j++
Step 10. for i=0 ; i<n–j ; i++
Step 11. diff[i][j]=diff[i+1][j–1]–diff[i][j–1]
Step 12. End Loop i
Step 13. End Loop j
Step 14. i=0
Step 15. Repeat Step 16 until ax[i]<x
Step 16. i=i+1
Step 17. i=i–1 ;
Step 18. p=(x–ax[i])/h
Step 19. q=1–p
Step 20. y1=q*(ay[i])
Step 21. y2=q*(q*q–1)*diff[i–1][2]/6
Step 22. y3=q*(q*q–1)*(q*q–4)*(diff[i–2][4])/120
Step 23. py1=p*ay[i+1]
Step 24. py2=p*(p*p–1)*diff[i][2]/6
Step 25. py3=p*(p*p–1)*(p*p–4)*(diff[i–1][4])/120

Step 26. y=y1+y2+y3+y4+py1+py2+py3

Step 27. Print Output x, y

Step 28. End of Program

4.22.2. Flow-chart

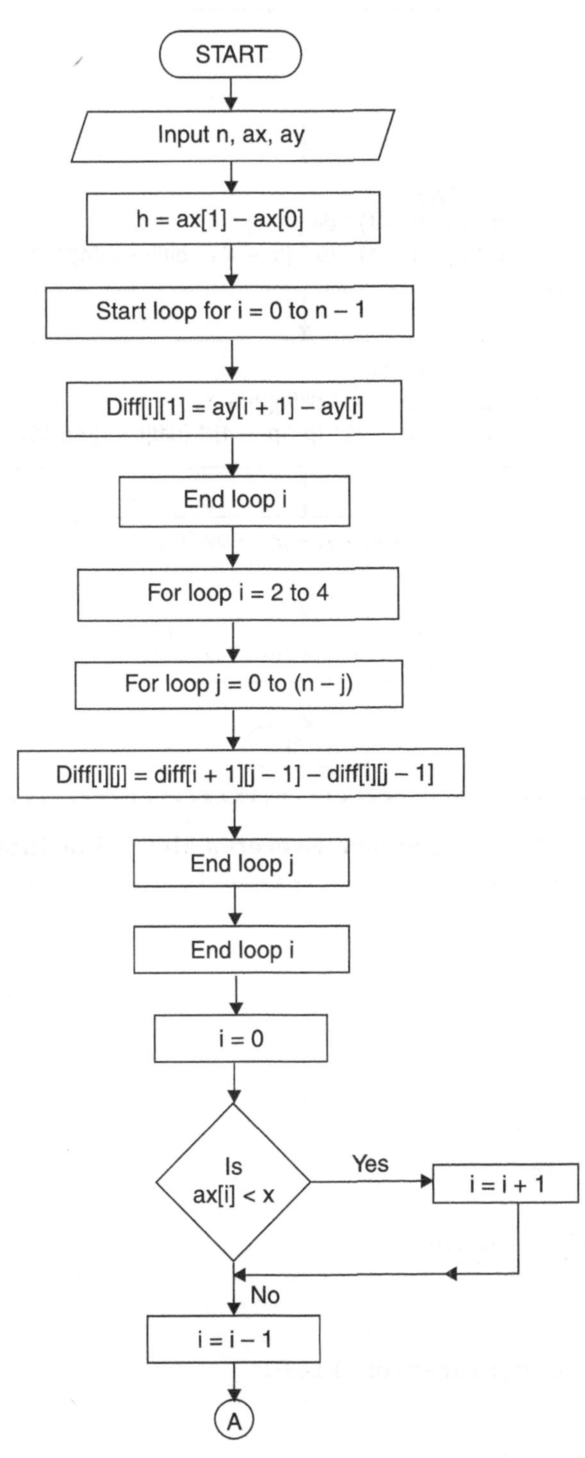

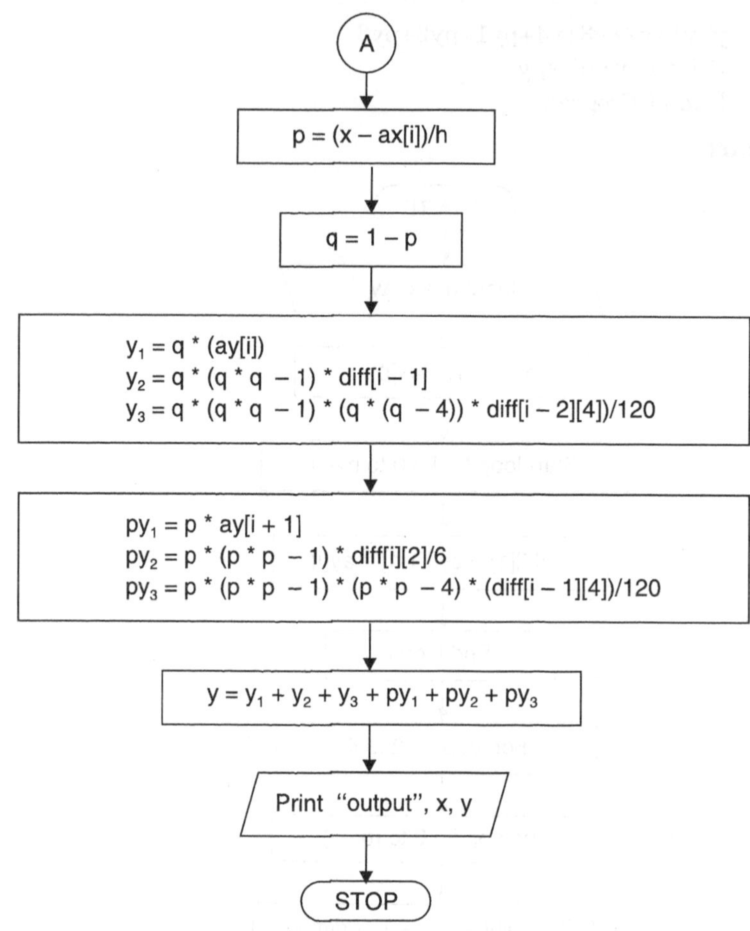


```
/* ***********************************************************************
```

4.22.3. Program to Implement Laplace Everett's Method of Interpolation

```
************************************************************************ */

//... HEADER FILES DECLARATION

# include <stdio.h>
# include <conio.h>
# include <math.h>
# include <process.h>
# include <string.h>

//... MAIN EXECUTION THREAD
void main()
     {

     //... Variable declaration Field
```

```
//... Integer Type

int n;
int i,j;

//... Floating Type
float ax[10];                              //... array limit 9
float ay[10];                              //... array limit 9
float x;
float nr,dr;
float y=0;                                 //... Initial value 0
float h;
float p,q;
float diff[20][20];                        //... array limit 19,19
float y1,y2,y3,y4;
float py1,py2,py3,py4;

//... Invoke Function Clear Screen

clrscr();

//... Input Section

printf ("\n Enter the number of terms - ");
scanf("%d",&n);
//... Input Sequel for array X

printf("\n\n Enter the value in the form of x - ");

//... Input Loop for Array X

for (i=0;i<n;i++)
      {
      Printf("\n\n Enter the value of x%d - ",i+1);
      scanf("%f",&ax[i]);
      }
//... Input Sequel for Array X

printf ("\n\n Enter the value in the form of y - ");

//... Input Loop Array Y

for (i=0;i<n;i++)
      {
```

```
        printf ("\n\n Enter the value of y%d - ",i+1);
        scanf("%f",&ay[i]);
        }

//... Inputting the required value querry

printf("\nEnter the value of x for ");
printf("\nwhich you want the value of y - ");
scanf("%f",&x);

//... Calculation and Processing Section
h=ax[1]-ax[0];
for(i=0;i<n-1;i++)
        {
        diff[i][1]=ay[i+1]-ay[i];
        }
for(j=2;j<=4;j++)
        {
        for(i=0;i<n-j;i++)
                {
                diff[i][j]=diff[i+1][j-1]-diff[i][j-1];
                }
        }
i=0;
do      {
        i++;
        }while(ax[i]<x);
i--;
p=(x-ax[i])/h;
q=1-p;
y1=q*(ay[i]);
y2=q*(q*q-1)*diff[i-1][2]/6;
y3=q*(q*q-1)*(q*q-4)*(diff[i-2][4])/120;
py1=p*ay[i+1];
py2=p*(p*p-1)*diff[i][2]/6;
py3=p*(p*p-1)*(p*p-4)*(diff[i-1][4])/120;

//... Taking sum

y=y1+y2+y3+y4+py1+py2+py3;
```

```
    //... Output Section
    printf("\n when x=%6.2f,y=%6.8f  ",x,y);
    //... Invoke User Watch Halt Function
    printf("\n\n\n Press Enter to Exit ");
    getch();
    }
//... Termination of Main Execution Thread
```

4.22.4. Output

```
Enter the number of terms - 7
Enter the value in the form of x -
Enter the value of x1 - 1.72
Enter the value of x2 - 1.73
Enter the value of x3 - 1.74
Enter the value of x4 - 1.75
Enter the value of x5 - 1.76
Enter the value of x6 - 1.77
Enter the value of x7 - 1.78
Enter the value in the form of y -
Enter the value of y1 - .1790661479
Enter the value of y2 - .1772844100
Enter the value of y3 - .1755204006
Enter the value of y4 - .1737739435
Enter the value of y5 - .1720448638
Enter the value of y6 - .1703329888
Enter the value of y7 - .1686381473
Enter the value of x for
which you want the value of y - 1.7475
When x = 1.7475, y = 0.17420892
Press Enter to Exit
```

EXAMPLES

Example 1. *Using Everett's formula, evaluate f(30) if*

$f(20) = 2854,\quad f(28) = 3162\quad f(36) = 7088,\quad f(44) = 7984.$

Sol. Take origin at 28.

$$\therefore \qquad a = 28,\ h = 8$$

$$a + hu = 30$$

$\Rightarrow \quad 28 + 8u = 30 \quad \Rightarrow \quad u = 0.25$

Also, $\quad w = 1 - u = 1 - 0.25 = 0.75$

Difference table is :

u	$f(u)$	$\Delta f(u)$	$\Delta^2 f(u)$	$\Delta^3 f(u)$
– 1	2854			
		308		
0	3162		3618	
		3926		– 6648
1	7088		– 3030	
		896		
2	7984			

By Everett's formula,

$$\therefore \quad f(.25) = \left\{(.25)\,(7088) + \frac{(1.25)\,(.25)\,(-.75)}{3\,!}\,(-3030) + ...\right\}$$

$$+ \left\{(0.75)\,(3162) + \frac{(1.75)\,(0.75)\,(-0.25)}{3\,!}\,(3618) + ...\right\}$$

$$= 4064$$

Hence $\quad f(30) = 4064.$

Example 2. *Find the value of f(27.4) from the following table:*

x :	25	26	27	28	29	30
$f(x)$:	4.000	3.846	3.704	3.571	3.448	3.333.

Sol. Here $u = \dfrac{27.4 - 27.0}{1} = 0.4 \because$ origin is at 27.0, $h = 1$

Also, $\quad w = 1 - u = 0.6$

Difference table is:

u	$10^3\, f(u)$	$10^3\, \Delta f(u)$	$10^3 \Delta^2 f(u)$	$10^3 \Delta^3 f(u)$	$10^3 \Delta^4 f(u)$
– 2	4000				
		– 154			
– 1	3846		12		
		– 142		– 3	
0	3704		9		4
		– 133		1	
1	3571		10		– 3
		– 123		– 2	
2	3448		8		
		– 115			
3	3333				

By Laplace Everett's formula,

$$f(.4) = \left\{(0.4)(3571) + \frac{(1.4)(0.4)(-0.6)}{3!}(10) + \frac{(2.4)(1.4)(0.4)(-0.6)(-1.6)}{5!}(-3) + ...\right\}$$

$$+ \left\{(0.6)(3704) + \frac{(1.6)(0.6)(-0.4)}{3!}(9) + \frac{(2.6)(1.6)(0.6)(-0.4)(-1.4)}{5!}(4)\right\}$$

$$= 3649.678336.$$

Hence $f(27.4) = 3649.678336$.

ASSIGNMENT

1. Given the table

x	21	22	23	24	25	26
$\log x$	1.3222	1.3424	1.3617	1.3802	1.3979	1.4150

Apply Laplace-Everett's formula to find the value of log 2375.

2. From the following table of values of x and $y = e^x$, interpolate the value of y when $x = 1.91$

x	1.7	1.8	1.9	2.0	2.1	2.2
$y = e^x$	5.4739	6.0496	6.6859	7.3891	8.1662	9.0250.

3. Given the table :

x	310	320	330	340	350	360
$\log x$	2.49136	2.50515	2.51851	2.53148	2.54407	2.55630.

Find the value of log 337.5 by Laplace Everett's formula.

4. Find y_{12} if $y_0 = 0$, $y_{10} = 43214$, $y_{20} = 86002$ and $y_{30} = 128372$.

5. Obtain the values of y_{25}, given that

$$y_{20} = 2854, \quad y_{24} = 3162, \quad y_{28} = 3544 \quad \text{and} \quad y_{32} = 3992$$

6. Find the value of e^{-x} when $x = 1.748$ from the following :

x	1.72	1.73	1.74	1.75	1.76	1.77
e^{-x}	0.1790	0.1773	0.1755	0.1738	0.1720	0.1703

7. Use Everett's formula to find the present value of the annuity for $n = 36$ from the table :

x	25	30	35	40	45	50
a_x	12.7834	13.7648	14.4982	15.0463	15.4558	15.7619.

8. Apply Everett's formula to find the value of $f(26)$ and $f(27)$ from the table :

x	15	20	25	30	35	40
$f(x)$	12.849	16.351	19.524	22.396	24.999	27.356.

9. The following table gives the values of e^x for certain equidistant values of x. Find the value of e^x when $x = 0.644$ using Everett's formula

x	0.61	0.62	0.63	0.64	0.65	0.66	0.67
$y = e^x$	1.840431	1.858928	1.877610	1.896481	1.915541	1.934792	1.954237.

10. The values of the elliptic integral,

$$k(m) = \int_0^{\pi/2} (1 - m \sin^2 \theta)^{-\frac{1}{2}} \, d\theta$$

for certain equidistant values of m are given below. Use Everett's or Bessel's formula to determine $k(0.25)$.

m	0.20	0.22	0.24	0.26	0.28	0.30
$k(m)$	1.659624	1.669850	1.680373	1.691208	1.702374	1.713889.

Answers

1. 3.3756	**2.** 6.7531	**3.** 2.52828	**4.** 56266
5. 3250.875	**6.** 0.1741	**7.** 14.620947	
8. 20.121431, 20.707077	**9.** 1.904082	**10.** 1.685750.	

4.23. INTERPOLATION BY UNEVENLY SPACED POINTS

The interpolation formulae derived sofar possess the disadvantage of being applicable only to equally spaced values of the argument. It is then desirable to develop interpolation formulae for unequally spaced values of x. We shall study two such formulae:

(1) Lagrange's interpolation formula

(2) Newton's general interpolation formula with divided differences.

4.24. LAGRANGE'S INTERPOLATION FORMULA

Let $f(x_0), f(x_1), \ldots\ldots, f(x_n)$ be $(n + 1)$ entries of a function $y = f(x)$, where $f(x)$ is assumed to be a polynomial corresponding to the arguments $x_0, x_1, x_2, \ldots\ldots, x_n$.

The polynomial $f(x)$ may be written as

$$f(x) = A_0 (x - x_1)(x - x_2) \ldots\ldots (x - x_n) + A_1(x - x_0)(x - x_2) \ldots\ldots (x - x_n) + \ldots\ldots + A_n (x - x_0)(x - x_1) \ldots\ldots (x - x_{n-1}) \quad \ldots(1)$$

where $A_0, A_1, \ldots\ldots, A_n$ are constants to be determined.

Putting $x = x_0, x_1, \ldots\ldots, x_n$ in (1), we get

$$f(x_0) = A_0 (x_0 - x_1)(x_0 - x_2) \ldots\ldots (x_0 - x_n)$$

$$\therefore \quad A_0 = \frac{f(x_0)}{(x_0 - x_1)(x_0 - x_2) \ldots\ldots (x_0 - x_n)} \quad \ldots(2)$$

$$f(x_1) = A_1 (x_1 - x_0)(x_1 - x_2) \ldots\ldots (x_1 - x_n)$$

$$\therefore \quad A_1 = \frac{f(x_1)}{(x_1 - x_0)(x_1 - x_2) \ldots\ldots (x_1 - x_n)} \quad \ldots(3)$$

$$\vdots \qquad \vdots \qquad \vdots$$

Similarly, $$A_n = \frac{f(x_n)}{(x_n - x_0)(x_n - x_1) \ldots\ldots (x_n - x_{n-1})} \quad \ldots(4)$$

Substituting the values of $A_0, A_1, \ldots\ldots, A_n$ in equation (1), we get

$$f(x) = \frac{(x - x_1)(x - x_2) \ldots\ldots (x - x_n)}{(x_0 - x_1)(x_0 - x_2) \ldots\ldots (x_0 - x_n)} f(x_0) + \frac{(x - x_0)(x - x_2) \ldots\ldots (x - x_n)}{(x_1 - x_0)(x_1 - x_2) \ldots\ldots (x_1 - x_n)} f(x_1) + \ldots\ldots + \frac{(x - x_0)(x - x_1) \ldots\ldots (x - x_{n-1})}{(x_n - x_0)(x_n - x_1) \ldots\ldots (x_n - x_{n-1})} f(x_n) \quad \ldots(5)$$

This is called **Lagrange's interpolation formula.** In eqn. (5), dividing both sides by $(x - x_0)(x - x_1) \ldots\ldots (x - x_n)$, Lagrange's formula may also be written as

$$\frac{f(x)}{(x - x_0)(x - x_1) \ldots\ldots (x - x_n)} = \frac{f(x_0)}{(x_0 - x_1)(x_0 - x_2) \ldots\ldots (x_0 - x_n)} \cdot \frac{1}{(x - x_0)} + \frac{f(x_1)}{(x_1 - x_0)(x_1 - x_2) \ldots\ldots (x_1 - x_n)} \cdot \frac{1}{(x - x_1)} + \ldots\ldots + \frac{f(x_n)}{(x_n - x_0)(x_n - x_1) \ldots\ldots (x_n - x_{n-1})} \cdot \frac{1}{(x - x_n)}. \quad \ldots(6)$$

4.24.1. Another Form of Lagrange's Formula

§ **Prove that** the Lagrange's formula can be put in the form

$$P_n(x) = \sum_{r=0}^{n} \frac{\phi(x) f(x_r)}{(x - x_r)\phi'(x_r)}$$

where $\phi(x) = \prod_{r=0}^{n} (x - x_r)$ and $\phi'(x_r) = \left[\frac{d}{dx}\{\phi(x)\}\right]_{x = x_r}$

We have the Lagrange's formula,

$$P_n(x) = \sum_{r=0}^{n} \frac{(x - x_0)(x - x_1)\dots(x - x_{r-1})(x - x_{r+1})\dots(x - x_n)}{(x_r - x_0)(x_r - x_1)\dots(x_r - x_{r-1})(x_r - x_{r+1})\dots(x_r - x_n)} f(x_r)$$

$$= \sum_{r=0}^{n} \left\{\frac{\phi(x)}{x - x_r}\right\}\left\{\frac{f(x_r)}{(x_r - x_0)(x_r - x_1)\dots(x_r - x_{r-1})(x_r - x_{r+1})\dots(x_r - x_n)}\right\} \quad \dots(1)$$

Now, $\phi(x) = \prod_{r=0}^{n} (x - x_r)$

$$= (x - x_0)(x - x_1) \dots\dots (x - x_{r-1})(x - x_r)(x - x_{r+1}) \dots\dots (x - x_n)$$

$$\therefore \quad \phi'(x) = (x - x_1)(x - x_2) \dots\dots (x - x_r) \dots\dots (x - x_n) + (x - x_0)(x - x_2) \dots\dots (x - x_r) \dots\dots (x - x_n) + \dots\dots + (x - x_0)(x - x_1) \dots\dots (x - x_{r-1})(x - x_{r+1}) \dots\dots (x - x_n) + \dots\dots + (x - x_0)(x - x_1) \dots\dots (x - x_r) \dots\dots (x - x_{n-1})$$

$$\Rightarrow \quad \phi'(x_r) = [\phi'(x)]_{x = x_r}$$

$$= (x_r - x_0)(x_r - x_1) \dots\dots (x_r - x_{r-1})(x_r - x_{r+1}) \dots\dots (x_r - x_n) \quad \dots(2)$$

Hence from (1), $P_n(x) = \sum_{r=0}^{n} \frac{\phi(x) f(x_r)}{(x - x_r)\phi'(x_r)}$ | Using (2)

4.24.2. Algorithm

Step 01. Start of the program
Step 02. Input no. of terms n
Step 03. Input the array ax
Step 04. Input the array ay
Step 05. for i=0 ; i<n ; i++
Step 06. nr=1
Step 07. dr=1
Step 08. for j=0 ; j<n ; j++
Step 09. if j !=i
a. r=nr*=(x-ax[j])
b.dr*=(ax[i]-ax[j])
Step 10. End Loop j
Step 11. y+=(nr/dr)*ay[i]

Step 12. End Loop i

Step 13. Print Output x, y

Step 14. End of Program

4.24.3. Flow-chart

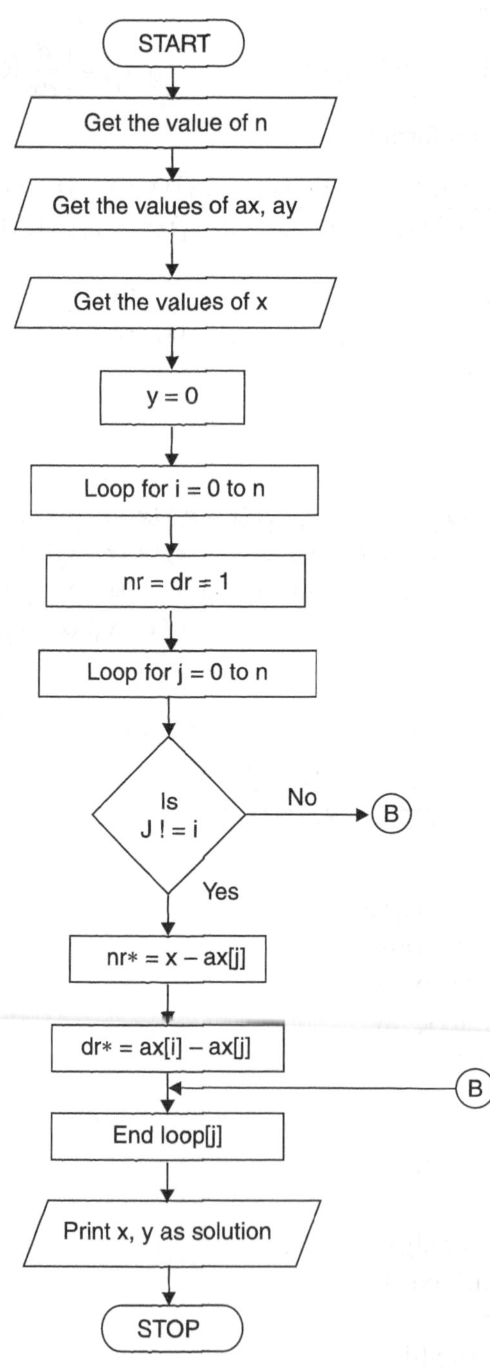

/* **

4.24.4. Program to Implement Lagrange's Method of Interpolation

** */

```
//... HEADER FILES DECLARATION

# include <stdio.h>
# include <conio.h>
# include <math.h>
# include <process.h>
# include <string.h>

//... MAIN EXECUTION THREAD

void main()
     {
     //... Variable declaration Field

     //... Integer Type

     int n;                                    //... No. of terms
     int i,j;                                  //... Loop Variables

     //... Floating Type
     float ax[100];                            //... array limit 99
     float ay[100];                            //... array limit 99
     float x=0;                                //... User Querry
     float y=0;                                //... Initial value 0
     float nr;                                 //... Calc. section
     float dr;                                 //... Calc. section

     //... Invoke Function Clear Screen

     clrscr();

     //... Input Section

     printf("\n Enter the number of terms - ");
     scanf("%d",&n);
     //... Input Sequel for array X

     printf("\n\n Enter the value in the form of  x - ");

     //... Input Loop for X

     for (i=0;i<n;i++)
```

```
        {
        printf ("\n\n Enter the value of  x%d - ", i+1);
        scanf("%f",&ax[i]);
        }

//... Input Sequel for array Y
printf("\n\n Enter the value in the form of y - ");
//... Input Loop for Y

for (i=0;i<n;i++)
        {
        printf("\n\n Enter the value of y%d - ", i+1);
        scanf ("%f",&ay[i]);
        }

//... Inputting the required value querry
printf("\n Enter the value of x for ");
printf("\n which you want the value of y - ");
scanf("%f",&x);

//... Calculation & Processing Section
for(i=0;i<n;i++)
        {
        nr=1;
        dr=1;
        for(j=0;j<n;j++)
        {
                if(j!=i)
                        {
                        nr=nr*(x-ax[j]);
                        dr=dr*(ax[i]-ax[j]);
                        }
                y+=(nr/dr)*ay[i];
                }
```

```
        }
        //... Output Section
        printf("\n\n When x=%5.2f,y=%5.2f ",x,y);
        //... Invoke User Watch Halt Function
        printf("\n\n\n Press Enter to Exit");
        getch();
        }
   //... Termination of Main Execution Thread
```

4.24.5. Output

```
Enter the number of terms - 5
Enter the value in the form of x -
Enter the value of x1- 5
Enter the value of x2 - 7
Enter the value of x3 - 11
Enter the value of x4 - 13
Enter the value of x5 - 17
Enter the value in the form of y -
Enter the value of y1 - 150
Enter the value of y2 - 392
Enter the value of y3 - 1452
Enter the value of y4 - 2366
Enter the value of y5 - 5202
Enter the value of x for
Which you want the value of y - 9.0
When x = 9.00, y = 810.00
Press Enter to Exit
```

EXAMPLES

Example 1. *Using Lagrange's interpolation formula, find y(10) from the following table :*

x	*5*	*6*	*9*	*11*
y	*12*	*13*	*14*	*16*

Sol. Here $x_0 = 5,\quad x_1 = 6,\quad x_2 = 9,\quad x_3 = 11$

$$f(x_0) = 12,\quad f(x_1) = 13,\quad f(x_2) = 14,\quad f(x_3) = 16$$

Lagrange's formula is

$$f(x) = \frac{(x - x_1)(x - x_2)(x - x_3)}{(x_0 - x_1)(x_0 - x_2)(x_0 - x_3)} f(x_0) + \frac{(x - x_0)(x - x_2)(x - x_3)}{(x_1 - x_0)(x_1 - x_2)(x_1 - x_3)} f(x_1)$$

$$+ \frac{(x - x_0)(x - x_1)(x - x_3)}{(x_2 - x_0)(x_2 - x_1)(x_2 - x_3)} f(x_2) + \frac{(x - x_0)(x - x_1)(x - x_2)}{(x_3 - x_0)(x_3 - x_1)(x_3 - x_2)} f(x_3)$$

$$f(x) = \frac{(x-6)(x-9)(x-11)}{(5-6)(5-9)(5-11)}(12) + \frac{(x-5)(x-9)(x-11)}{(6-5)(6-9)(6-11)}(13)$$

$$+ \frac{(x-5)(x-6)(x-11)}{(9-5)(9-6)(9-11)}(14) + \frac{(x-5)(x-6)(x-9)}{(11-5)(11-6)(11-9)}(16)$$

$$= -\frac{1}{2}(x-6)(x-9)(x-11) + \frac{13}{15}(x-5)(x-9)(x-11) - \frac{7}{12}(x-5)(x-6)(x-11)$$

$$+ \frac{4}{15}(x-5)(x-6)(x-9)$$

Putting $x = 10$, we get

$$f(10) = -\frac{1}{2}(10-6)(10-9)(10-11) + \frac{13}{15}(10-5)(10-9)(10-11)$$

$$- \frac{7}{12}(10-5)(10-6)(10-11) + \frac{4}{15}(10-5)(10-6)(10-9)$$

$$= 14.66666667$$

Hence, $y(10) = 14.66666667$.

Example 2. *Compute the value of f(x) for x = 2.5 from the following table :*

x	:	1	2	3	4
$f(x)$	:	1	8	27	64

using Lagrange's interpolation method.

Sol. Here $x_0 = 1$, $x_1 = 2$, $x_2 = 3$, $x_3 = 4$

$f(x_0) = 1$, $f(x_1) = 8$, $f(x_2) = 27$, $f(x_3) = 64$

Lagrange's formula is

$$f(x) = \frac{(x - x_1)(x - x_2)(x - x_3)}{(x_0 - x_1)(x_0 - x_2)(x_0 - x_3)} f(x_0) + \frac{(x - x_0)(x - x_2)(x - x_3)}{(x_1 - x_0)(x_1 - x_2)(x_1 - x_3)} f(x_1)$$

$$+ \frac{(x - x_0)(x - x_1)(x - x_3)}{(x_2 - x_0)(x_2 - x_1)(x_2 - x_3)} f(x_2) + \frac{(x - x_0)(x - x_1)(x - x_2)}{(x_3 - x_0)(x_3 - x_1)(x_3 - x_2)} f(x_3)$$

$$= \frac{(x-2)(x-3)(x-4)}{(1-2)(1-3)(1-4)}(1) + \frac{(x-1)(x-3)(x-4)}{(2-1)(2-3)(2-4)}(8) + \frac{(x-1)(x-2)(x-4)}{(3-1)(3-2)(3-4)}(27)$$

$$+ \frac{(x-1)(x-2)(x-3)}{(4-1)(4-2)(4-3)}(64)$$

$$= -\frac{1}{6}(x-2)(x-3)(x-4) + 4(x-1)(x-3)(x-4) - \frac{27}{2}(x-1)(x-2)(x-4)$$

$$+ \frac{32}{3}(x-1)(x-2)(x-3)$$

Putting $x = 2.5$, we get

$$f(2.5) = -\frac{1}{6}(2.5-2)(2.5-3)(2.5-4) + 4(2.5-1)(2.5-3)(2.5-4)$$

$$-\frac{27}{2}(2.5-1)(2.5-2)(2.5-4) + \frac{32}{3}(2.5-1)(2.5-2)(2.5-3)$$

$$= 15.625.$$

Example 3. *Find the cubic Lagrange's interpolating polynomial from the following data:*

x :	0	1	2	5
$f(x)$:	2	3	12	147.

Sol. Here $x_0 = 0,\quad x_1 = 1,\quad x_2 = 2,\quad x_3 = 5$

$f(x_0) = 2,\quad f(x_1) = 3,\quad f(x_2) = 12,\quad f(x_3) = 147$

Lagrange's formula is

$$f(x) = \frac{(x-x_1)(x-x_2)(x-x_3)}{(x_0-x_1)(x_0-x_2)(x_0-x_3)} f(x_0) + \frac{(x-x_0)(x-x_2)(x-x_3)}{(x_1-x_0)(x_1-x_2)(x_1-x_3)} f(x_1)$$

$$+ \frac{(x-x_0)(x-x_1)(x-x_3)}{(x_2-x_0)(x_2-x_1)(x_2-x_3)} f(x_2) + \frac{(x-x_0)(x-x_1)(x-x_2)}{(x_3-x_0)(x_3-x_1)(x_3-x_2)} f(x_3)$$

$$= \frac{(x-1)(x-2)(x-5)}{(0-1)(0-2)(0-5)}(2) + \frac{(x-0)(x-2)(x-5)}{(1-0)(1-2)(1-5)}(3) + \frac{(x-0)(x-1)(x-5)}{(2-0)(2-1)(2-5)}(12)$$

$$+ \frac{(x-0)(x-1)(x-2)}{(5-0)(5-1)(5-2)}(147)$$

$$= -\frac{1}{5}(x-1)(x-2) + \frac{3}{4}x(x-2)(x-5) - 2x(x-1)(x-5) + \frac{49}{20}x(x-1)(x-2)$$

$$\Rightarrow f(x) = x^3 + x^2 - x + 2$$

Example 4. *Find the unique polynomial $P(x)$ of degree 2 such that :*

$P(1) = 1,\quad P(3) = 27,\quad P(4) = 64$

Use Lagrange method of interpolation.

Sol. Here, $x_0 = 1,\quad x_1 = 3,\quad x_2 = 4$

$f(x_0) = 1,\quad f(x_1) = 27,\quad f(x_2) = 64$

By Lagrange's interpolation formula

$$P(x) = \frac{(x-x_1)(x-x_2)}{(x_0-x_1)(x_0-x_2)} f(x_0) + \frac{(x-x_0)(x-x_2)}{(x_1-x_0)(x_1-x_2)} f(x_1) + \frac{(x-x_0)(x-x_1)}{(x_2-x_0)(x_2-x_1)} f(x_2)$$

$$= \frac{(x-3)(x-4)}{(1-3)(1-4)}(1) + \frac{(x-1)(x-4)}{(3-1)(3-4)}(27) + \frac{(x-1)(x-3)}{(4-1)(4-3)}(64)$$

$$= \frac{1}{6}(x^2 - 7x + 12) - \frac{27}{2}(x^2 - 5x + 4) + \frac{64}{3}(x^2 - 4x + 3) = 8x^2 - 19x + 12$$

Example 5. *The function $y = f(x)$ is given at the points (7, 3), (8, 1), (9, 1) and (10, 9). Find the value of y for $x = 9.5$ using Lagrange's interpolation formula.*

Sol. We are given

x :	7	8	9	10
$f(x)$:	3	1	1	9

Here, $x_0 = 7, \quad x_1 = 8, \quad x_2 = 9, \quad x_3 = 10$

$f(x_0) = 3, \quad f(x_1) = 1, \quad f(x_2) = 1, \quad f(x_3) = 9$

Lagrange's interpolation formula is

$$f(x) = \frac{(x-x_1)(x-x_2)(x-x_3)}{(x_0-x_1)(x_0-x_2)(x_0-x_3)} f(x_0) + \frac{(x-x_0)(x-x_2)(x-x_3)}{(x_1-x_0)(x_1-x_2)(x_1-x_3)} f(x_1)$$

$$+ \frac{(x-x_0)(x-x_1)(x-x_3)}{(x_2-x_0)(x_2-x_1)(x_2-x_3)} f(x_2) + \frac{(x-x_0)(x-x_1)(x-x_2)}{(x_3-x_0)(x_3-x_1)(x_3-x_2)} f(x_3)$$

$$= \frac{(x-8)(x-9)(x-10)}{(7-8)(7-9)(7-10)}(3) + \frac{(x-7)(x-9)(x-10)}{(8-7)(8-9)(8-10)}(1) + \frac{(x-7)(x-8)(x-10)}{(9-7)(9-8)(9-10)}(1)$$

$$+ \frac{(x-7)(x-8)(x-9)}{(10-7)(10-8)(10-9)}(9)$$

$$= -\frac{1}{2}(x-8)(x-9)(x-10) + \frac{1}{2}(x-7)(x-9)(x-10) - \frac{1}{2}(x-7)(x-8)(x-10)$$

$$+ \frac{3}{2}(x-7)(x-8)(x-9) \qquad \text{...(1)}$$

Putting $x = 9.5$ in eqn. (1), we get

$$f(9.5) = -\frac{1}{2}(9.5-8)(9.5-9)(9.5-10) + \frac{1}{2}(9.5-7)(9.5-9)(9.5-10)$$

$$- \frac{1}{2}(9.5-7)(9.5-8)(9.5-10) + \frac{3}{2}(9.5-7)(9.5-8)(9.5-9) = 3.625.$$

Example 6. *Use Lagrange's interpolation formula to fit a polynomial to the data:*

x :	– 1	0	2	3
u_x :	– 8	3	1	12

Hence or otherwise find the value of u_1.

Sol. Here,

$x_0 = -1, \quad x_1 = 0, \quad x_2 = 2, \quad x_3 = 3$

$f(x_0) = -8, \quad f(x_1) = 3, \quad f(x_2) = 1, \quad f(x_3) = 12$

Lagrange's interpolation formula is

$$f(x) = \frac{(x-x_1)(x-x_2)(x-x_3)}{(x_0-x_1)(x_0-x_2)(x_0-x_3)} f(x_0) + \frac{(x-x_0)(x-x_2)(x-x_3)}{(x_1-x_0)(x_1-x_2)(x_1-x_3)} f(x_1)$$

$$+ \frac{(x-x_0)(x-x_1)(x-x_3)}{(x_2-x_0)(x_2-x_1)(x_2-x_3)} f(x_2) + \frac{(x-x_0)(x-x_1)(x-x_2)}{(x_3-x_0)(x_3-x_1)(x_3-x_2)} f(x_3)$$

$$= \frac{(x-0)(x-2)(x-3)}{(-1-0)(-1-2)(-1-3)}(-8) + \frac{(x+1)(x-2)(x-3)}{(0+1)(0-2)(0-3)}(3) + \frac{(x+1)(x-0)(x-3)}{(2+1)(2-0)(2-3)}(1)$$

$$+ \frac{(x+1)(x-0)(x-2)}{(3+1)(3-0)(3-2)}(12)$$

$$= \frac{2}{3}x(x-2)(x-3) + \frac{1}{2}(x+1)(x-2)(x-3) - \frac{1}{6}(x+1)x(x-3) + (x+1)x(x-2)$$

$$\Rightarrow \quad f(x) = 2x^3 - 6x^2 + 3x + 3$$

Hence, $u_x = 2x^3 - 6x^2 + 3x + 3$ ...(1)

Putting $x = 1$ in (1), we get

$$u_1 = 2(1)^3 - 6(1)^2 + 3(1) + 3 = 2.$$

Example 7. *By means of Lagrange's formula, prove that*

(i) $y_0 = \frac{1}{2}(y_1 + y_{-1}) - \frac{1}{8}\left[\frac{1}{2}(y_3 - y_1) - \frac{1}{2}(y_{-1} - y_{-3})\right]$

(ii) $y_3 = 0.05\,(y_0 + y_6) - 0.3\,(y_1 + y_5) + 0.75\,(y_2 + y_4)$

(iii) $y_1 = y_3 - 0.3\,(y_5 - y_{-3}) + 0.2\,(y_{-3} - y_{-5})$.

Sol. (*i*) For the arguments – 3, – 1, 1, 3, the Lagrange's formula is

$$y_x = \frac{(x+1)(x-1)(x-3)}{(-3+1)(-3-1)(-3-3)}y_{-3} + \frac{(x+3)(x-1)(x-3)}{(-1+3)(-1-1)(-1-3)}y_{-1} + \frac{(x+3)(x+1)(x-3)}{(1+3)(1+1)(1-3)}y_1$$

$$+ \frac{(x+3)(x+1)(x-1)}{(3+3)(3+1)(3-1)}y_3$$

$$= \frac{(x+1)(x-1)(x-3)}{(-48)}y_{-3} + \frac{(x+3)(x-1)(x-3)}{16}y_{-1} + \frac{(x+3)(x+1)(x-3)}{(-16)}y_1$$

$$+ \frac{(x+3)(x+1)(x-1)}{48}y_3 \quad \text{...(1)}$$

Putting $x = 0$ in (1), we get

$$y_0 = -\frac{1}{16}y_{-3} + \frac{9}{16}y_{-1} + \frac{9}{16}y_1 - \frac{1}{16}y_3$$

$$= \frac{1}{2}(y_1 + y_{-1}) - \frac{1}{8}\left[\frac{1}{2}(y_3 - y_1) - \frac{1}{2}(y_{-1} - y_{-3})\right]$$

(*ii*) For the arguments 0, 1, 2, 4, 5, 6, the Lagrange's formula is

$$y_x = \frac{(x-1)(x-2)(x-4)(x-5)(x-6)}{(0-1)(0-2)(0-4)(0-5)(0-6)}y_0 + \frac{(x-0)(x-2)(x-4)(x-5)(x-6)}{(1-0)(1-2)(1-4)(1-5)(1-6)}y_1$$

$$+ \frac{(x-0)(x-1)(x-4)(x-5)(x-6)}{(2-0)(2-1)(2-4)(2-5)(2-6)}y_2 + \frac{(x-0)(x-1)(x-2)(x-5)(x-6)}{(4-0)(4-1)(4-2)(4-5)(4-6)}y_4$$

$$+ \frac{(x-0)(x-1)(x-2)(x-4)(x-6)}{(5-0)(5-1)(5-2)(5-4)(5-6)}y_5 + \frac{(x-0)(x-1)(x-2)(x-4)(x-5)}{(6-0)(6-1)(6-2)(6-4)(6-5)}y_6 \quad \text{...(1)}$$

Putting $x = 3$ in (1), we get

$$y_3 = 0.05\, y_0 - 0.3\, y_1 + 0.75\, y_2 + 0.75\, y_4 - 0.3\, y_5 + 0.05\, y_6$$
$$= 0.05\,(y_0 + y_6) - 0.3(y_1 + y_5) + 0.75\,(y_2 + y_4).$$

(*iii*) For the arguments $-5, -3, 3, 5$, the Lagrange's formula is

$$y_x = \frac{(x+3)(x-3)(x-5)}{(-5+3)(-5-3)(-5-5)}\, y_{-5} + \frac{(x+5)(x-3)(x-5)}{(-3+5)(-3-3)(-3-5)}\, y_{-3}$$
$$+ \frac{(x+5)(x+3)(x-5)}{(3+5)(3+3)(3-5)}\, y_3 + \frac{(x+5)(x+3)(x-3)}{(5+5)(5+3)(5-3)}\, y_5 \quad ...(1)$$

Putting $x = 1$ in eqn. (1), we get

$$y_1 = -0.2\, y_{-5} + 0.5 y_{-3} + y_3 - 0.3\, y_5 = y_3 - 0.3\,(y_5 - y_{-3}) + 0.2\,(y_{-3} - y_{-5}).$$

Example 8. *Prove that Lagrange's formula can be expressed in the form*

$$\begin{vmatrix} P_n(x) & 1 & x & x^2 & \ldots & \ldots & x^n \\ f(x_0) & 1 & x_0 & x_0^2 & \ldots & \ldots & x_0^n \\ f(x_1) & 1 & x_1 & x_1^2 & \ldots & \ldots & x_1^n \\ \ldots & \ldots & \ldots & \ldots & \ldots & \ldots & \ldots \\ f(x_n) & 1 & x_n & x_n^2 & \ldots & \ldots & x_n^n \end{vmatrix} = 0 \quad \textit{where } P_n(x) = f(x).$$

Sol. Let $P_n(x) = a_0 + a_1 x + a_2 x^2 + \ldots + a_n x^n$ ...(1)

Putting $x = x_0, x_1, \ldots, x_n$, and $P_n(x_i) = f(x_i), i = 0, 1, 2, \ldots, n$

$$f(x_0) = a_0 + a_1 x_0 + a_2 x_0^2 + \ldots + a_n x_0^n \quad ...(2)$$
$$f(x_1) = a_0 + a_1 x_1 + a_2 x_1^2 + \ldots + a_n x_1^n \quad ...(3)$$
$$\ldots \quad \ldots \quad \ldots \quad \ldots \quad \ldots \quad \ldots$$
$$f(x_n) = a_0 + a_1 x_n + a_2 x_n^2 + \ldots + a_n x_n^n \quad ...(n+2)$$

Eliminating $a_0, a_1, a_2, \ldots\ldots, a_n$ from these equations, we get

$$\begin{vmatrix} -P_n(x) & 1 & x & x^2 & \ldots & \ldots & x^n \\ -f(x_0) & 1 & x_0 & x_0^2 & \ldots & \ldots & x_0^n \\ -f(x_1) & 1 & x_1 & x_1^2 & \ldots & \ldots & x_1^n \\ \ldots & \ldots & \ldots & \ldots & \ldots & \ldots & \ldots \\ -f(x_n) & 1 & x_n & x_n^2 & \ldots & \ldots & x_n^n \end{vmatrix} = 0$$

or

$$\begin{vmatrix} P_n(x) & 1 & x & x^2 & \ldots & \ldots & x^n \\ f(x_0) & 1 & x_0 & x_0^2 & \ldots & \ldots & x_0^n \\ f(x_1) & 1 & x_1 & x_1^2 & \ldots & \ldots & x_1^n \\ \ldots & \ldots & \ldots & \ldots & \ldots & \ldots & \ldots \\ f(x_n) & 1 & x_n & x_n^2 & \ldots & \ldots & x_n^n \end{vmatrix} = 0$$

ASSIGNMENT

1. Apply Lagrange's formula to find $f(5)$ and $f(6)$ given that

$$f(2) = 4, f(1) = 2, f(3) = 8, f(7) = 128$$

Explain why the result differs from those obtained by completing the series of powers of 2?

2. Values of $f(x)$ for values of x are given as

$$f(1) = 4, f(2) = 5, f(7) = 5, f(8) = 4$$

Find $f(6)$ and also the value of x for which $f(x)$ is maximum or minimum.

3. Using Lagrange interpolation formula, calculate $f(3)$ from the following table:

x :	0	1	2	4	5	6
$f(x)$:	1	14	15	5	6	19

4. Compute $f(27)$ from the following data using Lagrange's interpolation formula.

x :	14	17	31	35
$f(x)$:	68.7	64.0	44.0	39.1

5. Find the value of tan 33° by Lagrange's formula if
tan 30° = 0.5774, tan 32° = 0.6249, tan 35° = 0.7002, tan 38° = 0.7813.

6. (*i*) Use Lagrange's formula to find $f(6)$ from the following table :

x :	2	5	7	10	12
$f(x)$:	18	180	448	1210	2028.

(*ii*) Apply Lagrange's formula to find $f(15)$, if

x :	10	12	14	16	18	20
$f(x)$:	2420	1942	1497	1109	790	540.

7. Derive the Lagrange's interpolation formula for unequal intervals. Find the value of $f(2.6)$ from the given table (Use above formula).

x :	– 2	– 1	1	2	6
$f(x)$:	– 4	14	– 4	– 16	196

8. If $y_0, y_1, ..., y_9$ are consecutive terms of a series, prove that

$$y_5 = \frac{1}{70}[56(y_4 + y_6) - 28(y_3 + y_7) + 8(y_2 + y_8) - (y_1 + y_9)]$$

9. Using the following table, find $f(x)$ as a polynomial in x :

x :	– 1	0	3	6	7
$f(x)$:	3	– 6	39	822	1611.

10. If $y(1) = -3, y(3) = 9, y(4) = 30$, and $y(6) = 132$, find the four-point Lagrange interpolation polynomial that takes the same values as the function y at the given points.

11. Given the table of values

x :	150	152	154	156
$y = \sqrt{x}$:	12.247	12.329	12.410	12.490

Evaluate $\sqrt{155}$ using Lagrange's interpolation formula.

12. Use Lagrange's method to find a polynomial $p(x)$ of lowest possible degree such that $p(n) = 2^n$ for $n = 0, 1, 2, 3, 4$.

13. Values of $f(x)$ are given at a, b and c. Show that the maximum is obtained by

$$x = \frac{f(a)(b^2 - c^2) + f(b)(c^2 - a^2) + f(c)(a^2 - b^2)}{f(a)(b - c) + f(b)(c - a) + f(c)(a - b)}.$$

14. Let $f(x) = \log_e (1 + x)$, $x_0 = 1$ and $x_1 = 1.1$. Use Lagrange interpolation to calculate an approximate value of $f(1.04)$ and obtain a bound on truncation error.

$$\left[\textbf{Hint.} \text{ Truncation error} = \frac{(x-1)(x-1.1)}{2}(-\sin\xi) \text{ where } 1 < \xi < 1.1\right]$$

15. (*i*) Determine by Lagrange's formula, the percentage number of criminals under 35 years:

Age	*% number of criminals*
under 25 years	52
under 30 years	67.3
under 40 years	84.1
under 50 years	94.4

(*ii*) Find a Lagrange's interpolating polynomial for the data given below :

$$x_0 = 1, \quad x_1 = 2.5, \quad x_2 = 4 \text{ and } \quad x_3 = 5.5$$

$$f(x_0) = 4, \quad f(x_1) = 7.5, \quad f(x_2) = 13 \quad \text{and} \quad f(x_3) = 17.5$$

Also, find the value of $f(5)$.

Answers

1. 37.8, 73; 2^x is not a polynomial **2.** 5.66; $x = 4.5$ **3.** 10

4. 49.31046 **5.** 0.64942084 **6.** (*i*) 293.99856 (*ii*) 1294.8437

7. – 17.248 **9.** $x^4 - 3x^3 + 5x^2 - 6$ **10.** $x^3 - 3x^2 + 5x - 6$ **11.** 12.45

12. $\frac{x^4}{24} - \frac{x^3}{12} + \frac{11}{24}x^2 + \frac{7x}{12} + 1$ **14.** 0.7126, 0.00089

15. (*i*) 77.405 (*ii*) $-\frac{4}{27}x^3 + \frac{14}{9}x^2 - \frac{5}{3}x + \frac{115}{27}$; 16.2962963.

4.25. ERROR IN LAGRANGE'S INTERPOLATION FORMULA

Remainder,

$$y(x) - L_n(x) = R_n(x) = \frac{\Pi_{n+1}(x)}{(n+1)!} y^{(n+1)}(\xi), \; a < \xi < b$$

where Lagrange's formula is for the class of functions having continuous derivatives of order up to $(n + 1)$ on $[a, b]$.

Quantity $E_L = \max\limits_{[a,b]} | R_n(x) |$ may be taken as an estimate of error.

Let assume

$$| y^{(n+1)}(\xi) | \le M_{n+1}, \; a \le \xi \le b$$

then,

$$E_L \le \frac{M_{n+1}}{(n+1)!} \max\limits_{[a,b]} | \Pi_{n+1}(x) |.$$

EXAMPLES

Example 1. *Show that the truncation error of quadratic interpolation in an equidistant table is bounded by* $\frac{h^3}{9\sqrt{3}}$ *max* $| f'''(\xi) |$ *where h is the step size and f is the tabulated function.*

Sol. Let x_{i-1}, x_i, x_{i+1} denote three consecutive equispaced points with step size h. The truncation error of the quadratic Lagrange interpolation is bounded by

$$| E_2(f ; x) | \le \frac{M_3}{6} \max | (x - x_{i-1})(x - x_i)(x - x_{i+1}) |$$

where $x_{i-1} \le x \le x_{i+1}$ and $M_3 = \max\limits_{a \le x \le b} | f'''(x) |$

Substitute $t = \dfrac{x - x_i}{h}$ then,

$$x - x_{i-1} = x - (x_i - h) = x - x_i + h = th + h = (t + 1)h$$

$$x - x_{i+1} = x - (x_i + h) = x - x_i - h = th - h = (t - 1)h$$

and $\quad (x - x_{i-1})(x - x_i)(x - x_{i+1}) = (t + 1)\, t(t - 1)h^3 = t(t^2 - 1)h^3 = g(t)$

Setting $g'(t) = 0$, we get

$$3t^2 - 1 = 0 \quad \Rightarrow \quad t = \pm \frac{1}{\sqrt{3}}.$$

For both these values of t, we obtain

$$\max | (x - x_{i-1})(x - x_i)(x - x_{i+1}) | = h^3 \max_{-1 \le t \le 1} | t(t^2 - 1) | = \frac{2h^3}{3\sqrt{3}}$$

Hence, the truncation error of the quadratic interpolation is bounded by

$$| E_2(f ; x) | \le \frac{h^3}{9\sqrt{3}} M_3$$

or, $$| E_2(f ; x) | \le \frac{h^3}{9\sqrt{3}} \max | f'''(\xi) |.$$

Example 2. *Determine the step size that can be used in the tabulation of $f(x) = \sin x$ in the interval $\left[0, \frac{\pi}{4}\right]$ at equally spaced nodal points so that the truncation error of the quadratic interpolation is less than 5×10^{-8}.*

Sol. From Ex. 1, we have

$$| E_2(f ; x) | \le \frac{h^3}{9\sqrt{3}} M_3$$

For $\quad f(x) = \sin x$, we get $f'''(x) = -\cos x$ and $M_3 = \max\limits_{0 \le x \le \pi/4} |\cos x| = 1$

Hence the step size h is given by

$$\frac{h^3}{9\sqrt{3}} \le 5 \times 10^{-8} \quad \text{or} \quad h \approx 0.009$$

Example 3. *Using Lagrange's interpolation formula, find the value of sin* $\left(\frac{\pi}{6}\right)$ *from the following data :*

x	:	0	$\pi/4$	$\pi/2$
$y = \sin x$	:	0	0.70711	1.0

Also estimate the error in the solution.

Sol. $$\sin\left(\frac{\pi}{6}\right) = \frac{\left(\frac{\pi}{6}-0\right)\left(\frac{\pi}{6}-\frac{\pi}{2}\right)}{\left(\frac{\pi}{4}-0\right)\left(\frac{\pi}{4}-\frac{\pi}{2}\right)}(0.70711) + \frac{\left(\frac{\pi}{6}-0\right)\left(\frac{\pi}{6}-\frac{\pi}{4}\right)}{\left(\frac{\pi}{2}-0\right)\left(\frac{\pi}{2}-\frac{\pi}{4}\right)}(1) = 0.51743$$

Now, $y(x) = \sin x, \quad y'(x) = \cos x, \quad y''(x) = -\sin x, \quad y'''(x) = -\cos x$

Hence, $| y'''(\xi) | < 1$

when $x = \pi/6$.

$$| R_n(x) | \leq \left| \frac{\left(\frac{\pi}{6}-0\right)\left(\frac{\pi}{6}-\frac{\pi}{4}\right)\left(\frac{\pi}{6}-\frac{\pi}{2}\right)}{3!} \right| = 0.02392$$

where agrees with the actual error in problem.

4.26. EXPRESSION OF RATIONAL FUNCTION AS A SUM OF PARTIAL FRACTIONS

Let $$f(x) = \frac{3x^2 + x + 1}{(x-1)(x-2)(x-3)}$$

Consider $\phi(x) = 3x^2 + x + 1$ and tabulate its values for $x = 1, 2, 3$, we get

x	:	1	2	3
$3x^2 + x + 1$	:	5	15	31

Using Lagrange's interpolation formula, we get

$$f(x) = \frac{(x-2)(x-3)}{(1-2)(1-3)}(5) + \frac{(x-1)(x-3)}{-1}(15) + \frac{(x-1)(x-2)}{2}(31)$$

$$= \frac{5}{2}(x-2)(x-3) - 15(x-1)(x-3) + \frac{31}{2}(x-1)(x-2)$$

$$= \frac{5}{2(x-1)} - \frac{15}{x-2} + \frac{31}{2(x-3)}.$$

4.27. INVERSE INTERPOLATION

The process of estimating the value of x for the value of y not in the table is called *inverse interpolation.*

When values of x are unevenly spaced, Lagrange's method is used by interchanging x and y.

Example. *From the given table:*

x	:	20	25	30	35
$y(x)$	:	0.342	0.423	0.5	0.65

Find the value of x for y(x) = 0.390.

Sol. By inverse interpolation formula,

$$x = \frac{(y-y_1)(y-y_2)(y-y_3)}{(y_0-y_1)(y_0-y_2)(y_0-y_3)}x_0 + \frac{(y-y_0)(y-y_2)(y-y_3)}{(y_1-y_0)(y_1-y_2)(y_1-y_3)}x_1$$

$$+ \frac{(y-y_0)(y-y_1)(y-y_3)}{(y_2-y_0)(y_2-y_1)(y_2-y_3)}x_2 + \frac{(y-y_0)(y-y_1)(y-y_2)}{(y_3-y_0)(y_3-y_1)(y_3-y_2)}x_3$$

$$= \frac{(.39-.423)(.39-.5)(.39-.65)}{(.342-.423)(.342-.5)(.342-.65)}(20) + \frac{(.39-.342)(.39-.5)(.39-.65)}{(.423-.342))(.423-.5)(.423-.65)}(25)$$

$$+ \frac{(.39-.342)(.39-.423)(.39-.65)}{(.5-.342)(.5-.423)(.5-.65)}(30) + \frac{(.39-.342)(.39-.423)(.39-.5)}{(.65-.342)(.65-.423)(.65-.5)}(35)$$

$= 22.84057797.$

4.28. DIVIDED DIFFERENCES

We seek an interpolation polynomial which has the property that a polynomial of higher degree may be derived from it by simply adding new terms.

Newton's general interpolation formula is one such formula and it employs divided differences.

If (x_0, y_0), (x_1, y_1), (x_2, y_2) ...... be given points then the first divided difference for the arguments x_0, x_1 is defined by

$$\underset{x_1}{\Delta} y_0 = [x_0, x_1] = \frac{y_1 - y_0}{x_1 - x_0}$$

Similarly, $[x_1, x_2] = \dfrac{y_2 - y_1}{x_2 - x_1}$ and so on.

The second divided difference for x_0, x_1, x_2 is defined as

$$\underset{x_1, x_2}{\Delta^2} y_0 = [x_0, x_1, x_2] = \frac{[x_1, x_2] - [x_0, x_1]}{x_2 - x_0}$$

Third divided difference for x_0, x_1, x_2, x_3 is defined as

$$[x_0, x_1, x_2, x_3] = \frac{[x_1, x_2, x_3] - [x_0, x_1, x_2]}{x_3 - x_0} \quad \text{and so on.}$$

4.29. PROPERTIES OF DIVIDED DIFFERENCES

1. The divided differences are symmetrical in their arguments *i.e.*, independent of the order of arguments.

$$[x_0, x_1] = \frac{y_1}{x_1 - x_0} + \frac{y_0}{x_0 - x_1} = [x_1, x_0]$$

Also, $[x_0, x_1, x_2] = \dfrac{y_0}{(x_0 - x_1)(x_0 - x_2)} + \dfrac{y_1}{(x_1 - x_0)(x_1 - x_2)} + \dfrac{y_2}{(x_2 - x_0)(x_2 - x_1)}$

$= [x_2, x_0, x_1]$ or $[x_1, x_2, x_0]$

2. The nth divided differences of a polynomial of nth degree are constant.

Let the arguments be equally spaced so that

$$x_1 - x_0 = x_2 - x_1 = ... = x_n - x_{n-1} = h$$

then, $$[x_0, x_1] = \frac{y_1 - y_0}{x_1 - x_0} = \frac{\Delta y_0}{h}$$

$$[x_0, x_1, x_2] = \frac{[x_1, x_2] - [x_0, x_1]}{(x_2 - x_0)} = \frac{1}{2h}\left(\frac{\Delta y_1}{h} - \frac{\Delta y_0}{h}\right) = \frac{1}{2!}\cdot\frac{1}{h^2}(\Delta^2 y_0)$$

In general,

$$[x_0, x_1, x_2, ..., x_n] = \frac{1}{n!}\cdot\frac{1}{h^n}\Delta^n y_0$$

If tabulated function is a nth degree polynomial. $\therefore$ $\Delta^n y_0$ = constant

$\therefore$ n^{th} divided differences will also be constant.

4.30. NEWTON'S DIVIDED DIFFERENCE INTERPOLATION FORMULA

(U.P.T.U. 2009)

Let $y_0, y_1, ..., y_n$ be the values of $y = f(x)$ corresponding to the arguments $x_0, x_1, ..., x_n$ then from the definition of divided differences, we have

$$[x, x_0] = \frac{y - y_0}{x - x_0}$$

so that, $$y = y_0 + (x - x_0)[x, x_0] \quad ...(1)$$

Again, $$[x, x_0, x_1] = \frac{[x, x_0] - [x_0, x_1]}{x - x_1}$$

which gives, $$[x, x_0] = [x_0, x_1] + (x - x_1)[x, x_0, x_1] \quad ...(2)$$

From (1) and (2), $$y = y_0 + (x - x_0)[x_0, x_1] + (x - x_0)(x - x_1)[x, x_0, x_1] \quad ...(3)$$

Also $$[x, x_0, x_1, x_2] = \frac{[x, x_0, x_1] - [x_0, x_1, x_2]}{x - x_2}$$

which gives $$[x, x_0, x_1] = [x_0, x_1, x_2] + (x - x_2)[x, x_0, x_1, x_2] \quad ...(4)$$

From (3) and (4), $$y = y_0 + (x - x_0)[x_0, x_1] + (x - x_0)(x - x_1)[x_0, x_1, x_2] + (x - x_0)(x - x_1)(x - x_2)[x, x_0, x_1, x_2]$$

Proceeding in this manner, we get

$$y = f(x) = y_0 + (x - x_0)[x_0, x_1] + (x - x_0)(x - x_1)[x_0, x_1, x_2] + (x - x_0)(x - x_1)(x - x_2)[x_0, x_1, x_2, x_3] + ... + (x - x_0)(x - x_1)(x - x_2) ..... (x - x_{n-1})[x_0, x_1, x_2, x_3, ..., x_n] + (x - x_0)(x - x_1)(x - x_2) ..... (x - x_n)[x, x_0, x_1, x_2, ..., x_n]$$

which is called Newton's general interpolation formula with divided differences, the last term being the remainder term after $(n + 1)$ terms.

Newton's divided difference formula can also be written as

$$y = y_0 + (x - x_0)\Delta y_0 + (x - x_0)(x - x_1)\Delta^2 y_0 + (x - x_0)(x - x_1)(x - x_2)\Delta^3 y_0 + (x - x_0)(x - x_1)(x - x_2)(x - x_3)\Delta^4 y_0 + ... + (x - x_0)(x - x_1) ..... (x - x_{n-1})\Delta^n y_0$$

4.31. RELATION BETWEEN DIVIDED DIFFERENCES AND ORDINARY DIFFERENCES

Let the arguments $x_0, x_1, x_2, \ldots\ldots, x_n$ be equally spaced such that

$$x_1 - x_0 = x_2 - x_1 = \ldots = x_n - x_{n-1} = h$$

$$\therefore \quad x_1 = x_0 + h$$

$$x_2 = x_0 + 2h$$

$$\ldots\ldots\ldots\ldots\ldots$$

$$x_n = x_0 + nh$$

Now
$$\underset{x_1}{\Delta} f(x_0) = \frac{f(x_1) - f(x_0)}{x_1 - x_0} = \frac{f(x_0 + h) - f(x_0)}{h} = \frac{\Delta f(x_0)}{h} \quad \ldots(1)$$

$$\underset{x_1 x_2}{\Delta^2} f(x_0) = \frac{1}{x_2 - x_0} [f(x_1, x_2) - f(x_0, x_1)]$$

$$= \frac{1}{x_2 - x_0} \left[\frac{f(x_2) - f(x_1)}{x_2 - x_1} - \frac{f(x_1) - f(x_0)}{x_1 - x_0} \right]$$

$$= \frac{1}{2h} \left[\frac{f(x_0 + 2h) - f(x_0 + h)}{h} - \frac{f(x_0 + h) - f(x_0)}{h} \right]$$

$$= \frac{1}{2h^2} [f(x_0 + 2h) - 2f(x_0 + h) + f(x_0)] = \frac{\Delta^2 f(x_0)}{2!.h^2} \quad \ldots(2)$$

$$\underset{x_1, x_2, x_3}{\Delta^3} f(x_0) = \frac{1}{x_2 - x_0} [f(x_1, x_2, x_3) - f(x_0, x_1, x_2)]$$

$$= \frac{1}{3h} \left[\frac{\Delta^2 f(x_1)}{2h^2} - \frac{\Delta^2 f(x_0)}{2h^2} \right] = \frac{\Delta^2 f(x_1) - \Delta^2 f(x_0)}{6h^3} \quad \text{[From (1)]}$$

$$= \frac{\Delta^3 f(x_0)}{3!\, h^3}$$

$$\ldots \qquad \ldots \qquad \ldots$$

$$\underset{x_1, \ldots\ldots, x_n}{\Delta^n} f(x_0) = \frac{\Delta^n f(x_0)}{n!\, h^n}.$$

4.32. MERITS AND DEMERITS OF LAGRANGE'S FORMULA

1. The formula is simple and easy to remember.

2. There is no need to construct the divided difference table and we can directly interpolate the unknown value with the help of given observations.

3. The calculations in the formula are more complicated than in the divided difference formula.

4. The application of the formula is not speedy.

5. There is always a chance of commiting some error due to a no. of (+)ve and (–)ve sign in the denominator and numerator of each term.

6. The calculations provide no check whether the functional values used are taken correctly or not whereas the differences used in a difference formula provide a check on the functional values.

EXAMPLES

Example 1. (*i*) *Find the third divided difference with arguments 2, 4, 9, 10 of the function* $f(x) = x^3 - 2x$.

(*ii*) *If* $f(x) = \dfrac{1}{x^2}$, *find the first divided differences* $f(a, b)$, $f(a, b, c)$, $f(a, b, c, d)$.

(*iii*) *If* $f(x) = g(x)\,h(x)$, *prove that* $f(x_1, x_2) = g(x_1)\,h(x_1, x_2) + g(x_1, x_2)\,h(x_2)$.

Sol. (*i*)

x	$f(x)$	$\Delta f(x)$	$\Delta^2 f(x)$	$\Delta^3 f(x)$
2	4			
		$\dfrac{56-4}{4-2} = 26$		
4	56		$\dfrac{131-26}{9-2} = 15$	
		$\dfrac{711-56}{9-4} = 131$		$\dfrac{23-15}{10-2} = 1$
9	711		$\dfrac{269-131}{10-4} = 23$	
		$\dfrac{980-711}{10-9} = 269$		
10	980			

Hence third divided difference is 1.

(*ii*)

x	$f(x) = \dfrac{1}{x^2}$	$\Delta f(x)$	$\Delta^2 f(x)$	$\Delta^3 f(x)$
a	$\dfrac{1}{a^2}$			
		$\dfrac{\left(\dfrac{1}{b^2} - \dfrac{1}{a^2}\right)}{b-a} = \boxed{-\left(\dfrac{a+b}{a^2b^2}\right)}$		
b	$\dfrac{1}{b^2}$		$\boxed{\dfrac{ab+bc+ca}{a^2b^2c^2}}$	
		$-\left(\dfrac{b+c}{b^2c^2}\right)$		$\boxed{-\left(\dfrac{abc+acd+abd+bcd}{a^2b^2c^2d^2}\right)}$
c	$\dfrac{1}{c^2}$		$\dfrac{bc+cd+db}{b^2c^2d^2}$	
		$-\left(\dfrac{c+d}{c^2d^2}\right)$		
d	$\dfrac{1}{d^2}$			

From the above divided difference table, we observe that first divided differences,

$$f(a, b) = -\left(\frac{a+b}{a^2b^2}\right)$$

$$f(a, b, c) = \frac{ab + bc + ca}{a^2b^2c^2} \quad \text{and} \quad f(a, b, c, d) = -\left(\frac{abc + acd + abd + bcd}{a^2b^2c^2d^2}\right)$$

(*iii*)

$$\text{RHS} = g(x_1)\,\frac{h(x_2) - h(x_1)}{x_2 - x_1} + \frac{g(x_2) - g(x_1)}{x_2 - x_1}\,h(x_2)$$

$$= \frac{1}{x_2 - x_1}\,[\{g(x_1)\,h(x_2) - g(x_1)h(x_1)\} + \{g(x_2)\,h(x_2) - g(x_1)\,h(x_2)\}]$$

$$= \frac{g\,(x_2)\,h\,(x_2) - g\,(x_1)\,h\,(x_1)}{x_2 - x_1} = \underset{x_2}{\Delta}\,g(x_1)\,h(x_1) = \underset{x_2}{\Delta}\,f(x_1) = f(x_1, x_2) = \text{LHS}.$$

Example 2. (*i*) *Prove that* $\underset{bcd}{\Delta}^3\left(\frac{1}{a}\right) = -\frac{1}{abcd}$

(*ii*) *Show that the* n^{th} *divided differences* $[x_0, x_1, \ldots\ldots, x_n]$ *for* $u_x = \frac{1}{x}$ *is* $\left[\frac{(-1)^n}{x_0\,x_1\,\ldots\ldots\,x_n}\right]$.

Sol. (*i*)

x	$f(x)$	$\Delta f(x)$	$\Delta^2 f(x)$	$\Delta^3 f(x)$
a	$\frac{1}{a}$			
		$\frac{\frac{1}{b} - \frac{1}{a}}{b - a} = -\frac{1}{ba}$		
b	$\frac{1}{b}$		$(-1)^2\,\frac{1}{abc}$	
		$\frac{\frac{1}{c} - \frac{1}{b}}{c - b} = -\frac{1}{bc}$		$(-1)^3\,\frac{1}{abcd}$
c	$\frac{1}{c}$		$(-1)^2\,\frac{1}{bdc}$	
		$\frac{\frac{1}{d} - \frac{1}{c}}{d - c} = -\frac{1}{dc}$		
d	$\frac{1}{d}$			

From the table, we observe that $\underset{bcd}{\Delta}^3\left(\frac{1}{a}\right) = -\frac{1}{abcd}$. ...(1)

(*ii*) From (1), we see that

$$\underset{bcd}{\Delta^3}\left(\frac{1}{a}\right) = -\frac{1}{abcd} = (-1)^3 f(a, b, c, d)$$

$\therefore$ In general,

$$\underset{x_0, x_1, \ldots, x_n}{\Delta^n}\left(\frac{1}{x}\right) = (-1)^n f(x_0, x_1, x_2, \ldots, x_n) = \left[\frac{(-1)^n}{x_0\, x_1\, x_2 \ldots x_n}\right].$$

Example 3. *Using Newton's divided difference formula, find a polynomial function satisfying the following data:*

x:	*– 4*	*– 1*	*0*	*2*	*5*
f(x):	*1245*	*33*	*5*	*9*	*1335*

Hence find f(1).

Sol. The divided difference table is

x	$f(x)$	$\Delta f(x)$	$\Delta^2 f(x)$	$\Delta^3 f(x)$	$\Delta^4 f(x)$
– 4	1245				
		– 404			
– 1	33		94		
		– 28		– 14	
0	5		10		3
		2		13	
2	9		88		
		442			
5	1335				

Applying Newton's divided difference formula

$$f(x) = 1245 + (x + 4)(-404) + (x + 4)(x + 1)\,94$$
$$+ (x + 4)(x + 1)(x - 0)(-14) + (x + 4)(x + 1)x(x - 2)(3)$$
$$= 3x^4 - 5x^3 + 6x^2 - 14x + 5$$

Hence, $f(1) = 3 - 5 + 6 - 14 + 5 = -5$.

Example 4. *By means of Newton's divided difference formula, find the values of f(8) and f(15) from the following table:*

x:	*4*	*5*	*7*	*10*	*11*	*13*
f(x):	*48*	*100*	*294*	*900*	*1210*	*2028.*

[G.B.T.U. 2011, U.P.T.U. (MCA) 2009]

Sol. Newton's divided difference formula, using the arguments 4, 5, 7, 10, 11 and 13 is

$$f(x) = f(4) + (x - 4)\underset{5}{\Delta} f(4) + (x - 4)(x - 5)\underset{5,7}{\Delta^2} f(4) + (x - 4)(x - 5)(x - 7)\underset{5,7,10}{\Delta^3} f(4) + \ldots (1)$$

The divided difference table is as under:

x	$f(x)$	$\Delta f(x)$	$\Delta^2 f(x)$	$\Delta^3 f(x)$	$\Delta^4 f(x)$
4	$\boxed{48}$				
		$\frac{100-48}{5-4} = \boxed{52}$			
5	100		$\frac{97-52}{7-4} = \boxed{15}$		
		$\frac{294-100}{7-5} = 97$		$\frac{21-15}{10-4} = \boxed{1}$	
7	294		$\frac{202-97}{10-5} = 21$		0
		$\frac{900-294}{10-7} = 202$		$\frac{27-21}{11-5} = 1$	
10	900		$\frac{310-202}{11-7} = 27$		0
		$\frac{1210-900}{11-10} = 310$		$\frac{33-27}{13-7} = 1$	
11	1210		$\frac{409-310}{13-10} = 33$		
		$\frac{2028-1210}{13-11} = 409$			
13	2028				

Substituting the values of the divided differences in (1),

$$f(x) = 48 + (x-4) \times 52 + (x-4)(x-5) \times 15 + (x-5)(x-4)(x-7) \times 1$$

Putting $x = 8$ and 15, we get

$$f(8) = 448 \quad \text{and} \quad f(15) = 3150.$$

Example 5. *Given the following table, find $f(x)$ as a polynomial in powers of $(x - 5)$*

x:	0	2	3	4	7	9
$f(x)$:	4	26	58	112	466	922.

Sol. Divided difference table is

x	$f(x)$	$\Delta f(x)$	$\Delta^2 f(x)$	$\Delta^3 f(x)$
0	$\boxed{4}$			
		$\boxed{11}$		
2	26		$\boxed{7}$	
		32		$\boxed{1}$
3	58		11	
		54		1
4	112		16	
		118		1
7	466		22	
		228		
9	922			

By Newton's divided difference formula, we get

$$f(x) = 4 + (x - 0)(11) + (x - 0)(x - 2)7 + (x - 0)(x - 2)(x - 3)1$$
$$= x^3 + 2x^2 + 3x + 4$$

In order to express it in power of $(x - 5)$, we use synthetic division, as

5	1	2	3	4
		5	35	190
5	1	7	38	194
		5	60	
5	1	12	98	
		5		
	1	17		

$$\therefore \quad 2x^2 + x^3 + 3x + 4 = (x - 5)^3 + 17(x - 5)^2 + 98\,(x - 5) + 194.$$

Example 6. *Given $\log_{10} 654 = 2.8156$, $\log_{10} 658 = 2.8182$, $\log_{10} 659 = 2.8189$ and $\log_{10} 661 = 2.8202$, find by divided difference formula the value of $\log_{10} 656$.*

Sol. The divided difference table is as under:

x	$10^5\ f(x)$	$10^5\ \Delta f(x)$	$10^5\ \Delta^2 f(x)$	$10^5\ \Delta^3 f(x)$
654	281560			
		$\frac{260}{4} = 65$		
658	281820		$\frac{70-65}{5} = 1$	
		$\frac{70}{1} = 70$		$\frac{-1.66-1}{7} = -0.38$
659	281890		$\frac{65-70}{3} = -1.66$	
		$\frac{130}{2} = 65$		
661	282020			

For the arguments 654, 658, 659 and 661, the divided difference formula is

$$f(x) = f(654) + (x - 654) \underset{658}{\Delta} f(654) + (x - 655)\,(x - 658) \underset{658,\,659}{\Delta^2} f(654)$$
$$+ (x - 654)\,(x - 658)\,(x - 659) \underset{658,\,659,\,661}{\Delta^3} f(654) \qquad \ldots(1)$$

From (1),

$$10^5 f(x) = 281560 + (x - 654)\,(65) + (x - 654)\,(x - 658)\,(1)$$
$$+ (x - 654)\,(x - 658)\,(x - 659)\,(0.38)$$

Putting $x = 656$, we get

$$10^5 f(656) = 281560 + (2)\,(65) + (2)\,(-2)\,(1) + (2)\,(-2)\,(-3)\,(0.38) = 281690.56$$

$$\therefore \quad f(656) = 2.8169056$$

Hence, $\log_{10} 656 = 2.8169056$.

Example 7. *Find f '(10) from the following data:*

x:	3	5	11	27	34
$f(x)$:	− 13	23	899	17315	35606.

Sol. Divided difference table is

x	$f(x)$	$\Delta f(x)$	$\Delta^2 f(x)$	$\Delta^3 f(x)$	$\Delta^4 f(x)$
3	− 13				
		18			
5	23		16		
		146		1	
11	899		40		0
		1026		1	
27	17315		69		
		2613			
34	35606				

By Newton's divided difference formula,

$$f(x) = -13 + (x-3)\,18 + (x-3)(x-5)16 + (x-3)(x-5)(x-11)1$$

$$\therefore \qquad f'(x) = 3x^2 - 6x - 7$$

Put $x = 10$, $f'(10) = 3(10)^2 - 6(10) - 7 = 233.$

Example 8. *Given that* $\log_{10} 2 = 0.3010$, $\log_{10} 3 = 0.4771$, $\log_{10} 7 = 0.8451$, *find the value of* $\log_{10} 33$.

Sol. $\log 30 = 1.4771,$

$$\log 32 = 5 \log 2 = 5 \times 0.3010 = 1.5050$$

$$\log 36 = 2(\log 2 + \log 3) = 2 \times (0.3010 + 0.4771) = 1.5562$$

$$\log 35 = \log \frac{70}{2} = \log 70 - \log 2 = 1.8451 - 0.3010 = 1.5441.$$

Divided difference table is as under:

x	$10^4 \log_{10} x$	$10^4 \Delta \log_{10} x$	$10^4 \Delta^2 \log_{10} x$	$10^4 \Delta^3 \log_{10} x$
30	14771			
		$\frac{279}{2} = 139.5$		
32	15050		$\frac{9.2}{5} = -1.84$	
		$\frac{391}{3} = 130.3$		$\frac{0.48}{6} = -0.08$
35	15441		$-\frac{9.3}{7} = -2.32$	
		$\frac{121}{1} = 121$		
36	15562			

Applying Newton's divided difference formula, we get

$$10^4 \log_{10} x = 14771 + (x-30)(139.5) + (x-30)(x-32)(-1.84) + (x-30)(x-32)(x-35)(-0.08)$$

Putting $x = 33$

$$10^4 \log_{10} 33 = 15184.46$$

$$\therefore \quad \log_{10} 33 = 1.5184.$$

Example 9. *The mode of a certain frequency curve $y = f(x)$ is very near to $x = 9$ and the values of frequency density $f(x)$ for $x = 8.9$, 9.0 and 9.3 are respectively equal to 0.30, 0.35 and 0.25. Calculate the approximate value of mode.*

Sol. Divided difference table is as under:

x	$100\ f(x)$	$100\Delta f(x)$	$100\Delta^2 f(x)$
8.9	30		
		$\frac{5}{0.9} = \frac{50}{9}$	
9.0	35		$-\frac{350}{9 \times 0.4} = -\frac{3500}{36}$
		$-\frac{10}{0.3} = -\frac{100}{3}$	
9.3	25		

Applying Newton's divided difference formula

$$100\ f(x) = 30 + (x - 8.9) \times \frac{50}{9} + (x - 8.9)(x - 9)\left(-\frac{3500}{36}\right)$$

$$\therefore \quad f(x) = -0.9722x^2 + 17.45833x - 17.597217$$

$$f'(x) = -1.9444\,x + 17.45833$$

Putting $f'(x) = 0$, we get $x = \frac{17.45833}{1.9444} = 8.9788$

Also, $f''(x) = -1.9444$ *i.e.*, (–)ve

$\therefore$ $f(x)$ is maximum at $x = 8.9788$. Hence mode is 8.9788.

ASSIGNMENT

1. Construct Newton's interpolation polynomial for the data shown in the following table:

x:	0	2	3	4
$f(x)$:	7	11	28	63

[*U.P.T.U. MCA (SUM) 2009*]

2. (*i*) Given the values:

x:	5	7	11	13	17
$f(x)$:	150	392	1452	2366	5202

Evaluate $f(9)$ using Newton's divided difference formula.

(*ii*) Apply Newton's divided difference formula to find the value of $f(8)$ if

$$f(1) = 3,\ f(3) = 31,\ f(6) = 223,\ f(10) = 1011,\ f(11) = 1343.$$

3. Obtain the Newton's divided difference interpolating polynomial and hence find $f(6)$, $f(5)$ and $f(8)$.

x:	3	7	9	10
$f(x)$:	168	120	72	63

[*G.B.T.U. 2012, U.P.T.U. 2007*]

4. Given that

x:	1	3	4	6	7
y_x:	1	27	81	729	2187

Find y_5. Why does it differ from 3^5 ?

5. Use Newton's divided difference formula to find the interpolating polynomial and hence evaluate $y(9.5)$ from the given data:

x:	7	8	9	10
y:	3	1	1	9

[*G.B.T.U. 2011 ; G.B.T.U. (C.O.) 2011*]

6. (*i*) The following table is given:

x:	0	1	2	5
y:	2	3	12	147

What is the form of the function?

(*ii*) Develop the divided-difference table from the data given below and obtain the interpolation polynomial $f(x)$:

x:	1	3	5	7	11
$f(x)$:	5	11	17	23	29

Also, find the value of $f(19.5)$. (*U.P.T.U. 2009*)

7. Find the function u_x in powers of $x - 1$ given that $u_0 = 8$, $u_1 = 11$, $u_4 = 68$, $u_5 = 123$.

8. For the following table, find $f(x)$ as a polynomial in x using Newton's divided difference formula.

x:	5	6	9	11
$f(x)$:	12	13	14	16

(*U.P.T.U. 2006*)

9. Find the Newton's divided difference interpolation polynomial for:

x:	0.5	1.5	3.0	5.0	6.5	8.0
$f(x)$:	1.625	5.875	31.0	131.0	282.125	521.0

10. Using Newton's divided difference formula, calculate $f(6)$ from the following data:

x:	1	2	7	8
$f(x)$:	1	5	5	4

11. (*i*) Using Newton divided difference method, find the interpolating polynomial and hence compute $f(3)$ from the following table: [*M.T.U. 2014, G.B.T.U. 2013*]

x:	0	1	2	4	5	6
$f(x)$:	1	14	15	5	6	19

(*ii*) Use Newton's divided difference method to compute $f(5.5)$ from the following data:

x:	0	1	4	5	6
$f(x)$:	1	14	15	6	3

(*G.B.T.U. 2010*)

12. Given the data $f(1) = 4$, $f(2) = 5$, $f(7) = 5$, $f(8) = 4$. Find the the value of $f(6)$ and also the value of x for which $f(x)$ is maximum or minimum. (*M.T.U. 2013*)

13. For the following table, find $f(x)$ as a polynomial in x using Newton's divided difference formula:

x:	− 1	0	3	6	9
$f(x)$:	3	− 6	39	822	1611

Hence compute $f(1)$. (*M.T.U. 2012; U.P.T.U. 2009*)

14. Using the Newton's divided difference formula, find a polynomial which takes the values 3, 12, 15, − 21 when x has the values 3, 2, 1, − 1 respectively. (*U.P.T.U. 2008*)

15. Find Newton's divided differences polynomial for the following data:

x:	-3	-1	0	3	5
$f(x)$:	-30	-22	-12	330	3458

(M.T.U. 2013)

16. Compute $f'(3)$ from the following table:

x:	1	2	4	8	10
$f(x)$:	0	1	5	21	27

(G.B.T.U. 2011)

17. Find $f'''(5)$ from the data given below:

x:	2	4	9	13	16	21	29
$f(x)$:	57	1345	66340	402052	1118209	4287844	21242820

Answers

1. $x^3 - 2x + 7$ **2.** (*i*) 810 (*ii*) 521

3. $x^3 - 21x^2 + 119x - 27$; 147, 168, 93 **4.** 208.82222, 3^x is not a polynomial

5. $x^3 - 23x^2 + 174x - 431$, 3.625

6. (*i*) $x^3 + x^2 - x + 2$ (*ii*) $-$ 112.3955078; $\frac{-x^4}{320} + \frac{x^3}{20} - \frac{43x^2}{160} + \frac{71}{20}x + \frac{107}{64}$

7. $(x-1)^3 + 2(x-1)^2 + 4(x-1) + 11$ **8.** $\frac{x^3}{20} - \frac{7x^2}{6} + \frac{557x}{60} - 11.5$

9. $x^3 + x + 1$ **10.** 6.2381

11. (*i*) $x^3 - 9x^2 + 21x + 1$, 10 (*ii*) 3.096875 **12.** 5.66, $x = 4.5$

13. $f(x) = -\frac{257}{270}x^4 + \frac{1703}{135}x^3 - \frac{377}{30}x^2 - \frac{527}{15}x - 6$, $-$ 42.037

14. $f(x) = x^3 - 9x^2 + 17x + 6$ **15.** $5x^4 + 9x^3 - 27x^2 - 21x - 12$

16. 1.97916 **17.** 1626.

4.33. HERMITE'S INTERPOLATION FORMULA

So far we have considered the interpolation formulae which make use only of a certain number of function values. We now derive an interpolation formula in which both the function and its first derivative are to be assigned at each point of interpolation. This is called **Hermite's interpolation formula** or **osculating interpolation formula.**

Let the set of data points (x_i, y_i, y_i'), $0 \le i \le n$ be given. A polynomial of the least degree say $H(x)$ is to be determined such that

$$H(x_i) = y_i \quad \text{and} \quad H'(x_i) = y_i' \; ; i = 0, 1, 2, \ldots n \tag{1}$$

$H(x)$ is called Hermite's interpolating polynomial.

Since there are $2n + 2$ conditions to be satisfied, $H(x)$ must be a polynomial of degree $\le 2n + 1$.

The required polynomial may be written as

$$H(x) = \sum_{i=0}^{n} u_i(x)\, y_i + \sum_{i=0}^{n} v_i(x)\, y_i' \qquad \ldots(2)$$

where $u_i(x)$ and $v_i(x)$ are polynomials in x of degree $\le (2n + 1)$ and satisfy

$$(i)\ u_i(x_j) = \begin{Bmatrix} 0, & i \neq j \\ 1, & i = j \end{Bmatrix} \quad ...(3\ (i))$$

$$(ii)\ v_i(x_j) = 0 \quad \forall\ i, j \quad ...(3\ (ii))$$

$$(iii)\ u_i'(x_j) = 0 \quad \forall\ i, j \quad ...(3\ (iii))$$

$$(iv)\ v_i'(x_j) = \begin{Bmatrix} 0, & i \neq j \\ 1, & i = j \end{Bmatrix} \quad ...(3\ (iv))$$

Using the Lagrange fundamental polynomials $L_i(x)$, we choose

$$u_i(x) = A_i(x)\ [L_i(x)]^2$$

and

$$v_i(x) = B_i(x)\ [L_i(x)]^2 \quad ...(4)$$

where $L_i(x)$ is defined as

$$L_i(x) = \frac{(x - x_0)(x - x_1) \ldots (x - x_{i-1})(x - x_{i+1}) \ldots (x - x_n)}{(x_i - x_0)(x_i - x_1) \ldots (x_i - x_{i-1})(x_i - x_{i+1}) \ldots (x_i - x_n)}$$

Since $L_i^2(x)$ is a polynomial of degree $2n$, $A_i(x)$ and $B_i(x)$ must be linear polynomials.

Let $\quad A_i(x) = a_i x + b_i$

and $\quad B_i(x) = c_i x + d_i$ so that from (4),

$$u_i(x) = (a_i x + b_i)\ [L_i(x)]^2$$

$$v_i(x) = (c_i x + d_i)\ [L_i(x)]^2 \quad ...(5)$$

using conditions $3(i)$ and $3(ii)$ in (5), we get

$$a_i x + b_i = 1 \quad ...(6\ (i))$$

and

$$c_i x + d_i = 0 \quad ...(6\ (ii)) \quad |\ \text{since } [L_i(x_i)]^2 = 1$$

Again, using conditions 3 (iii) and 3 (iv) in (5), we get

$$a_i + 2L_i'(x_i) = 0 \quad ...(6\ (iii))$$

and

$$c_i = 1 \quad ...(6\ (iv))$$

From equations 6 (i), 6 (ii), 6 (iii) and 6 (iv), we deduce

$$\left.\begin{aligned} a_i &= -\ 2L_i'(x_i) \\ b_i &= 1 + 2x_i L_i'(x_i) \\ c_i &= 1 \\ \text{and} \quad d_i &= -\ x_i \end{aligned}\right\} \quad ...(7)$$

Hence, from (5),

$$u_i(x) = [-\ 2x\ L_i'(x_i) + 1 + 2x_i L_i'(x_i)]\ [L_i(x)]^2$$

$$= [1 - 2(x - x_i)\ L_i'(x_i)]\ [L_i(x)]^2$$

and

$$v_i(x) = (x - x_i)\ [L_i(x)]^2$$

Therefore from (2),

$$\boxed{H(x) = \sum_{i=0}^{n} [1 - 2(x - x_i)\ L_i'(x_i)]\ [L_i(x)]^2\ y_i + \sum_{i=0}^{n} (x - x_i)\ [L_i(x)]^2\ y_i'}$$

which is the required *Hermite's interpolation formula.*

EXAMPLES

Example 1. *Apply Hermite's interpolation formula to find a cubic polynomial which meets the following specifications.*

x_i	y_i	y_i'
0	0	0
1	1	1

Sol. Hermite interpolation formula is

$$H(x) = \sum_{i=0}^{1} [1 - 2(x - x_i) L_i'(x_i)] [L_i(x)]^2 y_i + \sum_{i=0}^{1} (x - x_i) [L_i(x)]^2 y_i'$$

$$= [1 - 2(x - x_0) L_0'(x_0)] [L_0(x)]^2 y_0 + [1 - 2(x - x_1) L_1'(x_1)] [L_1(x)]^2 y_1 + (x - x_0) [L_0(x)]^2 y_0' + (x - x_1) [L_1(x)]^2 y_1' \quad ...(1)$$

Now, $$L_0(x) = \frac{x - x_1}{x_0 - x_1} = \frac{x - 1}{0 - 1} = 1 - x$$

$$L_1(x) = \frac{x - x_0}{x_1 - x_0} = \frac{x - 0}{1 - 0} = x$$

$\therefore$ $L_0'(x) = -1$ and $L_1'(x) = 1$

Hence, $L_0'(x_0) = -1$ and $L_1'(x_1) = 1$

$\therefore$ From (1),

$$H(x) = [1 - 2(x - 0)(-1)] [(1 - x)^2 (0)] + [1 - 2(x - 1)(1)] x^2 (1) + (x - 0)(1 - x)^2 (0) + (x - 1) x^2 (1)$$

$$= x^2 - 2x^2(x - 1) + x^2(x - 1) = 2x^2 - x^3.$$

Example 2. *Apply Hermite's formula to find a polynomial which meets these specifications*

x_k	y_k	y_k'
0	0	0
1	1	0
2	0	0

Sol. Hermite's interpolation formula is

$$H(x) = \sum_{i=0}^{2} [1 - 2(x - x_i) L_i'(x_i)] [L_i(x)]^2 y_i + \sum_{i=0}^{2} (x - x_i) [L_i(x)]^2 y_i'$$

$$= [1 - 2(x - x_0) L_0'(x_0)] [L_0(x)]^2 y_0 + [1 - 2(x - x_1) L_1'(x_1)] [L_1(x)]^2 y_1 + [1 - 2(x - x_2) L_2'(x_2)] [L_2(x)]^2 y_2 + (x - x_0) [L_0(x)]^2 y_0' + (x - x_1) [L_1(x)]^2 y_1' + (x - x_2) [L_2(x)]^2 y_2' \quad ...(1)$$

Now, $$L_0(x) = \frac{(x - x_1)(x - x_2)}{(x_0 - x_1)(x_0 - x_2)} = \frac{(x - 1)(x - 2)}{(0 - 1)(0 - 2)} = \frac{1}{2}(x^2 - 3x + 2)$$

$$L_1(x) = \frac{(x - x_0)(x - x_2)}{(x_1 - x_0)(x_1 - x_2)} = \frac{(x - 0)(x - 2)}{(1 - 0)(1 - 2)} = 2x - x^2$$

$$L_2(x) = \frac{(x - x_0)(x - x_1)}{(x_2 - x_0)(x_2 - x_1)} = \frac{(x - 0)(x - 1)}{(2 - 0)(2 - 1)} = \frac{1}{2}(x^2 - x)$$

$\therefore$ $$L_0'(x) = \frac{2x - 3}{2}, \quad L_1'(x) = 2 - 2x, \; L_2'(x) = \frac{2x - 1}{2}$$

Hence, $$L_0'(x_0) = -\frac{3}{2}, L_1'(x_1) = 0, \quad L_2'(x_2) = \frac{3}{2}$$

$\therefore$ From (1),

$$H(x) = \left[1 - 2(x - 0)\left(-\frac{3}{2}\right)\right]\frac{1}{4}(x^2 - 3x + 2)^2 (0) + [1 - 2(x - 1)(0)](2x - x^2)^2 (1)$$

$$+ \left[1 - 2(x - 2)\left(\frac{3}{2}\right)\right]\frac{1}{4}(x^2 - x)^2 (0) + (x - 0)\frac{1}{4}(x^2 - 3x + 2)^2 (0)$$

$$+ (x - 1)(2x - x^2)^2 (0) + (x - 2)\frac{1}{4}(x^2 - x)^2 (0)$$

$$= (2x - x^2)^2 = x^4 - 4x^3 + 4x^2.$$

Example 3. *A switching path between parallel railroad tracks is to be a cubic polynomial joining positions (0, 0) and (4, 2) and tangent to the lines y = 0 and y = 2 as shown in the figure. Apply Hermite's interpolation formula to obtain this polynomial.*

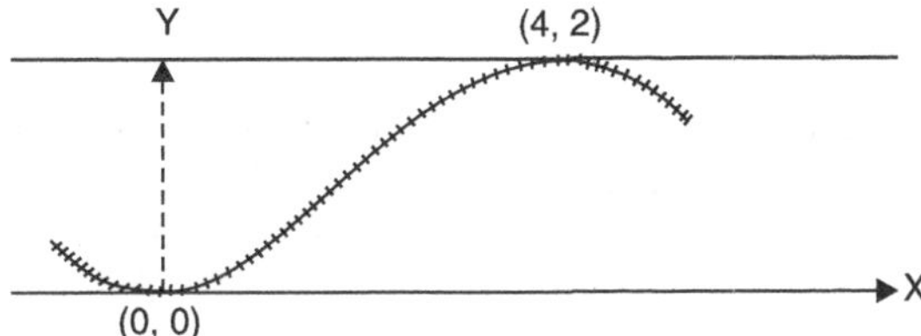

Sol. Since tangents are parallel to X-axis, $y' = 0$ in both the cases.

$\therefore$ We have the table of values,

x	y	y'
0	0	0
4	2	0

Hermite interpolation formula is

$$H(x) = \sum_{i=0}^{1} [1 - 2(x - x_i) L_i'(x_i)][L_i(x)]^2 y_i + \sum_{i=0}^{1} (x - x_i)[L_i(x)]^2 y_i' \qquad ...(1)$$

Now, $$L_0(x) = \frac{x - x_1}{x_0 - x_1} = \frac{x - 4}{0 - 4} = 1 - \frac{x}{4}$$

$$L_1(x) = \frac{x - x_0}{x_1 - x_0} = \frac{x - 0}{4 - 0} = \frac{x}{4}$$

$\therefore$ $$L_0'(x) = -\frac{1}{4} \text{ and } L_1'(x) = \frac{1}{4}$$

Hence, $$L_0'(x_0) = -\frac{1}{4} \text{ and } L_1'(x_1) = \frac{1}{4}$$

$$\therefore \text{ From (1), } H(x) = \left[1 - 2(x-0)\left(-\frac{1}{4}\right)\right]\left(1-\frac{x}{4}\right)^2 (0) + \left[1-2(x-4)\left(\frac{1}{4}\right)\right]\left(\frac{x}{4}\right)^2 (2)$$

$$+ (x-0)\left(1-\frac{x}{4}\right)^2 (0) + (x-4)\left(\frac{x}{4}\right)^2 (0)$$

$$= \left[1-\left(\frac{x-4}{2}\right)\right]\frac{x^2}{8} = \frac{(6-x)x^2}{16} = \frac{1}{16}(6x^2 - x^3).$$

ASSIGNMENT

1. Apply Hermite's interpolation formula to find $f(x)$ at $x = 0.5$ which meets the following requirement :

x_i	$f(x_i)$	$f'(x_i)$
– 1	1	– 5
0	1	1
1	3	7

Also find $f(-0.5)$.

2. Apply Hermite's interpolating formula to obtain a polynomial of degree 4 for the following data :

x_i	y_i	y_i'
0	1	0
1	0	0
2	9	24

3. Apply Hermite's formula to find a polynomial which meets the following specifications :

x_i	y_i	y_i'
– 1	– 1	0
0	0	0
1	1	0

4. Apply osculating interpolation formula to find a polynomial which meets the following requirements :

x_i	y_i	y_i'
0	1	0
1	0	0
2	9	0

5. Apply Hermite's formula to interpolate for sin 1.05 from the following data :

x	$\sin x$	$\cos x$
1.00	0.84147	0.54030
1.10	0.89121	0.45360

6. Find $y = f(x)$ by Hermite's interpolation from the table:

x_i	y_i	y_i'
− 1	1	− 5
0	1	1
1	3	7

Compute y_2 and y_2'.

7. Compute $\sqrt{e}$ by Hermite's formula for the function $f(x) = e^x$ at the points 0 and 1. Compare the value with the value obtained by using Lagrange's interpolation.

8. Show that

$$f\left(\frac{a+b}{2}\right) = \frac{f(a)+f(b)}{2} + \frac{(b-a)\,[f'(a)-f'(b)]}{8}$$

by Hermite's interpolation.

9. Apply Hermite's interpolation to find $f(1.05)$ given:

x	f	f'
1	1.0	0.5
1.1	1.04881	0.47673

10. Apply Hermite's interpolation to find log 2.05 given that

x	$\log x$	$\frac{1}{x}$
2.0	0.69315	0.5
2.1	0.74194	0.47619

11. Determine the Hermite polynomial of degree 5 which fits the following data and hence find an approximate value of $\log_e 2.7$.

x	$y = \log_e x$	$y' = \frac{1}{x}$
2.0	0.69315	0.5
2.5	0.91629	0.4
3.0	1.09861	0.33333

12. Using Hermite's interpolation formula, estimate the value of l_n (3.2) from the following table :

x	3	3.5	4.0
$y = l_n(x)$	1.09861	1.25276	1.38629
$y' = \frac{1}{x}$	0.33333	0.28571	0.25000

13. (*i*) Construct the Hermite interpolation polynomial that fits the data:

x	$f(x)$	$f'(x)$
1	7.389	14.778
2	54.598	109.196

Estimate the value of $f(1.5)$.

(*ii*) Consider the cubic polynomial

$$P(x) = c_0 + c_1x + c_2x^2 + c_3x^3.$$

Fit the data in problem 13(*i*) and find P(x). Are these polynomials different? Comment.

14. (*i*) Construct the Hermite interpolation polynomial that fits the data

x	$f(x)$	$f'(x)$
2	29	50
3	105	105

Interpolate $f(x)$ at $x = 2.5$.

(*ii*) Fit the cubic polynomial $P(x) = c_0 + c_1x + c_2x^2 + c_3x^3$ to the data given in problem 14(*i*). Are these polynomials same?

15. (*i*) Construct the Hermite interpolation polynomial that fits the data:

x	$f(x)$	$f'(x)$
0	0	1
0.5	0.4794	0.8776
1.0	0.8415	0.5403

Estimate the value of $f(0.75)$.

(*ii*) Construct the Hermite interpolation polynomial that fits the data:

x	$y(x)$	$y'(x)$
0	4	− 5
1	− 6	− 14
2	− 22	− 17

Interpolate $y(x)$ at $x = 0.5$ and 1.5.

16. Obtain the unique polynomial $p(x)$ of degree 3 or less corresponding to a function $f(x)$ where $f(0) = 1, f'(0) = 2, f(1) = 5, f'(1) = 4$.

Answers

1. $f(x) = 2x^4 - x^2 + x + 1, \frac{11}{8}, \frac{3}{8}$.

2. $x^4 - 2x^2 + 1$.

3. $\frac{1}{2}(5x^3 - 3x^5)$.

4. $x^2 (x^2 - 4x + 4)$.

5. 0.86742375.

6. $1 + x - x^2 + 2x^4, y_2 = 31, y_2' = 61$

7. $(1 + 3x)(1 - x)^2 + (2 - x)ex^2$; 1.644 ; 1.859.

9. 1.02470.

10. 0.71784.

11. 0.993252.

12. 1.16314.

13. (*i*) $29.556\, x^3 - 85.793\, x^2 + 97.696\, x - 34.07$; 19.19125.

(*ii*) Same polynomial as in (*i*).

14. (*i*) $3x^3 + 5x^2 - 6x - 3$, 60.125.

(*ii*) Same polynomial as in (1).

15. (*i*) $0.0068\, x^5 + 0.002\, x^4 - 0.1671\, x^3 - 0.0002\, x^2 + x$; 0.6816.

(*ii*) $x^3 - 6x^2 - 5x + 4$; 0.125, − 13.625.

16. $p(x) = -2x^3 + 4x^2 + 2x + 1$.

4.34. SPLINE INTERPOLATION [*G.B.T.U. (MCA) 2010*]

When computers were not available, the draftsman used a device to draw a smooth curve through a given set of points such that the slope and curvature are also continuous along the curve *i.e.*, $f(x)$, $f'(x)$ and $f''(x)$ are continuous on the curve. Such a device was called a **spline** and plotting of the curve was called **spline fitting.**

The given interval $[a, b]$ is subdivided into n subintervals $[x_0, x_1]$, $[x_1, x_2]$,......, $[x_{n-1}, x_n]$ where $a = x_0 < x_1 < x_2 < \ldots\ldots < x_n = b$. The nodes (knots) $x_1, x_2, \ldots\ldots, x_{n-1}$ are called internal nodes.

4.35. SPLINE FUNCTION

A spline function of degree n with knots (nodes) x_i, $i = 0, 1, \ldots\ldots, n$ is a function $F(x)$ satisfying the properties

(*i*) $F(x_i) = f(x_i)$; $i = 0, 1, \ldots\ldots, n$.

(*ii*) on each subinterval $[x_{i-1}, x_i]$, $1 \le i \le n$, $F(x)$ is a polynomial in x of degree atmost n.

(*iii*) $F(x)$ and its first $(n-1)$ derivatives are continuous on $[a, b]$

(*iv*) $F(x)$ is a polynomial of degree one for $x < a$ and $x > b$.

4.36. CUBIC SPLINE INTERPOLATION [*G.B.T.U. (MCA) SUM 2009*]

A cubic spline satisfies the following properties:

(*i*) $F(x_i) = f_i$, $i = 0, 1, \ldots\ldots, n$

(*ii*) On each subinterval $[x_{i-1}, x_i]$, $1 \le i \le n$, $F(x)$ is a third degree polynomial.

(*iii*) $F(x)$, $F'(x)$ and $F''(x)$ are continuous on $[a, b]$.

Since $F(x)$ is piecewise cubic, polynomial $F''(x)$ is a linear function of x in the interval $x_{i-1} \le x \le x_i$ and hence can be written as

$$F''(x) = \frac{x_i - x}{x_i - x_{i-1}} F''(x_{i-1}) + \frac{x - x_{i-1}}{x_i - x_{i-1}} F''(x_i) \qquad \ldots(1)$$

For equally spaced intervals,

$$x_i - x_{i-1} = h \; ; \; 1 \le i \le n$$

From (1), $$F''(x) = \frac{1}{h} [(x_i - x) F''(x_{i-1}) + (x - x_{i-1}) F''(x_i)] \qquad \ldots(2)$$

Integrating equation (2) twice, we get

$$F(x) = \frac{1}{h}\left[\frac{(x_i - x)^3}{6} F''(x_{i-1}) + \frac{(x - x_{i-1})^3}{6} F''(x_i)\right]$$
$$+ c_1(x_i - x) + c_2(x - x_{i-1}) \qquad \ldots(3)$$

where c_1 and c_2 are arbitrary constants which are to be determined by conditions

$$F(x_i) = f_i \; ; \; i = 0, 1, 2, \ldots\ldots, n$$

Then, $$f_i = \frac{1}{h}\left[\frac{h^3}{6} F''(x_i)\right] + c_2 h$$

$$\Rightarrow \qquad c_2 = \frac{f_i}{h} - \frac{h}{6} F''(x_i) \qquad \text{...(A)}$$

and
$$f_{i-1} = \frac{1}{h}\left[\frac{h^3}{6} F''(x_{i-1})\right] + c_1 h$$

$$\Rightarrow \qquad c_1 = \frac{f_{i-1}}{h} - \frac{h}{6} F''(x_{i-1}) \qquad \text{...(B)}$$

Putting the values of c_1 and c_2 in equation (3), we get

$$F(x) = \frac{1}{h}\left[\frac{(x_i - x)^3}{6} F''(x_{i-1}) + \frac{(x - x_{i-1})^3}{6} F''(x_i)\right.$$
$$\left. + (x_i - x)\left\{f_{i-1} - \frac{h^2}{6} F''(x_{i-1})\right\} + (x - x_{i-1})\left\{f_i - \frac{h^2}{6} F''(x_i)\right\}\right] \qquad \text{...(4)}$$

Denoting $F''(x_i) = M_i$, we have

$$F(x) = \frac{1}{6h}[(x_i - x)^3 M_{i-1} + (x - x_{i-1})^3 M_i$$
$$+ (x_i - x)\{6f_{i-1} - h^2 M_{i-1}\} + (x - x_{i-1})\{6f_i - h^2 M_i\}] \qquad \text{...(5)}$$

Now, $F'(x) = \frac{1}{6h}[-3(x_i - x)^2 M_{i-1} + 3(x - x_{i-1})^2 M_i + 6(f_i - f_{i-1}) + h^2 M_{i-1} - h^2 M_i]$ ...(6)

Now, we require that the derivative $F'(x)$ be continuous at $x = x_i \pm \varepsilon$ as $\varepsilon \to 0$

(*i*)
$$F'(x_{i-1} + 0) = \frac{1}{6h}[-3h^2 M_{i-1} + h^2 M_{i-1} - h^2 M_i + 6(f_i - f_{i-1})]$$
$$= \frac{1}{6h}[-h^2 M_i - 2h^2 M_{i-1} + 6(f_i - f_{i-1})] \qquad \text{...(7)}$$

Again in the interval $[x_{i-2}, x_{i-1}]$,

$$F'(x) = \frac{1}{6h}[-3(x_{i-1} - x)^2 M_{i-2} + 3(x - x_{i-2})^2 M_{i-1} + 6(f_{i-1} - f_{i-2})$$
$$+ h^2 M_{i-2} - h^2 M_{i-1}] \qquad \text{...(8)}$$

(*ii*) From (8),

$$F'(x_{i-1} - 0) = \frac{1}{6h}[3h^2 M_{i-1} + 6f_{i-1} - 6f_{i-2} + h^2 M_{i-2} - h^2 M_{i-1}]$$
$$= \frac{1}{6h}[2h^2 M_{i-1} + h^2 M_{i-2} + 6f_{i-1} - 6f_{i-2}] \qquad \text{...(9)}$$

As $F'(x)$ is continuous at x_{i-1},

$$\therefore \qquad F'(x_{i-1} - 0) = F'(x_{i-1} + 0)$$

$$\therefore \qquad 2h^2 M_{i-1} + h^2 M_{i-2} + 6f_{i-1} - 6f_{i-2} = -h^2 M_i - 2h^2 M_{i-1} + 6f_i - 6f_{i-1}$$

or
$$h^2 (M_i + 4M_{i-1} + M_{i-2}) = 6(f_i - 2f_{i-1} + f_{i-2})$$

For the interval $[x_{i-1}, x_i]$,

we have $$h^2 [M_{i+1} + 4M_i + M_{i-1}] = 6(f_{i+1} - 2f_i + f_{i-1}) \quad ...(10)$$

where $i = 1, 2, ..., n$

This gives a system of $(n - 1)$ linear equations with $(n + 1)$ unknowns $M_0, M_1, ..., M_n$.

Two additional conditions may be taken in one of the following forms:

(*i*) $\mathbf{M_0 = M_n = 0}$ **(Natural spline)**

(*ii*) $\mathbf{M_0 = M_n, M_1 = M_{n+1}, f_0 = f_n, f_1 = f_{n+1}, h_1 = h_{n+1}}$

A spline satisfying above conditions is called a **periodic spline.**

(*iii*) For a **non-periodic spline,** we use the conditions

$F'(a) = f'(a) = f_0'$ and $F'(b) = f'(b) = f_n'$

Splines usually provide a better approximation of the behaviour of functions that have abrupt local changes. Further, splines perform better than higher order polynomial approximations.

4.37. STEPS TO OBTAIN CUBIC SPLINE FOR GIVEN DATA

Step 1. For interval (x_{i-1}, x_i), Write cubic spline as

$$F(x) = \frac{1}{6h} [(x_i - x)^3 M_{i-1} + (x - x_{i-1})^3 M_i + (x_i - x) \{6f_{i-1} - h^2M_{i-1}\} + (x - x_{i-1})\{6f_i - h^2M_i\}]$$

Step 2. If not given, choose $M_0 = 0 = M_3$ (for the interval $0 \le x \le 3$)

Step 3. For $i = 1, 2, ..., n$, choose values of M_1 and M_2 s.t.

$$h^2[M_{i+1} + 4M_i + M_{i-1}] = 6[f_{i+1} - 2f_i + f_{i-1}]$$

exists for two sub intervals $0 \le x \le 1$ and $1 \le x \le 2$ respectively, where h is the interval of differencing.

Step 4. Find $F(x)$ for different sub-intervals and tabulate at last.

EXAMPLES

Example 1. *Obtain the cubic spline for the following data:*

x:	*0*	*1*	*2*	*3*
y:	*2*	*– 6*	*– 8*	*2.*

Sol. For the interval (x_{i-1}, x_i), the cubic spline is

$$F(x) = \frac{1}{6h} [(x_i - x)^3 M_{i-1} + (x - x_{i-1})^3 M_i + (x_i - x) \{6f_{i-1} - h^2M_{i-1}\} + (x - x_{i-1}) \{6f_i - h^2M_i\}]$$

With $M_0 = M_3 = 0$ and for $i = 1, 2, ..., n$; we also have

$$h^2[M_{i-1} + 4 M_i + M_{i+1}] = 6 [f_{i+1} - 2f_i + f_{i-1}]$$

Here $h = 1$

$\therefore$ $\quad M_0 + 4M_1 + M_2 = 6(f_2 - 2f_1 + f_0)$ | For $0 \le x \le 1$

and $\quad M_1 + 4M_2 + M_3 = 6(f_3 - 2f_2 + f_1)$ | For $1 \le x \le 2$

Here, $\quad M_2 + 4M_1 + M_0 = 6[- 8 - 2(- 6) + 2] = 36$

and $\quad M_3 + 4M_2 + M_1 = 6 [2 - 2 (- 8) + (- 6) = 72$

Putting $M_0 = M_3 = 0$, we get

$$M_2 + 4M_1 = 36$$
$$4M_2 + M_1 = 72$$

Solving, we get $M_1 = 4.8, M_2 = 16.8$

Hence for $0 \le x \le 1$,

$$F(x) = \frac{1}{6}[(1-x)^3 M_0 + (x-0)^3 M_1 + (1-x)(6f_0 - M_0) + (x-0)(6f_1 - M_1)]$$

$$= \frac{1}{6}[x^3(4.8) + (1-x)(12) + x(-36-4.8)] = 0.8x^3 - 8.8x + 2$$

For $1 \le x \le 2$,

$$F(x) = \frac{1}{6}[(2-x)^3 M_1 + (x-1)^3 M_2 + (2-x)\{6f_1 - M_1\} + (x-1)\{6f_2 - M_2\}]$$

$$= \frac{1}{6}[(2-x)^3(4.8) + (x-1)^3(16.8) + (2-x)\{-36-4.8\} + (x-1)\{-48-16.8\}]$$

$$= 2x^3 - 3.6x^2 - 5.2x + 0.8$$

For $2 \le x \le 3$,

$$F(x) = \frac{1}{6}[(3-x)^3 M_2 + (x-2)^3 M_3 + (3-x)\{6f_2 - h^2M_2\} + (x-2)\{6f_3 - h^2M_3\}]$$

$$= \frac{1}{6}[(3-x)^3(16.8) + (3-x)\{-48-16.8\} + (x-2)(12)] \quad | \text{ Using } M_3 = 0$$

$$\Rightarrow \quad F(x) = \frac{1}{6}[(27 - x^3 - 27x + 9x^2)(16.8) - 64.8(3-x) + 12x - 24]$$

$$= \frac{1}{6}[-16.8x^3 + 151.2x^2 - 376.8x + 235.2]$$

$$= -2.8x^3 + 25.2x^2 - 62.8x + 39.2$$

Therefore cubic splines in different intervals are tabulated as below:

Interval	*Cubic spline*
[0, 1]	$0.8x^3 - 8.8x + 2$
[1, 2]	$2x^3 - 3.6x^2 - 5.2x + 0.8$
[2, 3]	$-2.8x^3 + 25.2x^2 - 62.8x + 39.2$.

Example 2. *Obtain cubic spline for every subinterval from the given data:*

x:	*0*	*1*	*2*	*3*
f(x):	*1*	*2*	*33*	*244*

with the end conditions $M_0 = M_3 = 0$. Hence find an estimate of f(2.5).

Sol. For the inerval (x_{i-1}, x_i), the cubic spline is

$$F(x) = \frac{1}{6h}[(x_i - x)^3 M_{i-1} + (x - x_{i-1})^3 M_i + (x_i - x)\{6f_{i-1} - h^2M_{i-1}\} + (x - x_{i-1})\{6f_i - h^2M_i\}] \quad ...(1)$$

For $i = 1, 2, \ldots\ldots, n$, we have

$$h^2 [M_{i-1} + 4M_i + M_{i+1}] = 6[f_{i+1} - 2f_i + f_{i-1}] \qquad \ldots(2)$$

and $$M_0 = M_3 = 0 \qquad \ldots(3)$$

Here $h = 1$

$\therefore$ From (2), For $0 \le x \le 1$,

$$M_0 + 4M_1 + M_2 = 6(f_2 - 2f_1 + f_0) \qquad \ldots(4)$$

and for $1 \le x \le 2$,

$$M_1 + 4M_2 + M_3 = 6(f_3 - 2f_2 + f_1) \qquad \ldots(5)$$

From (4), we get

$$M_0 + 4M_1 + M_2 = 6[33 - 4 + 1] = 180 \qquad \ldots(6)$$

and $$M_1 + 4M_2 + M_3 = 6[244 - 66 + 2] = 1080 \qquad \ldots(7)$$

Using (3), equations (6) and (7) reduce to

$$4M_1 + M_2 = 180 \quad \text{and} \quad M_1 + 4M_2 = 1080$$

Solving, we get

$$M_1 = -24 \text{ and } M_2 = 276 \qquad \ldots(8)$$

Hence **for $0 \le x \le 1$,**

$$F(x) = \frac{1}{6} [(1 - x)^3 M_0 + (x - 0)^3 M_1 + (1 - x) \{6f_0 - M_0\} + (x - 0) \{6f_1 - M_1\}]$$

$| \because h = 1$

$$= \frac{1}{6} [x^3 (-24) + (1 - x) \{6\} + x(12 + 24)]$$

$$= \frac{1}{6} [-24x^3 + 6 - 6x + 36x] = -4x^3 + 5x + 1$$

For $1 \le x \le 2$,

$$F(x) = \frac{1}{6} [(2 - x)^3 M_1 + (x - 1)^3 M_2 + (2 - x) \{6f_1 - M_1\} + (x - 1) \{6f_2 - M_2\}]$$

$$= \frac{1}{6} [(2 - x)^3 (-24) + (x - 1)^3 (276) + (2 - x) (12 + 24) + (x - 1) \{198 - 276\}]$$

$$= \frac{1}{6} [(2 - x)^3 (-24) + 276 (x - 1)^3 + 36(2 - x) - 78(x - 1)]$$

$$= 50x^3 - 162 x^2 + 167 x - 53$$

For $2 \le x \le 3$,

$$F(x) = \frac{1}{6} [(3 - x)^3 M_2 + (x - 2)^3 M_3 + (3 - x) (6f_2 - M_2) + (x - 2) (6f_3 - M_3)]$$

$$= \frac{1}{6} [(3 - x)^3 (276) + (x - 2)^3 (0) + (3 - x) (198 - 276) + (x - 2) \{(6 \times 244) - 0\}]$$

$$= \frac{1}{6}[(27 - x^3 - 27x + 9x^2)(276) + (3 - x)(-78) + 1464(x - 2)]$$

$$= -46x^3 + 414x^2 - 985x + 715$$

Therefore, the cubic splines in different intervals are tabulated as below:

Interval	*Cubic Spline*
[0, 1]	$-4x^3 + 5x + 1$
[1, 2]	$50x^3 - 162x^2 + 167x - 53$
[2, 3]	$-46x^3 + 414x^2 - 985x + 715$

An estimate at $x = 2.5$ is

$$f(2.5) = -46(2.5)^3 + 414(2.5)^2 - 985(2.5) + 715 = 121.25.$$

ASSIGNMENT

1. Fit the following four points by the cubic splines:

x	1	2	3	4
y	1	5	11	8

Use the end conditions $y''(1) = 0 = y''(4)$. Hence compute $y(1.5.)$

2. Obtain (1.5) from the following data using cubic spline.

x	1	2	3
y	– 8	– 1	18

3. Obtain the cubic spline approximation valid in [3, 4] for the function given in the tabular form

x	1	2	3	4
$f(x)$	3	10	29	65

Under the natural spline conditions : M(1) = 0 = M(4)

4. Obtain the cubic spline fit for the data :

x	0	1	2	3
$f(x)$	1	4	10	8

under the end conditions $f''(0) = 0 = f''(3)$ and valid in the interval [1, 2].
Hence obtain the estimate of $f(1.5)$.

5. Find the natural cubic spline that fits the data :

x	1	2	3	4
$f(x)$	0	1	0	0

6. Evaluate

$$I = \int_0^1 \frac{1}{1+x}\, dx \text{ using the cubic spline method.}$$

[**Hint :** Use the table of values:

x	0	$\frac{1}{3}$	$\frac{2}{3}$	1
$f(x)$	1	$\frac{3}{4}$	$\frac{3}{5}$	$\frac{1}{2}$

Answers

1. $M_1 = \frac{34}{5}, \quad M_2 = -\frac{76}{5}$

$$F(x) = \begin{cases} \dfrac{17x^3 - 51x^2 + 94x - 45}{15}, & 1 \le x \le 2 \\ \dfrac{-55x^3 + 381x^2 - 770x + 531}{15}, & 2 \le x \le 3 \\ \dfrac{38x^3 - 456x^2 + 1741x - 1980}{15}, & 3 \le x \le 4 \end{cases}$$

$F(1.5) = 2.575$

2. $F(x) = 3(x-1)^3 + 4x - 12$; $F(1.5) = -5.625$

3. $M_1 = \frac{62}{5}, \quad M_2 = \frac{112}{5}, \quad F(x) = \frac{-56x^3 + 672x^2 - 2092x + 2175}{15}$

4. $M_1 = 8, \quad M_2 = -14, \quad F(x) = \frac{-11x^3 + 45x^2 - 40x + 18}{3}$; $F(1.5) = 7.375$

5. $M_1 = -\frac{18}{5}, \quad M_2 = \frac{12}{5}$

$$F(x) = \begin{cases} \dfrac{-3x^3 + 9x^2 - x - 5}{5}, & 1 \le x \le 2 \\ \dfrac{5x^3 - 39x^2 + 95x - 69}{5}, & 2 \le x \le 3 \\ \dfrac{-2x^3 + 24x^2 - 94x + 120}{5}, & 3 \le x \le 4 \end{cases}$$

6. $$F(x) = \begin{cases} 0.63x^3 - 0.82x + 1 ; & 0 \le x \le \frac{1}{3} \\ -0.45x^3 + 1.08x^2 - 1.18x + 1.04 ; & \frac{1}{3} \le x \le \frac{2}{3} \\ -0.18x^3 + 0.54x^2 - 0.82x + 0.96 ; & \frac{2}{3} \le x \le 1 \end{cases}$$

$I = 0.695$

❑❑❑

5

Curve-Fitting and Approximation

5.1. CURVE FITTING

Let there be two variables x and y which give us a set of n pairs of numerical values (x_1, y_1), (x_2, y_2),......., (x_n, y_n). In order to have an approximate idea about the relationship of these two variables, we plot these n paired points on a graph thus, we get a diagram showing the simultaneous variation in values of both the variables called *scatter or dot diagram.* From scatter diagram, we get only an approximate non-mathematical relation between two variables. Curve fitting means an exact relationship between two variables by algebraic equations, infact this relationship is the equation of the curve. Therefore, curve fitting means to form an equation of the curve from the given data. Curve fitting is considered of immense importance both from the point of view of theoretical and practical statistics.

Theoretically, it is useful in the study of correlation and regression. Practically, it enables us to represent the relationship between two variables by simple algebraic expressions *e.g.*, polynomials, exponential or logarithmic functions.

It is also used to estimate the values of one variable corresponding to the specified values of the other variable.

The constants occurring in the equation of approximate curve can be found by following methods :

(*i*) Graphical method (*ii*) Method of group averages

(*iii*) Method of least squares (*iv*) Method of moments.

Out of the above four methods, we will only discuss and study here *method of least squares.*

5.2. METHOD OF LEAST SQUARES

Method of least squares provides a unique set of values to the constants and hence suggests a curve of best fit to the given data.

Suppose we have m-paired observations (x_1, y_1), (x_2, y_2), ..., (x_m, y_m) of two variables x and y. It is required to fit a polynomial of degree n of the type

$$y = a + bx + cx^2 + \ldots\ldots + kx^n \qquad \ldots(1)$$

of these values. We have to determine the constants $a, b, c, \ldots, k$ such that it represents the curve of best fit of that degree.

In case $m = n$, we get in general a unique set of values satisfying the given system of equations.

But if $m > n$ then, we get m equations by putting different values of x and y in equation (1) and we want to find only the values of n constants. Thus there may be no such solution to satisfy all m equations.

Therefore we try to find out those values of $a, b, c, \ldots\ldots, k$ which satisfy all the equations as nearly as possible. We apply the method of least squares in such cases.

Putting $x_1, x_2, \ldots, x_m$ for x in (1), we get

$$y_1' = a + bx_1 + cx_1^2 + \ldots\ldots + kx_1^n$$
$$y_2' = a + bx_2 + cx_2^2 + \ldots\ldots + kx_2^n$$
$$\vdots \qquad \vdots$$
$$y_m' = a + bx_m + cx_m^2 + \ldots\ldots + kx_m^n$$

where $y_1', y_2', \ldots\ldots, y_m'$ are the expected values of y for $x = x_1, x_2, \ldots\ldots, x_m$ respectively. The values $y_1, y_2, \ldots\ldots, y_m$ are called observed values of y corresponding to $x = x_1, x_2, \ldots\ldots, x_m$ respectively.

The expected values are different from observed values, the difference $y_r - y_r'$ for different values of r are called *residuals*.

Introduce a new quantity U such that

$$U = \Sigma(y_r - y_r')^2 = \Sigma(y_r - a - bx_r - cx_r^2 - \ldots\ldots - kx_r^n)^2$$

The constants $a, b, c, \ldots\ldots, k$ are chosen in such a way that the sum of the squares of residuals is minimum.

Now the condition for U to be maximum or minimum is $\frac{\partial U}{\partial a} = 0 = \frac{\partial U}{\partial b} = \frac{\partial U}{\partial c} = \ldots\ldots = \frac{\partial U}{\partial k}$.

On simplifying these relations, we get

$$\Sigma y = ma + b\Sigma x + \ldots\ldots + k\Sigma x^n$$
$$\Sigma xy = a\Sigma x + b\Sigma x^2 + \ldots\ldots + k\ \Sigma x^{n+1}$$
$$\Sigma x^2 y = a\Sigma x^2 + b\Sigma x^3 + \ldots\ldots + k\ \Sigma x^{n+2}$$
$$\vdots \qquad \vdots$$
$$\Sigma x^n y = a\Sigma x^n + b\Sigma x^{n+1} + \ldots\ldots + k\ \Sigma x^{2n}$$

These are known as *Normal equations* and can be solved as simultaneous equations to give the values of the constants $a, b, c, \ldots\ldots, k$. These equations are $(n + 1)$ in number.

If we calculate the second order partial derivatives and these values are put, they give a positive value of the function, so U is minimum.

This method does not help us to choose the degree of the curve to be fitted but helps us in finding the values of the constants when the form of the curve has already been chosen.

5.3. FITTING A STRAIGHT LINE

Let (x_i, y_i), $i = 1, 2, \ldots\ldots, n$ be n sets of observations of related data and $y = a + bx$ ...(1) be the straight line to be fitted. The residual at $x = x_i$ is

$$E_i = y_i - f(x_i) = y_i - a - bx_i$$

Introduce a new quantity U such that

$$U = \sum_{i=1}^{n} E_i^2 = \sum_{i=1}^{n} (y_i - a - bx_i)^2$$

By the principle of Least squares, U is minimum

$$\therefore \quad \frac{\partial U}{\partial a} = 0 \quad \text{and} \quad \frac{\partial U}{\partial b} = 0$$

$$\therefore \quad 2\sum_{i=1}^{n} (y_i - a - bx_i)(-1) = 0 \quad \text{or} \quad \boxed{\Sigma y = na + b\Sigma x} \qquad ...(2)$$

and

$$2\sum_{i=1}^{n} (y_i - a - bx_i)(-x_i) = 0 \quad \text{or} \quad \boxed{\Sigma xy = a\Sigma x + b\Sigma x^2} \qquad ...(3)$$

Since x_i, y_i are known, equations (2) and (3) result two equations in a and b. Solving these, the best values for a and b can be known and hence equation (1).

Note. In case of change of origin,

if n is odd then, $$u = \frac{x - (\text{middle term})}{\text{interval } (h)}$$

but if n is even then $$u = \frac{x - (\text{mean of two middle terms})}{\frac{1}{2}(\text{interval})}.$$

5.4. ALGORITHM FOR FITTING A STRAIGHT LINE OF THE FORM y = a + bx FOR A GIVEN SET OF DATA POINTS

Step 01. Start of the program.
Step 02. Input no. of terms observ
Step 03. Input the array ax
Step 04. Input the array ay
Step 05. for i=0 to observ
Step 06. sum1+=x[i]
Step 07. sum2+=y[i]
Step 08. xy[i]=x[i]*y[i];
Step 09. sum3+=xy[i]
Step 10. End Loop i
Step 11. for i = 0 to observ
Step 12. x2[i]=x[i]*x[i]
Step 13. sum4+=x2[i]
Step 14. End of Loop i
Step 15. temp1=(sum2*sum4)-(sum3*sum1)
Step 16. a=temp1/((observ *sum4)-(sum1*sum1))
Step 17. b=(sum2-observ*a)/sum1
Step 18. Print output a,b
Step 19. Print "line is : y = a+bx"
Step 20. End of Program

5.5. FLOW CHART FOR FITTING A STRAIGHT LINE y = a + bx FOR A GIVEN SET OF DATA POINTS

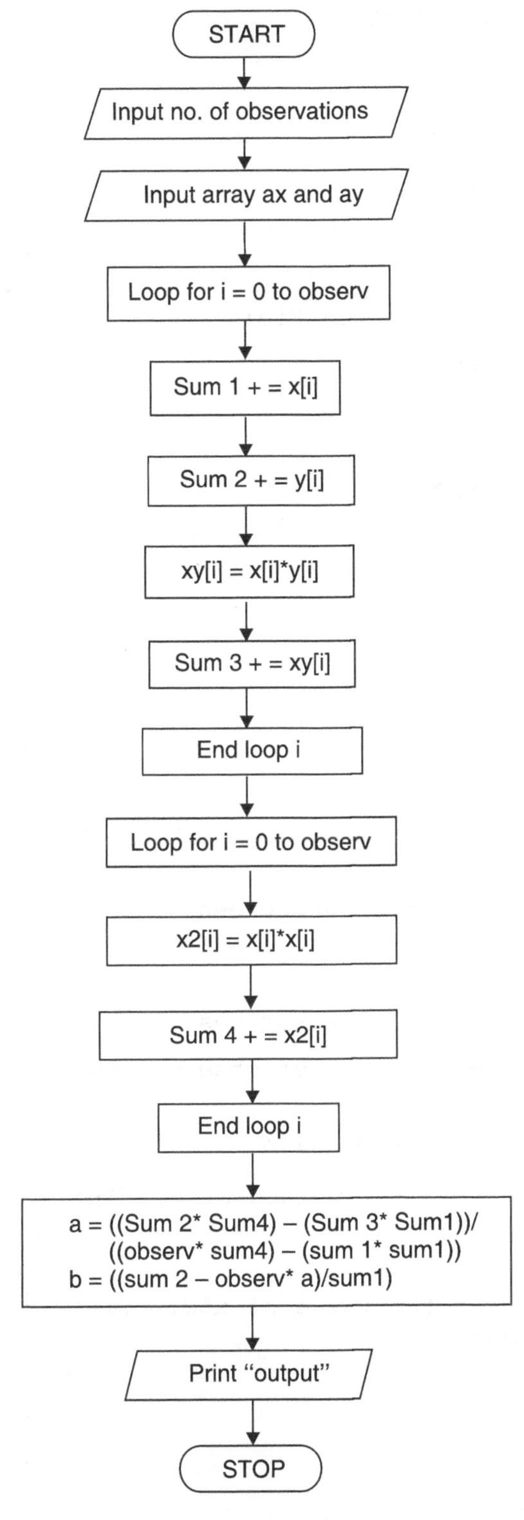

5.6. PROGRAM TO IMPLEMENT CURVE FITTING TO FIT A STRAIGHT LINE

```
//... HEADER FILE DECLARATION

# include <stdio.h>
# include <conio.h>
# include <math.h>

//... Main Execution Thread

void main()
     {
     //... Variable Declaration Field
     //... Integer Type

     int i=0;
     int observ;

     //... Floating Type
     float x[10];
     float y[10];
     float xy[10];
     float x2[10];
     float sum1=0.0;
     float sum2=0.0;
     float sum3=0.0;
     float sum4=0.0;

     //... Double Type
     double a;
     double b;
     //... Invoke Function Clear Screen
     clrscr ();
     //... Input Section

     //... Input Number of Observations

     printf("\n\n Enter the no. of observations - ");
     scanf("%d" ,&observ);
     //... Input Sequel For Array X

     printf("\n\n\n Enter the values of x - \n");
     for (;i<observ;i++)
     {
     printf("\n\n Enter the Value of x%d: ",i+1);
     scanf("%f" ,&x[i]);

     sum1 +=x[i];
```

```
}

//... Input Sequel For Array Y

printf("\n\n Enter the values of y - \n");
for(i=0;i<observ;i++)

{

printf("\n\n Enter the value of y%d:",i+1);

scanf("%f",&y[i]);

sum2+=y[i];

}

//... Processing and Calculation Section

for(i=0;i<observ;i++)

{
xy[i]=x[i]*y[i];

sum3 +=xy[i];

}

for(i=0;i<observ; i++)
{
x2[i]=x[i]*x[i];
sum4+ =x2[i];
}
a=(sum2*sum4-sum3*sum1)/(observ*sum4-sum1*sum1);

b=(sum2-observ*a)/sum1;
//... Output Section

printf("\n\n\n\n Equation of the STRAIGHT LINE");

printf("of the form y = a + b*x is:");
printf("\n\n\n \t\t\t Y = %.2f + (%.2f) X", a,b);

//... Invoke User Watch Halt Function

printf("\n\n\n Press Enter to Exit");
getch();
}
//... Termination of Main Execution Thread
```

EXAMPLES

Example 1. *By the method of least squares, find the straight line that best fits the following data :*

x : 1 2 3 4 5

y : 14 27 40 55 68.

Sol. Let the straight line of best fit be $y = a + bx$ ...(1)

Normal equations are $\Sigma y = ma + b\Sigma x$ ...(2)

and $\Sigma xy = a\Sigma x + b\Sigma x^2$ ...(3)

Here $m = 5$

Table is as below :

x	y	xy	x^2
1	14	14	1
2	27	54	4
3	40	120	9
4	55	220	16
5	68	340	25
$\Sigma x = 15$	$\Sigma y = 204$	$\Sigma xy = 748$	$\Sigma x^2 = 55$

Substituting in (2) and (3), we get

$$204 = 5a + 15b$$

$$748 = 15a + 55b$$

Solving, we get $a = 0$, $b = 13.6$

Hence required straight line is $\boxed{y = 13.6x}$

Example 2. *Fit a straight line to the following data :*

x : 0 1 2 3 4

y : 1 1.8 3.3 4.5 6.3.

Sol. Let the straight line obtained from the given data be $y = a + bx$ then the normal equations are

$$\Sigma y = ma + b\ \Sigma x \quad ...(1)$$

$$\Sigma xy = a\Sigma x + b\Sigma x^2 \quad ...(2)$$

Here $m = 5$

x	y	xy	x^2
0	1	0	0
1	1.8	1.8	1
2	3.3	6.6	4
3	4.5	13.5	9
4	6.3	25.2	16
$\Sigma x = 10$	$\Sigma y = 16.9$	$\Sigma xy = 47.1$	$\Sigma x^2 = 30$

From (1) and (2), $16.9 = 5a + 10b$

and $47.1 = 10a + 30b$

Solving, we get $a = 0.72, b = 1.33$

$\therefore$ Required line is $\boxed{y = 0.72 + 1.33\,x.}$

Example 3. *Fit a straight line to the following data regarding x as the independent variable :*

x :	1	2	3	4	5	6
y :	1200	900	600	200	110	50.

Sol. Let the equation of the straight line to be fitted be $y = a + bx$

Here $m = 6$

x	y	x^2	xy
1	1200	1	1200
2	900	4	1800
3	600	9	1800
4	200	16	800
5	110	25	550
6	50	36	300
$\Sigma x = 21$	$\Sigma y = 3060$	$\Sigma x^2 = 91$	$\Sigma xy = 6450$

From normal equations, we get

$$3060 = 6a + 21b,\ 6450 = 21a + 91b$$

Solving, we get $a = 1361.97, b = -243.42$

$\therefore$ Required line is

$$\boxed{y = 1361.97 - 243.42\,x.}$$

Example 4. *Show that the line of fit to the following data is given by* $y = 0.7x + 11.285$:

x :	0	5	10	15	20	25
y :	12	15	17	22	24	30.

Sol. Since m is even,

Let $x_0 = 12.5 \quad h = 5 \quad y_0 = 20$ (say)

Then let, $u = \dfrac{x - 12.5}{2.5}$ and $v = y - 20$

x	y	u	v	uv	u^2
0	12	– 5	– 8	40	25
5	15	– 3	– 5	15	9
10	17	– 1	– 3	3	1
15	22	1	2	2	1
20	24	3	4	12	9
25	30	5	10	50	25
Total		$\Sigma u = 0$	$\Sigma v = 0$	$\Sigma uv = 122$	$\Sigma u^2 = 70$

Normal equations are $0 = 6a$ and $122 = 70b$

$\Rightarrow$ $a = 0, \quad b = 1.743$

Line of fit is $v = 1.743u$

Put $u = \dfrac{x - 12.5}{2.5}$ and $v = y - 20$, we get

$$\boxed{y = 0.7x + 11.285.}$$

Example 5. *Fit a straight line to the following data :*

x :	71	68	73	69	67	65	66	67
y :	69	72	70	70	68	67	68	64.

Sol. Let the equation of the straight line to be fitted be

$$y = a + bx \quad ...(1)$$

Normal equations are

$$\Sigma y = ma + b\Sigma x \quad ...(2)$$

and $$\Sigma xy = a\Sigma x + b\Sigma x^2 \quad ...(3)$$

Here $m = 8$. Table is as below :

x	y	xy	x^2
71	69	4899	5041
68	72	4896	4624
73	70	5110	5329
69	70	4830	4761
67	68	4556	4489
65	67	4355	4225
66	68	4488	4356
67	64	4288	4489
$\Sigma x = 546$	$\Sigma y = 548$	$\Sigma xy = 37422$	$\Sigma x^2 = 37314$

Substituting these values in equations (2) and (3), we get

$$548 = 8a + 546b$$

$$37422 = 546a + 37314b$$

Solving, we get

$$a = 39.5454, \quad b = 0.4242$$

Hence the required line of best fit is

$$\boxed{y = 39.5454 + 0.4242\, x.}$$

Example 6. *Show that the best fitting linear function for the points $(x_1, y_1), (x_2, y_2), \ldots\ldots, (x_n, y_n)$ may be expressed in the form*

$$\begin{vmatrix} x & y & 1 \\ \Sigma x_i & \Sigma y_i & n \\ \Sigma x_i^2 & \Sigma x_i y_i & \Sigma x_i \end{vmatrix} = 0 \qquad (i = 1, 2, \ldots\ldots, n)$$

Show that the line passes through the mean point $(\bar{x}, \bar{y})$.

Sol. Let the best fitting linear function be $y = a + bx$ ...(1)

Then the normal equations are

$$\Sigma y_i = na + b\Sigma x_i \quad ...(2)$$

and

$$\Sigma x_i y_i = a\Sigma x_i + b\Sigma x_i^2 \quad ...(3)$$

Equations (1), (2), (3) may be rewritten as

$$bx - y + a = 0$$

$$b\Sigma x_i - \Sigma y_i + na = 0$$

and

$$b\Sigma x_i^2 - \Sigma x_i y_i + a\Sigma x_i = 0$$

Eliminating a and b between these equations

$$\begin{vmatrix} x & y & 1 \\ \Sigma x_i & \Sigma y_i & n \\ \Sigma x_i^2 & \Sigma x_i y_i & \Sigma x_i \end{vmatrix} = 0 \quad ...(4)$$

which is the required best fitting linear function for the mean point $(\bar{x}, \bar{y})$,

$$\bar{x} = \frac{1}{n}\Sigma x_i \quad \bar{y} = \frac{1}{n}\Sigma y_i .$$

Clearly, the line (4) posses through point $(\bar{x}, \bar{y})$ as two rows of determinant being equal make it zero.

ASSIGNMENT

1. (*a*) Differentiate between interpolation and curve fitting.
   (*b*) Explain least square fit for curve fitting by taking suitable example.
   (*c*) Write a C program to determine the best fit straight line to given set of values (x_i, y_i), $i = 1, 2, ..., 10$, according to least squares principle.
   (*d*) Differentiate between interpolating polynomial and least squares polynomial obtained for a set of data.
2. Find the best values of a and b so that $y = a + bx$ fits the given data :

x	0	1	2	3	4
y	1.0	2.9	4.8	6.7	8.6

3. Fit a straight line approximate to the data :

x	1	2	3	4
y	3	7	13	21

4. A simply supported beam carries a concentrated load P(*lb*) at its mid-point. Corresponding to various values of P, the maximum deflection Y (*in*) is measured. The data are given below. Find a law of the type $Y = a + bP$

P	100	120	140	160	180	200
Y	0.45	0.55	0.60	0.70	0.80	0.85

5. In the following table y in the weight of potassium bromide which will dissolve in 100 grams of water at temperature x^0. Find a linear law between x and y

$x^0(c)$	0	10	20	30	40	50	60	70
y gm	53.5	59.5	65.2	70.6	75.5	80.2	85.5	90

6. The weight of a calf taken at weekly intervals are given below. Fit a straight line using method of least squares and calculate the average rate of growth per week.

Age	1	2	3	4	5	6	7	8	9	10
Weight	52.5	58.7	65	70.2	75.4	81.1	87.2	95.5	102.2	108.4

7. Find the least square line for the data points

(– 1, 10), (0, 9), (1, 7), (2, 5), (3, 4), (4, 3), (5, 0) and (6, – 1).

8. Find the least square line $y = a + bx$ for the data :

x_i	– 2	– 1	0	1	2
y_i	1	2	3	3	4

9. If P is the pull required to lift a load W by means of a pulley block, find a linear law of the form $P = mW + c$ connecting P and W, using the data :

P	12	15	21	25
W	50	70	100	120

where P and W are taken in kg-wt.

10. Using the method of least squares, fit a straight line to the following data :

x	1	2	3	4	5
y	2	4	6	8	10

Answers

2. $y = 1 + 1.9x$ **3.** $y = -4 + 6x$ **4.** $Y = 0.004P + 0.048$

5. $y = 54.35 + 0.5184x^\circ$ **6.** $y = 45.74 + 6.16x$; 6.16

7. $y = -1.6071429x + 8.6428571$ **8.** $y = 2.6 + (0.7)\,x$ **9.** $P = 2.2759 + 0.1879\,W$

10. $y = 2x$.

5.7. FITTING OF AN EXPONENTIAL CURVE y = ae^{bx}

Taking logarithms on both sides, we get

$$\log_{10} y = \log_{10} a + bx \log_{10} e$$

i.e.,
$$\boxed{Y = A + Bx} \qquad (1)$$

where $Y = \log_{10} y$, $A = \log_{10} a$ and $B = b \log_{10} e$

The normal equations for (1) are $\Sigma Y = nA + B\Sigma x$ and $\Sigma xY = A\Sigma x + B\Sigma x^2$

Solving these, we get A and B.

Then $a = \text{antilog } A$ and $b = \dfrac{B}{\log_{10} e}$.

5.8. FITTING OF THE CURVE $y = ax^b$

Taking logarithm on both sides, we get

$$\log_{10} y = \log_{10} a + b \log_{10} x$$

i.e., $$\boxed{Y = A + bX} \quad ...(1)$$

where $Y = \log_{10} y$, $A = \log_{10} a$ and $X = \log_{10} x$.

The normal equations to (1) are $\Sigma Y = nA + b\Sigma X$

and $\Sigma XY = A\Sigma X + b\Sigma X^2$

which results A and b on solving and a = antilog A.

5.9. FITTING OF THE CURVE $y = ab^x$

Taking logarithm on both sides,

$$\log y = \log a + x \log b$$

$$\Rightarrow \quad \boxed{Y = A + Bx} \quad ...(1)$$

where $Y = \log y$, $A = \log a$, $B = \log b$.

This is a linear equation in Y and x.

For estimating A and B, normal equations are

$$\Sigma Y = nA + B\,\Sigma x$$

and $$\Sigma xY = A\,\Sigma x + B\,\Sigma x^2$$

where n is the number of pairs of values of x and y.

Ultimately, a = antilog (A) and b = antilog (B).

5.10. FITTING OF THE CURVE $pv^r = k$

$$pv^r = k \quad \Rightarrow \quad v = k^{1/r}\, p^{-1/r}$$

Taking logarithm on both sides,

$$\log v = \frac{1}{r} \log k - \frac{1}{r} \log p$$

$$\Rightarrow \quad \boxed{Y = A + BX}$$

where $Y = \log v$, $A = \frac{1}{r} \log k$, $B = -\frac{1}{r}$ and $X = \log p$

r and k are determined by above equations. Normal equations are obtained as that of the straight line.

5.11. FITTING OF THE CURVE OF TYPE $xy = b + ax$

$$xy = b + ax \quad \Rightarrow \quad y = \frac{b}{x} + a$$

$$\Rightarrow \quad Y = bX + a, \quad \text{where } X = \frac{1}{x}.$$

Normal equations are $\Sigma Y = na + b\Sigma X$ and $\Sigma XY = a\Sigma X + b\Sigma X^2$.

5.12. FITTING OF THE CURVE $y = ax^2 + \frac{b}{x}$

Let the n points be $(x_1, y_1), (x_2, y_2), \ldots, (x_n, y_n)$

Error of estimate for i^{th} point (x_i, y_i) is

$$E_i = \left(y_i - ax_i^2 - \frac{b}{x_i}\right)$$

By principle of Least squares, the values of a and b are such that

$$U = \sum_{i=1}^{n} E_i^2 = \sum_{i=1}^{n} \left(y_i - ax_i^2 - \frac{b}{x_i}\right)^2 \text{ is minimum.}$$

Normal equations are given by

$$\frac{\partial U}{\partial a} = 0$$

$$\Rightarrow \quad \sum_{i=1}^{n} x_i^2 y_i = a\sum_{i=1}^{n} x_i^4 + b\sum_{i=1}^{n} x_i$$

and

$$\frac{\partial U}{\partial b} = 0$$

$$\Rightarrow \quad \sum_{i=1}^{n} \frac{y_i}{x_i} = a\sum_{i=1}^{n} x_i + b\sum_{i=1}^{n} \frac{1}{x_i^2}$$

or Dropping the suffix i, normal equations are

$$\boxed{\Sigma x^2 y = a\,\Sigma x^4 + b\Sigma x} \quad \text{and} \quad \boxed{\sum \frac{y}{x} = a\,\Sigma x + b\sum \frac{1}{x^2}}.$$

5.13. FITTING OF THE CURVE $y = ax + bx^2$

Error of estimate for i^{th} point (x_i, y_i) is $E_i = (y_i - ax_i - bx_i^2)$

By principle of Least squares, the values of a and b are such that

$$U = \sum_{i=1}^{n} E_i^2 = \sum_{i=1}^{n} (y_i - ax_i - bx_i^2)^2 \text{ is minimum.}$$

Normal equations are given by $\frac{\partial U}{\partial a} = 0$

$$\Rightarrow \quad \sum_{i=1}^{n} x_i y_i = a\sum_{i=1}^{n} x_i^2 + b\sum_{i=1}^{n} x_i^3$$

and

$$\frac{\partial U}{\partial b} = 0$$

$$\Rightarrow \qquad \sum_{i=1}^{n} x_i^2 y_i = a \sum_{i=1}^{n} x_i^3 + b \sum_{i=1}^{n} x_i^4$$

or Dropping the suffix i, normal equations are

$$\boxed{\Sigma xy = a\,\Sigma x^2 + b\Sigma x^3} \quad \text{and} \quad \boxed{\Sigma x^2 y = a\,\Sigma x^3 + b\Sigma x^4.}$$

5.14. FITTING OF THE CURVE $y = ax + \frac{b}{x}$

Error of estimate for i^{th} point (x_i, y_i) is

$$E_i = y_i - ax_i - \frac{b}{x_i}$$

By principle of Least squares the values of a and b are such that

$$U = \sum_{i=1}^{n} E_i^2 = \sum_{i=1}^{n} \left(y_i - ax_i - \frac{b}{x_i}\right)^2 \text{ is minimum.}$$

Normal equations are given by

$$\frac{\partial U}{\partial a} = 0$$

$$\Rightarrow \qquad 2\sum_{i=1}^{n} \left(y_i - ax_i - \frac{b}{x_i}\right)(-x_i) = 0$$

$$\Rightarrow \qquad \sum_{i=1}^{n} x_i y_i = a \sum_{i=1}^{n} x_i^2 + nb \qquad ...(1)$$

and

$$\frac{\partial U}{\partial b} = 0$$

$$\Rightarrow \qquad 2\sum_{i=1}^{n} \left(y_i - ax_i - \frac{b}{x_i}\right)\left(-\frac{1}{x_i}\right) = 0$$

$$\Rightarrow \qquad \sum_{i=1}^{n} \frac{y_i}{x_i} = na + b \sum_{i=1}^{n} \frac{1}{x_i^2} \qquad ...(2)$$

Dropping the suffix i, normal equations are

$$\boxed{\Sigma xy = a\Sigma x^2 + nb} \quad \text{and} \quad \boxed{\sum \frac{y}{x} = na + b\sum \frac{1}{x^2}}$$

where n is the no. of pairs of values of x and y.

5.15. FITTING OF THE CURVE $y = a + \frac{b}{x} + \frac{c}{x^2}$

Normal equations are

$$\Sigma y = ma + b\sum \frac{1}{x} + c\sum \frac{1}{x^2}$$

$$\sum \frac{y}{x} = a \sum \frac{1}{x} + b \sum \frac{1}{x^2} + c \sum \frac{1}{x^3}$$

$$\sum \frac{y}{x^2} = a \sum \frac{1}{x^2} + b \sum \frac{1}{x^3} + c \sum \frac{1}{x^4}$$

where m is number of pairs of values of x and y.

5.16. FITTING OF THE CURVE $y = \frac{c_0}{x} + c_1\sqrt{x}$

Error of estimate for i^{th} point (x_i, y_i) is

$$E_i = y_i - \frac{c_0}{x_i} - c_1\sqrt{x_i}$$

By principle of Least squares, the values of a and b are such that

$$U = \sum_{i=1}^{n} E_i^2 = \sum_{i=1}^{n} \left(y_i - \frac{c_0}{x_i} - c_i\sqrt{x_i}\right)^2 \text{ is minimum.}$$

Normal equations are given by

$$\frac{\partial U}{\partial c_0} = 0 \quad \text{and} \quad \frac{\partial U}{\partial c_1} = 0$$

Now, $$\frac{\partial U}{\partial c_0} = 0$$

$$\Rightarrow \quad 2\sum_{i=1}^{n} \left(y_i - \frac{c_0}{x_i} - c_1\sqrt{x_i}\right)\left(-\frac{1}{x_i}\right) = 0$$

$$\Rightarrow \quad \sum_{i=1}^{n} \frac{y_i}{x_i} = c_0 \sum_{i=1}^{n} \frac{1}{x_i^2} + c_1 \sum_{i=1}^{n} \frac{1}{\sqrt{x_i}} \qquad \text{...(1)}$$

Also, $$\frac{\partial U}{\partial c_1} = 0$$

$$\Rightarrow \quad 2\sum_{i=1}^{n} \left(y_i - \frac{c_0}{x_i} - c_1\sqrt{x_i}\right)(-\sqrt{x_i}) = 0$$

$$\Rightarrow \quad \sum_{i=1}^{n} y_i\sqrt{x_i} = c_0 \sum_{i=1}^{n} \frac{1}{\sqrt{x_i}} + c_1 \sum_{i=1}^{n} x_i \qquad \text{...(2)}$$

Dropping suffix i, normal equations (1) and (2) become

$$\sum \frac{y}{x} = c_0 \sum \frac{1}{x^2} + c_1 \sum \frac{1}{\sqrt{x}}$$

and $$\sum y\sqrt{x} = c_0 \sum \frac{1}{\sqrt{x}} + c_1\, \Sigma x.$$

5.17. FITTING OF THE CURVE $2^x = ax^2 + bx + c$

Normal equations are

$$\Sigma\, 2^x x^2 = a\Sigma x^4 + b\Sigma x^3 + c\Sigma x^2$$

$$\Sigma\, 2^x x = a\Sigma x^3 + b\Sigma x^2 + c\Sigma x$$

and $$\Sigma\, 2^x = a\Sigma x^2 + b\Sigma x + mc$$

where m is number of points (x_i, y_i)

5.18. FITTING OF THE CURVE $y = ae^{-3x} + be^{-2x}$

Normal equations are

$$\Sigma ye^{-3x} = a\, \Sigma e^{-6x} + b\, \Sigma e^{-5x}$$

and $$\Sigma ye^{-2x} = a\, \Sigma e^{-5x} + b\, \Sigma e^{-4x}$$

EXAMPLES

Example 1. *Find the curve of best fit of the type $y = ae^{bx}$ to the following data by the method of Least squares :*

x :	1	5	7	9	12
y :	10	15	12	15	21.

Sol. The curve to be fitted is $y = ae^{bx}$

or $$Y = A + Bx, \quad \text{where } Y = \log_{10} y,\ A = \log_{10} a, \text{ and } B = b \log_{10} e$$

$\therefore$ The normal equations are $\Sigma Y = 5A + B\Sigma x$

and $$\Sigma xY = A\Sigma x + B\Sigma x^2$$

x	y	$Y = \log_{10} y$	x^2	xy
1	10	1.0000	1	1
5	15	1.1761	25	5.8805
7	12	1.0792	49	7.5544
9	15	1.1761	81	10.5849
12	21	1.3222	144	15.8664
$\Sigma x = 34$		$\Sigma Y = 5.7536$	$\Sigma x^2 = 300$	$\Sigma xY = 40.8862$

Substituting the above values in the normal equations, we get

$$5.7536 = 5A + 34B$$

and $$40.8862 = 34A + 300B$$

On solving $A = 0.9766$; $B = 0.02561$

$$\therefore \quad a = \text{antilog}_{10} A = 9.4754;\ b = \frac{B}{\log_{10} e} = 0.059$$

Hence the required curve is $\boxed{y = 9.4754e^{0.059x}}$.

Example 2. *For the data given below, find the equation to the best fitting exponential curve of the form $y = ae^{bx}$*

x :	1	2	3	4	5	6
y :	1.6	4.5	13.8	40.2	125	300.

Sol. $y = ae^{bx}$

Take log, $\log y = \log a + bx \log e$

which is of the form $Y = A + Bx$

where $Y = \log y$, $A = \log a$, $B = b \log e$

x	y	$Y = \log y$	x^2	xy
1	1.6	0.2041	1	0.2041
2	4.5	0.6532	4	1.3064
3	13.8	1.1399	9	3.4197
4	40.2	1.6042	16	6.4168
5	125	2.0969	25	10.4845
6	300	2.4771	36	14.8626
$\Sigma x = 21$		$\Sigma Y = 8.1754$	$\Sigma x^2 = 91$	$\Sigma xY = 36.6941$

Normal equations are

and
$$\left.\begin{aligned} \Sigma Y &= mA + B\Sigma x \\ \Sigma xY &= A\Sigma x + B\Sigma x^2 \end{aligned}\right\} \quad ...(1)$$

Here $m = 6$

$\therefore$ From (1), $8.1754 = 6A + 21B$, $36.6941 = 21A + 91B$

$\Rightarrow$ $A = -0.2534$, $B = 0.4617$

$\therefore$ $a = \text{antilog } A = \text{antilog } (-0.2534) = \text{antilog } (\bar{1}.7466) = 0.5580$

and
$$b = \frac{B}{\log e} = \frac{0.4617}{0.4343} = 1.0631$$

Hence required equation is

$$\boxed{y = 0.5580\, e^{1.0631\, x}.}$$

Example 3. *Determine the constants a and b by the method of Least squares such that $y = ae^{bx}$ fits the following data :*

x	2	4	6	8	10
y	4.077	11.084	30.128	81.897	222.62

Sol. $y = ae^{bx}$

Taking log on both sides

$$\log y = \log a + bx \log e$$

or $Y = A + BX,$

where $Y = \log y$, $A = \log a$, $B = b \log_{10} e$, $X = x$.

Normal equations are

$$\Sigma Y = mA + B\Sigma X \quad ...(1)$$

and
$$\Sigma XY = A\Sigma X + B\Sigma X^2. \quad ...(2)$$

Here $m = 5$.

Table is as follows:

x	y	X	Y	XY	X^2
2	4.077	2	0.61034	1.22068	4
4	11.084	4	1.04469	4.17876	16
6	30.128	6	1.47897	8.87382	36
8	81.897	8	1.91326	15.30608	64
10	222.62	10	2.347564	23.47564	100
		$\Sigma X = 30$	$\Sigma Y = 7.394824$	$\Sigma XY = 53.05498$	$\Sigma X^2 = 220$

Substituting these values in equations (1) and (2), we get

$$7.394824 = 5A + 30B$$

and $$53.05498 = 30A + 220B.$$

Solving, we get $A = 0.1760594$

and $B = 0.2171509$

$\therefore$ $a = \text{antilog (A)}$

$= \text{antilog } (0.1760594) = 1.49989$

and $$b = \frac{B}{\log_{10} e} = \frac{0.2171509}{0.4342945} = 0.50001$$

Hence the required equation is

$$\boxed{y = 1.49989\, e^{0.50001x}.}$$

Example 4. *Obtain a relation of the form $y = ab^x$ for the following data by the method of least squares :*

x	2	3	4	5	6
y	8.3	15.4	33.1	65.2	126.4

Sol. The curve to be fitted is $y = ab^x$

or $Y = A + Bx,$

where $A = \log_{10} a$, $B = \log_{10} b$ and $Y = \log_{10} y$.

$\therefore$ The normal equations are $\Sigma Y = 5A + B\Sigma x$

and $\Sigma XY = A\Sigma x + B\Sigma x^2$.

x	y	$Y = \log_{10} y$	x^2	xY
2	8.3	0.9191	4	1.8382
3	15.4	1.1872	9	3.5616
4	33.1	1.5198	16	6.0792
5	65.2	1.8142	25	9.0710
6	127.4	2.1052	36	12.6312
$\Sigma x = 20$		$\Sigma Y = 7.5455$	$\Sigma x^2 = 90$	$\Sigma xY = 33.1812$

Substituting the above values, we get

$$7.5455 = 5A + 20B \quad \text{and} \quad 33.1812 = 20A + 90B.$$

On solving $\quad A = 0.31$ and $B = 0.3$

$\therefore \quad a = \text{antilog } A = 2.04$

and $\quad b = \text{antilog } B = 1.995.$

Hence the required curve is

$$\boxed{y = 2.04(1.995)^x.}$$

Example 5. *Obtain the least squares fit of the form*

$f(t) = a\, e^{-3t} + be^{-2t}$ for the data:

t :	0.1	0.2	0.3	0.4
$f(t)$:	0.76	0.58	0.44	0.35

Sol. Normal equations to the curve $f(t) = a\, e^{-3t} + be^{-2t}$ are :

$$\Sigma f(t)\, e^{-3t} = a\, \Sigma\, e^{-6t} + b\, \Sigma\, e^{-5t} \qquad ...(1)$$

$$\Sigma f(t)\, e^{-2t} = a\, \Sigma\, e^{-5t} + b\, \Sigma\, e^{-4t} \qquad ...(2)$$

See art. 5.18

Table of values is

t	$f(t)$	e^{-4t}	e^{-5t}	e^{-6t}	$f(t)\, e^{-2t}$	$f(t)\, e^{-3t}$
0.1	0.76	0.6703	0.6065	0.5488	0.6222	0.5630
0.2	0.58	0.4493	0.3679	0.3012	0.3888	0.3183
0.3	0.44	0.3012	0.2231	0.1653	0.2415	0.1789
0.4	0.35	0.2019	0.1353	0.0907	0.1573	0.1054
Total		Σe^{-4t} = 1.6227	Σe^{-5t} = 1.3328	Σe^{-6t} = 1.106	$\Sigma f(t)\, e^{-2t}$ = 1.4098	$\Sigma f(t)\, e^{-3t}$ = 1.1656

Substituting values in (1) and (2), we get

$$1.106\, a + 1.3328\, b = 1.1656$$

$$1.3328\, a + 1.6227\, b = 1.4098$$

On solving, we get $\quad a = 0.6778, \quad b = 0.3121.$

Hence the least squares fit is $f(t) = 0.6778\, e^{-3t} + 0.3121 e^{-2t}$.

Example 6. *By the method of least squares, find the curve $y = ax + bx^2$ that best fits the following data :*

x	1	2	3	4	5
y	1.8	5.1	8.9	14.1	19.8

Sol. Error of estimate for i^{th} point (x_i, y_i) is $E_i = (y_i - ax_i - bx_i^2)$

By method of least squares, the values of a and b are such that

$$U = \sum_{i=1}^{5} E_i^2 = \sum_{i=1}^{5} (y_i - ax_i - bx_i^2)^2 \text{ is minimum.}$$

Normal equations are given by

$$\frac{\partial U}{\partial a} = 0$$

$$\Rightarrow \qquad \sum_{i=1}^{5} x_i y_i = a \sum_{i=1}^{5} x_i^2 + b \sum_{i=1}^{5} x_i^3$$

and

$$\frac{\partial U}{\partial b} = 0$$

$$\Rightarrow \qquad \sum_{i=1}^{5} x_i^2 y_i = a \sum_{i=1}^{5} x_i^3 + b \sum_{i=1}^{5} x_i^4$$

Dropping the suffix i, Normal equations are

$$\Sigma xy = a\Sigma x^2 + b\Sigma x^3 \qquad \ldots(1)$$

and

$$\Sigma x^2 y = a\Sigma x^3 + b\Sigma x^4 \qquad \ldots(2)$$

Let us form a table as below:

x	y	x^2	x^3	x^4	xy	x^2y
1	1.8	1	1	1	1.8	1.8
2	5.1	4	8	16	10.2	20.4
3	8.9	9	27	81	26.7	80.1
4	14.1	16	64	256	56.4	225.6
5	19.8	25	125	625	99	495
Total		$\Sigma x^2 = 55$	$\Sigma x^3 = 225$	$\Sigma x^4 = 979$	$\Sigma xy = 194.1$	$\Sigma x^2y = 822.9$

Substituting these values in equations (1) and (2), we get

$$194.1 = 55\,a + 225\,b$$

and

$$822.9 = 225\,a + 979\,b$$

$$\Rightarrow \qquad a = \frac{83.85}{55} \simeq 1.52 \quad \text{and} \quad b = \frac{317.4}{664} \simeq 0.49$$

Hence required parabolic curve is $y = 1.52\,x + 0.49\,x^2$.

Example 7. *Fit the curve $pv^{\gamma} = k$ to the following data:*

p (kg/cm²)	*0.5*	*1*	*1.5*	*2*	*2.5*	*3*
v (litres)	*1620*	*1000*	*750*	*620*	*520*	*460*

Sol.

$$pv^{\gamma} = k$$

$$v = \left(\frac{k}{p}\right)^{1/\gamma} = k^{1/\gamma}\, p^{-1/\gamma}$$

Taking log,

$$\log v = \frac{1}{\gamma} \log k - \frac{1}{\gamma} \log p$$

which is of the form

$$Y = A + BX$$

where $Y = \log v$, $X = \log p$, $A = \dfrac{1}{\gamma} \log k$ and $B = -\dfrac{1}{\gamma}$

p	v	X	Y	XY	X^2
0.5	1620	–0 .30103	3.20952	– 0.96616	0.09062
1	1000	0	3	0	0
1.5	750	0.17609	2.87506	0.50627	0.03101
2	620	0.30103	2.79239	0.84059	0.09062
2.5	520	0.39794	2.716	1.08080	0.15836
3	460	0.47712	2.66276	1.27046	0.22764
Total		$\Sigma X = 1.05115$	$\Sigma Y = 17.25573$	$\Sigma XY = 2.73196$	$\Sigma X^2 = .59825$

Here $m = 6$

Normal equations are

$$17.25573 = 6A + 1.05115\ B$$

and

$$2.73196 = 1.05115\ A + 0.59825\ B$$

Solving these, we get

$$A = 2.99911 \quad \text{and} \quad B = -\ 0.70298$$

$\therefore$

$$\gamma = -\frac{1}{B} = \frac{1}{0.70298} = 1.42252$$

Again,

$$\log k = \gamma A = 4.26629$$

$\therefore$

$$k = \text{antilog}\ (4.26629) = 18462.48$$

Hence required curve is

$$\boxed{pv^{1.42252} = 18462.48}$$

Example 8. *Given the following experimental values :*

x :	0	1	2	3
y :	2	4	10	15

Fit by the method of least squares a parabola of the type $y = a + bx^2$.

Sol. Error of estimate for i^{th} point (x_i, y_i) is $E_i = (y_i - a - bx_i^2)$

By method of least squares, the values of a, b are chosen such that

$$U = \sum_{i=1}^{4} E_i^2 = \sum_{i=1}^{4} (y_i - a - bx_i^2)^2 \text{ is minimum.}$$

Normal equation are given by

$$\frac{\partial U}{\partial a} = 0 \Rightarrow \Sigma y = ma + b\Sigma x^2 \qquad \text{...(1)}$$

and

$$\frac{\partial U}{\partial b} = 0 \quad \Sigma x^2 y = a\Sigma x^2 + b\Sigma x^4 \qquad \text{...(2)}$$

x	y	x^2	x^2y	x^4
0	2	0	0	0
1	4	1	4	1
2	10	4	40	16
3	15	9	135	81
Total	$\Sigma y = 31$	$\Sigma x^2 = 14$	$\Sigma x^2y = 179$	$\Sigma x^4 = 98$

Here $m = 4$

From (1) and (2), $31 = 4a + 14b$ and $179 = 14a + 98b$

Solving for a and b, we get $a = 2.71,\ b = 1.44$

Hence the required curve is $y = 2.71 + 1.44\,x^2$.

Example 9. *The pressure of the gas corresponding to various volumes V is measured, given by the following data :*

V (cm³) :	*50*	*60*	*70*	*90*	*100*
P (kg cm⁻²) :	*64.7*	*51.3*	*40.5*	*25.9*	*78*

Fit the data to the equation $PV^{\gamma} = C$.

Sol. $PV^{\gamma} = C$

$\Rightarrow$ $P = CV^{-\gamma}$

Take log on both sides,

$$\log P = \log C - \gamma \log V$$

$$\Rightarrow \quad Y = A + BX$$

where $Y = \log P,\ A = \log C,\ B = -\gamma,\ X = \log V$

Normal equations are

$$\Sigma Y = mA + B\Sigma X \quad \text{...(1)}$$

and

$$\Sigma XY = A\Sigma X + B\Sigma X^2 \quad \text{...(2)}$$

Here $m = 5$

Table is as below:

V	*P*	*X = log V*	*Y = log P*	*XY*	*X²*
50	64.7	1.69897	1.81090	3.07666	2.88650
60	51.3	1.77815	1.71012	3.04085	3.16182
70	40.5	1.84510	1.60746	2.96592	3.40439
90	25.9	1.95424	1.41330	2.76193	3.81905
100	78	2	1.89209	3.78418	4
		$\Sigma X = 9.27646$	$\Sigma Y = 8.43387$	$\Sigma XY = 15.62954$	$\Sigma X^2 = 17.27176$

From Normal equations, we have

$$8.43387 = 5A + 9.27646\ B$$

and

$$15.62954 = 9.27646\ A + 17.27176\ B$$

Solving these, we get

$$A = 2.22476,\ B = -0.28997$$

$$\therefore \quad \gamma = -B = 0.28997$$

$$C = \text{antilog}\ (A) = \text{antilog}\ (2.22476) = 167.78765$$

Hence the required equation of curve is

$$PV^{0.28997} = 167.78765.$$

Example 10. *Use the method of Least squares to fit the curve :* $y = \frac{c_0}{x} + c_1\sqrt{x}$ *to the following table of values:*

x :	0.1	0.2	0.4	0.5	1	2
y :	21	11	7	6	5	6.

Sol. As derived in art. 5.16, normal equations to the curve

$$y = \frac{c_0}{x} + c_1\sqrt{x} \text{ are}$$

$$\sum \frac{y}{x} = c_0 \sum \frac{1}{x^2} + c_1 \sum \frac{1}{\sqrt{x}} \quad \text{...(1)}$$

and $$\sum y\sqrt{x} = c_0 \sum \frac{1}{\sqrt{x}} + c_1 \sum x \quad \text{...(2)}$$

Table is as below:

x	y	y/x	$y\sqrt{x}$	$\frac{1}{\sqrt{x}}$	$\frac{1}{x^2}$
0.1	21	210	6.64078	3.16228	100
0.2	11	55	4.91935	2.23607	25
0.4	7	17.5	4.42719	1.58114	6.25
0.5	6	12	4.24264	1.41421	4
1	5	5	5	1	1
2	6	3	8.48528	0.70711	0.25
$\Sigma x = 4.2$		$\Sigma(y/x) = 302.5$	$\Sigma y\sqrt{x} = 33.71524$	$\sum\frac{1}{\sqrt{x}} = 10.10081$	$\sum\frac{1}{x^2} = 136.5$

From equations (1) and (2), we have

$$302.5 = 136.5\, c_0 + 10.10081\, c_1$$

and $$33.71524 = 10.10081\, c_0 + 4.2\, c_1$$

Solving these, we get

$$c_0 = 1.97327 \quad \text{and} \quad c_1 = 3.28182$$

Hence the required equation of curve is

$$y = \frac{1.97327}{x} + 3.28182\sqrt{x}.$$

ASSIGNMENT

1. (*i*) Using the method of least squares, fit the non-linear curve of the form $y = ae^{bx}$ to the following data:

x	0	2	4
y	5.012	10	31.62

(*ii*) The voltage V across a capacitor at time t seconds is given by the following table. Use the principle of least squares to fit a curve of the form $V = ae^{kt}$ to the data:

t	0	2	4	6	8
V	150	63	28	12	5.6

2. (*i*) State some important curve-fitting procedures.

(*ii*) Derive the least square equations for fitting a curve of the type $y = ax + \frac{b}{x}$ to a set of n points (x_i, y_i) ; $i = 1, 2, ..., n$.

3. (*i*) Fit a curve $y = ax^b$ to the following data:

x	1	2	3	4	5	6
y	2.98	4.26	5.21	6.1	6.8	7.5

(*ii*) Fit a least square geometric curve $y = ax^b$ to the following data:

x	1	2	3	4	5
y	0.5	2	4.5	8	12.5

(*iii*) Fit a curve of the form $y = ax^b$ to the data given below:

x	1	2	3	4	5
y	7.1	27.8	62.1	110	161

4. (*i*) Fit a curve of the form $y = ab^x$ in least square sence to the data given below:

x	2	3	4	5	6
y	144	172.8	207.4	248.8	298.5

(*ii*) Fit an exponential curve of the form $y = ab^x$ to the following data:

x	1	2	3	4	5	6	7	8
y	1	1.2	1.8	2.5	3.6	4.7	6.6	9.1

5. The presssure and volume of a gas are related by the equation $pv^a = b$ where a and b are constants. Fit this equation to the following set of data:

p (kg/cm^2)	0.5	1	1.5	2	2.5	3
v (litres)	1.62	1	0.75	0.62	0.52	0.46

6. Determine the constants of the curve $y = ax + bx^2$ for the following data:

x	0	1	2	3	4
y	2.1	2.4	2.6	2.7	3.4

7. Fit a curve of the type $xy = ax + b$ to the following data:

x	1	3	5	7	9	10
y	36	29	28	26	24	15

8. It is known that the variables x and y hold the relation of the form $y = ax + \frac{b}{x}$.

Fit the curve to the given data:

x	1	2	3	4	5	6	7	8
y	5.43	6.28	8.23	10.32	12.63	14.86	17.27	19.51

9. Derive the least square equations for fitting a curve of the type $y = ax^2 + \frac{b}{x}$ to a set of n points.

Hence fit a curve of this type to the data:

x	1	2	3	4
y	– 1.51	0.99	3.88	7.66

10. Derive the least squares approximations of the type $ax^2 + bx + c$ to the function 2^x at the points $x_i = 0, 1, 2, 3, 4$.

11. A person runs the same race track for 5 consecutive days and is timed as follows:

Day (x)	1	2	3	4	5
Time (y)	15.3	15.1	15	14.5	14

Make a least square fit to the above data using a function $a + \frac{b}{x} + \frac{c}{x^2}$.

12. Use the method of least squares to fit the curve $y = c_0\, x + \frac{c_1}{\sqrt{x}}$ for the following data:

x	0.2	0.3	0.5	1	2
y	16	14	11	6	3

13. Experiments with a periodic process gave the following data :

$t°$	0	50	100	150	200	250	300	350
y	0.754	1.762	2.041	1.412	0.303	– 0.484	– 0.38	0.520

Estimate the parameters a and b in the model $y = b + a \sin t$ using the least squares approximation.

14. A physicist wants to approximate the following data:

x	0	0.5	1	2
$f(x)$	0	0.57	1.46	5.05

using a function $a\, e^{bx} + c$. He believes that $b \approx 1$. Compute the values of a and c that give the best least squares approximation assuming that $b = 1$.

15. Determine the normal equations if the cubic polynomial $y = a_0 + a_1x + a_2x^2 + a_3x^3$ is fitted to the data (x_i, y_i) ; $0 \le i \le m$.

Answers

1. (*i*) $y = 4.642\, e^{0.46x}$ (*ii*) $V = 146.3\, e^{-0.4118t}$

3. (*i*) $y = 2.978\, x^{0.5143}$ (*ii*) $y = 0.5012\, x^{1.9977}$ (*iii*) $y = 7.173x^{1.952}$

4. (*i*) $y = 99.86\,(1.2)^x$ (*ii*) $y = 0.6823\,(1.384)^x$ **5.** $pv^{1.42} = 0.99$

6. $a = 1.97,\ b = -0.298$ **7.** $xy = 16.18x + 40.78$ **8.** $y = 2.395x + \dfrac{3.09}{x}$

9. $y = 0.509x^2 - \dfrac{2.04}{x}$ **10.** $y = 1.143x^2 - 0.971x + 1.286$

11. $y = 13.0065 + \dfrac{6.7512}{x} - \dfrac{4.4738}{x^2}$ **12.** $y = -1.1836\, x + \dfrac{7.5961}{\sqrt{x}}$

13. $a = 1.312810,\ b = 0.752575$ **14.** $a = 0.784976,\quad b = -0.733298$

15. $\Sigma y = m\, a_0 + a_1\, \Sigma x + a_2\, \Sigma x^2 + a_3\, \Sigma x^3$

$\Sigma xy = a_0\, \Sigma x + a_1\, \Sigma x^2 + a_2\, \Sigma x^3 + a_3\, \Sigma x^4$

$\Sigma x^2 y = a_0\, \Sigma x^2 + a_1\, \Sigma x^3 + a_2\, \Sigma x^4 + a_3\, \Sigma x^5$

$\Sigma x^3 y = a_0\, \Sigma x^3 + a_1\, \Sigma x^4 + a_2\, \Sigma x^5 + a_3\, \Sigma x^6.$

5.19. MOST PLAUSIBLE SOLUTION OF A SYSTEM OF LINEAR EQUATIONS

Consider a set of m equations in n variables $x, y, z, \ldots\ldots, t$;

$$\left.\begin{array}{l} a_1x + b_1y + c_1z + \ldots\ldots + k_1t = l_1 \\ a_2x + b_2y + c_2z + \ldots\ldots + k_2t = l_2 \\ \quad\vdots \qquad \vdots \qquad\quad \vdots \quad \vdots \qquad \vdots \quad \vdots \\ a_mx + b_my + c_mz + \ldots\ldots + k_mt = l_m \end{array}\right\} \qquad \ldots(1)$$

where $a_i, b_i, c_i \ldots\ldots, k_i, l_i$; $i = 1, 2, \ldots\ldots, m$ are constants.

In case $m = n$, the system of equation (1) can be solved uniquely by using algebra.

In case $m > n$, we find the values of $x, y, z, \ldots\ldots, t$ which will satisfy the system (1) as nearly as possible using normal equations.

On solving normal equations simultaneously, they give the values of $x, y, z, \ldots\ldots, t$; known as the best or *most plausible values.*

On calculating the second order partial derivatives and substituting values of $x, y, z, \ldots\ldots, t$ so obtained, we will observe that the expression will be positive.

EXAMPLES

Example 1. *Find the most plausible values of x and y from the following equations :*

$$3x + y = 4.95,\ x + y = 3.00,\ 2x - y = 0.5,\ x + 3y = 7.25.$$

Sol. Let

$$S = (3x + y - 4.95)^2 + (x + y - 3)^2 + (2x - y - 0.5)^2 + (x + 3y - 7.25)^2 \qquad \ldots(1)$$

Differentiating S partially w.r.t. x and y separately and equating to zero, we have

$$\frac{\partial S}{\partial x} = 0 = 2(3x + y - 4.95)\,(3) + 2(x + y - 3) + 2(2x - y - 0.5)\,(2) + 2(x + 3y - 7.25)$$

$$\Rightarrow \qquad 30x + 10y = 52.2$$

or $$3x + y = 5.22 \qquad \ldots(2)$$

and $$\frac{\partial S}{\partial y} = 0 = 2(3x + y - 4.95) + 2(x + y - 3) + 2(2x - y - 0.5)(-1) + 2(x + 3y - 7.25)(3)$$

$$\Rightarrow \qquad 10x + 24y = 58.4$$

or $$x + 2.4y = 5.84 \qquad \ldots(3)$$

Solving equations (2) and (3), we get

$$x = 1.07871 \quad \text{and} \quad y = 1.98387.$$

Example 2. *Three independent measurements on each of the angles A, B and C of a triangle are as follows :*

A	*B*	*C*
39.5°	*60.3°*	*80.1°*
39.3°	*63.2°*	*80.3°*
39.6°	*69.1°*	*80.4°*

Obtain the best estimate of the three angles when the sum of the angles is taken to be 180°.

Sol. Let the three measurements of angles A, B, C be x_1, x_2, x_3 ; y_1, y_2, y_3 and z_1, z_2, z_3 respectively. Further suppose the best estimates of the angle A, B and C be α, β, γ respectively where $\gamma = 180° - (\alpha + \beta)$

According to Least squares method,

$$S = \sum_{i=1}^{3} (x_i - \alpha)^2 + \sum_{i=1}^{3} (y_i - \beta)^2 + \sum_{i=1}^{3} (z_i - 180 + \alpha + \beta)^2 \qquad \ldots(1)$$

and $$\frac{\partial S}{\partial \alpha} = 0 = -2\sum_{i=1}^{3} (x_i - \alpha) + 2\sum_{i=1}^{3} (z_i - 180 + \alpha + \beta)$$

$$\frac{\partial S}{\partial \beta} = 0 = -2\sum_{i=1}^{3} (y_i - \beta) + 2\sum_{i=1}^{3} (z_i - 180 + \alpha + \beta)$$

or $$\begin{cases} -\Sigma x + 3\alpha + \Sigma z - 540 + 3\alpha + 3\beta = 0 \\ -\Sigma y + 3\beta + \Sigma z - 540 + 3\alpha + 3\beta = 0 \end{cases}$$

or $$\begin{cases} 6\alpha + 3\beta = 540 + \Sigma x - \Sigma z = 417.6 & \ldots(2) \\ 3\alpha + 6\beta = 540 + \Sigma y - \Sigma z = 481.8 & \ldots(3) \end{cases}$$

Solving equations (2) and (3), we get

$$\alpha = 39.2667, \beta = 60.6667, \gamma = 80.0666$$

ASSIGNMENT

1. Find the most plausible values of x and y from the following equations:
   $$x + y = 3, x - y = 2, x + 2y = 4, x - 2y = 1$$
2. Find the most plausible values of x and y from the equations:
   $$x + y = 3.31, \quad 2x - y = 0.03, \quad x + 3y = 7.73, \quad 3x + y = 5.47$$
3. Find the most plausible values of x, y and z from the follwoing equations:
   $$x - y + 2z = 3, 3x + 2y - 5z = 5,$$
   $$4x + y + 4z = 21, -x + 3y + 3z = 14$$

4. Find the most plausible values of x, y and z from the following equations:

(i) $x + y = 3.01$, $2x - y = 0.03$, $x + 3y = 7.02$ and $3x + y = 4.97$

(ii) $x + 2y = 4$, $x = y + 2$, $x + y - 3 = 0$, $x - 2y = 1$

(iii) $x + 2.5y = 21$, $4x + 1.2y = 42.04$, $3.2x - y = 28$ and $1.5x + 6.3y = 40$

(iv) $x - 5y + 4 = 0$, $2x - 3y + 5 = 0$, $x + 2y - 3 = 0$, $4x + 3y + 1 = 0$.

5. Find the most plausible values of x, y and z from the following equations:

(i) $3x + 2y - 5z = 13$
$x - y + 2z = -2$
$4x + y + 4z = 3$
$-x + 3y + 3z = 0$

(ii) $x + 2y + z = 1$
$2x + y + z = 4$
$-x + y + 2z = 3$
$4x + 2y - 5z = -7$

(iii) $x - y + 2z = 3$, $3x + 2y - 5z = 5$, $4x + y + 4z = 21$, $-x + 3y + 3z = 14$.

Answers

1. $x = 2.5$, $y = 0.7$

2. $x = 1.42$, $y = 1.24$

3. $x = 2.47$, $y = 3.55$, $z = 1.92$

4. (i) $x = 0.999$, $y = 2.004$ (ii) $x = 2.5$, $y = 0.7$

(iii) $x = 5.5$, $y = 4.7$ (iv) $x = -\dfrac{819}{1025}, y = \dfrac{881}{1025}$

5. (i) $x = 1.54$, $y = 1.27$, $z = -1.08$ (ii) $x = 1.16$, $y = -0.76$, $z = 2.8$

(iii) $x = 6.9$, $y = 3.6$, $z = 4.14$.

5.20. POLYNOMIAL FIT : NON-LINEAR REGRESSION

Let
$$y = a + bx + cx^2 \quad \text{...(1)}$$
be a second degree parabolic curve of regression of y on x to be fitted for the data (x_i, y_i), $i = 1, 2, \ldots\ldots, n$.

Residual at $x = x_i$ is
$$E_i = y_i - f(x_i) = y_i - a - bx_i - cx_i^2$$

Now, let
$$U = \sum_{i=1}^{n} E_i^2 = \sum_{i=1}^{n} (y_i - a - bx_i - cx_i^2)^2$$

By principle of Least squares, U should be minimum for the best values of a, b and c.

For this,
$$\frac{\partial U}{\partial a} = 0, \quad \frac{\partial U}{\partial b} = 0 \text{ and } \frac{\partial U}{\partial c} = 0$$

$$\frac{\partial U}{\partial a} = 0 \quad \Rightarrow \quad 2\sum_{i=1}^{n} (y_i - a - bx_i - cx_i^2)(-1) = 0$$

$$\Rightarrow \quad \boxed{\Sigma y = na + b\Sigma x + c\Sigma x^2} \quad \text{...(1)}$$

$$\frac{\partial U}{\partial b} = 0 \quad \Rightarrow \quad 2\sum_{i=1}^{n} (y_i - a - bx_i - cx_i^2)(-x_i) = 0$$

$$\Rightarrow \quad \boxed{\Sigma xy = a\Sigma x + b\Sigma x^2 + c\Sigma x^3} \quad \text{...(2)}$$

$$\frac{\partial U}{\partial c} = 0 \quad \Rightarrow \quad 2\sum_{i=1}^{n} (y_i - a - bx_i - cx_i^2)(-x_i^2) = 0$$

$$\Rightarrow \boxed{\Sigma x^2 y = a\Sigma x^2 + b\Sigma x^3 + c\Sigma x^4} \qquad ...(3)$$

Equations (1), (2) and (3) are the normal equations for fitting a second degree parabolic curve of regression of y on x. Here n is the no. of pairs of values of x and y.

EXAMPLES

Example 1. (*a*) *Fit a second degree parabola to the following data :*

x:	0.0	1.0	2.0
y:	1.0	6.0	17.0

(*b*) *Fit a second degree curve of regression of y on x to the following data :*

x:	1.0	2.0	3.0	4.0
y:	6.0	11.0	18.0	27

(*c*) *Fit a second degree parabola in the following data :*

x:	0.0	1.0	2.0	3.0	4.0
y:	1.0	4.0	10.0	17.0	30.0

Sol. The equation of second degree parabola is given by

$$y = a + bx + cx^2 \qquad ...(1)$$

Normal equations are

$$\Sigma y = ma + b\Sigma x + c\Sigma x^2 \qquad ...(2)$$

$$\Sigma xy = a\Sigma x + b\Sigma x^2 + c\Sigma x^3 \qquad ...(3)$$

and

$$\Sigma x^2 y = a\Sigma x^2 + b\Sigma x^3 + c\Sigma x^4 \qquad ...(4)$$

(*a*) Here $m = 3$

Table is as follows:

x	y	x^2	x^3	x^4	xy	x^2y
0	1	0	0	0	0	0
1	6	1	1	1	6	6
2	17	4	8	16	34	68
Total	24	5	9	17	40	74

Substituting in eqns. (2), (3) and (4), we get

$$24 = 3a + 3b + 5c \qquad ...(5)$$

$$40 = 3a + 5b + 9c \qquad ...(6)$$

$$74 = 5a + 9b + 17c \qquad ...(7)$$

Solving eqns. (5), (6) and (7), we get

$$a = 1, b = 2, c = 3$$

Hence the required second degree parabola is

$$y = 1 + 2x + 3x^2$$

(*b*) Here $m = 4$

Table is as follows:

x	y	x^2	x^3	x^4	xy	x^2y
1	6	1	1	1	6	6
2	11	4	8	16	22	44
3	18	9	27	81	54	162
4	27	16	64	256	108	432
$\Sigma x = 10$	$\Sigma y = 62$	$\Sigma x^2 = 30$	$\Sigma x^3 = 100$	$\Sigma x^4 = 354$	$\Sigma xy = 190$	$\Sigma x^2y = 644$

Substituting values in eqns. (2), (3) and (4), we get

$$62 = 4a + 10b + 30c \quad \text{...(8)}$$

$$190 = 10a + 30b + 100c \quad \text{...(9)}$$

$$644 = 30a + 100b + 354c \quad \text{...(10)}$$

Solving equations (8), (9) and (10), we get

$$a = 3, b = 2, c = 1$$

Hence the required second degree parabola is

$$y = 3 + 2x + x^2$$

(*c*) Here $m = 5$

Table is as follows:

x	y	x^2	x^3	x^4	xy	x^2y
0.0	1.0	0	0	0	0	0
1.0	4.0	1	1	1	4	4
2.0	10.0	4	8	16	20	40
3.0	17.0	9	27	81	51	153
4.0	30.0	16	64	256	120	480
$\Sigma x = 10$	$\Sigma y = 62$	$\Sigma x^2 = 30$	$\Sigma x^3 = 100$	$\Sigma x^4 = 354$	$\Sigma xy = 195$	$\Sigma x^2y = 677$

Substituting values in eqns. (2), (3) and (4), we get

$$62 = 5a + 10b + 30c \quad \text{...(11)}$$

$$195 = 10a + 30b + 100c \quad \text{...(12)}$$

$$677 = 30a + 100b + 354c \quad \text{...(13)}$$

Solving eqns. (11), (12) and (13), we get

$$a = 1.2, b = 1.1 \text{ and } c = 1.5$$

Hence the required second degree parabola is

$$y = 1.2 + 1.1x + 1.5x^2$$

Example 2. *Fit a parabola $y = ax^2 + bx + c$ in least square sense to the data*

x :	*10*	*12*	*15*	*23*	*20*
y :	*14*	*17*	*23*	*25*	*21.*

Sol. The normal equations to the curve are

$$\left.\begin{aligned}\Sigma y &= a\Sigma x^2 + b\Sigma x + 5c\\ \Sigma xy &= a\Sigma x^3 + b\Sigma x^2 + c\Sigma x\\ \text{and}\quad \Sigma x^2 y &= a\Sigma x^4 + b\Sigma x^3 + c\Sigma x^2\end{aligned}\right\} \quad ...(1)$$

The values of Σx, Σx^2,...... etc., are calculated by means of the following table:

x	y	x^2	x^3	x^4	xy	x^2y
10	14	100	1000	10000	140	1400
12	17	144	1728	20736	204	2448
15	23	225	3375	50625	345	5175
23	25	529	12167	279841	575	13225
20	21	400	8000	160000	420	8400
$\Sigma x = 80$	$\Sigma y = 100$	$\Sigma x^2 = 1398$	$\Sigma x^3 = 26270$	$\Sigma x^4 = 521202$	$\Sigma xy = 1684$	$\Sigma x^2y = 30648$

Substituting the obtained values from the table in normal equation (1), we have

$$100 = 1398a + 80b + 5c$$

$$1684 = 26270a + 1398b + 80c$$

$$30648 = 521202a + 26270b + 1398c$$

On solving, $a = -0.07,\ b = 3.03,\ c = -8.89$

$\therefore$ The required equation is $y = -0.07x^2 + 3.03x - 8.89$.

Example 3. *Fit a parabolic curve of regression of y on x to the following data:*

x :	1.0	1.5	2.0	2.5	3.0	3.5	4.0
y :	1.1	1.3	1.6	2.0	2.7	3.4	4.1

Sol. Here $m = 7$ (odd)

Let $u = \dfrac{x - 2.5}{0.5} = 2x - 5$ and $v = y$

Results in tabular form are

x	y	u	v	u^2	uv	u^2v	u^3	u^4
1.0	1.1	– 3	1.1	9	– 3.3	9.9	– 27	81
1.5	1.3	– 2	1.3	4	– 2.6	5.2	– 8	16
2.0	1.6	1	1.6	1	1.6	1.6	– 1	1
2.5	2.0	0	2.0	0	0	0	0	0
3.0	2.7	1	2.7	1	2.7	2.7	1	1
3.5	3.4	2	3.4	4	6.8	13.6	8	16
4.0	4.1	3	4.1	9	12.3	36.9	27	81
Total		0	16.2	28	14.3	69.9	0	196

Let the curve to be fitted be $v = a + bu + cu^2$ so that the normal equations are

$$\Sigma v = 7a + b\Sigma u + c\Sigma u^2$$

$$\Sigma uv = a\Sigma u + b\Sigma u^2 + c\Sigma u^3$$

and $$\Sigma u^2 v = a\Sigma u^2 + b\Sigma u^3 + c\Sigma u^4$$

$\Rightarrow$ $$16.2 = 7a + 28c, \quad 14.3 = 28b, \quad 69.9 = 28a + 196c$$

Solving, we get $a = 2.07, \quad b = 0.511, \quad c = 0.061$

Hence the curve of fit is

$$v = 2.07 + 0.511u + 0.061u^2$$

$\Rightarrow$ $$y = 2.07 + 0.511\,(2x - 5) + 0.061\,(2x - 5)^2$$

$$= 1.04 - 0.193x + 0.243x^2.$$

Example 4. *Fit a second degree parabola to the following data by Least squares method:*

x :	1929	1930	1931	1932	1933	1934	1935	1936	1937
y :	352	356	357	358	360	361	361	360	359.

Sol. Here $m = 9$ (odd)

$\therefore$ Let $x_0 = 1933, \quad h = 1, \quad y_0 = 357$

then $$u = \frac{x - 1933}{1} = x - 1933, \quad v = y - 357$$

and the equation $y = a + bx + cx^2$ is transformed to

$$v = a' + b'u + c'u^2$$

x	u	y	v	uv	u^2	u^2v	u^3	u^4
1929	– 4	352	– 5	20	16	– 80	– 64	256
1930	– 3	356	– 1	3	9	– 9	– 27	81
1931	– 2	357	0	0	4	0	– 8	16
1932	– 1	358	1	– 1	1	1	– 1	1
1933	0	360	3	0	0	0	0	0
1934	1	361	4	4	1	4	1	1
1935	2	361	4	8	4	16	8	16
1936	3	360	3	9	9	27	27	81
1937	4	359	2	8	16	32	64	256
Total	$\Sigma u = 0$		$\Sigma v = 11$	$\Sigma uv = 51$	$\Sigma u^2 = 60$	$\Sigma u^2 v = -9$	$\Sigma u^3 = 0$	$\Sigma u^4 = 708$

Putting the above values in normal equations, we get

$$11 = 9a' + 60c', \quad 51 = 60b', \quad -9 = 60a' + 708c'$$

$\Rightarrow$ $$a' = 3, \quad b' = 0.85, \quad c' = -0.27.$$

Fitted parabola in u and v is given by

$$v = 3 + 0.85\,u - 0.27\,u^2$$

Putting $u = x - 1933$ and $v = y - 357$

$$y - 357 = 3 + 0.85\,(x - 1933) - 0.27\,(x - 1933)^2$$

$\Rightarrow$ $$y = -0.27x^2 + 1044.67x - 1010135.08$$

which is the required equation.

Example 5. *Fit a second degree parabola to the following data by Least squares method :*

x : 1 2 3 4 5

y : 1090 1220 1390 1625 1915

Sol. Here $m = 5$ (odd)

Let $u = x - 3, \quad v = y - 1220$

x	y	u	v	u^2	u^2v	uv	u^3	u^4
1	1090	– 2	– 130	4	– 520	260	– 8	16
2	1220	– 1	0	1	0	0	– 1	1
3	1390	0	170	0	0	0	0	0
4	1625	1	405	1	405	405	1	1
5	1915	2	695	4	2780	1390	8	16
Total		$\Sigma u = 0$	$\Sigma v = 1140$	$\Sigma u^2 = 10$	$\Sigma u^2v = 2665$	$\Sigma uv = 2055$	$\Sigma u^3 = 0$	$\Sigma u^4 = 34$

Putting these values in normal equations, we get

$$1140 = 5a' + 10c', \quad 2055 = 10b', \quad 2655 = 10a' + 34c'$$

$\Rightarrow$ $a' = 173, \quad b' = 205.5, \quad c' = 27.5$

$\therefore$ $v = 173 + 205.5u + 27.5u^2$ ...(1)

Put $u = x - 3$ and $v = y - 1220$

From (1), $y - 1220 = 173 + 205.5\,(x - 3) + 27.5\,(x - 3)^2$

$\Rightarrow$ $y = 27.5x^2 + 40.5x + 1024.$

Example 6. *Fit a second degree parabola to the following data taking y as dependent variable:*

x	1	2	3	4	5	6	7	8	9
y	2	6	7	8	10	11	11	10	9

Sol. Normal equations to fit a second degree parabola of the form $y = a + bx + cx^2$ are

and
$$\left.\begin{aligned} \Sigma y &= ma + b\Sigma x + c\Sigma x^2 \\ \Sigma xy &= a\Sigma x + b\Sigma x^2 + c\Sigma x^3 \\ \Sigma x^2 y &= a\Sigma x^2 + b\Sigma x^3 + c\Sigma x^4 \end{aligned}\right\} \quad ...(1)$$

Here, $m = 9$

x	y	x^2	x^3	x^4	xy	x^2y
1	2	1	1	1	2	2
2	6	4	8	16	12	24
3	7	9	27	81	21	63
4	8	16	64	256	32	128
5	10	25	125	625	50	250
6	11	36	216	1296	66	396
7	11	49	343	2401	77	539
8	10	64	512	4096	80	640
9	9	81	729	6561	81	729
$\Sigma x = 45$	$\Sigma y = 74$	$\Sigma x^2 = 285$	$\Sigma x^3 = 2025$	$\Sigma x^4 = 15333$	$\Sigma xy = 421$	$\Sigma x^2y = 2771$

Putting in (1), we get

$$74 = 9a + 45b + 285c$$
$$421 = 45a + 285b + 2025c$$
$$2771 = 285a + 2025b + 15333c$$

Solving the above equations, we get

$$a = -1, \qquad b = 3.55, \qquad c = -0.27$$

Hence the required equation of second degree parabola is

$$y = -1 + 3.55x - 0.27x^2.$$

Example 7. *Employ the method of least squares to fit a parabola $y = a + bx + cx^2$ in the following data :*

(x, y) : $(-1, 2), (0, 0), (0, 1), (1, 2)$

Sol. Normal equations to the parabola $y = a + bx + cx^2$ are

$$\Sigma y = ma + b\Sigma x + c\Sigma x^2 \qquad ...(1)$$
$$\Sigma xy = a\Sigma x + b\Sigma x^2 + c\Sigma x^3 \qquad ...(2)$$
and
$$\Sigma x^2 y = a\Sigma x^2 + b\Sigma x^3 + c\Sigma x^4 \qquad ...(3)$$

Here $m = 4$

The table is as follows:

x	y	x^2	x^3	x^4	xy	x^2y
-1	2	1	-1	1	-2	2
0	0	0	0	0	0	0
0	1	0	0	0	0	0
1	2	1	1	1	2	2
$\Sigma x = 0$	$\Sigma y = 5$	$\Sigma x^2 = 2$	$\Sigma x^3 = 0$	$\Sigma x^4 = 2$	$\Sigma xy = 0$	$\Sigma x^2y = 4$

Substituting these values in equations (1), (2) and (3) ; we get

$$5 = 4a + 2c \qquad ...(4)$$
$$0 = 2b \qquad ...(5)$$
and
$$4 = 2a + 2c \qquad ...(6)$$

Solving (4), (5) and (6), we get

$$a = 0.5, b = 0 \text{ and } c = 1.5$$

Hence the required second degree parabola is

$$y = 0.5 + 1.5x^2$$

5.21. ALGORITHM OF SECOND DEGREE PARABOLIC CURVE FITTING

```
1.  Input n
2.  For i=0,3
3.  For j=0,4
4.  u(i,j)=0
5.  Next j
```

```
 6.  Next i
 7.  u(0,0)=n
 8.  For i=0,n
 9.  Input x,y
10.  x2=x*x
11.  u(0,1)+=x
12.  u(0,2)+=x2
13.  u(1,2)+=x*x2
14.  u(2,2)+=x2*x2
15.  u(0,3)+=y
16.  u(1,3)+=x*y
17.  u(2,3)+=x2*y
18.  Next i
19.  u(1,1)=u(0,2)
20.  u(2,1)=u(1,2)
21.  u(1,0)=u(0,1)
22.  u(2,0)=u(1,1)
23.  For j=0,3
24.  For i=0,3
25.  If i!=j then
                 goto step 26
           ELSE
                 goto step 24
26.  y=u(i,j)/u(j,j)
27.  For k=0,4
28.  u(i,k)-=u(j,k)*p
29.  Next k
30.  Next i
31.  Next j
32.  a=u(0,3)/u(0,0)
33.  b=u(1,3)/u(1,1)
34.  c=u(2,3)/u(2,2)
35.  Print a,b,c
36.  Stop
```

5.22. FLOW CHART OF SECOND DEGREE PARABOLIC CURVE FITTING

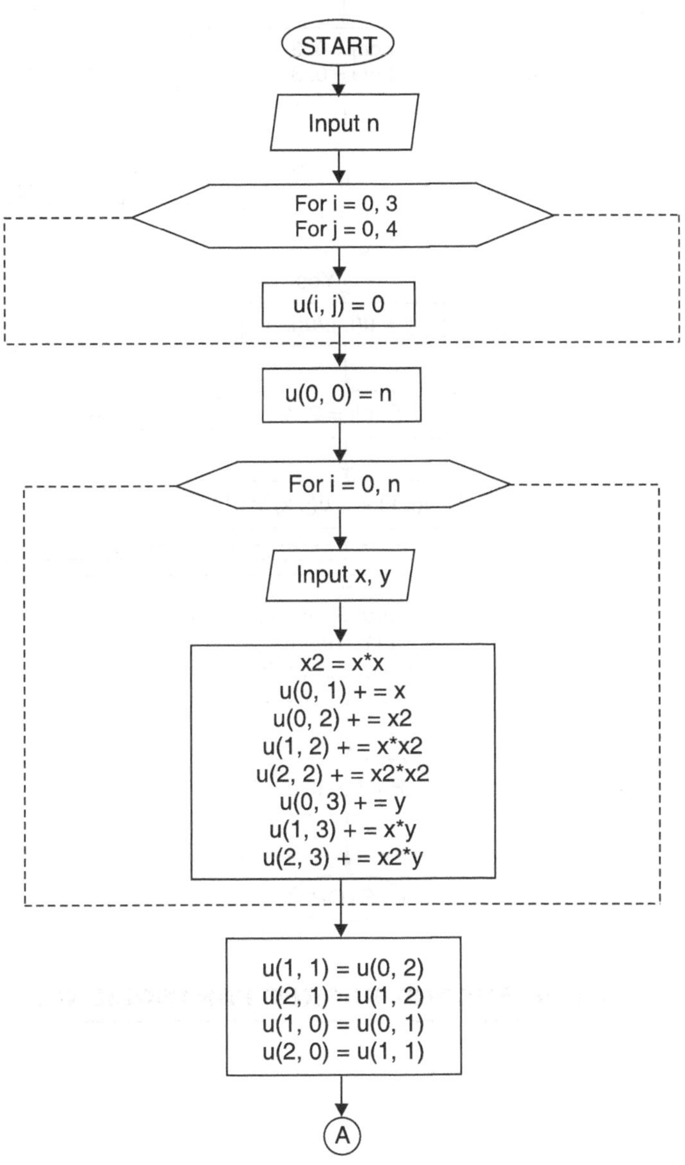

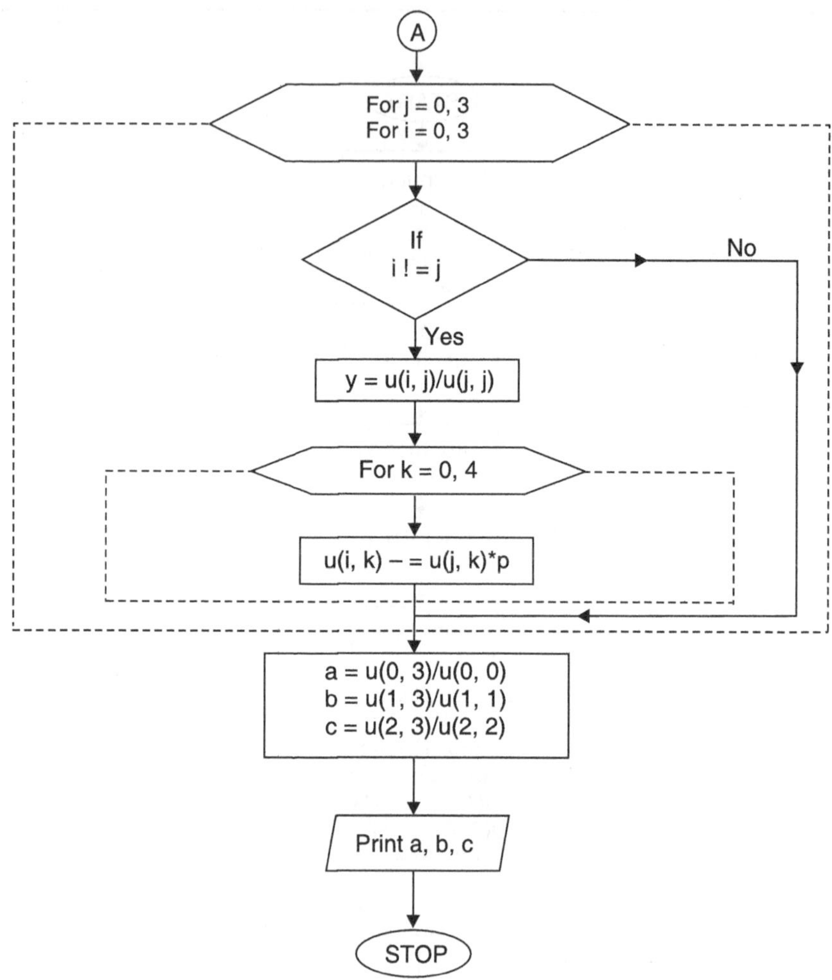

5.23. PROGRAM IN 'C' FOR SECOND DEGREE PARABOLIC CURVE FITTING

```
#include<stdio.h>
main()
{
 int i,j,k,n;
 float u[3][4], x,y,x2,p,a,b,c;
 printf("\nEnter the value of data set n:");
 scanf("%d",&n);
 for(i=0; i<3; i++)
 for(j=0; j<4; j++)
 u[i][j]=0;
```

```
u[0][0]=n;
printf("\nEnter the value of x & y :\n");
for(i=0; i<n; i++)
    {
    scanf("%f%f", &x, &y);
    x2=x*x;
    u[0][1]+=x;
    u[0][2]+=x2;
    u[1][2]+=x*x2;
    u[2][2]+=x2*x2;
    u[0][3]+=y;
    u[1][3]+=x*y;
    u[2][3]+=x2*y;
    }
u[1][1]=u[0][2];
u[2][1]=u[1][2];
u[1][0]=u[0][1];
u[2][0]=u[1][1];
/* Finding the value of a,b,c */
for (j=0;j<3;j++)
for (i=0;i<3;i++)
    if(i!=j)
        {
        p=u[i][j]/u[j][j];
        for(k=0;k;k++)
        u[i][k]-=u[j][k]*p;
        }
a=u[0][3]/u[0][0];
b=u[1][3]/u[1][1];
c=u[2][3]/u[2][2];
printf("\na=%f b=%f  c=%f ", a,b,c);
printf("\n\nEquation of parabola is: y=a+bx+cx^2 \n");
printf("\ny=%f+(%f)x+(%f)x^2",a,b,c);
return;
}
```

5.23.1. Output

```
Enter the value of data set n : 5
Enter the value of x & y :
1 10.9
2 12.2
```

```
3 13.9
4 16.3
5 19.2
a=10.239998 b=0.398574 c=0.278571
Equation of parabola is: y = a+bx+cx^2
y=10.239998+(0.398574)x+(0.278571)x^2
```

5.24. MULTIPLE LINEAR REGRESSION

Now we proceed to discuss the case where the dependent variable is a function of two or more linear or non-linear independent variables. Consider such a linear function as

$$y = a + bx + cz \qquad ...(1)$$

The sum of the squares of residual is

$$U = \sum_{i=1}^{n} (y_i - a - bx_i - cz_i)^2 \qquad ...(2)$$

Differentiating U partially w.r.t. a, b, c ; we get

$$\frac{\partial U}{\partial a} = 0 \Rightarrow 2\sum_{i=1}^{n} (y_i - a - bx_i - cz_i)(-1) = 0$$

$$\frac{\partial U}{\partial b} = 0 \Rightarrow 2\sum_{i=1}^{n} (y_i - a - bx_i - cz_i)(-x_i) = 0$$

and

$$\frac{\partial U}{\partial c} = 0 \Rightarrow 2\sum_{i=1}^{n} (y_i - a - bx_i - cz_i)(-z_i) = 0$$

which on simplification and omitting the suffix i, yields.

$$\Sigma y = ma + b\Sigma x + c\Sigma z$$

$$\Sigma xy = a\Sigma x + b\Sigma x^2 + c\Sigma xz$$

$$\Sigma yz = a\Sigma z + b\Sigma xz + c\Sigma z^2$$

Solving the above three equations, we get values of a, b and c. Consequently, we get the linear function $y = a + bx + cz$ called **regression plane.**

5.25. ALGORITHM OF MULTIPLE LINEAR REGRESSION

We have to fit $y = a + bx + cz$.

1. Read data x_i, y_i, z_i where $1 \le i \le n$
2. Obtain sum Σx_i, Σy_i, Σz_i, $\Sigma y_i x_i$, $\Sigma y_i z_i$, $\Sigma x_i z_i$, Σx_i^2, Σz_i^2
3. Compute a, b, c by normal equations

$$\Sigma y_i = na + b\Sigma x_i + c\Sigma z_i$$

$$\Sigma x_i y_i = a\Sigma x_i + b\Sigma x_i^2 + c\Sigma z_i x_i$$

$$\Sigma y_i z_i = a\Sigma z_i + b\Sigma x_i z_i + c\Sigma z_i^2$$

4. Print the equation $y = a + bx + cz$.
5. Find the required estimated value.

EXAMPLES

Example 1. *Obtain a regression plane by using multiple linear regression to fit the data given below :*

x :	1	2	3	4
z :	0	1	2	3
y :	12	18	24	30

Sol. Let $y = a + bx + cz$ be the required regression plane where a, b, c are the constants to be determined by following equations :

$$\Sigma y = ma + b\Sigma x + c\Sigma z$$

$$\Sigma yx = a\Sigma x + b\Sigma x^2 + c\Sigma zx$$

and $$\Sigma yz = a\Sigma z + b\Sigma zx + c\Sigma z^2$$

Here $m = 4$

x	z	y	x^2	z^2	yx	zx	yz
1	0	12	1	0	12	0	0
2	1	18	4	1	36	2	18
3	2	24	9	4	72	6	48
4	3	30	16	9	120	12	90
$\Sigma x = 10$	$\Sigma z = 6$	$\Sigma y = 84$	$\Sigma x^2 = 30$	$\Sigma z^2 = 14$	$\Sigma yx = 240$	$\Sigma zx = 20$	$\Sigma yz = 156$

Substitution yields, $84 = 4a + 10b + 6c$

$$240 = 10a + 30b + 20c$$

and $$156 = 6a + 20b + 14c$$

Solving, we get $a = 10, b = 2, c = 4$

Hence the required regression plane is

$$y = 10 + 2x + 4z$$

Example 2. *Find the multiple linear regression of X_1 on X_2 and X_3 from the data relating to three variables:*

X_1	4	6	7	9	13	15
X_2	15	12	8	6	4	3
X_3	30	24	20	14	10	4

Sol. Let $X_1 = a + bX_2 + cX_3$ be the required regression plane where a, b, c are the constants, determined by the following normal equations

$$\Sigma X_1 = ma + b\Sigma X_2 + c\Sigma X_3$$
$$\Sigma X_1X_2 = a\Sigma X_2 + b\Sigma X_2^2 + c\Sigma X_2X_3$$
$$\Sigma X_1X_3 = a\Sigma X_3 + b\Sigma X_2X_3 + c\Sigma X_3^2$$

Here $m = 6$

X_1	X_2	X_3	X_1X_2	X_2^2	X_2X_3	X_1X_3	X_3^2
4	15	30	60	225	450	120	900
6	12	24	72	144	288	144	576
7	8	20	56	64	160	140	400
9	6	14	54	36	84	126	196
13	4	10	52	16	40	130	100
15	3	4	45	9	12	60	16
Total 54	48	102	339	494	1034	720	2188

Substituting the values, we get

$$54 = 6a + 48b + 102c$$
$$339 = 48a + 102b + 1034c$$
$$720 = 102a + 1034b + 2188c$$

On solving, we get, $a = 16.413$, $b = -0.00536$, $c = -0.4335$

Hence $X_1 = 16.413 - 0.00536X_2 - 0.4335X_3$

ASSIGNMENT

1. Fit a second degree parabola to the following data taking x as the independent variable:

x	0	1	2	3	4
y	1	5	10	22	38

2. Fit a second degree parabola to the following data by Least squares method:

x	0	1	2	3	4
y	1	1.8	1.3	2.5	6.3

3. The profit of a certain company in X^{th} year of its life are given by:

x	1	2	3	4	5
y	1250	1400	1650	1950	2300

Taking $u = x - 3$ and $v = \dfrac{y - 1650}{50}$, show that the parabola of second degree of v on u is $v + 0.086 = 5.3\,u + 0.643u^2$ and deduce that the parabola of second degree of y on x is

$$y = 1144 + 72x + 32.15x^2$$

4. The following table gives the results of the measurements of train resistances, V is the velocity in miles per hour, R is the resistance in pounds per ton:

V	20	40	60	80	100	120
R	5.5	9.1	14.9	22.8	33.3	46

If R is related to V by the relation $R = a + bV + cV^2$; find a, b and c by using the method of least squares.

5. Determine the constants a, b and c by the method of least squares such that $y = ax^2 + bx + c$ fits the following data:

x	2	4	6	8	10
y	4.01	11.08	30.12	81.89	222.62

6. (*i*) Explain Multiple Regression Algorithm by suitable example.

(*ii*) What do you understand by multiple regression analysis ? Explain it by example.

(*iii*) Multiple linear regression has been approximated by quadratic equation:

$$y = a_2x^2 + a_1x + a_0$$

Applying least square minimizing technique, how a_2, a_1, a_0 are to be computed? Discuss.

Answers

1. $y = 1.43 + 0.24x + 2.21x^2$

2. $y = 1.42 - 1.07x + 0.55x^2$

4. $R = 4.35 + 0.00241\,V + 0.0028705\,V^2$

5. $a = 5.358035714$, $b = -38.89492857$, $c = 67.56$.

5.26. APPROXIMATION OF FUNCTIONS

The problem of approximating a function is an important problem in numerical analysis due to its wide application in the development of software for digital computers. The functions which are commonly used for approximating given functions are polynomials, trigonometric functions, exponential functions and rational functions. However from application point of view, the polynomial functions are mostly used.

The criteria to be considered before choosing an approximation are :

(*i*) The error in the approximation should not be large for some arguments and small for others. It should be uniformly spread out over the useful range of arguments.

(*ii*) As the function will be repeatedly used, it would be worthwhile to express it in a form which would minimise computing time.

The weierstrass approximation theorem which states "If the function $f(x)$ is continuous on a finite interval $[a, b]$ then for any given $\varepsilon > 0$, $\exists$ a (+) ve integer $n = n(\varepsilon)$ and a polynomial $p(x)$ of degree n s.t.

$$|f(x) - P(x)| < \varepsilon \quad \forall\, x \in [a, b]\text{"}$$

guarantees the existence of a polynomial function P(x) which approximates any continuous function $f(x)$ defined on a finite interval $[a, b]$.

The error of approximation is defined as

$$E(f : c_0, c_1, \ldots, c_n) = \| f(x) - \{c_0 \, \phi_0 (x) + \ldots + c_n \, \phi_n(x)\} \| \quad \ldots(1)$$

where $\| \cdot \|$ is a well-defined norm. The problem of approximation is to determine the parameters $c_0, c_1, \ldots, c_n$ such that this error is least in some sense.

By using different norms, we obtain different types of approximations. The most commonly used norms are given below:

***(i)* For discrete data**

***(a)* L^p – norm.** It is defined as $\| x \| = \left(\sum_{i=1}^{n} | x_i |^p \right)^{\frac{1}{p}}, \quad p \geq 1$

where $x = \{x_i\}$ is a sequence of real or complex numbers.

***(b)* Euclidean or square norm.** It is defined as $\| x \| = \left(\sum_{i=1}^{n} | x_i |^2 \right)^{\frac{1}{2}}$.

***(c)* Uniform norm.** It is defined as $\| x \| = \max_{1 \leq i \leq n} | x_i |$

***(ii)* For continuous data**

***(a)* L^p – norm.** It is defined as

$$\| f \| = \left(\int_a^b W(x) \, | f(x) |^p \, dx \right)^{\frac{1}{p}}, \quad p \geq 1$$

where $f(x)$ is continuous on $[a, b]$, $| f(x) |^p$ is integrable on $[a, b]$ and $W(x) > 0$ is the weight function.

***(b)* Euclidean or square norm.** It is defined as

$$\| f \| = \left(\int_a^b W(x) \, f^2(x) \, dx \right)^{\frac{1}{2}}$$

***(c)* Uniform norm.** It is defined as

$$\| f \| = \max_{a \leq x \leq b} | f(x) |$$

When the Euclidean norm is used, we obtain the least squares approximation and when uniform norm is used, we obtain the uniform approximation.

5.27. TAYLOR SERIES APPROXIMATION

Taylor's series for a function $f(x)$ in an interval $[a, b]$ near $x = x_0$ is

$$f(x) = f(x_0) + (x - x_0) f'(x_0) + \frac{(x - x_0)^2}{2!} f''(x_0) + \ldots + \frac{(x - x_0)^n}{n!} f^{(n)}(x_0) + R_n$$

where R_n is the remainder term given by

$$\frac{(x - x_0)^{n+1}}{n + 1!} f^{(n+1)}(\xi); \quad x_0 < \xi < x$$

R_n gives the truncation error if only first n terms in Taylor's series are used to represent the function.

Truncation error $= \dfrac{\left|(x - x_0)^{n+1}\right| \left| f^{(n+1)}(\xi) \right|}{n+1!}$

$$\mathrm{T_E} \le \frac{\left|(x - x_0)^{n+1}\right|}{n+1!} \mathrm{M}$$

where $\mathrm{M} = \max. \mid f^{(n+1)}(\xi) \mid \quad \forall\, x \in [a, b]$

This series representation is useful in many applications.

For example, we have

$$\cos x = 1 - \frac{x^2}{2!} + \frac{x^4}{4!} - \frac{x^6}{6!} + \ldots + (-1)^n \frac{x^{2n}}{2n!}$$

in which $\mid \mathrm{T_E} \mid \le \dfrac{x^{2n+2}}{2n+2!}$

For $\mid x \mid < \dfrac{\pi}{2}$, the series converges fast. If an error less than $\dfrac{1}{2} \times 10^{-6}$ is required, one need to take only the first six terms. Given any angle, it should be transformed to make $\mid x \mid < \dfrac{\pi}{2}$.

5.28. LEAST SQUARES APPROXIMATION

Suppose a function $f(x)$ is given at n distinct points x_i as $f(x_i) = f_i$, $1 \le i \le n$. In interpolation, we seek a polynomial $\mathrm{P}(x)$ of degree $(n - 1)$ such that $\mathrm{P}(x_i) = f_i$. If the degree of $\mathrm{P}(x)$ is specified beforehand, it may not be possible to make the curve $y = \mathrm{P}(x)$ pass through all the n points (x_i, f_i). The procedure, given by *Gauss*, called the least square approximation is used in such cases.

EXAMPLES

Example 1. *Obtain a linear polynomial approximation to the function $f(x) = x^3$ on the interval [0, 1] using the least squares approximation with W(x) = 1.*

Sol. Consider a linear polynomial $\mathrm{P}(x) = a + bx$ where a and b are arbitrary parameters.

We have, $\mathrm{U}(a, b)$ = sum of the squares of the errors

$$= \int_0^1 [x^3 - (a + bx)]^2 \, dx$$

$$= \int_0^1 [x^6 - 2(ax^3 + bx^4) + a^2 + b^2x^2 + 2abx] \, dx$$

$$= \left[\frac{x^7}{7} - 2\left(\frac{ax^4}{4} + b\frac{x^5}{5} \right) + a^2x + b^2\frac{x^3}{3} + abx^2 \right]_0^1$$

$$= \frac{1}{7} - 2\left(\frac{a}{4} + \frac{b}{5}\right) + a^2 + ab + \frac{b^2}{3}$$

which is to be minimum.

Necessary conditions for U(a, b) to be minimum are

$$\frac{\partial U}{\partial a} = -\frac{1}{2} + 2a + b = 0$$

$$\frac{\partial U}{\partial b} = -\frac{2}{5} + a + \frac{2}{3}b = 0$$

Solving these equations, we get

$$a = -\frac{1}{5}, \quad b = \frac{9}{10}$$

Hence the desired linear polynomial approximation is

$$p(x) = -\frac{1}{5} + \frac{9}{10}x = \frac{9x - 2}{10}$$

Example 2. *Obtain an approximation in least squares sense in the form of polynomials of the degree 2 to the function: $f(x) = x^3$ in the interval [0, 2].*

Sol. Let the least square polynomial approximation of degree 2 be $P(x) = a + bx + cx^2$ where a, b, c are arbitrary constants.

$$U(a, b, c) = \int_0^2 [x^3 - (a + bx + cx^2)]^2\, dx \quad \ldots(1)$$

which is to be minimum.

Normal equations are,

$$\frac{\partial U}{\partial a} = 0 = \int_0^2 2(x^3 - a - bx - cx^2).\,(-1)\, dx$$

$$\Rightarrow \quad \int_0^2 (x^3 - a - bx - cx^2)\, dx = 0$$

$$\Rightarrow \quad \left(\frac{x^4}{4} - ax - \frac{bx^2}{2} - \frac{cx^3}{3}\right)_0^2 = 0$$

$$\Rightarrow \quad 4 - 2a - 2b - \frac{8}{3}c = 0 \quad \ldots(2)$$

$$\frac{\partial U}{\partial b} = 0 = \int_0^2 2(x^3 - a - bx - cx^2)(-x)\, dx$$

$$\Rightarrow \quad \int_0^2 (x^4 - ax - bx^2 - cx^3)\, dx = 0$$

$$\Rightarrow \quad \left(\frac{x^5}{5} - \frac{ax^2}{2} - \frac{bx^3}{3} - \frac{cx^4}{4}\right)_0^2 = 0$$

$$\Rightarrow \quad \frac{32}{5} - 2a - \frac{8}{3}b - 4c = 0 \quad \ldots(3)$$

and $$\frac{\partial U}{\partial c} = 0 = \int_0^2 2(x^3 - a - bx - cx^2)(-x^2)\,dx$$

$$\Rightarrow \quad \int_0^2 (x^5 - ax^2 - bx^3 - cx^4)\,dx = 0$$

$$\Rightarrow \quad \left(\frac{x^6}{6} - a\frac{x^3}{3} - b\frac{x^4}{4} - c\frac{x^5}{5}\right)_0^2 = 0$$

$$\Rightarrow \quad \frac{32}{3} - \frac{8}{3}a - 4b - \frac{32}{5}c = 0 \qquad \ldots(4)$$

Solving (2), (3) and (4), we get

$$a = 0.4, \quad b = -2.4, \quad c = 3$$

Hence the required second degree polynomial is

$$P(x) = 0.4 - 2.4x + 3x^2.$$

ASSIGNMENT

1. Obtain the least square polynomials of degree one and two for $f(x) = x^{1/2}$ on [0, 1].
2. Obtain an approximation in the sense of the principle of least squares in the form of a polynomial of second degree to the function $f(x) = \dfrac{1}{1+x^2}$ in the range $-1 \le x \le 1$.
3. Find the least squares approximating polynomial of degree 2 for the function $f(x) = \sin \pi x$ on the interval [0, 1].
4. Obtain a linear polynomial approximation to the function $f(x) = x^3$ on the interval [0, 2] using the least square approximation with $W(x) = 1$.
5. Construct a least squares quadratic approximation to the function $y(x) = \sin x$ on $\left[0, \frac{\pi}{2}\right]$ w.r.t. the weight function $W(x) = 1$.
6. Find the best parabola which fits $f(x) = \cos x$ in $\left(\frac{-\pi}{2}, \frac{\pi}{2}\right)$.
7. Explain approximation of function by Taylor series by taking suitable example.

Answers

1. (*i*) $\frac{4}{15}(1 + 3x)$, $\frac{1}{35}(6 + 48x - 20x^2)$
2. $\frac{3}{4}(2\pi - 5) + \frac{15}{4}(3 - \pi)x^2$
3. $-0.050465 + 4.12251x - 4.12251x^2$
4. $-1.6 + 3.6x$
5. $\left(\frac{18}{\pi} + \frac{96}{\pi^2} - \frac{480}{\pi^3}\right) + \left(-\frac{144}{\pi^2} - \frac{1344}{\pi^3} + \frac{5760}{\pi^4}\right)x + \left(\frac{240}{\pi^3} + \frac{2880}{\pi^4} - \frac{11520}{\pi^5}\right)x^2$
6. $y = 0.67 - 0.04\,x^2$.

5.29. ORTHOGONAL POLYNOMIALS

Approximation of function by least squares method possesses the disadvantage of solving a large linear system of equations which exhibit ill-conditioning also. Hence the method which employs orthogonal polynomials is currently in use. It has the advantage that it does not require a linear system to be solved.

We choose the approximation in the form

$$y(x) = a_0 f_0(x) + a_1 f_1(x) + \ldots + a_n f_n(x)$$

where $f_j(x)$ is a polynomial in x of degree j.

Then, we write $\quad U = \int_a^b W(x)\,[y(x) - \{a_0 f_0(x) + a_1 f_1(x) + \ldots + a_n f_n(x)\}]^2\,dx$

For U to be minimum, we must have

$$\frac{\partial U}{\partial a_0} = 0, \quad \frac{\partial U}{\partial a_1} = 0, \quad \ldots, \quad \frac{\partial U}{\partial a_n} = 0$$

From which, we obtain,

$$a_j = \frac{\int_a^b W(x)\, y(x)\, f_j(x)\, dx}{\int_a^b W(x)\, f_j^2(x)\, dx}, \quad 0 \le j \le n$$

$f_j(x)$ are called orthogonal polynomial and are said to be orthogonal *w.r.t.* W(x), the weight function. They are obtained by **Gram-Schmidt orthogonalization process.**

Orthogonal polynomials	$f_j(x)$	*Interval*	$w(x)$
Legendre	$P_n(x)$	$(-1, 1)$	1
Hermite	$H_n(x)$	$(-\infty, \infty)$	e^{-x^2}
Laguerre	$L_n(x)$	$[0, \infty)$	e^{-x}
Chebyshev of first kind	$T_n(x)$	$[-1, 1]$	$\frac{1}{\sqrt{1-x^2}}$
Chebyshev of second kind	$U_n(x)$	$[-1, 1]$	$\sqrt{1-x^2}$

5.30. GRAM-SCHMIDT ORTHOGONALIZATION PROCESS

There exists a procedure for constructing the orthogonal polynomials ϕ_i with the leading term x^i corresponding to any interval $[a, b]$ and any weight function W. This is known as Gram-Schmidt orthogonalization process. It is described below :

Step 1. Take $\phi_0(x) = 1$

Step 2. Any linear polynomial $\phi_1(x)$ with leading term x can be expressed as

$$\phi_1(x) = x + k_{1,0}\, \phi_0(x) \text{ for some constant } k_{1,0}.$$

Value of $k_{1,0}$ is chosen to ensure that ϕ_0 and ϕ_1 are orthogonal. This requires,

$$\int_a^b W(x)\, \phi_0(x)\, [x + k_{1,0}\, \phi_0(x)]\, dx = 0$$

$$\Rightarrow \qquad k_{1,0} = -\frac{\int_a^b W(x)\, \phi_0(x)\, x\, dx}{\int_a^b W(x)\, \phi_0^2(x)\, dx}$$

Similarly, $$k_{2,0} = -\frac{\int_a^b W(x)\,\phi_0(x)\,x^2\,dx}{\int_a^b W(x)\,\phi_0^2(x)\,dx}$$

The requirement that ϕ_1 and ϕ_2 are orthogonal leads to

$$k_{2,1} = \frac{\int_a^b W(x)\,\phi_1(x)\,x^2\,dx}{\int_a^b W(x)\,\phi_1^2(x)\,dx}$$

The general step of the procedure is given by

$$\phi_i(x) = x^i\, k_{i,0}\,\phi_0(x) + k_{i,1}\,\phi_1(x) + \ldots + k_{i,i-1}\,\phi_{i-1}(x)$$

where $k_{i,j}$ are chosen to ensure that ϕ_i is orthogonal to ϕ_j $(0 \le j \le i - 1)$. This condition yields to

$$k_{i,j} = \frac{\int_a^b W(x)\,\phi_j(x)\,x^i\,dx}{\int_a^b W(x)\,\phi_j^2(x)\,dx}$$

Example. *Using Gram-Schmidt orthogonalization process, compute the first two orthogonal polynomials $P_0(x)$, $P_1(x)$ which are orthogonal on interval [0, 1] w.r.t. the weight function $W(x) = 1$.*

Using these polynomials, obtain least squares approximation of first degree for $f(x) = x^{1/2}$ on interval [0, 1].

Sol. $$P_0(x) = 1$$

$$P_1(x) = x + k_{1,0}\,P_0(x) = x + k_{1,0}$$

where $$k_{1,0} = -\frac{\int_0^1 1.1.x\,dx}{\int_0^1 1.1\,dx} = -\frac{1}{2}$$

Hence, $$P_1(x) = x - \frac{1}{2}$$

Using these polynomials, we have

$$U = \int_0^1 [x^{1/2} - \{a_0\,P_0(x) + a_1\,P_1(x)\}]^2\,dx$$

which is to be minimum.

This requires

$$\frac{\partial U}{\partial a_0} = 0 = \frac{\partial U}{\partial a_1}$$

$$\Rightarrow \qquad a_0 = \frac{\int_0^1 x^{1/2}\,P_0(x)\,dx}{\int_0^1 P_0^2(x)\,dx} = \frac{\int_0^1 x^{1/2}\,dx}{\int_0^1 dx} = \frac{2}{3}$$

and
$$a_1 = \frac{\int_0^1 x^{1/2}\, P_1(x)\, dx}{\int_0^1 P_1^2(x)\, dx} = \frac{\int_0^1 x^{1/2}\left(x - \frac{1}{2}\right) dx}{\int_0^1 \left(x - \frac{1}{2}\right)^2 dx} = \frac{4}{5}$$

Hence the required least squares approximation is

$$x^{1/2} \approx \frac{2}{3}\, P_0(x) + \frac{4}{5}\, P_1(x) \approx \frac{4}{15}\,(1 + 3x).$$

5.31. LEGENDRE AND CHEBYSHEV POLYNOMIALS

In the theory of approximation of functions, we often use the well known orthogonal polynomials, Legendre and Chebyshev polynomials as the coordinate functions while applying the method of least squares.

Chebyshev polynomials are also used in the economization of power series.

5.32. LEGENDRE POLYNOMIALS

$P_n(x)$ is a Legendre polynomial in x of degree n and satisfies the Legendre differential equation

$$(1 - x^2)\,\frac{d^2y}{dx^2} - 2x\,\frac{dy}{dx} + n\,(n + 1)\,y = 0$$

we have
$$P_n(-x) = (-1)^n\, P_n(x).$$

From this, we conclude that $P_n(x)$ is an even function of x if n is even and an odd function of x if n is odd.

Legendre polynomials satisfy the recurrence relation

$$(n + 1)\, P_{n+1}\,(x) = (2n + 1)\, xP_n(x) - nP_{n-1}(x)$$
$$P_0(x) = 1,\ P_1(x) = x$$

we have

$$P_n(x) = \frac{1 \cdot 3 \cdot 5 \ldots\ldots (2n - 1)}{n\,!}\left[x^n - \frac{n(n-1)}{2(2n-1)}\, x^{n-2} + \frac{n(n-1)(n-2)(n-3)}{2.4.(2n-1)\,(2n-3)}\, x^{n-4} - \ldots\ldots\right]$$

In particular,

$$P_2(x) = \frac{3x^2 - 1}{2},\quad P_3(x) = \frac{5x^3 - 3x}{2}$$

$$P_4(x) = \frac{35x^4 - 30x^2 + 3}{8},\quad P_5(x) = \frac{63x^5 - 70x^3 + 15x}{8}$$

Legendre polynomials $P_n(x)$ are orthogonal on the interval [–1, 1] w.r.t. the weight function $W(x) = 1$

We have

$$\int_{-1}^1 P_m(x)\, P_n(x)\, dx = \begin{cases} 0\ , & \text{if } m \neq n \\ \dfrac{2}{2n+1}\ , & \text{if } m \neq n \end{cases}$$

5.33. CHEBYSHEV POLYNOMIALS

Chebyshev polynomial of first kind of degree n over the interval [– 1, 1] is denoted by $T_n(x)$ and is defined by the relation

$$T_n(x) = \cos(n \cos^{-1} x) = \cos n\theta$$

where $\theta = \cos^{-1} x$ or $x = \cos\theta$

we have, $T_0(x) = 1$ and $T_1(x) = x$

Chebyshev polynomial of second kind of degree n over the interval [– 1, 1] is denoted by $U_n(x)$ and is defined by the relation

$$U_n(x) = \sin(n \cos^{-1} x) = \sin n\theta$$

where $\theta = \cos^{-1} x$ or $x = \cos\theta$

Note 1. Chebyshev's polynomials are also known as Tchebichef or Tchebicheff or Tchebysheff.

Note 2. Sometimes the Chebyshev polynomial of the second kind is defined by

$$U_n(x) = \frac{\sin\{(n+1)\cos^{-1} x\}}{\sqrt{1-x^2}} = \frac{U_{n+1}(x)}{\sqrt{1-x^2}}.$$

5.34. SPECIAL VALUES OF CHEBYSHEV POLYNOMIALS

$$T_0(x) = \cos 0 = 1$$

$$T_1(x) = \cos(\cos^{-1} x) = x$$

$$T_2(x) = \cos(2\cos^{-1} x) = 2\cos^2(\cos^{-1} x) - 1 = 2x^2 - 1$$

$$T_3(x) = \cos(3\cos^{-1} x) = 4\cos^3(\cos^{-1} x) - 3\cos(\cos^{-1} x) = 4x^3 - 3x$$

$$T_4(x) = \cos(4\cos^{-1} x) = 2\cos^2(2\cos^{-1} x) - 1 = 2(2x^2-1)^2 - 1 = 8x^4 - 8x^2 + 1$$

$$T_5(x) = \cos(5\cos^{-1} x) = \cos(3\cos^{-1} x)\cos(2\cos^{-1} x) - \sin(3\cos^{-1} x)\sin(2\cos^{-1} x)$$

$$= 16x^5 - 20x^3 + 5x$$

Similarly, $T_6(x) = 32x^6 - 48x^4 + 18x^2 - 1$ and so on.

5.35. ORTHOGONAL PROPERTIES

To prove:

$$\text{(1)} \int_{-1}^{1} \frac{T_n(x)\,T_m(x)}{\sqrt{1-x^2}}\,dx = \begin{cases} 0; & \text{if } m \neq n \\ \pi/2; & \text{if } m = n \neq 0 \\ \pi; & \text{if } m = n = 0 \end{cases}$$

$$\text{(2)} \int_{-1}^{1} \frac{U_n(x)\,U_m(x)}{\sqrt{1-x^2}}\,dx = \begin{cases} 0; & \text{if } m \neq n \\ \pi/2; & \text{if } m = n \neq 0 \\ 0; & \text{if } m = n = 0 \end{cases}.$$

5.36. RECURRENCE RELATIONS

1. $T_{n+1}(x) - 2x\,T_n(x) + T_{n-1}(x) = 0.$
2. $(1 - x^2)\,T_n'(x) = -nxT_n(x) + n\,T_{n-1}(x).$
3. $U_{n+1}(x) - 2x\,U_n(x) + U_{n-1}(x) = 0.$
4. $(1 - x^2)\,U_n'(x) = -nx\,U_n(x) + nU_{n-1}(x).$

5.37. ALITER TO FIND CHEBYSHEV POLYNOMIALS

The recurrence relation

$$T_{n+1}(x) = 2x\, T_n(x) - T_{n-1}(x) \quad \ldots(1)$$

Can also be used to compute all $T_n(x)$ successively since we know $T_0(x)$ and $T_1(x)$.

$$T_0(x) = 1, \quad T_1(x) = x$$

Putting $n = 1$ in (1), we have

$$T_2(x) = 2xT_1(x) - T_0(x) = 2x^2 - 1$$

Putting $n = 2$ in (1), we get

$$T_3(x) = 2x\, T_2(x) - T_1(x) = 2x\,(2x^2 - 1) - x = 4x^3 - 3x$$

Putting $n = 3$ in (1), we get

$$T_4(x) = 2x\, T_3(x) - T_2(x) = 2x\,(4x^3 - 3x) - (2x^2 - 1)$$
$$= 8x^4 - 6x^2 - 2x^2 + 1 = 8x^4 - 8x^2 + 1$$

Putting $n = 4$ in (1), we get

$$T_5(x) = 2x\, T_4(x) - T_3(x) = 2x\,(8x^4 - 8x^2 + 1) - (4x^3 - 3x)$$
$$= 16x^5 - 20x^3 + 5x$$

Similarly,
$$T_6(x) = 2x\, T_5(x) - T_4(x) = 2x\,(16x^5 - 20x^3 + 5x) - (8x^4 - 8x^2 + 1)$$
$$= 32x^6 - 48x^4 + 18x^2 - 1.$$

5.38. EXPRESSION OF POWERS OF X IN TERMS OF CHEBYSHEV POLYNOMIALS

$$1 = T_0(x)$$
$$x = T_1(x)$$
$$x^2 = \frac{1}{2}\,[T_0(x) + T_2(x)]$$
$$x^3 = \frac{1}{4}\,[3\,T_1(x) + T_3(x)]$$
$$x^4 = \frac{1}{8}\,[3\,T_0(x) + 4T_2(x) + T_4(x)]$$
$$x^5 = \frac{1}{16}\,[10\,T_1(x) + 5T_3(x) + T_5(x)]$$
$$x^6 = \frac{1}{32}\,[10\,T_0(x) + 15T_2(x) + 6T_4(x) + T_6(x)]$$

and so on.

Above expressions will be useful in the economization of power series.

5.39. PROPERTIES OF CHEBYSHEV POLYNOMIALS

(*i*) $T_n(x)$ is a polynomial of degree n. We have $T_n(-x) = (-1)^n\, T_n(x)$ so that $T_n(x)$ is an even function of x if n is even and it is an odd function of x if n is odd.

(*ii*) $T_n(x)$ has n simple zeros.

$$x_k = \cos\left(\frac{2k-1}{2n}\pi\right),\ k = 1, 2, \ldots\ldots, n \text{ on the interval } [-1, 1]$$

(*iii*) $T_n(x)$ assumes extreme values at $(n + 1)$ points $x_k = \cos\frac{k\pi}{n}$, $k = 0, 1, 2, \ldots\ldots, n$ and the extreme value at x_k is $(-1)^k$.

(*iv*) $|\ T_n(x)\ | \le 1, x \in [-1, 1]$

(*v*) $T_n(x)$ are orthogonal on the interval $[-1, 1]$ w.r.t. the weight function

$$W(x) = \frac{1}{\sqrt{1-x^2}}$$

(*vi*) If $p_n(x)$ is any monic polynomial of degree n and $\tilde{T}_n(x) = \frac{T_n(x)}{2^{n-1}}$ is the monic Chebyshev polynomial, then

$$\max_{-1\le x\le 1} |\tilde{T}_n(x)| \le \max_{-1\le x\le 1} |p_n(x)|.$$

5.40. CHEBYSHEV POLYNOMIAL APPROXIMATION

Let $f(x)$ be a continuous function defined on the interval $[-1, 1]$ and let $c_0 + c_1x + c_2x^2 + \ldots\ldots + c_nx^n$ be the required **minimax** (or uniform) polynomial approximation for $f(x)$.

Suppose $f(x) = \frac{a_0}{2} + \sum_{i=1}^{\infty} a_i\, T_i(x)$ is the Chebyshev series expansion for $f(x)$.

Then the truncated series or the partial sum

$$P_n(x) = \frac{a_0}{2} + \sum_{i=1}^{n} a_i\, T_i(x) \qquad \ldots(1)$$

is very nearly the solution to the problem

$$\max_{-1\le x\le 1}\left| f(x) - \sum_{i=0}^{n} c_i\, x^i \right| = \min_{-1\le x\le 1}\left| f(x) - \sum_{i=0}^{n} c_i\, x^i \right|$$

i.e., the partial sum (1) is nearly the best uniform approximation to $f(x)$.

Reason. Suppose we write

$$f(x) = \frac{a_0}{2} + a_1T_1(x) + a_2T_2(x) + \ldots\ldots + a_nT_n(x) + a_{n+1}T_{n+1}(x) + \text{remainder} \qquad \ldots(2)$$

Neglecting the remainder, we obtain from (2),

$$f(x) - \left[\frac{a_0}{2} + \sum_{i=1}^{n} a_iT_i(x)\right] = a_{n+1}T_{n+1}(x) \qquad \ldots(3)$$

Since $T_{n+1}(x)$ has $n + 2$ equal maxima and minima which alternate in sign, therefore by Chebyshev equioscillation theorem, the polynomial (1) of degree n is the best uniform approximation to $f(x)$.

5.41. LANCZOS ECONOMIZATION OF POWER SERIES

First we express the given function $f(x)$ as a power series in x in the form

$$f(x) = \sum_{i=0}^{\infty} a_i x^i , \; -1 \le x \le 1 \qquad ...(1)$$

Then we change each power of x in (1) in terms of Chebyshev polynomials and we obtain

$$f(x) = \sum_{i=0}^{\infty} c_i \mathrm{T}_i(x) \qquad ...(2)$$

as the Chebyshev series expansion for $f(x)$ on [– 1, 1]. It has been found that for a large no. of functions $f(x)$, the series (2) converges more rapidly than the power series given by eqn. (1). If we truncate series (2) at $\mathrm{T}_n(x)$, then the partial sum

$$\mathrm{P}_n(x) = \sum_{i=0}^{n} c_i \mathrm{T}_i(x) \qquad ...(3)$$

is a good uniform approximation to $f(x)$ in the sense

$$\max_{-1 \le x \le 1} | f(x) - \mathrm{P}_n(x) | \le | c_{n+1} | + | c_{n+2} | + \ldots\ldots \le \varepsilon \quad \text{(say)}$$

For a given ε, it is possible to find the no. of terms that should be retained in eqn. (3). This process is known as **Lanczos economization.** Replacing each $\mathrm{T}_i(x)$ in eqn. (3) by its polynomial form and rearranging the terms, we get the required economized polynomial approximation for $f(x)$.

EXAMPLES

Example 1. *Express* $2\,T_0(x) - \frac{1}{4} T_2(x) + \frac{1}{8} T_4(x)$ *as polynomials in x.*

Sol. $2\mathrm{T}_0(x) - \frac{1}{4}\mathrm{T}_2(x) + \frac{1}{8}\mathrm{T}_4(x)$

$$= 2(1) - \frac{1}{4}(2x^2 - 1) + \frac{1}{8}(8x^4 - 8x^2 + 1) = 2 - \frac{1}{2}x^2 + \frac{1}{4} + x^4 - x^2 + \frac{1}{8}$$

$$= x^4 - \frac{3}{4}x^2 + \frac{19}{8}.$$

Example 2. *Express* $1 - x^2 + 2x^4$ *as sum of Chebyshev polynomials.*

Sol.

$$1 - x^2 + 2x^4 = 1 - x^2 + 2\left[\frac{1}{8}\{3\mathrm{T}_0(x) + 4\mathrm{T}_2(x) + \mathrm{T}_4(x)\}\right]$$

$$= 1 - x^2 + \frac{3}{4}\mathrm{T}_0(x) + \mathrm{T}_2(x) + \frac{1}{4}\mathrm{T}_4(x)$$

$$= 1 - \frac{1}{2}[\mathrm{T}_0(x) + \mathrm{T}_2(x)] + \frac{3}{4}\mathrm{T}_0(x) + \mathrm{T}_2(x) + \frac{1}{4}\mathrm{T}_4(x)$$

$$= \mathrm{T}_0(x) - \frac{1}{2}\mathrm{T}_0(x) - \frac{1}{2}\mathrm{T}_2(x) + \frac{3}{4}\mathrm{T}_0(x) + \mathrm{T}_2(x) + \frac{1}{4}\mathrm{T}_4(x)$$

$$= \frac{5}{4}\mathrm{T}_0(x) + \frac{1}{2}\mathrm{T}_2(x) + \frac{1}{4}\mathrm{T}_4(x).$$

Example 3. *Find the best lower order approximation to the cubic $2x^3 + 3x^2$.*

Sol. We know that

$$x^3 = \frac{1}{4}[3T_1(x) + T_3(x)]$$

$$2x^3 + 3x^2 = 2\left[\frac{1}{4}\{3T_1(x) + T_3(x)\}\right] + 3x^2$$

$$= \frac{3}{2}T_1(x) + \frac{1}{2}T_3(x) + 3x^2 = 3x^2 + \frac{3}{2}x + \frac{1}{2}T_3(x) \qquad [\because \ T_1(x) = x]$$

Since $|T_3(x)| \le 1, -1 \le x \le 1$ therefore, the polynomial $3x^2 + \frac{3}{2}x$ is the required lower order approximation to the given cubic with a max. error $\pm \frac{1}{2}$ in range $[-1, 1]$.

Example 4. *Find the best uniform approximation of degree 3 or less to x^4 on $[-1, 1]$.*

Sol. Expressing x^4 in terms of Chebyshev polynomials, we get

$$x^4 = \frac{3}{8}T_0 + \frac{1}{2}T_2 + \frac{1}{8}T_4 \qquad ...(1)$$

Since T_4 is a polynomial of degree 4, therefore we approximate $f(x)$ by $\frac{3}{8}T_0 + \frac{1}{2}T_2$.

The error of approximation $\varepsilon(x)$ is given by

$$\varepsilon(x) = x^4 - \left(\frac{3}{8}T_0 + \frac{1}{2}T_2\right) = \frac{1}{8}T_4$$

Hence the uniform polynomial approximation of degree 3 or less to x^4 is

$$\frac{3}{8}T_0 + \frac{1}{2}T_2 = \frac{3}{8} + \frac{1}{2}(2x^2 - 1) = x^2 - \frac{1}{8}.$$

Example 5. *Economize the power series : $\sin x \approx x - \frac{x^3}{6} + \frac{x^5}{120} - \frac{x^7}{5040} + ...$ to three significant digit accuracy.*

Sol. Truncated series is

$$\sin x \approx x - \frac{x^3}{6} + \frac{x^5}{120} \qquad ...(1)$$

which is obtained by truncating the last term since $\frac{1}{5040} = 0.000198$ will produce a change in the fourth decimal place only.

Converting the powers of x in (1) into Chebyshev polynomials, we get

$$\sin x \approx T_1(x) - \frac{1}{6}\left[\frac{1}{4}\{3T_1(x) + T_3(x)\}\right] + \frac{1}{120}\left[\frac{1}{16}\{10T_1(x) + 5T_3(x) + T_5(x)\}\right]$$

$$\approx T_1(x) - \frac{1}{24}[3T_1(x) + T_3(x)] + \frac{1}{120 \times 16}[10T_1(x) + 5T_3(x) + T_5(x)]$$

$$\approx \frac{169}{192} T_1(x) - \frac{5}{128} T_3(x) + \frac{1}{1920} T_5(x) \qquad ...(2)$$

Truncated series is

$$\sin x \approx \frac{169}{192} T_1(x) - \frac{5}{128} T_3(x)$$

which is obtained by truncating the last term since $\frac{1}{1920} = 0.00052$ will produce a change in the fourth decimal place only.

Economized series is

$$\sin x \approx \frac{169}{192} x - \frac{5}{128}(4x^3 - 3x)$$

$$= \frac{383}{384} x - \frac{5}{32} x^3 = 0.9974x - 0.1526x^3$$

which gives sin x to three significant digit accuracy.

Example 6. *Using the Chebyshev polynomials, obtain the least squares approximation of second degree for $f(x) = x^4$ on [– 1, 1].*

Sol. Let $f(x) \approx P(x) = C_0T_0(x) + C_1T_1(x) + C_2T_2(x)$

We have

$$U(C_0, C_1, C_2) = \int_{-1}^{1} \frac{1}{\sqrt{1-x^2}} (x^4 - C_0T_0 - C_1T_1 - C_2T_2)^2 \, dx$$

which is to be minimum.

Normal equations are given by

$$\frac{\partial U}{\partial C_0} = 0 \Rightarrow \int_{-1}^{1} (x^4 - C_0T_0 - C_1T_1 - C_2T_2) \frac{T_0}{\sqrt{1-x^2}} \, dx = 0$$

$$\frac{\partial U}{\partial C_1} = 0 \Rightarrow \int_{-1}^{1} (x^4 - C_0T_0 - C_1T_1 - C_2T_2) \frac{T_1}{\sqrt{1-x^2}} \, dx = 0$$

and

$$\frac{\partial U}{\partial C_2} = 0 \Rightarrow \int_{-1}^{1} (x^4 - C_0T_0 - C_1T_1 - C_2T_2) \frac{T_2}{\sqrt{1-x^2}} \, dx = 0$$

We find that

$$C_0 = \frac{1}{\pi} \int_{-1}^{1} \frac{x^4 T_0}{\sqrt{1-x^2}} \, dx = \frac{3}{8}$$

$$C_1 = \frac{2}{\pi} \int_{-1}^{1} \frac{x^4 T_1}{\sqrt{1-x^2}} \, dx = 0$$

$$C_2 = \frac{2}{\pi} \int_{-1}^{1} \frac{x^4 T_2}{\sqrt{1-x^2}} \, dx = \frac{1}{2}$$

Hence the required approximation is $f(x) = \frac{3}{8} T_0 + \frac{1}{2} T_2$.

Example 7. *Find a uniform polynomial approximation of degree four or less to e^x on [– 1, 1] using Lanczos economization with a tolerance of ε = 0.02.*

Sol. We have

$$f(x) = e^x = 1 + x + \frac{x^2}{2} + \frac{x^3}{6} + \frac{x^4}{24} + \frac{x^5}{120} + \ldots\ldots$$

Since $\frac{1}{120} = 0.008\ldots\ldots$, therefore

$$e^x = 1 + x + \frac{x^2}{2} + \frac{x^3}{6} + \frac{x^4}{24} \quad \ldots(1)$$

with a tolerance of ε = 0.02.

Changing each power of x in (1) in terms of Chebyshev polynomials, we get

$$e^x = T_0 + T_1 + \frac{1}{4}(T_0 + T_2) + \frac{1}{24}(3T_1 + T_3) + \frac{1}{192}(3T_0 + 4T_2 + T_4)$$

$$= \frac{81}{64}T_0 + \frac{9}{8}T_1 + \frac{13}{48}T_2 + \frac{1}{24}T_3 + \frac{1}{192}T_4 \quad \ldots(2)$$

We have $\frac{1}{192} = 0.005 \ldots\ldots$

∴ The magnitude of last term on RHS of (2) is less than 0.02.

Hence the required economized polynomial approximation for e^x is given by

$$e^x = \frac{81}{64}T_0 + \frac{9}{8}T_1 + \frac{13}{48}T_2 + \frac{1}{24}T_3$$

or

$$e^x = \frac{x^3}{6} + \frac{13}{24}x^2 + x + \frac{191}{192}.$$

Example 8. *The function f is defined by* $f(x) = \frac{1}{x}\int_0^x \frac{1 - e^{-t^2}}{t^2}\,dt$

Approximate f by a polynomial $P(x) = a + bx + cx^2$ such that

$$\max_{|x| \le 1} |f(x) - P(x)| \le 5 \times 10^{-3}.$$

Sol. The given function

$$f(x) = \frac{1}{x}\int_0^x \left(1 - \frac{t^2}{2} + \frac{t^4}{6} - \frac{t^6}{24} + \frac{t^8}{120} - \frac{t^{10}}{720} + \ldots\ldots\right) dt$$

$$= 1 - \frac{x^2}{6} + \frac{x^4}{30} - \frac{x^6}{168} + \frac{x^8}{1080} - \frac{x^{10}}{7920} + \ldots\ldots \quad \ldots(1)$$

The tolerable error is $5 \times 10^{-3} \approx 0.005$.

Truncating the series (1) at x^8, we get

$$P(x) = 1 - \frac{x^2}{6} + \frac{x^4}{30} - \frac{x^6}{168} + \frac{x^8}{1080}$$

$$= T_0 - \frac{1}{12}(T_2 + T_0) + \frac{1}{240}(T_4 + 4T_2 + 3T_0) - \frac{1}{5376}(T_6 + 6T_4 + 15T_2 + 10T_0)$$

$$+ \frac{1}{138240}(T_8 + 8T_6 + 28T_4 + 56T_2 + 35T_0)$$

$$= 0.92755973\ T_0 - 0.06905175\ T_2 + 0.003253\ T_4 - 0.000128\ T_6 + 0.000007\ T_8 \quad ...(2)$$

Truncating RHS of (2) at T_2, we obtain the required polynomial

$$P(x) = 0.92755973\ T_0 - 0.06905175\ T_2$$
$$= 0.99661148 - 0.13810350x^2 = 0.9966 - 0.1381x^2$$

The maximum absolute error in the neglected terms is obviously less than the tolerable error.

Example 9. *Suppose we want to approximate the function* $f(x) = \dfrac{1}{3+x}$ *on the interval* $-1 \le x \le 1$ *with a polynomial P(x) such that*

$$\max_{|x| \le 1} | f(x) - P(x) | \le 0.021$$

(i) Show that there does not exist a first degree polynomial satisfying this condition.

(ii) Show that there exists a second degree polynomial satisfying this condition.

Sol.
$$f(x) = \frac{1}{3+x} = \frac{1}{3}\left(1+\frac{x}{3}\right)^{-1}$$
$$= \frac{1}{3} - \frac{1}{9}x + \frac{1}{27}x^2 - \frac{1}{81}x^3 + \ldots ; -1 \le x \le 1.$$

We approximate $f(x)$ by a second degree polynomial $P_2(x) = \dfrac{1}{3} - \dfrac{1}{9}x + \dfrac{1}{27}x^2$

with an error of approximation $= \dfrac{1}{81} \approx 0.0123$

If we approximate $f(x)$ by the first degree polynomial $P_1(x) = \dfrac{1}{3} - \dfrac{1}{9}x$ then the error of approximation $= \dfrac{1}{27} \approx 0.04$ which is more than the tolerable error 0.021.

However, changing $P_2(x)$ interms of Chebyshev polynomials, we get

$$P_2(x) = \frac{1}{3}T_0 - \frac{1}{9}T_1 + \frac{1}{54}(T_0 + T_2)$$
$$= \frac{19}{54}T_0 - \frac{1}{9}T_1 + \frac{1}{54}T_2$$

If we truncate $P_2(x)$ at T_1 then the max. error of approximation is $\dfrac{1}{54}$ and the total error becomes $\dfrac{1}{54} + \dfrac{1}{81} = \dfrac{5}{162} \approx 0.03$ which is again more than the tolerable error 0.021.

Hence $\exists$ no first degree polynomial satisfying the given accuracy.

However $P_2(x) = \dfrac{1}{3} - \dfrac{1}{9}x + \dfrac{1}{27}x^2$ is the required second degree polynomial of approximation for $f(x) = \dfrac{1}{3+x}$ satisfying the given accuracy.

Example 10. *Find a polynomial P(x) of degree as low as possible such that*

$$\max_{|x| \le 1} \left| e^{x^2} - P(x) \right| \le 0.05.$$

Sol.

$$e^{x^2} = 1 + x^2 + \frac{x^4}{2} + \frac{x^6}{6} + \frac{x^8}{24} + \frac{x^{10}}{120} + \ldots$$

$$\approx 1 + x^2 + \frac{x^4}{2} + \frac{x^6}{6} + \frac{x^8}{24} = \text{P}(x) \qquad \ldots(1)$$

with error in the leading term $= \dfrac{1}{120} \approx 0.0083.$

Expressing P(x) as sum of Chebyshev polynomials, we get

$$\text{P}(x) = \frac{1}{3072} (5379\ \text{T}_0 + 2600\ \text{T}_2 + 316\ \text{T}_4 + 24\ \text{T}_6 + \text{T}_8)$$

We have $\left| \dfrac{1}{3072} (24\ \text{T}_6 + \text{T}_8) \right| \le 0.008138$ $\quad \left| \because \dfrac{25}{3072} = 0.008138 \text{ since } |x| \le 1 \right.$

which is also less than 0.05.

Hence we get the required approximation

$$e^{x^2} \simeq \frac{1}{3072} (5379\ \text{T}_0 + 2600\ \text{T}_2 + 316\ \text{T}_4)$$

$$= \frac{1}{3072} [5379 + 2600\ (2x^2 - 1) + 316\ (8x^4 - 8x^2 + 1)]$$

$$= \frac{1}{3072} (3095 + 2672\ x^2 + 2528\ x^4)$$

$$= 1.0075 + 0.8698\ x^2 + 0.8229\ x^4.$$

ASSIGNMENT

1. Express $1 + x - x^2 + x^3$ as sum of Chebyshev polynomials.
2. Prove that $x^2 = \dfrac{1}{2} [\text{T}_0(x) + \text{T}_2(x)]$
3. Express $\text{T}_0(x) + 2\text{T}_1(x) + \text{T}_2(x)$ as polynomials in x.
4. Obtain the best lower degree approximation to the cubic $x^3 + 2x^2$.
5. Economize the series $\cos x = 1 - \dfrac{x^2}{2} + \dfrac{x^4}{24} - \dfrac{x^6}{720}$.
6. Explain approximation of function by Chebyshev polynomial with suitable example.
7. Economize the series

$$f(x) = 1 - \frac{x}{2} - \frac{x^2}{8} - \frac{x^3}{16}$$

Answers

1. $\frac{1}{2}T_0(x) + \frac{7}{4}T_1(x) - \frac{1}{2}T_2(x) + \frac{1}{4}T_3(x)$ 3. $2x + 2x^2$ 4. $2x^2 + \frac{3}{4}x$

5. $\frac{191}{192} - \frac{x^2}{2}$ 7. $\frac{15}{16} - \frac{1}{2}x$.

5.42. RATIONAL APPROXIMATION

When the function $f(x)$ is such that it retains a finite value as $x \to \infty$, polynomial approximations for $f(x)$ give very poor results. Polynomial approximation is not always the best approximation when $f(x)$ is a rational function.

Rational approximation for a function $f(x)$ is written in the form

$$f(x) = R_{n,m}(x) = \frac{a_0 + a_1 x + \ldots + a_n x^n}{b_0 + b_1 x + \ldots + b_m x^m} = \frac{\sum_{i=0}^{n} a_i x^i}{\sum_{j=0}^{m} b_j x^j} \quad \ldots(1)$$

Since we can always divide both numerator and denominator in (1) by b_0, we take $b_0 = 1$. b_0 will generally not be zero so that the approximation does not become undefined at $x = 0$.

We generally use rational approximations to compute the values of the functions like e^x, $\sin x$, $\cos x$ etc. for large values of argument x. This approximation is also called **Pade approximation.**

This is illustrated through the following examples.

EXAMPLES

Example 1. *Obtain the rational approximation for e^x of the form $\frac{a_0 + a_1 x}{1 + b_1 x}$.*

Sol. We have

$$e^x - \left(\frac{a_0 + a_1 x}{1 + b_1 x}\right) = \frac{\left(1 + x + \frac{x^2}{2} + \ldots\right)(1 + b_1 x) - (a_0 + a_1 x)}{1 + b_1 x}$$

Set $\left(1 + x + \frac{x^2}{2} + \ldots\right)(1 + b_1 x) - (a_0 + a_1 x) = \sum_{j=0}^{\infty} d_j x^j$

To determine the three constants a_0, a_1 and b_1, put $d_j = 0, j = 0, 1, 2$, we get

$$1 - a_0 = 0$$
$$1 + b_1 - a_1 = 0$$
$$b_1 + \frac{1}{2} = 0$$

$\Rightarrow$ $a_0 = 1, \quad b_1 = -\frac{1}{2}, \quad a_1 = \frac{1}{2}$

$$\therefore \qquad e^x \simeq \frac{1+\frac{1}{2}x}{1-\frac{1}{2}x} + O(x^3)$$

Example 2. *Obtain the rational approximation of the form* $\frac{a_0 + a_1x + a_2x^2}{1+b_1x}$ *to the function* e^x.

Sol. We have,

$$e^x - \left(\frac{a_0 + a_1x + a_2x^2}{1+b_1x}\right) = \frac{\left(1+x+\frac{x^2}{2}+\frac{x^3}{6}+\ldots\right)(1+b_1x) - (a_0 + a_1x + a_2x^2)}{1+b_1x}$$

Set $\qquad \left(1+x+\frac{x^2}{2}+\frac{x^3}{6}+\ldots\right)(1 + b_1x) - (a_0 + a_1x + a_2x^2) = \sum_{j=0}^{\infty} d_jx^j$

To determine the constants a_0, a_1, a_2 and b_1, we put $d_j = 0$, $j = 0, 1, 2, 3$, we get

$$1 - a_0 = 0$$

$$b_1 + 1 - a_1 = 0$$

$$b_1 + \frac{1}{2} - a_2 = 0$$

$$\frac{1}{2}b_1 + \frac{1}{6} = 0$$

$$\Rightarrow \qquad a_0 = 1, \quad a_1 = \frac{2}{3}, \quad a_2 = \frac{1}{6}, \quad b_1 = -\frac{1}{3}$$

$$\therefore \qquad e^x \simeq \frac{1+\frac{2}{3}x+\frac{1}{6}x^2}{1-\frac{1}{3}x} + O(x^4).$$

ASSIGNMENT

1. Obtain the rational approximation for e^x of the form $\frac{a_0 + a_1x + a_2x^2}{1+b_1x+b_2x^2}$.

2. Obtain the rational approximation of the form $\frac{a_0 + a_1x}{1+b_1x+b_2x^2}$ to the function e^x.

Answers

1. $e^x \simeq \frac{1+\frac{1}{2}x+\frac{1}{12}x^2}{1-\frac{1}{2}x+\frac{1}{12}x^2} + O(x^5)$

2. $e^x \simeq \frac{1+\frac{1}{3}x}{1-\frac{2}{3}x+\frac{1}{6}x^2} + O(x^4)$.

❑❑❑

UNIT-III

Differentiation: Methods based on Interpolation and Finite Differences, Richardson Extrapolation.

Integration: Error Analysis of Trepezoidal and Simpson Methods, Newton Cotes Integration Methods, Gaussian Integration Methods: Gauss Legendre Method, Lobatto Integration Method and Radau Integration Method. Error Terms in Integration Methods.

6

Numerical Differentiation and Integration

6.1. INTRODUCTION

Consider a function of a single variable $y = f(x)$. If $f(x)$ is defined as an expression, its derivative or integral may often be determined using the techniques of calculus.

However, when $f(x)$ is a complicated function or when it is given in a tabular form, we use numerical methods.

In this chapter, we will discuss numerical methods for approximating the derivative(s) $f^{(r)}(x)$, $r \geq 1$ of a given function $f(x)$ and for the evaluation of the integral $\int_a^b f(x)\,dx$ where a, b may be finite or infinite.

The accuracy attainable by these methods would depend on the given function and the order of the polynomial used. If the polynomial fitted is exact then the error would be theoretically zero. In practice, however, rounding errors will introduce errors in the calculated values.

The error introduced in obtaining derivatives is in general much worse than that introduced in determining integrals. It may be observed that any errors in approximating a function are amplified while taking the derivative whereas they are smoothed out in integration.

Thus numerical differentiation should be avoided if an alternative exists.

6.2. NUMERICAL DIFFERENTIATION [*M.T.U. 2012, U.P.T.U. 2008*]

In the case of numerical data, the functional form of $f(x)$ is not known in general. First we have to find an appropriate form of $f(x)$ and then obtain its derivatives. So "**Numerical differentiation**" is concerned with the method of finding the successive derivatives of a function at a given argument, using the given table of entries corresponding to a set of arguments, equally or unequally spaced. Using the theory of interpolation, a suitable interpolating polynomial can be chosen to represent the function to a good degree of approximation in the given interval of the argument.

For the proper choice of interpolation formula, the criterion is same as in case of interpolation problems. In case of equidistant values of x, if the derivative is to be found at a point near the beginning or the end of the given set of values, we should use Newton's forward or backward difference formula accordingly. Also if the derivative is to be found at a point near the middle of the given set of values, then we should use any one of the central difference formulae. However, if the values of the function are not known at equidistant values of x, we shall use Newton's divided difference or Lagrange's formula.

6.3. FORMULAE FOR DERIVATIVES

(1) Newton's forward difference interpolation formula is

$$y = y_0 + u\,\Delta y_0 + \frac{u(u-1)}{2!}\Delta^2 y_0 + \frac{u(u-1)(u-2)}{3!}\Delta^3 y_0 + \cdots \qquad \ldots(1)$$

where

$$u = \frac{x-a}{h} \qquad \ldots(2)$$

Differentiating eqn. (1) with respect to u, we get

$$\frac{dy}{du} = \Delta y_0 + \frac{2u-1}{2}\Delta^2 y_0 + \frac{3u^2-6u+2}{6}\Delta^3 y_0 + \cdots \qquad \ldots(3)$$

Differentiating eqn. (2) with respect to x, we get

$$\frac{du}{dx} = \frac{1}{h} \qquad \ldots(4)$$

We know that

$$\frac{dy}{dx} = \frac{dy}{du}\cdot\frac{du}{dx} = \frac{1}{h}\left[\Delta y_0 + \left(\frac{2u-1}{2}\right)\Delta^2 y_0 + \left(\frac{3u^2-6u+2}{6}\right)\Delta^3 y_0 + \cdots\right] \qquad \ldots(5)$$

Expression (5) provides the value of $\frac{dy}{dx}$ at any x which is not tabulated.

Formula (5) becomes simple for tabulated values of x, in particular when $x = a$ and $u = 0$

Putting $u = 0$ in (5), we get

$$\left(\frac{dy}{dx}\right)_{x=a} = \frac{1}{h}\left[\Delta y_0 - \frac{1}{2}\Delta^2 y_0 + \frac{1}{3}\Delta^3 y_0 - \frac{1}{4}\Delta^4 y_0 + \frac{1}{5}\Delta^5 y_0 - \ldots\right] \qquad \ldots(6)$$

(M.T.U. 2013)

Differentiating eqn. (5) with respect to x, we get

$$\frac{d^2y}{dx^2} = \frac{d}{dx}\left(\frac{dy}{dx}\right) = \frac{d}{du}\left(\frac{dy}{dx}\right)\frac{du}{dx}$$

$$= \frac{1}{h}\left[\Delta^2 y_0 + (u-1)\,\Delta^3 y_0 + \left(\frac{6u^2-18u+11}{12}\right)\Delta^4 y_0 + \ldots\right]\frac{1}{h}$$

$$= \frac{1}{h^2}\left[\Delta^2 y_0 + (u-1)\,\Delta^3 y_0 + \left(\frac{6u^2-18u+11}{12}\right)\Delta^4 y_0 + \ldots\right] \qquad \ldots(7)$$

Putting $u = 0$ in (7), we get

$$\left(\frac{d^2y}{dx^2}\right)_{x=a} = \frac{1}{h^2}\left(\Delta^2 y_0 - \Delta^3 y_0 + \frac{11}{12}\Delta^4 y_0 - \ldots\right) \qquad \ldots(8)$$

Similarly, we get

$$\left(\frac{d^3y}{dx^3}\right)_{x=a} = \frac{1}{h^3}\left(\Delta^3 y_0 - \frac{3}{2}\Delta^4 y_0 + \ldots\right) \qquad \ldots(9)$$

and so on.

Formulae for computing higher derivatives may be obtained by successive differentiation.

Aliter : We know that

$$E = e^{hD} \Rightarrow 1 + \Delta = e^{hD}$$

$$\therefore \quad hD = \log(1+\Delta) = \Delta - \frac{\Delta^2}{2} + \frac{\Delta^3}{3} - \frac{\Delta^4}{4} + \ldots$$

$$\Rightarrow \quad D = \frac{1}{h}\left[\Delta - \frac{1}{2}\Delta^2 + \frac{1}{3}\Delta^3 - \frac{1}{4}\Delta^4 + \ldots\right]$$

[U.P.T.U. (MCA) 2007]

Similarly, $$D^2 = \frac{1}{h^2}\left(\Delta - \frac{1}{2}\Delta^2 + \frac{1}{3}\Delta^3 - \frac{1}{4}\Delta^4 + \ldots\right)^2 = \frac{1}{h^2}\left(\Delta^2 - \Delta^3 + \frac{11}{12}\Delta^4 - \frac{5}{6}\Delta^5 + \ldots\right)$$

and $$D^3 = \frac{1}{h^3}\left(\Delta^3 - \frac{3}{2}\Delta^4 + \ldots\right)$$

(2) Newton's backward difference interpolation formula is

$$y = y_n + u\,\nabla y_n + \frac{u(u+1)}{2!}\nabla^2 y_n + \frac{u(u+1)(u+2)}{3!}\nabla^3 y_n + \ldots \quad \ldots(10)$$

where $u = \dfrac{x - x_n}{h}$ ...(11)

Differentiating (10) with respect to, u, we get

$$\frac{dy}{du} = \nabla y_n + \left(\frac{2u+1}{2}\right)\nabla^2 y_n + \left(\frac{3u^2+6u+2}{6}\right)\nabla^3 y_n + \ldots \quad \ldots(12)$$

Differentiating (11) with respect to x, we get

$$\frac{du}{dx} = \frac{1}{h} \quad \ldots(13)$$

Now,

$$\frac{dy}{dx} = \frac{dy}{du}\cdot\frac{du}{dx}$$

$$= \frac{1}{h}\left[\nabla y_n + \left(\frac{2u+1}{2}\right)\nabla^2 y_n + \left(\frac{3u^2+6u+2}{6}\right)\nabla^3 y_n + \ldots\right] \quad \ldots(14)$$

Expression (14) provides us the value of $\dfrac{dy}{dx}$ at any x which is not tabulated.

At $x = x_n$, we have $u = 0$

$\therefore$ Putting $u = 0$ in (14), we get

$$\boxed{\left(\frac{dy}{dx}\right)_{x=x_n} = \frac{1}{h}\left(\nabla y_n + \frac{1}{2}\nabla^2 y_n + \frac{1}{3}\nabla^3 y_n + \frac{1}{4}\nabla^4 y_n + \ldots\right)} \quad \ldots(15)$$

Differentiating (14) with respect to x, we get

$$\frac{d^2y}{dx^2} = \frac{d}{du}\left(\frac{dy}{dx}\right)\frac{du}{dx}$$

$$= \frac{1}{h^2}\left[\nabla^2 y_n + (u+1)\nabla^3 y_n + \left(\frac{6u^2+18u+11}{12}\right)\nabla^4 y_n + \ldots\right] \quad \ldots(16)$$

Putting $u = 0$ in (16), we get

$$\left(\frac{d^2y}{dx^2}\right)_{x=x_n} = \frac{1}{h^2}\left(\nabla^2 y_n + \nabla^3 y_n + \frac{11}{12}\nabla^4 y_n + \ldots\right) \quad \ldots(17)$$

Similarly, we get

$$\left(\frac{d^3y}{dx^3}\right)_{x=x_n} = \frac{1}{h^3}\left(\nabla^3 y_n + \frac{3}{2}\nabla^4 y_n + \ldots\right) \quad \ldots(18)$$

and so on.

Formulae for computing higher derivatives may be obtained by successive differentiation.

Aliter: We know that

$$E^{-1} = 1 - \nabla$$

$$e^{-hD} = 1 - \nabla$$

$$\therefore \quad -hD = \log(1 - \nabla) = -\left(\nabla + \frac{1}{2}\nabla^2 + \frac{1}{3}\nabla^3 + \frac{1}{4}\nabla^4 + \ldots\right)$$

$$\Rightarrow \quad D = \frac{1}{h}\left(\nabla + \frac{1}{2}\nabla^2 + \frac{1}{3}\nabla^3 + \frac{1}{4}\nabla^4 + \ldots\right)$$

Also, $$D^2 = \frac{1}{h^2}\left(\nabla + \frac{1}{2}\nabla^2 + \frac{1}{3}\nabla^3 + \ldots\right)^2 = \frac{1}{h^2}\left(\nabla^2 + \nabla^3 + \frac{11}{12}\nabla^4 + \ldots\right)$$

Similarly, $$D^3 = \frac{1}{h^3}\left(\nabla^3 + \frac{3}{2}\nabla^4 + \ldots\right) \text{ and so on.}$$

(3) Stirling's central difference interpolation formula is

$$y = y_0 + \frac{u}{1!}\left(\frac{\Delta y_0 + \Delta y_{-1}}{2}\right) + \frac{u^2}{2!}\Delta^2 y_{-1} + \frac{u(u^2 - 1^2)}{3!}\left(\frac{\Delta^3 y_{-1} + \Delta^3 y_{-2}}{2}\right)$$

$$+ \frac{u^2(u^2 - 1^2)}{4!}\Delta^4 y_{-2} + \frac{u(u^2 - 1^2)(u^2 - 2^2)}{5!}\left(\frac{\Delta^5 y_{-2} + \Delta^5 y_{-3}}{2}\right) + \ldots \quad \ldots(19)$$

where $$u = \frac{x - a}{h} \quad \ldots(20)$$

Differentiating eqn. (19) with respect to u, we get

$$\frac{dy}{du} = \frac{\Delta y_0 + \Delta y_{-1}}{2} + u\Delta^2 y_{-1} + \left(\frac{3u^2 - 1}{6}\right)\left(\frac{\Delta^3 y_{-1} + \Delta^3 y_{-2}}{2}\right)$$

$$+ \left(\frac{4u^3 - 2u}{4!}\right)\Delta^4 y_{-2} + \left(\frac{5u^4 - 15u^2 + 4}{5!}\right)\left(\frac{\Delta^5 y_{-2} + \Delta^5 y_{-3}}{2}\right) + \ldots \quad \ldots(21)$$

Differentiating eqn. (20) with respect to x, we get

$$\frac{du}{dx} = \frac{1}{h} \quad \ldots(22)$$

Now,

$$\frac{dy}{dx} = \frac{dy}{du} \cdot \frac{du}{dx}$$

$$= \frac{1}{h}\left[\frac{\Delta y_0 + \Delta y_{-1}}{2} + u\,\Delta^2 y_{-1} + \left(\frac{3u^2 - 1}{6}\right)\left(\frac{\Delta^3 y_{-1} + \Delta^3 y_{-2}}{2}\right) + \left(\frac{4u^3 - 2u}{4!}\right)\Delta^4 y_{-2} + \left(\frac{5u^4 - 15u^2 + 4}{5!}\right)\left(\frac{\Delta^5 y_{-2} + \Delta^5 y_{-3}}{2}\right) + \ldots\right] \quad \ldots(23)$$

Expression (23) provides us the value of $\frac{dy}{dx}$ at any x which is not tabulated.

Put $x = a$, we have $u = 0$

$\therefore$ Putting $u = 0$ in (23), we get

$$\left(\frac{dy}{dx}\right)_{x=a} = \frac{1}{h}\left[\left(\frac{\Delta y_0 + \Delta y_{-1}}{2}\right) - \frac{1}{6}\left(\frac{\Delta^3 y_{-1} + \Delta^3 y_{-2}}{2}\right) + \frac{1}{30}\left(\frac{\Delta^5 y_{-2} + \Delta^5 y_{-3}}{2}\right) - \ldots\right] \quad \ldots(24)$$

Differentiating eqn. (23) with respect to x, we get

$$\frac{d^2y}{dx^2} = \frac{d}{du}\left(\frac{dy}{dx}\right)\frac{du}{dx}$$

$$= \frac{1}{h^2}\left[\Delta^2 y_{-1} + u\left(\frac{\Delta^3 y_{-1} + \Delta^3 y_{-2}}{2}\right) + \left(\frac{6u^2 - 1}{12}\right)\Delta^4 y_{-2} + \left(\frac{2u^3 - 3u}{12}\right)\left(\frac{\Delta^5 y_{-2} + \Delta^5 y_{-3}}{2}\right) + \ldots\right] \quad \ldots(25)$$

Putting $u = 0$ in (25), we get

$$\left(\frac{d^2y}{dx^2}\right)_{x=a} = \frac{1}{h^2}\left(\Delta^2 y_{-1} - \frac{1}{12}\Delta^4 y_{-2} + \frac{1}{90}\Delta^6 y_{-3} - \ldots\right) \quad \ldots(26)$$

and so on.

Formulae for computing higher derivatives may be obtained by successive differentiation.

(4) Bessel's central difference interpolation formula is

$$y = \left(\frac{y_0 + y_1}{2}\right) + \left(u - \frac{1}{2}\right)\Delta y_0 + \frac{u(u-1)}{2!}\left(\frac{\Delta^2 y_{-1} + \Delta^2 y_0}{2}\right) + \frac{u(u-1)\left(u - \frac{1}{2}\right)}{3!}\Delta^3 y_{-1}$$

$$+ \frac{(u+1)\,u(u-1)(u-2)}{4!}\left(\frac{\Delta^4 y_{-2} + \Delta^4 y_{-1}}{2}\right) + \frac{(u+1)\,u(u-1)(u-2)\left(u - \frac{1}{2}\right)}{5!}\Delta^5 y_{-2}$$

$$+ \frac{(u+2)(u+1)\,u(u-1)(u-2)(u-3)}{6!}\left(\frac{\Delta^6 y_{-3} + \Delta^6 y_{-2}}{2}\right) + \ldots \quad \ldots(27)$$

where $u = \frac{x - a}{h}$ ...(28)

Differentiating eqn. (27) with respect to u, we get

$$\frac{dy}{du} = \Delta y_0 + \left(\frac{2u-1}{2!}\right)\left(\frac{\Delta^2 y_{-1} + \Delta^2 y_0}{2}\right) + \left(\frac{3u^2 - 3u + \frac{1}{2}}{3!}\right) \Delta^3 y_{-1}$$

$$+ \left(\frac{4u^3 - 6u^2 - 2u + 2}{4!}\right)\left(\frac{\Delta^4 y_{-2} + \Delta^4 y_{-1}}{2}\right) + \left(\frac{5u^4 - 10u^3 + 5u - 1}{5!}\right) \Delta^5 y_{-2}$$

$$+ \left(\frac{6u^5 - 15u^4 - 20u^3 + 45u^2 + 8u - 12}{6!}\right)\left(\frac{\Delta^6 y_{-3} + \Delta^6 y_{-2}}{2}\right) + \ldots \quad \ldots(29)$$

Differentiating eqn. (28) with respect to x, we get

$$\frac{du}{dx} = \frac{1}{h}$$

Now, $$\frac{dy}{dx} = \frac{dy}{du} \cdot \frac{du}{dx}$$

$$= \frac{1}{h}\left[\Delta y_0 + \left(\frac{2u-1}{2!}\right)\left(\frac{\Delta^2 y_{-1} + \Delta^2 y_0}{2}\right) + \left(\frac{3u^2 - 3u + \frac{1}{2}}{3!}\right) \Delta^3 y_{-1}\right.$$

$$+ \left(\frac{4u^3 - 6u^2 - 2u + 2}{4!}\right)\left(\frac{\Delta^4 y_{-2} + \Delta^4 y_{-1}}{2}\right) + \left(\frac{5u^4 - 10u^3 + 5u - 1}{5!}\right) \Delta^5 y_{-2}$$

$$\left. + \left(\frac{6u^5 - 15u^4 - 20u^3 + 45u^2 + 8u - 12}{6!}\right)\left(\frac{\Delta^6 y_{-3} + \Delta^6 y_{-2}}{2}\right) + \ldots\right] \quad \ldots(30)$$

Expression (30) provides us the value of $\frac{dy}{dx}$ at any x which is not tabulated.

Put $x = a$, we have $u = 0$

$\therefore$ Putting $u = 0$ in (30), we get

$$\left(\frac{dy}{dx}\right)_{x=a} = \frac{1}{h}\left[\Delta y_0 - \frac{1}{2}\left(\frac{\Delta^2 y_{-1} + \Delta^2 y_0}{2}\right) + \frac{1}{12}\Delta^3 y_{-1} + \frac{1}{12}\left(\frac{\Delta^4 y_{-2} + \Delta^4 y_{-1}}{2}\right)\right.$$

$$\left. - \frac{1}{120}\Delta^5 y_{-2} - \frac{1}{60}\left(\frac{\Delta^6 y_{-3} + \Delta^6 y_{-2}}{2}\right) + \ldots\right] \quad \ldots(31)$$

Differentiating eqn. (30) with respect to x, we get

$$\frac{d^2 y}{dx^2} = \frac{d}{dx}\left(\frac{dy}{dx}\right) = \frac{d}{du}\left(\frac{dy}{dx}\right)\frac{du}{dx}$$

$$= \frac{1}{h^2}\left[\left(\frac{\Delta^2 y_{-1} + \Delta^2 y_0}{2}\right) + \left(\frac{2u-1}{2}\right)\Delta^3 y_{-1} + \left(\frac{6u^2-6u-1}{12}\right)\left(\frac{\Delta^4 y_{-2} + \Delta^4 y_{-1}}{2}\right)\right.$$

$$+ \left(\frac{4u^3-6u^2+1}{24}\right)\Delta^5 y_{-2}$$

$$\left. + \left(\frac{15u^4 - 30u^3 - 30u^2 + 45u + 4}{360}\right)\left(\frac{\Delta^6 y_{-3} + \Delta^6 y_{-2}}{2}\right) + \ldots\right] \quad \ldots(32)$$

Putting $u = 0$ in eqn. (32), we get

$$\left(\frac{d^2y}{dx^2}\right)_{x=a} = \frac{1}{h^2}\left[\left(\frac{\Delta^2 y_{-1} + \Delta^2 y_0}{2}\right) - \frac{1}{2}\Delta^3 y_{-1} - \frac{1}{12}\left(\frac{\Delta^4 y_{-2} + \Delta^4 y_{-1}}{2}\right)\right.$$

$$\left. + \frac{1}{24}\Delta^5 y_{-2} + \frac{1}{90}\left(\frac{\Delta^6 y_{-3} + \Delta^6 y_{-2}}{2}\right) + \ldots\right] \quad \ldots(33)$$

and so on.

(5) For unequally spaced values of the argument

(*i*) Newton's divided difference formula is

$$f(x) = f(x_0) + (x - x_0)\,\Delta f(x_0) + (x - x_0)(x - x_1)\,\Delta^2 f(x_0) + (x - x_0)(x - x_1)$$
$$(x - x_2)\,\Delta^3 f(x_0) + (x - x_0)(x - x_1)\,(x - x_2)(x - x_3)\,\Delta^4 f(x_0) + \ldots \quad \ldots(34)$$

$f'(x)$ is given by

$$f'(x) = \Delta f(x_0) + \{2x - (x_0 + x_1)\}\,\Delta^2 f(x_0) + \{3x^2 - 2x(x_0 + x_1 + x_2)$$
$$+ (x_0x_1 + x_1x_2 + x_2x_0)\}\,\Delta^3 f(x_0) + \ldots \quad \ldots(35)$$

(*ii*) Lagrange's interpolation formula is

$$f(x) = \frac{(x - x_1)(x - x_2)\ldots(x - x_n)}{(x_0 - x_1)(x_0 - x_2)\ldots(x_0 - x_n)}\,f(x_0) + \frac{(x - x_0)(x - x_2)\ldots(x - x_n)}{(x_1 - x_0)(x_1 - x_2)\ldots(x_1 - x_n)}\,f(x_1) + \ldots$$
$$\ldots(36)$$

$f'(x)$ can be obtained by differentiating $f(x)$ in eqn. (36).

Note 1. Formula (8) can be extended as

$$\left(\frac{d^2y}{dx^2}\right)_{x=a} = \frac{1}{h^2}\left(\Delta^2 - \Delta^3 + \frac{11}{12}\Delta^4 - \frac{5}{6}\Delta^5 + \frac{137}{180}\Delta^6 - \frac{7}{10}\Delta^7 + \frac{363}{560}\Delta^8 + \ldots\right) y_0$$

2. Formula (17) can be extended as

$$\left(\frac{d^2y}{dx^2}\right)_{x=x_n} = \frac{1}{h^2}\left(\nabla^2 + \nabla^3 + \frac{11}{12}\nabla^4 + \frac{5}{6}\nabla^5 + \frac{137}{180}\nabla^6 + \frac{7}{10}\nabla^7 + \frac{363}{560}\nabla^8 + \ldots\right) y_n.$$

6.4. MAXIMA AND MINIMA OF A TABULATED FUNCTION

Since maxima and minima of $y = f(x)$ can be found by equating $\frac{dy}{dx}$ to zero and solving the equation for the argument x, the same method can be used to determine maxima and minima of tabulated function by differentiating the interpolating polynomial.

e.g. if Newton's forward difference formula is used, we have

$$y = y_0 + u\,\Delta y_0 + \frac{u(u-1)}{2!}\Delta^2 y_0 + \frac{u(u-1)(u-2)}{3!}\Delta^3 y_0 + \ldots \qquad \ldots(1)$$

Differentiating (1) with respect to u, we get

$$\frac{dy}{du} = \Delta y_0 + \frac{2u-1}{2!}\Delta^2 y_0 + \frac{3u^2-6u+2}{3!}\Delta^3 y_0 + \ldots$$

For maxima or minima,

$$\frac{dy}{du} = 0$$

$$\Rightarrow \qquad \Delta y_0 + \frac{2u-1}{2!}\Delta^2 y_0 + \frac{3u^2-6u+2}{3!}\Delta^3 y_0 + \ldots = 0 \qquad \ldots(2)$$

If we terminate LHS series after third differences for convenience, eqn. (2) being a quadratic in u gives two values of u.

Corresponding to these values, $x = a + uh$ will give the corresponding x at which function may be maximum or minimum.

For maximum, $\frac{d^2y}{du^2}$ = (–)ve; For minimum, $\frac{d^2y}{du^2}$ = (+)ve.

EXAMPLES

Example 1. *Find* $\frac{dy}{dx}$ *at* $x = 0.1$ *from the following table:*

x :	*0.1*	*0.2*	*0.3*	*0.4*
y :	*0.9975*	*0.9900*	*0.9776*	*0.9604.*

Sol. Take $a = 0.1$. The difference table is

x	y	Δy	$\Delta^2 y$	$\Delta^3 y$
0.1	0.9975			
		0.0075		
0.2	0.9900		– 0.0049	
		– 0.0124		0.0001
0.3	0.9776		– 0.0048	
		– 0.0172		
0.4	0.9604			

Here $\qquad h = 0.1$ and $y_0 = 0.9975$

$$\left[\frac{dy}{dx}\right]_{x=0.1} = \frac{1}{h}\left[\Delta y_0 - \frac{1}{2}\Delta^2 y_0 + \frac{1}{3}\Delta^3 y_0\right]$$

$$= \frac{1}{0.1}\left[-0.0075 - \frac{1}{2}(-0.0049) + \frac{1}{3}(0.0001)\right] = -0.050167.$$

Example 2. *The table given below reveals the velocity 'v' of a body during the time 't' specified. Find its acceleration at t = 1.1.*

t :	1.0	1.1	1.2	1.3	1.4
v :	43.1	47.7	52.1	56.4	60.8.

Sol. The difference table is

t	v	Δv	$\Delta^2 v$	$\Delta^3 v$	$\Delta^4 v$
1.0	43.1				
		4.6			
1.1	47.7		– 0.2		
		4.4		0.1	
1.2	52.1		– 0.1		0.1
		4.3		0.2	
1.3	56.4		0.1		
		4.4			
1.4	60.8				

Let $a = 1.1$,

$\therefore$ $v_0 = 47.7$ and $h = 0.1$

Acceleration at $t = 1.1$ is given by

$$\left[\frac{dv}{dt}\right]_{t=1.1} = \frac{1}{h}\left[\Delta v_0 - \frac{1}{2}\Delta^2 v_0 + \frac{1}{3}\Delta^3 v_0\right] = \frac{1}{0.1}\left[4.4 - \frac{1}{2}(-0.1) + \frac{1}{3}(0.2)\right]$$

$$= 45.1667$$

Hence the required acceleration is **45.1667.**

Example 3. *Find f '(1.1) and f "(1.1) from the following table :*

x :	1.0	1.2	1.4	1.6	1.8	2.0
$f(x)$:	0.0	0.1280	0.5540	1.2960	2.4320	4.000.

Sol. Since we are to find $f'(x)$ and $f''(x)$ for non-tabular value of x, we proceed as follows :

Newton's forward difference formula is

$$y = y_0 + u\,\Delta y_0 + \frac{u(u-1)}{2!}\Delta^2 y_0 + \frac{u(u-1)(u-2)}{3!}\Delta^3 y_0 + \frac{u(u-1)(u-2)(u-3)}{4!}\Delta^4 y_0 + \ldots \quad \ldots(1)$$

where $$u = \frac{x-a}{h} \quad \ldots(2)$$

Differentiating eqn. (1) with respect to u, we get

$$\frac{dy}{du} = \Delta y_0 + \left(\frac{2u-1}{2}\right)\Delta^2 y_0 + \left(\frac{3u^2-6u+2}{6}\right)\Delta^3 y_0 + \left(\frac{2u^3-9u^2+11u-3}{12}\right)\Delta^4 y_0 + \ldots \quad \ldots(3)$$

Differentiating eqn. (2) with respect to x

$$\frac{du}{dx} = \frac{1}{h} \quad \ldots(4)$$

$$\therefore \quad \frac{dy}{dx} = \frac{dy}{du} \cdot \frac{du}{dx}$$

$$= \frac{1}{h}\left[\Delta y_0 + \left(\frac{2u-1}{2}\right)\Delta^2 y_0 + \left(\frac{3u^2-6u+2}{6}\right)\Delta^3 y_0 + \left(\frac{2u^3-9u^2+11u-3}{12}\right)\Delta^4 y_0 + \ldots\right] \quad \ldots(5)$$

Also, at $x = 1.1$, $u = \frac{1.1 - 1.0}{0.2} = \frac{1}{2}$ | Here $a = 1.0$ and $h = 0.2$

Forward difference table is as follows:

x	$f(x) = y$	Δy	$\Delta^2 y$	$\Delta^3 y$	$\Delta^4 y$	$\Delta^5 y$
1.0	0.0					
		0.1280				
1.2	0.1280		0.298			
		0.4260		0.018		
1.4	0.5540		0.316		0.06	
		0.7420		0.078		– 0.1
1.6	1.2960		0.394		– 0.04	
		1.1360		0.038		
1.8	2.4320		0.432			
		1.5680				
2.0	4.000					

From eqn. (5),

$$\frac{dy}{dx} = \frac{1}{h}\left[\Delta y_0 + \left(\frac{2u-1}{2}\right)\Delta^2 y_0 + \left(\frac{3u^2-6u+2}{6}\right)\Delta^3 y_0 + \left(\frac{2u^3-9u^2+11u-3}{12}\right)\Delta^4 y_0 + \left(\frac{5u^4-40u^3+105u^2-100u+24}{120}\right)\Delta^5 y_0 + \ldots\right] \quad \ldots(6)$$

At $x = 1.1$, we get

$$f'(1.1) = \left(\frac{dy}{dx}\right)_{x=1.1} = \frac{1}{0.2}\left[0.1280 + \left\{\frac{2\left(\frac{1}{2}\right)-1}{2}\right\}(0.298)\right.$$

$$+\left\{\frac{3\left(\frac{1}{2}\right)^2-6\left(\frac{1}{2}\right)+2}{6}\right\}(0.018)+\left\{\frac{2\left(\frac{1}{2}\right)^3-9\left(\frac{1}{2}\right)^2+11\left(\frac{1}{2}\right)-3}{12}\right\}(.06)$$

$$\left.+\left\{\frac{5\left(\frac{1}{2}\right)^4-40\left(\frac{1}{2}\right)^3+105\left(\frac{1}{2}\right)^2-100\left(\frac{1}{2}\right)+24}{120}\right\}(-0.1)\right]$$

$$= 0.66724.$$

Differentiating eqn. (6), with respect to x, we get

$$\frac{d^2y}{dx^2} = \frac{d}{du}\left(\frac{dy}{du}\right)\frac{du}{dx} = \frac{1}{h^2}\left[\Delta^2 y_0 + (u-1)\,\Delta^3 y_0 + \left(\frac{6u^2-18u+11}{12}\right)\Delta^4 y_0\right.$$

$$\left.+\left(\frac{2u^3-12u^2+21u-10}{12}\right)\Delta^5 y_0 + \ldots\right]$$

At $x = 1.1$, we get

$$f''(1.1) = \left(\frac{d^2y}{dx^2}\right)_{x=1.1} = 8.13125.$$

Example 4. *The distance covered by an athlete for the 50 metre race is given in the following table:*

Time (sec) :	*0*	*1*	*2*	*3*	*4*	*5*	*6*
Distance (metre):	*0*	*2.5*	*8.5*	*15.5*	*24.5*	*36.5*	*50*

Determine the speed of the athlete at $t = 5$ sec. correct to two decimals. (U.P.T.U. 2009)

Sol. Here we are to find derivative at $t = 5$ which is near the end of the table hence we shall use formula obtained from Newton's backward difference formula. Backward difference table is as follows:

t	s	∇s	$\nabla^2 s$	$\nabla^3 s$	$\nabla^4 s$	$\nabla^5 s$	$\nabla^6 s$
0	0						
		2.5					
1	2.5		3.5				
		6		– 2.5			
2	8.5		1		3.5		
		7		1		– 3.5	
3	15.5		2		0		1
		9		1		– 2.5	
4	24.5		3		– 2.5		
		12		– 1.5			
5	36.5		1.5				
		13.5					
6	50						

Speed of athlete at $t = 5$ sec is given by

$$\left(\frac{ds}{dt}\right)_{t=5} = \frac{1}{h}\left[\nabla s_5 + \frac{1}{2}\nabla^2 s_5 + \frac{1}{3}\nabla^3 s_5 + \frac{1}{4}\nabla^4 s_5 + \frac{1}{5}\nabla^5 s_5\right]$$

$$= \frac{1}{1}\left[12 + \frac{1}{2}(3) + \frac{1}{3}(1) + \frac{1}{4}(0) + \frac{1}{5}(-3.5)\right]$$

$$= 13.1333 \approx 13.13 \text{ metre/sec.}$$

Example 5. *A rod is rotating in a plane. The following table gives the angle θ (in radians) through which the rod has turned for various values of time t (in seconds)*

t :	*0*	*0.2*	*0.4*	*0.6*	*0.8*	*1.0*	*1.2*
θ :	*0*	*0.12*	*0.49*	*1.12*	*2.02*	*3.20*	*4.67.*

Calculate the angular velocity and angular acceleration of the rod at t = 0.6 sec.

[G.B.T.U. (C.O.) 2011)

Sol. Forward difference table is

t	θ	$\Delta\theta$	$\Delta^2\theta$	$\Delta^3\theta$	$\Delta^4\theta$
0	0				
		0.12			
0.2	0.12		0.25		
		0.37		0.01	
0.4	0.49		0.26		0
		0.63		0.01	
0.6	1.12		0.27		0
		0.9		0.01	
0.8	2.02		0.28		0
		1.18		0.01	
1.0	3.20		0.29		
		1.47			
1.2	4.67				

Here $a = 0.6$

$\therefore$ $\theta_0 = 1.12$ and $h = 0.2$

Since we are to find derivatives at $t = 0.6$ sec which is in the middle of the table, hence we shall use formula obtained from Stirling's or Bessel's central difference formula.

Let us choose formula obtained from Bessel's central difference formula.

Angular velocity at $t = 0.6$ sec is given by

$$\left(\frac{d\theta}{dt}\right)_{t=0.6} = \frac{1}{h}\left[\Delta\theta_0 - \frac{1}{2}\left(\frac{\Delta^2\theta_{-1} + \Delta^2\theta_0}{2}\right) + \frac{1}{12}\Delta^3\theta_{-1}\right]$$

$$= \frac{1}{0.2}\left[0.9 - \frac{1}{2}\left(\frac{0.27 + 0.28}{2}\right) + \frac{1}{12}(0.01)\right] = 3.81667 \text{ rad./sec.}$$

Angular acceleration at $t = 0.6$ sec is given by

$$\left(\frac{d^2\theta}{dt^2}\right)_{t=0.6} = \frac{1}{h^2}\left[\left(\frac{\Delta^2\theta_{-1} + \Delta^2\theta_0}{2}\right) - \frac{1}{2}\Delta^3\theta_{-1}\right]$$

$$= \frac{1}{(0.2)^2}\left[\left(\frac{0.27 + 0.28}{2}\right) - \frac{1}{2}(0.01)\right] = 6.75 \text{ rad./sec}^2.$$

Note. In case we choose formula obtained from Stirling's formula, at $t = 0.6$ sec.,

angular velocity $$\left(\frac{d\theta}{dt}\right) = \frac{1}{h}\left[\left(\frac{\Delta\theta_0 + \Delta\theta_{-1}}{2}\right) - \frac{1}{6}\left(\frac{\Delta^3\theta_{-1} + \Delta^3\theta_{-2}}{2}\right)\right]$$

$$= \frac{1}{0.2}\left[\left(\frac{0.9 + 0.63}{2}\right) - \frac{1}{6}\left(\frac{0.01 + 0.01}{2}\right)\right] = 3.81667 \text{ rad./sec.}$$

and angular acceleration $$\left(\frac{d^2\theta}{dt^2}\right) = \frac{1}{h^2}(\Delta^2\theta_{-1}) = \frac{1}{(0.2)^2}(0.27) = 6.75 \text{ rad./sec}^2.$$

Example 6. *From the following table of values of x and y, obtain* $\frac{dy}{dx}$ *and* $\frac{d^2y}{dx^2}$ *for* $x = 1.2$, *2.2 and 1.6*

x :	1.0	1.2	1.4	1.6	1.8	2.0	2.2
y :	2.7183	3.3201	4.0552	4.9530	6.0496	7.3891	9.0250.

Sol. The forward difference table is

x	y	Δy	$\Delta^2 y$	$\Delta^3 y$	$\Delta^4 y$	$\Delta^5 y$	$\Delta^6 y$
1.0	2.7183						
		0.6018					
1.2	3.3201		0.1333				
		0.7351		0.0294			
1.4	4.0552		0.1627		0.0067		
		0.8978		0.0361		0.0013	
1.6	4.9530		0.1988		0.0080		0.0001
		1.0966		0.0441		0.0014	
1.8	6.0496		0.2429		0.0094		
		1.3395		0.0535			
2.0	7.3891		0.2964				
		1.6359					
2.2	9.0250						

(*i*) Here $a = 1.2$

$\therefore \quad y_0 = 3.3201; \quad h = 0.2$

$$\left[\frac{dy}{dx}\right]_{x=1.2} = \frac{1}{0.2}\left[0.7351 - \frac{1}{2}(0.1627) + \frac{1}{3}(0.0361) - \frac{1}{4}(0.008) + \frac{1}{5}(0.0014)\right]$$

$$= 3.3205$$

$$\left[\frac{d^2y}{dx^2}\right]_{x=1.2} = \frac{1}{(0.2)^2}\left[0.1627 - 0.0361 + \frac{11}{12}(0.0080) - \frac{5}{6}(0.0014)\right] = 3.318$$

(*ii*) Here $a = 2.2,$

$\therefore \quad y_n = 9.02 \quad \text{and} \quad h = 0.2$

$$\left[\frac{dy}{dx}\right]_{x=2.2} = \frac{1}{0.2}\left[1.6359 + \frac{1}{2}(0.2964) + \frac{1}{3}(0.0535) + \frac{1}{4}(0.0094) + \frac{1}{5}(0.0014)\frac{1}{6}(0.0001)\right]$$

$$= 9.0228$$

$$\left[\frac{d^2y}{dx^2}\right]_{x=2.2} = \frac{1}{0.04}\left[0.2964 + 0.0535 + \frac{11}{12}(0.0094) + \frac{5}{6}(0.0014)\frac{137}{180}(0.0001)\right] = 8.9939.$$

(*iii*) Here $a = 1.6$

$\therefore \quad y_0 = 4.9530, y_{-1} = 4.0552$

$y_{-2} = 3.3201, y_{-3} = 2.7183 \quad \text{and} \quad h = 0.2$

By using Stirling formula for derivatives, we get

$$\left[\frac{dy}{dx}\right]_{x=1.6} = \frac{1}{0.2}\left[\left(\frac{1.0966 + 0.8978}{2}\right) - \frac{1}{6}\left(\frac{0.0441 + 0.0361}{2}\right) + \frac{1}{30}\left(\frac{0.0014 + 0.0013}{2}\right)\right] = 4.9530$$

and $$\left[\frac{d^2y}{dx^2}\right]_{x=1.6} = \frac{1}{0.04}\left[0.1988 - \frac{1}{12}(0.0080) + \frac{1}{90}(0.0001)\right] = 4.9525.$$

Example 7. *The table below gives the result of an observation. θ is the observed temperature in degrees centigrade of a vessel of cooling water, t is the time in minutes from the beginning of observations:*

t:	1	3	5	7	9
θ:	85.3	74.5	67.0	60.5	54.3

Find the approximate rate of cooling at t = 3 and 3.5.

Sol. Forward difference table is

t	θ	$\Delta\theta$	$\Delta^2\theta$	$\Delta^3\theta$	$\Delta^4\theta$
1	85.3				
		− 10.8			
3	74.5		3.3		
		− 7.5		− 2.3	
5	67.0		1.0		1.6
		− 6.5		− 0.7	
7	60.5		0.3		
		− 6.2			
9	54.3				

(*i*) When $t = 3$, $\theta_0 = 74.5$. Here $h = 2$

Rate of cooling $= \dfrac{d\theta}{dt}$

$$\therefore \quad \left(\frac{d\theta}{dt}\right)_{t=3} = \frac{1}{h}\left[\Delta\theta_0 - \frac{1}{2}\Delta^2\theta_0 + \frac{1}{3}\Delta^3\theta_0 - \frac{1}{4}\Delta^4\theta_0\right]$$

$$= \frac{1}{2}\left[-7.5 - \frac{1}{2}(1) + \frac{1}{3}(-0.7)\right] = -4.11667°\text{C/min.}$$

(*ii*) $t = 3.5$ is the non-tabular value of t so, we have from Newton's forward difference formula,

$$\frac{d\theta}{dt} = \frac{1}{h}\left[\Delta\theta_0 + \left(\frac{2u-1}{2}\right)\Delta^2\theta_0 + \left(\frac{3u^2-6u+2}{6}\right)\Delta^3\theta_0 + \left(\frac{2u^3-9u^2+11u-3}{12}\right)\Delta^4\theta_0 + \ldots\right] \quad \ldots(1)$$

At $t = 3.5$, $\quad u = \dfrac{3.5-3.0}{2} = \dfrac{0.5}{2} = 0.25$ | Here $a = 3.0$ and $h = 2$

From (1),

$$\left(\frac{d\theta}{dt}\right)_{t=3.5} = \frac{1}{2}\left[-7.5 + \left\{\frac{2(0.25)-1}{2}\right\}(1) + \left\{\frac{3(0.25)^2-6(0.25)+2}{6}\right\}(-0.7)\right]$$

$$= -3.9151°\text{C/min.}$$

Example 8. *Find x for which y is maximum and find this value of y*

x:	1.2	1.3	1.4	1.5	1.6
y:	0.9320	0.9636	0.9855	0.9975	0.9996.

Sol. The difference table is as follows:

x	y	Δy	$\Delta^2 y$	$\Delta^3 y$	$\Delta^4 y$
1.2	0.9320				
		0.0316			
1.3	0.9636		– 0.0097		
		0.0219		– 0.0002	
1.4	0.9855		– 0.0099		0.0002
		0.0120		0	
1.5	0.9975		– 0.0099		
		0.0021			
1.6	0.9996				

Let $y_0 = 0.9320$ and $a = 1.2$

By Newton's forward difference formula,

$$y = y_0 + u\,\Delta y_0 + \frac{u(u-1)}{2}\Delta^2 y_0 + \ldots$$

$$= 0.9320 + 0.0316\,u + \frac{u(u-1)}{2}(-0.0097) \qquad | \text{ Neglecting higher differences}$$

$$\frac{dy}{du} = 0.0316 + \left(\frac{2u-1}{2}\right)(-0.0097)$$

At a maximum, $\frac{dy}{du} = 0$

$$\Rightarrow \qquad 0.0316 = \left(u - \frac{1}{2}\right)(0.0097) \quad \Rightarrow \quad u = 3.76$$

$$\therefore \qquad x = a + hu = 1.2 + (0.1)(3.76) = 1.576$$

To find $y_{max.}$, we use backward difference formula,

$$x = x_n + hu$$

$$\Rightarrow \qquad 1.576 = 1.6 + (0.1)u \quad \Rightarrow \quad u = -0.24$$

$$y(1.576) = y_n + u\,\nabla y_n + \frac{u(u+1)}{2}\nabla^2 y_n + \frac{u(u+1)(u+2)}{3!}\nabla^3 y_n$$

$$= 0.9996 - (0.24 \times 0.0021) + \frac{(-0.24)(1-0.24)}{2}(-0.0099)$$

$$= 0.9999988 = 0.9999 \text{ nearly}$$

$\therefore$ Maximum y = 0.9999 **approximately.**

Example 9. *Derive the formula* $y_0' = (y_{-2} - 8y_{-1} + 8y_1 - y_2)/12h$ *for numerical differentiation at mid-point of a table.* (U.P.T.U. 2009)

Sol. Take $a = 0$ Difference table is

x	y	Δy	$\Delta^2 y$	$\Delta^3 y$	$\Delta^4 y$
-2	y_{-2}				
		$y_{-1} - y_{-2}$			
-1	y_{-1}		$y_0 - 2y_{-1} + y_{-2}$		
		$y_0 - y_{-1}$		$y_1 - 3y_0 + 3y_{-1} - y_{-2}$	
0	y_0		$y_1 - 2y_0 + y_{-1}$		$y_2 - 4y_1 + 6y_0 - 4y_{-1} + y_{-2}$
		$y_1 - y_0$		$y_2 - 3y_1 + 3y_0 - y_{-1}$	
1	y_1		$y_2 - 2y_1 + y_0$		
		$y_2 - y_1$			
2	y_2				

By using Stirling's formula for first derivative, we get

$$y_0' = \frac{1}{h}\left[\left(\frac{\Delta y_0 + \Delta y_{-1}}{2}\right) - \frac{1}{6}\left(\frac{\Delta^3 y_{-1} + \Delta^3 y_{-2}}{2}\right) + \ldots\right]$$

$$= \frac{1}{h}\left[\left(\frac{y_1 - y_0 + y_0 - y_{-1}}{2}\right) - \frac{1}{12}(y_2 - 3y_1 + 3y_0 - y_{-1} + y_1 - 3y_0 + 3y_{-1} - y_{-2})\right]$$

$$= \frac{1}{h}\left[\left(\frac{y_1 - y_{-1}}{2}\right) - \frac{1}{12}(y_2 - 2y_1 + 2y_{-1} - y_{-2})\right]$$

$$\Rightarrow \quad y_0' = \frac{1}{12h}[8y_1 - 8y_{-1} - y_2 + y_{-2}]$$

Example 10. *State the three different finite difference approximations to the first derivative $f'(x_0)$ together with the order of their truncation errors. Derive the forward difference approximation and its leading error term.*

Sol. (*i*) Newton's forward difference approximation is given by

$$f(x) = f_0 + u\,\Delta f_0 + \frac{u(u-1)}{2}\Delta^2 f_0$$

where $u = \dfrac{x - x_0}{h}$ and $E = \dfrac{1}{6}u(u-1)(u-2)h^3 f'''(\xi)$

We have, $f'(x) = \dfrac{df}{du}\cdot\dfrac{du}{dx} = \dfrac{1}{h}\left[\Delta f_0 + \dfrac{1}{2}(2u-1)\Delta^2 f_0\right]$

and $|E'(x_0)| = |E'(u=0)| \le \dfrac{h^2}{3} M_3$ where $M_3 = \max\limits_{x_0 \le x \le x_2} |f'''(x)|$

(*ii*) Newton's backward difference approximation is given by

$$f(x) = f_2 + u\,\nabla f_2 + \frac{1}{2}u(u+1)\nabla^2 f_2$$

where $u = \dfrac{x - x_2}{h}$ and $E = \dfrac{1}{6} u(u+1)(u+2) h^3 f'''(\xi)$

We have, $$f'(x) = \frac{1}{h}\left[\nabla f_2 + \frac{1}{2}(2u+1)\nabla^2 f_2\right]$$

and $$|E'(x_2)| = |E'(u=0)| \le \frac{h^2}{3} M_3$$

(*iii*) Central difference approximation is given by

$$f(x) = f_0 + \frac{u}{2}(\delta f_{1/2} + \delta f_{-1/2}) \quad \text{where} \quad u = \frac{x - x_0}{h}.$$

We have $$f'(x) = \frac{1}{2h}(\delta f_{1/2} + \delta f_{-1/2}) = \frac{1}{2h}[(f_1 - f_0) + (f_0 - f_{-1})] = \frac{1}{2h}(f_1 - f_{-1})$$

and $$|E'(x)| \le \frac{h^2}{6} M_3.$$

ASSIGNMENT

1. (*i*) Find $y'(0)$ and $y''(0)$ from the given table:

x:	0	1	2	3	4	5
y:	4	8	15	7	6	2

(*ii*) Find the first and second derivatives for the function tabulated below at the point $x = 3.0$:

x:	3	3.2	3.4	3.6	3.8	4.0
y:	–14	–10.032	–5.296	0.256	6.672	14

2. (*i*) From the following table, estimate $y'(1.05)$:

x:	1	1.05	1.10	1.15	1.20	1.25
y:	1.1	1.1347	1.1688	1.1564	1.2344	1.2345

(*G.B.T.U. 2013*)

(*ii*) Find the derivative of $f(x)$ at $x = 0.4$ from the following table:

x:	0.1	0.2	0.3	0.4
$f(x)$:	1.10517	1.22140	1.34986	1.49182

(*M.T.U. 2013*)

3. Find $\dfrac{d}{dx}(J_0)$ and $\dfrac{d^2}{dx^2}(J_0)$ at $x = 0.1$ from the following table:

x:	0.0	0.1	0.2	0.3	0.4
$J_0(x)$:	1	0.9975	0.99	0.9776	0.9604.

4. (*i*) Find the numerical value of $y'(10°)$ for $y = \sin x$ given that:

sin 0° = 0.000, sin 10° = 0.1736, sin 20° = 0.3420, sin 30° = 0.5000, sin 40° = 0.6428.

(*ii*) Compute $y'(1.1)$ from the following table:

x:	1.0	1.1	1.2	1.3	1.4	1.5
$y(x)$:	7.989	8.403	8.781	9.129	9.451	9.750

(*G.B.T.U. 2012*)

5. (*i*) Find $f'(1.5)$ and $f''(1.5)$ from the following table:

x:	0.0	0.5	1.0	1.5	2.0
$f(x)$:	0.3989	0.3521	0.2420	0.1245	0.0540

[*U.P.T.U. (MCA) 2006*]

(*ii*) The population of a certain town is given below. Find the rate of growth of the population in 1961:

Year:	1931	1941	1951	1961	1971
Population: (*in lacs*)	40.62	60.80	71.95	103.56	132.65

(*M.T.U. 2012*)

6. Find first and second derivative of the function tabulated below at $x = 0.6$

[*G.B.T.U. (C.O.) 2010*]

x:	0.4	0.5	0.6	0.7	0.8
y:	1.5836	1.7974	2.0442	2.3275	2.6511.

7. Find the values of $f'(5)$, $f''(5)$ and $f''(0.5)$ from the following table:

(*G.B.T.U. 2012, U.P.T.U. 2007*)

x:	0	1	2	3	4	5
$f(x)$:	4930	5026	5122	5217	5312	5407

8. (*i*) A slider in a machine moves along a fixed straight rod. Its distance x cm along the rod is given below for various values of the time t seconds. Find the velocity of the slider and its acceleration when $t = 0.3$ second.

t:	0	0.1	0.2	0.3	0.4	0.5	0.6
x:	30.13	31.62	32.87	33.64	33.95	33.81	33.24.

(*ii*) A slider in a machine moves along fixed straight rod. Its distances x (m.) along the rod are given at various times (sec.)

t:	1	1.1	1.2	1.3	1.4	1.5
x:	16.40	19.01	21.96	25.29	29.03	33.21

Find the velocity of the slider at $t = 1.1$ sec.

9. A slider in a machine moves along a fixed straight rod. Its distance x(in cm) along the rod is given at various times t (in secs).

t:	0	0.1	0.2	0.3	0.4	0.5	0.6
x:	30.28	31.43	32.98	33.54	33.97	33.48	32.13

Evaluate $\frac{dx}{dt}$ at $t = 0.1$ and at $t = 0.5$.

10. Given the following table:

x:	1	1.05	1.1	1.15	1.2	1.25	1.3
$f(x) = \sqrt{x}$:	1	1.0247	1.04881	1.07238	1.09544	1.11803	1.14014

Apply the above results to find $f'(1)$, $f''(1)$ and $f'''(1)$.

11. (*i*) Using Newton's divided difference formula, find $f'(10)$ from the following data:

x:	3	5	11	27	34
$f(x)$:	– 13	23	899	17315	35606

(*ii*) Given the following data, find $y'(6)$:

x:	0	2	3	4	7	8
$f(x)$:	4	26	58	112	466	922

(*U.P.T.U. 2008*)

(*iii*) Find $f'(6)$ from the following table:

x:	0	1	3	4	5	7	9
$f(y)$:	150	108	0	–54	–100	–144	–84

12. (*i*) From the table below, for what value of x, y is minimum? Also find this value of y.

x:	3	4	5	6	7	8
y:	0.205	0.240	0.259	0.262	0.250	0.224.

(*ii*) Find the minimum value of y from the following table:

x:	0.2	0.3	0.4	0.5	0.6	0.7
y:	0.9182	0.8975	0.8873	0.8862	0.8935	0.9086

13. If $y = f(x)$ and y_n denotes $f(x_0 + nh)$, prove that, if powers of h above h^6 be neglected,

$$\left(\frac{dy}{dx}\right)_{x=x_0} = \frac{3}{4h}\left[y_1 - y_{-1} - \frac{1}{5}(y_2 - y_{-2}) + \frac{1}{45}(y_3 - y_{-3})\right]$$ (*U.P.T.U. 2006*)

14. The following table gives values of pressure P and specific volume V of saturated steam:

P:	105	42.7	25.3	16.7	13
V:	2	4	6	8	10

Find

(*a*) the rate of change of pressure w.r.t. volume at V = 2

(*b*) the rate of change of volume w.r.t. pressure at P = 105.

15. y is a function of x satisfying the equation $xy'' + ay' + (x - b)y = 0$, where a and b are integers. Find the values of constants a and b if y is given by the following table:

x:	0.8	1	1.2	1.4	1.6	1.8	2	2.2
y:	1.73036	1.95532	2.19756	2.45693	2.73309	3.02549	2.3333	3.65563.

16. (*a*) When does the need of numerical differentiation arise? (*U.P.T.U. 2008*)

(*b*) Prove that $D = \frac{1}{h}\left(\Delta - \frac{\Delta^2}{2} + \frac{\Delta^3}{3} - \ldots\right)$, the symbols used have usual meanings.

[*U.P.T.U.* (*MCA*) *2007*]

Answers

1. (*i*) – 27.9, 117.67 (*ii*) 18, 18

2. (*i*) 3.5856 (*ii*) 1.4913 **3.** – 0.05, – 0.5

4. (*i*) 0.9848 (*ii*) 3.945833

5. (*i*) – 0.2051, 0.194 (*ii*) 5.167 lacs/year **6.** 2.64442, 3.6475

7. 94.15, – 3.4166, 1.6458 **8.** (*i*) 5.33 cm/sec, – 45.6 cm/sec^2 (*ii*) 27.7 m/sec.

9. 32.44166 cm/sec., – 24.05833 cm/sec. **10.** 0.50024, – 0.256, 0.4

11. (*i*) 232.869 (*ii*) 125.4744 (*iii*) – 23

12. (*i*) 5.6875, 0.2628 (*ii*) 0.4623

14. (*a*) – 52.4 (*b*) – 0.01908 **15.** $a = 8, b = 6$.

6.5. ERRORS IN NUMERICAL DIFFERENTIATION

In numerical differentiation, the error in the higher order derivatives occurs due to the reason that, although the tabulated function and its approximating polynomial would agree at the set of data points, their slopes at these points may vary considerably. Numerical differentiation is, therefore, an unsatisfactory process and should be used only in rare cases.

The numerical computation of derivatives involves two types of errors: **truncation errors** and **rounding errors.**

The truncation error is caused by replacing the tabulated function by means of an interpolating polynomial.

Truncation error in first derivative is

$$= \frac{1}{6h}\left|\frac{\Delta^3 y_{-2} + \Delta^3 y_{-1}}{2}\right|.$$

Truncation error in second derivative is

$$= \frac{1}{12h^2}|\Delta^4 y_{-2}|.$$

The rounding error is $\propto \frac{1}{h}$ in case of first derivatives while it is $\propto \frac{1}{h^2}$ in case of second derivatives, and so on.

Max. Rounding error in first derivative is $= \frac{3}{2}\frac{\varepsilon}{h}$

Max. Rounding error in second derivative is $= \frac{4\varepsilon}{h^2}$

where ε is the maximum error in the value of y_i.

Example. *Assume the table of values given in previous. Example 6 on page no. 355 and the function values are correct to the accuracy given, estimate the errors in $\frac{dy}{dx}$ at $x = 1.6$.*

Sol. Since the values are correct to four decimals, it follows that $\varepsilon = 0.5 \times 10^{-4}$

$$\text{Truncation error} = \frac{1}{6h}\left|\frac{\Delta^3 y_{-1} + \Delta^3 y_0}{2}\right|$$

$$= \frac{1}{1.2}\left(\frac{0.0361 + 0.0441}{2}\right) \quad \text{| See difference table in Example 6}$$

$$= 0.03342$$

$$\text{Rounding error} = \frac{3\varepsilon}{2h} = \frac{3 \times 0.5 \times 10^{-4}}{2 \times 0.2} = 0.00038.$$

6.6. EXTRAPOLATION METHODS

Higher order differentiation methods require a large number of tabular points and hence a large number of function evaluations. As a result, rounding errors may increase which make numerical results meaningless.

To get highly accurate results, we may combine the computed values obtained by using a certain method with different step-sizes. These techniques of combining two computed values thus obtained is called the extrapolation methods.

6.7. RICHARDSON'S EXTRAPOLATION METHOD

To improve the accuracy of the derivative of a function, which is computed by starting with an arbitrarily selected value of h, Richardson's extrapolation method is often employed.

If the local truncation error associated with the method is known as a power series in h then by repeating the extrapolation procedure a number of times, we can obtain the methods of any arbitrary order. The application of this method becomes simplified when the step lengths form a geometric sequence.

Suppose we use two-point formula

$$y'(x) = \frac{y(x+h) - y(x-h)}{2h} + \text{E}_\text{T} = \text{F}(h) + \text{E}_\text{T} \qquad ...(1)$$

to compute the derivative of a function $y(x)$. Here E_T is the truncation error.

Using Taylor's series expansion, we see

$$E_T = c_1h^2 + c_2h^4 + c_3h^6 + \ldots \qquad \ldots(2)$$

The basic idea of Richardson's extrapolation is to combine two computed values of $y'(x)$ using the same method but with two different step sizes usually h and $\frac{h}{2}$ to yield a higher order method. Thus, we have

$$\left.\begin{aligned} y'(x) &= F(h) + c_1h^2 + c_2h^4 + \ldots \\ \text{and} \quad y'(x) &= F\left(\frac{h}{2}\right) + c_1\frac{h^2}{4} + c_2\frac{h^4}{16} + \ldots \end{aligned}\right\} \qquad \ldots(3)$$

Here, c_i are constants, independent of h while $F(h)$ and $F\left(\frac{h}{2}\right)$ represent approximate values of derivatives. Eliminating c_1 from above two equations, we get

$$y'(x) = \frac{4F\left(\frac{h}{2}\right) - F(h)}{3} + d_1h^4 + O(h^6) \qquad \ldots(4)$$

Let, $F_1\left(\frac{h}{2}\right) = \dfrac{4F\left(\frac{h}{2}\right) - F(h)}{3}$ then from (4),

$$y'(x) = F_1\left(\frac{h}{2}\right) + d_1h^4 + O(h^6).$$

Thus, we have obtained a fourth order accurate differentiation formula by combining two results which are second order accurate. Now repeating the above argument, we have

$$\left.\begin{aligned} y'(x) &= F_1\left(\frac{h}{2}\right) + d_1h^4 + O(h^6) \\ y'(x) &= F_1\left(\frac{h}{4}\right) + d_1\frac{h^4}{16} + O(h^6) \end{aligned}\right\} \qquad \ldots(5)$$

Eliminating d_1 from the above two equations, we get better approximation as

$$y'(x) = F_2\left(\frac{h}{4}\right) + O(h^6)$$

which is of sixth-order accurate, where

$$F_2\left(\frac{h}{4}\right) = \frac{4^2F_1\left(\frac{h}{2^2}\right) - F_1\left(\frac{h}{2}\right)}{4^2 - 1} \qquad \ldots(6)$$

This extrapolation procedure can be repeated further until the required accuracy is obtained which is called an extrapolation to the limit. Eqn. (6) can be generalized as

$$F_m\left(\frac{h}{2^m}\right) = \frac{4^mF_m\left(\frac{h}{2^m}\right) - F_{m-1}\left(\frac{h}{2^{m-1}}\right)}{4^m - 1}, \quad m = 1, 2, 3, \ldots$$

where $F_0(h) = F(h)$

Extrapolation Table

Order	*Second*	*Fourth*	*Sixth*	*Eighth*
h	$F(h)$			
		$F_1(h)$		
$\frac{h}{2}$	$F\left(\frac{h}{2}\right)$		$F_2(h)$	
		$F_1\left(\frac{h}{2}\right)$		$F_3(h)$
$\frac{h}{2^2}$	$F\left(\frac{h}{2^2}\right)$		$F_2\left(\frac{h}{2}\right)$	
		$F_1\left(\frac{h}{2^2}\right)$		
$\frac{h}{2^3}$	$F\left(\frac{h}{2^3}\right)$			

It is observed that the successive entries in a column give better approximation than the preceding entries. Similarly, the successive columns give better approximations than the preceding columns. The best results can be obtained from the lower diagonal terms. The extrapolation can be stopped when $| F_k(h) - F_{k-1}(h/2) | < \varepsilon$ for a given error tolerance ε.

Example. *Using Richardson's extrapolation limit, find $y'(0.05)$ to the function $y = -\frac{1}{x}$ with $h = 0.0128, 0.0064, 0.0032$.*

Sol. Let $h = 0.0128$,

$$F(h) = \frac{y(x+h) - y(x-h)}{2h} \qquad | \, x = 0.05$$

$$= \frac{-\frac{1}{x+h} + \frac{1}{x-h}}{2h} = 428.05289 \qquad \ldots(1)$$

Similarly,
$$F\left(\frac{h}{2}\right) = 406.66273 \qquad \left| \, \frac{h}{2} = 0.0064 \right.$$

Therefore,
$$F_1\left(\frac{h}{2}\right) = \frac{4F\left(\frac{h}{2}\right) - F(h)}{4-1} = 399.5327 \qquad \ldots(2)$$

which is accurate to $O(h^4)$. Halving the step size further, we get

$$F\left(\frac{h}{2^2}\right) = 401.64515 \qquad \left| \, \frac{h}{2^2} = 0.0032 \right.$$

and
$$F_1\left(\frac{h}{2^2}\right) = \frac{4F\left(\frac{h}{2^2}\right) - F\left(\frac{h}{2}\right)}{4-1} = 399.97263$$

Again, $$\mathrm{F}_2\left(\frac{h}{2^2}\right) = \frac{4^2\mathrm{F}_1\left(\frac{h}{2^2}\right) - \mathrm{F}_1\left(\frac{h}{2}\right)}{4^2 - 1} = 400.00195$$

The above computation can be summarized in the following table:

h	F	F_1	F_2
0.0128	428.0529		
		399.5327	
0.0064	406.6627		400.00195
		399.9726	
0.0032	401.6452		

Thus, after two steps, $y(0.05) = 400.00195$.

The exact value is $$y'(0.05) = \left(\frac{1}{x^2}\right)_{x=0.05} = 400$$

ASSIGNMENT

1. Using the Richardson extrapolation limit, find $y''(0.6)$ of the following tabulated function by applying the formula

$$\mathrm{F}(x) = \frac{1}{h^2}\,[y(x+h) - 2y(x) + y(x-h)]$$

with $h = 0.4, 0.2, 0.1$.

x:	0.2	0.4	0.5	0.6	0.7	0.8	1.0
$y(x)$:	1.42007	1.88124	2.12815	2.38676	2.65797	2.94289	3.55975

2. Given:

x:	− 1	1	2	3	4	5	7
$f(x)$:	1	1	16	81	256	625	2401

Using the formula $f'(x_1) = \dfrac{f(x_2) - f(x_0)}{2h}$ and the Richardson extrapolation, find $f'(3)$.

3. By use of repeated Richardson extrapolation, find $f'(1)$ from the following values:

x:	0.6	0.8	0.9	1	1.1	1.2	1.4
$f(x)$:	0.707178	0.859892	0.925863	0.984007	1.033743	1.074575	1.127986

Apply the approximate formula $f'(x_0) = \dfrac{f(x_0+h) - f(x_0-h)}{2h}$ with $h = 0.4, 0.2, 0.1$.

Answers

1. 1.25766 **2.** 108 **3.** 0.540299

6.8. NUMERICAL INTEGRATION

Given a set of tabulated values of the integrand $f(x)$, to determine the value of $\int_{x_0}^{x_n} f(x)\,dx$ is called numerical integration. We subdivide the given interval of integration into a large number of subintervals of equal width h and replace the function tabulated at the points of subdivision by any one of the interpolating polynomials like Newton-Gregory's, Stirling's, Bessel's over each of the subintervals and evaluate the integral. We have several formulae for numerical integration which we shall derive in the sequel.

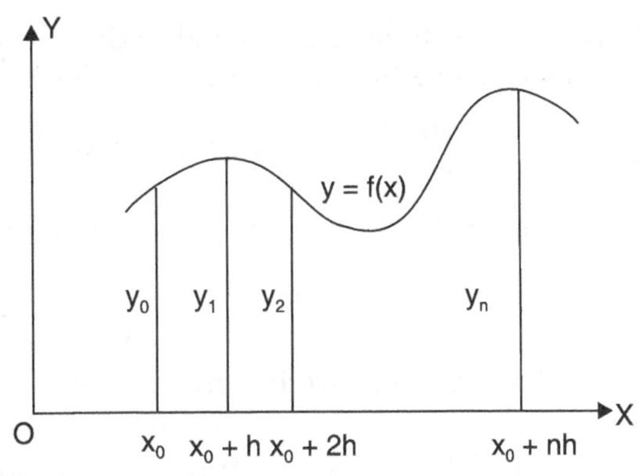

6.9. NEWTON-COTE'S QUADRATURE FORMULA

[*M.T.U. 2013, U.P.T.U. (MCA) 2009*]

Let $\quad I = \int_a^b y\,dx$, where y takes the values $y_0, y_1, y_2, \ldots\ldots, y_n$ for $x = x_0, x_1, x_2, \ldots\ldots, x_n$.

Let the interval of integration (a, b) be divided into n equal sub-intervals, each of width $h = \dfrac{b-a}{n}$ so that $x_0 = a, x_1 = x_0 + h, x_2 = x_0 + 2h, \ldots, x_n = x_0 + nh = b$.

$$\therefore \qquad I = \int_{x_0}^{x_0 + nh} f(x)\,dx$$

Since any x is given by $x = x_0 + rh$ and $dx = hdr$

$$\therefore \qquad I = h\int_0^n f(x_0 + rh)\,dr$$

$$= h\int_0^n \left[y_0 + r\Delta y_0 + \frac{r(r-1)}{2!}\Delta^2 y_0 + \frac{r(r-1)(r-2)}{3!}\Delta^3 y_0 + \ldots \right] dr$$

[By Newton's forward interpolation formula]

$$= h\left[ry_0 + \frac{r^2}{2}\Delta y_0 + \frac{1}{2}\left(\frac{r^3}{3} - \frac{r^2}{2}\right)\Delta^2 y_0 + \frac{1}{6}\left(\frac{r^4}{4} - r^3 + r^2\right)\Delta^3 y_0 + \ldots \right]_0^n$$

$$I = nh\left[y_0 + \frac{n}{2}\Delta y_0 + \frac{n(2n-3)}{12}\Delta^2 y_0 + \frac{n(n-2)^2}{24}\Delta^3 y_0 + \ldots \right] \qquad \ldots(1)$$

This is a **general quadrature formula** and is known as **Newton-Cote's quadrature formula.** A number of important deductions *viz.* Trapezoidal rule, Simpson's one-third and three-eighth rules, can be immediately deduced by putting $n = 1$, 2 and 3 respectively, in formula (1).

6.10. TRAPEZOIDAL RULE (n = 1) *[U.P.T.U. MCA (SUM) 2008]*

Putting $n = 1$ in formula (1) and taking the curve through (x_0, y_0) and (x_1, y_1) as a polynomial of degree one so that differences of order higher than one vanish, we get

$$\int_{x_0}^{x_0+h} f(x)\,dx = h\left(y_0 + \frac{1}{2}\Delta y_0\right) = \frac{h}{2}[2y_0 + (y_1 - y_0)] = \frac{h}{2}(y_0 + y_1)$$

Similarly, for the next sub-interval $(x_0 + h, x_0 + 2h)$, we get

$$\int_{x_0+h}^{x_0+2h} f(x)\,dx = \frac{h}{2}(y_1 + y_2), \ldots\ldots, \int_{x_0+(n-1)h}^{x_0+nh} f(x)\,dx = \frac{h}{2}(y_{n-1} + y_n)$$

Adding the above integrals, we get

$$\boxed{\int_{x_0}^{x_0+nh} f(x)\,dx = \frac{h}{2}[(y_0 + y_n) + 2(y_1 + y_2 + \ldots\ldots + y_{n-1})]}$$

which is known as **Trapezoidal rule.** By increasing the number of subintervals, thereby making h very small, we can improve the accuracy of the value of the given integral.

6.11. SIMPSON'S ONE-THIRD RULE (n = 2) *(G.B.T.U. 2013)*

Putting $n = 2$ in formula (1) and taking the curve through (x_0, y_0), (x_1, y_1) and (x_2, y_2) as a polynomial of degree two so that differences of order higher than two vanish, we get

$$\int_{x_0}^{x_0+2h} f(x)\,dx = 2h\left[y_0 + \Delta y_0 + \frac{1}{6}\Delta^2 y_0\right]$$

$$= \frac{2h}{6}[6y_0 + 6(y_1 - y_0) + (y_2 - 2y_1 + y_0)] = \frac{h}{3}(y_0 + 4y_1 + y_2)$$

Similarly, $\displaystyle\int_{x_0+2h}^{x_0+4h} f(x)\,dx = \frac{h}{3}(y_2 + 4y_3 + y_4), \ldots\ldots,$

$$\int_{x_0+(n-2)h}^{x_0+nh} f(x)\,dx = \frac{h}{3}(y_{n-2} + 4y_{n-1} + y_n)$$

Adding the above integrals, we get

$$\boxed{\int_{x_0}^{x_0+nh} f(x)\,dx = \frac{h}{3}[(y_0 + y_n) + 4(y_1 + y_3 + \ldots + y_{n-1}) + 2(y_2 + y_4 + \ldots + y_{n-2})]}$$

which is known as **Simpson's one-third rule.**

While using this formula, the given interval of integration must be divided into an even number of sub-intervals, since we find the area over two sub-intervals at a time.

6.12. SIMPSON'S THREE-EIGHTH RULE (n = 3)

[G.B.T.U. (MCA) 2010, G.B.T.U. 2009, 2010]

Putting $n = 3$ in formula (1) and taking the curve through (x_0, y_0), (x_1, y_1), (x_2, y_2) and (x_3, y_3) as a polynomial of degree three so that differences of order higher than three vanish, we get

$$\int_{x_0}^{x_0+3h} f(x)\,dx = 3h\left(y_0 + \frac{3}{2}\Delta y_0 + \frac{3}{4}\Delta^2 y_0 + \frac{1}{8}\Delta^3 y_0\right)$$

$$= \frac{3h}{8}[8y_0 + 12(y_1 - y_0) + 6(y_2 - 2y_1 + y_0) + (y_3 - 3y_2 + 3y_1 - y_0)]$$

$$= \frac{3h}{8}[y_0 + 3y_1 + 3y_2 + y_3]$$

Similarly, $\int_{x_0+3h}^{x_0+6h} f(x)\,dx = \frac{3h}{8}[y_3 + 3y_4 + 3y_5 + y_6], \ldots$

$$\int_{x_0+(n-3)h}^{x_0+6h} f(x)\,dx = \frac{3h}{8}[y_{n-3} + 3y_{n-2} + 3y_{n-1} + y_n]$$

Adding the above integrals, we get

$$\int_{x_0}^{x_0+nh} f(x)\,dx = \frac{3h}{8}[(y_0 + y_n) + 3(y_1 + y_2 + y_4 + y_5 + \ldots + y_{n-2} + y_{n-1}) + 2(y_3 + y_6 + \ldots + y_{n-3})]$$

which is known as **Simpson's three-eighth rule.**

While using this formula, the given interval of integration must be divided into sub-intervals whose number n is a multiple of 3.

6.13. BOOLE'S RULE

Putting $n = 4$ in formula (1) and neglecting all differences of order higher than four, we get

$$\int_{x_0}^{x_0+4h} f(x)\,dx$$

$$= h\int_0^4 \left[y_0 + r\Delta y_0 + \frac{r(r-1)}{2!}\Delta^2 y_0 + \frac{r(r-1)(r-2)}{3!}\Delta^3 y_0 + \frac{r(r-1)(r-2)(r-3)}{4!}\Delta^4 y_0\right] dr$$

| By Newton's forward interpolation formula

$$= 4h\left[y_0 + \frac{n}{2}\Delta y_0 + \frac{n(2n-3)}{12}\Delta^2 y_0 + \frac{n(n-2)^2}{24}\Delta^3 y_0 + \left(\frac{n^4}{5} - \frac{3n^3}{2} + \frac{11n^2}{3} - 3n\right)\frac{\Delta^4 y_0}{4!}\right]_0^4$$

$$= 4h\left[y_0 + 2\Delta y_0 + \frac{5}{3}\Delta^2 y_0 + \frac{3}{2}\Delta^3 y_0 + \frac{7}{90}\Delta^4 y_0\right]$$

$$= \frac{2h}{45}(7y_0 + 32y_1 + 12y_2 + 32y_3 + 7y_4)$$

Similarly, $\int_{x_0+4h}^{x_0+8h} f(x)\,dx = \frac{2h}{45}(7y_4 + 32y_5 + 12y_6 + 32y_7 + 7y_8)$ and so on.

Adding all these integrals from x_0 to $x_0 + nh$, where n is a multiple of 4, we get

$$\int_{x_0}^{x_0+nh} f(x)\,dx = \frac{2h}{45}[7y_0 + 32y_1 + 12y_2 + 32y_3 + 14y_4 + 32y_5 + 12y_6 + 32y_7 + 14y_8 + \ldots]$$

This is known as **Boole's rule.**

While applying Boole's rule, the **number of sub-intervals should be taken as a multiple of 4.**

6.14. WEDDLE'S RULE (n = 6)

Putting $n = 6$ in formula (1) and neglecting all differences of order higher than six, we get

$$\int_{x_0}^{x_0+6h} f(x)\,dx = h\int_0^6 \Bigg[y_0 + r\Delta y_0 + \frac{r(r-1)}{2!}\Delta^2 y_0 + \frac{r(r-1)(r-2)}{3!}\Delta^3 y_0 + \frac{r(r-1)(r-2)(r-3)}{4!}\Delta^4 y_0 + \frac{r(r-1)(r-2)(r-3)(r-4)}{5!}\Delta^5 y_0 + \frac{r(r-1)(r-2)(r-3)(r-4)(r-5)}{6!}\Delta^6 y_0 \Bigg] dr$$

$$= h\Bigg[ry_0 + \frac{r^2}{2}\Delta y_0 + \frac{1}{2}\left(\frac{r^3}{3} - \frac{r^2}{2}\right)\Delta^2 y_0 + \frac{1}{6}\left(\frac{r^4}{4} - r^3 + r^2\right)\Delta^3 y_0 + \frac{1}{24}\left(\frac{r^5}{5} - \frac{3r^4}{2} + \frac{11r^3}{3} - 3r^2\right)\Delta^4 y_0 + \frac{1}{120}\left(\frac{r^6}{6} - 2r^5 + \frac{35r^4}{4} - \frac{50r^3}{3} + 12r^2\right)\Delta^5 y_0 + \frac{1}{720}\left(\frac{r^7}{7} - \frac{5r^6}{2} + 17r^5 - \frac{225r^4}{4} + \frac{274r^3}{3} - 60r^2\right)\Delta^6 y_0 \Bigg]_0^6$$

$$= 6h\left[y_0 + 3\Delta y_0 + \frac{9}{2}\Delta^2 y_0 + 4\Delta^3 y_0 + \frac{41}{20}\Delta^4 y_0 + \frac{11}{20}\Delta^5 y_0 + \frac{41}{840}\Delta^6 y_0 \right]$$

$$= \frac{6h}{20}\left[20y_0 + 60\Delta y_0 + 90\Delta^2 y_0 + 80\Delta^3 y_0 + 41\Delta^4 y_0 + 11\Delta^5 y_0 + \frac{41}{42}\Delta^6 y_0 \right]$$

$$= \frac{3h}{10}\,[20y_0 + 60(y_1 - y_0) + 90(y_2 - 2y_1 + y_0) + 80(y_3 - 3y_2 + 3y_1 - y_0) + 41(y_4 - 4y_3 + 6y_2 - 4y_1 + y_0) + 11\,(y_5 - 5y_4 + 10y_3 - 10y_2 + 5y_1 - y_0) + (y_6 - 6y_5 + 15y_4 - 20y_3 + 15y_2 - 6y_1 + y_0)] \qquad \left[\because\ \frac{41}{42} \simeq 1\right]$$

$$= \frac{3h}{10}\,[y_0 + 5y_1 + y_2 + 6y_3 + y_4 + 5y_5 + y_6]$$

Similarly, $\displaystyle\int_{x_0+6h}^{x_0+12h} f(x)\,dx = \frac{3h}{10}\,[y_6 + 5y_7 + y_8 + 6y_9 + y_{10} + 5y_{11} + y_{12}]$

....

....

$$\int_{x_0+(n-6)h}^{x_0+nh} f(x)\,dx = \frac{3h}{10}\,[y_{n-6} + 5y_{n-5} + y_{n-4} + 6y_{n-3} + y_{n-2} + 5y_{n-1} + y_n]$$

Adding the above integrals, we get

$$\int_{x_0}^{x_0+nh} f(x)\,dx = \frac{3h}{10}\,[y_0 + 5y_1 + y_2 + 6y_3 + y_4 + 5y_5 + 2y_6 + 5y_7 + y_8 + 6y_9 + y_{10} + 5y_{11} + 2y_{12} + \ldots\ldots]$$

which is known as **Weddle's rule.** *Here* **n must be a multiple of 6.**

6.15. ERRORS IN QUADRATURE FORMULAE

If y_p is a polynomial representing the function $y = f(x)$ in the interval $[a, b]$ then error in the quadrature formulae is given by

$$E = \int_a^b f(x)\,dx - \int_a^b y_p\,dx \quad \text{...(1)}$$

6.15.1. Error in Trapezoidal Rule [U.P.T.U. (MCA) 2006, U.P.T.U. MCA (SUM) 2008]

Expanding $y = f(x)$ in the neighbourhood of $x = x_0$ by Taylor's series, we get

$$y = y_0 + (x - x_0)\,y_0' + \frac{(x - x_0)^2}{2!}\,y_0'' + \ldots \quad \text{...(2)}$$

$$\therefore \quad \int_{x_0}^{x_1} y\,dx = \int_{x_0}^{x_0+h}\left[y_0 + (x - x_0)\,y_0' + \frac{(x - x_0)^2}{2!}\,y_0'' + \ldots\right]dx$$

$$= hy_0 + \frac{h^2}{2!}\,y_0' + \frac{h^3}{3!}\,y_0'' + \ldots \quad \text{...(3)}$$

Now, area of the first trapezium in the interval $[x_0, x_1] = A_1 = \frac{h}{2}\,(y_0 + y_1)$ ...(4)

Putting $x = x_0 + h$, $y = y_1$ in (2),

$$y_1 = y_0 + hy_0' + \frac{h^2}{2!}\,y_0'' + \ldots \quad \text{...(5)}$$

From (4) and (5), we get

$$A_1 = \frac{h}{2}\left[y_0 + y_0 + hy_0' + \frac{h^2}{2!}\,y_0'' + \ldots\right] = hy_0 + \frac{h^2}{2!}\,y_0' + \frac{h^3}{2\,2!}\,y_0'' + \ldots \quad \text{...(6)}$$

Subtracting eqn. (6) from eqn. (3) gives the error in $[x_0, x_1]$,

$$\int_{x_0}^{x_1} y\,dx - A_1 = \left(\frac{1}{3!} - \frac{1}{2\,2!}\right)h^3\,y_0'' + \ldots \approx -\frac{h^3}{12}\,y_0'' \quad \text{| Neglecting other terms}$$

Similarly, the error in $[x_1, x_2]$ is $-\frac{h^3}{12}\,y_1''$ and in $[x_{n-1}, x_n]$ is $\frac{-h^3}{12}\,y_{n-1}''$.

Hence the total error is

$$E = \frac{-h^3}{12}\,(y_0'' + y_1'' + \ldots + y_{n-1}'')$$

Let $y''(\xi)$, $a < \xi < b$ be the maximum of $|\,y_0''\,|, |\,y_1''\,|, \ldots, |\,y_{n-1}''\,|$ then, we have

$$E < \frac{-nh^3}{12}\,y''(\xi) = -\frac{(b-a)}{12}\,h^2\,y''(\xi) \quad |\because\ b - a = nh$$

Hence the error in the Trapezoidal rule is of order h^2.

6.15.2. Error in Simpson's 1/3rd Rule. (U.P.T.U. 2008)

Integrating eqn. (2) w.r.t. x between the limits x_0 and x_2.

$$\int_{x_0}^{x_2} y\,dx = \int_{x_0}^{x_0+2h}\left[y_0 + (x - x_0)\,y_0' + \frac{(x - x_0)^2}{2!}\,y_0'' + \ldots\right]dx$$

$$= 2hy_0 + 2h^2y_0' + \frac{8h^3}{3!}\,y_0'' + \frac{16h^4}{4!}\,y_0''' + \frac{32h^5}{5!}\,y_0^{(iv)} + \ldots \quad \text{...(7)}$$

Now, $$A_1 = \frac{h}{3}(y_0 + 4y_1 + y_2) \qquad ...(8)$$

where A_1 is the area of the curve in the interval $[x_0, x_2]$.

Putting $x = x_0 + h$, $y = y_1$ in (2), we get

$$y_1 = y_0 + hy_0' + \frac{h^2}{2!} y_0'' + \frac{h^3}{3!} y_0''' + ... \qquad ...(9)$$

Putting $x = x_0 + 2h$, $y = y_2$ in (2), we get

$$y_2 = y_0 + 2h\, y_0' + \frac{4h^2}{2!} y_0'' + \frac{8h^3}{3!} y_0''' + ... \qquad ...(10)$$

Substituting eqns. (9) and (10) in eqn. (8), we get

$$A_1 = 2h\, y_0 + 2h^2 y_0' + \frac{4h^3}{3} y_0'' + \frac{2h^4}{3} y_0''' + \frac{5h^5}{18} y_0^{(iv)} + ... \qquad ...(11)$$

Now, the error in interval $[x_0, x_2]$ is given by

$$\int_{x_0}^{x_2} y\, dx - A_1 = \left(\frac{4}{15} - \frac{5}{18}\right) h^5 y_0^{(iv)} + ...$$

$$\approx -\frac{h^5}{90} y_0^{(iv)} \qquad | \text{ Neglecting terms of order } h^6, h^7, ...$$

Similarly, the principal part of error in interval $[x_2, x_4]$ is $= -\frac{h^5}{90} y_2^{(iv)}$ and so on.

Hence total principal error is

$$E = -\frac{h^5}{90}\left[y_0^{(iv)} + y_2^{(iv)} + ... + y_{2(n-1)}^{(iv)}\right]$$

Let $y^{(iv)}(\xi)$ be the maximum of $|y_0^{(iv)}|, |y_2^{(iv)}|, ..., |y_{2n-1}^{(iv)}|$.

Then, we have, $E < -\frac{h^5}{90} y^{(iv)}(\xi) = \frac{-(b-a)h^4}{180} y^{(iv)}(\xi)$

Hence, the error in the Simpson's (1/3)rd rule is of order h^4.

Note. Similarly, the principal part of the error for Simpson's (3/8)th rule is $-\frac{3h^5}{80} y^{(iv)}$ in the interval $[x_0, x_3]$ and that for weddle's rule is $-\frac{h^7}{140} y^{(vi)}$ in the interval $[x_0, x_6]$.

6.16. ALGORITHM OF TRAPEZOIDAL RULE

Step 01. Start of the program.
Step 02. Input Lower limit a
Step 03. Input Upper Limit b
Step 04. Input no. of sub intervals n
Step 05. h=(b-a)/n
Step 06. sum=0
Step 07. sum=fun(a)+fun(b)
Step 08. for i=1 ; i<n ; i++
Step 09. sum +=2*fun(a+i)
Step 10. End Loop i
Step 11. result =sum*h/2;

Step 12. Print Output result
Step 13. End of Program
Step 14. Start of Section fun
Step 15. temp = 1/(1+(x*x))
Step 16. Return temp
Step 17. End of Section fun.

6.17. FLOW CHART FOR TRAPEZOIDAL RULE

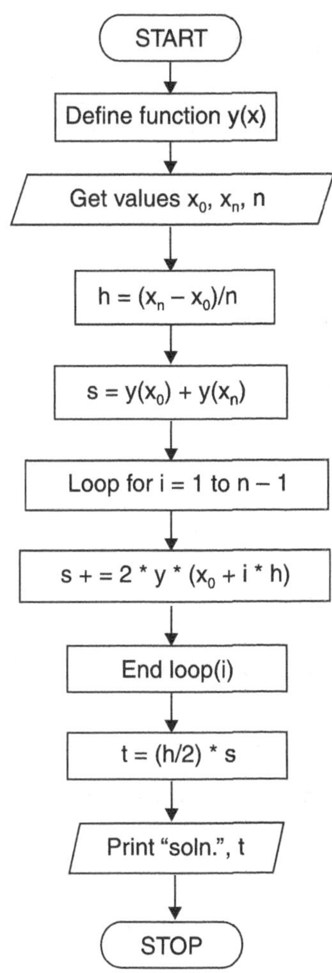


```
/* *****************************************************************
```

6.18. PROGRAM TO IMPLEMENT TRAPEZOIDAL METHOD OF NUMERICAL INTEGRATION

```
*****************************************************************  */
//... HEADER FILES DECLARATION

# include <stdio.h>
# include <conio.h>
```

```
# include <math.h>
# include <process.h>
# include <string.h>

//... Function Prototype Declaration

float fun(float);
//... Main Execution Thread

void main()
     {
     //... Variable Declaration Field
     //... Floating Type

     float result=1;
     float a,b;
     float h,sum;

     //... Integer Type

     int i,j;
     int n;

     //... Invoke Clear Screen Function
     clrscr();

     //... Input Section

     //... Input Range

     printf("\n\n Enter the range - ");
     printf("\n\n Lower Limit a - ");
     scanf("%f" ,&a);

     printf("\n\n Upper Limit b - ");
     scanf("%f" ,&b);

     //... Input No. of subintervals

     printf("\n\n Enter number of subintervals - ");
     scanf("%d" ,&n);

     //... Calculation and Processing Section

     h=(b-a)/n;

     sum=0;
     sum=fun(a)+fun(b);

     for(i=1;i<n;i++)
           {
           sum+=2*fun(a+i);
           }
     result=sum*h/2;

     //... Output Section
```

```
    printf("n\n\n\n Value of the integral is %6.4f\t",result);
    //...Invoke User Watch Halt Function
    printf("\n\n\n Press Enter to Exit");
    getch();
    }
//... Termination of Main Execution Thread
//... Function Body
float fun(float x)
    {
    float temp;
    temp = 1/(1+(x*x));
    return temp;
    }
//... Termination of Function Body
```

6.18.1. Output

```
Enter the range -
Lower Limit a - 0
Upper Limit b - 6
Enter number of subintervals - 6
Value of the integral is 1.4108
Press Enter to Exit
```

6.19. ALGORITHM OF SIMPSON'S 3/8th RULE

Step 01. Start of the program.
Step 02. Input Lower limit a
Step 03. Input Upper limit b
Step 04. Input number of subintervals n
Step 05. h = (b – a)/n
Step 06. sum = 0
Step 07. sum = fun(a) + fun (b)
Step 08. for i = 1 ; i < n ; i++
Step 09. if i%3=0 :
Step 10. sum + = 2*fun(a + i*h)
Step 11. else :
Step 12. sum + = 3*fun(a+(i)*h)
Step 13. End of loop i
Step 14. result = sum*3*h/8
Step 15. Print Output result
Step 16. End of Program
Step 17. Start of Section fun
Step 18. temp = 1/(1+(x*x))
Step 19. Return temp
Step 20. End of section fun

6.20. FLOW CHART OF SIMPSON'S 3/8th RULE

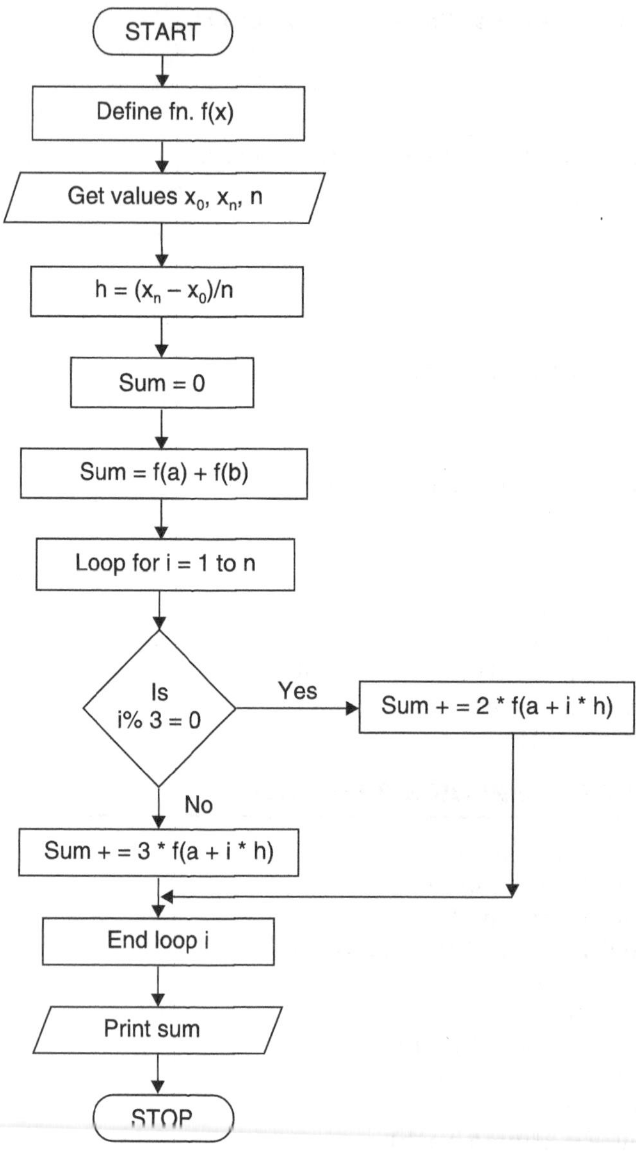


```
/**************************************************************************
```

6.21. PROGRAM TO IMPLEMENT SIMPSON'S 3/8th METHOD OF NUMERICAL INTEGRATION

```
**************************************************************************/
//... HEADER FILES DECLARATION
# include <stdio.h>
# include <conio.h>
# include <math.h>
```

```
# include <process.h>
# include <string.h>
//... Function Prototype Declaration

float fun(float);
//... Main Execution Thread

void main()
     {
     //... Variable Declaration Field

     //... Floating Type
     float result=1;
     float a,b;
     float h,sum;

     //...Integer Type

     int i,j;
     int n;

     //...Invoke Clear Screen Function

     clrscr();

     //...Input Section

     //...Input Range
     printf("\n\n Enter the range - ");
     printf("\n\n Lower Limit a - ");
     scanf("%f" ,&a);

     printf("\n\n Upper Limit b - ");
     scanf("%f" ,&b);

     //...Input No. of Subintervals
     printf("\n\n Enter number of subintervals - ");
     scanf("%d" ,&n);

     //...Calculation and Processing Section
     h=(b-a)/n;

     sum=0;
     sum=fun(a)+fun(b);

     for(i=1;i<n;i++)
           {
           if(i%3==0)
                 {
                 sum+=2*fun(a+i*h);
                 }
```

```
            else
                  {
                  sum+=3*fun(a+(i)*h);
                  }
            }
      result=sum*3*h/8;
      //... Output Section
      printf("\n\n\n\n Value of the integral is %6.4f\t",result);
      //... Invoke User Watch Halt Function
      printf("\n\n\n Press Enter to Exit");
      getch();
      }
//... Termination of Main Execution Thread
//... Function Body
float fun(float x)
      {
      float temp;
      temp=1/(1+(x*x));
      return temp;
      }
//... Termination of Function Body
```

6.21.1. Output

```
Enter the range -
Lower Limit a - 0
Upper Limit b - 6
Enter number of subintervals - 6
Value of the integral is 1.3571
Press Enter to Exit
```

6.22. ALGORITHM OF SIMPSON'S 1/3rd RULE

Step 01. Start of the program.
Step 02. Input Lower limit a
Step 03. Input Upper limit b
Step 04. Input No. of subintervals n
Step 05. h=(b–a)/n
Step 06. sum=0

Step 07. sum=fun(a)+4*fun(a+h)+fun(b)
Step 08. for i=3 ; i<n ; i + = 2
Step 09. sum + = 2*fun(a+(i – 1)*h) + 4*fun(a+i*h)
Step 10. End of loop i
Step 11. result=sum*h/3
Step 12. Print Output result
Step 13. End of Program
Step 14. Start of Section fun
Step 15. temp = 1/(1+(x*x))
Step 16. Return temp
Step 17. End of Section fun

6.23. FLOW CHART OF SIMPSON'S 1/3rd RULE

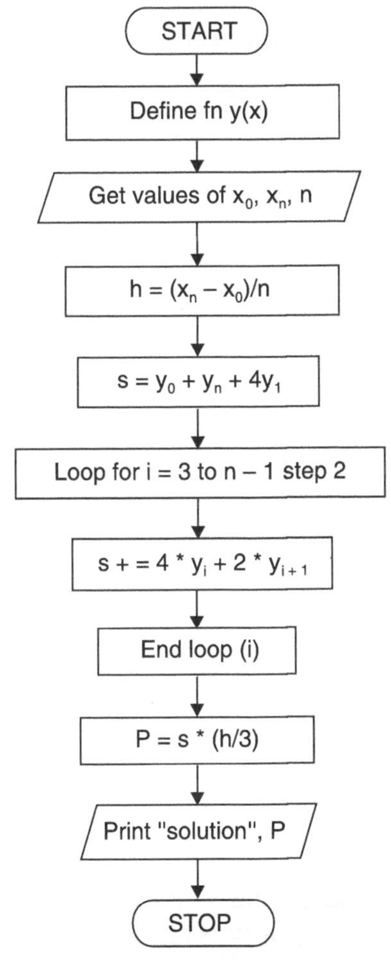

/**

6.24. PROGRAM TO IMPLEMENT SIMPSON'S 1/3rd METHOD OF NUMERICAL INTEGRATION

**/

```
//... HEADER FILES DECLARATION

# include <stdio.h>
# include <conio.h>
# include <math.h>
# include <process.h>
# include <string.h>

//... Function Prototype Declaration

float fun(float);

//... Main Execution Thread

void main()
     {
     //...Variable Declaration Field
     //... Floating Type
     float result=1;
     float a,b;
     float h,sum;

     //... Integer Type

     int i,j;
     int n;

     //... Invoke Clear Screen Function
     clrscr();

     //... Input Section

     //...Input Range
     printf("\n\n Enter the range - ");
     printf("\n\n Lower Limit a - ");
     scanf("%f" ,&a);

     printf("\n\n Upper Limit b - ");
```

```
    scanf("%f" ,&b);
    //... Input No. of Subintervals
    printf("\n\n Enter number of subintervals - ");
    scanf("%d",&n);

    //... Calculation and Processing Section

    h=(b-a)/n;

    sum=0;
    sum=fun(a)+4*fun(a+h)+fun(b);
    for(i=3;i<n;i+=2)
          {
          sum+=2*fun(a+(i-1)*h)+4*fun(a+i*h);
          }

    result=sum*h/3;

    //... Output Section

    printf("\n\n\n\n Value of the integral is %6.4f\t",result);

    //... Invoke User Watch Halt Function

    printf("\n\n\n Press Enter to Exit");

    getch();

    }

//... Termination of Main Execution Thread

//... Function Body

float fun(float x)
    {

    float temp;
    temp=1/(1+(x*x));
    return temp;

    }

//... Termination of Function Body
```

6.24.1. Output

```
Enter the range -
Lower Limit a - 0
Upper Limit b - 6
Enter number of subintervals - 6
Value of the integral is 1.3662
Press Enter to Exit
```

EXAMPLES

Example 1. *Compute* $I_p = \int_0^1 \frac{x^p}{x^3 + 10}\, dx$ *for p = 0, 1.*

Use Trapezoidal rule with number of points 3, 5 and 9.

Sol. For $p = 0$

$$I_0 = \int_0^1 \frac{1}{x^3 + 10}\, dx$$

(*i*) Dividing the interval (0, 1) into 2 equal parts, each of width $h = \frac{1-0}{2} = \frac{1}{2}$, the values of $f(x) = \frac{1}{x^3 + 10}$ are given below:

x:	0	$\frac{1}{2}$	1
$f(x)$:	$\frac{1}{10}$	$\frac{8}{81}$	$\frac{1}{11}$

By Trapezoidal rule,

$$I_0 = \frac{h}{2}\,[(y_0 + y_2) + 2y_1] = \frac{1}{4}\left[\left(\frac{1}{10} + \frac{1}{11}\right) + \frac{16}{81}\right] = 0.0971099$$

(*ii*) Dividing the interval (0, 1) into 4 equal parts, each of width $h = \frac{1-0}{4} = \frac{1}{4}$, the values of $f(x) = \frac{1}{x^3 + 10}$ are given below:

x:	0	$\frac{1}{4}$	$\frac{1}{2}$	$\frac{3}{4}$	1
$f(x)$:	$\frac{1}{10}$	$\frac{64}{641}$	$\frac{8}{81}$	$\frac{64}{667}$	$\frac{1}{11}$

By Trapezoidal rule,

$$I_0 = \frac{h}{2}\,[(y_0 + y_4) + 2(y_1 + y_2 + y_3)]$$

$$= \frac{1}{8}\left[\left(\frac{1}{10} + \frac{1}{11}\right) + 2\left(\frac{64}{641} + \frac{8}{81} + \frac{64}{667}\right)\right] = 0.0975039$$

(*iii*) Dividing the interval (0, 1) into 8 equal parts, each of width $h = \frac{1}{8}$, the values of $f(x) = \frac{1}{x^3 + 10}$ are given below:

x:	0	$\frac{1}{8}$	$\frac{1}{4}$	$\frac{3}{8}$	$\frac{1}{2}$	$\frac{5}{8}$	$\frac{3}{4}$	$\frac{7}{8}$	1
$f(x)$:	$\frac{1}{10}$	$\frac{512}{5121}$	$\frac{64}{641}$	$\frac{512}{5147}$	$\frac{8}{81}$	$\frac{512}{5245}$	$\frac{64}{667}$	$\frac{512}{5463}$	$\frac{1}{11}$

By Trapezoidal rule,

$$I_0 = \frac{h}{2} [(y_0 + y_8) + 2 (y_1 + y_2 + y_3 + y_4 + y_5 + y_6 + y_7)]$$

$$= \frac{1}{16}\left[\left(\frac{1}{10}+\frac{1}{11}\right)+2\left(\frac{512}{5121}+\frac{64}{641}+\frac{512}{5147}+\frac{8}{81}+\frac{512}{5245}+\frac{64}{667}+\frac{512}{5463}\right)\right]$$

$$= 0.0976012$$

Repeating the above process for $p = 1$ so that

$$I_1 = \int_0^1 \frac{x}{x^3 + 10}\, dx$$

and dividing the interval (0, 1) into 2, 4 and 8 equal parts respectively, we get I_1 as 0.0480733, 0.0481145 and 0.0481164 respectively.

Example 2. *Evaluate* $\int_0^1 \frac{dx}{1+x^2}$ *using*

(*i*) *Simpson's* $\frac{1}{3}$ *rule taking* $h = \frac{1}{4}$ [U.P.T.U. (MCA) 2007]

(*ii*) *Simpson's* $\frac{3}{8}$ *rule taking* $h = \frac{1}{6}$ [G.B.T.U. 2010, U.P.T.U. (MCA) 2006]

Hence compute an approximate value of π *in each case.*

Sol. (*i*) The values of $f(x) = \frac{1}{1+x^2}$ at $x = 0, \frac{1}{4}, \frac{2}{4}, \frac{3}{4}, 1$ are given below:

x:	0	$\frac{1}{4}$	$\frac{1}{2}$	$\frac{3}{4}$	1
$f(x)$:	1	$\frac{16}{17}$	0.8	0.64	0.5
	y_0	y_1	y_2	y_3	y_4

By Simpson's $\frac{1}{3}$ rule,

$$\int_0^1 \frac{dx}{1+x^2} = \frac{h}{3} [(y_0 + y_4) + 4(y_1 + y_3) + 2y_2]$$

$$= \frac{1}{12}\left[(1 + 0.5) + 4\left\{\frac{16}{17} + 0.64\right\} + 2(0.8)\right] = 0.785392156$$

Also
$$\int_0^1 \frac{dx}{1+x^2} = \left[\tan^{-1} x\right]_0^1 = \tan^{-1} 1 = \frac{\pi}{4}$$

$\therefore$
$$\frac{\pi}{4} \simeq 0.785392156 \Rightarrow \pi \simeq 3.1415686$$

(*ii*) The values of $f(x) = \frac{1}{1+x^2}$ at $x = 0, \frac{1}{6}, \frac{2}{6}, \frac{3}{6}, \frac{4}{6}, \frac{5}{6}, 1$ are given below:

x:	0	$\frac{1}{6}$	$\frac{2}{6}$	$\frac{3}{6}$	$\frac{4}{6}$	$\frac{5}{6}$	1
$f(x)$:	1	$\frac{36}{37}$	$\frac{9}{10}$	$\frac{4}{5}$	$\frac{9}{13}$	$\frac{36}{61}$	$\frac{1}{2}$
	y_0	y_1	y_2	y_3	y_4	y_5	y_6

By Simpson's $\frac{3}{8}$ rule,

$$\int_0^1 \frac{dx}{1+x^2} = \frac{3h}{8}\,[(y_0 + y_6) + 3(y_1 + y_2 + y_4 + y_5) + 2y_3]$$

$$= \frac{3\left(\frac{1}{6}\right)}{8}\left[\left(1+\frac{1}{2}\right) + 3\left\{\frac{36}{37} + \frac{9}{10} + \frac{9}{13} + \frac{36}{61}\right\} + 2\left(\frac{4}{5}\right)\right] = 0.785395862$$

Also, $\int_0^1 \frac{dx}{1+x^2} = \frac{\pi}{4}$

$$\therefore \qquad \frac{\pi}{4} = 0.785395862 \quad \Rightarrow \quad \pi = 3.141583$$

Example 3. *Evaluate* $\int_0^6 \frac{dx}{1+x^2}$ *by using*

(*i*) *Simpson's one-third rule* [M.T.U. (MCA) 2012]

(*ii*) *Simpson's three-eighth rule*

(*iii*) *Trapezoidal rule.*

Sol. Divide the interval (0, 6) into six parts each of width $h = 1$.

The values of $f(x) = \frac{1}{1+x^2}$ are given below:

x:	0	1	2	3	4	5	6
$f(x)$:	1	0.5	0.2	0.1	$\frac{1}{17}$	$\frac{1}{26}$	$\frac{1}{37}$
	y_0	y_1	y_2	y_3	y_4	y_5	y_6

(*i*) By Simpson's one-third rule,

$$\int_0^6 \frac{dx}{1+x^2} = \frac{h}{3}\,[(y_0 + y_6) + 4(y_1 + y_3 + y_5) + 2(y_2 + y_4)]$$

$$= \frac{1}{3}\left[\left(1+\frac{1}{37}\right) + 4\left(0.5 + 0.1 + \frac{1}{26}\right) + 2\left(0.2 + \frac{1}{17}\right)\right] = 1.366173413.$$

(*ii*) By Simpson's three-eighth rule,

$$\int_0^6 \frac{dx}{1+x^2} = \frac{3h}{8}\,[(y_0 + y_6) + 3(y_1 + y_2 + y_4 + y_5) + 2y_3]$$

$$= \frac{3}{8}\left[\left(1+\frac{1}{37}\right)+3\left(0.5+0.2+\frac{1}{17}+\frac{1}{26}\right)+2(0.1)\right] = 1.357080836.$$

(*iii*) By Trapezoidal rule,

$$\int_0^6 \frac{dx}{1+x^2} = \frac{h}{2}\,[(y_0 + y_6) + 2(y_1 + y_2 + y_3 + y_4 + y_5)]$$

$$= \frac{1}{2}\left[\left(1+\frac{1}{37}\right)+2\left(0.5+0.2+0.1+\frac{1}{17}+\frac{1}{26}\right)\right] = 1.410798581.$$

Example 4. *The speed, v metres per second, of a car, t seconds after it starts, is shown in the following table:*

t	*0*	*12*	*24*	*36*	*48*	*60*	*72*	*84*	*96*	*108*	*120*
v	*0*	*3.60*	*10.08*	*18.90*	*21.60*	*18.54*	*10.26*	*5.40*	*4.50*	*5.40*	*9.00*

Using Simpson's $\left(\frac{1}{3}\right)^{rd}$ *rule, find the distance travelled by the car in 2 minutes.*

Sol. If s metres is the distance covered in t seconds, then

$$\frac{ds}{dt} = v$$

$$\therefore \qquad \Big[s\Big]_{t=0}^{t=120} = \int_0^{120} v\,dt$$

Since the number of sub-intervals is **10 (even)**, hence, by using Simpson's $1/3^{rd}$ rule,

$$\int_0^{120} v\,dt = \frac{h}{3}\,[(v_0 + v_{10}) + 4(v_1 + v_3 + v_5 + v_7 + v_9) + 2(v_2 + v_4 + v_6 + v_8)]$$

$$= \frac{12}{3}\,[(0 + 9) + 4(3.6 + 18.9 + 18.54 + 5.4 + 5.4)$$

$$+ 2(10.08 + 21.6 + 10.26 + 4.5)]$$

$$= 1236.96 \text{ metres.}$$

Hence, the distance travelled by car in 2 minutes is 1236.96 metres.

Example 5. *Evaluate* $\int_{0.6}^{2} y\,dx$, *where y is given by the following table:*

x:	*0.6*	*0.8*	*1.0*	*1.2*	*1.4*	*1.6*	*1.8*	*2.0*
y:	*1.23*	*1.58*	*2.03*	*4.32*	*6.25*	*8.36*	*10.23*	*12.45.*

Sol. Here the no. of sub-intervals is 7 which is neither even nor a multiple of 3. Also this number is neither a multiple of 4 nor a multiple of 6 hence using Trapezoidal rule, we get

$$\int_{0.6}^{2} y\,dx = \frac{h}{2}\,[(y_0 + y_7) + 2(y_1 + y_2 + y_3 + y_4 + y_5 + y_6)]$$

$$= \frac{0.2}{2}\,[(1.23 + 12.45) + 2(1.58 + 2.03 + 4.32 + 6.25 + 8.36 + 10.23)]$$

| Here $h = 0.2$

$$= 7.922.$$

Example 6. *Find, from the following table, the area bounded by the curve and the x-axis from x = 7.47 to x = 7.52.*

x:	*7.47*	*7.48*	*7.49*	*7.50*	*7.51*	*7.52*
f(x):	*1.93*	*1.95*	*1.98*	*2.01*	*2.03*	*2.06.*

Sol. We know that

$$\text{Area} = \int_{7.47}^{7.52} f(x)\,dx \text{ with } h = 0.01, \text{ the trapezoidal rule gives,}$$

$$\text{Area} = \frac{0.01}{2}\,[(1.93 + 2.06) + 2(1.95 + 1.98 + 2.01 + 2.03)] = 0.09965.$$

Example 7. *Using Simpson's 3/8th rule on integration, evaluate*

$$\int_0^6 \frac{1}{1+x}\,dx$$ [G.B.T.U. 2009; G.B.T.U. (M.Tech.) 2011]

Sol. The table of values is as follows: (Here $h = 1$)

x:	0	1	2	3	4	5	6
$f(x) = \frac{1}{1+x}$:	1	$\frac{1}{2}$	$\frac{1}{3}$	$\frac{1}{4}$	$\frac{1}{5}$	$\frac{1}{6}$	$\frac{1}{7}$
	y_0	y_1	y_2	y_3	y_4	y_5	y_6

By Simpson's 3/8th rule,

$$\int_0^6 \frac{1}{1+x}\,dx = \frac{3h}{8}\,[(y_0 + y_6) + 3\,(y_1 + y_2 + y_4 + y_5) + 2y_3]$$

$$= \frac{3}{8}\left[\left(1+\frac{1}{7}\right) + 3\left(\frac{1}{2}+\frac{1}{3}+\frac{1}{5}+\frac{1}{6}\right) + 2\left(\frac{1}{4}\right)\right] = 1.96607.$$

Example 8. *Evaluate* $\int_0^1 \frac{dx}{1+x}$ *by dividing the interval of integration into 8 equal parts. Hence find* $\log_e 2$ *approximately.* [U.P.T.U. (MCA) 2008]

Sol. Since the interval of integration is divided into an even number of sub-intervals, we shall use Simpson's one-third rule.

Here, $$y = \frac{1}{1+x} = f(x)$$

$$y_0 = f(0) = \frac{1}{1+0} = 1, \quad y_1 = f\left(\frac{1}{8}\right) = \frac{1}{1+\frac{1}{8}} = \frac{8}{9}, \qquad y_2 = f\left(\frac{2}{8}\right) = \frac{4}{5}$$

$$y_3 = f\left(\frac{3}{8}\right) = \frac{8}{11}, \qquad y_4 = f\left(\frac{4}{8}\right) = \frac{2}{3}, \qquad y_5 = f\left(\frac{5}{8}\right) = \frac{8}{13}$$

$$y_6 = f\left(\frac{6}{8}\right) = \frac{4}{7}, \qquad y_7 = f\left(\frac{7}{8}\right) = \frac{8}{15} \qquad \text{and} \quad y_8 = f(1) = \frac{1}{2}$$

Hence the table of values is

x:	0	$\frac{1}{8}$	$\frac{2}{8}$	$\frac{3}{8}$	$\frac{4}{8}$	$\frac{5}{8}$	$\frac{6}{8}$	$\frac{7}{8}$	1
y:	1	$\frac{8}{9}$	$\frac{4}{5}$	$\frac{8}{11}$	$\frac{2}{3}$	$\frac{8}{13}$	$\frac{4}{7}$	$\frac{8}{15}$	$\frac{1}{2}$
	y_0	y_1	y_2	y_3	y_4	y_5	y_6	y_7	y_8

By Simpson's 1/3rd rule,

$$\int_0^1 \frac{dx}{1+x} = \frac{h}{3}\ [(y_0 + y_8) + 4(y_1 + y_3 + y_5 + y_7) + 2(y_2 + y_4 + y_6)]$$

$$= \frac{1}{24}\left[\left(1+\frac{1}{2}\right) + 4\left(\frac{8}{9}+\frac{8}{11}+\frac{8}{13}+\frac{8}{15}\right) + 2\left(\frac{4}{5}+\frac{2}{3}+\frac{4}{7}\right)\right] \qquad | \text{ Here } h = 1/8$$

$$= 0.69315453$$

Since, $\displaystyle\int_0^1 \frac{dx}{1+x} = \Big[\log_e(1+x)\Big]_0^1 = \log_e 2$

$\therefore$ $\log_e 2 = 0.69315453.$

Example 9. *Evaluate* $\int_1^2 e^{-\frac{1}{2}x}\, dx$ *using four intervals.*

Sol. The table of values is

x:	1	1.25	1.5	1.75	2
$y = e^{-x/2}$:	0.60653	0.53526	0.47237	0.41686	0.36788
	y_0	y_1	y_2	y_3	y_4

Since we have four (even) sub-intervals here, we will use Simpson's 1/3rd rule.

$$\therefore \quad \int_1^2 e^{-\frac{1}{2}x}\, dx = \frac{h}{3}\ [(y_0 + y_4) + 4(y_1 + y_3) + 2y_2]$$

$$= \frac{0.25}{3}\ [(0.60653 + 0.36788) + 4(0.53526) + 0.41686) + 2(0.47237)]$$

$$= 0.4773025.$$

Example 10. *Use Simpson's rule for evaluating* $\int_{-0.6}^{0.3} f(x)\, dx$ *from the table given below:*

x:	– 0.6	– 0.5	– 0.4	– 0.3	– 0.2	– 0.1	0	0.1	0.2	0.3
$f(x)$:	4	2	5	3	– 2	1	6	4	2	8

Sol. Since the no. of sub-intervals is 9(a multiple of 3) hence we will use Simpson's 3/8th rule here.

$$\therefore \quad \int_{-0.6}^{0.3} f(x)\,dx = \frac{3(0.1)}{8}\,[(4+8)+3\{2+5+(-2)+1+4+2\}+2(3+6)] = 2.475.$$

Example 11. *A train is moving at the speed of 30 m / sec. Suddenly brakes are applied. The speed of the train per second after t seconds is given by*

Time (t):	*0*	*5*	*10*	*15*	*20*	*25*	*30*	*35*	*40*	*45*
Speed (v):	*30*	*24*	*19*	*16*	*13*	*11*	*10*	*8*	*7*	*5*

Apply Simpson's three-eighth rule to determine the distance moved by the train in 45 seconds.

Sol. If s metres is the distance covered in t seconds, then

$$\frac{ds}{dt} = v$$

$$\Rightarrow \quad \Big[s\Big]_{t=0}^{t=45} = \int_0^{45} v\,dt \qquad \text{...(1)}$$

Since the no. of sub-intervals is **9 (a multiple of 3)** hence by using Simpson's $\left(\frac{3}{8}\right)^{\text{th}}$ rule,

$$\int_0^{45} v\,dt = \frac{3h}{8}\,[(v_0+v_9)+3(v_1+v_2+v_4+v_5+v_7+v_8)+2(v_3+v_6)]$$

$$= \frac{15}{8}\,[(30+5)+3(24+19+13+11+8+7)+2(16+10)]$$

$$= 624.375 \text{ metres.}$$

Hence the distance moved by the train in 45 seconds is **624.375** metres.

Example 12. *Find* $\int_0^6 \frac{e^x}{1+x}\,dx$ *approximately using Simpson's 3/8th rule on integration.*

[U.P.T.U. MCA (C.O.) 2008, U.P.T.U. (MCA) 2009, U.P.T.U. 2006]

Sol. Divide the given integral of integration into 6 equal sub-intervals, the arguments are 0, 1, 2, 3, 4, 5, 6; $h = 1$.

$$f(x) = \frac{e^x}{1+x}\,; \qquad y_0 = f(0) = 1$$

$$y_1 = f(1) = \frac{e}{2}, \qquad y_2 = f(2) = \frac{e^2}{3}, \qquad y_3 = f(3) = \frac{e^3}{4},$$

$$y_4 = f(4) = \frac{e^4}{5}, \qquad y_5 = f(5) = \frac{e^5}{6}, \qquad y_6 = f(6) = \frac{e^6}{7}$$

The table is as below:

x:	0	1	2	3	4	5	6
y:	1	$\frac{e}{2}$	$\frac{e^2}{3}$	$\frac{e^3}{4}$	$\frac{e^4}{5}$	$\frac{e^5}{6}$	$\frac{e^6}{7}$
	y_0	y_1	y_2	y_3	y_4	y_5	y_6

Applying Simpson's three-eighth rule, we have

$$\int_0^6 \frac{e^x}{1+x}\,dx = \frac{3h}{8}\,[(y_0 + y_6) + 3(y_1 + y_2 + y_4 + y_5) + 2y_3]$$

$$= \frac{3}{8}\left[\left(1+\frac{e^6}{7}\right)+3\left(\frac{e}{2}+\frac{e^2}{3}+\frac{e^4}{5}+\frac{e^5}{6}\right)+2\,\frac{e^3}{4}\right]$$

$$= \frac{3}{8}\,[(1 + 57.6327) + 3(1.3591 + 2.463 + 10.9196 + 24.7355 + 2(5.0214)]$$

$$= 70.1652.$$

Note. It is not possible to evaluate $\int_0^6 \frac{e^x}{1+x}\,dx$ by using usual calculus method. Numerical integration comes to our rescue in such situations.

Example 13. *Evaluate* $\int_0^4 \frac{dx}{1+x^2}$ *using Boole's rule taking*

(i) $h = 1$ *(ii)* $h = 0.5$

Compare the results with the actual value and indicate the error in both.

Sol. (*i*) Dividing the given interval into 4 equal sub-intervals (*i.e.*, $h = 1$), the table is as below:

$x:$	0	1	2	3	4
$y:$	1	$\frac{1}{2}$	$\frac{1}{5}$	$\frac{1}{10}$	$\frac{1}{17}$
	y_0	y_1	y_2	y_3	y_4

using Boole's rule,

$$\int_0^4 y\,dx = \frac{2h}{45}\,[7y_0 + 32y_1 + 12y_2 + 32y_3 + 7y_4]$$

$$= \frac{2(1)}{45}\left[7(1)+32\left(\frac{1}{2}\right)+12\left(\frac{1}{5}\right)+32\left(\frac{1}{10}\right)+7\left(\frac{1}{17}\right)\right] = 1.289412 \text{ (approx.)}$$

$$\therefore \quad \int_0^4 \frac{dx}{1+x^2} = 1.289412.$$

(*ii*) Dividing the given interval into 8 equal sub-intervals (*i.e.*, $h = 0.5$), the table is as below:

$x:$	0	.5	1	1.5	2	2.5	3	3.5	4
$y:$	1	0.8	0.5	$\frac{4}{13}$	.2	$\frac{4}{29}$	.1	$\frac{4}{53}$	$\frac{1}{17}$
	y_0	y_1	y_2	y_3	y_4	y_5	y_6	y_7	y_8

using Boole's rule,

$$\int_0^4 y dx = \frac{2h}{45}[7(y_0)+32(y_1)+12(y_2)+32(y_3)+7(y_4)$$

$$+7(y_4)+32(y_5)+12(y_6)+32(y_7)+7(y_8)]$$

$$= \frac{1}{45}\left[7(1)+32(0.8)+12(0.5)+32\left(\frac{4}{13}\right)+7(0.2)+7(0.2)+32\left(\frac{4}{29}\right)+12(0.1)\right.$$

$$\left.+32\left(\frac{4}{53}\right)+7\left(\frac{1}{17}\right)\right]$$

$$= 1.326373$$

$$\therefore \qquad \int_0^4 \frac{dx}{1+x^2} = 1.326373$$

But the actual value is

$$\int_0^4 \frac{dx}{1+x^2} = \left(\tan^{-1} x\right)_0^4 = \tan^{-1}(4) = 1.325818$$

Error in I result $= \left(\dfrac{1.325818 - 1.289412}{1.325818}\right) \times 100 = 2.746\%$

Error in II result $= \left(\dfrac{1.325818 - 1.326373}{1.325818}\right) \times 100 = -0.0419\%$.

Example 14. *A river is 80 m wide. The depth 'y' of the river at a distance 'x' from one bank is given by the following table:*

x:	0	10	20	30	40	50	60	70	80
y:	0	4	7	9	12	15	14	8	3

Find the approximate area of cross-section of the river using

(*i*) *Boole's rule.* [U.P.T.U. (SUM) 2004]

(*ii*) *Simpson's* $\frac{1}{3}$*rd rule.*

Sol. The required area of the cross-section of the river

$$= \int_0^{80} y\, dx \qquad ...(1)$$

Here no. of sub-intervals is 8.

(*i*) *By Boole's rule,*

$$\int_0^{80} y\,dx = \frac{2h}{45}[7y_0 + 32y_1 + 12y_2 + 32y_3 + 7y_4 + 7y_4 + 32y_5 + 12y_6 + 32y_7 + 7y_8]$$

$$= \frac{2(10)}{45}[7(0) + 32(4) + 12(7) + 32(9) + 7(12) + 7(12) + 32(15)$$

$$+ 12(14) + 32(8) + 7(3)]$$

$$= 708$$

Hence the required area of the cross-section of the river = 708 sq. m.

(*ii*) *By Simpson's* $\frac{1}{3}$*rd rule*

$$\int_0^{80} y\,dx = \frac{h}{3}[(y_0 + y_8) + 4(y_1 + y_3 + y_5 + y_7) + 2(y_2 + y_4 + y_6)]$$

$$= \frac{10}{3}[(0 + 3) + 4(4 + 9 + 15 + 8) + 2(7 + 12 + 14)] = 710$$

Hence the required area of the cross section of the river = 710 sq. m.

Example 15. *Evaluate* $\int_{0.2}^{1.4} (\sin x - \log_e x + e^x)\, dx$ *approximately using Weddle's rule correct to 4 decimals.*

Sol. Let $f(x) = \sin x - \log x + e^x$. We shall divide the given interval of integration into 12 equal parts so that the arguments are : 0.2, 0.3, 0.4, 0.5, 0.6, 0.7, 0.8, 0.9, 1.0, 1.1, 1.2, 1.3, 1.4.

The corresponding entries are

$y_0 = f(0.2) = 3.0295$, $y_1 = f(0.3) = 2.8494$, $y_2 = f(0.4) = 2.7975$,
$y_3 = f(0.5) = 2.8213$, $y_4 = f(0.6) = 2.8976$, $y_5 = f(0.7) = 3.0147$
$y_6 = f(0.8) = 3.1661$, $y_7 = f(0.9) = 3.3483$, $y_8 = f(1) = 3.5598$,
$y_9 = f(1.1) = 3.8001$, $y_{10} = f(1.2) = 4.0698$, $y_{11} = f(1.3) = 4.3705$
$y_{12} = f(1.4) = 4.7042$

Now, by Weddle's rule,

$$\int_{0.2}^{1.4} f(x)\, dx = \frac{3h}{10}[y_0 + 5y_1 + y_2 + 6y_3 + y_4 + 5y_5 + y_6 + y_6 + 5y_7 + y_8 + 6y_9 + y_{10} + 5y_{11} + y_{12}]$$

$$= \frac{3}{10}(0.1)[3.0295 + 14.2470 + 2.7975 + 16.9278 + 2.8976 + 15.0735 + 3.1661 + 3.1661 + 16.7415 + 3.5598 + 22.8006 + 4.0698 + 21.8525 + 4.7042]$$

$$= 4.051.$$

Example 16. *A solid of revolution is formed by rotating about x-axis, the lines x = 0 and x = 1 and a curve through the points with the following co-ordinates.*

x:	*0*	*0.25*	*0.5*	*0.75*	*1*
y:	*1*	*0.9896*	*0.9589*	*0.9089*	*0.8415*

Estimate the volume of the solid formed using Simpson's rule.

Sol. If V is the volume of the solid formed then we know that

$$V = \pi \int_0^1 y^2\, dx$$

Hence we need the values of y^2 and these are tabulated below correct to four decimal places

x	0	0.25	0.5	0.75	1
y^2	1	0.9793	0.9195	0.8261	0.7081

With $h = 0.25$, Simpson's rule gives

$$V = \pi \frac{(0.25)}{3}[(1 + 0.7081) + 4(0.9793 + 0.8261) + 2(0.9195)] = 2.8192.$$

Example 17. *A tank is discharging water through an orifice at a depth of x metre below the surface of the water whose area is A m*^{2}*. Following are the values of x for the corresponding values of A.*

A:	*1.257*	*1.39*	*1.52*	*1.65*	*1.809*	*1.962*	*2.123*	*2.295*	*2.462*	*2.650*	*2.827*
x:	*1.5*	*1.65*	*1.8*	*1.95*	*2.1*	*2.25*	*2.4*	*2.55*	*2.7*	*2.85*	*3*

Using the formula (0.018) $T = \int_{1.5}^{3.0} \frac{A}{\sqrt{x}}\, dx$, *calculate T, the time (in seconds) for the level of the water to drop from 3.0 m to 1.5 m above the orifice.*

Sol. Here $h = 0.15$

The table of values of x and the corresponding values of $\frac{A}{\sqrt{x}}$ is

x	1.5	1.65	1.8	1.95	2.1	2.25	2.4	2.55	2.7	2.85	3
$y = \frac{A}{\sqrt{x}}$	1.025	1.081	1.132	1.182	1.249	1.308	1.375	1.438	1.498	1.571	1.632

Using Simpson's 1/3rd rule, we get

$$\int_{1.5}^{3} \frac{A}{\sqrt{x}}\, dx = \frac{0.15}{3}[(1.025+1.632) + 4(1.081 + 1.182 + 1.308 + 1.438 + 1.571)$$
$$+ 2(1.132 + 1.249 + 1.375 + 1.498)]$$
$$= 1.9743$$

Using the formula

$$(0.018)T = \int_{1.5}^{3} \frac{A}{\sqrt{x}}\, dx$$

We get $0.018T = 1.9743 \Rightarrow T = 110$ sec. (approximately).

Example 18. *Using the following table of values, approximate by Simpson's rule, the arc length of the graph* $y = \frac{1}{x}$ *between the points (1, 1) and* $\left(5, \frac{1}{5}\right)$

x	:	1	2	3	4	5
$\sqrt{\frac{1+x^4}{x^4}}$	:	1.414	1.031	1.007	1.002	1.001.

Sol. The given curve is

$$y = \frac{1}{x}$$

$$\therefore \quad \frac{dy}{dx} = -\frac{1}{x^2}$$

$$\therefore \quad \frac{ds}{dx} = \sqrt{1+\left(\frac{dy}{dx}\right)^2} = \sqrt{1+\frac{1}{x^4}} = \sqrt{\frac{1+x^4}{x^4}}$$

$\therefore$ The arc length of the curve between the points (1, 1) and $\left(5, \frac{1}{5}\right)$

$$= \int_{1}^{5} \sqrt{\frac{1+x^4}{x^4}}\, dx$$

$$= \frac{1}{3}[(1.414 + 1.001) + 4(1.031 + 1.002) + 2(1.007)] = 4.187$$

Example 19. *From the following values of $y = f(x)$ in the given range of values of x, find the position of the centroid of the area under the curve and the x-axis*

x :	0	$\frac{1}{4}$	$\frac{1}{2}$	$\frac{3}{4}$	1
y :	1	4	8	4	1

Also find

(i) the volume of solid obtained by revolving the above area about x-axis.

(ii) the moment of inertia of the area about x-axis.

Sol. Centroid of the plane area under the curve $y = f(x)$ is given by $(\bar{x}, \bar{y})$ where

$$\bar{x} = \frac{\int_0^1 xy\,dx}{\int_0^1 y\,dx}$$

and

$$\bar{y} = \frac{\int_0^1 \frac{y}{2}\cdot y\,dx}{\int_0^1 y\,dx} = \frac{\int_0^1 \frac{y^2}{2}\,dx}{\int_0^1 y\,dx} \quad \ldots(1)$$

From the given data, we obtain

x	:	0	$\frac{1}{4}$	$\frac{1}{2}$	$\frac{3}{4}$	1
y	:	1	4	8	4	1
xy	:	0	1	4	3	1
$\frac{y^2}{2}$	:	$\frac{1}{2}$	8	32	8	$\frac{1}{2}$

∴ By Simpson's rule,

$$\int_0^1 xy\,dx = \frac{(1/4)}{3}[(0 + 1) + 4(1 + 3) + 2(4)] = \frac{25}{12}$$

$$\int_0^1 \frac{y^2}{2}\,dx = \frac{1}{12}\left[\left(\frac{1}{2}+\frac{1}{2}\right) + 4(8+8) + 2(32)\right] = \frac{129}{12}$$

$$\int_0^1 y\,dx = \frac{1}{12}[(1 + 1) + 4(4 + 4) + 2(8)] = \frac{50}{12}$$

From (1),
$$\bar{x} = \frac{25/12}{50/12} = \frac{1}{2} = 0.5\;;\quad \bar{y} = \frac{129/12}{50/12} = \frac{129}{50} = 2.58$$

∴ Centroid is the point (0.5, 2.58).

(*i*) We know that

$$\text{V} = \text{Volume} = \pi\int_0^1 y^2\,dx$$

∴ Reqd. volume
$$= \pi.2\int_0^1 \frac{y^2}{2}dx = 2\pi \times \frac{129}{12} = 67.5442$$

(*ii*) We know that moment of inertia of the area about x-axis is given by

$$\text{M.I.} = \frac{1}{3}\rho\int_a^b y^3\,dx$$

where ρ is the mass per unit area.

Table for y^3 is

x :	0	$\frac{1}{4}$	$\frac{1}{2}$	$\frac{3}{4}$	1
y :	1	4	8	4	1
y^3 :	1	64	512	64	1

$$\int_0^1 y^3\,dx = \frac{1}{12}[(1+1)+4(64+64)+2(512)] = \frac{769}{6}$$

$$\therefore \quad \text{Reqd. M.I.} = \frac{1}{3}\rho\left(\frac{769}{6}\right) = \frac{769}{18}\rho = 42.7222\,\rho.$$

Example 20. *A reservoir discharging water through sluices at a depth h below the water surface, has a surface area A for various values of h as given below :*

h (in metres) :	*10*	*11*	*12*	*13*	*14*
A (in sq. metres) :	*950*	*1070*	*1200*	*1350*	*1530*

If t denotes time in minutes, the rate of fall of the surface is given by

$$\frac{dh}{dt} = -\frac{48}{A}\sqrt{h}$$

Estimate the time taken for the water level to fall from 14 to 10 m above the sluices.

Sol. From $\quad \dfrac{dh}{dt} = -\dfrac{48}{A}\sqrt{h}$, we have

$$dt = -\frac{A}{48}\frac{dh}{\sqrt{h}}$$

Integration yields,

$$t = -\frac{1}{48}\int_{14}^{10}\frac{A}{\sqrt{h}}\,dh = \frac{1}{48}\int_{10}^{14}\frac{A}{\sqrt{h}}\,dh$$

Here, $y = \dfrac{A}{\sqrt{h}}$. The table of values is as below :

h :	10	11	12	13	14
A :	950	1070	1200	1350	1530
$\frac{A}{\sqrt{h}}$:	300.4164	322.6171	346.4102	374.4226	408.9097

Applying Simpson's $\frac{1}{3}$rd rule, we have

$$\text{time } t = \frac{1}{48}\cdot\frac{1}{3}[(300.4164+408.9097)+4(322.6171+374.4226)+2(346.4102)]$$

$$= 29.0993 \text{ minutes.}$$

ASSIGNMENT

1. (*i*) Evaluate $\int_1^2 \frac{1}{x}\, dx$ by Simpson's 1/3rd rule with four strips and determine the error by direct integration. [*G.B.T.U. (MCA) 2010*]

   (*ii*) Evaluate the integral $\int_0^1 e^{x+1}\, dx$ using Simpson's 1/3 rule by dividing the interval of integration into 8 equal parts. (*G.B.T.U. 2013, 2011*)

2. Compute $\int_0^{\pi/2} \sin x\, dx$ using Simpson's three-eighth rule of integration, taking $h = \frac{\pi}{18}$. (*U.P.T.U. 2007*)

3. Evaluate $\int_4^{5.2} \log_e x\, dx$ by Simpson's 3/8th rule. [*G.B.T.U. (C.O.) 2011*]

4. (*i*) Find the value of $\int_0^{\pi/2} \sqrt{1 - 0.162 \sin^2 x}\; dx$ using Simpson's one-third rule taking 6 sub-intervals. (*U.P.T.U. 2007*)

   (*ii*) Find the approximate value of the following integral using Simpson's rule by dividing the interval into six equal parts: $\int_0^{\pi} \sqrt{1 + 3\cos^2 x}\; dx$. (*M.T.U. 2012*)

5. (*i*) Use Simpson's 1/3 rule to evaluate the integral of $f(x) = \frac{\sin(x)}{x}$ with respect to x between $x = 0$ and $x = 1$ with a value of $h = 0.25$. [*G.B.T.U. MCA (SUM) 2010*]

   (*ii*) Evaluate $\int_0^8 x \sec x\, dx$ using eight intervals by Trapezoidal rule. (*U.P.T.U. 2009*)

   (*iii*) State the need and scope of numerical integration. Use the Trapezoidal rule to estimate the integral $\int_0^2 e^{x^2}\, dx$ taking the number of intervals 10. [*G.B.T.U. (C.O.) 2010, U.P.T.U. 2008*]

6. (*a*) Evaluate using Trapezoidal rule

   (*i*) $\int_0^{\pi} t \sin t\, dt$ (*ii*) $\int_{-2}^{2} \frac{t\, dt}{5 + 2t}$

   (*b*) Evaluate the integral $\int_0^{2\pi} e^{-t} \sin 10\, t\, dt$ using (*i*) Simpson's 3/8 rule. (*M.T.U. 2012*)

   (*ii*) Simpson's rule with eight intervals. (*U.P.T.U. 2014*)

7. (*i*) Evaluate $\int_0^4 e^x\, dx$ by Simpson's rule, given that $e = 2.72$, $e^2 = 7.39$, $e^3 = 20.09$, $e^4 = 54.6$ and compare it with the actual value.

   (*ii*) Using Simpson's 1/3 rule, evaluate $\int_0^3 (2x - x^2)\, dx$ by taking $n = 6$. (*G.B.T.U. 2013*)

8. (*i*) The velocities of a car running on a straight road at intervals of 2 minutes are given below:

Time (*in minutes*:	0	2	4	6	8	10	12
Velocity (*in km/hr*:	0	22	30	27	18	7	0

   Apply Simpson's rule to find the distance covered by the car. (*G.B.T.U. 2011*) (*ii*) The velocity v of a particle at distance s from a point on its path is given by the table below:

s (*in meter*):	0	10	20	30	40	50	60
v (*m/sec*):	47	58	64	65	61	52	38

Estimate the time taken to travel 60 meters by using Simpson's $\frac{1}{3}$ rule.

(*U.P.T.U. 2007, G.B.T.U. (C.O.) 2011*]

(*iii*) The velocity 'v' of a particle at distance 's' from a point on its linear path is given in the following table:

s (*m*):	0	2.5	5	7.5	10	12.5	15	17.5	20
v (*m/sec*):	16	19	21	22	20	17	13	11	9

Apply Simpson's rule to estimate the time taken by the particle to traverse the distance of 20 meters. (*G.B.T.U. 2011*)

9. The velocity of a train which starts from rest is given by the following table, time being reckoned in minutes from the start and speed in kilometres per hour:

Minutes:	0	2	4	6	8	10	12	14	16	18	20
Speed (km/hr):	0	10	18	25	29	32	20	11	5	2	0

Estimate the total distance in 20 minutes. $\left[\textbf{Hint.}\text{ Here step-size } h = \frac{2}{60}\right]$

10. A rocket is launched from the ground. Its acceleration is registered during the first 80 seconds and is given in the table below. Using Simpson's 1/3rd rule, find the velocity of the rocket at t = 80 seconds. (*G.B.T.U. 2012*)

t(*sec*):	0	10	20	30	40	50	60	70	80
f(*cm/sec*^{2}):	30	31.63	33.34	35.47	37.75	40.33	43.25	46.69	50.67.

11. (*i*) Find an approximate value of $\log_e 5$ by calculating to 4 decimal places, by Simpson's 1/3rd rule, $\int_0^5 \frac{dx}{4x+5}$ dividing the range into 10 equal parts.

(*ii*) Find the value of $\log_e 2$ from $\int_0^1 \frac{x^2}{1+x^3}\, dx$ using Simpson's 1/3rd rule by dividing the range of integration into four equal parts. Also find the error.

12. In an experiment, a quantity G was measured as follows:

G(20) = 95.9, G(21) = 96.85, G(22) = 97.77, G(23) = 98.68, G(24) = 99.56,

G(25) = 100.41, G(26) = 101.24.

Compute $\int_{20}^{26} G(x)\, dx$ by Simpson's rule.

13. Using the data of the following table, compute the integral $\int_{0.5}^{1.1} xy\, dx$ by Simpson's rule:

x:	0.5	0.6	0.7	0.8	0.9	1.0	1.1
y:	0.4804	0.5669	0.6490	0.7262	0.7985	0.8658	0.9281

14. Apply Simpson's 1/3rd rule to evaluate the integral $I = \int_0^1 e^x\, dx$ by choosing step size $h = 0.1$

Show that this step size is sufficient to obtain the result correct to five decimal places.

15. (*i*) Use Simpson's rule dividing the range into ten equal parts to show that:

$$\int_0^1 \frac{\log(1+x^2)}{1+x^2}\,dx = 0.173$$

(*ii*) Evaluate $\int_0^2 \frac{dx}{x^2+x+1}$ to three decimals, dividing the range of integration into 8 equal parts.

(*U.P.T.U. 2007*)

(*iii*) Compute the value of I given by $I = \int_{0.2}^{1.5} e^{-x^2}\,dx$ using Simpson's $\left(\frac{1}{3}\right)^{rd}$ rule with four subdivisions.

16. (*i*) Using 3/8th Simpson's rule, Evaluate: $\int_0^6 \frac{dx}{1+x^4}$.

(*ii*) Evaluate $\int_0^9 \frac{1}{1+x^3}\,dx$ by using Simpson's three-eighth rule. [*G.B.T.U. (M.Tech.) 2010*]

(*iii*) Using Simpson's 1/3rd formula, evaluate $\int_0^1 \frac{dx}{x^3+x+1}$ choose with steplength 0.25.

(*U.P.T.U. 2009*)

17. A solid of revolution is formed by revolving the area $y = f(x)$ from $x = 1$ to $x = 3$ about the x-axis. The following table gives relation between x and y for this curve:

x:	1	1.5	2	2.5	3
y:	1	0.9896	0.9589	0.9089	0.8415

Using Simpson's one-third rule, estimate the volume of the solid formed. (*M.T.U. 2013*)

18. (*i*) Find the distance between two stations from the following data consisting of the speeds $v(t)$ of an electric train at various times t after leaving one station until it stops at the next station. Apply Simpson's rule:

v (miles/hr):	0	13	33	39.5	40	40	36	15	0
t (min):	0	0.5	1	1.5	2	2.5	3	3.5	4

$\left[\textbf{Hint.}\text{ Here } h = \frac{1}{120}\right]$ (*G.B.T.U. 2012*)

(*ii*) The speed of a train at various times after leaving one station until it stops at another station are given in the following table:

Speed (in mph):	0	13	33	39.5	40	40	36	15	0
Time (in minutes):	0	0.5	1	1.5	2	2.5	3	3.25	3.5

Find the distance between the two stations using trapezoidal rule, Simpson's $\frac{1}{3}$ rule and Simpson's $\frac{3}{8}$ rule. (*M.T.U. 2013*)

$$\left[\textbf{Hint.}\text{ Since time interval is not same, hence, } s = \int_0^{3.5} v\,dt = \int_0^3 v\,dt + \int_3^{3.5} v\,dt \quad (\text{taking } h = 0.5 \text{ and } 0.25)\right]$$

19. A curve is drawn to pass through the points given by the following table:

x:	1	1.5	2	2.5	3	3.5	4
y:	2	2.4	2.7	2.8	3	2.6	2.1

Find

(*i*) Centre of gravity of the area. (*ii*) Volume of the solid of revolution.

(*iii*) The area bounded by the curve, the x-axis and lines $x = 1$, $x = 4$.

20. (*i*) Obtain the global truncation error term of trapezoidal method of integration.

(*ii*) Derive an expression for error estimation in Simpson's one-third rule. (*U.P.T.U. 2008*)

(*iii*) Derive Simpson's 3/8th rule. [*U.P.T.U. (MCA) 2009; U.P.T.U. 2009*]

21. Find by Weddle's rule, the value of $I = \int_{0.4}^{1.6} \frac{x}{\sinh x}\, dx$

by taking 12 sub-intervals.

Answers

1. (*i*) 0.69325 ; 0.0001 (*ii*) 4.67078 **2.** 0.974353 **3.** 1.8278

4. (*i*) 1.505103 (*ii*) 5.4059

5. (*i*) 0.946058 (*ii*) – 6.435936 (*iii*) 17.1702

6. (*a*) (*i*) 3.14 (*ii*) – 0.747 (*b*) (*i*) – 0.24245 (*ii*) 0.39466

7. (*i*) 53.87, 53.60 (*ii*) 0

8. (*i*) $3\frac{5}{9}$ km (*ii*) 1.063521 sec (*iii*) 1.26164 sec **9.** 5.156 km **10.** 30.87 m/sec

11. (*i*) 1.61 (*ii*) 0.693255; 0.0001078 **12.** 591.85333 **13.** 0.358487

14. 1.718282782 **15.** (*ii*) 0.824 (*iii*) 0.658596

16. (*i*) 1.019286497 (*ii*) 1.124955 (*iii*) 0.6305

17. 5.638478 **18.** (*i*) 1.8 miles (*ii*) 1.666 miles, 1.666 miles, 1.6671875 miles

19. (*i*) (2.53, 1.31) (*ii*) 64.07 (*iii*) 7.7833 **21.** 1.0101996

6.25. EULER-MACLAURIN'S FORMULA

This formula is based on the expansion of operators. Suppose $\Delta F(x) = f(x)$, then an operator Δ^{-1}, called inverse operator, is defined as

$$F(x) = \Delta^{-1} f(x) \quad ...(1)$$

Also, $\Delta F(x) = f(x)$ gives $F(x_1) - F(x_0) = f(x_0)$

Similarly, $F(x_2) - F(x_1) = f(x_1)$

$$\vdots \qquad \vdots \qquad \vdots$$

$$F(x_n) - F(x_{n-1}) = f(x_{n-1})$$

On adding, $$F(x_n) - F(x_0) = \sum_{i=0}^{n-1} f(x_i) \quad ...(2)$$

where $x_0, x_1, ..., x_n$ are the $(n + 1)$ equidistant values of x with difference h.

From (1), $F(x) = (E-1)^{-1} f(x) = (e^{hD}-1)^{-1} f(x)$

$$= \left[\left(1 + hD + \frac{h^2D^2}{2!} + \frac{h^3D^3}{3!} + \ldots\ldots\right) - 1\right]^{-1} f(x)$$

$$= \left[hD + \frac{h^2D^2}{2!} + \frac{h^3D^3}{3!} + \ldots\ldots\right]^{-1} f(x) = (hD)^{-1}\left[1 + \left(\frac{hD}{2!} + \frac{h^2D^2}{3!} + \ldots\ldots\right)\right]^{-1} f(x)$$

$$= \frac{1}{h} D^{-1}\left[1 - \left(\frac{hD}{2!} + \frac{h^2D^2}{3!} + \ldots\ldots\right) + \frac{(-1)(-2)}{2!}\left(\frac{hD}{2!} + \frac{h^2D^2}{3!} + \ldots\ldots\right)^2 + \ldots\ldots\right] f(x)$$

$$= \frac{1}{h} D^{-1}\left[1 - \frac{hD}{2} + \frac{h^2D^2}{12} - \frac{h^4D^4}{720} + \ldots\ldots\right] f(x)$$

$$F(x) = \frac{1}{h}\int f(x)\,dx - \frac{1}{2} f(x) + \frac{h}{12} f'(x) - \frac{h^3}{720} f'''(x) + \ldots\ldots \quad \ldots(3)$$

Putting $x = x_n$ and $x = x_0$ in (3) and then subtracting, we get

$$F(x_n) - F(x_0) = \frac{1}{h}\int_{x_0}^{x_n} f(x)\,dx - \frac{1}{2}[f(x_n) - f(x_0)] + \frac{h}{12}[f'(x_n) - f'(x_0)] - \frac{h^3}{720}[f'''(x_n) - f'''(x_0)] + \ldots\ldots$$

$$\Rightarrow \quad \sum_{i=0}^{n-1} f(x_i) = \frac{1}{h}\int_{x_0}^{x_n} f(x)\,dx - \frac{1}{2}[f(x_n) - f(x_0)] + \frac{h}{12}[f'(x_n) - f'(x_0)] - \frac{h^3}{720}[f'''(x_n) - f'''(x_0)] + \ldots\ldots \quad | \text{ Using (2)}$$

$$\Rightarrow \quad \frac{1}{h}\int_{x_0}^{x_n} f(x)\,dx = \sum_{i=0}^{n-1} f(x_i) + \frac{1}{2}[f(x_n) - f(x_0)] - \frac{h}{12}[f'(x_n) - f'(x_0)] + \frac{h^3}{720}[f'''(x_n) - f'''(x_0)] - \ldots\ldots \quad \ldots(4)$$

or $$\int_{x_0}^{x_n} y\,dx = \frac{h}{2}[y_0 + 2y_1 + 2y_2 + \ldots\ldots + y_n] - \frac{h^2}{12}(y_n' - y_0') + \frac{h^4}{720}(y_n''' - y_0''') - \ldots\ldots$$

or $$\int_{x_0}^{x_n} y\,dx = \frac{h}{2}[(y_0 + y_n) + 2(y_1 + y_2 + \ldots\ldots + y_{n-1})] - \frac{h^2}{12}(y_n' - y_0') + \frac{h^4}{720}(y_n''' - y_0''') - \ldots\ldots \quad \ldots(5)$$

which is called **Euler-Maclaurin's formula.** The first term on the R.H.S. of (5) represents the approximate value of the integral obtained from trapezoidal rule and the other terms denote the successive corrections to this value.

This formula is often used to find the sum of a series of the form

$y(x_0) + y(x_0 + h) + y(x_0 + 2h) + \ldots\ldots + y(x_0 + nh)$.

6.26. GAUSSIAN QUADRATURE FORMULA

Consider the numerical evaluation of the integral

$$\int_a^b f(x)\,dx \qquad ...(1)$$

So far, we studied some integration formulae which require values of the function at equally spaced points of the interval. Gauss derived a formula which uses the same number of function values but with different spacing and gives better accuracy.

Gauss's formula is expressed in the form

$$\int_{-1}^{1} F(u)\,du = W_1 F(u_1) + W_2 F(u_2) + \ldots\ldots + W_n F(u_n) = \sum_{i=1}^{n} W_i F(u_i) \qquad ...(2)$$

where W_i and u_i are called the weights and abscissae respectively. The formula has an advantage that the abscissae and weights are symmetrical with respect to the middle point of the interval.

In equation (2), there are altogether $2n$ arbitrary parameters and therefore the weights and abscissae can be determined s.t. the formula is exact when $F(u)$ is a polynomial of degree not exceeding $2n - 1$. Hence, we start with

$$F(u) = C_0 + C_1 u + C_2 u^2 + C_3 u^3 + \ldots\ldots + C_{2n-1} u^{2n-1} \qquad ...(3)$$

Then from (2),

$$\int_{-1}^{1} F(u)\,du = \int_{-1}^{1} (C_0 + C_1 u + C_2 u^2 + C_3 u^3 + \ldots\ldots + C_{2n-1} u^{2n-1})\,du$$

$$= 2C_0 + \frac{2}{3} C_2 + \frac{2}{5} C_4 + \ldots\ldots. \qquad ...(4)$$

Set $u = u_i$ in (3), we get

$$F(u_i) = C_0 + C_1 u_i + C_2 u_i^2 + C_3 u_i^3 + \ldots\ldots + C_{2n-1} u_i^{2n-1}$$

From (2),

$$\begin{aligned}\int_{-1}^{1} F(u)\,du &= W_1 (C_0 + C_1 u_1 + C_2 u_1^2 + \ldots\ldots.. + C_{2n-1} u_1^{2n-1}) \\ &+ W_2 (C_0 + C_1 u_2 + C_2 u_2^2 + \ldots\ldots + C_{2n-1} u_2^{2n-1}) \\ &+ W_3 (C_0 + C_1 u_3 + C_2 u_3^2 + \ldots\ldots + C_{2n-1} u_3^{2n-1}) + \ldots\ldots \\ &+ W_n (C_0 + C_1 u_n + C_2 u_n^2 + \ldots\ldots + C_{2n-1} u_n^{2n-1})\end{aligned}$$

which can be written as

$$\begin{aligned}\int_{-1}^{1} F(u)\,du &= C_0 (W_1 + W_2 + \ldots\ldots. + W_n) + C_1 (W_1 u_1 + W_2 u_2 + W_3 u_3 + \ldots\ldots + W_n u_n) \\ &+ C_2 (W_1 u_1^2 + W_2 u_2^2 + W_3 u_3^2 + \ldots\ldots + W_n u_n^2) + \ldots\ldots \\ &+ C_{2n-1} (W_1 u_1^{2n-1} + W_2 u_2^{2n-1} + W_3 u_3^{2n-1} + \ldots\ldots + W_n u_n^{2n-1})\end{aligned} \qquad ...(5)$$

Now equations (4) and (5) are identical for all values of C_i and hence comparing the coefficients of C_i, we obtain $2n$ equations

$$\left.\begin{aligned} W_1 + W_2 + W_3 + \ldots\ldots + W_n &= 2 \\ W_1 u_1 + W_2 u_2 + W_3 u_3 + \ldots\ldots + W_n u_n &= 0 \\ W_1 u_1^2 + W_2 u_2^2 + W_3 u_3^2 + \ldots\ldots + W_n u_n^2 &= \frac{2}{3} \\ \vdots \qquad\qquad \vdots \qquad\qquad & \vdots \\ W_1 u_1^{2n-1} + W_2 u_2^{2n-1} + W_3 u_3^{2n-1} + \ldots\ldots + W_n u_n^{2n-1} &= 0 \end{aligned}\right\} \quad \ldots(6)$$

in $2n$ unknowns W_i and u_i $(i = 1, 2, \ldots\ldots, n)$.

The abscissae u_i and the weights W_i are extensively tabulated for different values of n. The table up to $n = 5$ is given below :

n	$\pm u_i$	W_i
2	0.57735, 02692	1.0
	0.0	0.88888 88889
3	0.77459 66692	0.55555 55556
4	0.33998 10436	0.65214 51549
	0.86113 63116	0.34785 48451
	0.0	0.56888 88889
5	0.53846 93101	0.47862 86705
	0.90617 98459	0.23692 68851

In general case, the limits of integral in (1) have to be changed to those in (2) by transformation

$$x = \frac{1}{2} u (b - a) + \frac{1}{2}(a + b).$$

6.27. NUMERICAL EVALUATION OF SINGULAR INTEGRALS

The various numerical integration formulae, we have discussed so far are valid if integrand $f(x)$ can be expanded by a polynomial or alternatively be expanded in a Taylor's series in the interval $[a, b]$. In a case where function has a singularity, the preceding formulae cannot be applied and special methods will have to be adopted.

6.27.1. Evaluation of Principal value integrals

Consider, $$\mathrm{I}(f) = \int_a^b \frac{f(x)}{x - t}\, dx \quad \ldots(1)$$

which is singular at $t = x$.

Its Principal value,

$$\mathrm{P(I)} = \lim_{\varepsilon \to 0} \left[\int_a^{t-\varepsilon} \frac{f(x)}{x - t}\, dx + \int_{t+\varepsilon}^b \frac{f(x)}{x - t}\, dx \right];\ a < t < b \quad \ldots(2)$$

$$= \mathrm{I}(f) \text{ (for } t < a \quad \text{or} \quad t > b)$$

Set $\qquad x = a + uh$ and $t = a + kh$ in (1), we get

$$\mathrm{P(I)} = \mathrm{P} \int_0^p \frac{f(a + hu)}{u - k}\, du \quad \ldots(3)$$

Replacing $f(a + hu)$ by Newton's forward difference formula at $x = a$ and simplifying, we get

$$I(f) = \sum_{j=0}^{\infty} \frac{\Delta^j f(a)}{j!} C_j \qquad ...(4)$$

where the constants C_j are given by

$$C_j = P \int_0^p \frac{(u)_j}{u-k} du \qquad ...(5)$$

In (5), $(u)_0 = 1$, $(u)_1 = u$, $(u)_2 = u(u-1)$ etc.

Various approximate formulae can be obtained by truncating the series on RHS of (4).

Eqn. (4) may be written as

$$I_n(f) = \sum_{j=0}^{n} \frac{\Delta^j f(a)}{j!} C_j \qquad ...(6)$$

We obtain rules of orders 1, 2, 3, ... etc. by setting $n = 1, 2, 3, ...$ respectively.

(*i*) **Two point rule** ($n = 1$) : $I_1(f) = \sum_{j=0}^{1} \frac{\Delta^j f(a)}{j!} C_j$

$$= C_0 f(a) + C_1 \Delta f(a)$$

$$= (C_0 - C_1) f(a) + C_1 f(a+h) \qquad ...(7)$$

(*ii*) **Three-point rule** ($n = 2$) :

$$I_2(f) = \sum_{j=0}^{2} \frac{\Delta^j f(a)}{j!} C_j = C_0 f(a) + C_1 \Delta f(a) + C_2 \Delta^2 f(a)$$

$$= \left(C_0 - C_1 + \frac{1}{2} C_2\right) f(a) + (C_1 - C_2) f(a+h) + \frac{1}{2} C_2 f(a+2h) \qquad ...(8)$$

In above relations (7) and (8), values of C_j are given by,

$$C_0 = \log_e \left|\frac{p-k}{k}\right|, \quad C_1 = p + C_0 k, \quad C_2 = \frac{1}{2} p^2 + p(k-1) + C_0 k(k-1).$$

6.28. ROMBERG INTEGRATION

We modify the trapezoidal rule to find a better approximation to the value of an integral $\int_a^b y \, dx$.

$$\text{Error in trapezoidal rule } E = -\left(\frac{b-a}{12}\right) h^2 y''(\xi) \, ; \, a < \xi < b$$

If we put $c = -\left(\frac{b-a}{12}\right) y''(\xi)$ then,

$$\text{error } E = ch^2 \qquad ...(1)$$

Suppose, we evaluate $I = \int_a^b y\, dx$ by the trapezoidal rule with two different sub-intervals h_1 and h_2. Let I_1, I_2 be the approximations with errors E_1 and E_2 respectively. Then,

$$\left.\begin{aligned} I &= I_1 + E_1 = I_1 + ch_1^2 \\ \text{and} \quad I &= I_2 + E_2 = I_2 + ch_2^2 \end{aligned}\right\} \quad ...(2)$$

$\therefore$ We get $I_1 + ch_1^2 = I_2 + ch_2^2$

$$\Rightarrow \quad c = \frac{I_1 - I_2}{h_2^2 - h_1^2}$$

$$\therefore \quad I = I_1 + \left(\frac{I_1 - I_2}{h_2^2 - h_1^2}\right) h_1^2 = \frac{I_1 h_2^2 - I_2 h_1^2}{h_2^2 - h_1^2} \quad ...(3)$$

This will be a better approximation to I_1 than I_1 or I_2. The above method is called **Richardson's method.**

If we take, $h_1 = h$ and $h_2 = \frac{1}{2}h$ in (3), we get

$$I = \frac{I_1\left(\frac{h}{2}\right)^2 - I_2 h^2}{\left(\frac{h}{2}\right)^2 - h^2} = \frac{4I_2 - I_1}{3}$$

$$\Rightarrow \quad I = I_2 + \frac{1}{3}(I_2 - I_1) \quad ...(4)$$

If we apply the trapezoidal rule several times successively, every time halving h, we get a sequence of results $A_1, A_2, A_3, A_4,...$ in which the error is reduced by $\frac{1}{4}$ every time.

Let the formula (4) be applied to each pair of A_i's and denote the results by $B_1, B_2, B_3,...$ etc.

Again applying (4) to each pair of B_i's, we get the next results $C_1, C_2, C_3,...$ etc.

We continue this process until two successive values are very close to each other.

This refinement of Richardson's method is called **Romberg integration.** An obvious advantage of this method is that the accuracy of the computed value is known at each step.

The values of the integral in Romberg integration can be tabulated as follows:

$I(h)$			
	$I(h, h/2)$		
$I(h/2)$		$I(h, h/2, h/4)$	
	$I(h/2, h/4)$		$I(h, h/2, h/4, h/8)$
$I(h/4)$		$I(h/2, h/4, h/8)$	
	$I(h/4, h/8)$		
$I(h/8)$			

6.29. GAUSS-LEGENDRE TWO AND THREE POINT FORMULAE

Consider the integral in the form

$$\int_{-1}^{1} w(x)\, f(x)\, dx = \sum_{k=0}^{n} \lambda_k\, f(x_k) \qquad ...(1)$$

where $w(x) > 0, -1 \le x \le 1$ is the weight function. Let the weight function be $w(x) = 1$ then by (1)

$$\int_{-1}^{1} f(x)\, dx = \sum_{k=0}^{n} \lambda_k\, f(x_k) \qquad ...(2)$$

Here all the nodes x_k and weights λ_k are unknown.

(*a*) **Two point formula** when $n = 1$, from (2),

$$\int_{-1}^{1} f(x)\, dx = \lambda_0\, f(x_0) + \lambda_1\, f(x_1) \qquad ...(3)$$

The method has four unknowns, x_0, x_1, λ_0 and λ_1. Making the method exact for $f(x) = 1, x, x^2, x^3$, we get

$$f(x) = 1 \quad \Rightarrow \quad 2 = \lambda_0 + \lambda_1 \qquad ...(4)$$

$$f(x) = x \quad \Rightarrow \quad 0 = \lambda_0\, x_0 + \lambda_1\, x_1 \qquad ...(5)$$

$$f(x) = x^2 \quad \Rightarrow \quad \frac{2}{3} = \lambda_0\, x_0^2 + \lambda_1\, x_1^2 \qquad ...(6)$$

$$f(x) = x^3 \quad \Rightarrow \quad 0 = \lambda_0\, x_0^3 + \lambda_1\, x_1^3 \qquad ...(7)$$

From (5) and (7),

$$\lambda_1 x_1 (x_1 - x_0)(x_1 + x_0) = 0$$

$$\Rightarrow \quad x_1 = -x_0 \qquad | \because \ \lambda_1 \neq 0, x_1 \neq x_0$$

From (5), $\lambda_1 = \lambda_0$

From (4), $\lambda_1 = \lambda_0 = 1$

From (6), $x_0^2 = \dfrac{1}{3} \Rightarrow x_0 = \pm \dfrac{1}{\sqrt{3}}$ and $x_1 = \mp \dfrac{1}{\sqrt{3}}$

Hence the two-point Gauss-Legendre method is given by

$$\int_{-1}^{1} f(x)\, dx = f\left(-\frac{1}{\sqrt{3}}\right) + f\left(\frac{1}{\sqrt{3}}\right)$$

The error constant, $C = \displaystyle\int_{-1}^{1} x^4\, dx - \left(\frac{1}{9} + \frac{1}{9}\right) = \frac{8}{45}$

and the error term $R_4 = \dfrac{C}{4!} f^{(iv)}(\xi) = \dfrac{1}{135} f^{(iv)}(\xi)\,; -1 < \xi < 1$

(*b*) **Three point formula.** When $n = 2$, from (2),

$$\int_{-1}^{1} f(x)\, dx = \lambda_0\, f(x_0) + \lambda_1\, f(x_1) + \lambda_2\, f(x_2)$$

The method has 6 unknowns and it can be made exact for polynomials of degree up to 5. For $f(x) = x^i$, $0 \le i \le 5$, we get the system of equations

$$\lambda_0 + \lambda_1 + \lambda_2 = 2$$

$$\lambda_0 x_0 + \lambda_1 x_1 + \lambda_2 x_2 = 0$$

$$\lambda_0 x_0^2 + \lambda_1 x_1^2 + \lambda_2 x_2^2 = \frac{2}{3}$$

$$\lambda_0 x_0^3 + \lambda_1 x_1^3 + \lambda_2 x_2^3 = 0$$

$$\lambda_0 x_0^4 + \lambda_1 x_1^4 + \lambda_2 x_2^4 = \frac{2}{5}$$

$$\lambda_0 x_0^5 + \lambda_1 x_1^5 + \lambda_2 x_2^5 = 0$$

Solving above, we get $x_0 = \pm \sqrt{\frac{3}{5}}$, $x_1 = 0$, $x_2 = \mp \sqrt{\frac{3}{5}}$

$$\lambda_0 = \frac{5}{9}, \lambda_1 = \frac{8}{9}, \lambda_2 = \frac{5}{9}$$

Hence the three point Gauss Legendre method is given by

$$\int_{-1}^{1} f(x)\, dx = \frac{5}{9} f\left(-\sqrt{\frac{3}{5}}\right) + \frac{8}{9} f(0) + \frac{5}{9} f\left(\sqrt{\frac{3}{5}}\right)$$

The error constant, $$C = \int_{-1}^{1} x^6\, dx - \frac{1}{9}\left[5\left(-\sqrt{\frac{3}{5}}\right)^6 + 0 + 5\left(\sqrt{\frac{3}{5}}\right)^6\right] = \frac{8}{175}$$

The error in the method is $= R_6 = \frac{C}{6!} f^{(vi)}(\xi) = \frac{1}{15750} f^{(vi)}(\xi)\, ; -1 < \xi < 1.$

6.30. LOBATTO INTEGRATION METHODS

The Lobatte integration methods are of Gauss type with two nodes preassigned. Consider the quadrature formula

$$\int_{-1}^{1} \omega(x) f(x)\, dx \approx \sum_{k=1}^{m} a_k f(n_k) + \sum_{k=1}^{n} \lambda_k f(x_k)$$

In case of Lobatto method, we preassign

$$\omega(x) = 1, \eta_1 = -1, \eta_m = 1, a_i = 0, i = 2, 3, \ldots, m-1.$$

The integration formula can be written as

$$\int_{-1}^{1} f(x)\, dx = \lambda_0 f(-1) + \lambda_n f(1) + \sum_{k=1}^{n-1} \lambda_k f(x_k)$$

Since there are $(n-1)$ nodes and $(n+1)$ weights hence $2n$ unknowns, this method can be made exact for polynomials of degree up to $2n - 1$.

For $n = 2$, we have

$$\int_{-1}^{1} f(x)\, dx = \lambda_0 f(-1) + \lambda_1 f(x_1) + \lambda_2 f(1) \qquad \ldots(1)$$

Making the formula exact for $f(x) = 1, x, x^2$ and x^3, we get

$$f(x) = 1 \quad \Rightarrow \quad \lambda_0 + \lambda_1 + \lambda_2 = 2 \qquad ...(2)$$

$$f(x) = x \quad \Rightarrow \quad -\lambda_0 + \lambda_1 x_1 + \lambda_2 = 0 \qquad ...(3)$$

$$f(x) = x^2 \quad \Rightarrow \quad \lambda_0 + \lambda_1 x_1^2 + \lambda_2 = \frac{2}{3} \qquad ...(4)$$

$$f(x) = x^3 \quad \Rightarrow \quad -\lambda_0 + \lambda_1 x_1^3 + \lambda_2 = 0 \qquad ...(5)$$

Subtracting (2) from (4), we get

$$\lambda_1 x_1 (x_1^2 - 1) = 0$$

$$\Rightarrow \quad x_1 = 0 \qquad | \text{ Since } x_1 \neq \pm 1$$

From (3) and (4) and solving, we get

$$\lambda_0 = \lambda_2 = \frac{1}{3}$$

From (2), $\lambda_1 = \dfrac{4}{3}$

$\therefore$ Lobatto method is given by

$$\int_{-1}^{1} f(x)\, dx = \frac{1}{3}[f(-1) + 4f(0) + f(1)]$$

and the error constant is given by

$$C = \int_{-1}^{1} x^4\, dx - \frac{1}{3}[1 + 0 + 1] = -\frac{4}{15}$$

Therefore the error in the method is

$$R_4 = \frac{C}{4!} f^{(iv)}(\xi) = -\frac{1}{90} f^{(iv)}(\xi) \; ; -1 < \xi < 1$$

Similarly for $n = 3$,

Lobatto method is obtained as

$$\int_{-1}^{1} f(x)\, dx = \frac{1}{6}\left[f(-1) + 5f\left(-\frac{\sqrt{5}}{5}\right) + 5f\left(\frac{\sqrt{5}}{5}\right) + f(1)\right]$$

and the error constant is

$$C = \int_{-1}^{1} x^6\, dx - \frac{1}{6}\left[1 + 5\left(\frac{1}{125}\right) + 5\left(\frac{1}{125}\right) + 1\right] = -\frac{32}{525}$$

Therefore the error in the method is

$$R_6 = \frac{C}{6!} f^{(vi)}(\xi) = -\frac{32}{525\,(6!)} f^{(vi)}(\xi) \; ; -1 < \xi < 1$$

Nodes and Weights for Lobatto integration method

n	nodes x_k	weights λ_k
2	$\pm$ 1.00000000	0.33333333
	0.00000000	1.33333333
3	$\pm$ 1.00000000	0.16666667
	$\pm$ 0.44721360	0.83333333
4	$\pm$ 1.00000000	0.10000000
	$\pm$ 0.65465367	0.54444444
	0.00000000	0.71111111
5	$\pm$ 1.00000000	0.06666667
	$\pm$ 0.76505532	0.37847496
	$\pm$ 0.28523152	0.55485837

6.31. RADAU INTEGRATION METHODS

Radau integration methods are of Gauss type with one node preassigned.

Consider the quadrature formula

$$\int_{-1}^{1} \omega(x)\, f(x)\, dx \approx \sum_{k=1}^{m} a_k f(\eta_k) + \sum_{k=1}^{n} \lambda_k f(x_k)$$

In case of Radau formula, we preassign $\omega(x) = 1$, $\eta_1 = -1$, $a_i = 0$, $i = 2, 3, \ldots, m$.

The integration formula can be written as

$$\int_{-1}^{1} f(x)\, dx = \lambda_0 f(-1) + \sum_{k=1}^{n} \lambda_k f_k \qquad \ldots(1)$$

Since there are n nodes and $(n + 1)$ weights hence $(2n + 1)$ unknowns, this method can be made exact for polynomials of degree up to $2n$.

For $n = 1$, we have

$$\int_{-1}^{1} f(x)\, dx = \lambda_0 f(-1) + \lambda_1 f(x_1) \qquad \ldots(2)$$

The method has three unknowns and it can be made exact for polynomials of degree up to 2.

For $f(x) = 1, x, x^2$, we get

$$f(x) = 1 \;\Rightarrow\; \lambda_0 + \lambda_1 = 2 \qquad \ldots(3)$$

$$f(x) = x \;\Rightarrow\; -\lambda_0 + \lambda_1 x_1 = 0 \qquad \ldots(4)$$

$$f(x) = x^2 \;\Rightarrow\; \lambda_0 + \lambda_1 x_1^2 = \frac{2}{3} \qquad \ldots(5)$$

Adding (3) and (4), $\lambda_1(1 + x_1) = 2$

Adding (4) and (5), $\lambda_1 x_1(1 + x_1) = \dfrac{2}{3}$

Dividing, we get $x_1 = \dfrac{1}{3}$ hence, $\lambda_1 = \dfrac{3}{2}$

From (3), we get $\lambda_0 = 2 - \lambda_1 = \dfrac{1}{2}$

From (2), the method becomes,

$$\int_{-1}^{1} f(x)\,dx = \frac{1}{2}\left[f(-1) + 3f\left(\frac{1}{3}\right)\right]$$

The error constant is given by

$$C = \int_{-1}^{1} x^3\,dx - \frac{1}{2}\left[-1 + 3\left(\frac{1}{27}\right)\right] = \frac{4}{9}$$

Therefore the error in the method becomes

$$R_3 = \frac{C}{3!} f^{(iii)}(\xi) = \frac{2}{27} f'''(\xi), -1 < \xi < 1$$

Similarly, for $n = 2$,
Radau method is obtained as

$$\int_{-1}^{1} f(x)\,dx = \frac{1}{18}\left[4f(-1) + (16 + \sqrt{6})f\left(\frac{1-\sqrt{6}}{5}\right) + (16 - \sqrt{6})f\left(\frac{1+\sqrt{6}}{5}\right)\right]$$

The error constant is given by $C = \dfrac{8}{75}$

The error term is given by $R_5 = \dfrac{C}{5!} f^{(v)}(\xi) = \dfrac{8}{75\,(5!)} f^{(v)}(\xi); -1 < \xi < 1$

Nodes and weights for Radau Integration method

n	*nodes* x_k	*weights* λ_k
1	–1.0000000	0.5000000
	0.3333333	1.5000000
2	– 1.000000	0.2222222
	– 0.2898979	1.0249717
	0.6898979	0.7528061
3	– 1.0000000	0.1250000
	– 0.5753189	0.6576886
	0.1810663	0.7763870
	0.8228241	0.4409244
4	– 1.0000000	0.0800000
	– 0.7204803	0.4462078
	0.1671809	0.6236530
	0.4463140	0.5627120
	0.8857916	0.2874271
5	– 1.0000000	0.0555556
	– 0.8029298	0.3196408
	– 0.3909286	0.4853872
	0.1240504	0.5209268
	0.6039732	0.4169013
	0.9203803	0.2015884

EXAMPLES

Example 1. *Apply Euler-Maclaurin formula to evaluate*

$$\frac{1}{51^2}+\frac{1}{53^2}+\frac{1}{55^2}+\ldots\ldots+\frac{1}{99^2}.$$

Sol. Take $y = \frac{1}{x^2}$, $x_0 = 51$, $h = 2$, $n = 24$, we have

$$y' = -\frac{2}{x^3}, \qquad y''' = -\frac{24}{x^5}$$

Then from Euler-Maclaurin's formula,

$$\int_{51}^{99}\frac{dx}{x^2} = \frac{2}{2}\left[\frac{1}{51^2}+\frac{2}{53^2}+\frac{2}{55^2}+\ldots\ldots+\frac{2}{97^2}+\frac{1}{99^2}\right]$$
$$-\frac{(2)^2}{12}\left[\frac{(-2)}{(99)^3}-\frac{(-2)}{(51)^3}\right]+\frac{(2)^4}{720}\left[\frac{(-24)}{(99)^5}-\frac{(-24)}{(51)^5}\right]$$

$$\therefore \quad \frac{1}{51^2}+\frac{2}{53^2}+\frac{2}{55^2}+\ldots\ldots+\frac{2}{97^2}+\frac{1}{99^2} = \int_{51}^{99}\frac{dx}{x^2}$$
$$+\frac{2}{3}\left[\frac{1}{(51)^3}-\frac{1}{(99)^3}\right]-\frac{8}{15}\left[\frac{1}{(51)^5}-\frac{1}{(99)^5}\right]+\ldots\ldots$$

$$\Rightarrow \quad 2\left[\frac{1}{51^2}+\frac{1}{53^2}+\frac{1}{55^2}+\ldots\ldots+\frac{1}{99^2}\right]$$
$$=\int_{51}^{99}\frac{dx}{x^2}+\left(\frac{1}{51^2}+\frac{1}{99^2}\right)+\frac{2}{3}\left[\frac{1}{(51)^3}-\frac{1}{(99)^3}\right]-\frac{8}{15}\left[\frac{1}{(51)^5}-\frac{1}{(99)^5}\right]+\ldots\ldots$$

$$\Rightarrow \quad \frac{1}{(51)^2}+\frac{1}{(53)^2}+\frac{1}{(55)^2}+\ldots\ldots+\frac{1}{(99)^2}$$
$$=\frac{1}{2}\int_{51}^{99}\frac{dx}{x^2}+\frac{1}{2}\left[\frac{1}{(51)^2}+\frac{1}{(99)^2}\right]+\frac{1}{3}\left[\frac{1}{(51)^3}-\frac{1}{(99)^3}\right]-\frac{4}{15}\left[\frac{1}{(51)^5}-\frac{1}{(99)^5}\right]+\ldots\ldots$$
$$=\frac{1}{2}\left(-\frac{1}{x}\right)_{51}^{99}+\frac{1}{2}\left[\frac{1}{(51)^2}+\frac{1}{(99)^2}\right]+\frac{1}{3}\left[\frac{1}{(51)^3}-\frac{1}{(99)^3}\right]-\frac{4}{15}\left[\frac{1}{(51)^5}-\frac{1}{(99)^5}\right]+\ldots\ldots.$$
$$= 0.00475 + 0.000243 + 0.0000022 + \ldots\ldots = 0.00499 \text{ approximately.}$$

Example 2. *Using Euler-Maclaurin's formula, find the value of* $\log_e 2$ *from* $\int_0^1 \frac{dx}{1+x}$.

Sol. Take $y = \frac{1}{1+x}$, $x_0 = 0$, $n = 10$, $h = 0.1$,

we have $y' = -\frac{1}{(1+x)^2}$ and $y''' = \frac{-6}{(1+x)^4}$

Then from Euler-Maclaurin's formula, we have

$$\int_0^1 \frac{dx}{1+x} = \frac{0.1}{2}\left[\frac{1}{1+0}+\frac{2}{1+0.1}+\frac{2}{1+0.2}+\frac{2}{1+0.3}+\frac{2}{1+0.4}+\frac{2}{1+0.5}+\frac{2}{1+0.6}\right.$$

$$\left.+\frac{2}{1+0.7}+\frac{2}{1+0.8}+\frac{2}{1+0.9}+\frac{1}{1+1}\right]$$

$$-\frac{(0.1)^2}{12}\left[\frac{(-1)}{(1+1)^2}-\frac{(-1)}{(1+0)^2}\right]+\frac{(0.1)^4}{720}\left[\frac{(-6)}{(1+1)^4}-\frac{(-6)}{(1+0)^4}\right]$$

$$= 0.693773 - 0.000625 + 0.000001 = 0.693149$$

Also, $\displaystyle\int_0^1 \frac{dx}{1+x} = \Big|\log(1+x)\Big|_0^1 = \log 2$

Hence $\log_e 2 = 0.693149.$

Example 3. *Evaluate* $\displaystyle\int_0^{\pi/2} \sin x\, dx$ *using the Euler-Maclaurin formula.*

Sol. $\displaystyle\int_0^{\pi/2} \sin x\, dx = \frac{h}{2}\,[y_0 + 2y_1 + 2y_2 + \ldots\ldots. + 2y_{n-1} + y_n] + \frac{h^2}{12} + \frac{h^4}{720} + \frac{h^6}{30240} + \ldots\ldots$

To evaluate the integral, let us take $h = \dfrac{\pi}{4}$.

Then we obtain,

$$\int_0^{\pi/2} \sin x\, dx = \frac{\pi}{8}\,(0 + 2 + 0) + \frac{\pi^2}{192} + \frac{\pi^4}{184320} + \ldots\ldots$$

$$= \frac{\pi}{4} + \frac{\pi^2}{192} + \frac{\pi^4}{184320} \text{ (approximately)}$$

$$= 0.785398 + 0.051404 + 0.000528 = 0.837330$$

If we take $h = \dfrac{\pi}{8}$, we get

$$\int_0^{\pi/2} \sin x\, dx = \frac{\pi}{16}\,[0 + 2(0.382683 + 0.707117 + 0.923879) + 1]$$

$$= 0.987119 + 0.012851 + 0.000033 = 1.000003.$$

Example 4. *Use Euler-Maclaurin's formula to prove that*

$$\sum_1^n x^2 = \frac{n\,(n+1)\,(2n+1)}{6}.$$

Sol. By Euler–Maclaurin's formula,

$$\int_{x_0}^{x_n} y\, dx = \frac{h}{2}\,[y_0 + 2y_1 + 2y_2 + \ldots\ldots\ldots + 2y_{n-1} + y_n] - \frac{h^2}{12}\,(y_n' - y_0') + \frac{h^4}{720}(y_n''' - y_0''')$$

$$- \frac{h^6}{30240}\,(y_n^{(v)} - y_0^{(v)}) + \ldots..$$

$$\Rightarrow \quad \frac{1}{2}y_0 + y_1 + y_2 + \ldots\ldots + y_{n-1} + \frac{1}{2}y_n$$

$$= \frac{1}{h}\int_{x_0}^{x_n} y\,dx + \frac{h}{12}(y_n' - y_0') - \frac{h^3}{720}(y_n''' - y_0''') + \frac{h^5}{30240}(y_n^{(v)} - y_0^{(v)}) - \ldots\ldots \quad \ldots(1)$$

Here $y(x) = x^2$, $y'(x) = 2x$ and $h = 1$

$\therefore$ From (1),

$$\text{Sum} = \int_1^n x^2\,dx + \frac{1}{2}(n^2 + 1) + \frac{1}{12}(2n - 2) \qquad \because \frac{1}{2}y_0 = \frac{1}{2}, \frac{1}{2}y_n = \frac{n^2}{2}$$

$$= \frac{1}{3}(n^3 - 1) + \frac{1}{2}(n^2 + 1) + \frac{1}{6}(n - 1) = \frac{n(n+1)(2n+1)}{6}.$$

Example 5. *Find* $\int_0^1 x\,dx$ *by Gaussian formula.*

Sol. Let us change the limits as

$$x = \frac{1}{2}u(1 - 0) + \frac{1}{2}(1 + 0) = \frac{1}{2}(u + 1)$$

This gives,

$$I = \frac{1}{4}\int_{-1}^{1}(u + 1)\,du = \frac{1}{4}\sum_{i=1}^{n} W_i\,F(u_i)$$

where $F(u_i) = u_i + 1$

For simplicity, let $n = 4$ and using the abscissae and weights corresponding to $n = 4$ in the table, we get

$$I = \frac{1}{4}[(-0.86114 + 1)(0.34785) + (-0.33998 + 1)(0.65214)$$
$$+ (0.33998 + 1)(0.65214) + (0.86114 + 1)(0.34785)]$$

$$= 0.49999 \ldots..$$

where the abscissae and weights have been rounded to 5 decimal places.

Example 6. *Show that the integration formula* $\int_0^h f(x)\,dx = hf\left(\frac{h}{2}\right)$ *is exact for all polynomials of degree less than or equal to 1. Obtain an estimate for the truncation error.*

If $|f''(x)| < 1$ *for all x, then find the step size h so that the truncation error is less than* 10^{-3}.

Sol. If $f(x) = k$ (a constant or zero degree polynomial) then the result is obvious since

$$\int_0^h f(x)\,dx = kh \quad \ldots(1)$$

and

$$hf\left(\frac{h}{2}\right) = hk \quad \ldots(2)$$

$\therefore$ From (1) and (2),

$$\int_0^h f(x)\,dx = hf\left(\frac{h}{2}\right)$$

If $f(x)$ is a polynomial of degree one then $f(x) = ax + b$

$$\int_0^h f(x)\,dx = \int_0^h (ax+b)\,dx = \frac{ah^2}{2} + bh \qquad ...(3)$$

$$hf\left(\frac{h}{2}\right) = h\left(\frac{ah}{2} + b\right) = \frac{ah^2}{2} + bh \qquad ...(4)$$

From (3) and (4), we have the result.

Now, $$\int_0^h y\,dx = \int_0^h \left[y_0 + (x - x_0)\,y_0{}' + \frac{(x-x_0)^2}{2}\,y_0{}'' + ...\right] dx$$

$$= hy_0 + \frac{h^2}{2!}\,y_0{}' + \frac{h^3}{3!}\,y_0{}'' + ... \qquad \text{(where } x - x_0 = h) \qquad ...(5)$$

Also, $$hf\left(\frac{h}{2}\right) = h\left[y_0 + \frac{h}{2}\,y_0{}' + \frac{\left(\frac{h}{2}\right)^2}{2!}\,y_0{}'' + ...\right] \qquad ...(6)$$

(5) – (6) gives the truncation error $= h^3\left(\frac{1}{6} - \frac{1}{8}\right) y_0{}''$ (nearly)

Now, $$\left|\frac{h^3}{24}\,y_0{}''\right| < \frac{1}{24}h^3$$

$\Rightarrow$ $$\frac{1}{24}\,h^3 < 10^{-3} \qquad \text{or} \qquad |\,h^3\,| < 24 \times 10^{-3} = 0.024$$

$\Rightarrow$ $$-\sqrt[3]{0.024} < h < \sqrt[3]{0.024}\,.$$

Example 7. *Find λ such that the quadrature formula $\int_0^1 \frac{f(x)}{\sqrt{x}}\,dx \approx Af(0) + Bf(\lambda) + Cf(1)$ may be exact for polynomials of degree 3.*

Sol. $$\int_0^1 \frac{f(x)}{\sqrt{x}}\,dx = Af(0) + Bf(\lambda) + Cf(1)$$

Set $f(x) = 1, x, x^2$ and x^3 in turn,

$$2 = A + B + C \qquad ...(1) \qquad\qquad \frac{2}{3} = B\lambda + C \qquad ...(2)$$

$$\frac{2}{5} = B\lambda^2 + C \qquad ...(3) \qquad\qquad \frac{2}{7} = B\lambda^3 + C \qquad ...(4)$$

Subtracting (2) from (3), we get

$$B\lambda(\lambda - 1) = -\frac{4}{15}$$

Subtracting (3) from (4), we get

$$B\lambda^2(\lambda - 1) = -\frac{4}{35}$$

$$\therefore \qquad \lambda = \frac{3}{7}.$$

Example 8. *Determine W_0, W_1 and W_2 as functions of α such that the error R in*

$$\int_{-1}^{1} f(x)\,dx = W_0 f(-\alpha) + W_1 f(0) + W_2 f(\alpha) + R, \ \alpha \neq 0$$

Vanishes when f(x) is an arbitrary polynomial of degree at most 3. Show that the precision is five when $\alpha = \sqrt{\frac{3}{5}}$ and three otherwise. Compute the error R when $\alpha = \sqrt{\frac{3}{5}}$.

Sol. $\int_{-1}^{1} f(x)\,dx = W_0 f(-\alpha) + W_1 f(0) + W_2 f(\alpha)$ is exact for $f(x) = 1, x, x^2, x^3$.

$$f(x) = 1 \quad \Rightarrow \quad W_0 + W_1 + W_2 = 2$$

$$f(x) = x \quad \Rightarrow \quad W_0 = W_2$$

$$f(x) = x^2 \quad \Rightarrow \quad 2W_0\alpha^2 = \frac{2}{3}$$

$$f(x) = x^3 \quad \Rightarrow \quad W_0 = W_2$$

Solving, we find

$$W_0 = W_2 = \frac{1}{3\alpha^2}, \qquad W_1 = 2\left(1 - \frac{1}{3\alpha^2}\right)$$

Choosing $f(x) = x^4$, we get

$$\frac{2}{5} = 2W_0\alpha^4 = \frac{2}{3}\alpha^2$$

$$\Rightarrow \qquad \alpha = \sqrt{\frac{3}{5}}$$

With this value, $f(x) = x^5$ gives exact value.

$\therefore$ The precision is 5.

If $\alpha \neq \sqrt{\frac{3}{5}}$ the precision is 3.

With $\alpha = \sqrt{\frac{3}{5}}$, we have

$$\int_{-1}^{1} f(x)\,dx = \frac{5}{9}\left[f\left(-\sqrt{\frac{3}{5}}\right) + f\left(\sqrt{\frac{3}{5}}\right)\right] + \frac{8}{9} f(0) + R$$

Hence the error term R is given by

$$R = \frac{2}{7!} f^{(vi)}(0) + \text{terms involving higher order derivatives} = \frac{f^{(vi)}(0)}{2520}.$$

Example 9. *Determine a, b and c such that the formula*

$$\int_0^h f(x)\, dx = h\left\{af(0) + bf\left(\frac{h}{3}\right) + cf(h)\right\}$$

is exact for polynomials of as high order as possible and determine the order of truncation error.

Sol. Making the method exact for polynomials of degree upto 2, we get

For $f(x) = 1$: $\quad h = h(a + b + c) \quad \Rightarrow \quad a + b + c = 1$

For $f(x) = x$: $\quad \frac{h^2}{2} = h\left(\frac{bh}{3} + ch\right) \quad \Rightarrow \quad \frac{b}{3} + c = \frac{1}{2}$

For $f(x) = x^2$: $\quad \frac{h^3}{3} = h\left(\frac{bh^2}{9} + ch^2\right) \quad \Rightarrow \quad \frac{b}{9} + c = \frac{1}{3}$

Solving above eqns., we get $\quad a = 0, b = \frac{3}{4}, c = \frac{1}{4}$

Truncation error of the formula $= \frac{c}{3!} f'''(\xi)\,; \qquad 0 < \xi < h$

and $$c = \int_0^h x^3\, dx - h\left(\frac{bh^3}{27} + ch^3\right) = -\frac{h^4}{36}$$

Hence, Truncation error $= -\frac{h^4}{216} f'''(\xi) = O(h^4)$.

Example 10. *Use Romberg Integration to compute*

$$I = \int_0^1 \frac{1}{1+x}\, dx \text{ correct to three decimal places.}$$

Sol. Let $h = 0.5$. Then, by trapezoidal rule,

$$I(h) = 0.7084,\ I\left(\frac{1}{2}h\right) = 0.6970 \text{ and } I\left(\frac{1}{4}h\right) = 0.6941$$

Now, $$I\left(h, \frac{h}{2}\right) = I\left(\frac{h}{2}\right) + \frac{1}{3}\left[I\left(\frac{h}{2}\right) - I(h)\right] = 0.6932$$

and $$I\left(\frac{h}{2}, \frac{h}{4}\right) = I\left(\frac{h}{4}\right) + \frac{1}{3}\left[I\left(\frac{h}{4}\right) - I\left(\frac{h}{2}\right)\right] = 0.6931$$

Finally, $\text{I}\left(h, \frac{1}{2}h, \frac{1}{4}h\right) = 0.6931 + \frac{1}{3}(0.6931 - 0.6932) = 0.6931$

The table of values is

0.7084		
	0.6932	
0.6970		0.6931
	0.6931	
0.6941		

Hence, I = 0.6931

Example 11. *Evaluate* $I = \int_0^1 \frac{dx}{2x^2 + 2x + 1}$ *using the Lobatto 3-point and Radau 3-point formulae. Compare with exact solution.*

Sol. Using the transformation $x = \frac{t+1}{2}$, we obtain

$$\text{I} = \int_{-1}^{1} \frac{dt}{(t+1)^2 + 2t + 4} = \int_{-1}^{1} f(t)\, dt$$

Lobatto 3-point formula gives the solution as

$$\text{I} = \frac{1}{3}[f(-1) + 4f(0) + f(1)] = \frac{1}{3}\left[\frac{1}{2} + \frac{4}{5} + \frac{1}{10}\right] = 0.46667.$$

Radau 3-point formula gives the solution as

$$\begin{aligned} \text{I} &= 0.22222f(-1) + 1.02497f(-0.28990) + 0.75281f(0.68990) \\ &= 0.11111 + 0.26118 + 0.09141 = 0.4637 \end{aligned}$$

The exact solution is $\text{I} = \tan^{-1}(3) - \frac{\pi}{4} = 0.46365.$

ASSIGNMENT

1. Using Euler-Maclaurin's formula; evaluate

   (*i*) $\frac{1}{400} + \frac{1}{402} + \frac{1}{404} + \ldots\ldots + \frac{1}{500}$ (*ii*) $\frac{1}{(201)^2} + \frac{1}{(203)^2} + \frac{1}{(205)^2} + \ldots\ldots + \frac{1}{(299)^2}.$

2. Prove that $\sum_{1}^{n} x^3 = \left\{\frac{n(n+1)}{2}\right\}^2$ applying Euler-Maclaurin's formula.

3. Use Euler-Maclaurin's formula to find the value of π from the formula

   $$\frac{\pi}{4} = \int_0^1 \frac{dx}{1+x^2}.$$

4. Find the sum of the fourth powers of first n natural numbers by means of Euler-Maclaurin's formula.

OR

Prove that, $$\sum_{0}^{n} i^4 = \frac{n^5}{5} + \frac{n^4}{2} + \frac{n^3}{3} + \frac{n}{30}.$$

5. Show that $$\sum_{i=1}^{n} i^7 + \sum_{i=1}^{n} i^5 = 2\left(\sum_{i=1}^{n} i^3\right)^2.$$

6. Obtain the approximate value of

$$I = \int_{-1}^{1} e^{-x^2} \cos x \, dx$$

Using

(*i*) Gauss-Legendre integration method for $n = 2, 3$.

(*ii*) Radau integration method for $n = 2, 3$.

(*iii*) Lobatto integration method for $n = 2, 3$.

Answers

1. (*i*) 0.01138 (*ii*) 0.00083

6. (*i*) $n = 2$, three points, I = 1.324708
$n = 3$, four points, I = 1.311354
(*ii*) $n = 2$, three points, I = 1.307951
$n = 3$, four points, I = 1.312610
(*iii*) $n = 2$, three points, I = 1.465844
$n = 3$, four points, I = 1.296610

❑❑❑

UNIT-IV

Solution of Simultaneous Linear Algebraic Equation: Gauss Elimination Method, ill Conditioned Systems. Condition Number, Successive Over Relaxation Method, Rate of Convergence.

Solution of Ordinary Differential Equations: Single Step Methods-Runge-Kutta Second Order, Third Order and Fourth Order Methods, Multi Step Method-Predictor-Corrector Method.

Statistical Techniques: Statistical Hypotheses, Test of Hypotheses, Type-I and Type-II Errors, Level of Significance, Test involving Normal Distribution.

7

Solution of Simultaneous Linear Algebraic Equations

7.1. INTRODUCTION

The systems of simultaneous linear equations arise, both directly in modelling physical situations and indirectly in the numerical solution of other mathematical models.

Problems such as determining the potential in certain electrical networks, stresses in a building frame, flow rates in a hydraulic system etc., are all reduced to solving a set of algebraic equations simultaneously.

Linear algebraic systems are also involved in the optimization theory, least squares fitting of data, numerical solution of boundary value problems for ordinary and partial differential equations, statistical inference etc.

Consider a non-homogeneous system of n simultaneous linear algebraic equations in n unknowns as

$$\begin{matrix} a_{11}x_1 + a_{12}x_2 + a_{13}x_3 + \ldots + a_{1n}x_n = b_1 \\ a_{21}x_1 + a_{22}x_2 + a_{23}x_3 + \ldots + a_{2n}x_n = b_2 \\ a_{31}x_1 + a_{32}x_2 + a_{33}x_3 + \ldots + a_{3n}x_n = b_3 \\ \vdots \qquad \vdots \qquad \vdots \qquad \vdots \\ a_{n1}x_1 + a_{n2}x_2 + a_{n3}x_3 + \ldots + a_{nn}x_n = b_n \end{matrix} \qquad \ldots(1)$$

Using matrix notation, the above system (1) can be written as

$$AX = B \qquad \ldots(2)$$

where,

$$A = \begin{bmatrix} a_{11} & a_{12} & a_{13} & \cdots & a_{1n} \\ a_{21} & a_{22} & a_{23} & \cdots & a_{2n} \\ a_{31} & a_{32} & a_{33} & \cdots & a_{3n} \\ \vdots & \vdots & \vdots & \vdots & \vdots \\ a_{n1} & a_{n2} & a_{n3} & \cdots & a_{nn} \end{bmatrix} \quad X = \begin{bmatrix} x_1 \\ x_2 \\ x_3 \\ \vdots \\ x_n \end{bmatrix} \quad \text{and} \quad B = \begin{bmatrix} b_1 \\ b_2 \\ b_3 \\ \vdots \\ b_n \end{bmatrix}$$

By finding a solution of the system, we mean to obtain the values of n unknowns x_1, x_2, x_3, ..., x_n such that they satisfy the given equations. If B = O, then the system is called homogeneous.

The methods of solution of linear algebraic eqns. (1) may be classified into two types:

(*i*) **Direct methods.** These methods yield the exact solution after a finite number of steps in absence of round-off errors. In these methods, the amount of computation involved can be specified in advance. They are independent of the desired accuracy.

(*ii*) **Iterative methods.** These methods give a sequence of approximations which converges when the number of steps tend to infinity.

In some cases, both the direct and iterative methods are combined. First, we may use a direct method and then the solution may be improved by using iterative methods.

In this chapter, we will study direct and iterative methods to solve the system (1).

7.2. DIRECT METHODS

Consider a system of linear equations

$$AX = B \quad \text{...(1)}$$

where A is coefficient matrix, X is column matrix of unknowns and B is column matrix of constants. The necessary and sufficient condition for the system (1) to be consistent is

$$\rho(A) = \rho(A : B)$$

where $\rho(A)$ denotes the rank of A and $\rho(A : B)$ denotes the rank of augmented matrix (A : B).

Further if $\rho(A) = \rho(A : B)$ = no. of unknowns, the system (1) will have unique solution and if $\rho(A) = \rho(A : B) <$ no. of unknowns, the system (1) will have infinite no. of solutions.

Again, the system (1) of equations can also be solved by using the inverse of matrix.

If A is non singular square matrix then premultiplying (1) by A^{-1}, we get

$$A^{-1}(AX) = A^{-1}B$$

$$\Rightarrow \quad X = A^{-1}B$$

The inverse of A can be obtained by either $A^{-1} = \dfrac{\text{adj. A}}{|A|}$ or by using elementary row operations or by using Cayley-Hamilton theorem.

Also, Cramer's rule can be used to solve (1). But this method is satisfactory only for a small number of simultaneous equations. Although this method involves simple calculation yet large amount of computation is required to evaluate large order determinants. For an $n \times n$ system, the method involves evaluation of $(n + 1)$ determinants each of nth order. Each determinant involves large no. of multiplications. The addition or subtraction time on computers is usually small compared to the time taken for multiplications or divisions time. The method which requires the least multiplication time is the one which is preferred. In addition to this, there are no simple methods to evaluate large order determinants. For example, to evaluate 10×10 determinants, we will have to carry out 10 times evaluation of determinants, each one of which require the evaluation of 9×9 determinants etc. and they naturally need large amount of computation. In view of above, the Cramer's rule is impractical for large systems of equations.

Similarly, the computation of inverse of a matrix is the main problem on computers and it becomes tougher for large system. Hence the method of finding unknowns by $X = A^{-1}B$ is also not practical for large systems.

To avoid these unnecessary computations, some simpler and less time consuming procedures were developed and suggested. One of the most important methods is the so called Gauss-algorithm which is a systematic elimination method.

7.3. GAUSS ELIMINATION METHOD

This method is one of the most widely used simplest step-by-step elimination method given by C.F. Gauss (1777–1855). This is a direct method with a fixed number of arithmetic operations. It is quite efficient and straight forward but the round off errors become significant for a large set of equations.

In this method, the solution to the given system of equations is obtained in two stages.

In the first stage, the unknowns are eliminated successively by transforming the given system into an equivalent system with upper triangular coefficient matrix using elementary row operations. In the second stage, the unknowns are found by back substitution.

Consider a system of n equations in n unknowns

$$\left.\begin{array}{l} a_{11}x_1 + a_{12}x_2 + \ldots + a_{1n}x_n = b_1 \\ a_{21}x_1 + a_{22}x_2 + \ldots + a_{2n}x_n = b_2 \\ a_{31}x_1 + a_{32}x_2 + \ldots + a_{3n}x_n = b_3 \\ \ldots\ldots\ldots\ldots\ldots\ldots\ldots\ldots\ldots\ldots \\ a_{n1}x_1 + a_{n2}x_2 + \ldots + a_{nn}x_n = b_n \end{array}\right\} \qquad \ldots(1)$$

By elementary row operations, we transform (1) into the form

$$\left.\begin{array}{r} c_{11}x_1 + c_{12}x_2 + \ldots + c_{1n}x_n = d_1 \\ c_{22}x_2 + \ldots + c_{2n}x_n = d_2 \\ \ldots\ldots\ldots\ldots\ldots\ldots\ldots\ldots\ldots\ldots \\ c_{nn}x_n = d_n \end{array}\right\} \qquad \ldots(2)$$

The coefficient matrix in (2) is an upper triangular matrix. Hence the solution can be obtained by back substitution

$$x_n = \frac{d_n}{c_{nn}}, \quad x_{n-1} = \frac{d_{n-1} - c_{n-1,n}\, x_n}{c_{n-1,n-1}} \text{ etc.}$$

Therefore, the Gauss elimination method gives

$$[A : B] \xrightarrow{\text{Gauss elimination}} [U : B']$$

where $[A : B]$ is the augmented matrix.

The elements a_{ii} $(1 \le i \le n)$ of the coefficient matrix corresponding to the given system of equations are called **pivot** elements.

If any one of the pivot elements vanishes or becomes very small (close to zero) compared to other elements in that column, then we attempt to rearrange the remaining rows so as to obtain a non-vanishing pivot or to avoid the division by a very small number. This strategy is called **pivoting.**

The problems of failure of entire process, if the pivot is zero, and that of occurrence of round-off errors if the pivot is close to zero can be avoided by adopting pivoting procedure.

Pivoting is of two types—

(1) Partial pivoting. If a_{11} in system (1) of equations is either zero or very small compared to the other coefficients of the equation, then we find the largest available coefficient in the columns below the pivotal equation and then interchange the two rows.

In this way, we obtain a new pivotal equation with a non-zero pivot. Since we search only the columns below for the largest element in this case, such a process is called partial pivoting.

However, this process can be understood easily by taking a suitable example *e.g.*

Consider a simple system of equations

$$\begin{aligned} 10^{-5}\, x_1 + x_2 &= 1 \\ x_1 + x_2 &= 2 \end{aligned}$$

Assuming that we require the solution accurate to only four decimal places, let us solve the above system using Gauss elimination method with or without partial pivoting.

Without partial pivoting, the solution by Gauss elimination method gives $x_1 = 0$, $x_2 = 1$ while if we use partial pivoting, the above system will take the form

$$x_1 + x_2 = 2$$
$$10^{-5} x_1 + x_2 = 1$$

Again, using Gauss elimination method, the solution is found to be $x_1 = 1$ and $x_2 = 1$ which is a meaningful and perfect result.

(2) Complete pivoting. If we are not interested in the elimination of x, y, z in a particular order then at each stage, we can choose the numerically largest coefficient of the entire coefficient matrix. This requires an interchange of equations and also an interchange of position of the variables. This modified procedure is called complete pivoting. It produces an additional reduction in the effect of rounding errors.

Complete pivoting involves more complexity in computations since interchange of columns means change of order of unknowns which requires more programming effort.

In comparison, partial pivoting is easily adopted in programming. Due to this reason, complete pivoting is rarely used although it may yield slightly improved numerical stability.

Note. If the matrix is diagonally dominant or real, symmetric and positive definite then no pivoting is necessary.

7.3.1. Algorithm of Gauss Elimination Method

```
1.  Input n
2.  m=n+1
3.  For i=0, n-1
4.  For j=0, m-1
5.  Input a(i, j)
6.  Next j
7.  Next i
8.  For i=0, n-1
9.  If a(i, i)=0 then step 10
       ELSE
       goto step 8
10. For k=i, j=0, m-1
11. d(k+1, j)=a(k+1, j)
12. a(k+1, j)=a(k, j)
13. a(k, j)=d(k+1, j)
14. Print a(k, j)
15. Print a(k+1, j)
16. Next k
17. For j=0, m-1
18. b(i, j)=a(i, j)/a(i, i)*1
19. Next j
```

```
For j = 0, m-1, 1 = i
a(i, j)=b(1, j)
Next j
For k=i+1, n-1
For j=0, m-1
c(k, j)=a(k, j)-a (i, j)*a(k, i)
Next j
For j=0, m-1 p=k
a(p, j)=c(p, j)
Next j
Next k
Next i
For i=0, n-1
For j=0, m-1
Print a(i, j)
Next j
Next i
x(n-1)=a(n-1, m-1)
For i=n-2, 0, -1 k=m-1
For j=m-2, i+1, - 1
d(i, j)=a(i, j) *x(j)
s=s-d(i, j)
Next j
x(i)=a(i, k)+s
s=0
Next i
For i=0, n-1 j=m-1
print x(i)
Next i
Stop
```

7.3.2. Flow Chart of Gauss Elimination Method

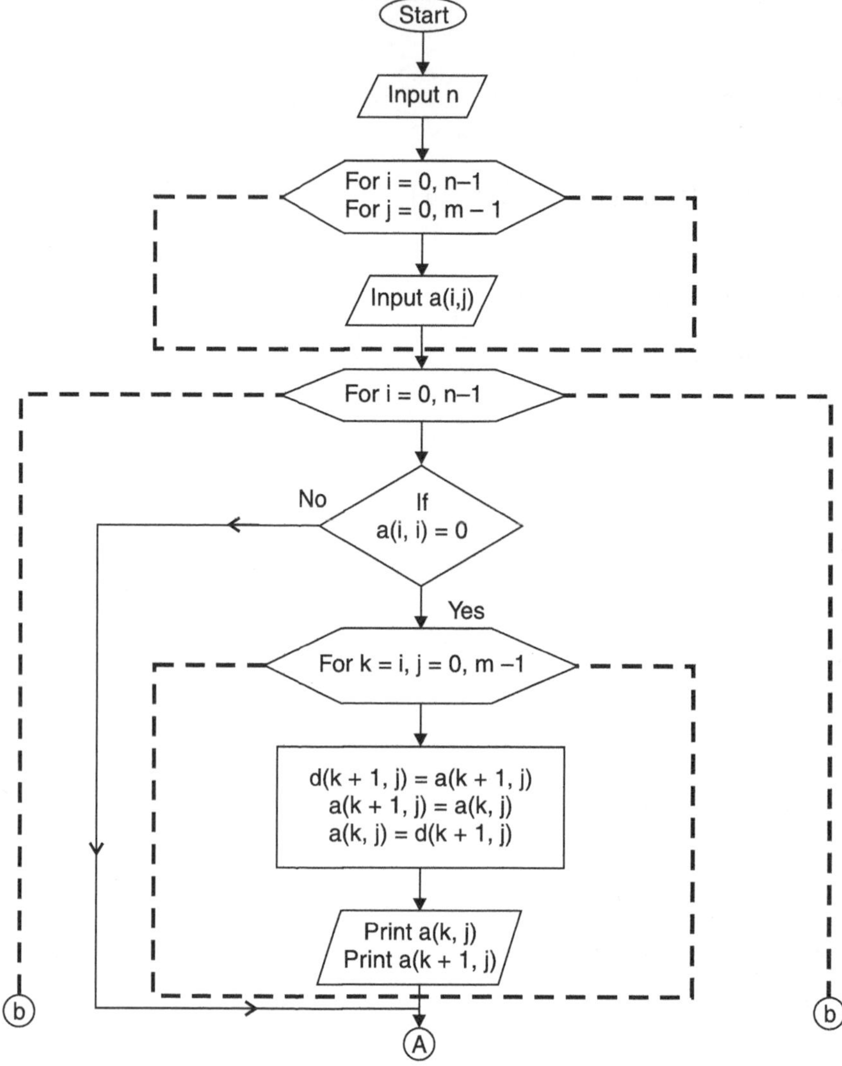

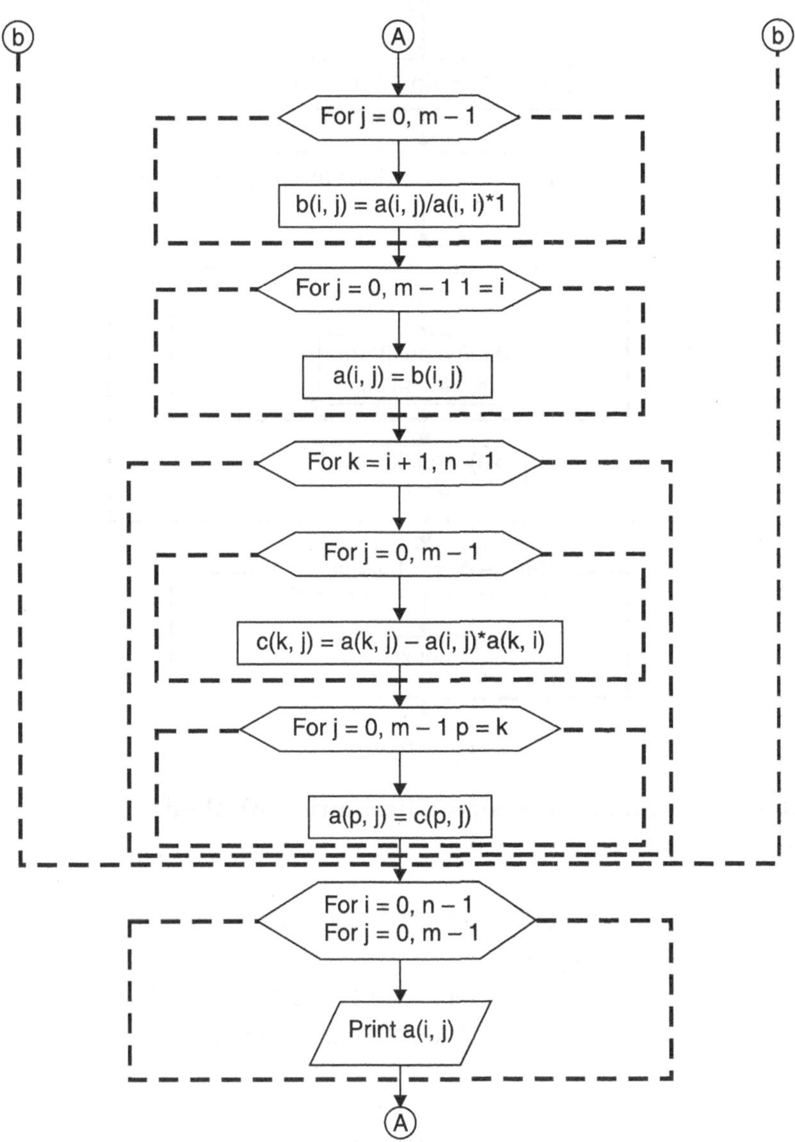
b
A
b
For j = 0, m – 1
b(i, j) = a(i, j)/a(i, i)*1
For j = 0, m – 1 1 = i
a(i, j) = b(i, j)
For k = i + 1, n – 1
For j = 0, m – 1
c(k, j) = a(k, j) – a(i, j)*a(k, i)
For j = 0, m – 1 p = k
a(p, j) = c(p, j)
For i = 0, n – 1
For j = 0, m – 1
Print a(i, j)
A

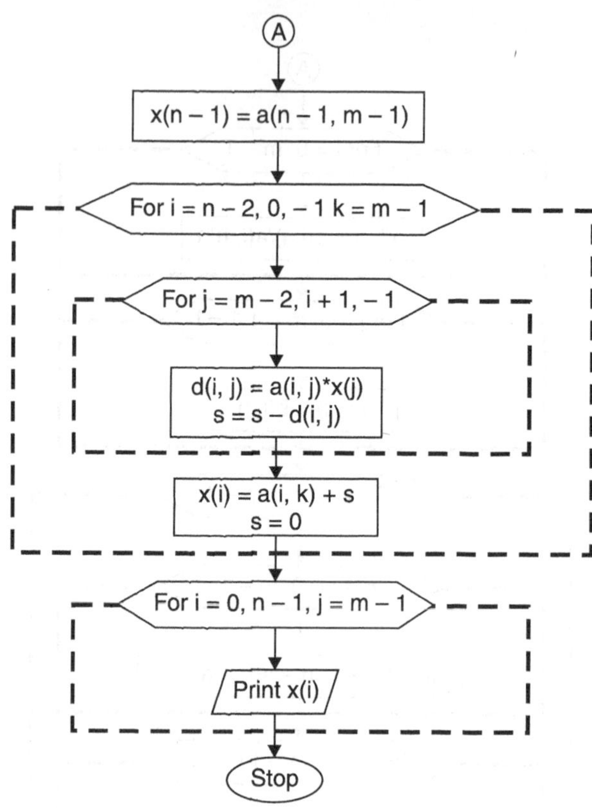

7.3.3. Computer Programme for Gauss Elimination Method

```
# include<stdio.h>
main ( )
{
    int n, i, j, k, m, l, p;
    float a[10] [10], b[10] [10], c[10] [10], d[10] [10], x[10], s=0;
    printf ("\nGIVE THE SIZE OF GIVEN MATRIX=");
    scanf("%d", &n) ;
m=n+1 ;
printf ("\nGIVE THE ELEMENTS OF MATRIX & RHS :\n") ;
for (i=0, i<=n-1; i++)
    {
       for(j=0 ; j<=m-1 ; j++)
       scanf ("%f", &a[i][j]) ;
    }
for (i=0 ; i<=n-1 ; i++)
    {
    if (a[i][i]==0)
    {
    printf ("\n Matrix element changed row to row is :\n") ;
```

```
    for (k=i, j=0; j<=m-1 ; j++)
    {
    d[k+1] [j]=a[k+1][j] ;
    a[k+1] [j] = a[k] [j] ;
    a[k] [j] = d[k+1] [j] ;
    printf ("a[%d] [%d] = %f\t", k, j, a[k] [j]) ;
    printf ("a[%d] [%d] = %f\n", k+1, j, a[k+1] [j]) ;
    }
}
for (j=0; j<=m-1 ; j++)
b[i] [j] = a[i] [j]/a [i] [i]*1.0 ;
for (j=0, 1=i ; j<=m-1 ; j++)
a[1][j]=b[1] [j] ;
for (k=i+1 ; k<=n-1 ; k++)
    {
    for (j=0 ; j<=m-1 ; j++)
    c[k] [j]=a[k] [j]-a[i] [j]*a[k] [i] ;
    for (j=0, p=k ; j<=m-1 ; j++)
     a[p][j]=c[p][j] ;
    }
}
printf ("\n Matrix after calculation is : \n") ;
for (i=0 ; i<=n-1 ; i++)
    {
    for (j=0 ; j<=m-1 ; j++)
    printf ("%. 3f\t", a[i] [j] ) ;
    printf ("\n") ;
    }
x[n-1]=a[n-1] [m-1] ;
for (k=m-1, i=n-2; i>=0 ; i - -)
    {
for (j=m-2 ; j>=i+1 ; j - -)
    {
    d[i] [j] = a[i] [j]*x[j] ;
    s=s-d[i] [j] ;
    }
x[i]=a[i] [k]+s ;
s=0 ;
}
printf ("\n Solution of given system is : \n") ;
for (j=m-1, i=0 ; i<=n-1 ; i++)
    {
    printf ("X[%d]=%.3f", i, x[i]) ;
```

```
printf ("\n");
}
return ;
}
```

7.3.4. Output

```
Give the size of given matrix = 3
Give the Elements of Matrix and RHS:
    1     1     1     1
    4     3   - 1     6
    3     5     3     4
Matrix after calculation is:
  1.000       1.000       1.000       1.000
- 0.000       1.000       5.000     - 2.000
- 0.000     - 0.000       1.000     - 0.500
Solution of given system is:
              X[0] = 1.000
              X[1] = 0.500
              X[2] = - 0.500
```

EXAMPLES

Example 1. *Use Gauss elimination method to solve the following system of equations:*

$$2x + y + z = 10$$
$$3x + 2y + 3z = 18$$
$$x + 4y + 9z = 16.$$

Sol. Eliminating x from the second and third equations, we get

$$2x + y + z = 10 \qquad \text{...(1)}$$
$$y + 3z = 6 \qquad \text{...(2)}$$
$$7y + 17z = 22 \qquad \text{...(3)}$$

Now, eliminating y from (3), we get

$$\left.\begin{aligned} 2x + y + z &= 10 \\ y + 3z &= 6 \\ -4z &= -20 \end{aligned}\right\} \qquad \text{...(4)}$$

which is upper triangular form.

Solving the above system (4), using back substitution, we get

$$x = 7, y = -9, z = 5.$$

Example 2. *Solve the following system of equations by Gauss Elimination method:*

$$\begin{bmatrix} 1 & 2 & 3 & 4 \\ 7 & 10 & 5 & 2 \\ 13 & 6 & 2 & -3 \\ 11 & 14 & 8 & -1 \end{bmatrix} \begin{bmatrix} x_1 \\ x_2 \\ x_3 \\ x_4 \end{bmatrix} = \begin{bmatrix} 10 \\ 40 \\ 34 \\ 64 \end{bmatrix}.$$

Sol. Augmented matrix

$$[A \,\vdots\, B] = \left[\begin{array}{cccc|c} 1 & 2 & 3 & 4 & 10 \\ 7 & 10 & 5 & 2 & 40 \\ 13 & 6 & 2 & -3 & 34 \\ 11 & 14 & 8 & -1 & 64 \end{array}\right]$$

Operating $R_{21}(-7)$, $R_{31}(-13)$, $R_{41}(-11)$

$$\sim \left[\begin{array}{cccc|c} 1 & 2 & 3 & 4 & 10 \\ 0 & -4 & -16 & -26 & -30 \\ 0 & -20 & -37 & -55 & -96 \\ 0 & -8 & -25 & -45 & -46 \end{array}\right]$$

Operating $R_{32}(-5)$, $R_{42}(-2)$

$$\sim \left[\begin{array}{cccc|c} 1 & 2 & 3 & 4 & 10 \\ 0 & -4 & -16 & -26 & -30 \\ 0 & 0 & 43 & 75 & 54 \\ 0 & 0 & 7 & 7 & 16 \end{array}\right]$$

Operating $R_{43}\left(-\dfrac{7}{43}\right)$

$$\sim \left[\begin{array}{cccc|c} 1 & 2 & 3 & 4 & 10 \\ 0 & -4 & -16 & -26 & -30 \\ 0 & 0 & 43 & 75 & 54 \\ 0 & 0 & 0 & -\dfrac{224}{43} & \dfrac{224}{43} \end{array}\right]$$

Equivalent system is

$$\begin{aligned} x_1 + 2x_2 + 3x_3 + 4x_4 &= 10 \\ -4x_2 - 16x_3 - 26x_4 &= -30 \\ 43x_3 + 75x_4 &= 54 \\ \frac{-224}{43}x_4 &= \frac{224}{43} \end{aligned}$$

Solving above using back substitution, we get

$$x_4 = -1,\ x_3 = 3,\ x_2 = 2,\ x_1 = 1.$$

Example 3. *Solve the equations*

$$\begin{aligned} 10x_1 - x_2 + 2x_3 &= 4 \\ x_1 + 10x_2 - x_3 &= 3 \\ 2x_1 + 3x_2 + 20x_3 &= 7 \end{aligned}$$

using Gauss Elimination method.

Sol. The given system is diagonally dominant and therefore no pivoting is necessary. Augmented matrix is

$$[A : B] = \left[\begin{array}{ccc|c} 10 & -1 & 2 & 4 \\ 1 & 10 & -1 & 3 \\ 2 & 3 & 20 & 7 \end{array}\right]$$

Operating $R_{21}\left(-\frac{1}{10}\right), R_{31}\left(-\frac{1}{5}\right)$

$$\sim \left[\begin{array}{ccc|c} 10 & -1 & 2 & 4 \\ 0 & \frac{101}{10} & \frac{-6}{5} & \frac{13}{5} \\ 0 & \frac{16}{5} & \frac{98}{5} & \frac{31}{5} \end{array}\right]$$

Operating $R_{32}\left(-\frac{32}{101}\right)$

$$\sim \left[\begin{array}{ccc|c} 10 & -1 & 2 & 4 \\ 0 & \frac{101}{10} & \frac{-6}{5} & \frac{13}{5} \\ 0 & 0 & \frac{20180}{1010} & \frac{5430}{1010} \end{array}\right]$$

The equivalent system is

$$10x_1 - x_2 + 2x_3 = 4$$

$$\frac{101}{10} x_2 - \frac{6}{5} x_3 = \frac{13}{5}$$

$$\frac{20180}{1010} x_3 = \frac{5430}{1010}$$

Using back substitution, we get

$$x_1 = 0.375, x_2 = 0.289, x_3 = 0.269.$$

Example 4. *Solve the following equations by Gauss Elimination method:*

$$3x - y + 2z = 12$$
$$x + 2y + 3z = 11$$
$$2x - 2y - z = 2.$$

Sol. Here, we will rearrange the equations so that the system becomes diagonally dominant. Then, Augmented matrix is

$$[A : B] = \left[\begin{array}{ccc|c} 3 & -1 & 2 & 12 \\ 2 & -2 & -1 & 2 \\ 1 & 2 & 3 & 11 \end{array}\right]$$

Operating $R_{21}\left(-\frac{2}{3}\right)$, $R_{31}\left(-\frac{1}{3}\right)$,

$$\sim \left[\begin{array}{ccc|c} 3 & -1 & 2 & 12 \\ 0 & -\frac{4}{3} & -\frac{7}{3} & -6 \\ 0 & \frac{7}{3} & \frac{7}{3} & 7 \end{array}\right]$$

Operating $R_{32}\left(\frac{7}{4}\right)$,

$$\sim \left[\begin{array}{ccc|c} 3 & -1 & 2 & 12 \\ 0 & -\frac{4}{3} & -\frac{7}{3} & -6 \\ 0 & 0 & -\frac{7}{4} & -\frac{7}{2} \end{array}\right]$$

Equivalent system is

$$3x - y + 2z = 12$$

$$-\frac{4}{3}y - \frac{7}{3}z = -6$$

$$-\frac{7}{4}z = -\frac{7}{2}$$

Using back substitution, we get the solution

$$z = 2, y = 1 \quad \text{and} \quad x = 3.$$

Example 5. *Solve the following system of equations using Gauss Elimination method with partial pivoting.*

$$x + y + z = 7$$

$$3x + 3y + 4z = 24$$

$$2x + y + 3z = 16.$$

Sol. In matrix form, the given system can be written as

$$\begin{bmatrix} 1 & 1 & 1 \\ 3 & 3 & 4 \\ 2 & 1 & 3 \end{bmatrix} \begin{bmatrix} x \\ y \\ z \end{bmatrix} = \begin{bmatrix} 7 \\ 24 \\ 16 \end{bmatrix} \qquad ...(1)$$

To start with, we observe that the pivot element $a_{11} = 1 (\neq 0)$. However, a glance at the first column reveals that the numerically largest element is 3 which is in second row. Hence we interchange the first row with the second row and eqn. (1) becomes

$$\begin{bmatrix} 3 & 3 & 4 \\ 1 & 1 & 1 \\ 2 & 1 & 3 \end{bmatrix} \begin{bmatrix} x \\ y \\ z \end{bmatrix} = \begin{bmatrix} 24 \\ 7 \\ 16 \end{bmatrix} \qquad ...(2)$$

after partial pivoting.

Eliminating x from the last two rows, we get

$$\begin{bmatrix} 3 & 3 & 4 \\ 0 & 0 & -\frac{1}{3} \\ 0 & -1 & \frac{1}{3} \end{bmatrix} \begin{bmatrix} x \\ y \\ z \end{bmatrix} = \begin{bmatrix} 24 \\ -1 \\ 0 \end{bmatrix} \quad ...(3)$$

The second row in eqn. (3) cannot be used as the pivot row as $a_{22} = 0$. Therefore, interchanging second and third rows, we get

$$\begin{bmatrix} 3 & 3 & 4 \\ 0 & -1 & 1/3 \\ 0 & 0 & -1/3 \end{bmatrix} \begin{bmatrix} x \\ y \\ z \end{bmatrix} = \begin{bmatrix} 24 \\ 0 \\ -1 \end{bmatrix} \quad ...(4)$$

which is an upper triangular form.

Using back substitution, we find

$$z = 3, y = 1, x = 3.$$

Note. In partial pivoting, we observe that the unknown column vector remains unaltered while the right hand side column vector gets changed.

Example 6. *Solve the system of equations*

$$x + y + z = 6$$
$$3x + (3 + \varepsilon) y + 4z = 20$$
$$2x + y + 3z = 13$$

using Gauss Elimination method where ε *is small such that* $1 \pm \varepsilon^2 \approx 1$. *What happens if we do not use partial pivoting at second step?*

Sol. We have the eqns.

$$x + y + z = 6 \quad ...(1)$$
$$3x + (3 + \varepsilon) y + 4z = 20 \quad ...(2)$$
$$2x + y + 3z = 13 \quad ...(3)$$

Eliminating x from eqns. (2) and (3), we get

$$x + y + z = 6 \quad ...(1)$$
$$\varepsilon y + z = 2 \quad ...(4)$$
$$-y + z = 1 \quad ...(5)$$

Here, the pivot in eqn. (4) is ε which is a very small number.

Using partial pivoting, we write the system as

$$x + y + z = 6 \quad ...(1)$$
$$-y + z = 1 \quad ...(5)$$
$$\varepsilon y + z = 2 \quad ...(4)$$

Eliminating y from (4), we get

$$x + y + z = 6 \quad ...(1)$$
$$-y + z = 1 \quad ...(5)$$
$$(1 + \varepsilon) z = 2 + \varepsilon \quad ...(6)$$

Using back substitution, we obtain the solution as

$$z = \frac{2+\varepsilon}{1+\varepsilon}, y = \frac{1}{1+\varepsilon}, x = \frac{3+5\varepsilon}{1+\varepsilon}$$

If we do not use partial pivoting in the second step, the solution will be

$$z = \frac{1+(2/\varepsilon)}{1+(1/\varepsilon)}, \quad y = \frac{1}{\varepsilon}\left[2 - \frac{1+(2/\varepsilon)}{1+(1/\varepsilon)}\right] \quad \text{and} \quad x = 6 - y - z$$

which may be very inaccurate if ε is of the order of the round-off error.

ASSIGNMENT

1. Solve the following system of equations by Gauss Elimination method:

(*i*)
$$5x_1 - x_2 = 9$$
$$-x_1 + 5x_2 - x_3 = 4$$
$$-x_2 + 5x_3 = -6$$

(*ii*)
$$x_1 + x_2 + x_3 = 6$$
$$3x_1 + 3x_2 + 4x_3 = 20$$
$$2x_1 + x_2 + 3x_3 = 13$$

(*iii*)
$$3x + y - z = 3$$
$$2x - 8y + z = -5$$
$$x - 2y + 9z = 8$$

(*iv*)
$$3.15x - 1.96y + 3.85z = 12.95$$
$$2.13x + 5.12y - 2.89z = -8.61$$
$$5.92x + 3.05y + 2.15z = 6.88$$

(*v*)
$$2x + 3y - z = 5$$
$$4x + 4y - 3z = 3$$
$$-2x + 3y - z = 1$$

(*vi*)
$$5x_1 - x_2 + x_3 = 10$$
$$2x_1 + 4x_2 = 12$$
$$x_1 + x_2 + 5x_3 = -1$$

(*vii*)
$$4.12x - 9.68y + 2.01z = 4.93$$
$$1.88x - 4.62y + 5.50z = 3.11$$
$$1.10x - 0.96y + 2.72z = 4.02$$

(*viii*)
$$3x + 4y + 5z = 40$$
$$2x - 3y + 4z = 13$$
$$x + y + z = 9$$

(*ix*)
$$x + 2y + z = 3$$
$$2x + 3y + 3z = 10$$
$$3x - y + 2z = 13$$

(*x*)
$$2x_1 + 8x_2 + 2x_3 = 14$$
$$x_1 + 6x_2 - x_3 = 13$$
$$2x_1 - x_2 + 2x_3 = 5.$$

2. With partial pivoting, solve the following system of equations using Gauss Elimination method:

(*i*)
$$0x_1 + 4x_2 + 2x_3 + 8x_4 = 24$$
$$4x_1 + 10x_2 + 5x_3 + 4x_4 = 32$$
$$4x_1 + 5x_2 + 6.5x_3 + 2x_4 = 26$$
$$9x_1 + 4x_2 + 4x_3 + 0x_4 = 21$$

(*ii*)
$$\begin{bmatrix} 2 & 1 & 1 & -2 \\ 4 & 0 & 2 & 1 \\ 3 & 2 & 2 & 0 \\ 1 & 3 & 2 & -1 \end{bmatrix} \begin{bmatrix} x_1 \\ x_2 \\ x_3 \\ x_4 \end{bmatrix} = \begin{bmatrix} -10 \\ 8 \\ 7 \\ -5 \end{bmatrix}$$

(*iii*)
$$2x + y - z = -1$$
$$x - 2y + 3z = 9$$
$$3x - y + 5z = 14$$

(*iv*)
$$0.61x_1 + 1.23x_2 + 1.72x_3 = 0.792$$
$$1.02x_1 + 2.15x_2 - 5.51x_3 = 12.0$$
$$-4.34x_1 + 11.2x_2 - 4.25x_3 = 16.3$$

(*v*)
$$10x_1 - 7x_2 + 3x_3 + 5x_4 = 6$$
$$-6x_1 + 8x_2 - x_3 - 4x_4 = 5$$
$$3x_1 + x_2 + 4x_3 + 11x_4 = 2$$
$$5x_1 - 9x_2 - 2x_3 + 4x_4 = 7$$

(*vi*)
$$28x + 4y - z = 32$$
$$x + 3y + 10z = 24$$
$$2x + 17y + 4z = 35$$

(*vii*)
$$\begin{aligned} x_1 + x_2 + x_3 + x_4 &= 2 \\ x_1 + x_2 + 3x_3 - 2x_4 &= -6 \\ 2x_1 + 3x_2 - x_3 + 2x_4 &= 7 \\ x_1 + 2x_2 + x_3 - x_4 &= -2 \end{aligned}$$

(*viii*)
$$\begin{bmatrix} 2 & 2 & 1 \\ 4 & 2 & 3 \\ 1 & 1 & 1 \end{bmatrix} \begin{bmatrix} x_1 \\ x_2 \\ x_3 \end{bmatrix} = \begin{bmatrix} 1 \\ 2 \\ 3 \end{bmatrix}$$

(*ix*)
$$\begin{bmatrix} 2 & 1 & 1 & 2 \\ 4 & 0 & 2 & 1 \\ 3 & 2 & 2 & 0 \\ 1 & 3 & 2 & 0 \end{bmatrix} \begin{bmatrix} x_1 \\ x_2 \\ x_3 \\ x_4 \end{bmatrix} = \begin{bmatrix} 2 \\ 3 \\ -1 \\ -4 \end{bmatrix}.$$

3. Solve the system
$$\begin{aligned} 0.0002x + 0.3003y &= 0.1002 \\ 2.0000x + 3.0000y &= 2.0000 \end{aligned}$$
by Gauss Elimination method
(*i*) Without pivoting (*ii*) With partial pivoting.

4. Solve the system of equations
$$\begin{aligned} 10x + y + z &= 12 \\ 2x + 10y + z &= 13 \\ x + y + 5z &= 7 \end{aligned}$$
by Gauss Elimination method.

5. Solve the given system of equations
$$\begin{aligned} x_1 + x_2 - 2x_3 &= 3 \\ 4x_1 - 2x_2 + x_3 &= 5 \\ 3x_1 - x_2 + 3x_3 &= 8 \end{aligned}$$
using Gaussian Elimination with partial pivoting.

6. Solve the system of equations
$$\begin{aligned} x_1 - 3x_2 + 2x_3 &= 3 \\ 2x_1 + 6x_2 + 8x_3 &= -1 \\ 4x_1 - 3x_2 + x_3 &= 4.25 \end{aligned}$$
using the Gauss Elimination method with partial pivoting.

7. Solve the following simultaneous equations by Gauss Elimination method
$$\begin{aligned} 3x_1 + 2x_2 + x_3 &= 10 \\ 2x_1 + 3x_2 + 2x_3 &= 14 \\ x_1 + 2x_2 + 3x_3 &= 14. \end{aligned}$$

8. Solve the given system of equations using Gauss Elimination method with partial pivoting
$$\begin{aligned} x - y + 3z &= 13 \\ 4x - 2y + z &= 15 \\ -3x - y + 4z &= 8. \end{aligned}$$

9. Solve the simultaneous equations
$$\begin{aligned} x + 0.01y - 0.02z &= 3.3354 \\ 0.02x + y - 0.05z &= 4.8241 \\ 0.03x - 0.01y + z &= 7.3417 \end{aligned}$$
by Gauss Elimination method.

10. Solve the following system of linear equations by Gauss Elimination method:

(*i*)
$$\begin{aligned} 3x + y + z &= 6 \\ x + 2y + 3z &= 8 \\ 2x + y + 4z &= 8 \end{aligned}$$

(*ii*)
$$\begin{aligned} 5x - 2y + z &= 4 \\ 7x + y - 5z &= 8 \\ 3x + 7y + 4z &= 10. \end{aligned}$$

Answers

1. (*i*) $x_1 = 2, x_2 = 1, x_3 = -1$ (*ii*) $x_1 = 3, x_2 = 1, x_3 = 2$
   (*iii*) $x = 1, y = 1, z = 1$ (*iv*) $x = 1.708864, y = -1.8005692, z = 1.0488215$
   (*v*) $x = 1, y = 2, z = 3$ (*vi*) $x_1 = \frac{23}{9}, x_2 = \frac{31}{18}, x_3 = -\frac{19}{18}$
   (*vii*) $x = 4.2097, y = 1.3337, z = 0.2468$ (*viii*) $x = 1, y = 3, z = 5$
   (*ix*) $x = 2, y = -1, z = 3$ (*x*) $x_1 = 5, x_2 = 1, x_3 = -2$
2. (*i*) $x_1 = 1, x_2 = 1, x_3 = 2, x_4 = 2$ (*ii*) $x_1 = 5, x_2 = 6, x_3 = -10, x_4 = 8$
   (*iii*) $x = 1, y = -1, z = 2$ (*iv*) $x_1 = 1.59, x_2 = 1.6, x_3 = -1.25$
   (*v*) $x_1 = 5, x_2 = 4, x_3 = -7, x_4 = 1$ (*vi*) $x = 0.9935941, y = 1.5069778, z = 1.8485472$
   (*vii*) $x_1 = 1, x_2 = 0, x_3 = -1, x_4 = 2$ (*viii*) $x_1 = -9/2, x_2 = 5/2, x_3 = 5$
   (*ix*) $x_1 = 1, x_2 = -1, x_3 = -1, x_4 = 1$
3. (*i*) $x = .5005, y = 0.3330$ (Without pivoting)
   (*ii*) $x = 0.5, y = 1/3$ (With pivoting)
4. $x = 1, y = 1, z = 1$
5. $x_1 = \frac{22}{9}, x_2 = 3, x_3 = \frac{11}{9}$
6. $x_1 = 1/2, x_2 = -2/3, x_3 = 1/4$
7. $x_1 = 1, x_2 = 2, x_3 = 3$
8. $x = 2, y = -2, z = 3$
9. $x = 3.4280884, y = 5.1151375, z = 7.1919862$
10. (*i*) $x = 1, y = 2, z = 1$ (*ii*) $x = \frac{122}{109}, y = \frac{284}{327}, z = \frac{46}{327}$.

7.4. ILL-CONDITIONED SYSTEM OF EQUATIONS

A system of equations AX = B is said to be ill-conditioned if it is highly sensitive to small changes in A and B, *i.e.*, small change in A or B cause a large change in the solution of the system. In it, even the small round-off errors effect the solutions very badly. Unfortunately, it is quite difficult to recognize an ill-conditioned system. For example, consider the following two almost identical systems

$$\left.\begin{aligned} 2x + y &= 2 \\ 2x + 1.01y &= 2.01 \end{aligned}\right\} \quad \text{and} \quad \left.\begin{aligned} 2x + y &= 2 \\ 2.01x + y &= 2.05 \end{aligned}\right\}$$

Respective solutions are $\left(\frac{1}{2}, 1\right)$ and $(5, -8)$.

It is clear that the solutions differ too much. Hence the system is **ill-conditioned.**

EXAMPLES

Example 1. *Show that the following system of linear equations is ill-conditioned*

$$7x - 10y = 1$$
$$5x + 7y = 0.7.$$

Sol. On solving the given equations, we get $x = 0$ and $y = 0.1$.

Now, we make slight changes in the given system of equations. The new system becomes

$$7x + 10y = 1.01$$
$$5x + 7y = 0.69$$

Here we get the solution as $x = -0.17, y = 0.22$

Hence the given system is ill-conditioned.

Example 2. *A system is described by the following simultaneous equations:*

$$x - 2y = -2$$
$$0.45x - 0.91y = -1$$

Discuss, whether the system is ill-conditioned system.

Sol. On solving the given equations, we get

$$x = 18, y = 10$$

Now, we make slight changes in the given system of equations. The new system becomes

$$x - 2y = -2$$
$$0.45x - 0.92y = -1$$

Here, we get the solution as

$$x = 8, y = 5$$

Hence the given system is ill-conditioned.

ASSIGNMENT

1. What do you understand by ill-conditioned system of equations ? Illustrate your answer with the help of suitable examples.
2. Consider the following system of equations:

$$100x - 200y = 100$$
$$-200x + 401y = -100$$

Determine, whether given system is ill-conditioned or not.

Answer

2. Yes.

7.5. REFINEMENT OF SOLUTION

To improve the accuracy of solution of an ill-conditioned system, we use an iterative procedure. Consider a system

$$\left.\begin{aligned} a_1x + b_1y + c_1z &= d_1 \\ a_2x + b_2y + c_2z &= d_2 \\ a_3x + b_3y + c_3z &= d_3 \end{aligned}\right\} \quad ...(1)$$

Let x_1, y_1, z_1 be an approximate solution.

Substituting in (1), we get new values d_1', d_2', d_3' on RHS.

The new system (1) becomes

$$\left.\begin{aligned} a_1x_1 + b_1y_1 + c_1z_1 &= d_1' \\ a_2x_1 + b_2y_1 + c_2z_1 &= d_2' \\ a_3x_1 + b_3y_1 + c_3z_1 &= d_3' \end{aligned}\right\} \quad ...(2)$$

Subtracting each eqn. in (2) from corresponding eqns. in (1), we get

$$\left.\begin{aligned} a_1\bar{x} + b_1\bar{y} + c_1\bar{z} &= e_1 \\ a_2\bar{x} + b_2\bar{y} + c_2\bar{z} &= e_2 \\ a_3\bar{x} + b_3\bar{y} + c_3\bar{z} &= e_3 \end{aligned}\right\} \qquad ...(3)$$

where, $\bar{x} = x - x_1$, $\bar{y} = y - y_1$, $\bar{z} = z - z_1$ and $e_i = d_i - d_i'$.

We now solve the system (3) for $\bar{x}$, $\bar{y}$, $\bar{z}$ giving $x = x_1 + \bar{x}$, $y = y_1 + \bar{y}$ and $z = z_1 + \bar{z}$ which will be better approximations for x, y and z. We can repeat the process for more refinement of the solution.

EXAMPLE

Example. *For the system of equations*

$$x + 2y + z = 8$$
$$2x - y + 2z = 6$$
$$3x + 2y - z = 4$$

an approximate solution is given by $x = 1$, $y = 1.8$ and $z = 2.8$. Improve this solution by the iterative method.

Sol. Substituting the approximate values, we get

$$\left.\begin{aligned} (1) + 2(1.8) + (2.8) &= 7.4 \\ 2(1) - (1.8) + 2(2.8) &= 5.8 \\ 3(1) + 2(1.8) - 2.8 &= 3.8 \end{aligned}\right\} \qquad ...(1)$$

Subtracting each eqn. in (1) from the corresponding given equations, we get

$$\left.\begin{aligned} \bar{x} + 2\bar{y} + \bar{z} &= 0.6 \\ 2\bar{x} - \bar{y} + 2\bar{z} &= 0.2 \\ 3\bar{x} + 2\bar{y} - \bar{z} &= 0.2 \end{aligned}\right\} \qquad ...(2)$$

where, $\bar{x} = x - 1$, $\bar{y} = y - 1.8$, $\bar{z} = z - 2.8$.

Solving the system (2), we get

$$\bar{x} = 0, \ \bar{y} = 0.2, \ \bar{z} = 0.2$$

This gives the better solution

$$x = 1, y = 1.8 + .2 = 2 \quad \text{and} \quad z = 2.8 + .2 = 3.$$

7.6. GAUSS-JORDAN ELIMINATION METHOD

This method is a modified form of Gauss-elimination method. In this method, the coefficient matrix is reduced to a diagonal matrix.

Although this method involves more arithmetical operations, the back substitution is not required as each of the final equivalent system of equations will contain only one unknown.

Hence by Gauss-Jordan method

$$[\mathrm{A} : b] \xrightarrow{\textit{Gauss Jordan}} [\mathrm{I} : d]$$

Generally, this method is not used for the solution of a system of equations as it is having more computations than the Gauss-elimination method.

7.6.1. Algorithm of Gauss-Jordan Method

```
 1. Input n
 2. For j=1,n
 3. For j=1,n+1
 4. Input a(i,j)
 5. Next j
 6. Next i
 7. For j=1,n
 8. For i=1,n
 9. If i!=j then step 10
      ELSE
     goto step 8
10. t=a  (i,j)/a(j,j)
11. For k=1,n+1
12. a(i,k)=a(i,k)-a(j,k)*t
13. Next k
14. Next i
15. Next j
16. For i=1,n
17. x(i)=a(i,n+1)/a(i,i)
18. Next i
19. For i=1,n
20. Print x(i)
21. Next i
22. Stop
```

7.6.2. Flow Chart of Gauss-Jordan Method

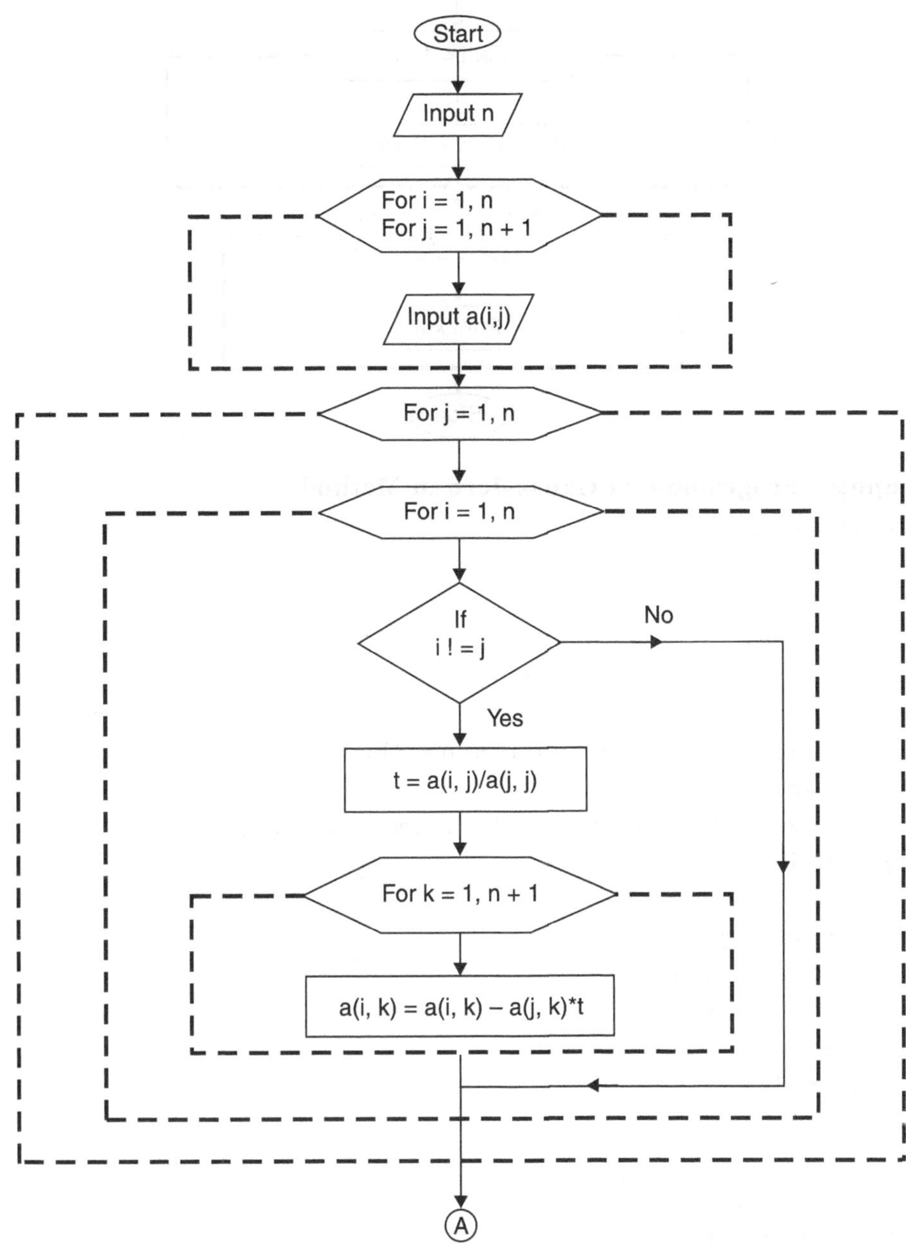

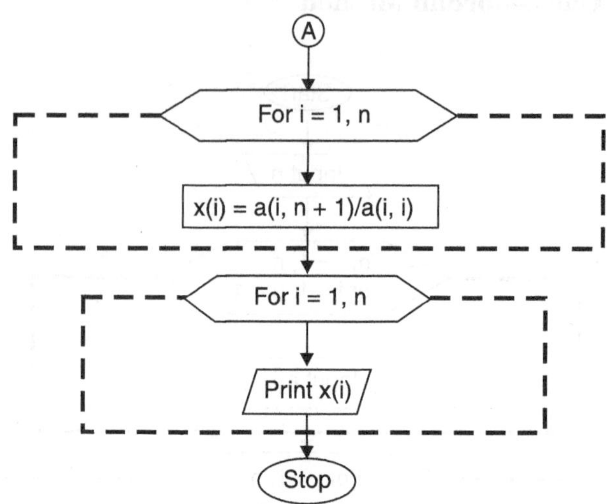

7.6.3. Computer Programme of Gauss-Jordan Method

```
#include<stdio.h>

main()
{
int i,j,k,n;
float  a[5][5],x[5],t;
printf("\nEnter the size of matrix n= ");
scanf ("%d" &n);
printf("\nEnter elements in matrix form & RHS\n");
for(i=1;i<=n;i++)
   {
   for(j=1;j<=n+1;j++)
   scanf("%f",&a[i][j]);
   }
for(j=1;j<=n;j++)
for  (i=1;i<=n;i++)
if(i!-j)
   {
   t=a[i][j]/a[j][j];
   for  (k=1;k<=n+1;k++)
     a[i][k]=a[i][k]-a[j][k]*t;
   }
else
   continue;
for(i=1;i<=n;i++)
x[i]=a[i][n+1]/a[i][i];
```

```
printf("\nSolution of given matrix is:\n");
for(i=1;i<=n;i++)
printf("X(%d)=%.3f\n",i,x[i]);
return;
}
```

7.6.4. Output

```
Enter the size of matrix n= 3
Enter elements in matrix form & RHS
      1    1    1    1
      4    3   -1    6
      3    5    3    4
Solution of given matrix is
X(1)=1.000
X(2)=0.500
X(3)=-0.500
```

EXAMPLES

Example 1. *Solve the following linear equations by using Gauss-Jordan method.*

$$2x_1 + 8x_2 + 2x_3 = 14$$
$$6x_1 + 6x_2 - x_3 = 13$$
$$2x_1 - x_2 + 2x_3 = 5$$

Sol. We have,

$$\left.\begin{aligned} 2x_1 + 8x_2 + 2x_3 &= 14 \\ 6x_1 + 6x_2 - x_3 &= 13 \\ 2x_1 - x_2 + 2x_3 &= 5 \end{aligned}\right\} \qquad ...(1)$$

In matrix notation, the given system (1) can be written as

$$\begin{bmatrix} 2 & 8 & 2 \\ 6 & 6 & -1 \\ 2 & -1 & 2 \end{bmatrix}\begin{bmatrix} x_1 \\ x_2 \\ x_3 \end{bmatrix} = \begin{bmatrix} 14 \\ 13 \\ 5 \end{bmatrix} \qquad ...(2)$$

Eliminating x_1 from second and third rows of (2), we get

$$\begin{bmatrix} 2 & 8 & 2 \\ 0 & -18 & -7 \\ 0 & -9 & 0 \end{bmatrix}\begin{bmatrix} x_1 \\ x_2 \\ x_3 \end{bmatrix} = \begin{bmatrix} 14 \\ -29 \\ -9 \end{bmatrix} \qquad ...(3)$$

Eliminating x_2 from the first and third rows using the second row, we get

$$\begin{bmatrix} 2 & 0 & -10/9 \\ 0 & -18 & -7 \\ 0 & 0 & 7/2 \end{bmatrix} \begin{bmatrix} x_1 \\ x_2 \\ x_3 \end{bmatrix} = \begin{bmatrix} 10/9 \\ -29 \\ 11/2 \end{bmatrix} \quad ...(4)$$

Eliminating x_3 from the first and second rows, we get

$$\begin{bmatrix} 2 & 0 & 0 \\ 0 & -18 & 0 \\ 0 & 0 & 7/2 \end{bmatrix} \begin{bmatrix} x_1 \\ x_2 \\ x_3 \end{bmatrix} = \begin{bmatrix} 20/7 \\ -18 \\ 11/2 \end{bmatrix} \quad ...(5)$$

From eqn. (5), we get the solution as

$$x_1 = \frac{10}{7}, x_2 = 1, x_3 = \frac{11}{7}.$$

Example 2. *Solve the equations by Gauss-Jordan method.*

$$10x + y + z = 12$$
$$2x + 10y + z = 13$$

and $$x + y + 5z = 7$$

Sol. In matrix form, the given system is

$$\begin{bmatrix} 10 & 1 & 1 \\ 2 & 10 & 1 \\ 1 & 1 & 5 \end{bmatrix} \begin{bmatrix} x \\ y \\ z \end{bmatrix} = \begin{bmatrix} 12 \\ 13 \\ 7 \end{bmatrix}$$

Augmented matrix is

$$[A : B] = \left[\begin{array}{ccc|c} 10 & 1 & 1 & 12 \\ 2 & 10 & 1 & 13 \\ 1 & 1 & 5 & 7 \end{array}\right]$$

Operating $R_{13}(-9)$

$$\sim \left[\begin{array}{ccc|c} 1 & -8 & -44 & -51 \\ 2 & 10 & 1 & 13 \\ 1 & 1 & 5 & 7 \end{array}\right]$$

Operating $R_{21}(-2)$, $R_{31}(-1)$

$$\sim \left[\begin{array}{ccc|c} 1 & -8 & -44 & -51 \\ 0 & 26 & 89 & 115 \\ 0 & 9 & 49 & 58 \end{array}\right]$$

Operating $R_2 - 3R_3$

$$\sim \left[\begin{array}{ccc|c} 1 & -8 & -44 & -51 \\ 0 & -1 & -58 & -59 \\ 0 & 9 & 49 & 58 \end{array}\right]$$

Operating R_2 (– 1)

$$\sim \left[\begin{array}{ccc|c} 1 & -8 & -44 & -51 \\ 0 & 1 & 58 & 59 \\ 0 & 9 & 49 & 58 \end{array}\right]$$

Operating R_{32} (–9), R_{12} (8)

$$\sim \left[\begin{array}{ccc|c} 1 & 0 & 420 & 421 \\ 0 & 1 & 58 & 59 \\ 0 & 0 & -473 & -473 \end{array}\right]$$

Operating $R_3 \left(-\frac{1}{473}\right)$

$$\sim \left[\begin{array}{ccc|c} 1 & 0 & 420 & 421 \\ 0 & 1 & 58 & 59 \\ 0 & 0 & 1 & 1 \end{array}\right]$$

Operating R_{13} (– 420), R_{23} (– 58),

$$\sim \left[\begin{array}{ccc|c} 1 & 0 & 0 & 1 \\ 0 & 1 & 0 & 1 \\ 0 & 0 & 1 & 1 \end{array}\right]$$

∴ The equivalent system of equations is

$$\begin{bmatrix} 1 & 0 & 0 \\ 0 & 1 & 0 \\ 0 & 0 & 1 \end{bmatrix} \begin{bmatrix} x \\ y \\ z \end{bmatrix} = \begin{bmatrix} 1 \\ 1 \\ 1 \end{bmatrix}$$

$$\Rightarrow \qquad x = 1, y = 1, z = 1.$$

ASSIGNMENT

1. Solve the following system(s) of linear equations by Gauss-Jordan elimination method.

(*i*) $10x_1 + x_2 + x_3 = 12$
$x_1 + 10x_2 - x_3 = 10$
$x_1 - 2x_2 + 10x_3 = 9$

(*ii*) $x + 2y + z - w = -2$
$2x + 3y - z + 2w = 7$
$x + y + 3z - 2w = -6$
$x + y + z + w = 2$

(*iii*) $x + 2y + z = 8$
$2x + 3y + 4z = 20$
$4x + 3y + 2z = 16$

(*iv*) $x_1 + x_2 + x_3 = 1$
$4x_1 + 3x_2 - x_3 = 6$
$3x_1 + 5x_2 + 3x_3 = 4$

(*v*) $10x + y + z = 12$
$x + 10y + z = 12$
$x + y + 10z = 12$

(*vi*) $10x_1 + x_2 - x_3 = 11.19$
$x_1 + 10x_2 + x_3 = 20.08$
$-x_1 + x_2 + 10x_3 = 35.61.$

Answers

1. (*i*) $x_1 = 1, x_2 = 1, x_3 = 1$

(*ii*) $x = 1, y = 0, z = -1, w = 2$

(*iii*) $x = 1, y = 2, z = 3$

(*iv*) $x_1 = 1, x_2 = \frac{1}{2}, x_3 = -\frac{1}{2}$

(*v*) $x = 1, y = 2, z = 1$

(*vi*) $x_1 = 1.32, x_2 = 1.5219, x_3 = 3.5408.$

7.7. TRIANGULARIZATION METHOD

This method is also known as the *LU decomposition method* or *the method of factorization*.

In this method, the coefficient matrix A of the system of equations AX = B is decomposed into the product of a lower triangular matrix L and an upper triangular matrix U so that

$$A = LU \qquad ...(1)$$

where $L = \begin{bmatrix} l_{11} & 0 & 0 & \dots & 0 \\ l_{21} & l_{22} & 0 & \dots & 0 \\ l_{31} & l_{32} & l_{33} & \dots & 0 \\ \vdots & \vdots & \vdots & \vdots & \vdots \\ l_{n1} & l_{n2} & l_{n3} & \dots & l_{mn} \end{bmatrix}$ and $U = \begin{bmatrix} u_{11} & u_{12} & u_{13} & \dots & u_{1n} \\ 0 & u_{22} & u_{23} & \dots & u_{2n} \\ 0 & 0 & u_{33} & \dots & u_{3n} \\ \vdots & \vdots & \vdots & \vdots & \vdots \\ 0 & 0 & 0 & \dots & u_{nn} \end{bmatrix}$

Using the matrix multiplication and comparing corresponding elements in (1), we obtain

$$l_{i1}\,u_{1j} + l_{i2}\,u_{2j} + \ldots\ldots + l_{in}\,u_{nj} = a_{ij},\ 1 \le j \le n$$

where $l_{ij} = 0,\ \ j > i \ \text{ and } \ u_{ij} = 0,\ \ i > j$

To produce a unique solution, it is convenient to choose either $u_{ii} = 1$ or $l_{ii} = 1$; $1 \le i \le n$.

(*i*) When we choose $l_{ii} = 1$, the method is called the **Doolittle's method.**

(*ii*) When we choose $u_{ii} = 1$, the method is called the **Crout's method.**

The given system of equations is

$$AX = B \qquad ...(2)$$

$$\Rightarrow \quad LUX = B \qquad ...(3) \mid \text{Using } (1)$$

Let UX = Y then eqn. (3) becomes

$$LY = B \qquad ...(4)$$

The unknowns $y_1, y_2, y_3, \ldots, y_n$ in (4) are determined by forward substitution and the unknowns $x_1, x_2, x_3, \ldots, x_n$ in UX = Y are obtained by back substitution.

Note 1. The method fails if any of the diagonal elements l_{ii} or u_{ii} is zero.

2. LU decomposition is guaranteed when the matrix A is positive definite.

EXAMPLES

Example 1. *Solve, by Crout's method, the following system of equations:*

$$x + y + z = 3$$
$$2x - y + 3z = 16$$
$$3x + y - z = -3.$$

[*U.P.T.U. (M. Tech.) 2010*]

Sol. We choose $u_{ii} = 1$ and write

$$A = LU$$

$$\begin{bmatrix} 1 & 1 & 1 \\ 2 & -1 & 3 \\ 3 & 1 & -1 \end{bmatrix} = \begin{bmatrix} l_{11} & 0 & 0 \\ l_{21} & l_{22} & 0 \\ l_{31} & l_{32} & l_{33} \end{bmatrix} \begin{bmatrix} 1 & u_{12} & u_{13} \\ 0 & 1 & u_{23} \\ 0 & 0 & 1 \end{bmatrix}$$

$$= \begin{bmatrix} l_{11} & l_{11}u_{12} & l_{11}u_{13} \\ l_{21} & l_{21}\,u_{12} + l_{22} & l_{21}u_{13} + l_{22}\,u_{23} \\ l_{31} & l_{31}u_{12} + l_{32} & l_{31}\,u_{13} + l_{32}\,u_{23} + l_{33} \end{bmatrix}$$

Equating, we get

$$l_{11} = 1, l_{21} = 2, l_{31} = 3$$

$$l_{11}\, u_{12} = 1 \quad \Rightarrow \quad u_{12} = 1$$

$$l_{11}\, u_{13} = 1 \quad \Rightarrow \quad u_{13} = 1$$

$$l_{21}\, u_{12} + l_{22} = -1 \quad \Rightarrow \quad l_{22} = -3$$

$$l_{31}\, u_{12} + l_{32} = 1 \quad \Rightarrow \quad l_{32} = -2$$

$$l_{31}\, u_{13} + l_{22}\, u_{23} = 3 \quad \Rightarrow \quad u_{23} = -\frac{1}{3}$$

$$l_{31}\, u_{13} + l_{32}\, u_{23} + l_{33} = -1 \quad \Rightarrow \quad l_{33} = -\frac{14}{3}$$

Thus, we get

$$A = LU = \begin{bmatrix} 1 & 0 & 0 \\ 2 & -3 & 0 \\ 3 & -2 & -\frac{14}{3} \end{bmatrix} \begin{bmatrix} 1 & 1 & 1 \\ 0 & 1 & -\frac{1}{3} \\ 0 & 0 & 1 \end{bmatrix}$$

The given system is

$$AX = B$$

$$\Rightarrow \qquad LUX = B \qquad \text{...(1)}$$

Let UX = Y so that (1) becomes

$$LY = B$$

$$\begin{bmatrix} 1 & 0 & 0 \\ 2 & -3 & 0 \\ 3 & -2 & -\frac{14}{3} \end{bmatrix} \begin{bmatrix} y_1 \\ y_2 \\ y_3 \end{bmatrix} = \begin{bmatrix} 3 \\ 16 \\ -3 \end{bmatrix}$$

which gives

$$y_1 = 3$$

$$2y_1 - 3y_2 = 16$$

$$3y_1 - 2y_2 - \frac{14}{3}\, y_3 = -3$$

$$\Rightarrow \qquad y_1 = 3, y_2 = -\frac{10}{3}, y_3 = 4$$ | By forward substitution

Now, $\qquad UX = Y$

$$\begin{bmatrix} 1 & 1 & 1 \\ 0 & 1 & -1/3 \\ 0 & 0 & 1 \end{bmatrix} \begin{bmatrix} x \\ y \\ z \end{bmatrix} = \begin{bmatrix} 3 \\ -10/3 \\ 4 \end{bmatrix}$$

which gives, $\qquad x + y + z = 3$

$$y - \frac{1}{3} z = -\frac{10}{3}$$

$$z = 4$$

By back substitution

$$x = 1, y = -2, z = 4.$$

Example 2. *Solve the following system of equations by the LU factorization method:*

$$2x + 3y + z = 9$$
$$x + 2y + 3z = 6$$
$$3x + y + 2z = 8.$$

Sol. We choose $l_{ii} = 1$ and write

$$\begin{bmatrix} 2 & 3 & 1 \\ 1 & 2 & 3 \\ 3 & 1 & 2 \end{bmatrix} = \begin{bmatrix} 1 & 0 & 0 \\ l_{21} & 1 & 0 \\ l_{31} & l_{32} & 1 \end{bmatrix} \begin{bmatrix} u_{11} & u_{12} & u_{13} \\ 0 & u_{22} & u_{23} \\ 0 & 0 & u_{33} \end{bmatrix}$$

$$= \begin{bmatrix} u_{11} & u_{12} & u_{13} \\ l_{21} u_{11} & l_{21} u_{12} + u_{22} & l_{21} u_{13} + u_{23} \\ l_{31} u_{11} & l_{31} u_{12} + l_{32} u_{22} & l_{31} u_{13} + l_{32} u_{23} + u_{33} \end{bmatrix}$$

Equating, we get

$$u_{11} = 2, \quad u_{12} = 3, \quad u_{13} = 1$$
$$l_{21} u_{11} = 1 \quad \Rightarrow \quad l_{21} = 1/2$$
$$l_{31} u_{11} = 3 \quad \Rightarrow \quad l_{31} = 3/2$$
$$l_{21} u_{12} + u_{22} = 2 \quad \Rightarrow \quad u_{22} = 1/2$$
$$l_{21} u_{13} + u_{23} = 3 \quad \Rightarrow \quad u_{23} = 5/2$$
$$l_{31} u_{12} + l_{32} u_{22} = 1 \quad \Rightarrow \quad l_{32} = -7$$
$$l_{31} u_{13} + l_{32} u_{23} + u_{33} = 2 \quad \Rightarrow \quad u_{33} = 18$$

Thus, we get

$$A = LU = \begin{bmatrix} 1 & 0 & 0 \\ 1/2 & 1 & 0 \\ 3/2 & -7 & 1 \end{bmatrix} \begin{bmatrix} 2 & 3 & 1 \\ 0 & 1/2 & 5/2 \\ 0 & 0 & 18 \end{bmatrix}$$

The given system is

$$AX = B$$

$$\Rightarrow \qquad LUX = B \qquad \text{...(1)}$$

Let $\quad UX = Y$ so that (1) becomes

$$LY = B$$

$$\begin{bmatrix} 1 & 0 & 0 \\ 1/2 & 1 & 0 \\ 3/2 & -7 & 1 \end{bmatrix} \begin{bmatrix} y_1 \\ y_2 \\ y_3 \end{bmatrix} = \begin{bmatrix} 9 \\ 6 \\ 8 \end{bmatrix}$$

which gives

$$y_1 = 9$$

$$\frac{1}{2} y_1 + y_2 = 6$$

$$\frac{3}{2} y_1 - 7 y_2 + y_3 = 8$$

$\Rightarrow$ $y_1 = 9, \quad y_2 = 3/2, \quad y_3 = 5$ | By forward substitution

Now, $UX = Y$

$$\begin{bmatrix} 2 & 3 & 1 \\ 0 & 1/2 & 5/2 \\ 0 & 0 & 18 \end{bmatrix} \begin{bmatrix} x \\ y \\ z \end{bmatrix} = \begin{bmatrix} 9 \\ 3/2 \\ 5 \end{bmatrix}$$

which gives,

$$2x + 3y + z = 9$$

$$\frac{1}{2} y + \frac{5}{2} z = \frac{3}{2}$$

$$18 z = 5$$

By back substitution

$$\Rightarrow \quad x = \frac{35}{18}, \quad y = \frac{29}{18}, \quad z = \frac{5}{18}$$

Note. We may also choose $u_{ii} = 1$ to get the solution.

Example 3. *Show that the LU decomposition method fails to solve the system of equations*

$$x_1 + x_2 - x_3 = 2$$
$$2x_1 + 2x_2 + 5x_3 = -3$$
$$3x_1 + 2x_2 - 3x_3 = 6$$

whose exact solution is (1, 0, – 1).

Sol. Case I. If we write (taking $l_{ii} = 1$)

$$\begin{bmatrix} 1 & 1 & -1 \\ 2 & 2 & 5 \\ 3 & 2 & -3 \end{bmatrix} = \begin{bmatrix} 1 & 0 & 0 \\ l_{21} & 1 & 0 \\ l_{31} & l_{32} & 1 \end{bmatrix} \begin{bmatrix} u_{11} & u_{12} & u_{13} \\ 0 & u_{22} & u_{23} \\ 0 & 0 & u_{33} \end{bmatrix}$$

We obtain,

$$u_{11} = 1, \quad u_{12} = 1, \quad u_{13} = -1$$
$$l_{21} u_{11} = 2 \quad \Rightarrow \quad l_{21} = 2$$
$$l_{21} u_{12} + u_{22} = 2 \quad \Rightarrow \quad u_{22} = 0$$

Hence LU decomposition method fails as the pivot $u_{22} = 0$.

Case II. If we write (taking $u_{ii} = 1$)

$$\begin{bmatrix} 1 & 1 & -1 \\ 2 & 2 & 5 \\ 3 & 2 & -3 \end{bmatrix} = \begin{bmatrix} l_{11} & 0 & 0 \\ l_{21} & l_{22} & 0 \\ l_{31} & l_{32} & l_{33} \end{bmatrix} \begin{bmatrix} 1 & u_{12} & u_{13} \\ 0 & 1 & u_{23} \\ 0 & 0 & 1 \end{bmatrix}$$

We obtain,

$$l_{11} = 1, \quad l_{21} = 2, \quad l_{31} = 3$$
$$l_{11} u_{12} = 1 \quad \Rightarrow \quad u_{12} = 1$$
$$l_{11} u_{13} = -1 \quad \Rightarrow \quad u_{13} = -1$$
$$l_{21} u_{12} + l_{22} = 2 \quad \Rightarrow \quad l_{22} = 0$$

Hence LU decomposition method fails as again the pivot $l_{22} = 0$.

ASSIGNMENT

1. Solve the following system(s) of linear equations by Crout's method.

(*i*) $x_1 + x_2 + x_3 = 1$
$4x_1 + 3x_2 - x_3 = 6$
$3x_1 + 5x_2 + 3x_3 = 4$

(*ii*) $10x + y + z = 12$
$2x + 10y + z = 13$
$2x + 2y + 10z = 14$

(*iii*) $3x - y + 2z = 12$
$x + 2y + 3z = 11$
$2x - 2y - z = 2$
[*M.T.U. 2012, G.B.T.U. 2011, 2013*]

(*iv*) $x_1 + x_2 + x_3 = 1$
$3x_1 + x_2 - 3x_3 = 5$
$x_1 - 2x_2 - 5x_3 = 10$ (*M.T.U. 2013*)

(*v*) $$\begin{bmatrix} 2 & 1 & -4 & 1 \\ -4 & 3 & 5 & -2 \\ 1 & -1 & 1 & -1 \\ 1 & 3 & -3 & 2 \end{bmatrix}\begin{bmatrix} x_1 \\ x_2 \\ x_3 \\ x_4 \end{bmatrix} = \begin{bmatrix} 4 \\ -10 \\ 2 \\ -1 \end{bmatrix}.$$ (*U.P.T.U. 2007*)

2. Solve the following system of linear equations by LU decomposition method.

(*i*) $x_1 + 2x_2 + 3x_3 = 14$
$2x_1 + 5x_2 + 2x_3 = 18$
$3x_1 + x_2 + 5x_3 = 20$

(*ii*) $$\begin{bmatrix} 2 & 1 & 1 & -2 \\ 4 & 0 & 2 & 1 \\ 3 & 2 & 2 & 0 \\ 1 & 3 & 2 & -1 \end{bmatrix}\begin{bmatrix} x_1 \\ x_2 \\ x_3 \\ x_4 \end{bmatrix} = \begin{bmatrix} -10 \\ 8 \\ 7 \\ -5 \end{bmatrix}$$ (*U.P.T.U. 2009*)

(*iii*) $5x - 2y + z = 4$
$7x + y - 5z = 8$
$3x + 7y + 4z = 10.$

3. Solve the following system of equations by triangularization method.

(*i*) $2x - 3y + 10z = 3$
$-x + 4y + 2z = 20$
$5x + 2y + z = -12$

(*ii*) $x_1 + 2x_2 - x_3 = 3$
$x_1 - x_2 + x_3 = -1$
$2x_1 - 2x_2 + 3x_3 = 2$

(*iii*) $4x_1 + x_2 + x_3 = 4$
$x_1 + 4x_2 - 2x_3 = 4$
$3x_1 + 2x_2 - 4x_3 = 6$

(*iv*) $x_1 + x_2 - x_3 = 2$
$2x_1 + 3x_2 + 5x_3 = -3$
$3x_1 + 2x_2 - 3x_3 = 6.$

4. Obtain the LU decomposition of the matrix

$$\begin{bmatrix} 2 & -6 & 10 \\ 1 & 5 & 1 \\ -1 & 15 & -5 \end{bmatrix}$$

so that for $1 \le i \le 3$,

(*i*) $u_{ii} = 2$ (*ii*) $l_{ii} = 2.$

Answers

1. (*i*) $x_1 = 1, x_2 = 0.5, x_3 = -0.5$ (*ii*) $x = 1, y = 1, z = 1$

(*iii*) $x = 3, y = 1, z = 2$ (*iv*) $x_1 = 6, x_2 = -7, x_3 = 2$

(*v*) $x_1 = 1, x_2 = -1, x_3 = -1, x_4 = -1$

2. (*i*) $x_1 = 1, x_2 = 2, x_3 = 3$ (*ii*) $x_1 = 5, x_2 = 6, x_3 = -10, x_4 = 8$

(*iii*) $x = 1.11926, y = 0.8685, z = 0.14067$

3. (*i*) $x = -4, y = 3, z = 2$ (*ii*) $x_1 = -1, x_2 = 4, x_3 = 4$ (*iii*) $x_1 = 1, x_2 = 5, x_3 = -5$
(*iv*) $x_1 = 1, x_2 = 0, x_3 = -1$

4. (*i*) $L = \begin{bmatrix} 1 & 0 & 0 \\ 1/2 & 4 & 0 \\ -1/2 & 6 & 3 \end{bmatrix}, U = \begin{bmatrix} 2 & -6 & 10 \\ 0 & 2 & -1 \\ 0 & 0 & 2 \end{bmatrix}$ (*ii*) $L = \begin{bmatrix} 2 & 0 & 0 \\ 1 & 2 & 0 \\ -1 & 3 & 2 \end{bmatrix}, U = \begin{bmatrix} 1 & -3 & 5 \\ 0 & 4 & -2 \\ 0 & 0 & 3 \end{bmatrix}$

7.8. CHOLESKY METHOD

This method is also called square-root method. Consider a system of equations

$$AX = B \quad ...(1)$$

If the coefficient matrix A is symmetric and positive definite then A can be decomposed as

$$A = LL^T \quad ...(2)$$

where L is a lower triangular matrix.

A may also be decomposed as $A = UU^T$ where U is an upper triangular matrix.

From (1) and (2),

$$LL^TX = B$$

$$\Rightarrow \quad LY = B \quad ...(3)$$

where $$L^TX = Y \quad ...(4)$$

The values y_i, $1 \le i \le n$ can be obtained by forward substitution and the solution x_i, $1 \le i \le n$ are obtained by back substitution.

Example. *Solve the following system of equations*

$$\begin{bmatrix} 1 & 2 & 3 \\ 2 & 8 & 22 \\ 3 & 22 & 82 \end{bmatrix} \begin{bmatrix} x_1 \\ x_2 \\ x_3 \end{bmatrix} = \begin{bmatrix} 5 \\ 6 \\ -10 \end{bmatrix}$$

using Cholesky method.

Sol. Let $$A = LL^T \qquad | \because \text{ A is symmetric}$$

$$\begin{bmatrix} 1 & 2 & 3 \\ 2 & 8 & 22 \\ 3 & 22 & 82 \end{bmatrix} = \begin{bmatrix} l_{11} & 0 & 0 \\ l_{21} & l_{22} & 0 \\ l_{31} & l_{32} & l_{33} \end{bmatrix} \begin{bmatrix} l_{11} & l_{21} & l_{31} \\ 0 & l_{22} & l_{32} \\ 0 & 0 & l_{33} \end{bmatrix}$$

$$= \begin{bmatrix} l_{11}^2 & l_{11}l_{21} & l_{11}l_{31} \\ l_{21}l_{11} & l_{21}^2 + l_{22}^2 & l_{21}l_{31} + l_{22}l_{32} \\ l_{31}l_{11} & l_{31}l_{21} + l_{32}l_{22} & l_{31}^2 + l_{32}^2 + l_{33}^2 \end{bmatrix}$$

Equating the corresponding elements, we get

$$l_{11}^2 = 1 \quad \Rightarrow \quad l_{11} = 1$$
$$l_{11}\,l_{21} = 2 \quad \Rightarrow \quad l_{21} = 2$$
$$l_{11}\,l_{31} = 3 \quad \Rightarrow \quad l_{31} = 3$$
$$l_{21}^2 + l_{22}^2 = 8 \quad \Rightarrow \quad l_{22} = 2$$

$$l_{31}\,l_{21} + l_{32}\,l_{22} = 22 \quad \Rightarrow \quad l_{32} = 8$$
$$l_{31}^2 + l_{32}^2 + l_{33}^2 = 82 \quad \Rightarrow \quad l_{33} = 3$$

Hence, $$L = \begin{bmatrix} 1 & 0 & 0 \\ 2 & 2 & 0 \\ 3 & 8 & 3 \end{bmatrix}$$

The given system can be written as $LL^TX = B$

or $LY = B$ where $L^TX = Y$

From $LY = B$, we get

$$\begin{bmatrix} 1 & 0 & 0 \\ 2 & 2 & 0 \\ 3 & 8 & 3 \end{bmatrix} \begin{bmatrix} y_1 \\ y_2 \\ y_3 \end{bmatrix} = \begin{bmatrix} 5 \\ 6 \\ -10 \end{bmatrix}$$

$\Rightarrow$ $y_1 = 5, y_2 = -2, y_3 = -3$ | By forward substitution

From $L^TX = Y$, we get

$$\begin{bmatrix} 1 & 2 & 3 \\ 0 & 2 & 8 \\ 0 & 0 & 3 \end{bmatrix} \begin{bmatrix} x_1 \\ x_2 \\ x_3 \end{bmatrix} = \begin{bmatrix} 5 \\ -2 \\ -3 \end{bmatrix}$$

$\Rightarrow$ $x_1 = 2, \quad x_2 = 3, \quad x_3 = -1.$ | By backward substitution

ASSIGNMENT

1. Solve the system of equations by the Cholesky method.

$$4x_1 - x_2 = 1$$
$$-x_1 + 4x_2 - x_3 = 0$$
$$-x_2 + 4x_3 = 0$$

Answer

1. $x_1 = \frac{15}{56}, \quad x_2 = \frac{1}{14}, \quad x_3 = \frac{1}{56}.$

7.9. ITERATIVE METHODS

The iterative or indirect methods start from an approximation to the true solution and if convergent, derive a sequence of closer approximations. The cycle of computations is repeated till the desired accuracy is attained. In these methods, the amount of computation depends on the accuracy required.

Generally, direct methods are preferred for the solution of a linear system of equations but in case of matrices having large number of zero elements, iterative methods are preferred since they preserve those elements.

The direct method discussed so far involve many subtractions. When the terms involved in subtractions are nearly equal, their difference is nearly zero and hence causes inaccuracies. The inaccuracies due to this inherent weakness of the direct methods cannot be completely avoided whereas the iterative methods are free from such inaccuracies.

The disadvantage of the iterative methods is that they can not be applied to all systems of equations. The sufficient condition for their use is that the system of equations should be diagonally dominant. In other words, after rearranging the equations, if necessary, the larger coefficients must be along the leading diagonal of the coefficient matrix. Successful use of iteration process requires that the moduli of diagonal coefficients of given systems should be large in comparison with the moduli of non-diagonal coefficients.

Among the iterative methods, we will first discuss Jacobi's method and then Gauss-Seidel method. It is known that for a given system of equations, the Gauss-Seidel method converges more rapidly than the Jacobi's method.

7.10. JACOBI'S ITERATIVE METHOD

OR

METHOD OF SIMULTANEOUS DISPLACEMENTS

Consider a system of n simultaneous linear equations in n unknowns as

$$\left.\begin{array}{l} a_{11}x_1 + a_{12}x_2 + a_{13}x_3 + \ldots + a_{1n}x_n = b_1 \\ a_{21}x_1 + a_{22}x_2 + a_{23}x_3 + \ldots + a_{2n}x_n = b_2 \\ \vdots \qquad \vdots \qquad \vdots \qquad \vdots \qquad \vdots \\ a_{n1}x_1 + a_{n2}x_2 + a_{n3}x_3 + \ldots + a_{nn}\,x_n = b_n \end{array}\right\} \qquad \ldots(1)$$

where a_{ii} is the largest coefficient in the ith equation $(1 \le i \le n)$.

System (1) of equations can be rewritten as

$$\left.\begin{array}{l} x_1 = \dfrac{b_1}{a_{11}} - \dfrac{a_{12}}{a_{11}}x_2 - \dfrac{a_{13}}{a_{11}}x_3 - \ldots - \dfrac{a_{1n}}{a_{11}}x_n \\[2ex] x_2 = \dfrac{b_2}{a_{22}} - \dfrac{a_{21}}{a_{22}}x_1 - \dfrac{a_{23}}{a_{22}}x_3 - \ldots - \dfrac{a_{2n}}{a_{22}}x_n \\ \vdots \qquad\qquad \vdots \qquad\qquad \vdots \qquad\qquad \vdots \\ x_n = \dfrac{b_n}{a_{nn}} - \dfrac{a_{n1}}{a_{nn}}x_1 - \dfrac{a_{n2}}{a_{nn}}x_2 - \ldots - \dfrac{a_{n(n-1)}}{a_{nn}}x_{n-1} \end{array}\right\} \qquad \ldots(2)$$

Let the first approximations to the unknowns $x_1, x_2, \ldots, x_n$ be $x_1^{(1)}, x_2^{(1)}, \ldots, x_n^{(1)}$. Put the first approximation in RHS of (2) to get the results as $x_1^{(2)}, x_2^{(2)}, x_3^{(2)}, \ldots, x_n^{(2)}$, a system of second approximations.

This entire process is repeated until the values of $x_1, x_2, \ldots, x_n$ are obtained to desired accuracy *i.e.*, until successive values of each of the unknowns are sufficiently close.

Jacobi's method, if suitable to a system of equations, converges for any value of initial approximations. Generally they are taken as $x_1^{(0)} = 0, x_2^{(0)} = 0, x_3^{(0)} = 0, \ldots$ and so on in absence of any better estimates.

EXAMPLE

Example. *Solve the following system of equations by Jacobi's method:*

$$8x - 3y + 2z = 20$$
$$6x + 3y + 12z = 35$$
$$4x + 11y - z = 33.$$

Sol. The coefficient matrix of the given system is not diagonally dominant. Hence we rearrange the equations such that the elements in the coefficient matrix are diagonally dominant.

$$\left.\begin{aligned} 8x - 3y + 2z &= 20 \\ 4x + 11y - z &= 33 \\ 6x + 3y + 12z &= 35 \end{aligned}\right\} \quad \text{...(1)}$$

Now, we write the equations in the form

$$\left.\begin{aligned} x &= \frac{1}{8}(20 + 3y - 2z) \\ y &= \frac{1}{11}(33 - 4x + z) \\ z &= \frac{1}{12}(35 - 6x - 3y) \end{aligned}\right\} \quad \text{...(2)}$$

We start from an initial approximation $x^{(0)} = 0$, $y^{(0)} = 0$ and $z^{(0)} = 0$. Substituting them in (2), we get

First approximation

$$x^{(1)} = \frac{1}{8}[20 + 3(0) - 2(0)] = 2.5$$

$$y^{(1)} = \frac{1}{11}[33 - 4(0) + (0)] = 3$$

$$z^{(1)} = \frac{1}{12}[35 - 6(0) - 3(0)] = 2.9166667$$

Second approximation

$$x^{(2)} = \frac{1}{8}[20 + 3y^{(1)} - 2z^{(1)}] = 2.895833$$

$$y^{(2)} = \frac{1}{11}[33 - 4x^{(1)} + z^{(1)}] = 2.3560606$$

$$z^{(2)} = \frac{1}{12}[35 - 6x^{(1)} - 3y^{(1)}] = 0.9166666$$

Third approximation

$$x^{(3)} = \frac{1}{8}[20 + 3y^{(2)} - 2z^{(2)}] = 3.1543561$$

$$y^{(3)} = \frac{1}{11}[33 - 4x^{(2)} + z^{(2)}] = 2.030303$$

$$z^{(3)} = \frac{1}{12}[35 - 6x^{(2)} - 3y^{(2)}] = 0.8797348$$

Proceeding in this way, after 12th approximation, we find that the two successive approximations are same up to four decimal places. Hence at this stage, we get

$$x = 3.0167,\ y = 1.9858 \text{ and } z = 0.9118.$$

7.11. GAUSS-SEIDEL ITERATIVE METHOD OR METHOD OF SUCCESSIVE DISPLACEMENTS

This method is only a slight modification of Jacobi's method.

Consider a system of n simultaneous linear eqns. in n unknowns as

$$\left.\begin{array}{l} a_{11}x_1 + a_{12}x_2 + a_{13}x_3 + \ldots + a_{1n}x_n = b_1 \\ a_{21}x_1 + a_{22}x_2 + a_{23}x_3 + \ldots + a_{2n}x_n = b_2 \\ \vdots \\ a_{n1}x_1 + a_{n2}x_2 + a_{n3}x_3 + \ldots\ldots + a_{nn}x_n = b_n \end{array}\right\} \qquad \ldots(1)$$

where a_{ii} is the largest coefficient in the ith equation $(1 \le i \le n)$.

We solve each equation of the system (1) for the unknown with the largest coefficient interms of the remaining unknown. System (1) can be written as

$$\left.\begin{array}{l} x_1 = \dfrac{b_1}{a_{11}} - \dfrac{a_{12}}{a_{11}} x_2 - \dfrac{a_{13}}{a_{11}} x_3 - \ldots - \dfrac{a_{1n}}{a_{11}} x_n \\ x_2 = \dfrac{b_2}{a_{22}} - \dfrac{a_{21}}{a_{22}} x_1 - \dfrac{a_{23}}{a_{22}} x_3 - \ldots - \dfrac{a_{2n}}{a_{22}} x_n \\ \vdots \\ x_n = \dfrac{b_n}{a_{nn}} - \dfrac{a_{n1}}{a_{nn}} x_1 - \dfrac{a_{n2}}{a_{nn}} x_2 - \ldots - \dfrac{a_{n(n-1)}}{a_{nn}} x_{n-1} \end{array}\right\} \qquad \ldots(2)$$

In the first equation of (2), we substitute the first approximation $x_1^{(1)}, x_2^{(1)}, x_3^{(1)}, \ldots, x_n^{(1)}$ into RHS. and denote the result as $x_1^{(2)}$.

In the second equation, we substitute $x_1^{(2)}, x_2^{(1)}, x_3^{(1)}, \ldots, x_n^{(1)}$ and denote the result as $x_2^{(2)}$. In the third equation, we substitute $x_1^{(2)}, x_2^{(2)}, x_3^{(1)}, \ldots, x_n^{(1)}$ and denote the result as $x_3^{(2)}$.

In this manner, we complete the first stage of iteration and the entire process is repeated till the values of $x_1, x_2, x_3, \ldots, x_n$ are obtained to the accuracy required.

This method uses an improved component as soon as it is available therefore it is also called the **method of successive displacements.**

For any choice of first approximation $x_j^{(1)}$ $(1 \le j \le n)$, Gauss-Seidel method converges if every equation of (2) satisfies the condition $\sum_{j=1, j \ne i}^{n} \left| \dfrac{a_{ij}}{a_{ii}} \right| \le 1, (1 \le i \le n)$, where '<' sign should be valid in case of at least one equation.

For any choice of first approximation $x_j^{(1)}$ $(1 \le j \le n)$, both Jacobi and Gauss-Seidel methods converge if every equation of (2) satisfies the condition $\sum_{j=1, j \ne i}^{n} \left| \dfrac{a_{ij}}{a_{ii}} \right| \le 1, (1 \le i \le n)$ where '<' sign should be valid in case of at least one equation.

The rate of convergence of Gauss-Seidel method is approximately twice that of Jacobi's method.

7.11.1. Algorithm of Gauss-Seidel Method

```
 1. Input n
 2. For i=1,n
 3. For j=1,n+1
 4. Input a(i,j)
 5. Next j
 6. Next i
 7. For i=1,n
 8. x(i)=0
 9. y(i)=0
10. Next i
11. itr=0
12. itr=itr+1
13. For i=1,n
14. x(i)=a(i,n+1)
15. For j=1,n
16. If i=j goto step 15
17. x(i)=x(i)-a(i,j)*x(j)
18. Next j
19. x(i)=x(i)/a(i,i)
20. Next i
21. For k=1,n
22. If abs(x(k)-y(k))>0.0001 goto step 23
      ELSE
      goto step 21
23. Print itr
24. For i=1,n
25. y(i)=x(i)
26. Print x(i)
27. Next i
28. GOTO step 12
29. Next k
30. Stop
```

7.11.2. Flow Chart of Gauss-Seidel Method

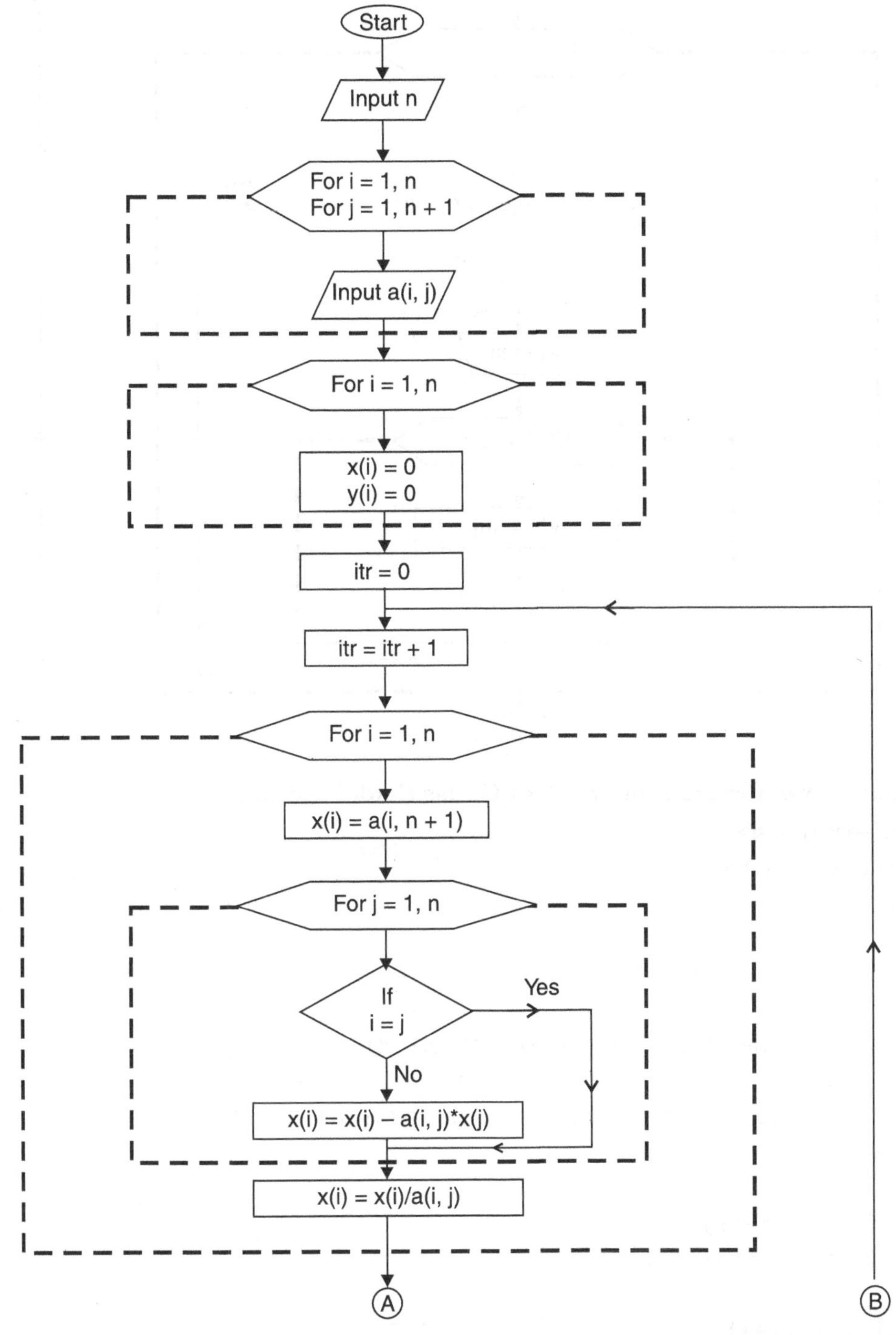

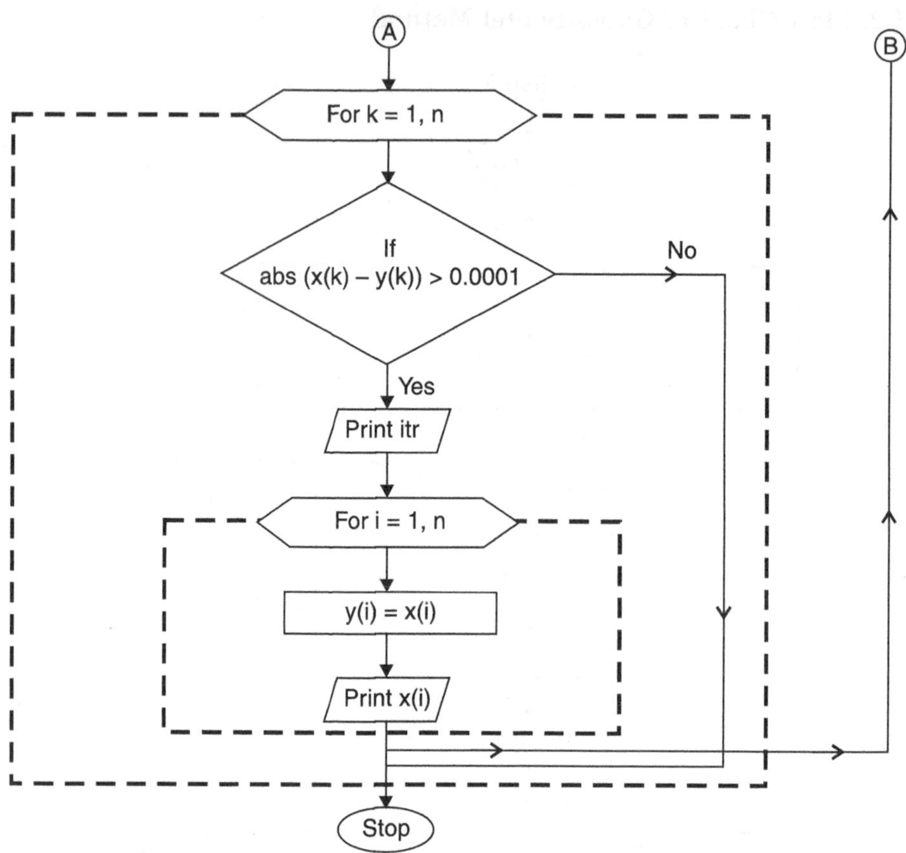

7.11.3. Computer Programme in 'C' of Gauss-Seidel Method

```
#include<math.h>
#include<stdio.h>
main()
{
float x[10],y[10],a[10][10];
int i,j,k,n,itr;
printf("\n ENTER THE SIZE OF MATRIX n: ");
scanf ("%d", &n);
printf("\n ENTER MATRIX ELEMENTS AND RHS:\n");
for(i=1;i<=n;i++)
   {
   for(j=1;j<=n+1;j++)
   scanf("%f",&a[i][j]);
   }
for(i=1;i<=n;i++)
   {
    x[i]=0.0;
    y[i]=0.0;
```

```
   }
 itr=0.0;
 top:
 itr=itr+1;
 for(i=1;i<=n;i++)
   {
   x[i]=a[i][n+1];
   for(j=1;j<=n;j++)
     {
     if (i==j)
       continue;
     else
     x[i]=x[i]-a[i][j]*x[j];
     }
     x[i]=x[i]/a[i][i];
   }
 for(k=1;k<=n;k++)
 if(fabs(x[k]-y[k])>0.0001)
   {
   printf("\n  ITERATION=%d}",itr);
   for(i=1;i<=n;i++)
     {
      y[i]=x[i];
      printf("\n x(%d)=%f",i,x[i]);
      }
      goto top;
     }
 else
 continue;
 return;
 }
```

7.11.4. Output

```
ENTER THE SIZE OF MATRIX N: 3
ENTER MATRIX ELEMENTS AND RHS :
     10   -1    2    4
      1   10   -1    3
      2    3   20    7
ITERATION=1
X(1)=0.400000
X(2)=0.260000
X(3)=0.271000
```

```
ITERATION=2
X(1)=0.371800
X(2)=0.289920
X(3)=0.269332
ITERATION=3
X(1)=0.375126
X(2)=0.289421
X(3)=0.269074
```

Notations used in the Program

(*i*) **n** is the number of unknowns/equations.

(*ii*) **a** is an array which contains values of augmented matrix.

(*iii*) **x** is an array which contains values of unknowns.

EXAMPLE

Example 1. *Use Gauss-Seidel iterative method to solve the following system of simultaneous equations:*

$$9x + 4y + z = -17$$
$$x - 2y - 6z = 14$$
$$x + 6y = 4$$

Perform four iterations. [U.P.T.U. (MCA) 2007]

Sol. The coefficient matrix of the given system is not diagonally dominant. Hence rearranging the equations as

$$9x + 4y + z = -17$$
$$x + 6y = 4$$
$$x - 2y - 6z = 14$$

Now, Gauss-Seidel's iterative method can be applied.

From the above equations, we get

$$x = \frac{1}{9}(-17 - 4y - z) \quad ...(1)$$

$$y = \frac{1}{6}(4 - x) \quad ...(2)$$

$$z = \frac{1}{6}(x - 2y - 14) \quad ...(3)$$

First approximation

Starting with $y = 0 = z$, we obtain

$$x^{(1)} = -\frac{17}{9} = -1.8888$$

Now, putting $x = -1.888$ and $z = 0$ in eqn. (2), we get

$$y^{(1)} = 0.9815$$

Again putting $x = -1.888$ and $y = 0.9815$ in eqn. (3), we get

$$z^{(1)} = -2.9753$$

Second approximation

$$x^{(2)} = \frac{1}{9}\{-17 - 4y^{(1)} - z^{(1)}\} = -1.9945$$

$$y^{(2)} = \frac{1}{6}\{4 - x^{(2)}\} = 0.9991$$

$$z^{(2)} = \frac{1}{6}\{x^{(2)} - 2y^{(2)} - 14\} = -2.9988$$

Third approximation

$$x^{(3)} = -1.9997$$
$$y^{(3)} = 0.9999$$
$$z^{(3)} = -2.9999$$

Fourth approximation

$$x^{(4)} = -1.9999 \approx -2$$
$$y^{(4)} = 0.9999 \approx 1$$
$$z^{(4)} = -2.9999 \approx -3$$

Hence after four iterations, we obtain

$$x = -2, y = 1, z = -3.$$

Example 2. *Solve the following system of equations using Gauss-Seidel iterative method:*

$$2x + 10y + z = 51$$
$$10x + y + 2z = 44$$
$$x + 2y + 10z = 61$$

[U.P.T.U. (MCA) 2009]

Sol. The given system is not diagonally dominant. Hence rearranging the equations as

$$10x + y + 2z = 44$$
$$2x + 10y + z = 51$$
$$x + 2y + 10z = 61$$

Now, Gauss-Seidel's iterative method can be applied.

From the above equations, we get

$$x = \frac{1}{10}(44 - y - 2z) \quad \text{...(1)}$$

$$y = \frac{1}{10}(51 - 2x - z) \quad \text{...(2)}$$

$$z = \frac{1}{10}(61 - x - 2y) \quad \text{...(3)}$$

First approximation.

Starting with $y = 0 = z$, we obtain from (1),

$$x^{(1)} = 4.4$$

Now, putting $x = 4.4$ and $z = 0$ in equation (2), we get

$$y^{(1)} = 4.22$$

Again, putting $x = 4.4$ and $y = 4.22$ in equation (3), we get

$$z^{(1)} = 4.816$$

Second approximation.

$$x^{(2)} = 3.0148$$
$$y^{(2)} = 4.01544$$
$$z^{(2)} = 4.995432$$

Third approximation

$$x^{(3)} = 2.9993696$$
$$y^{(3)} = 4.00058288$$
$$z^{(3)} = 4.999946464$$

Fourth approximation.

$$x^{(4)} = 2.999952419 \approx 3$$
$$y^{(4)} = 4.00001487 \approx 4$$
$$z^{(4)} = 5.000001784 \approx 5$$

Hence after four iterations, we obtain

$$x = 3, y = 4 \quad \text{and} \quad z = 5$$

Example 3. *Solve the following system of equations by Gauss-Seidel iterative method:*

$$20x + y - 2z = 17$$
$$3x + 20y - z = -18$$
$$2x - 3y + 20z = 25$$

[M.T.U. 2013; U.P.T.U. 2009]

Sol. The given system is diagonally dominant hence, from the given equations, we obtain

$$x = \frac{1}{20}(17 - y + 2z) \qquad ...(1)$$

$$y = \frac{1}{20}(-18 - 3x + z) \qquad ...(2)$$

$$z = \frac{1}{20}(25 - 2x + 3y) \qquad ...(3)$$

First Approximation

Starting with $y = 0 = z$, we obtain from (1),

$$x^{(1)} = 0.85$$

Now, putting $x = 0.85$, $z = 0$ in equation (2), we get

$$y^{(1)} = -1.0275$$

Again, putting $x = 0.85$ and $y = -1.0275$ in eqn. (3), we get

$$z^{(1)} = 1.010875$$

Second Approximation

$$x^{(2)} = 1.0024625$$
$$y^{(2)} = -0.999825625$$
$$z^{(2)} = 0.999779906$$

Third Approximation

$$x^{(3)} = 0.999969271 \approx 1$$
$$y^{(3)} = -1.000006395 \approx -1$$
$$z^{(3)} = 1.000002114 \approx 1$$

Hence after three approximations, we obtain

$$x = 1, y = -1, z = 1$$

ASSIGNMENT

1. Test if the following system of equations is diagonally dominant and hence solve this system using Gauss-Seidel method:

$$2x_1 + x_2 + 4x_3 = 7$$
$$3x_1 + x_2 + 2x_3 = 6$$
$$-x_1 + 4x_2 + 2x_3 = 5$$

(G.B.T.U. 2011)

2. Obtain the solution of the following system of equations using Gauss-Seidel iterative method:

$$2x - 7y - 10z = -17$$
$$5x + y + 3z = 14$$
$$x + 10y + 9z = 7$$

Perform three iterations. *[G.B.T.U. (MCA) 2011]*

3. Define diagonally dominant system of equations. Solve the following system of equations using Gauss-Seidel method:

$$10x + 15y + 3z = 14$$
$$-30x + y + 5z = 17$$
$$x + y + 4z = 3$$

(G.B.T.U. 2012)

4. Solve by Gauss-Seidel iterative method:

(i)
$$10x + 2y + z = 9$$
$$2x + 20y - 2z = -44$$
$$-2x + 3y + 10z = 22$$

(ii)
$$3x_1 + 2x_2 - x_3 = 7$$
$$x_1 - 3x_2 + 2x_3 = 4$$
$$-x_1 + x_2 - 3x_3 = -1$$

(iii)
$$x + 0.01y - 0.02z = 3.3354$$
$$0.02x + y - 0.05z = 4.8241$$
$$0.03x - 0.01y + z = 7.341$$

(iv)
$$10x_1 - x_2 + 2x_3 = 4$$
$$x_1 + 10x_2 + x_3 = 7$$
$$2x_1 + 3x_2 + 20x_3 = 13$$

(v)
$$6x_1 - 3x_2 + x_3 = 11$$
$$x_1 - 7x_2 + x_3 = 10$$
$$2x_1 + x_2 - 8x_3 = -15$$

(G.B.T.U. 2013, 2011)

(vi)
$$8x - 3y + 2z = 20$$
$$6x + 3y + 12z = 35$$
$$4x + 11y - z = 33$$

[G.B.T.U. (M. Tech.) 2010]

(vii)
$$27x + 6y - z = 85$$
$$6x + 15y + 2z = 72$$
$$x + y + 54z = 110$$

(M.T.U. 2012)

(viii)
$$83x + 11y - 4z = 95$$
$$7x + 52y + 13z = 104$$
$$3x + 8y + 29z = 71$$

(M.T.U. 2014)

5. Describe a method for solving a system of linear equations. Solve the following system of linear equations using Gauss-Seidel method:

$$23x_1 + 13x_2 + 3x_3 = 29$$
$$5x_1 + 23x_2 + 7x_3 = 37$$
$$11x_1 + x_2 + 23x_3 = 43.$$

(U.P.T.U. 2009)

6. Solve the following equations by Gauss-Seidel procedure:

$$9x_1 + 2x_2 + 4x_3 = 20$$
$$x_1 + 10x_2 + 4x_3 = 6$$
$$2x_1 - 4x_2 + 10x_3 = -15$$

The answer should be correct to 3 significant digits. *[U.P.T.U. MCA (SUM) 2009]*

7. Using Gauss-Seidel method, solve the following system of linear algebraic equations

$$10x_1 - 2x_2 - x_3 - x_4 = 3$$
$$-2x_1 + 10x_2 - x_3 - x_4 = 15$$
$$-x_1 - x_2 + 10x_3 - 2x_4 = 27$$
$$-x_1 - x_2 - 2x_3 + 10x_4 = -9$$

correct up to four decimal places. Perform seven iterations.

8. Solve the following system of equations using Jacobi's method:

$$5x - y + z = 10$$
$$2x + 4y = 12$$
$$x + y + 5z = -1$$

Start with the solution (2, 3, 0).

9. Solve the following system of equations by Jacobi's iteration method:

(*i*)
$$3x + 4y + 15z = 54.8$$
$$x + 12y + 3z = 39.66$$
$$10x + y - 2z = 7.74$$

(*ii*)
$$54x + y + z = 110$$
$$2x + 15y + 6z = 72$$
$$-x + 6y + 27z = 85$$

(*iii*)
$$10x_1 + 2x_2 + x_3 = 9$$
$$x_1 + 10x_2 - x_3 = -22$$
$$-2x_1 + 3x_2 + 10x_3 = 22$$

10. Solve by Jacobi's method:

(*i*)
$$30x - 2y + 3z = 75$$
$$x + 17y - 2z = 48$$
$$x + y + 9z = 15$$

(*ii*)
$$10x_1 - x_2 = 17$$
$$-x_1 + 10x_2 - x_3 = 24$$
$$-x_1 + 10x_3 - x_4 = 32$$
$$-x_3 + 10x_4 = 46$$

Answers

1. $x_1 = 1, x_2 = 1, x_3 = 1$

2. $x = 1, y = -3, z = 4$

3. $x = -0.4328, y = 1.1055, z = 0.5818$

4. (*i*) $x = 1, y = -2, z = 3$ (*ii*) $x_1 = 2.72, x_2 = -1.04, x_3 = -0.92$

(*iii*) $x = 3.429, y = 5.119, z = 7.289$ (*iv*) $x_1 = 0.3567, x_2 = 0.6120, x_3 = 0.5225$

(*v*) $x_1 = 1, x_2 = -1, x_3 = 2$ (*vi*) $x = 3.016, y = 1.985, z = 0.9118$

(*vii*) $x = 2.425, y = 3.573, z = 1.925$ (*viii*) $x = 1.057, y = 1.367, z = 1.961$.

5. $x_1 = 0.4765, x_2 = 1.0189, x_3 = 1.5973$

6. $x_1 = 2.74, x_2 = 0.987, x_3 = -1.65$

7. $x_1 = 1, x_2 = 2, x_3 = 3, x_4 = 0$

8. $x = 2.555, y = 1.722, z = -1.055$

9. (*i*) $x = 1.074, y = 2.524, z = 2.765$ (*ii*) $x = 1.926, y = 3.573, z = 2.425$

(*iii*) $x_1 = 1, x_2 = -2, x_3 = 3$

10. (*i*) $x = 2.580, y = 2.798, z = 1.069$ (*ii*) $x_1 = 2, x_2 = 3, x_3 = 4, x_4 = 5$

7.12. SUCCESSIVE OVER RELAXATION (SOR) METHOD

This method was invented by Gauss. R.V. Southwell revived and popularized it by applying in structural engineering. This method is a generalization of the Gauss-seidel method. This method is often used when the coefficient matrix of the system of equations is symmetric and has 'property A'*. This method is one of the most powerful acceleration technique for speeding up the convergence of iteration techniques.

*A real matrix B is said to have 'property A' iff there exists a permutation matrix P such PBP^T $= \begin{bmatrix} A_{11} & A_{12} \\ A_{21} & A_{22} \end{bmatrix}$ where A_{11} and A_{22} are diagonal matrices.

In this iterative method, initially assumed values of the unknowns are improved by reducing the so called **residuals** to zero or as close as possible to zero.

The residual of ith equation at m^{th} iteration is denoted by $R_i^{(m)}$ and is given by

$$R_i^{(m)} = b_i - a_{i1}\, x_1^{(m)} - a_{i2}\, x_2^{(m)} - \ldots\ldots - a_{in}\, x_n^{(m)}$$

where $x_j^{(m)}$ gives the value of x_j at m^{th} iteration.

To achieve the fast convergence, we take all the terms to one side and reorder the equations so that the largest negative coefficients in the equations appear on the diagonal. Now, if at any iteration, R_i is the largest residual in magnitude then we give an increment

$$dx_i = -\frac{R_i}{a_{ii}} \text{ to } x_i.$$

In other words, we replace x_i to $x_i + d\,x_i$ to reduce R_i to zero. Very often, we start with the initial values $x_1 = 0, x_2 = 0, x_3 = 0, \ldots, x_n = 0$.

The convergence conditions for iterative methods must be satisfied for convergence of relaxation method also.

Example. *Solve the following system of equations*

$$6x - 3y + z = 11$$
$$2x + y - 8z = -15$$
$$x - 7y + z = 10$$

by the relaxation method.

Sol. First of all, we transfer all the terms on one side and reorder the equations so that the largest coefficients in the equations appear on the diagonal.

Therefore,
$$\left.\begin{aligned} 0 &= 11 - 6x + 3y - z \\ 0 &= 10 - x + 7y - z \\ 0 &= -15 - 2x - y + 8z \end{aligned}\right\} \quad \ldots(1)$$

Starting with $x = 0, y = 0, z = 0$, we find the residuals, $R_1 = 11, R_2 = 10, R_3 = -15$ of which the largest residual in magnitude is R_3.

It indicates that the third equation has more error and it needs immediate attention for improvement.

We introduce a change dz in z such that

$$dz = -\frac{R_3}{a_{33}} = \frac{15}{8} = 1.875$$

Similarly, we find the new residuals of large magnitude and relax it to zero and so on. We will continue this process until all the residuals are zero or very small.

Following table is constructed after detailed calculations:

Iteration Number	*Residuals* R_1	R_2	R_3	*Maximum* R_i	*Difference* dx_i	*Variables* x	y	z
0	11	10	– 15	– 15	$\frac{15}{8} = 1.875$	0	0	0
1	9.125	8.125	0	9.125	$\frac{-9.125}{-6} = 1.5288$	0	0	1.875
2	0.0002	6.6042	– 3.0416	6.6042	$\frac{-6.6042}{7} = -0.9434$	1.5208	0	1.875
3	– 2.83	0.0004	– 2.0982	– 2.83	$\frac{2.83}{(-6)} = -0.4716$	1.5208	– 0.9434	1.875
4	– .0004	0.472	– 1.155	– 1.155	$\frac{1.155}{8} = 0.1443$	1.0492	– 0.9434	1.875
5	– .1447	0.3277	– 0.0006	0.3277	$\frac{-0.3277}{7} = -0.0468$	1.0492	– 0.9434	2.0193
6	– .2851	0.0001	0.0462	– 0.2851	$\frac{0.2851}{-6} = -0.0475$	1.0492	– 0.9902	2.0193
7	– .0001	0.0476	0.1412	0.1412	$-\frac{0.1412}{8} = -0.0176$	1.0017	– 0.9902	2.0193
8	.0175	0.0652	0.0004	0.0652	$-\frac{.0652}{7} = -.0093$	1.0017	– 0.9902	2.0017
9	– .0104	0.0001	0.0097	—	—	1.0017	– 0.9995	2.0017

At this stage, we observe that all the residuals R_1, R_2 and R_3 are small enough and therefore we may take the corresponding values of x, y, z at this iteration as the solution. Hence the numerical solution to the given system is given by

$$x = 1.0017,\ y = -0.9995,\ z = 2.0017$$

The exact solution is found to be

$$x = 1.0,\ y = -1.0,\ z = 2.0.$$

ASSIGNMENT

Solve by relaxation method, the following system of equations:

1.
$$x + 9y - z = 10$$
$$2x - y + 11z = 20$$
$$10x - 2y + z = 12$$

2.
$$27x + 6y - z = 85$$
$$6x + 15y + 2z = 72$$
$$x + y + 54z = 110$$

Answers

1. $x = 1.2624,\ y = 1.1591,\ z = 1.6940$ **2.** $x = 2.426,\ y = 3.572,\ z = 1.926$

7.13. VECTOR NORM

The non-negative quantity $\| \mathbf{x} \|$ is a measure of the size or length of a vector satisfying:

(*i*) $\| \mathbf{x} \| > 0$ for $\mathbf{x} \neq \mathbf{0}$ and $\| \mathbf{0} \| = 0$

(*ii*) $\| c\mathbf{x} \| = | c | \, \| \mathbf{x} \|$, for an arbitrary complex no. c.

(*iii*) $\| \mathbf{x} + \mathbf{y} \| \leq \| \mathbf{x} \| + \| \mathbf{y} \|$

The commonly used norms are

(*i*) **Absolute norm** (l_1 norm):

$$\| \mathbf{x} \|_1 = \sum_{i=1}^{n} | x_i |$$

(*ii*) **Euclidean norm:**

$$\| \mathbf{x} \|_2 = (\mathbf{x} * \mathbf{x})^{1/2} = \left(\sum_{i=1}^{n} | x_i |^2 \right)^{1/2}$$

(*iii*) **Maximum norm** (l_∞ norm):

$$\| \mathbf{x} \|_\infty = \max_{1 \leq i \leq n} | x_i |$$

7.14. MATRIX NORM

The matrix norm $\| \mathbf{A} \|$ is a non-negative number which satisfies the properties:

(*i*) $\| \mathbf{A} \| > 0$ if $\mathbf{A} \neq \mathbf{0}$ and $\| \mathbf{0} \| = 0$,

(*ii*) $\| c\mathbf{A} \| = | c | \, \| \mathbf{A} \|$ for an arbitrary complex no. c

(*iii*) $\| \mathbf{A} + \mathbf{B} \| \leq \| \mathbf{A} \| + \| \mathbf{B} \|$

(*iv*) $\| \mathbf{AB} \| \leq \| \mathbf{A} \| \, \| \mathbf{B} \|$

Most commonly used matrix norms are:

(*i*) **Frobenius or Euclidean norm**

$$\mathrm{F}(\mathbf{A}) = \left(\sum_{i,j=1}^{n} | a_{ij} |^2 \right)^{1/2}$$

(*ii*) **Maximum norm**

$$\| \mathbf{A} \| = \| \mathbf{A} \|_\infty = \max_i \sum_k | a_{ik} | \text{ (max. absolute row sum)}$$

$$\| \mathbf{A} \| = \| \mathbf{A} \|_1 = \max_k \sum_i | a_{ik} | \text{ (max. absolute column sum)}$$

(*iii*) **Hilbert norm or Spectral norm**

$$\| \mathbf{A} \|_2 = \sqrt{\lambda} \quad \text{where } \lambda = \rho(\mathbf{A} * \mathbf{A})$$

If $\mathbf{A}$ is Hermitain or real and symmetric then

$$\lambda = \rho(\mathbf{A}^2) = \rho^2(\mathbf{A})$$

so that $$\| \mathbf{A} \|_2 = \rho(\mathbf{A})$$

The matrix norm must be consistent with the vector norm for any vector **x** and matrix **A** *i.e.*,

$$\| \mathbf{A}x \| \leq \| \mathbf{A} \| \, \| x \|$$

7.15. CONDITION NUMBER

The quantity $k(\mathbf{A}) = \| \mathbf{A}^{-1} \| \, \| \mathbf{A} \|$ is called the condition number of the matrix **A** and is denoted by cond (**A**).

If $k(\mathbf{A})$ is small then small changes in **A** or **b** produce only small changes while if $k(\mathbf{A})$ is large, then system $\mathbf{Ax} = \mathbf{b}$ is said to be **ill-conditioned**. If $k(\mathbf{A})$ is near unity then the system is **well-conditioned.**

If $\| \cdot \|$ is spectral norm, then

$$k(\mathbf{A}) = \| \mathbf{A} \|_2 \, \| \mathbf{A}^{-1} \|_2 = \sqrt{\frac{\lambda}{\mu}}$$

where λ and μ are the largest and smallest eigen values in modulus of $\mathbf{A} * \mathbf{A}$. If **A** is Hermitian or real and symmetric then we have

$$k(\mathbf{A}) = \frac{\lambda *}{\mu *}$$

where λ^* and μ^* are the largest and smallest eigen values in modulus of **A**.

EXAMPLES

Example 1. *Determine the condition number of the matrix*

$$\mathbf{A} = \begin{bmatrix} 1 & 4 & 9 \\ 4 & 9 & 16 \\ 9 & 16 & 25 \end{bmatrix}$$

using the maximum absolute row sum norm.

Sol. We have, $$\mathbf{A}^{-1} = -\frac{1}{8}\begin{bmatrix} -31 & 44 & -17 \\ 44 & -56 & 20 \\ -17 & 20 & -7 \end{bmatrix}$$

$$\| \mathbf{A} \|_\infty = \text{max. absolute row sum norm for } \mathbf{A}$$

$$= \text{max. } \{14, 29, 50\} = 50$$

$$\| \mathbf{A}^{-1} \|_\infty = \text{max. absolute row sum norm for } \mathbf{A}^{-1}$$

$$= \text{max. } \left\{ \left(\frac{31}{8} + \frac{44}{8} + \frac{17}{8} \right), \left(\frac{44}{8} + \frac{56}{8} + \frac{20}{8} \right), \left(\frac{17}{8} + \frac{20}{8} + \frac{7}{8} \right) \right\}$$

$$= \text{max. } \left\{ \left(\frac{92}{8}, 15, \frac{44}{8} \right) \right\} = 15$$

$\therefore$ $$k(\mathbf{A}) = \| \mathbf{A} \|_\infty \, \| \mathbf{A}^{-1} \|_\infty = 750$$

Example 2. *Find the condition number of the system*

$$\begin{bmatrix} 2.1 & 1.8 \\ 6.2 & 5.3 \end{bmatrix} \begin{bmatrix} x_1 \\ x_2 \end{bmatrix} = \begin{bmatrix} 2.1 \\ 6.2 \end{bmatrix}$$

Sol. Using the spectral norm, we have

$$\mathbf{A}^*\mathbf{A} = \mathbf{A}^T\mathbf{A} = \begin{bmatrix} 42.85 & 36.64 \\ 36.64 & 31.33 \end{bmatrix}$$

Characteristic equation is

$$\lambda^2 - 74.18\,\lambda + 0.009 = 0$$

$$\Rightarrow \qquad \lambda_1 = 74.17998787$$

$$\lambda_2 = 0.000012132$$

which are the eigen values of $\mathbf{A}^*\mathbf{A}$.

Hence the condition number is

$$k(\mathbf{A}) = \sqrt{\frac{\lambda_1}{\lambda_2}} = 2472.73$$

Hence this system of equations is highly ill-conditioned and is very sensitive to round-off errors.

ASSIGNMENT

1. Determine the Euclidean and maximum absolute row sum norms of the matrix

$$\mathbf{A} = \begin{bmatrix} 1 & 7 & -4 \\ 4 & -4 & 9 \\ 12 & -1 & 3 \end{bmatrix}$$

2. Let

$$\mathbf{A}(\alpha) = \begin{bmatrix} 0.1\,\alpha & 0.1\,\alpha \\ 1.0 & 1.5 \end{bmatrix}$$

Determine α such that cond($\mathbf{A}(\alpha)$) is minimized. Use the maximum norm.

Answers

1. 18.25, 17

2. $\alpha = 12.5$, Min. Value of cond($\mathbf{A}(\alpha)$) = 11

❑❑❑

8

Numerical Solution of Ordinary Differential Equations

8.1. INTRODUCTION

A physical situation that concerns with the rate of change of one quantity with respect to another gives rise to a differential equation.

Consider the first order ordinary differential equation

$$\frac{dy}{dx} = f(x, y) \qquad \text{...(1)}$$

with the initial condition

$$y(x_0) = y_0 \qquad \text{...(2)}$$

Many analytical techniques exist for solving such equations. But these methods can be applied to solve only a selected class of differential equations.

However, a majority of differential equations appearing in physical problems cannot be solved analytically. Thus it becomes imperative to discuss their solution by numerical methods.

In numerical methods, we donot proceed in the hope of finding a relation between variables but we find the numerical values of the dependent variable for certain values of independent variable.

8.2. INITIAL-VALUE AND BOUNDARY-VALUE PROBLEMS *(M.T.U. 2012)*

Problems in which all the conditions are specified at the initial point only are called **initial-value problems**. For example, the problem given by eqns. (1) and (2) is an initial value problem.

Problems involving second and higher order differential equations, in which the conditions at two or more points are specified, are called **boundary-value problems**.

To obtain a unique solution of nth order ordinary differential equation, it is necessary to specify n values of the dependent variable and/or its derivative at specific values of independent variable.

8.3. SINGLE-STEP AND MULTI-STEP METHODS

The numerical solutions are obtained step-by-step through a series of equal intervals in the independent variable so that as soon as the solution y has been obtained at $x = x_i$, the next step consists of evaluating y_{i+1} at $x = x_{i+1}$. The methods which require only the numerical value y_i in order to compute the next value y_{i+1} for solving equation (1) given above are termed as **single-step methods.**

The methods which require not only the numerical value y_i but also at least one of the past values $y_{i-1}, y_{i-2}, ...$ are termed as **multi-step methods.**

8.4. COMPARISON OF SINGLE-STEP AND MULTI-STEP METHODS

The single-step method has obvious advantages over the multi-step methods that use several past values $(y_n, y_{n-1}, ..., y_{n-p})$ and that require initial values $(y_1, y_2, ..., y_n)$ that have to be calculated by another method.

The major disadvantage of single-step method is that they use many more evaluations of the derivative to attain the same degree of accuracy compared with the multi-step methods.

8.5. NUMERICAL METHODS OF SOLUTION OF O.D.E.

Here, we will discuss various numerical methods of solving ordinary differential equations.

We must know that these methods will yield the solution in one of the two forms:

(*a*) A series for y in terms of powers of x from which the value of y can be obtained by direct substitution.

(*b*) A set of tabulated values of x and y.

Picard's method belong to class (*a*) while those of Euler's, Runge-Kutta, Adams Bashforth, Milne's etc., belong to class (*b*). Methods which belong to class (*b*) are called **step-by-step methods** or **marching methods** because the values of y are computed by short steps ahead for equal intervals of the independent variable.

In Euler's and Runge-Kutta methods, the interval range h should be kept small hence they can be applied for tabulating y only over a limited range. To get functional values over a wide range, Adams Bashforth, Milne's etc., methods may be used since they use finite differences and require starting values usually obtained by Taylor's or R-K methods.

8.6. PICARD'S METHOD OF SUCCESSIVE APPROXIMATIONS

Emile Picard (1856–1941) was a distinguished Professor of Mathematics at the University of Paris, France. He was famous for his researches on the Theory of Functions.

Consider the differential equation

$$\frac{dy}{dx} = f(x, y); \quad y(x_0) = y_0 \qquad ...(1)$$

Integrating eqn. (1) between the limits x_0 and x and the corresponding limits y_0 and y, we get

$$\int_{y_0}^{y} dy = \int_{x_0}^{x} f(x, y)\, dx$$

$$\Rightarrow \qquad y - y_0 = \int_{x_0}^{x} f(x, y)\, dx$$

or,
$$y = y_0 + \int_{x_0}^{x} f(x, y)\, dx \qquad \text{...(2)}$$

In equation (2), the unknown function y appears under the integral sign. Such type of equation is called integral equation.

This equation can be solved by the method of successive approximations or iterations.

To obtain the first approximation, we replace y by y_0 in the RHS of eqn. (2).

Now, the first approximation is

$$y^{(1)} = y_0 + \int_{x_0}^{x} f(x, y_0)\, dx \qquad \text{...(3)}$$

The integrand is a function of x alone and can be integrated.

For a second approximation, replace y_0 by $y^{(1)}$ in $f(x, y_0)$ which gives

$$y^{(2)} = y_0 + \int_{x_0}^{x} f\{x, y^{(1)}\}\, dx \qquad \text{...(4)}$$

Proceeding in this way, we obtain $y^{(3)}, y^{(4)}, \ldots\ldots, y^{(n-1)}$ and $y^{(n)}$ where

$$y^{(n)} = y_0 + \int_{x_0}^{x} f\{x, y^{(n-1)}\}\, dx \text{ with } y(x_0) = y_0$$

As a matter of fact, the process is stopped when the two values of y *viz.* $y^{(n-1)}$ and $y^{(n)}$ are same to the desired degree of accuracy.

Picard's method is of theoretical value considerably. Practically, it is unsatisfactory because of the difficulties which arise in performing the necessary integrations. However, each step gives a better approximation of the required solution than the preceding one.

EXAMPLES

Example 1. *Use Picard's method to obtain y for x = 0.2. Given:*

$$\frac{dy}{dx} = x - y \text{ with initial condition } y = 1 \text{ when } x = 0.$$

Sol. Here $\quad f(x, y) = x - y, \quad x_0 = 0, y_0 = 1$

We have first approximation,

$$y^{(1)} = y_0 + \int_0^x f(x, y_0)\, dx = 1 + \int_0^x (x - 1)\, dx = 1 - x + \frac{x^2}{2}$$

Second approximation,

$$y^{(2)} = y_0 + \int_0^x f\{x, y^{(1)}\}\, dx = 1 + \int_0^x \{x - y^{(1)}\}\, dx$$

$$= 1 + \int_0^x \left(x - 1 + x - \frac{x^2}{2}\right) dx = 1 - x + x^2 - \frac{x^3}{6}$$

Third approximation,

$$y^{(3)} = y_0 + \int_0^x f\{x, y^{(2)}\}\,dx = 1 + \int_0^x \{x - y^{(2)}\}\,dx$$

$$= 1 + \int_0^x \left(x - 1 + x - x^2 + \frac{x^3}{6}\right) dx$$

$$= 1 - x + x^2 - \frac{x^3}{3} + \frac{x^4}{24}$$

Fourth approximation,

$$y^{(4)} = y_0 + \int_0^x f\{x, y^{(3)}\}\,dx = 1 + \int_0^x \{x - y^{(3)}\}\,dx$$

$$= 1 + \int_0^x \left(x - 1 + x - x^2 + \frac{x^3}{3} - \frac{x^4}{24}\right) dx$$

$$= 1 - x + x^2 - \frac{x^3}{3} + \frac{x^4}{12} - \frac{x^5}{120}$$

When $x = 0.2$, we get

$$y^{(1)} = 0.82,\ y^{(2)} = 0.83867,\ y^{(3)} = 0.83740,\ y^{(4)} = 0.83746$$

Since $y^{(3)}$ and $y^{(4)}$ are same upto four decimal places, therefore,

$$y(0.2) = 0.8374.$$

Example 2. *Using Picard's method of successive approximations, obtain a solution up to fifth approximation of the equation* $\frac{dy}{dx} = y + x$ *such that* $y = 1$ *when* $x = 0$.

Sol. We have,

$$f(x, y) = y + x,\ x_0 = 0,\ y_0 = 1$$

First approximation,

$$y^{(1)} = y_0 + \int_{x_0}^x f(x, y_0)\,dx = y_0 + \int_0^x (x + y_0)\,dx$$

$$= 1 + \int_0^x (x + 1)\,dx = 1 + x + \frac{x^2}{2}$$

Second approximation,

$$y^{(2)} = y_0 + \int_0^x f\{x, y^{(1)}\}\,dx = 1 + \int_0^x \{x + y^{(1)}\}\,dx$$

$$= 1 + \int_0^x \left(x + 1 + x + \frac{x^2}{2}\right) dx = 1 + x + x^2 + \frac{x^3}{6}$$

Third approximation,

$$y^{(3)} = y_0 + \int_0^x f\{x, y^{(2)}\}\,dx = 1 + \int_0^x \{x + y^{(2)}\}\,dx$$

$$= 1 + \int_0^x \left(x + 1 + x + x^2 + \frac{x^3}{6} \right) dx = 1 + x + x^2 + \frac{x^3}{3} + \frac{x^4}{24}$$

Fourth approximation,

$$y^{(4)} = y_0 + \int_0^x f\{x, y^{(3)}\} \, dx$$

$$= 1 + \int_0^x \left(x + 1 + x + x^2 + \frac{x^3}{3} + \frac{x^4}{24} \right) dx$$

$$= 1 + x + x^2 + \frac{x^3}{3} + \frac{x^4}{12} + \frac{x^5}{120}$$

Fifth approximation,

$$y^{(5)} = y_0 + \int_0^x f\{x, y^{(4)}\} \, dx$$

$$= 1 + \int_0^x \left(x + 1 + x + x^2 + \frac{x^3}{3} + \frac{x^4}{12} + \frac{x^5}{120} \right) dx$$

$$= 1 + x + x^2 + \frac{x^3}{3} + \frac{x^4}{12} + \frac{x^5}{60} + \frac{x^6}{720}$$

Example 3. *If* $\frac{dy}{dx} = \frac{y - x}{y + x}$, *find the value of y at x = 0.1 using Picard's method. Given that y(0) = 1.*

Sol. First approximation,

$$y^{(1)} = y_0 + \int_0^x \frac{y_0 - x}{y_0 + x} \, dx = 1 + \int_0^x \left(\frac{1 - x}{1 + x} \right) dx$$

$$= 1 + \int_0^x \left(\frac{2}{1 + x} - 1 \right) dx = 1 - x + 2 \log (1 + x)$$

Second approximation,

$$y^{(2)} = 1 + x - 2 \int_0^x \frac{x \, dx}{1 + 2 \log (1 + x)}$$

which is difficult to integrate.

Thus, when $x = 0.1$, $y^{(1)} = 1 - 0.1 + 2 \log (1.1) = 1.09062$

Here in this example, only I approximation can be obtained and so it gives the approximate value of y for $x = 0.1$.

Example 4. *Given the differential equation* $\frac{dy}{dx} = \frac{x^2}{y^2 + 1}$

with the initial condition y = 0 when x = 0. Use Picard's method to obtain y for x = 0.25, 0.5 and 1.0 correct to three decimal places.

Sol. The given initial value problem is

$$\frac{dy}{dx} = f(x, y) = \frac{x^2}{y^2+1} \qquad \text{where } y_0 = 0 \text{ at } x_0 = 0$$

We have first approximation,

$$y^{(1)} = y_0 + \int_{x_0}^{x} f(x, y_0)\, dx = 0 + \int_0^x \frac{x^2}{0+1}\, dx = \frac{1}{3}x^3 \qquad ...(1)$$

Second approximation,

$$y^{(2)} = y_0 + \int_{x_0}^{x} f\{x, y^{(1)}\}\, dx$$

$$= 0 + \int_0^x \frac{x^2}{\left(\frac{x^3}{3}\right)^2 + 1}\, dx = \tan^{-1}\frac{x^3}{3}$$

$$= \frac{1}{3}x^3 - \frac{1}{3}\left(\frac{1}{3}x^3\right)^3 + ... = \frac{1}{3}x^3 - \frac{1}{81}x^9 + ... \qquad ...(2)$$

From (1) and (2), we see that $y^{(1)}$ and $y^{(2)}$ agree to the first term $\frac{x^3}{3}$. To find the range of values of x so that the series with the term $\frac{1}{3}x^3$ alone will give the result correct to three decimal places, we put

$$\frac{1}{81}x^9 \le 0.0005$$

which gives, $\quad x^9 \le 0.0405 \quad \text{or} \quad x \le 0.7$

Hence, $\quad y(0.25) = \frac{1}{3}(0.25)^3 = 0.005 \quad$ and $\quad y(0.5) = \frac{1}{3}(0.5)^3 = 0.042$

To find $y(1.0)$, we make use of eqn. (2) which gives,

$$y(1.0) = \frac{1}{3} - \frac{1}{81} = 0.321.$$

8.7. PICARD'S METHOD FOR SIMULTANEOUS FIRST ORDER DIFFERENTIAL EQUATIONS

Let $\quad \frac{dy}{dx} = \phi(x, y, z) \quad \text{and} \quad \frac{dz}{dx} = f(x, y, z)$

be the simultaneous differential equations with initial conditions $y(x_0) = y_0$; $z(x_0) = z_0$.

Picard's method gives

$$y^{(1)} = y_0 + \int_{x_0}^{x} \phi(x, y_0, z_0)\, dx;\; z^{(1)} = z_0 + \int_{x_0}^{x} f(x, y_0, z_0)\, dx$$

$$y^{(2)} = y_0 + \int_{x_0}^{x} \phi\{x, y^{(1)}, z^{(1)}\}\, dx;\; z^{(2)} = z_0 + \int_{x_0}^{x} f\{x, y^{(1)}, z^{(1)}\}\, dx$$

and so on as successive approximations.

8.8. PICARD'S METHOD FOR SECOND ORDER DIFFERENTIAL EQUATIONS

Consider the second order differential equation

$$\frac{d^2y}{dx^2} = f\left(x, y, \frac{dy}{dx}\right)$$

By putting $\frac{dy}{dx} = z$, it can be reduced to two first order simultaneous differential equations:

$$\frac{dy}{dx} = z \quad \text{and} \quad \frac{dz}{dx} = f(x, y, z)$$

which can be solved easily as explained in art. 8.7.

EXAMPLES

Example 1. *Approximate y and z by using Picard's method for the particular solution of* $\frac{dy}{dx} = x + z,\ \frac{dz}{dx} = x - y^2$ *given that* $y = 2,\ z = 1$ *when* $x = 0$. (G.B.T.U. 2011)

Sol. Let $\phi(x, y, z) = x + z,\ f(x, y, z) = x - y^2$

Here, $x_0 = 0,\ y_0 = 2,\ z_0 = 1$

We have, $$\frac{dy}{dx} = \phi(x, y, z) \;\Rightarrow\; y = y_0 + \int_{x_0}^{x} \phi(x, y, z)\, dx \quad ...(1)$$

Also, $$\frac{dz}{dx} = f(x, y, z) \;\Rightarrow\; z = z_0 + \int_{x_0}^{x} f(x, y, z)\, dx \quad ...(2)$$

First approximation,

$$y^{(1)} = y_0 + \int_{x_0}^{x} \phi(x, y_0, z_0)\, dx = 2 + \int_0^x (x + z_0)\, dx$$

$$= 2 + \int_0^x (x + 1)\, dx = 2 + x + \frac{x^2}{2}$$

and $$z^{(1)} = z_0 + \int_{x_0}^{x} f(x, y_0, z_0)\, dx = 1 + \int_0^x (x - {y_0}^2)\, dx$$

$$= 1 + \int_0^x (x - 4)\, dx = 1 - 4x + \frac{x^2}{2}$$

Second approximation,

$$y^{(2)} = y_0 + \int_{x_0}^{x} \phi\{x, y^{(1)}, z^{(1)}\}\, dx = 2 + \int_0^x \{x + z^{(1)}\}\, dx$$

$$= 2 + \int_0^x \left(x + 1 - 4x + \frac{x^2}{2}\right) dx = 2 + x - \frac{3}{2}x^2 + \frac{x^3}{6}$$

$$z^{(2)} = z_0 + \int_{x_0}^{x} f\{x, y^{(1)}, z^{(1)}\}\, dx$$

$$= 1 + \int_0^x \left[x - \left(2 + x + \frac{x^2}{2}\right)^2\right] dx$$

$$= 1 - 4x - \frac{3}{2}x^2 - x^3 - \frac{x^4}{4} - \frac{x^5}{20}.$$

Example 2. *Solve by Picard's method, the differential equations* $\frac{dy}{dx} = z$, $\frac{dz}{dx} = x^3(y + z)$ *where* $y = 1$, $z = \frac{1}{2}$ *at* $x = 0$. *Obtain the values of y and z from III approximation when* $x = 0.2$ *and* $x = 0.5$.

Sol. Let $\phi(x, y, z) = z$, $f(x, y, z) = x^3(y + z)$

Here $x_0 = 0$, $y_0 = 1$, $z_0 = \frac{1}{2}$

First approximation,

$$y^{(1)} = y_0 + \int_0^x \phi(x, y_0, z_0)\, dx = 1 + \int_0^x z_0\, dx = 1 + \frac{1}{2}x$$

$$z^{(1)} = z_0 + \int_0^x f(x, y_0, z_0)\, dx = \frac{1}{2} + \int_0^x x^3(y_0 + z_0)\, dx = \frac{1}{2} + \frac{3}{8}x^4.$$

Second approximation,

$$y^{(2)} = 1 + \int_0^x z^{(1)}\, dx = 1 + \int_0^x \left(\frac{1}{2} + \frac{3}{8}x^4\right) dx = 1 + \frac{x}{2} + \frac{3}{40}x^5$$

$$z^{(2)} = \frac{1}{2} + \int_0^x x^3\{y^{(1)} + z^{(1)}\}\, dx$$

$$= \frac{1}{2} + \int_0^x x^3\left(\frac{3}{2} + \frac{x}{2} + \frac{3}{8}x^4\right) dx = \frac{1}{2} + \frac{3}{8}x^4 + \frac{x^5}{10} + \frac{3}{64}x^8$$

Third approximation,

$$y^{(3)} = 1 + \int_0^x z^{(2)}\, dx = 1 + \int_0^x \left(\frac{1}{2} + \frac{3x^4}{8} + \frac{x^5}{10} + \frac{3x^8}{64}\right) dx$$

$$= 1 + \frac{x}{2} + \frac{3}{40}x^5 + \frac{x^6}{60} + \frac{x^9}{192}$$

$$z^{(3)} = \frac{1}{2} + \int_0^x x^3\{y^{(2)} + z^{(2)}\}\, dx$$

$$= \frac{1}{2} + \int_0^x x^3 \left\{ \frac{3}{2} + \frac{x}{2} + \frac{3}{8} x^4 + \frac{7}{40} x^5 + \frac{3}{64} x^8 \right\} dx$$

$$= \frac{1}{2} + \frac{3}{8} x^4 + \frac{x^5}{10} + \frac{3}{64} x^8 + \frac{7}{360} x^9 + \frac{1}{256} x^{12}$$

When $x = 0.2$ $\quad y^{(3)} = 1 + 0.1 + \frac{3}{40}(0.2)^5 + \frac{(0.2)^6}{60} + \frac{1}{192}(0.2)^9$

$= 1.100024$ (leaving higher terms)

$$z^{(3)} = \frac{1}{2} + \frac{3}{8}(0.2)^4 + \frac{(0.2)^5}{10} + \frac{3}{64}(0.2)^8 + \frac{7}{360}(0.2)^9 + \frac{1}{256}(0.2)^{12}$$

$= 0.500632$ (leaving higher terms)

When $x = 0.5$ $\quad y^{(3)} = 1 + \frac{0.5}{2} + \frac{3}{40}(0.5)^5 + \frac{(0.5)^6}{60} + \frac{1}{192}(0.5)^9 = 1.25234375$

$$z^{(3)} = \frac{1}{2} + \frac{3}{8}(0.5)^4 + \frac{(0.5)^5}{10} + \frac{3}{64}(0.5)^8 + \frac{7}{360}(0.5)^9 + \frac{1}{256}(0.5)^{12}$$

$= 0.5234375.$

Example 3. *Use Picard's method to approximate y when x = 0.1 given that*

$$\frac{d^2y}{dx^2} + 2x \frac{dy}{dx} + y = 0 \text{ and } y = 0.5, \frac{dy}{dx} = 0.1 \text{ when } x = 0.$$

Sol. We have, $\quad \frac{d^2y}{dx^2} + 2x \frac{dy}{dx} + y = 0$ ...(1)

Let $\frac{dy}{dx} = z$ so that eqn. (1) becomes $\frac{dz}{dx} + 2xz + y = 0$

Now the equations to be solved are

$$\frac{dy}{dx} = f(x, y, z) = z \quad ...(2)$$

$$\frac{dz}{dx} = \phi(x, y, z) = -(2xz + y) \quad ...(3)$$

with the conditions $\quad y_0 = 0.5, z_0 = 0.1$ at $x_0 = 0$

First approximation

$$y^{(1)} = y_0 + \int_{x_0}^x f(x, y_0, z_0)\, dx = 0.5 + \int_0^x z_0\, dx = 0.5 + 0.1\, x$$

$$z^{(1)} = z_0 + \int_{x_0}^x \phi(x, y_0, z_0)\, dx = 0.1 + \int_0^x [-(2x\, z_0 + y_0)]\, dx$$

$$= 0.1 - \int_0^x (0.2x + 0.5)\, dx = 0.1 - 0.5x - 0.1x^2$$

Second approximation

$$y^{(2)} = y_0 + \int_0^x f\{x, y^{(1)}, z^{(1)}\}\, dx = 0.5 + \int_0^x z^{(1)}\, dx$$

$$= 0.5 + \int_0^x (0.1 - 0.5x - 0.1x^2)\, dx$$

$$= 0.5 + 0.1x - 0.25x^2 - \frac{0.1}{3} x^3$$

$$z^{(2)} = z_0 + \int_0^x \phi\, \{x, y^{(1)}, z^{(1)}\}\, dx = 0.1 - \int_0^x [2x\, z^{(1)} + y^{(1)}]\, dx$$

$$= 0.1 - \int_0^x [2x(0.1 - 0.5x - 0.1x^2) + (0.5 + 0.1x)]\, dx$$

$$= 0.1 - \int_0^x (0.3x - x^2 - 0.2x^3 + 0.5)\, dx$$

$$= 0.1 - 0.5x - 0.3\,\frac{x^2}{2} + \frac{x^3}{3} + \frac{0.1\,x^4}{2}$$

Third approximation

$$y^{(3)} = y_0 + \int_0^x f\{x, y^{(2)}, z^{(2)}\}\, dx = 0.5 + \int_0^x z^{(2)}\, dx$$

$$= 0.5 + \int_0^x \left(0.1 - 0.5x - 0.15x^2 + \frac{x^3}{3} + 0.05x^4\right) dx$$

$$= 0.5 + 0.1x - 0.25x^2 - 0.05x^3 + \frac{x^4}{12} + 0.01x^5$$

$$z^{(3)} = z_0 + \int_0^x \phi\, \{x, y^{(2)}, z^{(2)}\}\, dx = 0.1 - \int_0^x [2x\, z^{(2)} + y^{(2)}]\, dx$$

$$= 0.1 - \int_0^x \left[2x\left(0.1 - 0.5x - 0.15x^2 + \frac{x^3}{3} + 0.05x^4\right) + \left(0.5 + 0.1x - 0.25x^2 - \frac{0.1}{3}x^3\right)\right] dx$$

$$= 0.1 - 0.5x + 0.15x^2 - \frac{2.5}{6}x^3 + 0.2x^4 + \frac{2}{15}x^5 + \frac{0.1}{6}x^6$$

Now when $x = 0.1$, $y^{(1)} = 0.51$, $y^{(2)} = 0.50746667$, $y^{(3)} = 0.50745933$

Since $y^{(2)}$ and $y^{(3)}$ are same up to four decimal places hence $y(0.1) = 0.5074$.

ASSIGNMENT

1. Find the solution of $\frac{dy}{dx} = 1 + xy$, $y(0) = 1$ in the interval (0, 0.5) correct to 3 decimal places taking $h = 0.1$.

2. Solve numerically $\frac{dy}{dx} = 2x - y$, $y(0) = 0.9$ at $x = 0.4$ by Picard's method with three iterations and compare the result with the exact value.

3. Apply Picard's method to find the solution of the initial value problem $\frac{dy}{dx} = y - x, y(0) = 2$. Show that the iterative solution approaches the exact solution. *(M.T.U. 2012)*

4. Use Picard's method to approximate the value of y when $x = 0.1$ given that $y = 1$ when $x = 0$ and $\frac{dy}{dx} = 3x + y^2$. *(M.T.U. 2013)*

5. (*i*) For the differential equation $\frac{dy}{dx} = x - y^2$, $y(0) = 0$, calculate $y(0.2)$ by Picard's method to third approximations and round off the value at 4th place of decimals.

(*ii*) Find an approximate value of y when $x = 0.1$ if $\frac{dy}{dx} = x - y^2$ and $y = 1$ at $x = 0$ using Picard's method.

6. Employ Picard's method to find $y(0.2)$ and $y(0.4)$ given that $\frac{dy}{dx} = 1 + y^2$ and $y(0) = 0$.

7. Employ Picard's method to obtain the solution of $\frac{dy}{dx} = x^2 + y^2$ for $x = 0.4$ correct to four places of decimal given that $y = 0$ when $x = 0$.

8. Find $y(0.2)$ if $\frac{dy}{dx} = \log_{10}(x + y)$; $y(0) = 1$. Use Picard's method.

9. Solve by Picard's method: $\frac{d^2y}{dx^2} = x^3\left(\frac{dy}{dx} + y\right)$ where $y = 1$, $\frac{dy}{dx} = \frac{1}{2}$ when $x = 0$, obtain the results up to third approximation.

Answers

1.

x :	0	0.1	0.2	0.3	0.4	0.5
y :	1	1.105	1.222	1.355	1.505	1.677

2. 0.7432, 0.7439

3. $y = 2 + 2x + \frac{x^2}{2} + \frac{x^3}{6} - \frac{x^4}{24}$ (upto third approx.); exact solution: $y = 1 + x + e^x$

4. $y = 1 + x + \frac{5}{2}x^2 + \frac{4}{3}x^3 + \frac{3}{4}x^4 + \frac{9}{20}x^5$ (upto second approx.)

5. (*i*) 0.019984, 0.0200 (*ii*) 0.9138 **6.** 0.2027, 0.4227

7. 0.0213 **8.** 1.0082

9. $y^{(1)} = 1 + \frac{x}{2}, y^{(2)} = 1 + \frac{x}{2} + \frac{3x^5}{40}, y^{(3)} = 1 + \frac{x}{2} + \frac{3x^5}{40} + \frac{x^6}{60} + \frac{x^9}{192}$.

8.9. EULER'S METHOD

[G.B.T.U. (MCA) 2010]

It is the simplest one-step method and has a limited application because of its low accuracy. This method yields solution of an ordinary diff. eqn. in the form of a set of tabulated values.

In this method, we determine the change Δy is y corresponding to small increase in the argument x. Consider the differential equation

$$\frac{dy}{dx} = f(x, y), \quad y(x_0) = y_0 \qquad \text{...(1)}$$

Let $y = g(x)$ be the solution of (1). Let x_0, x_1, x_2 ...... be equidistant values of x.

In this method, we use the property that in a small interval, a curve is nearly a straight line. Thus at the point (x_0, y_0), we approximate the curve by the tangent at the point (x_0, y_0).

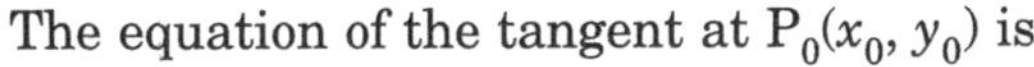

The equation of the tangent at $P_0(x_0, y_0)$ is

$$y - y_0 = \left(\frac{dy}{dx}\right)_{P_0} (x - x_0) = f(x_0, y_0)(x - x_0)$$

$$\Rightarrow \qquad y = y_0 + (x - x_0) f(x_0, y_0) \qquad \text{...(2)}$$

This gives the y-coordinate of any point on the tangent. Since the curve is approximated by the tangent in the interval (x_0, x_1), the value of y on the curve corresponding to $x = x_1$ is given by the above value of y in eqn. (2) approximately.

Putting $x = x_1 (= x_0 + h)$ in eqn. (2), we get

$$y_1 = y_0 + hf(x_0, y_0)$$

Thus Q_1 is (x_1, y_1)

Similarly, approximating the curve in the next interval (x_1, x_2) by a line through $Q_1(x_1, y_1)$ with slope $f(x_1, y_1)$, we get

$$y_2 = y_1 + hf(x_1, y_1)$$

In general, it can be shown that,

$$\boxed{y_{n+1} = y_n + hf(x_n, y_n)}$$

This is called Euler's formula.

A great disadvantage of this method lies in the fact that if $\frac{dy}{dx}$ changes rapidly over an interval, its value at the beginning of the interval may give a poor approximation as compared to its average value over the interval and thus the value of y calculated from Euler's method may be in much error from its true value. These errors accumulate in the succeeding intervals and the value of y becomes much erroroneous ultimately.

Note. In Euler's method, the curve of actual solution $y = g(x)$ is approximated by a sequence of short lines. The process is very slow. If h is not properly chosen, the curve $P_0Q_1Q_2$ ...... of short lines representing numerical solution deviates significantly from the curve of actual solution.

8.9.1. Algorithm of Euler's Method

```
Function F(x,y)=(x-y)/(x+y)
Input x0,y0,h,xn
n=((xn-x0)/h)+1
```

```
4. For i=1,n
5. y=y0+h*F(x0,y0)
6. x=x+h
7. Print x0,y0
8. If x<xn then
                x0=x
                y0=y
          ELSE
9. Next i
10. Stop
```

8.9.2. Flow Chart of Euler's Method

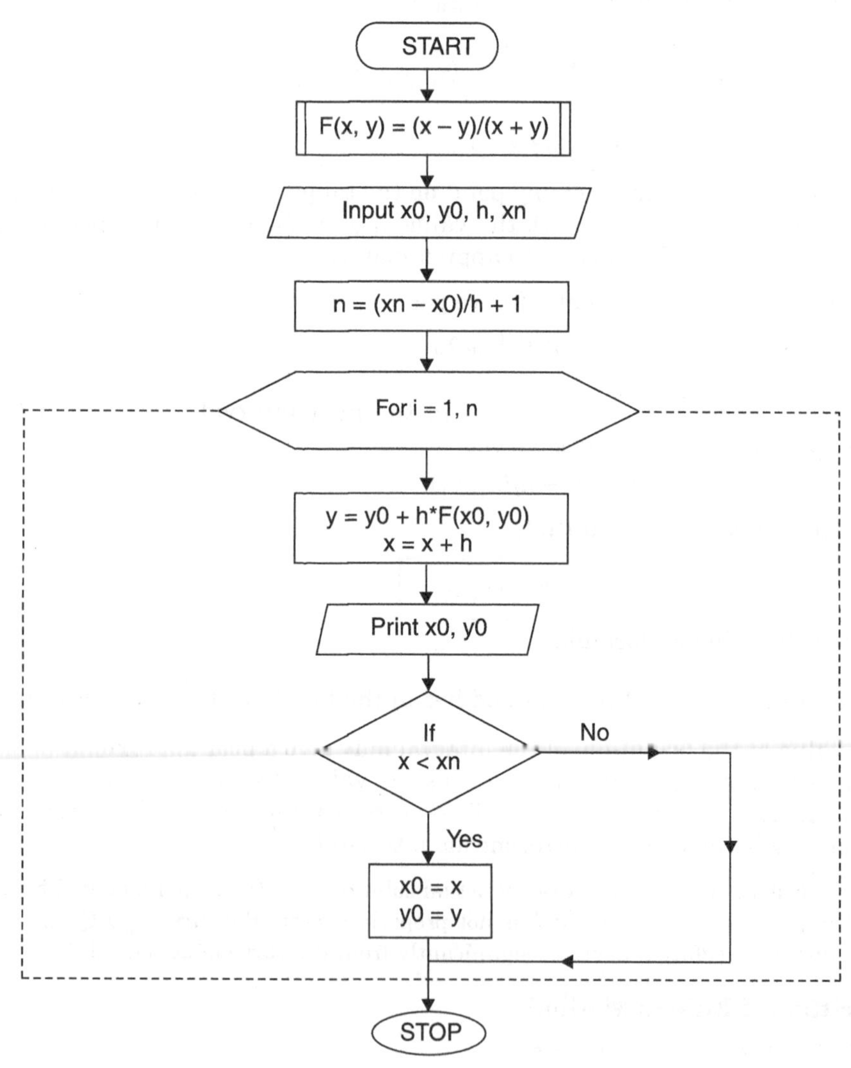

8.9.3. Program of Euler's Method

```
#include<stdio.h>
#define F(x,y)  (x-y)/(x+y)
main ( )
{
 int i,n;
 float x0,y0,h,xn,x,y;
 printf("\n Enter the values: x0,y0,h,xn: \n");
 scanf  ("%f%f%f%f",&x0,&y0,&h,&xn);
 n=(xn-x0)/h+1;
 for  (i=1;i<=n;i++)
       {
       y=y0+h*F(x0,y0);
       x=x0+h;
       printf("\n  X=%f  Y=%f",x0,y0);
         if(x<xn)
         {
         x0=x;
         y0=y;
         }
       }
return;
}
```

8.9.4. OUTPUT

```
Enter the values: x0,y0,h,xn:
0 1 0.02 0.1
X=0.000000 Y=1.000000
X=0.020000 Y=0.980000
X=0.040000 Y=0.960800
X=0.060000 Y=0.942399
X=0.080000 Y=0.924793
X=0.100000 Y=0.907978
```

8.10. IMPROVED EULER'S METHOD

The improved Euler's method gives greater improvement in accuracy over the original Euler's method. Here the core idea is that we use a line through (x_0, y_0) whose slope is the average of the slopes at (x_0, y_0) and $(x_1, y_1^{(1)})$ where $y_1^{(1)} = y_0 + hf(x_0, y_0)$. This line approximates the curve in the interval (x_0, x_1).

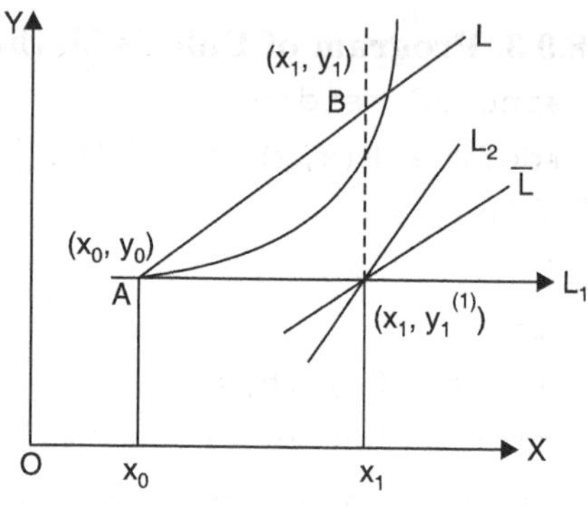

Geometrically, if L_1 is the tangent at (x_0, y_0), L_2 is a line through $(x_1, y_1^{(1)})$ of slope $f(x_1, y_1^{(1)})$ and $\bar{L}$ is the line through $(x_1, y_1^{(1)})$ but with a slope equal to the average of $f(x_0, y_0)$ and $f(x_1, y_1^{(1)})$ then the line L through (x_0, y_0) and parallel to $\bar{L}$ is used to approximate the curve in the interval (x_0, x_1). Thus the ordinate of the point B will give the value of y_1. Now, the eqn. of the line AL is given by

$$y_1 = y_0 + (x_1 - x_0)\left[\frac{f(x_0, y_0) + f(x_1, y_1^{(1)})}{2}\right]$$

$$= y_0 + h\left[\frac{f(x_0, y_0) + f(x_1, y_1^{(1)})}{2}\right] \qquad ...(1)$$

A generalized form of improved Euler's formula is

$$\boxed{y_1^{(n+1)} = y_0 + \frac{h}{2}\,[f(x_0, y_0) + f(x_1, y_1^{(n)})]} \; ; n = 0, 1, 2, ... \qquad ...(2)$$

where $y_1^{(n)}$ is the nth approximation to y_1.

The above iteration formula can be started by choosing $y_1^{(1)}$ from Euler's formula

$$y_1^{(1)} = y_0 + hf(x_0, y_0) \qquad ...(3)$$

Since this formula attempts to correct the values of y_{n+1} using the predicted value of y_{n+1} (by Euler's method), it is classified as a *one-step predictor-corrector method.*

8.10.1. Algorithm of Improved Euler's Method

```
1.  Function F(x)=(x-y)/(x+y)
2.  Input x(1),y(1),h,xn
3.  yp=y(1)+h*F(x(1),y(1))
4.  itr=(xn-x(1))/h
5.  Print x(1),y(1)
6.  For i=1,itr
7.  x(i+1)=x(i)+h
8.  For n=1,50
9.  yc(n+1)=y(i)+(h/2*(F(x(i),y(i))+F(x(i+1),yp))
10. Print n,yc(n+1)
11. p=yc (n+1)-yp
12. If abs(p)<.0001 then
            goto Step 14
     ELSE
            yp=yc(n+1)
13. Next n
14. y(i+1)=yc(n+1)
15. print x(i+1),yp
16. Next i
17. Stop
```

8.10.2. Flow Chart of Improved Euler's Method

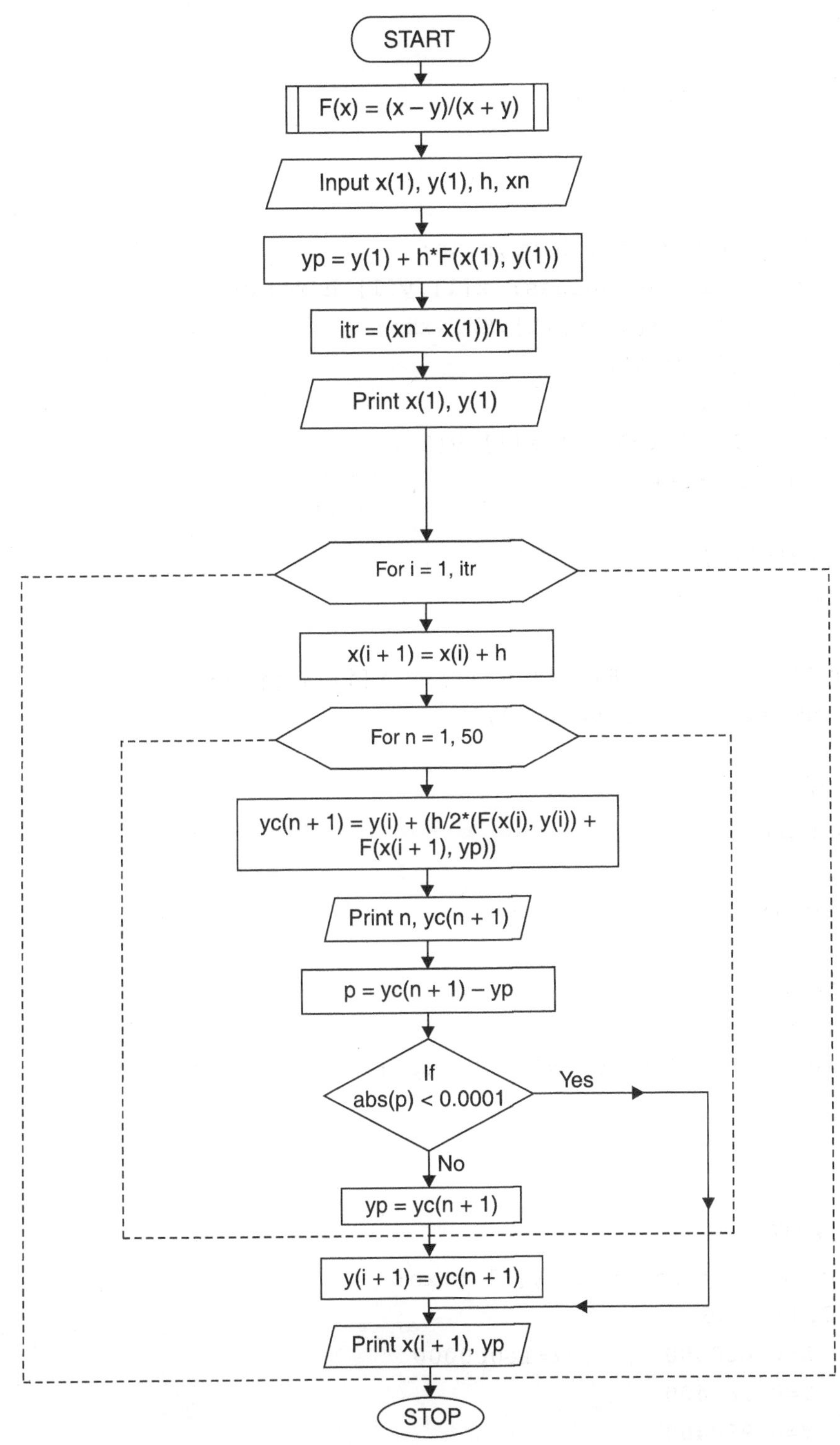

8.10.3. Program of Improved Euler's Method

```
#include<stdio.h>
#include<math.h>
#define F(x,y) (x-y)/(x+y)
main ()
{
 int i,n,itr ;
 float x[5],y[50],yc[50],h,yp,p,xn;
 printf("\n Enter the values: x[1],y[1],h,xn:\n");
 scanf("%f%f%f%f",&x[1],&y[1],&h,&xn);
 yp=y[1]+h*F(x[1],y[1]);
 itr=(xn-x[1])/h;
 printf("\n\n X=%f Y=%f\n",x[1],y[1];
 for (i=1;i<=itr;i++)
  {
   x[i+1]=x[i]+h;
   for (n=1;n<=50;n++)
    {
yc[n+1]=y[i]+(h/2.0)*(F(x[i],y[i])+F(x[i+1],yp));
printf("\nN=%d Y=%f",n,yc[n+1]);
p=yc[n+1]-yp;
if(fabs (p)<0.0001)
    goto next;
  else
     yp=yc[n+1];
    }
        next:
y[i+1]=yc[n+1];
printf("\n\n X=%f Y=%f\n",x[i+1], yp);
  }
return;
}
```

8.10.4. OUTPUT

```
Enter the values: x[1],y[1],h,xn:
0 1 0.02 0.06
      X=0.000000      Y=1.000000
N=1   Y=0.980400
N=2   Y=0.980400
```

```
        X=0.020000          Y=0.980400
N=1     Y=0.961584
N=2     Y=0.961598
        X=0.040000          Y=0.961584
N=1     Y=0.943572
N=2     Y=0.943593
        X=0.060000          Y=0.943572
```

8.11. MODIFIED EULER'S METHOD

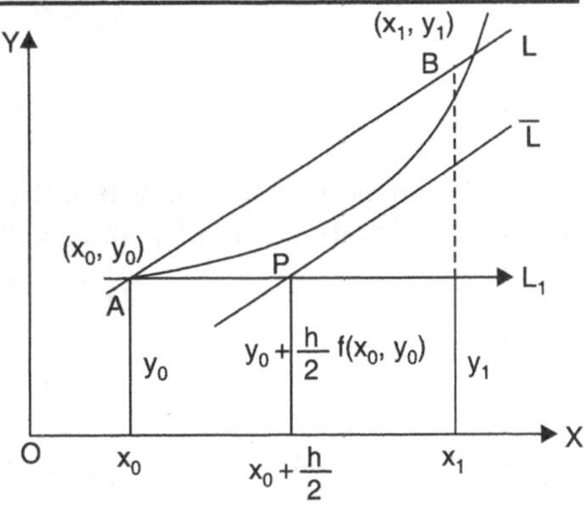

In this method, the curve in the interval (x_0, x_1), where $x_1 = x_0 + h$ is approximated by the line through (x_0, y_0) with slope $f\left\{x_0 + \frac{h}{2}, y_0 + \frac{h}{2} f(x_0, y_0)\right\}$, which is the slope at the middle point whose abscissa is the average of x_0 and x_1.

In the adjoining figure, line AL through $A(x_0, y_0)$ which is parallel to the line $P\bar{L}$ with slope $f\left\{x_0 + \frac{h}{2}, y_0 + \frac{h}{2} f(x_0, y_0)\right\}$ approximates the curve in the interval (x_0, x_1). The ordinate at $x = x_1$, meeting the line L at B, will give the value of y_1.

The equation for line AL is

$$y - y_0 = (x - x_0)\left[f\left\{x_0 + \frac{h}{2}, y_0 + \frac{h}{2} f(x_0, y_0)\right\}\right] \quad ...(1)$$

Putting $x = x_1$ in (1), we get

$$y_1 = y_0 + (x_1 - x_0)\left[f\left\{x_0 + \frac{h}{2}, y_0 + \frac{h}{2} f(x_0, y_0)\right\}\right]$$

$$\Rightarrow \quad y_1 = y_0 + h f\left\{x_0 + \frac{h}{2}, y_0 + \frac{h}{2} f(x_0, y_0)\right\}$$

Proceeding in the same way, we obtain

$$\boxed{y_{n+1} = y_n + h f\left\{x_n + \frac{h}{2}, y_n + \frac{h}{2} f(x_n, y_n)\right\}} \quad ...(2)$$

which is the generalized form of **modified Euler's formula.**

EXAMPLES

Example 1. *Given* $\frac{dy}{dx} = \frac{y-x}{y+x}$ *with $y = 1$ for $x = 0$. Find y approximately for $x = 0.1$ by Euler's method.*

Sol. We have

$$\frac{dy}{dx} = f(x, y) = \frac{y-x}{y+x}\ ; x_0 = 0, y_0 = 1, h = 0.1$$

Hence the approximate value of y at $x = 0.1$ is given by

$$y_1 = y_0 + hf(x_0, y_0) \qquad | \text{ Using } y_{n+1} = y_n + hf(x_n, y_n)$$

$$= 1 + (0.1)\left(\frac{1-0}{1+0}\right) = 1.1$$

Much better accuracy is obtained by breaking up the interval 0 to 0.1 into five steps. The approximate value of y at $x_A = 0.02$ is given by,

$$y_1 = y_0 + hf(x_0, y_0)$$

$$= 1 + (0.02)\left(\frac{1-0}{1+0}\right) = 1.02$$

At $x_B = 0.04$,

$$y_2 = y_1 + hf(x_1, y_1)$$

$$= 1.02 + (0.02)\left(\frac{1.02-0.02}{1.02+0.02}\right) = 1.0392$$

At $x_C = 0.06$,

$$y_3 = 1.0392 + (0.02)\left(\frac{1.0392-0.04}{1.0392+0.04}\right) = 1.0577$$

At $x_D = 0.08$,

$$y_4 = 1.0577 + (0.02)\left(\frac{1.0577-0.06}{1.0577+0.06}\right) = 1.0756$$

At $x_E = 0.1$,

$$y_5 = 1.0756 + (0.02)\left(\frac{1.0756-0.08}{1.0756+0.08}\right) = 1.0928$$

Hence $y = 1.0928$ when $x = 0.1$

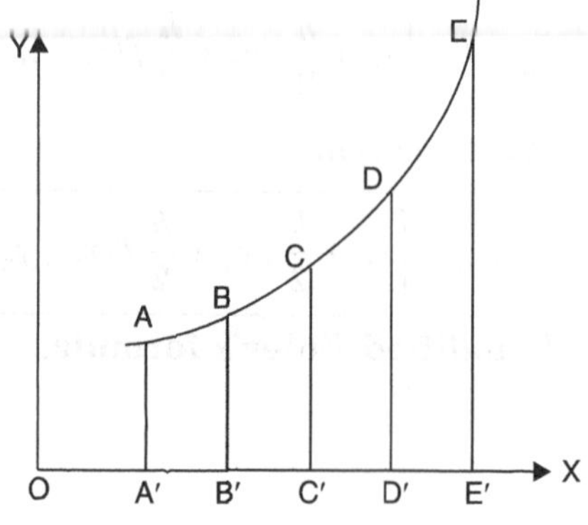

Example 2. *Solve the equation* $\frac{dy}{dx} = 1 - y$ *with the initial condition* $x = 0, y = 0$ *using Euler's algorithm and tabulate the solutions at* $x = 0.1, 0.2, 0.3$.

Sol. Here, $f(x, y) = 1 - y$

Taking $h = 0.1, x_0 = 0, y_0 = 0$, we obtain

$$y_1 = y_0 + hf(x_0, y_0) = 0 + (0.1)(1 - 0) = 0.1$$

$\therefore$ $y(0.1) = 0.1$

Again, $y_2 = y_1 + hf(x_1, y_1) = 0.1 + (0.1)(1 - 0.1) = 0.1 + 0.09 = 0.19$

$\therefore$ $y(0.2) = 0.19$

Again, $y_3 = y_2 + hf(x_2, y_2) = 0.19 + (0.1)(1 - 0.19) = 0.271$

$\therefore$ $y(0.3) = 0.271$

Tabulated values are

x	$y(x)$
0	0
0.1	0.1
0.2	0.19
0.3	0.271

Example 3. *Use Euler's method to obtain an approximate value of* $y(0.4)$ *for the equation* $y' = x + y$, $y(0) = 1$ *with* $h = 0.1$.

Sol. Here, $f(x, y) = x + y$

Taking $h = 0.1, x_0 = 0, y_0 = 1$, we obtain

$$y_1 = y_0 + h\, f(x_0, y_0) = 1 + (0.1)(0 + 1) = 1.1$$

$\therefore$ $y(0.1) = 1.1$

Again, $y_2 = y_1 + h\, f(x_1, y_1) = 1.1 + (0.1)(0.1 + 1.1) = 1.22$

$\therefore$ $y(0.2) = 1.22$

Again, $y_3 = y_2 + h\, f(x_2, y_2) = 1.22 + (0.1)(0.2 + 1.22) = 1.362$

$\therefore$ $y(0.3) = 1.362$

Again, $y_4 = y_3 + h\, f(x_3, y_3) = 1.362 + (0.1)(0.3 + 1.362) = 1.5282$

$\therefore$ $y(0.4) = 1.5282$

Example 4. *Solve the following differential equation using Euler's method from* $x = 0$ *to* $x = 0.2$ *when* $h = 0.05$.

$$\frac{dy}{dx} + xy = 0, \quad y(0) = 1$$

Sol. Here, $f(x, y) = -xy$

Taking $h = 0.05, x_0 = 0, y_0 = 1$, we obtain

$$y_1 = y_0 + h\, f(x_0, y_0) = 1 + (0.05)\{-(0 \times 1)\} = 1$$

$\therefore$ $y(0.05) = 1$

Again, $y_2 = y_1 + h\, f(x_1, y_1) = 1 + (0.05)\{-(0.05 \times 1)\} = 0.9975$

$\therefore$ $y(0.1) = 0.9975$

Again, $y_3 = y_2 + h\, f(x_2, y_2) = 0.9975 + (0.05)\{-(0.1 \times 0.9975)\} = 0.9925125$

$\therefore$ $y(0.15) = 0.9925125$

Again, $y_4 = y_3 + h\,f(x_3, y_3) = 0.9925125 + (0.05)\{-(0.15)(0.9925125)\}$
$= 0.985068656$

$\therefore \quad y(0.2) = 0.985068656$

Hence, in tabular form, we can write

x	0	0.05	0.10	0.15	0.2
y	1	1	0.9975	0.9925125	0.985068656

Example 5. *Find y(0.1) using improved Euler's method and then y(0.2) by using modified Euler's method, given that* $\frac{dy}{dx} = \log(x + y)$, $y(0) = 1.0$ (U.P.T.U. 2007)

Sol. Here $f(x, y) = \log(x + y)$

Also, $x_0 = 0, y_0 = 1, h = 0.1$

Using improved Euler's method, we get

$$y_1^{(1)} = y_0 + h\,f(x_0, y_0) = 1 + (0.1)\log(0 + 1) = 1$$

$$y_1^{(2)} = y_0 + \frac{h}{2}[f(x_0, y_0) + f\{x_1, y_1^{(1)}\}]$$

$$= 1 + \frac{(0.1)}{2}[0 + \log(0.1 + 1)] = 1.0047655$$

$$y_1^{(3)} = y_0 + \frac{h}{2}[f(x_0, y_0) + f\{x_1, y_1^{(2)}\}]$$

$$= 1 + \frac{(0.1)}{2}[0 + \log(0.1 + 1.0047655)] = 1.0049816$$

$$y_1^{(4)} = y_0 + \frac{h}{2}[f(x_0, y_0) + f\{x_1, y_1^{(3)}\}]$$

$$= 1 + \frac{(0.1)}{2}[0 + \log(0.1 + 1.0049816)] = 1.0049914$$

Since $y_1^{(3)}$ and $y_1^{(4)}$ are same up to four decimal places

$\therefore \quad y_1 = y(0.1) = 1.0049$

Again, $x_1 = 0.1, y_1 = 1.0049, h = 0.1$

Using modified Euler's method, we get

$$y_2 = y_1 + h\,f\left\{x_1 + \frac{h}{2}, y_1 + \frac{h}{2}f(x_1, y_1)\right\}$$

$$= 1.0049 + (0.1)\log\left\{x_1 + \frac{h}{2} + y_1 + \frac{h}{2}f(x_1, y_1)\right\}$$

$$= 1.0049 + (0.1)\log[0.1 + 0.05 + 1.0049 + (0.05)\log(0.1 + 1.0049)]$$

$$= 1.0197323$$

$\therefore \quad y(0.2) = 1.0197323$

Example 6. *Apply modified Euler's method to solve*

$$\frac{dy}{dx} = e^x + xy,\ y(0) = 0 \text{ to compute } y(0.1) \text{ and } y(0.2).$$

Sol. Here, $f(x, y) = e^x + xy$

We have, $x_0 = 0, y_0 = 0, h = 0.1$

Using modified Euler's method, we obtain

$$y_1 = y_0 + h\, f\left\{x_0 + \frac{h}{2}, y_0 + \frac{h}{2} f(x_0, y_0)\right\}$$

$$= 0 + (0.1)\ [e^{0.05} + (0.05)\ (0.05)\ (e^0 + 0)] = 0.105377$$

$\therefore$ $y(0.1) = 0.105377$

Again, $$y_2 = y_1 + h\, f\left\{x_1 + \frac{h}{2}, y_1 + \frac{h}{2} f(x_1, y_1)\right\}$$

$$= 0.105377 + (0.1)\ [e^{0.15} + (0.15)\ \{(0.105377) + (0.05)\ (e^{0.1} + 0.0105377)\}]$$

$$= 0.105377 + (0.1)\ [e^{0.15} + (0.15)\ (0.16116243)] = 0.22397786$$

$\therefore$ $y(0.2) = 0.22397786.$

ASSIGNMENT

1. Using Euler's method, compute $y(0.04)$ for the differential equation

   $\frac{dy}{dx} = -y;\quad y(0) = 1.\qquad$ Take $h = 0.01.$ *(U.P.T.U. 2007)*

2. Apply Euler's method to solve $\frac{dy}{dx} = x + y$; $y(0) = 0$ choosing $h = 0.2$ and compute $y(0.4)$, $y(0.6)$, $y(0.8)$ and $y(1.0)$.

3. If $\frac{dy}{dx} = 1 + y^2$, $y(0) = 1$, find $y(0.4)$ by using Euler's method. Take $h = 0.2$.

   [G.B.T.U. (C.O.) 2011]

4. Given that $\frac{dy}{dx} = \log_{10}(x + y)$; $y(0) = 1$

   Find $y(0.2)$ and $y(0.5)$ using improved Euler's method.

5. Using improved Euler's method, obtain a solution of the equation $\frac{dy}{dx} = x + |\sqrt{y}| = f(x, y)$ with initial condition $y = 1$ at $x = 0$ for the range $0 \le x \le 0.6$ in steps of 0.2.
6. Use Euler's modified method to obtain $y(0.25)$ given that $y' = 2xy$, $y(0) = 1$
7. Solve $y' = x^2 + y$, $y(0) = 1$ to obtain $y(0.02)$ and $y(0.04)$ using Euler's modified method.
8. Solve $\frac{dy}{dx} = y - \frac{2x}{y}$; $y(0) = 1$ in the range $0 \le x \le 0.2$ using

   (*i*) Improved Euler's method (*ii*) Modified Euler's method.

Answers

1. $y(0.04) = 0.960596$

2. $y(0.4) = 0.04, y(0.6) = 0.128, y(0.8) = 0.2736, y(1.0) = 0.48832$

3. $y(0.4) = 1.992$ **4.** $y(0.2) = 1.0082, y(0.5) = 1.0490$

5. $y(0.2) = 1.2309, y(0.4) = 1.5253, y(0.6) = 1.8861$

6. $y(0.25) = 1.0625$ **7.** $y(0.02) = 1.0202, y(0.04) = 1.0408$

8.

x	*Improved Euler's method*	*Modified Euler's method*
0	1	1
0.1	1.095	1.0954762
0.2	1.1828	1.1832984

8.12. TAYLOR'S METHOD

Consider the differential equation

$$\left.\begin{aligned} \frac{dy}{dx} &= f(x, y) \\ \text{with the initial condition } y(x_0) &= y_0. \end{aligned}\right\} \quad ...(1)$$

If $y(x)$ is the exact solution of (1) then $y(x)$ can be expanded into a Taylor's series about the point $x = x_0$ as

$$y(x) = y_0 + (x - x_0)\, y_0' + \frac{(x - x_0)^2}{2!}\, y_0'' + \frac{(x - x_0)^3}{3!}\, y_0''' + \ldots\ldots \quad ...(2)$$

where dashes denote differentiation w.r.t. x.

Differentiating (1) successively w.r.t. x, we get

$$y'' = \frac{\partial f}{\partial x} + \frac{\partial f}{\partial y}\frac{dy}{dx} = \frac{\partial f}{\partial x} + f\frac{\partial f}{\partial y} = \left(\frac{\partial}{\partial x} + f\frac{\partial}{\partial y}\right) f \quad ...(3)$$

$$\therefore \quad y''' = \frac{d}{dx}(y'') = \left(\frac{\partial}{\partial x} + f\frac{\partial}{\partial y}\right)\left(\frac{\partial f}{\partial x} + f\frac{\partial f}{\partial y}\right)$$

$$= \frac{\partial^2 f}{\partial x^2} + \frac{\partial f}{\partial x}\frac{\partial f}{\partial y} + f\frac{\partial^2 f}{\partial x \partial y} + f\frac{\partial^2 f}{\partial y \partial x} + f\left(\frac{\partial f}{\partial y}\right)^2 + f^2\frac{\partial^2 f}{\partial y^2} \quad ...(4)$$

and so on.

Putting $x = x_0$ and $y = y_0$ in the expressions for $y', y'', y''', \ldots\ldots.$ and substituting them in eqn. (2), we get a power series for $y(x)$ in powers of $x - x_0$.

i.e.,

$$\mathbf{y(x) = y_0 + (x - x_0)y_0' + \frac{(x - x_0)^2}{2!}\, y_0'' + \frac{(x - x_0)^3}{3!}\, y_0''' + \ldots\ldots.} \quad ...(5)$$

Putting $x = x_1\ (= x_0 + h)$ in (5), we get

$$\mathbf{y_1 = y(x_1) = y_0 + hy_0' + \frac{h^2}{2!}\, y_0'' + \frac{h^3}{3!}\, y_0''' + \ldots\ldots.} \quad ...(6)$$

Here y_0', y_0'', y_0''', ... can be found by using (1) and its successive differentiations (3) and (4) at $x = x_0$. The series (6) can be truncated at any stage if h is small.

After obtaining y_1, we can calculate y_1', y_1'', y_1''', ... from (1) at $x_1 = x_0 + h$.

Now, expanding $y(x)$ by Taylor's series about $x = x_1$, we get

$$y_2 = y_1 + hy'_1 + \frac{h^2}{2!} y_1'' + \frac{h^3}{3!} y_1''' + ...$$

Proceeding on, we get

$$y_n = y_{n-1} + hy_{n-1}' + \frac{h^2}{2!} y_{n-1}'' + \frac{h^3}{3!} y_{n-1}''' + ...$$

Practically, this method is not of much importance because of its need of partial derivatives.

Moreover if we are interested in a better approximation with a small truncation error, the evaluation of higher order derivatives is needed which are very much complicated in evaluation. Besides its impracticability, it is useful in judging the degree of accuracy of the approximations given by other methods.

We can determine the extent to which any other formula agrees with the Taylor's series expansion. Taylor's method is one of those methods which yield the solution of a differential equation in the form of a power series. This method suffers from a serious disadvantage that h should be small enough so that successive terms in the series diminishes quite rapidly.

8.13. TAYLOR'S METHOD FOR SIMULTANEOUS I ORDER DIFF. EQUATIONS

Simultaneous differential equations of the type

$$\frac{dy}{dx} = f(x, y, z) \quad ...(1)$$

and

$$\frac{dz}{dx} = \phi(x, y, z) \quad ...(2)$$

with initial conditions $y(x_0) = y_0$ and $z(x_0) = z_0$
can be solved by Taylor's method.

If h is the step-size then

$$y_1 = y(x_0 + h) \quad \text{and} \quad z_1 = z(x_0 + h)$$

Taylor's algorithm for (1) and (2) gives

$$y_1 = y_0 + hy_0' + \frac{h^2}{2!} y_0'' + \frac{h^3}{3!} y_0''' + ... \quad ...(3)$$

and

$$z_1 = z_0 + hz_0' + \frac{h^2}{2!} z_0'' + \frac{h^3}{3!} z_0''' + ... \quad ...(4)$$

Differentiating (1) and (2) successively, we get y'', y''', ..., z'', z''', ... etc. So the values y_0'', y_0''', ... and z_0'', z_0''', ... can be obtained.

Substituting them in (3) and (4), we get y_1, z_1 for the next step.

$$y_2 = y_1 + hy_1' + \frac{h^2}{2!} y_1'' + \frac{h^3}{3!} y_1''' + ...$$

and $$z_2 = z_1 + hz_1' + \frac{h^2}{2!} z_1'' + \frac{h^3}{3!} z_1''' + ...$$

Since y_1 and z_1 are known, y_1', y_1'', y_1'''......., z_1', z_1'', z_1''', ... can be calculated. Hence y_2 and z_2 can be obtained. Proceeding in this manner, we get other values of y, step by step.

EXAMPLES

Example 1. *Use Taylor's series method to solve*

$\frac{dy}{dx} = x + y$; *y(1) = 0 numerically upto x = 1.2 with h = 0.1. Compare the final result with the value of explicit solution.*

Sol. Here, $x_0 = 1, y_0 = 0$

$$\begin{aligned}
& y' = x + y && i.e., && y_0' = x_0 + y_0 = 1\\
\Rightarrow\ & y'' = 1 + y' && i.e., && y_0'' = 1 + y_0' = 2\\
\Rightarrow\ & y''' = y'' && i.e., && y_0''' = y_0'' = 2\\
\Rightarrow\ & y^{(iv)} = y''' && i.e., && y_0^{(iv)} = 2\\
\Rightarrow\ & y^{(v)} = y^{(iv)} && i.e., && y_0^{(v)} = 2
\end{aligned}$$

By Taylor's series, we have

$$y_1 = y_0 + hy_0' + \frac{h^2}{2!} y_0'' + \frac{h^3}{3!} y_0''' + \frac{h^4}{4!} y_0^{(iv)} + ...$$

$$y(1 + h) = 0 + (0.1)\, 1 + \frac{(0.1)^2}{2!}\, 2 + \frac{(0.1)^3}{3!}\, 2 + \frac{(0.1)^4}{4!}\, 2 + ...$$

$\Rightarrow$ $y(1.1) = 0.1103081 = 0.110$ (app.)

Also, $x_1 = x_0 + h = 1.1$

Again, $y_1' = x_1 + y_1 = 1.1 + 0.11 = 1.21$

$y_1'' = 1 + y_1' = 1 + 1.21 = 2.21$

$y_1''' = y_1'' = 2.21$

$y_1^{(iv)} = 2.21$

$y_1^{(v)} = 2.21$

Now, $$y(1.1 + h) = y_1 + hy_1' + \frac{h^2}{2!} y_1'' + \frac{h^3}{3!} y_1''' + ...$$

$$= 0\,.\,11 + (0.1)\,(1.21) + \frac{(0\,.1)^2}{2}\,(2.21) + ...$$

$\Rightarrow$ $y(1.2) = 0.232$ (app.)

The analytical solution of the given differential equation is

$$y = -x - 1 + 2e^{x-1}$$

when $x = 1.2$, we get

$$y = -1.2 - 1 + 2e^{0.2} = 0.242.$$

Example 2. *For the differential eqn.,* $\frac{dy}{dx} = -xy^2$, *y (0) = 2. Calculate y(0.2) by Taylor's series method retaining four non-zero terms only.*

Sol. Here $x_0 = 0, y_0 = 2$ Also $y' = -xy^2$

Taylor's series for $y(x)$ is given by

$$y(x) = y_0 + xy_0' + \frac{x^2}{2} y_0'' + \frac{x^3}{6} y_0''' + \frac{x^4}{24} y_0^{(iv)} + \frac{x^5}{120} y_0^{(v)} + \ldots\ldots. \quad \ldots(1)$$

The values of the derivatives y_0', y_0'', ..., etc. are obtained as follows :

$$\begin{aligned}
y' &= -xy^2 & y_0' &= -x_0y_0^2 = 0\\
y'' &= -y^2 - 2xyy' & y_0'' &= -2^2 - 0 = -4\\
y''' &= -4yy' - 2xy'^2 - 2xyy'' & y_0''' &= 0\\
y^{(iv)} &= -6y'^2 - 6y'y'' - 6xy'y'' - 2xyy''' & y_0^{(iv)} &= 48\\
y^{(v)} &= -24y'y'' - 8yy''' - 6xy''^2 & y_0^{(v)} &= 0\\
&\quad - 8xy'y''' - 2xyy^{(iv)} & &\\
y^{(vi)} &= -40y'y''' - 30y''^2 - 10\,yy^{(iv)} - 20xy''y''' & y_0^{(vi)} &= -1440\\
&\quad - 10xy'\,y^{(iv)} - 2xyy^{(v)}. & &
\end{aligned}$$

We stop here as we shall get four non-zero terms in the Taylor's series (1).

$$\therefore \quad y(x) = 2 + \frac{x^2}{2}(-4) + \frac{x^4}{24}(48) + \frac{x^6}{720}(-1440) + \ldots\ldots$$

$$= 2 - 2x^2 + 2x^4 - 2x^6 + \ldots\ldots.$$

$$\therefore \quad y(0.2) = 2 - 2(0.2)^2 + 2(0.2)^4 - 2\,(0.2)^6 + \ldots\ldots$$

$$= 2 - 0.08 + 0.0032 - 0.000128 = 1.923072$$

$$\simeq 1.9231 \quad \text{correct up to four decimal places.}$$

Example 3. *From the Taylor's series, for y(x), find y(0.1) correct to four decimal places if y(x) satisfies* $\frac{dy}{dx} = x - y^2$ *and y(0) = 1. Also find y(0.2).*

Sol. Here

$$\begin{aligned}
x_0 &= 0, & y_0 &= 1 \quad \ldots(1)\\
y' &= x - y^2 & y_0' &= 0 - 1 = -1\\
y'' &= 1 - 2yy' & y_0'' &= 3\\
y''' &= -2yy'' - 2y'^2 & y_0''' &= -8\\
y^{(iv)} &= -2yy''' - 6y'y'' & y_0^{(iv)} &= 34\\
y^{(v)} &= -2yy^{(iv)} - 8y'y''' - 6y''^2 & y_0^{(v)} &= -186\\
y^{(vi)} &= -2yy^{(v)} - 10y'y^{(iv)} - 20\,y''y''' & y_0^{(vi)} &= 1192\\
y^{(vii)} &= -2yy^{(vi)} - 12y'y^{(v)} - 50\,y''y^{(iv)} & y_0^{(vii)} &= -10996 \quad \text{(these two only for } y(0.2)\text{)}\\
&\quad - 20\,y'''^2 & &
\end{aligned}$$

Using these values, Taylor's series becomes

$$y(x) = 1 - x + \frac{3}{2}x^2 - \frac{4}{3}x^3 + \frac{17}{12}x^4 - \frac{31}{20}x^5 + \ldots\ldots \quad \ldots(2)$$

Put $x = 0.1$ in (2), we get

$y(0.1) = 0.91379 \simeq 0.9138$ (up to four decimal places)

To determine $y(0.2)$, we have

$$y(x) = 1 - x + \frac{3}{2}x^2 - \frac{4}{3}x^3 + \frac{17}{12}x^4 - \frac{31}{20}x^5 + \frac{1192}{720}x^6 - \frac{10996}{5040}x^7 + \ldots\ldots$$

$$= 0.8512 \quad \text{(correct to four decimal places)}.$$

Example 4. *Using Taylor's series, find the solution of the diff. equation $xy' = x - y$, $y(2) = 2$ at $x = 2.1$ correct to five decimal places.*

Sol. Here $x_0 = 2, y_0 = 2$

Also, $y' = 1 - \frac{y}{x}$ $\qquad y_0' = 0$

$$y'' = -\frac{y'}{x} + \frac{y}{x^2} \qquad y_0'' = -0 + \frac{2}{4} = \frac{1}{2}$$

$$y''' = -\frac{y''}{x} + \frac{2y'}{x^2} - \frac{2y}{x^3} \qquad y_0''' = \frac{-3}{4}$$

$$y^{(iv)} = -\frac{y'''}{x} + \frac{3y''}{x^2} - \frac{6y'}{x^3} + \frac{6y}{x^4} \qquad y_0^{(iv)} = \frac{3}{2} \text{ and so on.}$$

Putting these values in Taylor's series, we get

$$y(2 + h) = 2 + \frac{h^2}{4} - \frac{h^3}{8} + \frac{h^4}{16} + \ldots\ldots.$$

Put $h = 0.1$, we get

$y(2.1) = 2.00238$ (correct to 5 decimal places).

Example 5. *Find $y(1)$ for $\frac{dy}{dx} = 2y + 3e^x$, $y(0) = 0$. Also check the value.*

Sol. Here $x_0 = 0, y_0 = 0$

$$y'(x) = 2y + 3e^x \qquad y_0' = 3, y_0'' = 9,$$

$$y''(x) = 2y' + 3e^x \qquad y_0''' = 21, y_0^{(iv)} = 45$$

$\vdots \quad \vdots$

$\vdots \quad \vdots \qquad y_0^{(v)} = 93, y_0^{(vi)} = 189$

$$y^{(viii)}(x) = 2y^{(vii)} + 3e^x \qquad y_0^{(vii)} = 381, y_0^{(viii)} = 765$$

Now, $$y(h) = 3h + \frac{9}{2}h^2 + \frac{7}{2}h^3 + \frac{15}{8}h^4 + \frac{31}{40}h^5 + \frac{21}{80}h^6 + \frac{127}{1680}h^7 + \frac{17}{896}h^8 + \ldots\ldots.$$

Put $h = 1$, $y(1) = 14.01$

Exact solution.

$$\frac{dy}{dx} - 2y = 3e^x$$

Solution is $ye^{-2x} = -3e^{-x} + c$

$x = 0, y = 0 \qquad \therefore \quad c = 3$

$\therefore \qquad ye^{-2x} = -3e^{-x} + 3$

$\Rightarrow \qquad y = 3(e^{2x} - e^x)$

when $x = 1$,

$y = 3(e^2 - e) = 14.01$ correct to two decimal places.

Example 6. *Solve the simultaneous equations*

$$y' = 1 + xyz, \quad y(0) = 0$$
$$z' = x + y + z, \quad z(0) = 1.$$

Sol. Differentiating the given equations

$$y'' = yz + xy'z + xyz', \qquad y''' = 2y'z + 2yz' + 2xy'z' + xy''z + xyz''$$
$$z'' = 1 + y' + z', \qquad z''' = y'' + z''$$

with $x = 0, y = 0, \ z = 1$; we get $y' = 1, y'' = 0, y''' = 2$

Also $\quad z' = 1, z'' = 3, z''' = 3$

Hence, $\quad y(x) = x + \dfrac{x^3}{3}$ and $z(x) = 1 + x + \dfrac{3}{2}x^2 + \dfrac{1}{2}x^3.$

ASSIGNMENT

1. Compute y for $x = 0.1$ and 0.2 correct to four decimal places given: $y' = y - x$, $y(0) = 2$.
2. Solve by Taylor's method, $y' = x^2 + y^2$, $y(0) = 1$ compute $y(0.1)$.
3. Solve by Taylor's method : $y' = y - \dfrac{2x}{y}$; $y(0) = 1$. Also compute $y(0.1)$.
4. Using Taylor series method, solve $\dfrac{dy}{dx} = x^2 - y$, $y(0) = 1$ at $x = 0.1, 0.2, 0.3$ and 0.4. Compare the values with exact solution.
5. Solve $\dfrac{dy}{dx} = x + z$, $\dfrac{dz}{dx} = x - y^2$ with $y(0) = 2$, $z(0) = 1$ to get $y(0.1)$, $y(0.2)$, $z(0.1)$ and $z(0.2)$ approximately by Taylor's algorithm.
6. Given the differential equation $\dfrac{dy}{dx} = \dfrac{1}{x^2 + y}$ with $y(4) = 4$. Obtain $y(4.1)$ and $y(4.2)$ by Taylor's series method.

Answers

1. 2.2052, 2.4214
2. $y(x) = 1 + x + x^2 + \dfrac{4}{3}x^3 + \dfrac{7}{6}x^4 + \dfrac{6}{5}x^5 + \dfrac{37}{30}x^6$; 1.11146
3. $y(x) = 1 + x - \dfrac{x^2}{2} + \dfrac{x^3}{2} - \dfrac{5}{8}x^4$; 1.0954
4. $y(0.1) = 0.905125$, $\quad y(0.2) = 0.8212652$, $\quad y(0.3) = 0.7491509$, $\quad y(0.4) = 0.6896519$

   Exact solution. $\quad y(0.1) = 0.9051625$, $\quad y(0.2) = 0.8212692$

   $y(0.3) = 0.7491817$, $\quad y(0.4) = 0.6896799$
5. $y(0.1) = 2.0845$, $\quad z(0.1) = 0.5867$

   $y(0.2) = 2.1366338$, $\quad z(0.2) = 0.1549693$
6. 4.005, 4.0098.

8.14. RUNGE-KUTTA METHODS

More efficient methods in terms of accuracy were developed by two German Mathematicians **Carl Runge** (1856–1927) and **Wilhelm Kutta** (1867–1944). These methods are well-known as Runge-Kutta methods. They are distinguished by their orders in the sense that they agree with Taylor's series solution upto terms of h^r, where r is the order of the method.

These methods donot demand prior computation of higher derivatives of $y(x)$ as in Taylor's method. In place of these derivatives, extra values of the given function $f(x, y)$ are used.

Fourth order Runge-Kutta method is widely used for finding the numerical solutions of linear or non-linear ordinary differential equations.

Runge-Kutta methods are referred to a single step methods. The major disadvantage of Runge-Kutta methods is that they use many more evaluations of the derivative $f(x, y)$ to obtain the same accuracy compared with multi-step methods. A class of methods known as Runge-Kutta methods combines the advantage of high order accuracy with the property of being one step.

8.14.1. First Order Runge-Kutta Method

Consider the differential equation

$$\frac{dy}{dx} = f(x, y);\ y(x_0) = y_0 \qquad \text{...(1)}$$

Euler's method gives

$$y_1 = y_0 + hf(x_0, y_0) = y_0 + hy_0' \qquad \text{...(2)}$$

Expanding by Taylor's series, we get

$$y_1 = y(x_0 + h) = y_0 + hy_0' + \frac{h^2}{2!} y_0'' + \ldots \qquad \text{...(3)}$$

Comparing (2) and (3), it follows that Euler's method agrees with Taylor's series solution up to the term in h. Hence *Euler's method is the first order Runge-Kutta method.*

8.14.2. Second Order Runge-Kutta Method

Consider the differential equation

$$y' = f(x, y) \text{ with the initial condition } y(x_0) = y_0$$

Let h be the interval between equidistant values of x then in second order Runge-Kutta method, the first increment in y is computed from the formulae

$$\left.\begin{aligned} k_1 &= hf(x_0, y_0) \\ k_2 &= hf(x_0 + h, y_0 + k_1) \end{aligned}\right\}$$

$$\Delta y = \tfrac{1}{2}(k_1 + k_2)$$

taken in the given order.

Then,
$$x_1 = x_0 + h$$

$$y_1 = y_0 + \Delta y = y_0 + \tfrac{1}{2}(k_1 + k_2)$$

In a similar manner, the increment in y for the second interval is computed by means of the formulae,

$$\left.\begin{aligned} k_1 &= hf(x_1, y_1) \\ k_2 &= hf(x_1 + h, y_1 + k_1) \end{aligned}\right\}$$

$$\Delta y = \tfrac{1}{2}(k_1 + k_2)$$

and similarly for the next intervals.

The inherent error in the second order Runge-Kutta method is of order h^3.

8.14.3. Third Order Runge-Kutta Method

This method gives the approximate solution of the initial value problem

$$\frac{dy}{dx} = f(x, y);\ y(x_0) = y_0 \text{ as}$$

$$y_1 = y_0 + \Delta y \qquad \text{...(1)}$$

where
$$\Delta y = \frac{h}{6}(k_1 + 4k_2 + k_3)$$

Here,
$$k_1 = f(x_0, y_0)$$

$$k_2 = f\left\{x_0 + \frac{h}{2}, y_0 + \frac{k_1}{2}\right\}$$

$$k_3 = f(x_0 + h, y_0 + k');\ k' = hf(x_0 + h, y_0 + k_1)$$

Formula (1) can be generalised for successive approximations. Expression in (1) agrees with Taylor's series expansion for y_1 up to and including terms in h^3. This method is also known as **Runge's method.**

8.14.4. Fourth Order Runge-Kutta IV Method *[G.B.T.U. (MCA) 2010]*

It is one of the most widely used methods and is particularly suitable in cases when the computation of higher derivatives is complicated.

Consider the differential equation $y' = f(x, y)$ with the initial condition $y(x_0) = y_0$. Let h be the interval between equidistant values of x then the first increment in y is computed from the formulae

$$\left.\begin{aligned} k_1 &= hf(x_0, y_0) \\ k_2 &= hf\left(x_0 + \frac{h}{2}, y_0 + \frac{k_1}{2}\right) \\ k_3 &= hf\left(x_0 + \frac{h}{2}, y_0 + \frac{k_2}{2}\right) \\ k_4 &= hf(x_0 + h, y_0 + k_3) \\ \Delta y &= \frac{1}{6}(k_1 + 2k_2 + 2k_3 + k_4) \end{aligned}\right\} \qquad \text{....(1)}$$

taken in the given order.

Then, $\quad x_1 = x_0 + h \quad \text{and} \quad y_1 = y_0 + \Delta y$

In a similar manner, the increment in y for the second interval is computed by means of the formulae

$$k_1 = hf(x_1, y_1)$$
$$k_2 = hf\left(x_1 + \frac{h}{2}, y_1 + \frac{k_1}{2}\right)$$
$$k_3 = hf\left(x_1 + \frac{h}{2}, y_1 + \frac{k_2}{2}\right)$$
$$k_4 = hf(x_1 + h, y_1 + k_3)$$
$$\Delta y = \frac{1}{6}(k_1 + 2k_2 + 2k_3 + k_4)$$

and similarly for the next intervals.

This method is also termed as *Runge-Kutta's* method simply.

It is to be noted that the calculations for the first increment are exactly the same as for any other increment. The change in the formula for the different intervals is only in the values of x and y to be substituted. Hence to obtain Δy for the nth interval, we substitute $x_{n-1}, y_{n-1},$ in the expressions for $k_1, k_2,$ etc.

The inherent error in the fourth order Runge-Kutta method is of order h^5.

8.15. ALGORITHM OF RUNGE KUTTA IV ORDER METHOD

[*U.P.T.U. MCA(C.O.) 2005*]

```
Function F(x)=(x-y)/(x+y)
Input x0,y0,h,xn
n=(xn-x0)/h
x=x0
y=y0
For i=0, n
k1=h*F(x,y)
k2=h*F(x+h/2,y+k1/2)
k3=h*F(x+h/2,y+k2/2)
k4=h*F(x+h,y+k3)
k=(k1+(k2+k3)2+k4)/6
Print x,y
x=x+h
y=y+k
Next i
Stop
```

8.16. FLOW-CHART OF RUNGE-KUTTA IV ORDER METHOD

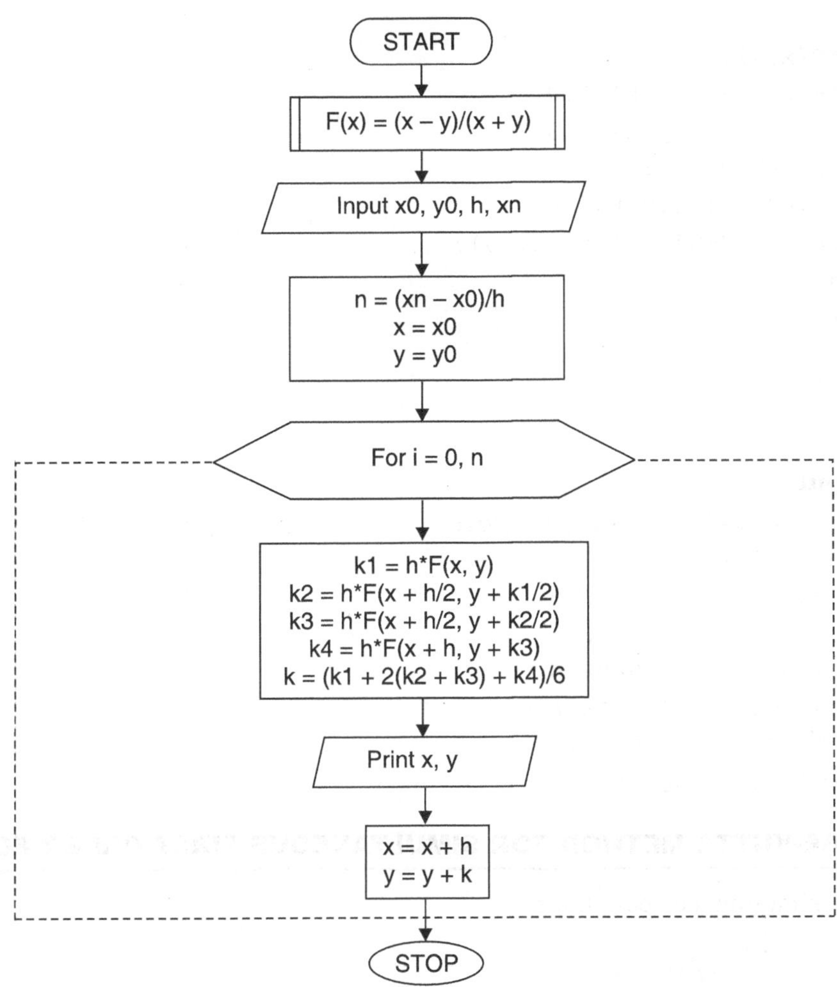

8.17. PROGRAM OF RUNGE-KUTTA IV ORDER METHOD *[U.P.T.U. MCA(C.O.) 2005]*

```
#include<stdio.h>
#define F(x,y)  (x-y)/(x+y)
main()
{
  int i,n;
  float x0,y0,h,xn,k1,k2,k3,k4,x,y,k;
  printf("\n Enter the values: x0,y0,h,xn:\n");
  scanf("%f%f%f%f", &x0,&y0,&h,&xn);
  n=(xn-x0)/h;
  x=x0;
```

```
    y=y0;
    for(i=0;i<=n;i++)
      {
      k1=h*F(x,y);
      k2=h*F(x+h/2.0,y+k1/2.0);
      k3=h*F(x+h/2.0,y+k2/2.0);
      k4=h*F(x+h,y+k3);
      k=(k1+(k2+k3)*2.0+k4)/6.0;
      printf("\n X=%f Y=%f", x, y);
      x=x+h;
      y=y+k;
    }
  return;
  }
```

8.17.1. Output

```
Enter the values: x0,y0,h,xn:
0 1 0.02 0.1
X=0.000000    Y=1.000000
X=0.020000    Y=0.980000
X=0.040000    Y=0.960816
X=0.060000    Y=0.942446
X=0.080000    Y=0.924885
X=0.100000    Y=0.908128
```

8.18. RUNGE-KUTTA METHOD FOR SIMULTANEOUS FIRST ORDER EQUATIONS

Consider the simultaneous equations

$$\frac{dy}{dx} = f_1(x, y, z) \qquad ...(1)$$

$$\frac{dz}{dx} = f_2(x, y, z) \qquad ...(2)$$

with the initial conditions $y(x_0) = y_0$ and $z(x_0) = z_0$. Now, starting from (x_0, y_0, z_0), the increments k and l in y and z are given by the following formulae:

$$k_1 = hf_1(x_0, y_0, z_0); \qquad l_1 = hf_2(x_0, y_0, z_0)$$

$$k_2 = hf_1\left(x_0 + \frac{h}{2}, y_0 + \frac{k_1}{2}, z_0 + \frac{l_1}{2}\right); \qquad l_2 = hf_2\left(x_0 + \frac{h}{2}, y_0 + \frac{k_1}{2}, z_0 + \frac{l_1}{2}\right)$$

$$k_3 = hf_1\left(x_0 + \frac{h}{2}, y_0 + \frac{k_2}{2}, z_0 + \frac{l_2}{2}\right); \qquad l_3 = hf_2\left(x_0 + \frac{h}{2}, y_0 + \frac{k_2}{2}, z_0 + \frac{l_2}{2}\right)$$

$$k_4 = hf_1(x_0 + h, y_0 + k_3, z_0 + l_3); \qquad l_4 = hf_2(x_0 + h, y_0 + k_3, z_0 + l_3)$$

$$k = \frac{1}{6}(k_1 + 2k_2 + 2k_3 + k_4); \qquad l = \frac{1}{6}(l_1 + 2l_2 + 2l_3 + l_4)$$

Hence $y_1 = y_0 + k$, $z_1 = z_0 + l$

To compute y_2, z_2, we simply replace x_0, y_0, z_0 by x_1, y_1, z_1 in the above formulae.

8.19. RUNGE-KUTTA METHOD FOR SECOND ORDER DIFFERENTIAL EQUATIONS

Consider a second order differential equation

$$\frac{d^2y}{dx^2} = \phi\left(x, y, \frac{dy}{dx}\right) \qquad ...(1)$$

with initial conditions $y(x_0) = y_0, y'(x_0) = y_0'$ ...(2)

Let $\frac{dy}{dx} = z$ so that $\frac{d^2y}{dx^2} = \frac{dz}{dx}$.

Substituting in equation (1), we get

$$\frac{dz}{dx} = \phi(x, y, z)$$

with initial conditions $y(x_0) = y_0, z(x_0) = z_0$

Hence, the problem is reduced to solving the simultaneous equations

$$\frac{dy}{dx} = z = f_1(x, y, z) \quad \text{and} \quad \frac{dz}{dx} = f_2(x, y, z)$$

subject to $y(x_0) = y_0, z(x_0) = z_0$.

Above simultaneous equations can be solved as explained in art. 8.18.

EXAMPLES

Example 1. *Solve the equation* $\frac{dy}{dx} = x + y$ *with initial condition* $y(0) = 1$ *by Runge-Kutta rule, from* $x = 0$ *to* $x = 0.4$ *with* $h = 0.1$. (M.T.U. 2014)

Sol. Here $f(x, y) = x + y, h = 0.1, x_0 = 0, y_0 = 1$

We have,

$$k_1 = hf(x_0, y_0) = 0.1\,(0 + 1) = 0.1$$

$$k_2 = hf\left(x_0 + \frac{h}{2},\ y_0 + \frac{k_1}{2}\right) = 0.1\,(0.05 + 1.05) = 0.11$$

$$k_3 = hf\left(x_0 + \frac{h}{2},\ y_0 + \frac{k_2}{2}\right) = 0.1105$$

$$k_4 = hf(x_0 + h,\ y_0 + k_3) = 0.12105$$

$$\therefore \quad \Delta y = \frac{1}{6}(k_1 + 2k_2 + 2k_3 + k_4) = 0.11034$$

Thus, $x_1 = x_0 + h = 0.1$ and $y_1 = y_0 + \Delta y = 1.11034$

Now for the second interval, we have

$$k_1 = hf(x_1, y_1) = 0.1\ (0.1 + 1.11034) = 0.121034$$

$$k_2 = hf\left(x_1 + \frac{h}{2}, y_1 + \frac{k_1}{2}\right) = 0.13208$$

$$k_3 = hf\left(x_1 + \frac{h}{2}, y_1 + \frac{k_2}{2}\right) = 0.13263$$

$$k_4 = hf(x_1 + h, y_1 + k_3) = 0.14429$$

$\therefore$ $$\Delta y = \frac{1}{6}(k_1 + 2k_2 + 2k_3 + k_4) = 0.132460$$

Hence $x_2 = 0.2$ and $y_2 = y_1 + \Delta y = 1.11034 + 0.13246 = 1.24280$

Similarly, for finding y_3, we have

$$k_1 = hf(x_2, y_2) = 0.14428,\ k_2 = 0.15649,\ k_3 = 0.15710,\ k_4 = 0.16999$$

$\therefore$ $$y_3 = 1.3997$$

and for $y_4 = y(0.4)$, we calculate

$$k_1 = 0.16997,\ k_2 = 0.18347,\ k_3 = 0.18414,\ k_4 = 0.19838$$

$\therefore$ $$y_4 = 1.5836.$$

Example 2. *Given* $\frac{dy}{dx} = y - x$, $y(0) = 2$. *Find* $y(0.1)$ *and* $y(0.2)$ *correct to four decimal places. (Use both second and fourth order methods)* [U.P.T.U. (MCA) 2009]

Sol. By second order Method

To find $y(0.1)$

Here $y' = f(x, y) = y - x,\ x_0 = 0,\ y_0 = 2$ and $h = 0.1$

Now, $k_1 = hf(x_0, y_0) = 0.1(2 - 0) = 0.2$

$$k_2 = hf(x_0 + h, y_0 + k_1) = 0.21$$

$\therefore$ $$\Delta y = \frac{1}{2}(k_1 + k_2) = 0.205$$

Thus, $x_1 = x_0 + h = 0.1$ and $y_1 = y_0 + \Delta y = 2.205$

To find $y(0.2)$ we note that,

$$x_1 = 0.1,\ y_1 = 2.205,\ h = 0.1$$

For second interval, we have

$$k_1 = hf(x_1, y_1) = 0.2105$$

$$k_2 = hf(x_1 + h, y_1 + k_1) = 0.22155$$

$\therefore$ $$\Delta y = \frac{1}{2}(k_1 + k_2) = 0.216025$$

Thus, $x_2 = x_1 + h = 0.2$ and $y_2 = y_1 + \Delta y = 2.4210$

Hence $y(0.1) = 2.205,\ y(0.2) = 2.421.$

By fourth order method

$$y' = f(x, y) = y - x,\ x_0 = 0,\ y_0 = 2 \text{ and } h = 0.1$$

$$k_1 = hf(x_0, y_0) = 0.1\,(2 - 0) = 0.2$$

$$k_2 = hf\left(x_0 + \frac{h}{2}, y_0 + \frac{k_1}{2}\right) = 0.205$$

$$k_3 = hf\left(x_0 + \frac{h}{2}, y_0 + \frac{k_2}{2}\right) = 0.20525$$

and $$k_4 = hf\,(x_0 + h, y_0 + k_3) = 0.210525$$

$\therefore$ $$\Delta y = \frac{1}{6}(k_1 + 2k_2 + 2k_3 + k_4) = 0.2052$$

Thus, $$x_1 = x_0 + h = 0 + 0.1 = 0.1$$

$$y_1 = y_0 + \Delta y = 2 + 0.2052 = 2.2052$$

Now to determine $y_2 = y(0.2)$, we note that

$$x_1 = x_0 + h = 0.1,\ y_1 = 2.2052,\ h = 0.1$$

For II interval, $$k_1 = hf\,(x_1, y_1) = 0.21052$$

$$k_2 = hf\left(x_1 + \frac{h}{2}, y_1 + \frac{k_1}{2}\right) = 0.21605$$

$$k_3 = hf\left(x_1 + h/2, y_1 + \frac{k_2}{2}\right) = 0.216323$$

and $$k_4 = hf\,(x_1 + h, y_1 + k_3) = 0.221523$$

$\therefore$ $$\Delta y = \frac{1}{6}(k_1 + 2k_2 + 2k_3 + k_4) = 0.21613$$

Thus, $$x_2 = x_1 + h = 0.1 + 0.1 = 0.2$$

and $$y_2 = y_1 + \Delta y = 2.2052 + 0.21613 = 2.4213$$

Hence, $y(0.1) = 2.2052$, $y(0.2) = 2.4213$.

Example 3. *Given the initial value problem:* $y' = 1 + y^2$, $y(0) = 0$

Find $y(0.6)$ *by Runge-Kutta fourth order method taking* $h = 0.2$. (U.P.T.U. 2008, 2006)

Sol. Here, $f(x, y) = 1 + y^2$, $h = 0.2$, $x_0 = 0$, $y_0 = 0$

We have, $$k_1 = h\,f\,(x_0, y_0) = 0.2$$

$$k_2 = h\,f\left(x_0 + \frac{h}{2}, y_0 + \frac{k_1}{2}\right) = 0.202$$

$$k_3 = h\,f\left(x_0 + \frac{h}{2}, y_0 + \frac{k_2}{2}\right) = 0.2020402$$

$$k_4 = h\,f\,(x_0 + h, y_0 + k_3) = 0.2081640$$

$\therefore$ $$\Delta y = \frac{1}{6}(k_1 + 2k_2 + 2k_3 + k_4) = 0.2027074$$

Thus, $y_1 = y(0.2) = y_0 + \Delta y = 0.2027074, x_1 = x_0 + h = 0.2$

Again, $f(x, y) = 1 + y^2, h = 0.2, x_1 = 0.2, y_1 = 0.2027074$

We have, $k_1 = h\,f(x_1, y_1) = 0.208218$

$$k_2 = h\,f\left(x_1 + \frac{h}{2}, y_1 + \frac{k_1}{2}\right) = 0.218827$$

$$k_3 = h\,f\left(x_1 + \frac{h}{2}, y_1 + \frac{k_2}{2}\right) = 0.219484$$

$$k_4 = h\,f(x_1 + h, y_1 + k_3) = 0.235649$$

$\therefore$ $\Delta y = \frac{1}{6}(k_1 + 2k_2 + 2k_3 + k_4) = 0.22008$

Thus, $y_2 = y(0.4) = y_1 + \Delta y = 0.4227874, x_2 = x_1 + h = 0.4$

Again, $f(x, y) = 1 + y^2, h = 0.2, x_2 = 0.4, y_2 = 0.4227874$

We have, $k_1 = h\,f(x_2, y_2) = 0.235749$

$$k_2 = h\,f\left(x_2 + \frac{h}{2}, y_2 + \frac{k_1}{2}\right) = 0.258463$$

$$k_3 = h\,f\left(x_2 + \frac{h}{2}, y_2 + \frac{k_2}{2}\right) = 0.260945$$

$$k_4 = h\,f(x_2 + h, y_2 + k_3) = 0.293498$$

$\therefore$ $\Delta y = \frac{1}{6}(k_1 + 2k_2 + 2k_3 + k_4) = 0.261344$

Thus, $y_3 = y(0.6) = y_2 + \Delta y = 0.6841314.$

Example 4. *Use the Runge-Kutta fourth order method to find the value of y when x = 1 given that y = 1 when x = 0 (taking n = 2) and* $\frac{dy}{dx} = \frac{y - x}{y + x}$. [U.P.T.U. (MCA) 2008]

Sol. Here, $f(x, y) = \frac{y - x}{y + x}, x_0 = 0, y_0 = 1, h = 0.5$

We have, $k_1 = h\,f(x_0, y_0) = 0.5$

$$k_2 = h\,f\left(x_0 + \frac{h}{2}, y_0 + \frac{k_1}{2}\right) = 0.333$$

$$k_3 = h\,f\left(x_0 + \frac{h}{2}, y_0 + \frac{k_2}{2}\right) = 0.3235$$

$$k_4 = h\,f(x_0 + h, y_0 + k_3) = 0.2258$$

$\therefore$ $\Delta y = \frac{1}{6}(k_1 + 2k_2 + 2k_3 + k_4) = 0.3398$

Thus, $y_1 = y(0.5) = y_0 + \Delta y = 1.3398, x_1 = x_0 + h = 0.5$

Again, $k_1 = h\,f(x_1, y_1) = 0.22823$

$$k_2 = h\,f\left(x_1 + \frac{h}{2}, y_1 + \frac{k_1}{2}\right) = 0.15969$$

$$k_3 = h\,f\left(x_1 + \frac{h}{2}, y_1 + \frac{k_2}{2}\right) = 0.15432$$

$$k_4 = h\,f(x_1 + h, y_1 + k_3) = 0.09906$$

$\therefore$ $$\Delta y = \frac{1}{6}(k_1 + 2k_2 + 2k_3 + k_4) = 0.159218$$

Thus, $y_2 = y(1.0) = y_1 + \Delta y = 1.499018.$

Example 5. *Use Runge-Kutta method of fourth order to approximate y when x = 0.1 given that y = 1 at x = 0 and* $\frac{dy}{dx} = 3x + y^2$. [U.P.T.U. MCA (C.O.) 2008]

Sol. Here, $f(x, y) = 3x + y^2, h = 0.1, x_0 = 0, y_0 = 1$

We have, $$k_1 = h\,f(x_0, y_0) = 0.1$$

$$k_2 = h\,f\left(x_0 + \frac{h}{2}, y_0 + \frac{k_1}{2}\right) = 0.12525$$

$$k_3 = h\,f\left(x_0 + \frac{h}{2}, y_0 + \frac{k_2}{2}\right) = 0.127917$$

$$k_4 = h\,f(x_0 + h, y_0 + k_3) = 0.15722$$

$\therefore$ $$\Delta y = \frac{1}{6}(k_1 + 2k_2 + 2k_3 + k_4) = 0.127259$$

Thus, $y(0.1) = y_0 + \Delta y = 1.127259.$

Example 6. *Find the value of y(1.1) using Runge-Kutta method of fourth order, given that* $\frac{dy}{dx} = y^2 + xy$, *y(1) = 1.0, take h = 0.05.* (G.B.T.U. 2011, 2012; M.T.U. 2013)

Sol. Here, $f(x, y) = y^2 + xy, x_0 = 1, y_0 = 1, h = 0.05$

We have, $$k_1 = h\,f(x_0, y_0) = 0.1$$

$$k_2 = h\,f\left(x_0 + \frac{h}{2}, y_0 + \frac{k_1}{2}\right) = 0.10894$$

$$k_3 = h\,f\left(x_0 + \frac{h}{2}, y_0 + \frac{k_2}{2}\right) = 0.109637$$

$$k_4 = h\,f(x_0 + h, y_0 + k_3) = 0.119821$$

$\therefore$ $$\Delta y = \frac{1}{6}(k_1 + 2k_2 + 2k_3 + k_4) = 0.109496$$

Thus, $y_1 = y(1.05) = y_0 + \Delta y = 1.109496, x_1 = x_0 + h = 1.05$

Again, $$k_1 = h\,f(x_1, y_1) = 0.119798$$

$$k_2 = h\,f\left(x_1 + \frac{h}{2}, y_1 + \frac{k_1}{2}\right) = 0.13123$$

$$k_3 = h\,f\left(x_1 + \frac{h}{2}, y_1 + \frac{k_2}{2}\right) = 0.13221$$

$$k_4 = h\,f(x_1 + h, y_1 + k_3) = 0.145385$$

$\therefore \quad \Delta y = \frac{1}{6}(k_1 + 2k_2 + 2k_3 + k_4) = 0.13201$

Thus, $\quad y_2 = y(1.1) = y_1 + \Delta y = 1.241506$

Example 7. *Use Runge-Kutta IV order method with $h = 0.1$ to find $x(0.1)$ and $x(0.2)$ where $\frac{dx}{dt} = t - x$ and $x(0) = 0$.*

Sol. Here, $\quad f(t, x) = t - x,\ t_0 = 0,\ x_0 = 0$

$$k_1 = hf(t_0, x_0) = 0$$

$$k_2 = hf\left(t_0 + \frac{h}{2}, x_0 + \frac{k_1}{2}\right) = 0.005$$

$$k_3 = hf\left(t_0 + \frac{h}{2}, x_0 + \frac{k_2}{2}\right) = 0.00475$$

$$k_4 = hf(t_0 + h, x_0 + k_3) = 0.009525$$

$\therefore \quad \Delta x = \frac{1}{6}(k_1 + 2k_2 + 2k_3 + k_4) = 0.0048375$

Thus, $\quad x(0.1) = x_0 + \Delta x = 0.0048375,\ t_1 = t_0 + h = 0.1$

Again, $\quad k_1 = hf(t_1, x_1) = 0.00951625$

$$k_2 = hf\left(t_1 + \frac{h}{2}, x_1 + \frac{k_1}{2}\right) = 0.014040$$

$$k_3 = hf\left(t_1 + \frac{h}{2}, x_1 + \frac{k_2}{2}\right) = 0.013814$$

$$k_4 = hf(t_1 + h, x_1 + k_3) = 0.018135$$

$\therefore \quad \Delta x = \frac{1}{6}(k_1 + 2k_2 + 2k_3 + k_4) = 0.013893$

Thus, $\quad x(0.2) = x_1 + \Delta x = 0.0187305.$

Example 8. *Solve the initial value problem $u' = -2tu^2$, $u(0) = 1$ with $h = 0.2$ on the interval $[0, 0.4]$. Use Runge-Kutta fourth order method and compare your result with exact solution.* [U.P.T.U. 2009, U.P.T.U. (MCA) 2006]

Sol. Here, $\quad f(t, u) = -2t\,u^2,\ t_0 = 0,\ u_0 = 1,\ h = 0.2$

We have, $\quad k_1 = h\,f(t_0, u_0) = 0$

$$k_2 = hf\left(t_0 + \frac{h}{2}, u_0 + \frac{k_1}{2}\right) = -0.04$$

$$k_3 = hf\left(t_0 + \frac{h}{2}, u_0 + \frac{k_2}{2}\right) = -0.038416$$

$$k_4 = hf(t_0 + h, u_0 + k_3) = -0.0739715$$

$\therefore \quad \Delta u = -0.03846725$

Thus, $\quad u_1 = u(0.2) = u_0 + \Delta u = 0.9615328$

Again, $k_1 = hf(t_1, u_1) = -0.0739636$

$$k_2 = hf\left(t_1 + \frac{h}{2}, u_1 + \frac{k_1}{2}\right) = -0.1025753$$

$$k_3 = hf\left(t_1 + \frac{h}{2}, u_1 + \frac{k_2}{2}\right) = -0.0994255$$

$$k_4 = hf(t_1 + h, u_1 + k_3) = -0.1189166$$

$\therefore$ $\Delta u = -0.0994803$

Thus, $u_2 = u(0.4) = u_1 + \Delta u = 0.8620525$

Absolute errors in numerical solutions are

$$\varepsilon(0.2) = |\ 0.961539 - 0.961533\ | = 0.000006$$

$$\varepsilon(0.4) = |\ 0.862069 - 0.862053\ | = 0.000016$$

Example 9. *Using Runge-Kutta method of fourth order, find y(0.8) correct to 4 decimal places if $y' = y - x^2$, $y(0.6) = 1.7379$, taking $h = 0.1$.* (U.P.T.U. 2007)

Sol. Here, $f(x, y) = y - x^2$, $x_0 = 0.6$, $h = 0.1$, $y_0 = 1.7379$

We have, $k_1 = hf(x_0, y_0) = h(y_0 - x_0^2) = 0.13779$

$$k_2 = hf\left(x_0 + \frac{h}{2}, y_0 + \frac{k_1}{2}\right) = h\left[\left(y_0 + \frac{k_1}{2}\right) - \left(x_0 + \frac{h}{2}\right)^2\right] = 0.1384295$$

$$k_3 = hf\left(x_0 + \frac{h}{2}, y_0 + \frac{k_2}{2}\right) = h\left[\left(y_0 + \frac{k_2}{2}\right) - \left(x_0 + \frac{h}{2}\right)^2\right]$$

$$= 0.138461475$$

$$k_4 = hf(x_0 + h, y_0 + k_3) = h[(y_0 + k_3) - (x_0 + h)^2] = 0.1386361475$$

$\therefore$ $$\Delta y = \frac{1}{6}(k_1 + 2k_2 + 2k_3 + k_4) = 0.138368$$

Thus, $y_1 = y(0.7) = y_0 + \Delta y = 1.876268$, $x_1 = x_0 + h = 0.7$

Now, $x_1 = 0.7$, $y_1 = y(0.7) = 1.876268$, $h = 0.1$

Again, $k_1 = hf(x_1, y_1) = h(y_1 - x_1^2) = 0.1386268$

$$k_2 = hf\left(x_1 + \frac{h}{2}, y_1 + \frac{k_1}{2}\right) = h\left[\left(y_1 + \frac{k_1}{2}\right) - \left(x_1 + \frac{h}{2}\right)^2\right] = 0.13830814$$

$$k_3 = hf\left(x_1 + \frac{h}{2}, y_1 + \frac{k_2}{2}\right) = h\left[\left(y_1 + \frac{k_2}{2}\right) - \left(x_1 + \frac{h}{2}\right)^2\right]$$

$$= 0.138292207$$

$$k_4 = hf(x_1 + h, y_1 + k_3) = h[(y_1 + k_3) - (x_1 + h)^2] = 0.1374560207$$

$\therefore$ $$\Delta y = \frac{1}{6}(k_1 + 2k_2 + 2k_3 + k_4) = 0.138213919$$

Thus, $y_2 = y(0.8) = y_1 + \Delta y = 2.0145$, $x_2 = x_1 + h = 0.8$.

Example 10. *Solve:* $y' = \frac{1}{x+y}$, *$y(0) = 1$ for $x = 0.5$ to $x = 1$ by Runge-Kutta method. Take $h = 0.5$.*

Sol. Here, $f(x, y) = \frac{1}{x+y}$, $x_0 = 0$, $h = 0.5$, $y_0 = 1$

We have, $$k_1 = hf(x_0, y_0) = h\left(\frac{1}{x_0 + y_0}\right) = 0.5$$

$$k_2 = hf\left(x_0 + \frac{h}{2}, y_0 + \frac{k_1}{2}\right) = h \frac{1}{\left(x_0 + \frac{h}{2} + y_0 + \frac{k_1}{2}\right)} = 0.3333$$

$$k_3 = hf\left(x_0 + \frac{h}{2}, y_0 + \frac{k_2}{2}\right) = h \cdot \frac{1}{\left(x_0 + \frac{h}{2} + y_0 + \frac{k_2}{2}\right)} = 0.3529$$

$$k_4 = hf(x_0 + h, y_0 + k_3) = h \frac{1}{(x_0 + h + y_0 + k_3)} = 0.2698$$

$\therefore$ $$\Delta y = \frac{1}{6}(k_1 + 2k_2 + 2k_3 + k_4) = 0.3570$$

Thus, $y_1 = y(0.5) = y_0 + \Delta y = 1.3570$, $x_1 = x_0 + h = 0.5$

Now, $x_1 = 0.5$, $y_1 = 1.3570$, $h = 0.5$

Again, $$k_1 = hf(x_1, y_1) = \frac{h}{x_1 + y_1} = 0.2692$$

$$k_2 = hf\left(x_1 + \frac{h}{2}, y_1 + \frac{k_1}{2}\right) = \frac{h}{x_1 + \frac{h}{2} + y_1 + \frac{k_1}{2}} = 0.2230$$

$$k_3 = hf\left(x_1 + \frac{h}{2}, y_1 + \frac{k_2}{2}\right) = \frac{h}{x_1 + \frac{h}{2} + y_1 + \frac{k_2}{2}} = 0.2254$$

$$k_4 = hf(x_1 + h, y_1 + k_3) = \frac{h}{x_1 + h + y_1 + k_3} = 0.1936$$

$\therefore$ $$\Delta y = \frac{1}{6}(k_1 + 2k_2 + 2k_3 + k_4) = 0.2266$$

Thus, $y_2 = y(1) = y_1 + \Delta y = 1.5836$, $x_2 = x_1 + h = 1$.

Example 11. *If $\frac{dy}{dx} = x + y^2$, use Runge-Kutta method of fouth order to find an approximate value of y for $x = 0.2$ given that $y = 1$ when $x = 0$. (Take $h = 0.1$)* (U.P.T.U. 2009)

Sol. Here, $f(x, y) = x + y^2$, $x_0 = 0$, $y_0 = 1$, $h = 0.1$

We have, $$k_1 = hf(x_0, y_0) = h(x_0 + y_0^2) = 0.1$$

$$k_2 = hf\left(x_0 + \frac{h}{2}, y_0 + \frac{k_1}{2}\right) = h\left[x_0 + \frac{h}{2} + \left(y_0 + \frac{k_1}{2}\right)^2\right] = 0.11525$$

$$k_3 = hf\left(x_0 + \frac{h}{2}, y_0 + \frac{k_2}{2}\right) = h\left[x_0 + \frac{h}{2} + \left(y_0 + \frac{k_2}{2}\right)^2\right] = 0.116857$$

$$k_4 = hf(x_0 + h, y_0 + k_3) = h[x_0 + h + (y_0 + k_3)^2] = 0.134737$$

$\therefore$ $$\Delta y = \frac{1}{6}(k_1 + 2k_2 + 2k_3 + k_4) = 0.116492$$

Thus, $y_1 = y(0.1) = y_0 + \Delta y = 1.116492, x_1 = x_0 + h = 0.1$

Now, $x_1 = 0.1, y_1 = 1.116492, h = 0.1$

Again, $k_1 = hf(x_1, y_1) = h(x_1 + y_1^2) = 0.134655$

$$k_2 = hf\left(x_1 + \frac{h}{2}, y_1 + \frac{k_1}{2}\right) = h\left[x_1 + \frac{h}{2} + \left(y_1 + \frac{k_1}{2}\right)^2\right] = 0.155143$$

$$k_3 = hf\left(x_1 + \frac{h}{2}, y_1 + \frac{k_2}{2}\right) = h\left[x_1 + \frac{h}{2} + \left(y_1 + \frac{k_2}{2}\right)^2\right] = 0.157579$$

$$k_4 = hf(x_1 + h, y_1 + k_3) = h[x_1 + h + (y_1 + k_3)^2] = 0.1823257$$

$\therefore$ $$\Delta y = \frac{1}{6}(k_1 + 2k_2 + 2k_3 + k_4) = 0.15707$$

Thus, $y_2 = y(0.2) = y_1 + \Delta y = 1.273562, \quad x_2 = x_1 + h = 0.2.$

Example 12. *Solve:* $\frac{dy}{dx} = yz + x, \frac{dz}{dx} = xz + y$ *; given that* $y(0) = 1, z(0) = -1$ *for* $y(0.1)$, $z(0.1)$.

Sol. Here, $f_1(x, y, z) = yz + x, f_2(x, y, z) = xz + y$

$$h = 0.1, x_0 = 0, y_0 = 1, z_0 = -1$$

$$k_1 = hf_1(x_0, y_0, z_0) = h(y_0 z_0 + x_0) = -0.1$$

$$l_1 = hf_2(x_0, y_0, z_0) = h(x_0 z_0 + y_0) = 0.1$$

$$k_2 = hf_1\left(x_0 + \frac{h}{2}, y_0 + \frac{k_1}{2}, z_0 + \frac{l_1}{2}\right) = -0.08525$$

$$l_2 = hf_2\left(x_0 + \frac{h}{2}, y_0 + \frac{k_1}{2}, z_0 + \frac{l_1}{2}\right) = 0.09025$$

$$k_3 = hf_1\left(x_0 + \frac{h}{2}, y_0 + \frac{k_2}{2}, z_0 + \frac{l_2}{2}\right) = -0.0864173$$

$$l_3 = hf_2\left(x_0 + \frac{h}{2}, y_0 + \frac{k_2}{2}, z_0 + \frac{l_2}{2}\right) = 0.090963125$$

$$k_4 = hf_1(x_0 + h, y_0 + k_3, z_0 + l_3) = -0.073048$$

$$l_4 = hf_2(x_0 + h, y_0 + k_3, z_0 + l_3) = 0.0822679$$

$\therefore$ $$k = \frac{1}{6}(k_1 + 2k_2 + 2k_3 + k_4) = -0.0860637$$

and $$l = \frac{1}{6}(l_1 + 2l_2 + 2l_3 + l_4) = 0.0907823$$

Thus, $$y_1 = y(0.1) = y_0 + k = 1 - 0.0860637 = 0.9139363$$

$$z_1 = z(0.1) = z_0 + l = -1 + 0.0907823 = -0.9092176.$$

ASSIGNMENT

1. Use Runge-Kutta method to approximate y when $x = 0.1$ given that $x = 0$ when $y = 1$ and $\frac{dy}{dx} = x + y$.
2. Use Runge-Kutta Fourth order formula to find $y(1.4)$ if $y(1) = 2$ and $\frac{dy}{dx} = xy$. Take $h = 0.2$.
3. Use Runge-Kutta method to find y when $x = 1.2$ in steps of 0.1 given that

$$\frac{dy}{dx} = x^2 + y^2 \quad \text{and} \quad y(1) = 1.5$$

4. Write the main steps to be followed in using the Runge-Kutta method of fourth order to solve an ordinary diff. equation of first order. Hence solve $\frac{dy}{dx} = x^3 + y^3$, $y(0) = 1$ and step length $h = 0.1$ up to three iterations.
5. Use classical Runge-Kutta method of fourth order to find the numerical solution at $x = 1.4$ for $\frac{dy}{dx} = y^2 + x^2$, $y(1) = 0$. Assume step size $h = 0.2$.
6. Given that $y' = x^2 - y$, $y(0) = 1$, find $y(0.1)$, $y(0.2)$ using Runge-Kutta method of fourth order.
7. (*i*) Estimate $y(1)$ if $2yy' = x^2$ and $y(0) = 2$ using Runge-Kutta method of fourth order by taking $h = 0.5$. Also compare the result with exact value. *(G.B.T.U. 2011)*

   (*ii*) Estimate $y(0.8)$ using Runge-Kutta method of fourth order (perform two iterations) for the differential equation $2y\frac{dy}{dx} = x^2$, $y(0) = 2$. Also compare the result with exact value.

   (G.B.T.U. 2013)
8. Using Runge-Kutta method, find $y(0.2)$ given that $\frac{dy}{dx} = 3x + \frac{1}{2}y$, $y(0) = 1$ taking $h = 0.1$.
9. Given that $\frac{dy}{dx} = 1 + xy$; $y(0) = 2$. Using Runge-Kutta fourth order method, find $y(0.1)$, $y(0.2)$.

   [G.B.T.U. MCA (SUM) 2010]
10. Use Runge-Kutta method of fourth order to solve the following differential equation in the interval [0, 0.4]:

$$\frac{dy}{dx} = \frac{y + x}{y - x}, \quad y(0) = 1. \quad \text{Take } h = 0.2.$$

[G.B.T.U. (C.O.) 2011]

11. Using Runge-Kutta method of fourth order, solve the following differential equation:

$$\frac{dy}{dx} = \frac{y^2 - x^2}{y^2 + x^2} \quad \text{with} \quad y(0) = 1 \quad \text{at } x = 0.2, 0.4.$$

(G.B.T.U. 2010)

12. Use Runge-Kutta formula of fourth order to find the numerical solution at $x = 0.6$ and 0.8 for the differential equation $y' = \sqrt{x + y}$, $y(0.4) = 0.41$. Assume the step length $h = 0.2$.

    [M.T.U. 2012, G.B.T.U. (MCA) 2011]

13. (*i*) Apply Runge-Kutta fourth order method to solve $10\,\frac{dy}{dx} = x^2 + y^2$; $y\,(0) = 1$ for $0 < x \le 0.4$ and $h = 0.1$. (*G.B.T.U. 2013, 2011*)

(*ii*) Apply Runge-Kutta method of fourth order to solve the initial value problem:

$$5\,\frac{dy}{dx} = x^2 + y^2, \quad y\,(0) = 1$$

and find y in the interval $0 \le x \le 0.2$, taking $h = 0.1$. (*G.B.T.U. 2012*)

14. Using Runge-Kutta method of fourth order, solve for $y(0.1)$, $y(0.2)$ and $y(0.3)$ given that $y' = xy + y^2$, $y(0) = 1$. [*M.T.U. (MCA) 2012, G.B.T.U. (C.O.) 2010*]

15. Using fourth order Runge-Kutta method, solve the initial value problem $\frac{d^2y}{dx^2} - x\,\frac{dy}{dx} + y^2 = 0$ with initial conditions $y = 1$ and $\frac{dy}{dx} = 0$ when $x = 0$ in the interval [0, 0.2] and step size $h = 0.1$. (*M.T.U. 2013*)

16. Solve $\frac{dy}{dx} = x + z$, $\frac{dz}{dx} = x - y^2$ for $y\,(0.1)$, $z\,(0.1)$ given that $y\,(0) = 2$, $z\,(0) = 1$ by Runge-Kutta IV order method.

Answers

1. 1.11034
2. $y(1.2) = 2.4921$, $y(1.4) = 3.2320$
3. $y(1.1) = 1.8955$, $y(1.2) = 2.5041$
4. 1.118057, 1.291457, 1.584057
5. $y(1.2) = 0.246326$, $y(1.4) = 0.622751489$
6. $y(0.1) = 0.9051627$, $y(0.2) = 0.8212695$
7. (*i*) 2.0816705

   (*ii*) $y(0.4) = 2.005326$, $y(0.8) = 2.042221$; $y(0.8)$ [Exact value] = 2.042221829
8. 1.1749
9. 2.110359, 2.24309
10. $y(0.2) = 1.23923$, $y(0.4) = 1.54892$
11. 1.195999, 1.375269
12. $y(0.6) = 0.61035$, $y\,(0.8) = 0.84899$
13. (*i*) $y(0.1) = 1.0101$, $y(0.2) = 1.0206$, $y(0.3) = 1.0317$, $y(0.4\,) = 1.0437$

   (*ii*)

x:	0	0.1	0.2
y:	1	1.020475	1.04221

14. $y(0.1) = 1.1168873$, $y(0.2) = 1.2773914$, $y(0.3) = 1.50412$
15.

x:	0	0.1	0.2
y:	1	0.995	0.98

16. 2.0845, 0.586.

8.20. PREDICTOR-CORRECTOR METHODS

In Runge-Kutta methods, we need only the information at (x_i, y_i) to calculate the value of y_{i+1} and no attention is paid for the nature of the solution at the earlier points.

To overcome this defect, Predictor-Corrector methods are useful. The technique of refining an initially crude predicted estimate of y_i by means of a more accurate corrector formula is called *Predictor-Corrector method.*

The modified Euler's method of solving the initial value problem,

$$y' = f(x, y), y(x_0) = y_0 \quad ...(1)$$

can be stated as

$$y_1^p = y_0 + hf(x_0, y_0) \quad ...(2)$$

$$y_1^c = y_0 + \frac{h}{2} [f(x_0, y_0) + f(x_1, y_1^p)] \quad ...(3)$$

Here we predict the value of y_1 by Euler's method and use it in (3) to get a corrected or improved value. This is a typical case of Predictor-Corrector method.

In this section, we will obtain two important Predictor-Corrector methods, namely, Milne's Simpson method and Adams-Moulton (or Adams-Bash forth) method. Both of these methods are of IV order and the error is of order h^5. These methods make use of four starting values of y namely, y_0, y_1, y_2 and y_3. Hence these methods are also called as *Multi-Step methods.*

8.21. MILNE'S METHOD

It is a simple and reasonably accurate method of solving differential equations numerically. To solve the differential equation $y' = f(x, y)$ by this method, first we get the approximate value of y_{n+1} by predictor formula and then improve this value using a corrector formula. These formula are derived from Newton's formula.

Newton's forward interpolation formula interms of y' and u is

$$y' = y_0' + u\Delta y_0' + \frac{u(u-1)}{2} \Delta^2 y_0' + \frac{u(u-1)(u-2)}{6} \Delta^3 y_0' + \frac{u(u-1)(u-2)(u-3)}{24} \Delta^4 y_0' + ... \quad ...(1)$$

where $\quad u = \frac{x - x_0}{h} \quad$ or $\quad x = x_0 + uh$

Now integrating (1) over the interval x_0 to $x_0 + 4h$ (or $u = 0$ to 4), we get

$$\int_{x_0}^{x_0+4h} y'\, dx = h\int_0^4 y'\, du \qquad | \because dx = hdu$$

or

$$y_4 - y_0 = h \int_0^4 \left[y_0' + u\Delta y_0' + \frac{u(u-1)}{2}\Delta^2 y_0' + \frac{u(u-1)(u-2)}{6}\Delta^3 y_0' + \frac{u(u-1)(u-2)(u-3)}{24}\Delta^4 y_0' + ...\right] du$$

$$= h\left(4y_0' + 8\Delta y_0' + \frac{20}{3}\Delta^2 y_0' + \frac{8}{3}\Delta^3 y_0' + \frac{28}{90}\Delta^4 y_0'\right)$$

| keeping up to IV differences

Here, y_0 and y_4 stand for values of y at $x = x_0$ and $x = x_0 + 4h$ respectively.

Substituting the values of I, II and III differences, we get

$$y_4 - y_0 = h\left(4y_0' + 8(E-1)y_0' + \frac{20}{3}(E-1)^2 y_0' + \frac{8}{3}(E-1)^3 y_0' + \frac{28}{90}\Delta^4 y_0'\right) \quad ...(2)$$

$$= \frac{4h}{3}(2y_1' - y_2' + 2y_3') + \frac{28}{90}h\Delta^4 y_0'$$

or

$$y_4 = y_0 + \frac{4h}{3}(2y_1' - y_2' + 2y_3') + \frac{28}{90}h\Delta^4 y_0' \quad ...(3)$$

This is ***Milne's Predictor (Extrapolation) formula.***

It is used to predict the value of y_4 when the value of y_0, y_1, y_2 and y_3 are known.

To obtain the corrector formula, we integrate (1) over the interval x_0 to $x_0 + 2h$ (or $u = 0$ to 2) and consequently.

$$y_2 - y_0 = h\left(2y_0' + 2\Delta y_0' + \frac{1}{3}\Delta^2 y_0' - \frac{1}{90}\Delta^4 y_0'\right)$$

Expressing the I, II and III differences interms of the function value by using $D \equiv E - 1$, we obtain,

$$y_2 - y_0 = \frac{h}{3}(y_0' + 4y_1' + y_2') - \frac{h}{90}\Delta^4 y_0'$$

$\Rightarrow$

$$y_2 = y_0 + \frac{h}{3}(y_0' + 4y_1' + y_2') - \frac{h}{90}\Delta^4 y_0' \quad ...(4)$$

This is ***Milne's corrector formula.***

The value of y_4 obtained from (3) and (4) can be put as

$$\boxed{y_{n+1} = y_{n-3} + \frac{4h}{3}(2y'_{n-2} - y'_{n-1} + 2y'_n)} \quad ...(5)$$

$$\boxed{y'_{n+1} = y_{n-1} + \frac{h}{3}(y'_{n-1} + 4y'_n + y'_{n+1})} \quad ...(6)$$

It is to be noted that we have considered the differences up to the third order because we fit up a polynomial of degree four.

The terms containing $\Delta^4 y_0'$ are not used explicitly in the formula but they give the principal parts of the errors in the two values of y_{n+1} as computed from (5) and (6).

We notice that this error in (6) is of opposite sign to that in (5) but it is very small in magnitude.

So we may take, $$(y_{n+1})_{\text{exact}} = y_{n+1} + \frac{28}{90}h\Delta^4 y'$$

and

$$(y_{n+1})_{\text{exact}} = y^{(1)}_{n+1} - \frac{h}{90}\Delta^4 y'$$

where y_{n+1} and $y^{(1)}_{n+1}$ denote the predicted and first corrected value of y at $x = x_{n+1}$.

Equating these two values, we get

$$y_{n+1} - y^{(1)}_{n+1} = -\frac{29}{90} h\Delta^4 y' = 29\ \delta$$

where $\delta = -\frac{h}{90}\ \Delta^4 y'$ denotes the principal part of the error in (6). Thus it gives

$$\delta = \frac{1}{29} [y_{n+1} - y^{(1)}_{n+1}]$$

Thus we observe that the error in (6) is $\frac{1}{29}$ th of the difference between the predicted and corrected values.

8.21.1. Algorithm of Milne's Predictor-Corrector Method

[*U.P.T.U. MCA(C.O.) 2003*]

```
 1. Function F(x,y)=x+y
 2. Input xn
 3. For i=0,3
 4. Input x(i),y(i)
 5. Next i
 6. h=x(1)-x(0)
 7. n=(xn-x(0))/h
 8. For i=3,n
 9. x(i+1)=x(i)+h
10. f=F(x(i),y(i))
11. f1=F(x(i-1),y(i-1))
12. f2=F(x(i-2),y(i-2))
13. yp=y(i-3)+4h/3(2f2-f1+2f)
14. yc=y(i-1)+h/3(f1+4f+F(x(i+1),yp))
15. If abs (yp-yc)<0.0005 then
     y(i+1)=yc
     print x(i+1), y(i+1)
    ELSE
     yp=yc
16. Next i
17. Stop
```

8.21.2. Flow Chart of Milne's Predictor Corrector Method

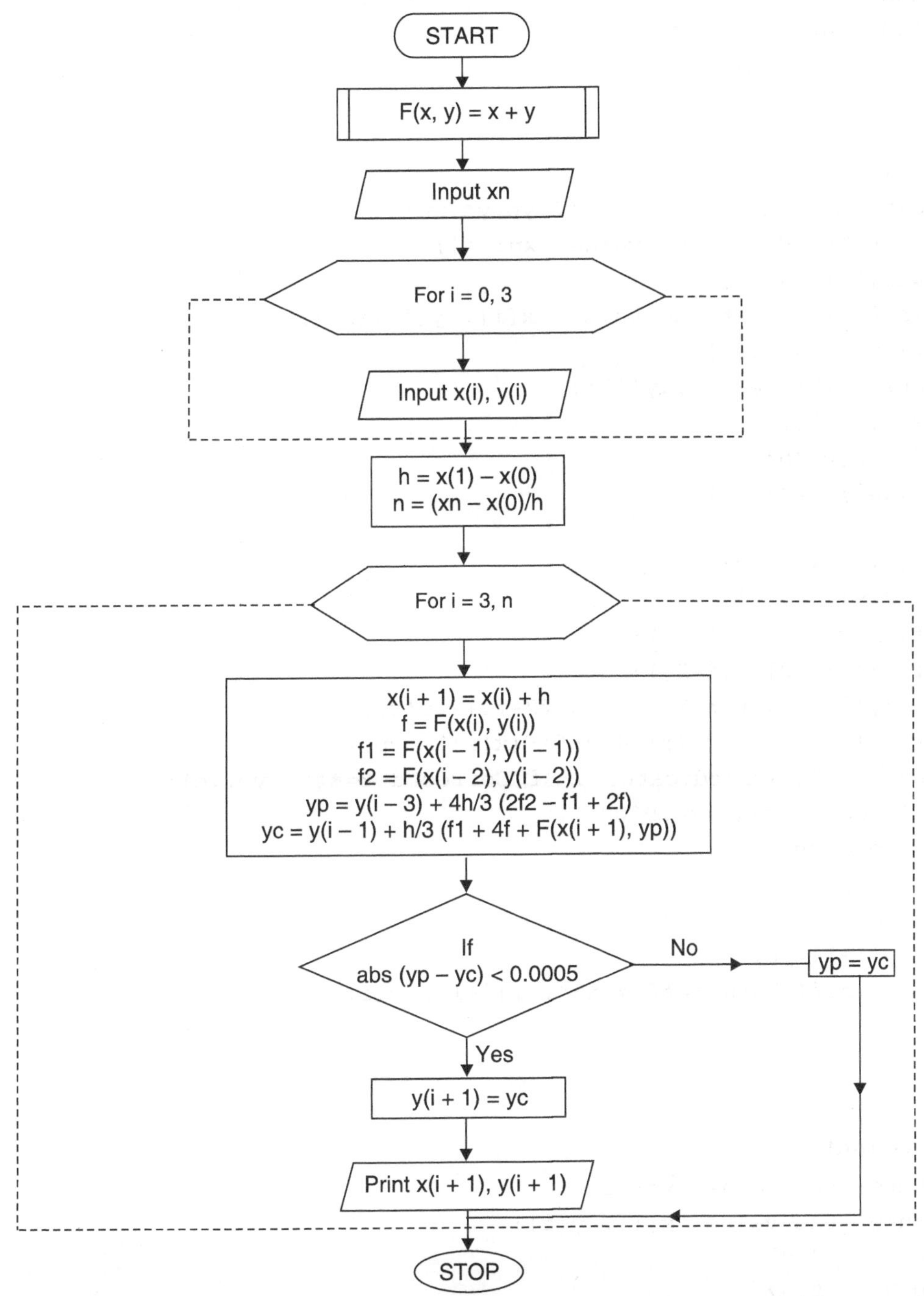

8.21.3. Program of Milne's Method

[U.P.T.U. (MCA) 2001]

```
#include<stdio.h>
#include<math.h>
#define F(x,y) x+y
main()
{
  int i,n;
  float x[20],y[20],h,f,f1,f2,yp,yc,xn;
  printf("\n Enter the value: xn: "};
  scanf{"%f",&xn);
  printf("\n Enter the value: x{i], y[i]:\n"};
  for(i=0;i<=3;i++)
  scanf("%f%f",&x[i],&y[i]);
  h=x[1]-x[0];
  n=(xn-x[0]/h;
  for(i=3;i<=n;i++)
   {
    x[i+1]=x[i]+h;
    f=F[x[i],y[i]);
    f1=F(x[i-1],y[i-1]);
    f2=F(x[i-2],y[i-2]);
    yp=y[i-3]+4.0*h/3.0*(2.0*f2-f1+2.0*f);
    yc=y[i-1]+h/3.0*(f1+4.0*f+F(x[i+1],yp));
    printf("\n\nPredicated Y=%f Correctd Y=%f", yp,yc);
    If(fabs (yp-yc)<0.00005)
      goto next;
      yp=yc;
      next;
      y[i+1]=yc;
      printf("\n\n X=%f Y=%f", x[i+1], y[i+1]);
  }
return;
}
```

8.21.4. Output

```
Enter the value: xn: 1
Enter the value: x[i], y[i]:
0.0    0.0
0.2    0.02
0.4    0.0906
0.6    0.2214
Predicted Y=0.423147 Corrected Y=0.429650
```

```
X=0.800000    Y=0.429650
Predicted Y=0.721307 Corrected Y=0.718820
X=1.000000    Y=0.718820
```

EXAMPLES

Example 1. *Using Milne predictor-corrector method, obtain y(0.4) from the given set of tabulated value and* $\frac{dy}{dx} = y^2 - x^2$.

x	0	0.1	0.2	0.3
y	1	1.11	1.25	1.42
f	1	1.22	1.52	1.92

Sol. Here, $x_0 = 0, x_1 = 0.1, x_2 = 0.2, x_3 = 0.3$

$y_0 = 1, y_1 = 1.11, y_2 = 1.25, y_3 = 1.42$

and $y_0' = 1, y_1' = 1.22, y_2' = 1.52, y_3' = 1.92, h = 0.1$

Using predictor formula,

$$y_4 = y_0 + \frac{4h}{3}(2y_1' - y_2' + 2y_3')$$

$$= 1 + \frac{4(0.1)}{3}[2(1.22) - 1.52 + 2(1.92)] = 1.63466$$

Using y_4, we obtain

$$y_4' = y_4^2 - x_4^2 = 2.51211$$

Now, applying corrector formula,

$$y_4^{(1)} = y_2 + \frac{h}{3}(y_2' + 4y_3' + y_4')$$

$$= 1.25 + \frac{(0.1)}{3}[1.52 + 4(1.92) + 2.51211] = 1.64040$$

Again, $$y_4^{(2)} = y_2 + \frac{h}{3}(y_2' + 4y_3' + y_4^{(1)'}) = 1.64103$$

Again, $$y_4^{(2)} = y_2 + \frac{h}{3}(y_2' + 4y_3' + y_4^{(2)'}) = 1.641099$$

Since $y_4^{(2)}$ and $y_4^{(3)}$ are same up to four decimal places hence, $y_4 = y(0.4) = 1.6410$

Example 2. *Find y(2) if y(x) is the solution of* $\frac{dy}{dx} = \frac{1}{2}(x + y)$ *where* $y(0) = 2$,

$$y(0.5) = 2.636,\ y(1) = 3.595,\ y(1.5) = 4.968$$

Sol. Let $x_0 = 0, x_1 = 0.5, x_2 = 1, x_3 = 1.5$ then we are given y_0, y_1, y_2, y_3 and we require y_4 corresponding to $x_4 = 2$.

By predictor formula, we get

$$y_4 = y_0 + \frac{4h}{3}(2y_1' - y_2' + 2y_3') \qquad ...(1)$$

we have, $$y' = \frac{1}{2}(x + y)$$

$\therefore$ $$y_1' = \frac{1}{2}(x_1 + y_1) = 1.568$$

Similarly $$y_2' = 2.2975, \quad y_3' = 3.234$$

$\therefore$ From (1), $$y_4 = 2 + \frac{4(0.5)}{3}[3.136 - 2.2975 + 6.468] = 6.871$$

$\Rightarrow$ $$y_4' = \frac{1}{2}(x_4 + y_4) = 4.4355$$

This is corrected by

$$y_4^{(1)} = y_2 + \frac{h}{3}(y_2' + 4y_3' + y_4')$$

$$= 3.595 + \frac{0.5}{3}[2.2975 + 12.936 + 4.4355] = 6.87317$$

Now, $$(y_4^{(1)})' = \frac{1}{2}[x_4 + y_4^{(1)}] = \frac{1}{2}(2 + 6.87317) = 4.43659$$

Again by the corrector formula, we get the second corrected value

$$y_4^{(2)} = y_2 + \frac{h}{3}[y_2' + 4y_3' + (y_4^{(1)})']$$

$$= 3.595 + \frac{0.5}{3}[2.2975 + 12.936 + 4.43659] = 6.87335$$

Hence, $$y_4 = y(2) = 6.873.$$

Example 3. *Using Milne's method, solve $y' = 1 + y^2$ with $y(0) = 0$, $y(0.2) = 0.2027$, $y(0.4) = 0.4228$, $y(0.6) = 0.6841$, obtain $y(0.8)$ and $y(1)$ and $y(-0.2)$.*

[G.B.T.U. 2011, G.B.T.U. (C.O.) 2011]

Sol. Here $x_0 = 0$, $x_1 = 0.2$, $x_2 = 0.4$, $x_3 = 0.6$, $h = 0.2$. We are also given y_0, y_1, y_2, y_3.

We have, $$y' = 1 + y^2$$

$\therefore$
$$y_1' = 1 + y_1^2 = 1 + (0.2027)^2 = 1.0411$$
$$y_2' = 1 + y_2^2 = 1 + (0.4228)^2 = 1.1788$$
$$y_3' = 1 + y_3^2 = 1 + (0.6841)^2 = 1.4680$$

By predictor formula, we get

$$y_4 = y_0 + \frac{4h}{3}(2y_1' - y_2' + 2y_3')$$

$$= 0 + \frac{0.8}{3}[2.0822 - 1.1788 + 2.936] = 1.0238$$

$$y_4' = 1 + y_4^2 = 1 + (1.0238)^2 = 2.0482$$

This is corrected by

$$y_4^{(1)} = y_2 + \frac{h}{3}(y_2' + 4y_3' + y_4')$$

$$= 0.4228 + \frac{0.2}{3}[1.1788 + 5.872 + 2.0482] = 1.0294$$

Now, $[y_4^{(1)}]' = 1 + [y_4^{(1)}]^2 = 1 + (1.0294)^2 = 2.0597$

The second corrected value is,

$$y_4^{(2)} = y_2 + \frac{h}{3}[y_2' + 4y_3' + y_4^{(1)\prime}]$$

$$= 0.4228 + \frac{0.2}{3}[1.1788 + 5.872 + 2.0597] = 1.0302$$

Again, $[y_4^{(2)}]' = 1 + [y_4^{(2)}]^2 = 1 + (1.0302)^2 = 2.0613$

Again, $y_4^{(3)} = 1.0303 = y_4^{(4)}$

hence, $y_4 = y(0.8) = 1.0303$

Now by predictor formula, also

$$y_5 = y_1 + \frac{4h}{3}(2y_2' - y_3' + 2y_4')$$

$$= 0.2027 + \frac{0.8}{3}[2.3576 - 1.468 + 4.123] \quad | \; y_4' = 1 + (1.0303)^2$$

$$= 1.5394$$

$$y_5' = 1 + y_5^2 = 3.3698$$

This is corrected by

$$y_5' = y_3 + \frac{h}{3}(y_3' + 4y_4' + y_5')$$

$$= 0.6841 + \frac{0.2}{3}(1.468 + 8.246 + 3.3698) = 1.5564$$

Now, $[y_5^{(1)}]' = 1 + (1.5564)^2 = 3.4224$

The second corrected value is

$$y_5^{(2)} = 1.55999$$

Now, $[y_5^{(2)}]' = 3.4333$

Also, $y_5^{(3)} = 1.5606$

Similarly $y_5^{(4)} = 1.5607 = y_5^{(5)}$

Hence, $y_5 = y(1.0) = 1.5607.$

To obtain $y(-0.2)$, we have

$$x_0 = 0.6, x_1 = 0.4, x_2 = 0.2, x_3 = 0$$

$$y_0 = 0.6841, y_1 = 0.4228, y_2 = 0.2027, y_3 = 0 \text{ and } h = -0.2$$

Now,

$$y_1' = 1 + y_1^2 = 1.17876$$

$$y_2' = 1 + y_2^2 = 1.04109$$

$$y_3' = 1 + y_3^2 = 1$$

By Milne's predictor formula,

$$y_4 = y_0 + \frac{4h}{3}(2y_1' - y_2' + 2y_3') = -0.20028$$

Using y_4, we get $y_4' = 1 + y_4^2 = 1.04011$

By Milne's corrector formula,

$$y_4^{(1)} = y_2 + \frac{h}{3}(y_2' + 4y_3' + y_4') = -0.20271$$

Again,

$$y_4^{(2)} = y_2 + \frac{h}{3}(y_2' + 4y_3' + y_4^{(1)\prime}) = -0.20278$$

Since $y_4^{(1)}$ and $y_4^{(2)}$ are same upto 4 decimal places

$$y_4 = y(-0.2) = -0.2027$$

Example 4. *Tabulate by Milne's method the numerical solution of* $\frac{dy}{dx} = x + y$ *with initial conditions* $x_0 = 0, y_0 = 1$ *from* $x = 0.20$ *to* $x = 0.30$.

Sol. To obtain the solution, first we shall find three consecutive values of y and y' corresponding to $x = 0.05, 0.10$ and 0.15 *i.e.*, taking $h = 0.05$

x	y	$y' = dy/dx$
0.00	1	1
0.05	1.0525	1.1025
0.10	1.1103	1.2103
0.15	1.1736	1.3236

(using $y = 2e^x - x - 1$ ...(1) as explicit solution of given equations)

In general form, Milne's predictor and corrector formula are

$$y_{n+1} = y_{n-3} + \frac{4h}{3}(2y'_{n-2} - y'_{n-1} + 2y_n') \quad ...(2)$$

and

$$y_{n+1}^{(1)} = y_{n-1} + \frac{h}{3}(y'_{n-1} + 4y_n' + y'_{n+1}) \quad ...(3)$$

Put $n = 3, h = 0.05$ in (2), we get by prediction formula,

$$y_4 = y_0 + \frac{4h}{3}(2y_1' - y_2' + 2y_3')$$

$$= 1 + \frac{4(0.05)}{3}[2.205 - 1.2103 + 2.6472]$$

$$= 1.2428 \text{ (predicted value)}$$

It is corrected by

$$y_4^{(1)} = y_2 + \frac{h}{3}(y_2' + 4y_3' + y_4')$$

$$= 1.1103 + \frac{0.05}{3}[1.2103 + 5.2944 + 1.4428] = 1.2428$$

which is the same as predicted value.

Put $x = 0.20$ and $y = 1.2428$ in $y' = x + y$, we get $y_4' = 1.4428$

Hence, $y = 1.2428$ when $x = 0.20$ and $y' = 1.4428$

Now, put $n = 4, h = 0.05$ in (2), we get

$$y_5 = y_1 + \frac{4h}{3}(2y_2' - y_3' + 2y_4')$$

$$= 1.0525 + \frac{4(0.05)}{3}[2.4206 - 1.3236 + 2.8856] = 1.3180$$

which is corrected by

$$y_5^{(1)} = y_3 + \frac{h}{3}(y_3' + 4y_4' + y_5')$$

$$= 1.1736 + \frac{0.05}{3}(1.3236 + 5.7712 + 1.568) = 1.3180$$

which is same as predicted value.

Thus, $y_5 = y_{0.25} = 1.3180$ and $y_5' = 1.5680$

Again putting $n = 5$, $h = 0.05$, we get

$y_6 = 1.3997$ which is corrected by

$y_6^{(1)} = 1.3997 = y_{0.30}$

The same as the predicted value.

$y_6 = 1.3997, y'_6 = 1.6997 \; (y' = x + y)$

Collecting the results in Tabular form, we get

x	y	$y' = dy/dx$
$x_4 = 0.20$	$y_4 = 1.2428$	$y_4' = 1.4428$
$x_5 = 0.25$	$y_5 = 1.3180$	$y_5' = 1.5680$
$x_6 = 0.30$	$y_6 = 1.3997$	$y_6' = 1.6997$

ASSIGNMENT

1. Apply Milne's method to solve the differential equation

$\frac{dy}{dx} = -xy^2$ at $x = 0.8$, given that

$y(0) = 2, y(0.2) = 1.923, y(0.4) = 1.724, y(0.6) = 1.471.$

2. Solve $10\dfrac{dy}{dx} = x^2 + y^2$, $y(0) = 1$ and compute $y(0.4)$ and $y(0.5)$ by Milne's method given

x :	0.1	0.2	0.3
y :	1.0101	1.0206	1.0317

3. Part of a numerical solution of the diff. equation $\dfrac{dy}{dx} = 0.2x + 0.1y$ is shown in the following table:

x :	0	0.05	0.10	0.15
y :	2	2.0103	2.0212	2.0323

Use Milne's method to find the next entry in the table.

4. Given $\dfrac{dy}{dx} = \dfrac{1}{2}(1 + x^2)\,y^2$ and $y(0) = 1$, $y(0.1) = 1.06$, $y(0.2) = 1.12$, $y(0.3) = 1.21$, evaluate $y(0.4)$ by Milne's Predictor-Corrector method.

5. The differential equation $\dfrac{dy}{dx} + \dfrac{1}{10}y^2 = x$ satisfies the following pairs of values of x and y :

x :	– 0.2	– 0.1	0.0	0.1	0.2
y :	1.04068	1.01513	1	0.99507	1.00013

Compute the values of y when $x = 0.3$ by Milne's method.

6. Solve the differential equation $\dfrac{dy}{dx} = y - x^2$ by Milne's method and compute y at $x = 0.80$ when:

x :	0	0.2	0.4	0.6
y :	1	1.12186	1.46820	1.73790

7. Solve numerically $\dfrac{dy}{dx} = 2e^x - y$ at $x = 0.4$ and 0.5 by Milne's method given:

x :	0	0.1	0.2	0.3
y :	2	2.010	2.040	2.090

8. Given : $\dfrac{dy}{dx} = 2 - xy^2$ and $y(0) = 1$. Show that by Milne's method, $y(1) = 1.6505$ taking $h = 0.2$. You may use Picard's method to obtain the values of $y(0.2)$, $y(0.4)$, $y(0.6)$.

9. Solve the initial value problem $\dfrac{dy}{dx} = 1 + xy^2$, $y(0) = 1$ for $x = 0.4$, 0.5 by using Milne's method. It is given that,

x :	0.1	0.2	0.3
y :	1.105	1.223	1.355

10. Derive Milne's predictor formula and find the solution of the equation $\dfrac{dy}{dx} = x - y^2$ for $y(0.8)$ and $y(1)$, given the starting values.

x :	0	0.2	0.4	0.6
y :	0	0.02	0.0795	0.1762

11. Given : $y(0) = 2$, $y(0.2) = 2.0933$, $y(0.4) = 2.1755$, $y(0.6) = 2.2493$, find $y(0.8)$ and $y(1.0)$ by solving $\dfrac{dy}{dx} = \dfrac{1}{x + y}$ by Milne's method.

Answers

1. $y_4^{(3)} = y(0.8) = 1.218$

2. $y(0.4) = 1.0438, y(0.5) = 1.0568$

3. 2.0444

4. $y(0.2) = 1.2797$

5. $y(0.3) = 1.0150$

6. $y(0.8) = 2.0111$

7. $y(0.4) = 2.162, y(0.5) = 2.256.$

9. $y(0.4) = 1.538, y(0.5) = 1.751$

10. $y(0.8) = 0.3046, y(1.0) = 0.4555$

11. $y(0.8) = 2.3164, y(1.0) = 2.3780$

8.22. ADAMS–MOULTON (OR ADAMS–BASHFORTH) FORMULA

Consider the initial value problem

$$\frac{dy}{dx} = f(x, y) \text{ with } y(x_0) = y_0 \quad \text{...(1)}$$

We compute $y_{-1} = y(x_0 - h), y_{-2} = y(x_0 - 2h), y_{-3} = y(x_0 - 3h), \ldots\ldots$

Now integrating (1) on both sides w.r.t. x in $[x_0, x_0 + h]$, we get

$$y_1 = y_0 + \int_{x_0}^{x_0 + h} f(x, y)\, dx \quad \text{...(2)}$$

Replacing $f(x, y)$ by Newton's backward interpolation formula, we get

$$y_1 = y_0 + h \int_0^1 \left\{ f_0 + u \nabla f_0 + \frac{u(u+1)}{2} \nabla^2 f_0 + \frac{u(u+1)(u+2)}{6} \nabla^3 f_0 + \ldots \right\} du$$

$\because x = x_0 + hu$
$\therefore dx = h\, du$
Limits of u are from 0 to 1

$$= y_0 + h \left(f_0 + \frac{1}{2} \nabla f_0 + \frac{5}{12} \nabla^2 f_0 + \frac{3}{8} \nabla^3 f_0 + \ldots \right) \quad \text{...(3)}$$

Neglecting the fourth order and higher order differences and using

$\nabla f_0 = f_0 - f_{-1}$

$\nabla^2 f_0 = f_0 - 2f_{-1} + f_{-2}$

$\nabla^3 f_0 = f_0 - 3f_{-1} + 3f_{-2} - f_{-3}$ in (3), we get after simplification,

$$y_1 = y_0 + \frac{h}{24} (55f_0 - 59f_{-1} + 37f_{-2} - 9f_{-3})$$

which is known as ***Adams–Bashforth or Adams–Moulton–Predictor formula*** and is denoted generally as

$$y^p_{n+1} = y_n + \frac{h}{24} (55f_n - 59f_{n-1} + 37f_{n-2} - 9f_{n-3})$$

or

$$y^p_{n+1} = y_0 + \frac{h}{24} (55y_n' - 59y'_{n-1} + 37y'_{n-2} - 9y'_{n-3})$$

Having found y_1, we find $f_1 = f(x_0 + h, y_1)$

To find *a* better value of y_1, we derive a corrector formula by substituting Newton's backward interpolation formula at f_1 in place of $f(x, y)$ in (2) *i.e.*,

$$y_1 = y_0 + \int_{x_0}^{x_0 + h} \left[f_1 + u \nabla f_1 + \frac{u(u+1)}{2} \nabla^2 f_1 + \frac{u(u+1)(u+2)}{6} \nabla^3 f_1 + \ldots \right] dx$$

$$= y_0 + h \int_{-1}^{0} \left[f_1 + u \nabla f_1 + \frac{(u^2 + u)}{2} \nabla^2 f_1 + \left(\frac{u^3 + 3u^2 + 2u}{6} \right) \nabla^3 f_1 + \ldots \right] du$$

$$\because x = x_1 + hu \quad \therefore dx = h\, du$$

$$= y_0 + h \left(f_1 - \frac{1}{2} \nabla f_1 - \frac{1}{12} \nabla^2 f_1 - \frac{1}{24} \nabla^3 f_1 - \ldots \right) \qquad \ldots(5)$$

Neglecting the fourth order and higher order differences and using

$\nabla f_1 = f_1 - f_0$, $\nabla^2 f_1 = f_1 - 2f_0 + f_{-1}$, $\nabla^3 f_1 = f_1 - 3f_0 + 3f_{-1} - f_{-2}$ in (5), we get

$$y_1 = y_0 + \frac{h}{24} (9f_1 + 19f_0 - 5f_{-1} + f_{-2})$$

which is known as ***Adams–Bashforth or Adams–Moulton Corrector formula*** and is denoted generally as

$$y^c_{n+1} = y_n + \frac{h}{24} (9f_{n+1} - 19f_n - 5f_{n-1} + f_{n-2})$$

or

$$y^c_{n+1} = y_n + \frac{h}{24} (9y'_{n+1} - 19y_n' - 5y'_{n-1} + y'_{n-2})$$

EXAMPLES

Example 1. *Using Adam's–Moulton–Bashforth method to find y (1.4) given:*

$$\frac{dy}{dx} = x^2 (1 + y),\ y(1) = 1,\ y(1.1) = 1.233,\ y(1.2) = 1.548 \text{ and } y(1.3) = 1.979$$

Sol. Here,

$$y' = x^2 (1 + y), \quad h = 0.1$$

$$x_0 = 1, x_1 = 1.1, x_2 = 1.2, x_3 = 1.3$$

$$y_0 = 1, y_1 = 1.233, y_2 = 1.548, y_3 = 1.979$$

Now, Adams–Bashforth predictor formula is

$$y_4^p = y_3 + \frac{h}{24} (55y_3' - 59y_2' + 37y_1' - 9y_0') \qquad \ldots(1)$$

Here,

$$y_0' = x_0^2 (1 + y_0) = 2$$

$$y_1' = x_1^2 (1 + y_1) = 2.70193$$

$$y_2' = x_2^2 (1 + y_2) = 3.66912$$

$$y_3' = x_3^2 (1 + y_3) = 5.03451$$

$\therefore$ From (1),

$$y_4^p = 1.979 + \left(\frac{0.1}{24}\right) [55(5.03451) - 59(3.66912) + 37(2.70193) - 9(2)]$$

$$= 2.5722974$$

Now,

$$(y_4')^p = x_4^2 (1 + y_4^p) = (1.4)^2 (1 + 2.5722974) = 7.0017029$$

Now, the corrector formula is

$$y_4^c = y_3 + \frac{h}{24} (9y_4'^p + 19y_3' - 5y_2' + y_1')$$

$$= 1.979 + \left(\frac{0.1}{24}\right) [9(7.0017029) + 19(5.03451) - 5(3.66912) + 2.70193]$$

$$= 2.5749473$$

$$\therefore \quad y(0.4) = 2.5749$$

Example 2. *Find y(0.1), y(0.2), y(0.3) from* $\frac{dy}{dx} = x^2 - y;\ y(0) = 1$ *by using Taylor's series method and hence obtain y(0.4) using Adams–Bashforth method.*

Sol. We have, $y' = x^2 - y,\ y(0) = 1$

By Taylor's series method, we have

$$y(0.1) = 0.905125,\ y(0.2) = 0.8212352,\ y(0.3) = 0.7491509$$

Hence, $x_0 = 0,\ x_1 = 0.1,\ x_2 = 0.2,\ x_3 = 0.3$

$y_0 = 1,\ y_1 = 0.905125,\ y_2 = 0.8212352,\ y_3 = 0.7491509$

Also, $y_0' = -1,\ y_1' = -0.895125,\ y_2' = -0.7812352$ and $y_3' = -0.6591509$

Now, Adams–Bashforth predictor formula is

$$y_4^p = y_3 + \frac{h}{24}(55y_3' - 59y_2' + 37y_1' - 9y_0')$$

$$= 0.7491509 + \left(\frac{0.1}{24}\right) [55(-0.6591509) - 59(-0.7812352) + 37(-0.895125) - 9(-1)]$$

$$= 0.6896507$$

Now, $y_4'^p = x_4^2 - y_4^p = (0.4)^2 - 0.6896507 = -0.5296507$

The corrector formula is

$$y_4^c = y_3 + \frac{h}{24}(9y_4'^p + 19y_3' - 5y_2' + y_1')$$

$$= 0.7491509 + \left(\frac{0.1}{24}\right) [9(-0.5296507) + 19(-0.6591509) - 5(-0.7812352) + (-0.895125)]$$

$$= 0.6896522$$

$$\therefore \quad y(0.4) = 0.6896522.$$

ASSIGNMENT

1. Using Adams–Bashforth formula, find $y(0.4)$ and $y(0.5)$ if y satisfies the differential equation

   $\frac{dy}{dx} = 3e^x + 2y$ with $y(0) = 0$.

   Compute y at $x = 0.1, 0.2, 0.3$ by means of Runge–Kutta method.

2. Determine $y(0.4)$ given the equation $\frac{dy}{dx} = \frac{1}{2}xy$ using Adams–Moulton method, given that

   $y(0) = 1,\ y(0.1) = 1.0025,\ y(0.2) = 1.0101,\ y(0.3) = 1.0228.$

3. Using Adams–Bashforth Predictor–Corrector method, find $y(1.4)$ given that

$$x^2y' + xy = 1\,;\, y(1) = 1,\, y(1.1) = 0.996,\, y(1.2) = 0.986,\, y(1.3) = 0.972$$

4. Compute $y(1)$ by Adam's method given

$$y' = x^2 - y^3\,,\, y(0) = 1,\, y(0.25) = 0.821028,\, y(0.5) = 0.741168,\, y(0.75) = 0.741043.$$

5. Given $y' = 2y - 1$, $y(0) = 1$. Compute y for $x = 0.1, 0.2, 0.3$ by the IV order Runge–Kutta method and $y(0.4)$ by Adam's method.

Answers

1. $y(0.4) = 2.2089$, $y(0.5) = 3.20798$
2. $y(0.4) = 1.0408$
3. $y(1.4) = 0.9996$
4. $y(1) = 0.8145958$
5. 1.1107, 1.2459, 1.4111, 1.61287

8.23. STABILITY

A numerical method for solving a mathematical problem is considered *stable* if the sensitivity of the numerical answer to the data is no greater than in the original mathematical problem. Stable problems are also called well-posed problems.

If a problem is not stable, it is called *unstable* or ill-posed.

A problem $f(x, y) = 0$ is said to be stable if the solution y depends in a continuous way on the variable x.

8.24. STABILITY IN THE SOLUTION OF ORDINARY DIFFERENTIAL EQUATION

The idea of stability may be defined as

(*i*) A computation is stable if it does not blow up.

(*ii*) Stability is a boundedness of the relative error.

Two types of stability considerations enter in the solution of ordinary differential equations.

(*a*) Inherent stability (*b*) Numerical stability

Inherent stability is determined by the mathematical formulations of the problem and is dependent on the eigen values of Jacobean Matrix of the differential equation.

Numerical stability is a function of the error propagation in the numerical method. Three types of errors occur in the application of numerical integration methods :

(*a*) Truncation error (*b*) Round off error (*c*) Propagation error.

8.25. STABILITY OF I ORDER LINEAR DIFF. EQUATION OF FORM $\frac{dy}{dx} = Ay$ WITH INITIAL CONDITION $y(x_0) = y_0$

The solution of this equation is

$$y(x) = y(x_0)\, e^{A(x - x_0)} \quad \ldots(1)$$

Let, $\quad y_n = y(x_n) + \varepsilon_n$ at $x_n = x_0 + nh$

ε_n being the total truncation error.

Let E(Ah) be the polynomial approximation to e^{-Ah} (for small Ah). Then the computed result of one step length is

$$y_{n+1} = \text{E}(Ah)\, y_n$$

while the correct solution is

$$y(x_{n+1}) = e^{Ah}\, y(x_n)$$

Thus,
$$\begin{aligned} y_{n+1} - y(x_{n+1}) &= \text{E}(Ah)\, y_n - e^{Ah}\, y(x_n) \\ &= \text{E}(Ah)\, [y(x_n) + \text{E}_n] - e^{Ah}\, y(x_n) \\ &= [\text{E}(Ah) - e^{Ah}]\, y(x_n) + \text{E}(Ah)\, \varepsilon_n \qquad \text{...(2)} \end{aligned}$$

Clearly, the error ε_n will be amplified if E(Ah) > 1 which is possible for sufficiently large Ah at $x_{n+k} = x_0 + (n + k)\, h$. It will have grown by factor $\text{E}^k(Ah)$. Thus meaningful results can be obtained only for E(Ah) < 1. If $|\, \text{E}(Ah)\, | < e^{Ah}$ then we say that the method is relatively stable for that value of Ah.

8.26. AUTOMATIC ERROR MONITORING

At first, the initial value problems for system of ODEs were solved with a fixed method and constant step size but now a days the general-purpose codes vary the step size/method. Estimating and controlling some measure of error by variation of step size/method inspires some confidence in the numerical solution and makes possible the solution of hard problems.

Consider the numerical solution of IVPs for ODEs of first order

$$y'(x) = f\{x, y(x)\} \qquad \text{...(1)}$$

For given initial value $y(a)$, we want to approximate $y(x)$ for $a \le x \le b$. On reaching $y_n \approx y(x_n)$, we take a step of size h_n in the direction of b to form an approximate solution at $x_{n+1} = x_n + h_n$. If a solution can change significantly on a scale that is very small compared to $b - a$, it may be impractical to solve the problem with a constant step-size that is small enough to resolve the fastest changes in $y(x)$ and if a constant step-size is too big, the computation may become unstable. Controlling the error by adjusting the step-size can often stabilize the integration.

There are two major factors affecting the choice of step-size. One is accuracy and the other is stability. Popular numerical methods produce results in qualitative agreement with the solution of the IVP only when step sizes/tolerances are sufficiently small. It is characteristic of a class of IVPs called "stiff" that the stability requirement is much more restrictive than the accuracy requirement. Implicit methods are used for stiff IVPs. The stability of the IVP itself governs the propagation of numerical errors. Reducing the tolerance results in the error being reduced proportionately. Monitoring the error inspires some confidence that the step-size is small enough both for resolving the behaviour of the solution and for the numerical method to behave as expected. This is what we mean by passive estimation of error.

It is evident that the accuracy of the calculation is strongly affected by the step-size. If h is chosen too large, the computed solution may be quite for from the true solution of the differential equation, if too small, then the calculation will become unnecessarily time-consuming and round-off errors may build up excessively because of the numerous arithmetic operations that are being carried out. If the true solution of the diff. eqn. is rapidly changing, then we will need a small value of h and if the solution changes slowly, then a larger value of h will do.

One way to get some control on h is to follow a policy of cutting the step-size in half whenever more than one or two iterations are necessary. Now we discuss estimation of single step truncation error.

The easiest example is Euler's method. The equation was

$$y(x_n + h) = y(x_n) + h\, y'(x_n) + \frac{h^2}{2} y''(\mathrm{X})$$

where X lies between x_n and $x_n + h$. In Euler's procedure, we drop the third term on the right, the "remainder term", and compute the solution from the rest of the equation. In doing this, we commit a single-step truncation error that is equal to

$$\mathrm{E} = h^2 \frac{y''(\mathrm{X})}{2} \ ; x_n < \mathrm{X} < x_n + h$$

Thus, Euler's method is exact (E = 0) if the solution is a polynomial of degree 1 or less ($y'' = 0$). Otherwise, the single-step error is proportional to h^2 so if we cut the step size in half, the local error is reduced to 1/4 of its former value, approximately and if we double h, the error is multiplied by about 4.

EXAMPLES

Example 1. (*i*) *Applying Euler's method to the equation* $\frac{dy}{dx} = \lambda y$*, given* $y(x_0) = y_0$*, determine its stability zone. What would be the range of stability when* $\lambda = -1$*?*

(*ii*) *Discuss the stability of Euler's method applied to the initial-value problem*

$$y' = \lambda y,\ y(0) = 1$$

Sol. (*i*) We have, $\quad y' = \lambda y,\ y(x_0) = y_0 \qquad \text{...(1)}$

By Euler's method, we have

$$y_n = y_{n-1} + h\, y'_{n-1} = (1 + \lambda h)\, y_{n-1}$$

$$\therefore \quad y_{n-1} = (1 + \lambda h)\, y_{n-2}$$

$$\vdots \qquad \vdots$$

$$y_1 = (1 + \lambda h)\, y_0$$

Multiplying all above eqns., we get

$$y_n = (1 + \lambda h)^n\, y_0 \qquad \text{...(2)}$$

Integrating (1), we get

$$y = c\, e^{\lambda x} \qquad \text{...(3)}$$

Applying condition $y(x_0) = y_0$, on (3),

$$y_0 = c\, e^{\lambda x_0} \qquad \text{...(4)}$$

From (3) and (4), $\quad y = y_0\, e^{\lambda(x - x_0)}$

In particular, the exact solution through (x_n, y_n) is

$$y_n = y_0\, e^{\lambda(x_n - x_0)} = y_0\, e^{\lambda n h}$$

$$= y_0 (e^{\lambda h})^n = y_0 \left[1 + \lambda h + \frac{(\lambda h)^2}{2!} + \dots\right]^n \qquad \text{...(5)}$$

Clearly, the numerical solution (2) agrees with exact solution (5) for small values of h.

$| 1 + \lambda h | < 1$ defines a stable zone.

When $\lambda = -1$, the method is stable if

$$| 1 + \lambda h | < 1$$

i.e., $$-1 < 1 - h < 1$$

or, $$-2 < -h < 0$$

i.e., $$0 < h < 2.$$

(*ii*) Here, $$y' = \lambda y, y(0) = 1 \quad ...(1)$$

Proceeding similarly as in (1), we get

$$y_n = (1 + \lambda h)^n \quad ...(2) \mid \because \; y_0 = 1$$

Integrating (1), we get

$$y = ce^{\lambda x} \quad ...(3)$$

Applying condition $y(0) = 1$, we get

$$1 = c \quad ...(4)$$

$\therefore$ $$y = e^{\lambda x} \quad ...(5) \mid \text{using (3) and (4)}$$

In particular, the exact solution through (x_n, y_n) is

$$y_n = e^{\lambda x_n} = (e^{\lambda h})^n \quad \mid \because \; x_n = x_0 + nh = nh$$

$$= \left[1 + \lambda h + \frac{(\lambda h)^2}{2!} + ...\right]^n \quad ...(6)$$

Again the numerical solution (2) agrees with exact solution (6) for small values of h.

(*a*) When λ is real, the method is stable if

$$| 1 + \lambda h | < 1 \quad i.e., \quad -2 < \lambda h < 0$$

(*b*) When λ is complex (say $\alpha + i\beta$) then the method is stable if

$$| 1 + (\alpha + i\beta) h | < 1$$

i.e., $$(1 + \alpha h)^2 + (\beta h)^2 < 1$$

i.e., $$(1 + x)^2 + y^2 < 1 \quad \text{where } x = \alpha h, y = \beta h$$

i.e., λh lies within the unit circle and the method is conditionally convergent.

(*c*) When λ is imaginary (say $i\beta$), then $| 1 + \lambda h | = 1$.

Hence we have a periodic stability.

Example 2. *How many terms are to be retained if we want to have an accuracy of 10^{-10} in solving $y' = x + y$, $y(0) = 1$, $x \in (0, 1)$ by Taylor's series method?*

Sol. $$y' = x + y$$

$\Rightarrow$ $$y'' = 1 + y', y''' = y'', ..., \text{and so on}$$

$\Rightarrow$ $$y^{(p+1)} = y^{(p)}, p = 2, 3...$$

$\therefore$ $$y'(0) = 1, y''(0) = 2, ..., y^{(p)}(0) = 2$$

Hence, $$y(x) = 1 + x + x^2 + ... + \frac{2}{p!} x^p + ...$$

In order to obtain results, which will be accurate up to 10^{-10} for $x \le 1$, we have,

$$\frac{1}{(p+1)!} < 5 \times 10^{-10}$$

$\Rightarrow$ $$p \approx 15$$

Hence about 15 terms are required to obtain the accuracy of 10^{-10} for solving $\frac{dy}{dx} = x + y$ by Taylor's series method when $x \le 1$.

Example 3. *Discuss stability of Euler's method for solving the differential equation.*

$$\frac{dy}{dx} = \lambda y$$

Sol.
$$\frac{dy}{dx} = \lambda y = f(x, y) \quad \text{...(1)}$$

True solution is $y(x) = ce^{\lambda x}$ so that

$$y(x_{n+1}) = y(x_n)e^{\lambda h}, \; h = x_{n+1} - x_n$$

Approximate solution using Euler's method is

$$\begin{aligned} y_{n+1} &= y_n + h\, f(x_n, y_n) = y_n + h\,\lambda\, y_n \\ &= (1 + h\lambda)\, y_n \end{aligned} \quad \text{...(2)}$$

Let
$$y_n = y(x_n) + \varepsilon_n$$

where ε_n is the total solution error.

$$\Rightarrow \quad \begin{aligned} y_{n+1} &= y(x_{n+1}) + \varepsilon_{n+1} = (1 + h\lambda)\, y_n \\ &= (1 + h\lambda)\, [y(x_n) + \varepsilon_n] \end{aligned}$$

Therefore,

$$y_{n+1} - y(x_{n+1}) = (1 + \lambda h)\, y(x_n) + (1 + \lambda h)\, \varepsilon_n - y(x_n)\, e^{\lambda h}$$

$$\Rightarrow \quad \varepsilon_{n+1} = (1 + \lambda h - e^{\lambda h})\, y(x_n) + (1 + \lambda h)\, \varepsilon_n \quad \text{...(3)}$$

The first term on RHS is the total truncation error while the second term is the contribution to the error from the previous step (inherited error).

Hence, we have $E(\lambda h) = 1 + \lambda h$

Where $E(\lambda h)$ is a polynomial approximation to $e^{\lambda h}$ for small λh.

Obviously, Euler's method is absolutely stable if $|\, 1 + \lambda h \,| < 1$ or $-2 < \lambda h < 0$; relatively stable if λh is greater than the solution of $\lambda h = -1 - e^{-\lambda h}$.

❑❑❑

9

Statistical Techniques

9.1. THE STATISTICAL METHODS

Statistical methods are devices by which complex and numerical data are so systematically treated as to present a comprehensible and intelligible view of them. In other words, the statistical method is a technique used to obtain, analyse and present numerical data.

9.2. LIMITATION OF STATISTICAL METHODS

There are certain limitations to the statistical methods.

1. Statistical laws are not exact laws like mathematical or chemical laws. They are derived by taking a majority of cases and are not true for every individual. Thus, the statistical inferences are uncertain.

2. Statistical technique applies only to data reducible to quantitative forms.

3. Statistical technique is the same for the social as for physical sciences.

4. Statistical results might lead to fallacious conclusions if they are quoted short of their context.

9.3. FREQUENCY CHARTS

To represent frequency distribution by means of a diagram makes the unwieldly data intelligible and conveys to the eye the general run of the observations. The graphs and diagrams have a more lasting effect on the brain. When data of two items is compared with one another it is always easier to compare through graphs and diagrams. Forecasting also becomes easier by the help of graphs. Graphs help us in interpolation of values of the variables.

However there are certain disadvantages also. Graphs do not give accurate measurements of the variables as are given by tables. The numerical value can be obtained to any number of decimal places but from graphs it can not be found, say to 2nd or 3rd places of decimals. Another disadvantage is that it is very difficult to have a proper selection of scale. By different scale it is possible that the facts may be misrepresented.

Generally the following types of graphs are used in representing frequency distributions :

(1) Histograms, (2) Frequency Polygon, (3) Frequency curve, (4) Cumulative frequency curve or the Ogive, (5) Historigrams, (6) Bar diagrams, (7) Area diagrams, (8) Circles or Pie diagrams, (9) Prisms, (10) Cartograms and map diagrams, (11) Pictograms.

9.3.1. Histograms

To draw the histograms of a given grouped frequency distribution, mark off along a horizontal base line all the class-intervals on a suitable scale. With the class-intervals as bases, draw rectangles with the areas proportional to the frequencies of the respective class-intervals. For equal class-intervals, the heights of the rectangles will be proportional to the frequencies. If the class-intervals are not equal, the heights of the rectangles will be proportional to the ratios of the frequencies to the width of the corresponding classes. A diagram with all these rectangles is a **Histogram.**

Consider a table:

Marks under	10	20	30	40	50	60	70	80	90	100
No. of students	2	6	16	20	23	31	32	37	48	50

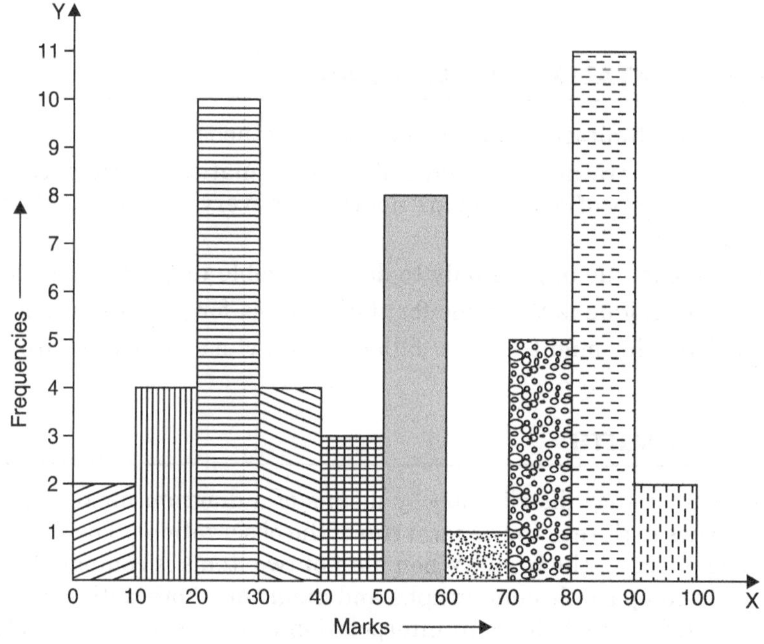

(Histogram for the table)

Histograms are also useful when the class-intervals are not of the same width. They are appropriate to cases in which the frequency changes rapidly.

9.3.2. Frequency Polygon

If the various points are obtained by plotting the central values of the class intervals as x co-ordinates and the respective frequencies as the y co-ordinates, and these points are joined by straight lines taken in order, they form a polygon called **frequency polygon.**

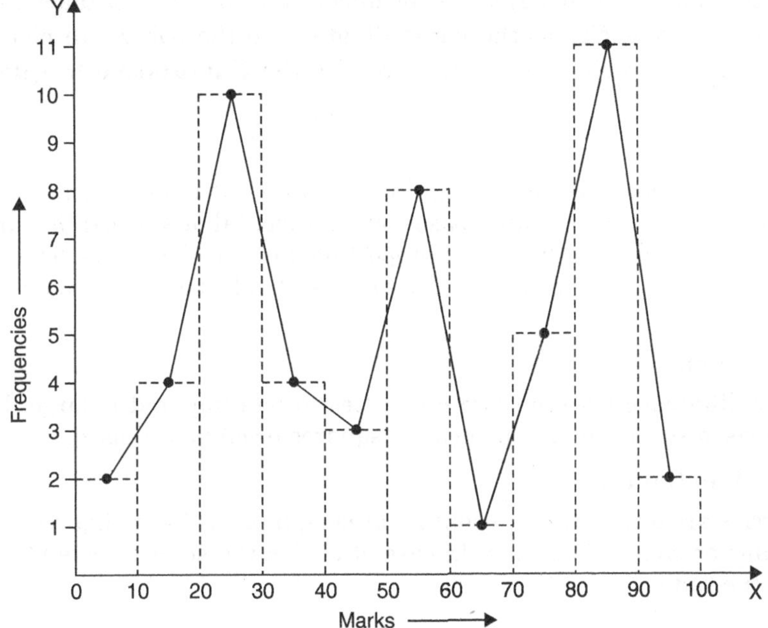

(Frequency Polygon)

In a frequency polygon the variables or individuals of each class are assumed to be concentrated at the mid-point of the class-interval.

Here in this diagram dotted is the **histogram** and a polygon with lines as sides is the **frequency polygon.**

9.3.3. Frequency Curve

If through the vertices of a frequency polygon, a smooth freehand curve is drawn we get the **frequency curve.** This is done usually when the class-intervals are of small widths.

9.3.4. Cumulative Frequency Curve or the Ogive

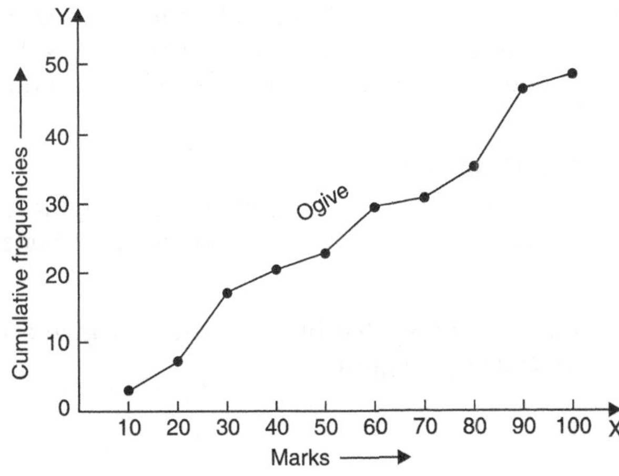

If from a cumulative frequency table, the upper limits of the class taken as x co-ordinates and the cumulative frequencies as the y co-ordinates and the points are plotted, then these points when joined by a freehand smooth curve give the **Cumulative frequency curve or the Ogive.**

9.3.5. Bar Diagrams

When the comparison of simple magnitude of different items is done the bar diagrams are widely used. In bar diagrams equal bases on a horizontal or vertical line are selected and rectangles are constructed with the length proportional to the given data. The width of bars is an arbitrary factor. The distance between two bars should be taken about one-half of the width of a bar.

9.3.6. Area Diagrams

When the difference between two quantities to be compared is large, bars would not show the comparison so clearly. In such cases, squares or circle are used.

9.3.7. Circle or Pie-diagrams

When circles are drawn to represent its area equivalent to the figures, they are said to form pie-diagrams or circles-diagrams. In case of circles the square roots of magnitudes are proportional to the radii.

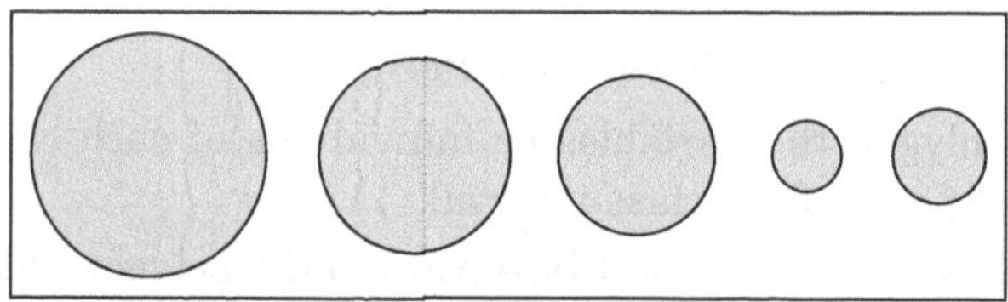

9.3.8. Subdivided Pie-diagram

Subdivided Pie-diagrams are used when comparison of the component parts is done with another and the total. The total value is equated to 360° and then the angles corresponding to component parts are calculated.

9.3.9. Prisms and Cubes

When the ratio between the two quantities to be compared is very great so that even area diagrams are not suitable, the data can be represented by spheres, prisms or cubes. Cubes are in common use. Cubes are constructed on sides which are taken in the ratio of cube roots of the given quantities.

9.3.10. Cartograms or Map Diagrams

Cartograms or map diagrams are most suitable for geographical datas. Rainfalls, temperature in different parts of the country are shown with dots, or shades in a particular map.

9.3.11. Pictograms

When numerical data are represented by pictures, they give a more attractive representation. Such pictures are called pictograms.

9.4. REGRESSION ANALYSIS

The term 'regression' was first used by Sir Francis Galton (1822–1911), a British Biometrician in connection with the height of parents and their offsprings. He found that the offspring of tall or short parents tend to regress to the average height. In other words, though tall fathers do tend to have tall sons yet the average height of tall fathers is more than the average height of their sons and the average height of short fathers is less than the average height of their sons.

The term 'regression' stands for some sort of functional relationship between two or more related variables. The only fundamental difference, if any, between problems of curve-fitting and regression is that in regression, any of the variables may be considered as independent or dependent while in curve-fitting, one variable cannot be dependent.

Regression measures the nature and extent of correlation. Regression is the estimation or prediction of unknown values of one variable from known values of another variable.

9.5. CURVE OF REGRESSION AND REGRESSION EQUATION

If two variates x and y are correlated *i.e.,* there exists an association or relationship between them, then the scatter diagram will be more or less concentrated round a curve. This curve is called the *curve of regression* and the relationship is said to be expressed by means of *curvilinear regression.*

The mathematical equation of the regression curve is called regression equation.

9.6. LINEAR REGRESSION

When the points of the scatter diagram concentrate round a straight line, the regression is called linear and this straight line is known as the line of regression.

Regression will be called non-linear if there exists a relationship other than a straight line between the variables under consideration.

9.7. LINES OF REGRESSION

A line of regression is the straight line which gives the best fit in the least square sense to the given frequency.

In case of n pairs (x_i, y_i); $i = 1, 2, ..., n$ from a bivariate data, we have no reason or justification to assume y as dependent variable and x as independent variable. Either of the two may be estimated for the given values of the other. Thus if we wish to estimate y for given values of x, we shall have the regression equation of the form $y = a + bx$, called the regression line of y on x. If we wish to estimate x for given values of y, we shall have the regression line of the form $x = \text{A} + \text{B}y$, called the regression line of x on y.

Thus it implies, in general, *we always have two lines of regression.*

If the line of regression is so chosen that the sum of squares of deviation parallel to the axis of y is minimised [*See Fig. (a)*], it is called *the line of regression of y on x* and it gives *the best estimate of y for any given value of x.*

If the line of regression is so chosen that the sum of squares of deviations parallel to the axis of x is minimised [*See Fig. (b)*], it is called *the line of regression of x on y* and it gives *the best estimate of x for any given value of y.*

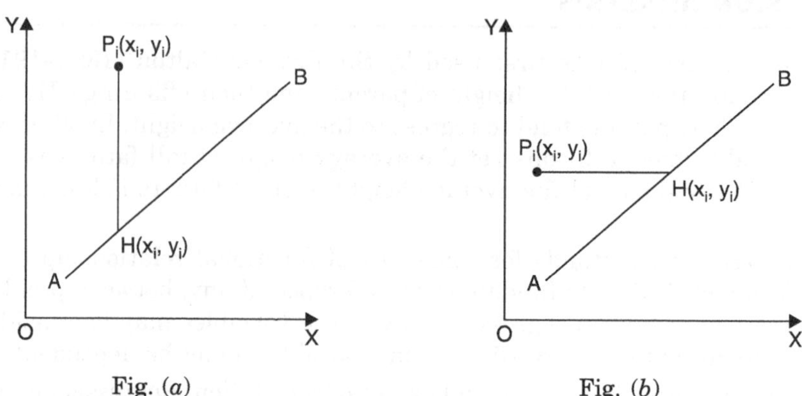

Fig. (*a*) Fig. (*b*)

The independent variable is called *predictor* or regresser or explanator and the dependent variable is called the *predictant* or regressed or explained variable.

9.8. DERIVATION OF LINES OF REGRESSION

9.8.1. Line of Regression of y on x

To obtain the line of regression of y on x, we shall assume y as dependent variable and x as independent variable.

Let $y = a + bx$ be the equation of regression line of y on x.

The residual for i^{th} point is $E_i = y_i - a - bx_i$.

Introduce a new quantity U such that

$$U = \sum_{i=1}^{n} E_i^2 = \sum_{i=1}^{n} (y_i - a - bx_i)^2 \quad \text{...(1)}$$

According to the *principle of Least squares*, the constants a and b are chosen in such a way that the sum of the squares of residuals is minimum.

Now, the condition for U to be maximum or minimum is

$$\frac{\partial U}{\partial a} = 0 \quad \text{and} \quad \frac{\partial U}{\partial b} = 0$$

From (1),
$$\frac{\partial U}{\partial a} = 2\sum_{i=1}^{n} (y_i - a - bx_i)(-1)$$

$$\frac{\partial U}{\partial a} = 0 \text{ gives } 2\sum_{i=1}^{n} (y_i - a - bx_i)(-1) = 0$$

$$\Rightarrow \quad \boxed{\Sigma y = na + b\,\Sigma x} \quad \text{...(2)}$$

Also,
$$\frac{\partial U}{\partial b} = 2\sum_{i=1}^{n} (y_i - a - bx_i)(-x_i)$$

$$\frac{\partial U}{\partial b} = 0 \text{ gives } 2\sum_{i=1}^{n} (y_i - a - bx_i)(-x_i) = 0$$

$$\Rightarrow \quad \boxed{\Sigma xy = a\,\Sigma x + b\,\Sigma x^2} \qquad ...(3)$$

Equations (2) and (3) are called *normal equations.*

Solving (2) and (3) for 'a' and 'b', we get

$$b = \frac{\Sigma xy - \frac{1}{n}\Sigma x\,\Sigma y}{\Sigma x^2 - \frac{1}{n}(\Sigma x)^2} = \frac{n\,\Sigma xy - \Sigma x\,\Sigma y}{n\,\Sigma x^2 - (\Sigma x)^2} \qquad ...(4)$$

and $$a = \frac{\Sigma y}{n} - b\frac{\Sigma x}{n} = \bar{y} - b\bar{x} \qquad ...(5)$$

Eqn. (5) gives $\bar{y} = a + b\bar{x}$

Hence $y = a + bx$ line passes through point $(\bar{x}, \bar{y})$

Putting $a = \bar{y} - b\bar{x}$ in equation of line $y = a + bx$, we get

$$\boxed{y - \bar{y} = b(x - \bar{x})} \qquad ...(6)$$

Equation (6) is called regression line of y on x. 'b' is called the regression coefficient of y on x and is usually denoted by b_{yx}.

Hence eqn. (6) can be rewritten as

$$y - \bar{y} = b_{yx}(x - \bar{x})$$

where $\bar{x}$ and $\bar{y}$ are mean values while

$$b_{yx} = \frac{n\,\Sigma xy - \Sigma x\,\Sigma y}{n\,\Sigma x^2 - (\Sigma x)^2}$$

In equation (3), shifting the origin to $(\bar{x}, \bar{y})$, we get

$$\Sigma(x - \bar{x})(y - \bar{y}) = a\,\Sigma(x - \bar{x}) + b(x - \bar{x})^2$$

$$\Rightarrow \quad nr\,\sigma_x\sigma_y = a(0) + bn\sigma_x^2$$

$\because\ \Sigma(x - \bar{x}) = 0,\ \frac{1}{n}\Sigma(x - \bar{x})^2 = \sigma_x^2$ and $\frac{\Sigma(x - \bar{x})(y - \bar{y})}{n\sigma_x\sigma_y} = r$

$$\Rightarrow \quad b = r\frac{\sigma_y}{\sigma_x}$$

Hence regression coefficient b_{yx} can also be defined as

$$\boxed{b_{yx} = r\frac{\sigma_y}{\sigma_x}}$$

where r is the coefficient of correlation, σ_x and σ_y are the standard deviations of x and y series respectively.

9.8.2. Line of Regression of x on y

Proceeding in the same way as 9.8.1, we can derive the regression line of x on y as

$$x - \bar{x} = b_{xy}(y - \bar{y})$$

where b_{xy} is the regression coefficient of x on y and is given by

$$b_{xy} = \frac{n\ \Sigma xy - \Sigma x\ \Sigma y}{n\ \Sigma y^2 - (\Sigma y)^2}$$

or

$$b_{xy} = r\ \frac{\sigma_x}{\sigma_y}$$

where the terms have their usual meanings.

Note. If $r = 0$, the two lines of regression become $y = \bar{y}$ and $x = \bar{x}$ which are two straight lines parallel to x and y axes respectively and passing through their means $\bar{y}$ and $\bar{x}$. They are mutually perpendicular. If $r = \pm 1$, the two lines of regression will coincide.

9.9. USE OF REGRESSION ANALYSIS

(*i*) In the field of Business, this tool of statistical analysis is widely used. Businessmen are interested in predicting future production, consumption, investment, prices, profits and sales etc.

(*ii*) In the field of economic planning and sociological studies, projections of population, birth rates, death rates and other similar variables are of great use.

9.10. COMPARISON OF CORRELATION AND REGRESSION ANALYSIS

Both the correlation and regression analysis helps us in studying the relationship between two variables yet they differ in their approach and objectives.

(*i*) Correlation studies are meant for studying the covariation of the two variables. They tell us whether the variables under study move in the same direction or in reverse directions. The degree of their covariation is also reflected in the correlation co-efficient but the correlation study does not provide the nature of relationship. It does not tell us about the relative movement in the variables and we cannot predict the value of one variable corresponding to the value of other variable. This is possible through regression analysis.

(*ii*) Regression presumes one variable as a cause and the other as its effect. The independent variable is supposed to be affecting the dependent variable and as such we can estimate the values of the dependent variable by projecting the relationship between them. However, correlation between two series is not necessarily a cause-effect relationship.

(*iii*) Coefficient of correlation cannot exceed unity but one of the regression coefficients can have a value higher than unity but the product of two regression coefficients can never exceed unity.

9.11. PROPERTIES OF REGRESSION CO-EFFICIENTS

Property I. Correlation co-efficient is the geometric mean between the regression co-efficients.

The co-efficients of regression are $\frac{r\sigma_y}{\sigma_x}$ and $\frac{r\sigma_x}{\sigma_y}$.

G.M. between them = $\sqrt{\frac{r\sigma_y}{\sigma_x} \times \frac{r\sigma_x}{\sigma_y}} = \sqrt{r^2} = r$ = co-efficient of correlation.

Property II. If one of the regression co-efficients is greater than unity, the other must be less than unity.

The two regression co-efficients are $b_{yx} = \frac{r\sigma_y}{\sigma_x}$ and $b_{xy} = \frac{r\sigma_x}{\sigma_y}$.

Let $\quad b_{yx} > 1$, then $\frac{1}{b_{yx}} < 1 \quad \ldots(1)$

Since $\quad b_{yx} \cdot b_{xy} = r^2 \le 1 \quad (\because \; -1 \le r \le 1)$

$\therefore \quad b_{xy} \le \frac{1}{b_{yx}} < 1. \quad$ | using (1)

Similarly, if $\quad b_{xy} > 1$, then $b_{yx} < 1$.

Property III. Arithmetic mean of regression co-efficients is greater than the correlation co-efficient.

We have to prove that

$$\frac{b_{yx} + b_{xy}}{2} > r$$

or
$$r\frac{\sigma_y}{\sigma_x} + r\frac{\sigma_x}{\sigma_y} > 2r$$

or
$$\sigma_x^2 + \sigma_y^2 > 2\sigma_x\sigma_y$$

or
$$(\sigma_x - \sigma_y)^2 > 0 \quad \text{which is true.}$$

Property IV. Regression co-efficients are independent of the origin but not of scale.

Proof. Let $\quad u = \frac{x-a}{h}, v = \frac{y-b}{k}$, where a, b, h and k are constants

$$b_{yx} = \frac{r\sigma_y}{\sigma_x} = r \cdot \frac{k\sigma_v}{h\sigma_u} = \frac{k}{h}\left(\frac{r\sigma_v}{\sigma_u}\right) = \frac{k}{h} b_{vu}$$

Similarly, $\quad b_{xy} = \frac{h}{k} b_{uv}$.

Thus, b_{yx} and b_{xy} are both independent of a and b but not of h and k.

Property V. The correlation co-efficient and the two regression co-efficients have same sign.

Proof. Regression co-efficient of y on $x = b_{yx} = r\frac{\sigma_y}{\sigma_x}$

Regression co-efficient of x on $y = b_{xy} = r \dfrac{\sigma_x}{\sigma_y}$

Since σ_x and σ_y are both positive ; b_{yx}, b_{xy} and r have same sign.

9.12. ANGLE BETWEEN TWO LINES OF REGRESSION

If θ is the acute angle between the two regression lines in the case of two variables x and y, show that

$$\tan\theta = \frac{1-r^2}{r} \cdot \frac{\sigma_x \sigma_y}{\sigma_x^2 + \sigma_y^2}, \qquad \text{where } r, \sigma_x, \sigma_y \text{ have their usual meanings.}$$

Explain the significance of the formula when r = 0 and r = ± 1.

Proof. Equations to the lines of regression of y on x and x on y are

$$y - \bar{y} = \frac{r\sigma_y}{\sigma_x}(x - \bar{x}) \qquad \text{and} \qquad x - \bar{x} = \frac{r\sigma_x}{\sigma_y}(y - \bar{y})$$

Their slopes are

$$m_1 = \frac{r\sigma_y}{\sigma_x} \qquad \text{and} \qquad m_2 = \frac{\sigma_y}{r\sigma_x}.$$

$$\therefore \qquad \tan\theta = \pm \frac{m_2 - m_1}{1 + m_2 m_1} = \pm \frac{\dfrac{\sigma_y}{r\sigma_x} - \dfrac{r\sigma_y}{\sigma_x}}{1 + \dfrac{\sigma_y^2}{\sigma_x^2}}$$

$$= \pm \frac{1-r^2}{r} \cdot \frac{\sigma_y}{\sigma_x} \cdot \frac{\sigma_x^2}{\sigma_x^2 + \sigma_y^2} = \pm \frac{1-r^2}{r} \cdot \frac{\sigma_x \sigma_y}{\sigma_x^2 + \sigma_y^2}$$

Since $r^2 \le 1$ and σ_x, σ_y are positive.

∴ +ve sign gives the acute angle between the lines.

Hence
$$\tan\theta = \frac{1-r^2}{r} \cdot \frac{\sigma_x \sigma_y}{\sigma_x^2 + \sigma_y^2}$$

when $r = 0$, $\theta = \dfrac{\pi}{2}$ ∴ The two lines of regression are perpendicular to each other.

Hence the estimated value of y is the same for all values of x and vice-versa.

When $r = \pm 1$, $\tan\theta = 0$ so that $\theta = 0$ or π

Hence the lines of regression coincide and there is perfect correlation between the two variates x and y.

9.13. ALGORITHM FOR LINEAR REGRESSION

```
Read n
sum x ← 0
sum xsq ← 0
sum y ← 0
sum xy ← 0
for i = 1 to n do
Read x,y
```

```
sum x ← sum x + x
sum xsq ← sum xsq + x^2
sum y ← sum y + y
sum xy ← sum xy + x × y
end for
denom ← n × sum x sq - sum x × sum x
a ← (sum y × sum x sq - sum x × sum xy)/denom
b ← (n × sum xy - sum x × sum y)/denom
Write b,a
Stop
```

9.14. PROGRAM TO IMPLEMENT LEAST SQUARE FIT OF A REGRESSION LINE OF Y ON X

```
#include<stdio.h>
#include<conio.h>
#include<math.h>
void main()
{
    int data,i;
    float x[10],y[10],xy[10],x2[10],z;
    float sum1=0.0,sum2=0.0,sum3=0.0,sum4=0.0;
    clrscr();

    printf("Enter the no. of data points:");
    scanf("%d",&data);
    printf("Enter the value of x: \n");
    for(i=0;i<data;i++)
    {
        printf("Value of x%d:",i+1);
        scanf("%f",&x[i]);
    }
    printf("\nEnter the value of f(x):\n");
    for(i=0;i<data;i++)
    {
        printf("Value of f(x%d):",i+1);
        scanf("%f",&y[i]);
    }
    for(i=0;i<data;i++)
    {
        xy[i]=x[i]*y[i];
        x2[i]=x[i]*x[i];
```

```
            sum1 +=xy[i];
            sum2 +=x2[i];
            sum3 +=x[i];
            sum4 +=y[i];
      }
      sum3 =sum3/2;
      sum4 =sum4/2;
      //printf("%.2f %.2f %.2f %.2f", sum1,sum2,sum3,sum4);
      sum1=(sum1/sum2);
      z=(sum1*sum3)-sum4;

      printf("\n\nThe REGRESSION LINE OF Y on X is :\n");
      printf("\t\t\t y=%.2f *x - (%.2f)",sum1,z);
      getch(1);
}
```

9.15. PROGRAM TO IMPLEMENT LEAST SQUARE FIT OF A REGRESSION LINE OF X ON Y

```
#include<stdio.h>
#include<conio.h>
#include<math.h>

void main()
{

      int data,i;
      float x[10],y[10],xy[10],y2[10],z;
      float sumx=0.0,sumy=0.0,sumxy=0.0,sumy2=0.0;
      clrscr();

      printf("Enter the no. of data points: ");
      scanf("%d",&data);

      printf("Enter the value of x: \n");
      for(i=0;i<data;i++)
      {
            printf("Value of x%d: ",i+1);
            scanf("%f",&x[i]);
      }

      printf("\nEnter the value of f(x): \n");
      for(i=0;i<data; i++)
```

```
    {
        printf("Value of f(x%d):", i+1);
        scanf("%f",&y[i]);
    }

    for(i=0;i<data;i++)
    {
        xy[i]=x[i]*y[i];
        y2[i]=y[i]*y[i];

        sumxy +=xy[i];
        sumy2 +=y2[i];
        sumx +=x[i];
        sumy +=y[i];
    }
    sumx =sumx/2;
    sumy =sumy/2;
    sumxy=(sumxy/sumy2);
    z=(sumxy*sumy)-sumx;

    printf("\n\nThe REGRESSION LINE OF X on Y is :\n");
    printf("\t\t\t x = %.2f *y - (%.2f)",sumxy, z);

    getch();
}
```

EXAMPLES

Example 1. *If the regression coefficients are 0.8 and 0.2, what would be the value of coefficient of correlation?*

Sol. We know that,

$$r^2 = b_{yx} \, . \, b_{xy} = 0.8 \times 0.2 = 0.16$$

Since r has the same sign as both the regression coefficients b_{yx} and b_{xy}

Hence $\quad r = \sqrt{0.16} = 0.4.$

Example 2. *Calculate linear regression coefficients from the following:*

x	→	*1*	*2*	*3*	*4*	*5*	*6*	*7*	*8*
y	→	*3*	*7*	*10*	*12*	*14*	*17*	*20*	*24*

Sol. Linear regression coefficients are given by

$$b_{yx} = \frac{n\,\Sigma xy - \Sigma x\,\Sigma y}{n\,\Sigma x^2 - (\Sigma x)^2}$$

and

$$b_{xy} = \frac{n\,\Sigma xy - \Sigma x\,\Sigma y}{n\,\Sigma y^2 - (\Sigma y)^2}$$

Let us prepare the following table:

x	y	x^2	y^2	xy
1	3	1	9	3
2	7	4	49	14
3	10	9	100	30
4	12	16	144	48
5	14	25	196	70
6	17	36	289	102
7	20	49	400	140
8	24	64	576	192
$\Sigma x = 36$	$\Sigma y = 107$	$\Sigma x^2 = 204$	$\Sigma y^2 = 1763$	$\Sigma xy = 599$

Here $n = 8$

$$\therefore \qquad b_{yx} = \frac{(8 \times 599) - (36 \times 107)}{(8 \times 204) - (36)^2} = \frac{4792 - 3852}{1632 - 1296} = \frac{940}{336} = 2.7976$$

and

$$b_{xy} = \frac{(8 \times 599) - (36 \times 107)}{(8 \times 1763) - (107)^2} = \frac{940}{2655} = 0.3540$$

Example 3. *The following table gives age (x) in years of cars and annual maintenance cost (y) in hundred rupees:*

X:	*1*	*3*	*5*	*7*	*9*
Y:	*15*	*18*	*21*	*23*	*22*

Estimate the maintenance cost for a 4 year old car after finding the regression equation.

Sol.

x	y	xy	x^2
1	15	15	1
3	18	54	9
5	21	105	25
7	23	161	49
9	22	198	81
$\Sigma x = 25$	$\Sigma y = 99$	$\Sigma xy = 533$	$\Sigma x^2 = 165$

Here, $\qquad n = 5$

$$\bar{x} = \frac{\Sigma x}{n} = \frac{25}{5} = 5, \ \bar{y} = \frac{\Sigma y}{n} = \frac{99}{5} = 19.8$$

$$\therefore \qquad b_{yx} = \frac{n\,\Sigma xy - \Sigma x\,\Sigma y}{n\,\Sigma x^2 - (\Sigma x)^2} = \frac{(5 \times 533) - (25 \times 99)}{(5 \times 165) - (25)^2} = 0.95$$

Regression line of y on x is given by

$$y - \bar{y} = b_{yx}\,(x - \bar{x})$$

$$\Rightarrow \qquad y - 19.8 = 0.95\,(x - 5)$$

$\Rightarrow$ $y = 0.95x + 15.05$

When $x = 4$ years, $y = (0.95 \times 4) + 15.05 = 18.85$ hundred rupees = ₹ 1885.

Example 4. *In a partially destroyed laboratory record of an analysis of a correlation data, the following results only are eligible:*

Variance of $x = 9$

Regression equations : $8x - 10y + 66 = 0$, $40x - 18y = 214$.

What were (a) the mean values of x and y (b) the standard deviation of y and the co-efficient of correlation between x and y.

Sol. (*a*) **Since both the lines of regression pass through the point** $(\bar{x}, \bar{y})$ therefore, we have

$$8\bar{x} - 10\bar{y} + 66 = 0 \quad \text{...(1)}$$

$$40\bar{x} - 18\bar{y} - 214 = 0 \quad \text{...(2)}$$

Multiplying (1) by 5, $40\bar{x} - 50\bar{y} + 330 = 0$ ...(3)

Subtracting (3) from (2), $32\bar{y} - 544 = 0$ $\therefore$ $\bar{y} = 17$

$\therefore$ From (1), $8\bar{x} - 170 + 66 = 0$ or $8\bar{x} = 104$ $\therefore$ $\bar{x} = 13$

Hence $\bar{x} = 13$, $\bar{y} = 17$

(*b*) Variance of $x = \sigma_x^2 = 9$ (given)

$\therefore$ $\sigma_x = 3$

The equations of lines of regression can be written as

$$y = 0.8x + 6.6 \quad \text{and} \quad x = 0.45y + 5.35$$

$\therefore$ The regression co-efficient of y on x is $\dfrac{r\sigma_y}{\sigma_x} = 0.8$ ...(4)

The regression co-efficient of x on y is $\dfrac{r\sigma_x}{\sigma_y} = 0.45$ ...(5)

Multiplying (4) and (5), $r^2 = 0.8 \times 0.45 = 0.36$ $\therefore$ $r = 0.6$

(+ve sign with square root is taken because regression co-efficients are +ve).

From (4), $\sigma_y = \dfrac{0.8\sigma_x}{r'} = \dfrac{0.8 \times 3}{0.6} = 4.$

Example 5. *The regression lines of y on x and x on y are respectively $y = ax + b$, $x = cy + d$. Show that*

$$\frac{\sigma_y}{\sigma_x} = \sqrt{\frac{a}{c}}, \ \bar{x} = \frac{bc + d}{1 - ac} \ \text{and} \ \bar{y} = \frac{ad + b}{1 - ac}.$$

Sol. The regression line of y on x is

$$y = ax + b \quad \text{...(1)}$$

$\therefore$ $b_{yx} = a$

The regression line of x on y is

$$x = cy + d \qquad \text{...(2)}$$

$\therefore$ $b_{xy} = c$

We know that, $$b_{yx} = r\,\frac{\sigma_y}{\sigma_x} \qquad \text{...(3)}$$

and $$b_{xy} = r\,\frac{\sigma_x}{\sigma_y} \qquad \text{...(4)}$$

Dividing eqn. (3) by (4), we get

$$\frac{b_{yx}}{b_{xy}} = \frac{\sigma_y^2}{\sigma_x^2} \Rightarrow \frac{a}{c} = \frac{\sigma_y^2}{\sigma_x^2} \Rightarrow \frac{\sigma_y}{\sigma_x} = \sqrt{\frac{a}{c}}$$

Since both the regression lines pass through the point $(\bar{x}, \bar{y})$ therefore,

$$\bar{y} = a\bar{x} + b \quad \text{and} \quad \bar{x} = c\bar{y} + d$$

$$\Rightarrow \quad a\bar{x} - \bar{y} = -b \qquad \text{...(5)}$$

$$\bar{x} - c\bar{y} = d \qquad \text{...(6)}$$

Multiplying equation (6) by a and then subtracting from (5), we get

$$(ac - 1)\,\bar{y} = -ad - b \Rightarrow \bar{y} = \frac{ad + b}{1 - ac}$$

Similarly, we get $$\bar{x} = \frac{bc + d}{1 - ac}.$$

Example 6. *For two random variables, x and y with the same mean, the two regression equations are*

$$y = ax + b \quad \textit{and} \quad x = \alpha y + \beta$$

Show that $\dfrac{b}{\beta} = \dfrac{1 - a}{1 - \alpha}$. *Find also the common mean.*

Sol. Here, $b_{yx} = a,\ b_{xy} = \alpha$

Let the common mean be m, then regression lines are

$$y - m = a\,(x - m)$$

$$\Rightarrow \quad y = ax + m\,(1 - a) \qquad \text{...(1)}$$

and $$x - m = \alpha(y - m)$$

$$\Rightarrow \quad x = \alpha y + m\,(1 - \alpha) \qquad \text{...(2)}$$

Comparing (1) and (2) with the given equations.

$$b = m\,(1 - a),\ \beta = m\,(1 - \alpha)$$

$$\therefore \quad \frac{b}{\beta} = \frac{1 - a}{1 - \alpha}$$

Again $$m = \frac{b}{1 - a} = \frac{\beta}{1 - \alpha}$$

Since regression lines pass through $(\bar{x}, \bar{y})$

$$\therefore \quad \bar{x} = \alpha\bar{y} + \beta \quad \text{and} \quad \bar{y} = a\bar{x} + b \text{ will hold.}$$

$$\Rightarrow \quad m = am + b,\ m = \alpha m + \beta$$

$$\Rightarrow \qquad am + b = \alpha m + \beta$$

$$\Rightarrow \qquad m = \frac{\beta - b}{a - \alpha}.$$

Example 7. *Obtain the line of regression of y on x for the data given below:*

x: *1.53* *1.78* *2.60* *2.95* *3.42*

y: *33.50* *36.30* *40.00* *45.80* *53.50.*

Sol. The line of regression of y on x is given by

$$y - \bar{y} = b_{yx}(x - \bar{x}) \qquad ...(1)$$

where b_{yx} is the coefficient of regression given by

$$b_{yx} = \frac{n\,\Sigma xy - \Sigma x\,\Sigma y}{n\,\Sigma x^2 - (\Sigma x)^2} \qquad ...(2)$$

Now we form the table as,

x	y	x^2	xy
1.53	33.50	2.3409	51.255
1.78	36.30	2.1684	64.614
2.60	40.00	6.76	104
2.95	45.80	8.7025	135.11
3.42	53.50	11.6964	182.97
$\Sigma x = 12.28$	$\Sigma y = 209.1$	$\Sigma x^2 = 32.6682$	$\Sigma xy = 537.949$

Here, $n = 5$

$$b_{yx} = \frac{(5 \times 537.949) - (12.28 \times 209.1)}{(5 \times 32.6682) - (12.28)^2} = \frac{121.997}{12.543} = 9.726$$

Also, $$\text{mean } \bar{x} = \frac{\Sigma x}{n} = \frac{12.28}{5} = 2.456$$

and $$\bar{y} = \frac{\Sigma y}{n} = \frac{209.1}{5} = 41.82$$

$\therefore$ From (1), we get

$$y - 41.82 = 9.726(x - 2.456) = 9.726x - 23.887$$

$$y = 17.932 + 9.726x$$

which is the required line of regression of y on x.

Example 8. *For 10 observations on price (x) and supply (y), the following data were obtained (in appropriate units):*

$$\Sigma x = 130, \quad \Sigma y = 220, \quad \Sigma x^2 = 2288, \quad \Sigma y^2 = 5506 \text{ and } \Sigma xy = 3467$$

Obtain the two lines of regression and estimate the supply when the price is 16 units.

Sol. Here, $$n = 10,\ \bar{x} = \frac{\Sigma x}{n} = 13 \text{ and } \bar{y} = \frac{\Sigma y}{n} = 22$$

Regression coefficient of y on x is

$$b_{yx} = \frac{n\,\Sigma xy - \Sigma x\,\Sigma y}{n\,\Sigma x^2 - (\Sigma x)^2} = \frac{(10 \times 3467) - (130 \times 220)}{(10 \times 2288) - (130)^2} = 1.015$$

$\therefore$ Regression line of y on x is

$$y - \bar{y} = b_{yx}(x - \bar{x})$$

$$y - 22 = 1.015(x - 13)$$

$$\Rightarrow \quad y = 1.015x + 8.805 \qquad ...(1)$$

Regression coefficient of x on y is

$$b_{xy} = \frac{n\,\Sigma xy - \Sigma x\,\Sigma y}{n\,\Sigma y^2 - (\Sigma y)^2}$$

$$= \frac{(10 \times 3467) - (130 \times 220)}{(10 \times 5506) - (220)^2} = \frac{6070}{6660} = 0.9114$$

Regression line of x on y is

$$x - \bar{x} = b_{xy}(y - \bar{y})$$

$$x - 13 = 0.9114(y - 22)$$

$$x = 0.9114y - 7.0508 \qquad ...(2)$$

Since we are to estimate supply (y) when price (x) is given therefore we are to use regression line of y on x here.

When $x = 16$ units,

$$y = 1.015(16) + 8.805 = 25.045 \text{ units.}$$

Example 9. *The following results were obtained from records of age (x) and systolic blood pressure (y) of a group of 10 men:*

	x	y
Mean	*53*	*142*
Variance	*130*	*165*

and $\Sigma(x - \bar{x})(y - \bar{y}) = 1220$

Find the approximate regression equation and use it to estimate the blood pressure of a man whose age is 45.

Sol. Given :

Mean	$\bar{x} = 53$	and $\bar{y} = 142$
Variance	$\sigma_x^2 = 130$	and $\sigma_y^2 = 165$
No. of men,	$n = 10$	

$$\Sigma(x - \bar{x})(y - \bar{y}) = 1220$$

$\therefore$ Coefficient of correlation,

$$r = \frac{\Sigma(x - \bar{x})(y - \bar{y})}{n\sigma_x\sigma_y} = \frac{1220}{10\sqrt{130 \times 165}} = \frac{122}{146.458} = 0.83.$$

Since we are to estimate blood pressure (y) of a 45 years old man, we will find regression line of y on x.

Regression coefficient $b_{yx} = r\,\dfrac{\sigma_y}{\sigma_x} = 0.83 \times \sqrt{\dfrac{165}{130}} = 0.935.$

Regression line of y on x is given by

$$y - \bar{y} = b_{yx}(x - \bar{x})$$

$$\Rightarrow \quad y - 142 = 0.935(x - 53) = 0.935x - 49.555$$

$$\Rightarrow \quad y = 0.935x + 92.445$$

when $x = 45$,

$$y = (0.935 \times 45) + 92.445 = 134.52.$$

Hence the required blood pressure = 134.52.

Example 10. *The following results were obtained from marks in Applied Mechanics and Engineering Mathematics in an examination:*

	Applied Mechanics (x)	*Engineering Mathematics (y)*
Mean	*47.5*	*39.5*
Standard Deviation	*16.8*	*10.8*

$r = 0.95.$

Find both the regression equations. Also estimate the value of y for x = 30.

Sol. $\bar{x} = 47.5, \quad \bar{y} = 39.5$

$\sigma_x = 16.8, \quad \sigma_y = 10.8 \quad$ and $\quad r = 0.95.$

Regression coefficients are

$$b_{yx} = r\,\frac{\sigma_y}{\sigma_x} = 0.95 \times \frac{10.8}{16.8} = 0.6107$$

and

$$b_{xy} = r\,\frac{\sigma_x}{\sigma_y} = 0.95 \times \frac{16.8}{10.8} = 1.477.$$

Regression line of y on x is

$$y - \bar{y} = b_{yx}(x - \bar{x})$$

$$\Rightarrow \quad y - 39.5 = 0.6107\,(x - 47.5) = 0.6107x - 29.008$$

$$y = 0.6107x + 10.49 \qquad \text{...(1)}$$

Regression line of x on y is

$$x - \bar{x} = b_{xy}\,(y - \bar{y})$$

$$\Rightarrow \quad x - 47.5 = 1.477\,(y - 39.5)$$

$$x = 1.477y - 10.8415 \qquad \text{...(2)}$$

Putting $x = 30$ in equation (1), we get

$$y = (0.6107)(30) + 10.49 = 18.321 + 10.49 = 28.81.$$

Example 11. *From the following data. Find the most likely value of y when x = 24:*

	y	*x*
Mean	*985.8*	*18.1*
S.D.	*36.4*	*2.0*

$r = 0.58.$

Sol. Given : $\bar{y} = 985.8, \quad \bar{x} = 18.1, \quad \sigma_y = 36.4, \quad \sigma_x = 2, \quad r = 0.58$

Regression coefficient,

$$b_{yx} = r\,\frac{\sigma_y}{\sigma_x} = (0.58)\,\frac{36.4}{2} = 10.556.$$

Regression line of y on x is

$$y - \bar{y} = b_{yx}(x - \bar{x})$$

$$\Rightarrow \quad y - 985.8 = 10.556(x - 18.1)$$

$$\Rightarrow \quad y = 10.556x + 794.73$$

when $x = 24$,

$$y = (10.556 \times 24) + 794.73 = 1048 \text{ (approximately).}$$

Example 12. *The equations of two regression lines, obtained in a correlation analysis of 60 observations are:*

$$5x = 6y + 24 \text{ and } 1000y = 768x - 3608.$$

What is the correlation coefficient ? Show that the ratio of coefficient of variability of x to that of y is $\frac{5}{24}$*. What is the ratio of variances of x and y?*

Sol. Regression line of x on y is

$$5x = 6y + 24$$

$$x = \frac{6}{5}y + \frac{24}{5}$$

$$\therefore \quad b_{xy} = \frac{6}{5} \quad \text{...(1)}$$

Regression line of y on x is

$$1000y = 768x - 3608$$

$$y = 0.768x - 3.608$$

$$\therefore \quad b_{yx} = 0.768 \quad \text{...(2)}$$

From (1), $$r\,\frac{\sigma_x}{\sigma_y} = \frac{6}{5} \quad \text{...(3)}$$

From (2), $$r\,\frac{\sigma_y}{\sigma_x} = 0.768 \quad \text{...(4)}$$

Multiplying equations (3) and (4), we get

$$r^2 = 0.9216 \quad \Rightarrow \quad r = 0.96 \quad \text{...(5)}$$

Dividing (4) by (3), we get

$$\frac{{\sigma_x}^2}{{\sigma_y}^2} = \frac{6}{5 \times 0.768} = 1.5625.$$

Taking square root, we get

$$\frac{\sigma_x}{\sigma_y} = 1.25 = \frac{5}{4} \quad \text{...(6)}$$

Since the regression lines pass through the point $(\bar{x}, \bar{y})$, we have

$$5\bar{x} = 6\bar{y} + 24$$

$$1000\bar{y} = 768\bar{x} - 3608.$$

Solving the above equations for $\bar{x}$ and $\bar{y}$, we get $\bar{x} = 6$, $\bar{y} = 1$.

Coefficient of variability of $x = \dfrac{\sigma_x}{\bar{x}}$,

Coefficient of variability of $y = \dfrac{\sigma_y}{\bar{y}}$.

$$\therefore \quad \text{Required ratio} = \frac{\sigma_x}{\bar{x}} \times \frac{\bar{y}}{\sigma_y} = \frac{\bar{y}}{\bar{x}}\left(\frac{\sigma_x}{\sigma_y}\right) = \frac{1}{6} \times \frac{5}{4} = \frac{5}{24}. \qquad | \text{ Using (6)}$$

Example 13. *The following data regarding the heights (y) and weights (x) of 100 college students are given:*

$\Sigma x = 15000$, $\Sigma x^2 = 2272500$, $\Sigma y = 6800$, $\Sigma y^2 = 463025$ *and* $\Sigma xy = 1022250$.

Find the equation of regression line of height on weight.

Sol. $\bar{x} = \dfrac{\Sigma x}{n} = \dfrac{15000}{100} = 150$, $\bar{y} = \dfrac{\Sigma y}{n} = \dfrac{6800}{100} = 68$

Regression coefficient of y on x,

$$b_{yx} = \frac{n\,\Sigma xy - \Sigma x\,\Sigma y}{n\,\Sigma x^2 - (\Sigma x)^2} = \frac{(100 \times 1022250) - (15000 \times 6800)}{(100 \times 2272500) - (15000)^2} = 0.1$$

Regression line of height (y) on weight (x) is given by

$$y - \bar{y} = b_{yx}(x - \bar{x})$$

$$\Rightarrow \quad y - 68 = 0.1(x - 150)$$

$$\Rightarrow \quad y = 0.1x + 53.$$

Example 14. *A study of prices of a certain commodity at Hapur and Kanpur yields the following data:*

	Hapur (₹)	*Kanpur (₹)*
Average price/kilo	*2.463*	*2.797*
Standard deviation	*0.326*	*0.207*

'r' between prices at Hapur and Kanpur is 0.774.

Estimate, from the above data, the most likely price at Hapur corresponding to the price of ₹ 3.052 per kilo at Kanpur.

Sol. Here, $\bar{x} = 2.463$, $\bar{y} = 2.797$, $\sigma_x = 0.326$, $\sigma_y = 0.207$ and $r = 0.774$

Regression coefficient $b_{xy} = r\,\dfrac{\sigma_x}{\sigma_y} = (0.774)\left(\dfrac{0.326}{0.207}\right) = 1.218956522$

Regression line of x on y is given by

$$x - \bar{x} = b_{xy}(y - \bar{y})$$

$$\Rightarrow \quad x - 2.463 = 1.218956522(y - 2.797)$$

$$x = 1.218956522y - 0.9464213$$

when $y = 3.052$, $\quad x = 1.218956522\ (3.052) - 0.9464213 = 2.7738$

Hence the most likely price at Hapur is ₹ 2.7738 per kilo, corresponding to the given price at Kanpur.

Example 15. *A panel of two judges, A and B, graded seven T.V. serial performances by awarding marks independently as shown in the following table:*

Performance	*1*	*2*	*3*	*4*	*5*	*6*	*7*
Marks by A	*46*	*42*	*44*	*40*	*43*	*41*	*45*
Marks by B	*40*	*38*	*36*	*35*	*39*	*37*	*41*

The eighth T.V. performance which judge B could not attend, was awarded 37 marks by judge A. If the judge B had also been present, how many marks would be expected to have been awarded by him to the eighth T.V. performance?

Use regression analysis to answer this question.

Sol. Let the marks awarded by judge A be denoted by x and the marks awarded by judge B be denoted by y.

Here, $n = 7$; $$\bar{x} = \frac{\Sigma x}{n} = \frac{46 + 42 + 44 + 40 + 43 + 41 + 45}{7} = 43$$

$$\bar{y} = \frac{\Sigma y}{n} = \frac{40 + 38 + 36 + 35 + 39 + 37 + 41}{7} = 38$$

Let us form the table as

x	y	xy	x^2
46	40	1840	2116
42	38	1596	1764
44	36	1584	1936
40	35	1400	1600
43	39	1677	1849
41	37	1517	1681
45	41	1845	2025
$\Sigma x = 301$	$\Sigma y = 266$	$\Sigma xy = 11459$	$\Sigma x^2 = 12971$

Regression coefficient,

$$b_{yx} = \frac{n\,\Sigma xy - \Sigma x\,\Sigma y}{n\,\Sigma x^2 - (\Sigma x)^2} = \frac{(7 \times 11459) - (301 \times 266)}{(7 \times 12971) - (301)^2} = 0.75$$

Regression line of y on x is given by

$$y - \bar{y} = b_{yx}(x - \bar{x})$$

$$y - 38 = 0.75(x - 43)$$

$$\Rightarrow \qquad y = 0.75x + 5.75$$

when $x = 37$,

$$y = 0.75(37) + 5.75 = 33.5 \text{ marks}$$

Hence, if judge B had also been present, 33.5 marks would be expected to have been awarded to the eighth T.V. performance.

Example 16. *Two variables x and y have zero means, the same variance σ^2 and zero correlation, show that:*

$$u = x \cos \alpha + y \sin \alpha \quad \text{and} \quad v = x \sin \alpha - y \cos \alpha$$

have the same variance σ^2 and zero correlation.

Sol. We are given that

$$r(x, y) = 0 \Rightarrow \text{Cov}(x, y) = 0, \quad \sigma_x^2 = \sigma_y^2 = \sigma^2$$

We have

$$\sigma_u^2 = \text{V}(x \cos \alpha + y \sin \alpha)$$
$$= \cos^2 \alpha \, \text{V}(x) + \sin^2 \alpha \, \text{V}(y) + 2 \sin \alpha \cos \alpha \, \text{Cov}(x, y)$$
$$= (\cos^2 \alpha + \sin^2 \alpha)\sigma^2 \qquad | \because \text{Cov}(x, y) = 0$$
$$= \sigma^2$$

Similarly,

$$\sigma_v^2 = \sigma^2$$

$$\text{Cov}(u, v) = \text{E}[(u - \bar{u})(v - \bar{v})]$$
$$= \text{E}[(x \cos \alpha + y \sin \alpha - \bar{x} \cos \alpha - \bar{y} \sin \alpha)(x \sin \alpha - y \cos \alpha - \bar{x} \sin \alpha + \bar{y} \cos \alpha)]$$
$$= \text{E}[(x \cos \alpha + y \sin \alpha)(x \sin \alpha - y \cos \alpha)] \qquad | \because \bar{x} = 0 = \bar{y}$$
$$= [\text{E}(x^2) - \text{E}(y^2)] \sin \alpha \cos \alpha + \text{E}(xy)(\sin^2 \alpha - \cos^2 \alpha)$$
$$= 0 \qquad | \because \sigma_x^2 = \sigma_y^2 = \sigma^2 \text{ and V}(xy) = 0$$

$$\therefore \quad r = \frac{\text{Cov}(u, v)}{\sigma_u \sigma_v} = 0.$$

ASSIGNMENT

1. (*i*) Discuss regression and its importance. Given the following data:

x:	1	5	3	2	1	1	7	3
y:	6	1	0	0	1	2	1	5

Find a regression line of x on y.

(*ii*) In a study between the amount of rainfall and the quantity of air pollution removed the following data were collected :

Daily rainfall : (*in .01 cm*)	4.3	4.5	5.9	5.6	6.1	5.2	3.8	2.1
Pollution removed : (*mg/m³*)	12.6	12.1	11.6	11.8	11.4	11.8	13.2	14.1

Find the regression line of y on x.

2. (*i*) Can Y = 5 + 2.8 X and X = 3 – 0.5 Y be the estimated regression equations of Y on X and X on Y respectively ? Explain your answer with suitable theoretical arguments.

(*ii*) Find the coefficient of correlation when the two regression equations are

$$\text{X} = -0.2\,\text{Y} + 4.2$$
$$\text{Y} = -0.8\,\text{X} + 8.4$$

3. If F is the pull required to lift a load W by means of a pulley block, fit a linear law of the form $F = mW + c$ connecting F and W, using the data

W :	50	70	100	120
F :	12	15	21	25

where F and W are in kg wt. Compute F when W = 150 kg wt.

4. A simply supported beam carries a concentrated load P (kg) at its mid-point. The following table gives maximum deflection y (cm) corresponding to various values of P :

P :	100	120	140	160	180	200
y :	0.45	0.55	0.60	0.70	0.80	0.85

Find a law of the form $y = a + bP$.

Also find the value of maximum deflection when P = 150 kg.

5. (*i*) The two regression equations of the variables x and y are $x = 19.13 - 0.87\,y$ and $y = 11.64 - 0.50x$. Find (*a*) mean of x's (*b*) mean of y's and (*c*) correlation coefficient between x and y.

(*ii*) Two random variables have the regression lines with equations $3x + 2y = 26$ and $6x + y = 31$. Find the mean values and the correlation coefficient between x and y.

(*iii*) In a partially destroyed laboratory data, only the equations giving the two lines of regression of y on x and x on y are available and are respectively

$$7x - 16y + 9 = 0$$
$$5y - 4x - 3 = 0$$

Calculate the coefficient of correlation, $\bar{x}$ and $\bar{y}$.

(*iv*) The regression equations calculated from a given set of observations for two random variables are

$$x = -0.4y + 6.4 \quad \text{and} \quad y = -0.6x + 4.6$$

Calculate (*i*) $\bar{x}$ (*ii*) $\bar{y}$ (*iii*) r.

6. Two lines of regression are given by

$$x + 2y - 5 = 0 \quad \text{and} \quad 2x + 3y - 8 = 0 \quad \text{and} \quad \sigma_x^2 = 12,$$

Calculate :

(*i*) the mean values of x and y

(*ii*) variance of y

(*iii*) the coefficient of correlation between x and y.

7. (*i*) Find both the lines of regression of following data :

x :	5.60	5.65	5.70	5.81	5.85
y :	5.80	5.70	5.80	5.79	6.01

(*ii*) Obtain regression line of x on y for the given data :

x :	1	2	3	4	5	6
y :	5.0	8.1	10.6	13.1	16.2	20.0

8. An analyst for a company was studying travelling expenses (y) in ₹ and duration (x) of these trips for 102 sales trip. He has found relation between x and y linear and data as follows :

$$\Sigma x = 510, \quad \Sigma y = 7140, \quad \Sigma x^2 = 4150, \quad \Sigma xy = 54900, \quad \Sigma y^2 = 740200$$

Calculate (*i*) Two regression lines

(*ii*) A given trip has to take 7 days. How much money should be allowed so that they will not run short of money?

9. Assuming that we conduct an experiment with 8 fields planted with corn, four fields having no nitrogen fertiliser and four fields having 80 kgs of nitrogen fertilizer. The resulting corn yields are shown in table in bushels per acre:

Field	:	1	2	3	4	5	6	7	8
Nitrogen (kgs) x	:	0	0	0	0	80	80	80	80
Corn yield y (acre)	:	120	360	60	180	1280	1120	1120	760

(*a*) Compute a linear regression equation of y on x.

(*b*) Predict corn yield for a field treated with 60 kgs of fertilizer.

10. The means of a bivariate frequency distribution are at (3, 4) and $r = 0.4$. The line of regression of y on x is parallel to the line $y = x$. Find the two lines of regression and estimate value of x when $y = 1$.

11. The following results were obtained in the analysis of data on yield of dry bark in ounces (y) and age in years (x) of 200 cinchona plants :

	x	y
Average :	9.2	16.5
Standard deviation :	2.1	4.2

Correlation coefficient = 0.84

Construct the two lines of regression and estimate the yield of dry bark of a plant of age 8 years.

12. Given N = 50, Mean of $y = 44$

Variance of x is $\frac{9}{16}$ of the variance of y.

Regression equation of x on y is $3y - 5x = -180$

Find (*i*) Mean of x (*ii*) Coeff. of correlation between x and y.

13. For an army personnel of strength 25, the regression of weight of kidneys (y) on weight of heart (x), both measured in ounces is

$$y - 0.399x - 6.934 = 0$$

and the regression of weight of heart on weight of kidney is $x - 1.212y + 2.461 = 0$.

Find the correlation coefficient between x and y and their mean values. Can you find out the standard deviation of x and y as well ?

14. A departmental store gives in-service training to its salesmen which is followed by a test. It is considering whether it should terminate the service of any salesman who does not do well in the test. The following data gives the test scores and sales made by 9 salesmen during a certain period :

Test scores :	14	19	24	21	26	22	15	20	19
Sales ('00 ₹) :	31	36	48	37	50	45	33	41	39

(*i*) Calculate the coefficient of correlation between the test scores and the sales.

(*ii*) Does it indicate that the termination of services of low test scores is justified ?

(*iii*) If the firm wants a minimum sales volume of ₹ 3000, what is the minimum test score that will ensure continuation of service ?

(*iv*) Also estimate the most probable sales volume of a salesman making a score of 28.

15. A panel of judges A and B graded 7 debators and independently awarded the following marks :

Debator :	1	2	3	4	5	6	7
Marks by A :	40	34	28	30	44	38	31
Marks by B :	32	39	26	30	38	34	28

An eighth debator was awarded 36 marks by judge A while judge B was not present. If judge B were also present, how many marks would you expect him to award to the eighth debator assuming that the same degree of relationship exists in their judgement.

Answers

1. (*i*) $72x = -20y + 247$ (*ii*) $y = -0.6842x + 15.5324$

2. (*i*) No (*ii*) $r = -0.4$

3. F = 0.18793W + 2.27595; F = 30.4654 kg wt.

4. $y = 0.04765 + 0.004071$ P; $y = 0.6583$ cm

5. (*i*) (*a*) 15.935 (*b*) 3.67 (*c*) – 0.659

(*ii*) $\bar{x} = 4$, $\bar{y} = 7$, $r = -0.5$ (*iii*) $r = 0.7395$, $\bar{x} = -0.1034$, $\bar{y} = 0.5172$

(*iv*) $\bar{x} = 6$, $\bar{y} = 1$, $r = -0.48989$

6. (*i*) $\bar{x} = 1$, $\bar{y} = 2$ (*ii*) 4 (*iii*) $-\frac{\sqrt{3}}{2}$

7. (*i*) Regression line of y on x: $y = 0.74306x + 1.56821$

Regression line of x on y: $x = 0.63602y + 2.0204$

(*ii*) $x = 0.34195y - 0.660355$.

8. (*i*) $y = 12x + 10$, $x = 0.07986y - 0.59068$ (*ii*) ₹ 94

9. (*a*) $y = 11.125x + 180$ (*b*) 847.5 acre

10. $y = x + 1$; $x = 0.16y + 2.36$; $x = 2.52$

11. $y = 1.68x + 1.044$, $x = 0.42y + 2.27$; $y = 14.484$

12. (*i*) 62.4 (*ii*) 0.8

13. $r = 0.70$, $\bar{x} = 11.5086$, $\bar{y} = 11.5261$, no

14. (*i*) 0.9476, high degree of correlation (*ii*) yes

(*iii*) 14.42 (*iv*) ₹ 5287

15. 33 marks.

9.16. STATISTICAL QUALITY CONTROL

A quality control system performs inspection, testing and analysis to ensure that the quality of the products produced is as per the laid down quality standards. It is called **"Statistical Quality Control"** when statistical techniques are employed to control, improve and maintain quality or to solve quality problems. Building an information system to satisfy the concept of prevention and control and improving upon product quality requires statistical thinking.

Statistical quality control (S.Q.C.) is systematic as compared to guess-work of haphazard process inspection and the mathematical statistical approach neutralizes personal bias and uncovers poor judgement. S.Q.C. consists of three general activities :

(1) Systematic collection and graphic recording of accurate data

(2) Analyzing the data

(3) Practical engineering or management action if the information obtained indicates significant deviations from the specified limits.

Modern techniques of statistical quality control and acceptance sampling have an important part to play in the improvement of quality, enhancement of productivity, creation of consumer confidence and development of industrial economy of the country.

Following statistical tools are generally used for the above purposes :

(*i*) **Frequency distribution:** Frequency distribution is a tabulation of the number of times a given quality characteristic occurs within the samples. Graphic representation of frequency distribution will show :

(*a*) Average quality (*b*) Spread of quality

(*c*) Comparison with specific requirements (*d*) Process capability.

(*ii*) **Control chart:** Control chart is a graphical representation of quality characteristics, which indicates whether the process is under control or not.

(*iii*) **Acceptance sampling:** Acceptance sampling is the process of evaluating a portion of the product/material in a lot for the purpose of accepting or rejecting the lot on the basis of conforming to a quality specification.

It reduces the time and cost of inspection and exerts more effective pressure on quality improvement than it is possible by 100% inspection.

It is used when assurance is desired for the quality of materials/products either produced or received.

(*iv*) **Analysis of data:** It includes analysis of tolerances, correlation, analysis of variance, analysis for engineering design, problem solving technique to eliminate cause to troubles. Statistical methods can be used in arriving at proper specification limits of product, in designing the product, in purchase of raw-material, semi-finished and finished products, manufacturing processes, inspection, packaging, sales and also after sales service.

9.17. ADVANTAGES OF STATISTICAL QUALITY CONTROL

1. Efficiency: The use of statistical quality control ensures rapid and efficient inspection at a minimum cost. It eliminates the need of 100% inspection of finished products because the acceptance sampling in S.Q.C. exerts more effective pressure for quality improvement than it.

2. Reduction of scrap: It uncovers the cause of excessive variability in manufactured products forecasting trouble before rejections occur and reducing the amount of spoiled work.

3. Easy detection of faults: In statistical quality control after plotting the control, charts ($\overline{X}$, R, P, C, U) etc. when the points fall above the upper control limits or below the lower control limit, it gives an indication of deterioration in quality. Necessary corrective action may be then taken immediately.

4. Adherence to specifications: So long as a statistical control continues, specifications can be accurately predicted for future by which it is possible to assess whether the production processes are capable of producing the products with the given set of specifications.

5. Increases output and reduces wasted machine and man hours.

6. Efficient utilization of personnel, machines and materials results in higher productivity.

7. Creates quality awareness in employees. However, it should be noted that statistical quality control is not a panacea for assuring product quality.

8. Provides a common language that may be used by all three groups designers, production personnel and inspectors in arriving at a rational solution of mutual problems.

9. Points out when and where 100% inspection, sorting or screening is required.

10. Elimination of bottlenecks in the process of manufacturing.

It simply furnishes 'perspective facts' upon which intelligent management and engineering action can be based. Without such action, the method is ineffective.

Even the application of standard procedures is also very dangerous without adequate study of the process.

9.18. REASONS FOR VARIATIONS IN THE QUALITY OF A PRODUCT

Two extremely similar things are rarely obtained in nature. This fact holds good for production processes as well. No production process is good enough to produce all items of products exactly alike. The variations are due to two main reasons :

(*i*) **Chance or random causes:** Variations due to chance causes are inevitable in any process or product. They are difficult to trace and to control also even under best conditions of production.

These variations may be due to some inherent characteristic of the process or machine which functions at random.

If the variations are due to chance factors alone, the observations will follow a "normal curve". The knowledge of the behaviour of chance variation is the foundation on which control chart analysis rests. The conditions which produce these variations are accordingly said to be **"under control"**. On the other hand, if the variations in the data do not conform to a pattern that might reasonably be produced by chance causes, then in this case, conditions producing the variations are said to be **"out of control"** as it may be concluded that one or more assignable causes are at work.

(*ii*) **Assignable causes:** The variations due to assignable causes possess greater magnitude as compared to those due to chance causes and can be easily traced or detected. The power of the shewhart control chart lies in its ability to separate out these assignable causes of quality variations *e.g.* in length thickness, weight or diameter of a component.

The variations due to assignable causes may be because of following factors :

(*i*) Differences among machines

(*ii*) Differences among workers

(*iii*) Differences among materials

(*iv*) Differences in each of these factors over time

(*v*) Differences in their relationship to one another.

These variations may also be caused due to change in working conditions, mistake on the part of operator etc.

9.19. TECHNIQUES OF STATISTICAL QUALITY CONTROL

To control the quality characteristics of the product, there are two main techniques :

1. Process Control: It is a process of monitoring and measuring variability in the performance of a process or a machine through the interpretation of statistical techniques and it is employed to manage in-process quality. This technique ensures the production of requisite standard product and makes use of control charts.

2. Product control: This technique is concerned with inspection of already produced goods to ascertain whether they are fit to be despatched or not. To achieve the objectives, it makes use of sampling inspection plans.

9.20. CONTROL CHART

A control chart is a graphical representation of the collected information. It detects the variation in processing and warns if there is any departure from the specified tolerance limits. In other words, control charts is a device which specifies the state of statistical control or is a device for attaining quality control or is a device to judge whether the statistical control has been attained.

The control limits on the chart are so placed as to disclose the presence or absence of the assignable causes of quality variation which makes the diagnosis possible and brings substantial improvements in product quality and reduction of spoilage and rework.

Moreover, by identifying chance variations, the control chart tells when to leave the process alone and thus prevents unnecessarily frequent adjustments that tend to increase the variability of the process rather than to decrease it.

There are many types of control charts designed for different control situations. Most commonly used control charts are

(*i*) **Control charts for variables:** They are useful to measure quality characteristics and to control fully automatic process. It includes $\overline{X}$ and R-charts and charts for $\overline{X}$ and σ.

(*ii*) **Control charts for attributes:** It includes P-chart for fraction defective. A fraction defective control chart discloses erratic fluctuations in the quality of inspection which may result in improvement in inspection practice and inspection standards.

It also includes C-chart for number of defects per unit.

9.21. OBJECTIVES OF CONTROL CHARTS

Control charts are based on statistical techniques.

1. $\overline{X}$ and R or $\overline{X}$ and σ charts are used in combination for control process. $\overline{X}$-chart shows the variation in the averages of samples. It is the most commonly used variables chart. R-chart shows the uniformity or consistency of the process *i.e.*, it shows the variations in the ranges of samples. It is a chart for measure of spread. σ-chart shows the variation of process.

2. To determine whether a given process can meet the existing specifications without a fundamental change in the production line or to tell whether the process is in control and if so, at what dispersion.

3. To secure information to be used in establishing or changing production procedures.

4. To secure information when it is necessary to widen the tolerances.

5. To provide a basis for current decisions or acceptance or rejection of manufactured or purchased product.

6. To secure information to be used in establishing or changing inspection procedure or acceptance procedure or both.

9.22. CONSTRUCTION OF CONTROL CHARTS FOR VARIABLES

First of all, a random sample of size n is taken during a manufacturing process over a period of time and quality measurements $x_1, x_2, \ldots\ldots, x_n$ are noted

Sample mean $$\bar{x} = \frac{x_1 + x_2 + \ldots\ldots + x_n}{n} = \frac{1}{n}\sum_{i=1}^{n} x_i$$

Sample range $\quad R = x_{\text{max.}} - x_{\text{min.}}$

If the process is found stable, k consecutive samples are selected and for each sample, $\bar{x}$ and R are calculated. Then we find $\bar{\bar{x}}$ and $\overline{R}$ as

$$\bar{\bar{x}} = \frac{\bar{x}_1 + \bar{x}_2 + \ldots\ldots + \bar{x}_k}{k} = \frac{1}{k}\sum_{i=1}^{k} \bar{x}_i$$

and $$\overline{R} = \frac{R_1 + R_2 + \ldots\ldots + R_k}{k} = \frac{1}{k}\sum_{i=1}^{k} R_i$$

For $\overline{X}$-chart

$$\text{Central line} = \begin{cases} \overline{\overline{x}}, \text{ when tolerance limits are not given} \\ \mu, \text{ when tolerance limits are given} \end{cases}$$

where $$\mu = \frac{1}{2}[\text{LCL} + \text{UCL}]$$

LCL is lower control limit and UCL is upper control limit

Now, LCL (for $\overline{X}$-chart) = $\overline{\overline{x}} - A_2\overline{R}$ and UCL (for $\overline{X}$-chart) = $\overline{\overline{x}} + A_2\overline{R}$ are set.

A_2 depends on sample size n and can be found from the following table :

Sample size (n)	2	3	4	5	6	7	8	9	10	11	12	13	14	15	16	17	18	19	20
A_2	1.88	1.02	0.73	0.58	0.48	0.42	0.37	0.34	0.31	0.29	0.27	0.25	0.24	0.22	0.21	0.20	0.19	0.19	0.18

For R-chart Central line (CL) = $\overline{R}$

Now, LCL (for R-chart) = $D_3\overline{R}$ UCL (for R-chart) = $D_4\overline{R}$ are set.

where D_3 and D_4 depend on sample size and are found from the following table :

Sample size (n)	D_3	D_4	d_2
2	0	3.27	1.13
3	0	2.57	1.69
4	0	2.28	2.06
5	0	2.11	2.33
6	0	2.00	2.53
7	0.08	1.92	2.70
8	0.14	1.86	2.85
9	0.18	1.82	2.97
10	0.22	1.78	3.08
11	0.26	1.74	3.17
12	0.28	1.72	3.26
13	0.31	1.69	3.34
14	0.33	1.67	3.41
15	0.35	1.65	3.47
16	0.36	1.64	3.53
17	0.38	1.62	3.59
18	0.39	1.61	3.64
19	0.40	1.60	3.69
20	0.41	1.59	3.74

To compute upper and lower process tolerance limits for the values of x, we have

$$\text{LTL} = \bar{\bar{x}} - \frac{3\bar{R}}{d_2} \qquad \text{UTL} = \bar{\bar{x}} + \frac{3\bar{R}}{d_2}$$

where d_2 is found from the above table.

Moreover, The process capability is given by $6\sigma = 6\frac{\bar{R}}{d_2}$ where σ is standard deviation.

While plotting the $\bar{X}$-chart the central line on the $\bar{X}$ chart should be drawn as a solid horizontal line at $\bar{X}$. The upper and lower control limits for $\bar{X}$ chart should be drawn as dotted horizontal lines at the computed values.

Similarly, for R-chart, the central line should be drawn as a solid horizontal line at $\bar{R}$. The upper control limit should be drawn as dotted horizontal line at the computed value of UCL_R. If the subgroup size is 7 or more, the lower control limit should be drawn as dotted horizontal line at LCL_R. However, if the subgroup size is ≤ 6, the lower control limit for R is zero.

Plot the averages of subgroups in $\bar{X}$-chart, in the order collected and ranges in R-chart which should be below the $\bar{X}$-chart so that the subgroups correspond to one-another in both the charts. Points outside the control limits are indicated with cross (×) on $\bar{X}$-chart and the points outside the limits on R chart by a circle (⊙).

9.23. CONTROL CHARTS FOR ATTRIBUTES

Following control charts will be discussed here

(*i*) P chart (*ii*) *np* chart (*iii*) C chart (*iv*) *u* chart.

As an alternative to $\bar{X}$ and R chart and as a substitute when characteristic is measured only by attribute, a control chart based on fraction defective p is used, called P-chart.

$$p = \frac{\text{No. of defective articles found in any inspection}}{\text{Total no. of articles actually inspected}}.$$

(*i*) **Control limits (3σ limits) on p-chart:** We know that for binomial distribution, the mean value of total number of defectives in a sample n is np and standard deviation is $\sqrt{npq}$ or $\sqrt{np(1-p)}$.

∴ Mean value of fraction defective is p and S.D.

$$\sigma_p = \frac{1}{n}\sqrt{np(1-p)} = \sqrt{\frac{p(1-p)}{n}}$$

$$\therefore \qquad \text{CL} = p$$

The upper and lower limits for P-chart are, $\quad UCL_P = p + 3\sigma_p = p + 3\sqrt{\frac{p(1-p)}{n}}$

and $\quad LCL_P = p - 3\sigma_p = p - 3\sqrt{\frac{p(1-p)}{n}}$.

Due to the lower inspection and maintenance costs of P-charts, they usually have a greater area of economical applications.

(*ii*) **Control limits for np chart:** Whenever subgroup size is variable, P-chart is used but if it is constant, the chart for actual number of defectives called *np* chart is used.

$$CL = n\bar{p} \quad \text{where} \quad \bar{p} = \frac{\Sigma np}{\Sigma n}$$

$$UCL_{np} = n\bar{p} + 3\sigma_{np} = n\bar{p} + 3\sqrt{n\bar{p}\,(1-\bar{p})} \qquad (\text{where } \sigma_{np} = n\sigma_p)$$

and

$$LCL_{np} = n\bar{p} - 3\sqrt{n\bar{p}\,(1-\bar{p})}.$$

Note. In case of $\overline{X}$ and R chart, it may not be necessary to draw lines connecting the points which represent the successive subgroups. But incase of P-chart, a line connecting the points is usually helpful in interpretation of the chart. Such a line assists in the interpretation of trends.

(*iii*) **Control limits for C chart**

(*a*) **Difference between a defect and defective**

An item is called defective if it fails to conform to the specifications in any of the characteristics. Each characteristic that does not meet the specifications is a defect. An item is defective if it contains atleast one defect. The *np* chart applies to the number of defectives in subgroups of constant size while C chart applies to the number of defects in a subgroup of constant size.

(*b*) **Basis for control limits on C chart**

Control limits on C chart are based on **Poisson distribution:** Hence two conditions must be satisfied. The first condition specifies that the area of opportunity for occurrence of defects should be fairly constant from period to period. Second condition specifies that opportunities for defects are large while the chances of a defect occurring in any one spot are small.

(*c*) **Calculation of control limits on C chart**

Standard deviation $\sigma_c = \sqrt{\overline{C}}$

Thus 3σ limits on a C chart are $UCL_c = \overline{C} + 3\sqrt{\overline{C}}$ and $LCL_c = \overline{C} - 3\sqrt{\overline{C}}$

and central line $CL = \overline{C}$

where

$$\overline{C} = \frac{\text{Number of defects in all samples}}{\text{Total number of samples}}.$$

(*iv*) **u chart:** When the subgroup size varies from sample to sample, it is necessary to use *u* charts. The control limits on *u* chart will however vary. If *c* is total number of defects found in any sample and *n* is number of inspection units in a sample,

$$\bar{u} = \frac{C}{n} = \frac{\text{Number of defects in a sample}}{\text{Number of units in a sample}}$$

The larger the number of units in a sample, the narrower the limits.

Formulae for control limits on *u* chart are:

$$UCL_u = \bar{u} + 3\sqrt{\frac{\bar{u}}{n}}\ ;\ LCL_u = \bar{u} - 3\sqrt{\frac{\bar{u}}{n}} \text{ and central line } CL = \bar{u}.$$

EXAMPLES

Example 1. *The following are the mean lengths and ranges of lengths of a finished product from 10 samples each of size 5. The specification limits for length are 200 ± 5 cm. Construct $\overline{X}$ and R-chart and examine whether the process is under control and state your recommendations.*

Sample No.	*1*	*2*	*3*	*4*	*5*	*6*	*7*	*8*	*9*	*10*
Mean ($\overline{X}$)	*201*	*198*	*202*	*200*	*203*	*204*	*199*	*196*	*199*	*201*
Range (R)	*5*	*0*	*7*	*3*	*3*	*7*	*2*	*8*	*5*	*6*

Assume for $n = 5$, $A_2 = 0.58$, $D_4 = 2.11$ *and* $D_3 = 0$.

Sol. (*i*) **Control limits for $\overline{X}$ chart:**

Central limit CL = 200 | ∵ Tolerance / specification limits are given ∴ $\mu = 200$

$$UCL_{\bar{x}} = \bar{\bar{x}} + A_2\overline{R} = \mu + A_2\overline{R}$$
$$LCL_{\bar{x}} = \bar{\bar{x}} - A_2\overline{R} = \mu - A_2\overline{R}$$

where
$$\overline{R} = \frac{R_1 + R_2 + \ldots\ldots + R_{10}}{10} = \frac{46}{10} = 4.6$$

Then,
$$UCL_{\overline{X}} = 200 + (0.58 \times 4.6) = 202.668$$
$$LCL_{\overline{X}} = 200 - (0.58 \times 4.6) = 197.332.$$

(*ii*) **Control limits for R chart:**

Central limit $CL = \overline{R} = 4.6$

$$UCL_R = D_4\overline{R} = 2.11 \times 4.6 = 9.706$$
$$LCL_R = D_3\overline{R} = 0 \times 4.6 = 0$$

The $\overline{X}$ and R-charts are drawn below:

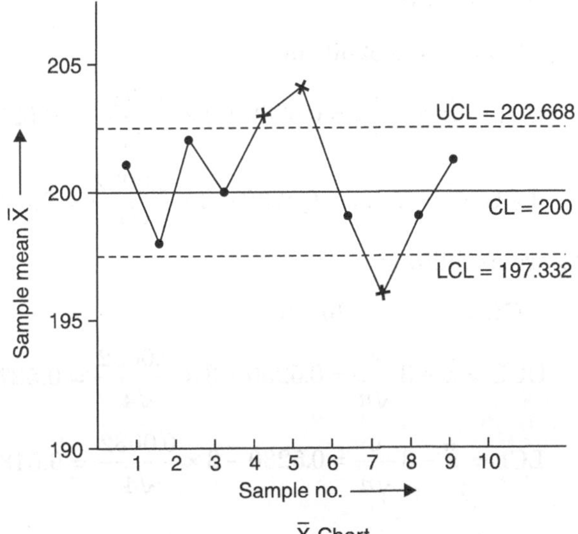

$\overline{X}$-Chart

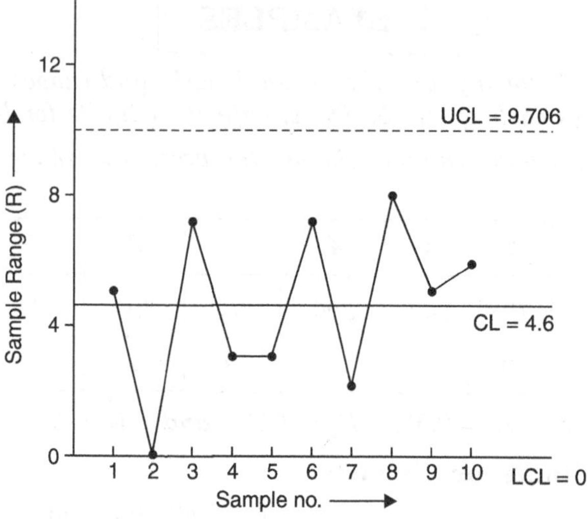

R-Chart

It is noted that all points lie within the control limits on R chart. Hence the process variability is under control. But in X-chart, points corresponding to sample number 5, 6 and 8 lie outside the control limits. Therefore the **process is not in statistical control.** The process should be halted and it is recommended to check for any assignable causes. Fluctuation will remain until these causes, if found, are removed.

Example 2. *A drilling machine bores holes with a mean diameter of 0.5230 cm and a standard deviation of 0.0032 cm. Calculate the 2-sigma and 3-sigma upper and lower control limits for means of sample of 4.*

Sol. Mean diameter $\bar{\bar{x}} = 0.5230$ cm

S.D. $\sigma = 0.0032$ cm

$n = 4$

(*i*) 2-sigma limits are as follows:

$$\text{CL} = \bar{\bar{x}} = 0.5230 \text{ cm}$$

$$\text{UCL} = \bar{\bar{x}} + 2\frac{\sigma}{\sqrt{n}} = 0.5230 + 2 \times \frac{0.0032}{\sqrt{4}} = 0.5262 \text{ cm}$$

$$\text{LCL} = \bar{\bar{x}} - 2\frac{\sigma}{\sqrt{n}} = 0.5230 - 2 \times \frac{0.0032}{\sqrt{4}} = 0.5198 \text{ cm.}$$

(*ii*) 3-sigma limits are as follows:

$$\text{CL} = \bar{\bar{x}} = 0.5230 \text{ cm}$$

$$\text{UCL} = \bar{\bar{x}} + 3\frac{\sigma}{\sqrt{n}} = 0.5230 + 3 \times \frac{0.0032}{\sqrt{4}} = 0.5278 \text{ cm}$$

$$\text{LCL} = \bar{\bar{x}} - 3\frac{\sigma}{\sqrt{n}} = 0.5230 - 3 \times \frac{0.0032}{\sqrt{4}} = 0.5182 \text{ cm.}$$

Example 3. *In a blade manufacturing factory, 1000 blades are examined daily. Draw the np chart for the following table and examine whether the process is under control?*

Date	: 1	2	3	4	5	6	7	8	9	10	11	12	13	14	15
No. of defective blades	: 9	10	12	8	7	15	10	12	10	8	7	13	14	15	16

Sol. Here, $n = 1000$

Σnp = total number of defectives = 166

Σn = total number inspected = 1000 × 15

$$\therefore \qquad \overline{p} = \frac{\Sigma np}{\Sigma n} = \frac{166}{1000 \times 15} = 0.011$$

$$\therefore \qquad n\overline{p} = 1000 \times 0.011 = 11$$

Control limits are $\quad \text{CL} = n\overline{p} = 11$

$$\text{UCL}_{np} = n\overline{p} + 3\sqrt{n\overline{p}\,(1-\overline{p})} = 11 + 3\sqrt{11(1-0.011)} = 20.894$$

$$\text{LCL}_{np} = n\overline{p} - 3\sqrt{n\overline{p}\,(1-\overline{p})} = 11 - 3\sqrt{11\,(1-0.011)} = 1.106$$

The *np* chart is drawn in the figure. Since all the points lie within the control limits, the process is under control.

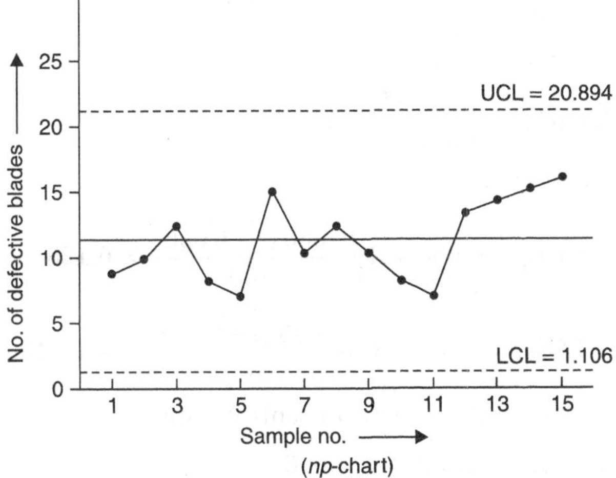

(*np*-chart)

Example 4. *In a manufacturing process, the number of defectives found in the inspection of 20 lots of 100 samples is given below:*

Lot no.	*No. of defectives*	*Lot no.*	*No. of defectives*
1	5	11	7
2	4	12	6
3	3	13	3
4	5	14	5
5	4	15	4
6	6	16	2
7	9	17	8
8	15	18	7
9	11	19	6
10	6	20	4

(i) Determine the control limits of p-chart and state whether the process is in control.

(ii) Determine the new value of mean fraction defective if some points are out of control. Compute the corresponding control limits and state whether the process is still in control or not.

(iii) Determine the sample size when a quality limit not worse than 9% is desirable and a 10% bad product will not be permitted more than three times in thousand.

Sol. (*i*)
$$\bar{p} = \frac{\text{Total number of defectives}}{\text{Total number of items inspected}} = \frac{120}{20 \times 100} = 0.06$$

$$\text{UCL}_\text{P} = \bar{p} + 3\sqrt{\frac{\bar{p}(1-\bar{p})}{n}} = 0.06 + 3\sqrt{\frac{0.06\,(1-0.06)}{100}} = 0.13095$$

$$\text{LCL}_\text{P} = \bar{p} - 3\sqrt{\frac{\bar{p}(1-\bar{p})}{n}} = 0.06 - 3\sqrt{\frac{0.06\,(1-0.06)}{100}} = -\,0.01095$$

Since the fraction defective cannot be (–) ve

$\therefore$ $\text{LCL}_\text{P} = 0$

After observing the values of defectives in the given example, it is clear that only 8th lot having fraction defective $\frac{15}{100} = 0.15$ will go above UCL_P.

(*ii*) After eliminating the 8th lot,

$$\text{Revised value of } \bar{p} = \frac{120 - 15}{100 \times 19} = 0.056$$

Revised control limits will be

$$\text{UCL}_\text{P} = 0.056 + 3\sqrt{\frac{0.056\,(1-0.056)}{100}} = 0.125$$

$$\text{LCL}_\text{P} = 0.056 - 3\sqrt{\frac{0.056\,(1-0.056)}{100}} = -\,0.013 \textit{ i.e., } \text{zero.}$$

It is clear that all the points are within control limits.

$\therefore$ Revised quality level $\bar{p} = 0.056$

(*iii*) Since a probability that a defective worse than 9% defective quality will not be permitted is more than 3 times in thousand (0.3%) is corresponding 3σ limits

$\therefore$
$$\bar{p} + 3p = 0.09$$

$$0.056 + 3\sqrt{\frac{0.056\,(1-0.056)}{n}} = 0.09 \;\Rightarrow\; \sqrt{\frac{0.056 \times 0.944}{n}} = \frac{0.034}{3}$$

Squaring,
$$\frac{0.056 \times 0.944}{n} = \left(\frac{0.034}{3}\right)^2 = (0.01133)^2$$

$$n = \frac{0.056 \times 0.944}{0.01133 \times 0.01133} = 333.$$

Example 5. *A control chart for defects per unit u uses probability limits corresponding to probabilities of 0.975 and 0.025. The central line on the control chart is at $\bar{u}$ = 2.0. The limits vary with the value of n. Determine the correct position of these upper and lower control limits when n = 5. (Assume σ = 1.96)*

Sol.
$$UCL_u = \bar{u} + \sigma\sqrt{\frac{\bar{u}}{n}} = 2 + 1.96\sqrt{\frac{2}{5}} = 3.239$$

$$LCL_u = 2 - 1.96\sqrt{\frac{2}{5}} = 0.761.$$

Example 6. *Determine the control limits for $\bar{X}$ and R charts if $\Sigma\bar{X}$ = 357.50, ΣR = 9.90, number of subgroups = 20. It is given that A_2 = 0.18, D_3 = 0.41, D_4 = 1.59 and d_2 = 3.736. Also find the process capability.*

Sol.
$$\bar{X} = \frac{\Sigma\bar{X}}{N} = \frac{357.50}{20} = 17.875$$

$$\bar{R} = \frac{\Sigma R}{N} = \frac{9.90}{20} = 0.495$$

$$UCL_{\bar{X}} = \bar{\bar{X}} + A_2\bar{R} = 17.875 + (0.18 \times 0.495) = 17.9641$$

$$LCL_{\bar{X}} = \bar{\bar{X}} - A_2\bar{R} = 17.875 - (0.18 \times 0.495) = 17.7859$$

$$UCL_R = D_4\bar{R} = 1.59 \times 0.495 = 0.78705$$

$$LCL_R = D_3\bar{R} = 0.41 \times 0.495 = 0.20295$$

$$\sigma = \frac{\bar{R}}{d_2} = \frac{0.495}{3.735} = 0.13253$$

∴ Process capability = 6σ = 6 × 0.13253 = 0.79518.

Example 7. *If the average fraction defective of a large sample of a product is 0.1537, Calculate the control limits given that sub-group size is 2000.*

Sol. Average fraction defective

$$\bar{p} = 0.1537$$

Sub-group size is 2000

∴ $n = 2000$

Central line $CL = n\bar{p} = 2000 \times 0.1537 = 307.4$

$$UCL_{np} = n\bar{p} + 3\sigma_{np} = n\bar{p} + 3\sqrt{n\bar{p}(1-\bar{p})}$$

$$= 307.4 + 3\sqrt{307.4\,(1 - 0.1537)} = 307.4 + 48.38774204$$

$$= 355.787742$$

and
$$LCL_{np} = n\bar{p} - 3\sqrt{n\bar{p}\,(1-\bar{p})} = 307.4 - 48.38774204$$

$$= 259.012258$$

ASSIGNMENT

1. A company manufactures screws to a nominal diameter 0.500 ± 0.030 cm. Five samples were taken randomly from the manufactured lots and 3 measurements were taken on each sample at different lengths. Following are the readings:

Sample no.	*Measurement per sample x(in cm)*		
	1	*2*	*3*
1	0.488	0.489	0.505
2	0.494	0.495	0.499
3	0.498	0.515	0.487
4	0.492	0.509	0.514
5	0.490	0.508	0.499

Calculate the control limits of $\overline{X}$ and R charts. Draw $\overline{X}$ and R charts and examine whether the process is in statistical control? [Take $A_2 = 1.02$, $D_4 = 2.57$, $D_3 = 0$ for $n = 3$]

2. Discuss how control charts can be used in quality control of industrial products. The average percentage of defectives in 27 samples of size 1500 each was found to be 13.7%. Construct P-chart for this situation. Explain how the control chart can be used to control quality.

[**Hint.** $\overline{p} = 0.137$]

3. The number of customer complaints received daily by an organization is given below :

Day :	1	2	3	4	5	6	7	8	9	10	11	12	13	14	15
Complaints :	2	3	0	1	9	2	0	0	4	2	0	7	0	2	4

Does it mean that the number of complaints is under statistical control ? Establish a control scheme for the future.

4. It was found that when a manufacturing process is under control, the average number of defectives per sample batch of 10 is 1.2. What limits would you set in a quality control chart based on the examination of defectives in sample batches of 10?

[**Hint.** $\overline{p} = 0.12$, $n\overline{p} = 1.2$]

5. The following data shows the value of sample mean $\overline{X}$ and range R for 10 samples of size 5 each. Calculate the values for central line and control limits for $\overline{X}$-chart and R chart and determine whether the process is under control.

Sample no. :	1	2	3	4	5	6	7	8	9	10
Mean $\overline{X}$ *:*	11.2	11.8	10.8	11.6	11	9.6	10.4	9.6	10.6	10
Range R :	7	4	8	5	7	4	8	4	7	9

Assume for $n = 5$, $A_2 = 0.577$, $D_3 = 0$ and $D_4 = 2.115$.

6. (*i*) What are statistical quality control techniques? Discuss the objectives and advantages of statistical quality control.

(*ii*) Give statistical quality control methods. Explain one of them with example.

7. The following table shows the number of missing rivets observed at the time of inspection of 12 aircrafts. Find the control limits for the number of defects chart and comment on the state of control.

Air craft number :	1	2	3	4	5	6	7	8	9	10	11	12
No. of missing rivets :	7	15	13	18	10	14	13	10	20	11	22	15

8. In a factory producing spark plug, the number of defectives found in inspection of 20 lots of 100 each is given below.

Lot No.	1	2	3	4	5	6	7	8	9	10	11	12	13	14	15	16	17	18	19	20
No. of defectives	5	10	12	8	6	4	6	3	3	5	4	7	8	3	3	4	5	8	6	10

Construct p-chart and state whether the process is in statistical control.

9. The data below given is the number of defective bearing in samples of size 150. Construct np-chart for these data. If any point(s) lie outside the control limits, assume that assignable cause can be found and determine the revised control limits :

Sample No.	1	2	3	4	5	6	7	8	9	10	11	12	13	14	15	16	17	18	19	20
No. of defectives	12	7	5	4	1	5	9	0	15	6	7	4	1	3	6	8	10	5	2	7

10. Write short notes on the following :

(*i*) Use of statistical techniques/methods in quality control

(*ii*) P-chart, np-chart and C-chart

Answers

1. $CL_{\overline{X}} = 0.4988$, $UCL_{\overline{X}} = 0.5172$, $LCL_{\overline{X}} = 0.4804$, $CL_R = 0.018$, $UCL_R = 0.0463$, $LCL_R = 0$. The process is in control.
2. $CL_P = 0.137$, $UCL_P = 0.164$, $LCL_P = 0.110$
3. $CL_C = 2.4$, $UCL_C = 7.05$, $LCL_C = 0$, the process is not under control.
4. $CL_{np} = 1.2$, $UCL_{np} = 2.175$, $LCL_{np} = 0.225$
5. $CL_{\overline{X}} = 10.66$, $UCL_{\overline{X}} = 14.295$, $LCL_{\overline{X}} = 7.025$, $CL_R = 0.3$, $UCL_R = 13.32$, $LCL_R = 0$; The process is under control
7. $UCL_C = 25.23$, $LCL_C = 2.77$. The process is in control.
8. Process is in statistical control. $UCL_p = 0.131$, $LCL_p = 0$
9. $CL_{np} = 5.36842$, $UCL_{np} = 12.19385$, $LCL_{np} = 0$.

9.24. POPULATION OR UNIVERSE

An aggregate of objects (animate or inanimate) under study is called **population or universe.** It is thus a collection of individuals or of their attributes (qualities) or of results of operations which can be numerically specified.

A universe containing a finite number of individuals or members is called a **finite inverse.** For example, the universe of the weights of students in a particular class.

A universe with infinite number of members is known as an **infinite universe.** For example, the universe of pressures at various points in the atmosphere.

In some cases, we may be even ignorant whether or not a particular universe is infinite, *e.g.*, the universe of stars.

The universe of concrete objects is an **existent universe.** The collection of all possible ways in which a specified event can happen is called a **hypothetical universe.** The universe of heads and tails obtained by tossing a coin an infinite number of times (provided that it does not wear out) is a hypothetical one.

9.25. SAMPLING

The statistician is often confronted with the problem of discussing universe of which he cannot examine every member *i.e.*, of which complete enumeration is impracticable. For example, if we want to have an idea of the average per capita income of the people of India, enumeration of every earning individual in the country is a very difficult task. Naturally, the question arises : What can be said about a universe of which we can examine only a limited number of members ? This question is the origin of the Theory of Sampling.

A finite subset of a universe is called a **sample.** A sample is thus a small portion of the universe. The number of individuals in a sample is called the **sample size.** The process of selecting a sample from a universe is called **sampling.**

The theory of sampling is a study of relationship existing between a population and samples drawn from the population. The fundamental objective of sampling is to get as much information as possible of the whole universe by examining only a part of it. An attempt is thus made through sampling to give the maximum information about the parent universe with the minimum effort.

Sampling is quite often used in our day-to-day practical life. For example, in a shop we assess the quality of sugar, rice or any other commodity by taking only a handful of it from the bag and then decide whether to purchase it or not. A housewife normally tests the cooked products to find if they are properly cooked and contain the proper quantity of salt or sugar, by taking a spoonful of it.

9.26. SAMPLING METHODOLOGIES

Sampling methodologies are classified under two general categories :

1. Probability sampling and 2. Non-probability sampling

In the former, the researcher knows the exact possibility of selecting each member of the population while in the latter, the chance of being included in the sample is not known. A probability sample tends to be more difficult and costly to conduct. However, probability samples are the only type of samples where the results can be generalized from the sample to the population. In addition, probability samples allow the researcher to calculate the precision of the estimates obtained from the sample and to specify the sampling error

Non-probability samples, in contrast, donot allow the study's findings to be generalized from the sample to the population. When discussing the results of a non-probability sample, the researchers must limit his/her findings to the persons or elements sampled.

This procedure also does not allow the researcher to calculate sampling statistics that provide information about the precision of the results. The advantage of non-probability sampling is the case in which it can be administered.

Non-probability samples tend to be less complicated and less time consuming than probability samples. If the researcher has no intention of generalizing beyond the sample, one of the non-probability sampling methodologies will provide the desired information.

9.27. NON-PROBABILITY SAMPLING

The three common types of non-probability samples are:

***(i)* Convenience Sampling:** As the name implies, convenience sampling involves choosing respondents at the convenience of the researcher. Examples of convenience sampling include people-in-the street interviews—the sampling of people to which the researcher has easy access, such as a class of students and studies that use people who have volunteered to be questioned as a result of an advertisement or another type of promotion. A drawback to this methodology is the lack of sampling accuracy. Because the probability of inclusion in the sample is unknown for each respondent, none of the reliability or sampling precision statistics can be calculated. Convenience samples, however, are employed by researchers because the time and cost of collecting information can be reduced.

***(ii)* Quota Sampling:** Quota sampling is often confused with stratified and cluster sampling—two probability sampling methodologies. All of these methodologies sample a population that has been subdivided into classes or categories.

The primary differences between the methodologies is that with stratified and cluster sampling, the classes are mutually exclusive and are isolated prior to sampling. Thus, the probability of being selected is known and members of the population selected to be sampled are not arbitrarily disqualified from being included in the results. In quota sampling, the classes cannot be isolated prior to sampling and respondents are categorized into the classes as the survey proceeds. As each class fills or reaches its quota, additional respondents that would have fallen into these classes are rejected or excluded from the results.

An example of a quota sample would be a survey in which the researcher desires to obtain a certain number of respondents from various income categories. Generally, researchers donot know the income of the persons they are sampling until they ask about income. Therefore, the researcher is unable to subdivide the population from which the sample is drawn into mutually exclusive income categories prior to drawing the sample.

***(iii)* Judgemental Sampling:** In judgemental or purposive sampling, the researcher employs his or her own expert judgement about who to include in the sample frame. Prior knowledge and research skill are used in selecting the respondents or elements to be sampled.

An example of this type of sample would be a study of potential users of a new recreational facility that is limited to those persons who live within two miles of the new facility. Expert judgement based on past experience indicates that most of the use of this type of facility comes from persons living within two miles. However, by limiting the sample to only this group, usage projections may not be reliable if the usage characteristics of the new facility vary from those previously experienced. As with all non-probability sampling methods, the degree and direction of error introduced by the researcher cannot be measured and statistics that measure the precision of the estimates cannot be calculated.

9.28. PROBABILITY SAMPLING

Five methodologies are most commonly used for conducting probability sampling.

***(i)* Simple Random Sampling:** Simple random sampling provides the base from which the other more complex sampling methodologies are derived.

To conduct a simple random sampling, the researcher must first prepare an exhaustive list (sampling frame) of all members of the population of interest. From this list, the sample is drawn so that each person or item has an equal chance of being drawn during each selection round. Samples may be drawn with or without replacement. In practice, however, most simple random sampling for survey research is done without replacement ; that is, a person or item selected for sampling is removed from the population for all subsequent selections. At any draw, the process for a simple random sample without replacement must provide an equal chance of inclusion to any member of the population not already drawn. To draw a simple random sample without introducing researcher bias, computerized sampling programs and random numbers tables are used to impartially select the members of the population to be sampled.

An example of a simple random sample would be a survey of County employees. An exhaustive list of all County employees as of a certain date could be obtained from the Department of Human Resources. If 100 names were selected from this list using a random number table or a computerized sampling program, then a simple random sample would be created. Such a random sampling procedure has the advantage of reducing bias and enables the researcher to estimate sampling errors and the precision of the estimates derived through statistical calculations.

***(ii)* Stratified Random Sampling.** Stratified random sampling involves categorizing the members of the population into mutually exclusive and collectively exhaustive groups. An independent simple random sample is then drawn from each group. Stratified sampling techniques can provide more precise estimates if the population being surveyed is more heterogeneous than the categorized groups, can enable the researcher to determine desired levels of sampling precision for each group, and can provide administrative efficiency.

An example of a stratified sample would be a sample conducted to determine the average income earned by families in the United States. To obtain more precise estimates of income, the researcher may want to stratify the sample by geographic region (northeast, mid-Atlantic, etc.) and/or stratify the sample by urban, suburban, and rural groupings. If the differences in income among the regions or groupings are greater than the income differences within the regions or groupings, precision of the estimates is improved. In addition, if the research organization has branch offices located in these regions, the administration of the survey can be decentralized and perhaps conducted in a more cost-efficient manner.

***(iii)* Cluster Sampling:** Cluster sampling is similar to stratified sampling because the population to be sampled is subdivided into mutually exclusive groups. However, in cluster sampling, the groups are defined so as to maintain the heterogeneity of the population. It is the researcher's goal to establish clusters that are representative of the population as a whole, although in practice this may be difficult to achieve. After the clusters are established, a simple random sample of the clusters is drawn and the members of the chosen clusters are sampled. If all of the elements (members) of the clusters selected are sampled, then the sampling procedure is defined as **one-stage cluster sampling.** If a random sample of the elements of each selected cluster is drawn, then the sampling procedure is defined as **two-stage cluster sampling.**

Cluster sampling is frequently employed when the researcher is unable to compile a comprehensive list of all the elements in the population of interest. A cluster sample might be used by a researcher attempting to measure the age distribution of persons residing in Mumbai. It would be much more difficult for the researcher to compile a list of every person residing in Mumbai than to compile a list of residential addresses. In this example, each address would represent a cluster of elements (persons) to be sampled. If the elements contained in the clusters are as heterogeneous as the population, then estimates derived from cluster sampling are as precise as those from simple random sampling. However, if the heterogeneity of the clusters is less than that of the population, the estimates will be less precise.

***(iv)* Systematic Sampling:** Systematic sampling, a form of one-stage cluster sampling, is often used in place of simple random sampling. In systematic sampling, the researcher selects every n^{th} member after randomly selecting the first through n^{th} element as the starting point. For example, if the researcher decides to sample every 20th member of the population, a 5 per cent sample, the starting point for the sample is randomly selected from the first 20 members. A systematic sample is a type of cluster sample because each of the first 20 members of the sampling frame defines a cluster that contains 5 percent of the population.

A researcher may choose to conduct a systematic sample instead of a simple random sample for several reasons. Systematic samples tend to be easier to draw and execute. The researcher does not have to jump backward and forward through the sampling frame to draw the members to be sampled. A systematic sample may spread the members selected for measurement more evenly across the entire population than simple random sampling. Therefore, in some cases, systematic sampling may be more representative of the population and more precise.

One of the most attractive aspects of systematic sampling is that this method can allow the researcher to draw a probability sample without complete prior knowledge of the sampling frame. For example, a survey of visitors to the County's publications desk could be conducted by sampling every 10th visitor after randomly selecting the first through 10th visitor as the starting point. By conducting the sample in this manner, it would not be necessary for the researcher to obtain a comprehensive list of visitors prior to drawing the sample.

As with other types of cluster sampling, systematic sampling is as precise as simple random sampling if the members contained in the clusters are as heterogeneous as the population. If this assumption is not valid, then systematic sampling will be less precise than simple random sampling. In conducting systematic sampling, it is also essential that the researcher does not introduce bias into the sample by selecting an inappropriate sampling interval. For instance, when conducting a sample of financial records, or other items that follow a calendar schedule, the researcher would not want to select "7" as the sampling interval because the sample would then be comprised of observations that were all on the same day of the week. Day-of-the-week influences may cause contamination of the sample, giving the researcher biased results.

***(v)* Multi-Stage Sampling:** Multi-stage sampling is like cluster sampling, but involves selecting a sample within each chosen cluster, rather than including all units in the cluster. Thus, multi-stage sampling involves selecting a sample in at least two stages. In the first stage, large groups or clusters are selected. These clusters are designed to contain more population units than are required for the final sample.

In the second stage, population units are chosen from selected clusters to derive a final sample. If more than two stages are used, the process of choosing population units within clusters continues until the final sample is achieved.

An example of multi-stage sampling is where, firstly, electoral sub-divisions (clusters) are sampled from a city or state. Secondly, blocks of houses are selected from within the electoral sub-divisions and, thirdly, individual houses are selected from within the selected blocks of houses.

The advantages of multi-stage sampling are convenience, economy and efficiency. Multi-stage sampling does not require a complete list of members in the target population, which greatly reduces sample preparation cost. The list of members is required only for those clusters used in the final stage. The main disadvantage of multi-stage sampling is the same as for cluster sampling: lower accuracy due to higher sampling error.

9.29. PARAMETERS OF STATISTICS

The statistical constants of the population such as mean, the variance etc. are known as the parameters. The statistical concepts of the sample from the members of the sample to estimate the parameters of the population from which the sample has been drawn is known as *statistic*.

Population mean and variance are denoted by μ and σ^2, while those of the samples are given by $\bar{x}$, s^2.

9.30. STANDARD ERROR

The standard deviation of the sampling distribution of a statistic is known as the **standard error (S.E.)**. It plays an important role in the theory of large samples and it forms a basis of the testing of hypothesis. If t is any statistic, for large sample. $z = \frac{t - E(t)}{S.E.(t)}$ is normally distributed with mean 0 and variance unity.

For large sample, the standard errors of some of the well known statistic are listed below:

n—sample size; σ^2—population variance; s^2—sample variance; p—population proportion; $Q = 1 - p$; n_1, n_2—are sizes of two independent random samples.

No.	*Statistic*	*Standard error*
1.	$\bar{x}$	$\sigma/\sqrt{n}$
2.	s	$\sqrt{\sigma^2/2n}$
3.	Difference of two sample means $\bar{x}_1 - \bar{x}_2$	$\sqrt{\frac{\sigma_1^2}{n_1} + \frac{\sigma_2^2}{n_2}}$
4.	Difference of two sample standard deviation $s_1 - s_2$	$\sqrt{\frac{\sigma_1^2}{2n_1} + \frac{\sigma_2^2}{2n_2}}$
5.	Difference of two sample proportions $p_1 - p_2$	$\sqrt{\frac{P_1Q_1}{n_1} + \frac{P_2Q_2}{n_2}}$
6.	Observed sample proportion p	$\sqrt{PQ/n}$

9.31. TEST OF SIGNIFICANCE

An important aspect of the sampling theory is to study the test of significance which will enable us to decide, on the basis of the results of the sample, whether

(*i*) *the deviation between the observed sample statistic and the hypothetical parameter value or*

(*ii*) *the deviation between two sample statistics is significant or might be attributed due to chance or the fluctuations of the sampling.*

9.32. TESTING OF STATISTICAL HYPOTHESIS

Step 1. Null hypothesis [*U.P.T.U. (MCA) 2007*]

For applying the tests of significance, we first set up a hypothesis which is a definite statement about the population parameter called Null Hypothesis. It is denoted by H_0.

Null hypothesis is the hypothesis which is tested for possible rejection under the assumption that it is true. First, we set up H_0 in clear terms.

Step 2. Alternative hypothesis

Any hypothesis which is complementary to the null hypothesis (H_0) is called an alternative hypothesis. It is denoted by H_1.

For example, if we want to test the null hypothesis that the population has a specified mean μ_0 then we have

$$H_0 : \mu = \mu_0$$

then the alternative hypothesis will be

(*i*) $H_1 : \mu \neq \mu_0$ (Two tailed alternative hypothesis)

(*ii*) $H_1 : \mu > \mu_0$ (right tailed alternative hypothesis (or) single tailed)

(*iii*) $H_1 : \mu < \mu_0$ (left tailed alternative hypothesis (or) single tailed)

Hence alternative hypothesis helps to know whether the test is two tailed test or one tailed test. Therefore, we set up H_1 for this decision.

Step 3. Level of significance [*U.P.T.U. (MCA) 2008, 2007*]

The probability of the value of the variate falling in the critical region is known as level of significance. A region corresponding to a statistic t in the sample space S which amounts to rejection of the null hypothesis H_0 is called as **critical region** or region of rejection while which amounts to acceptance of H_0 is called **acceptance region.** The probability α that a random value of the statistic t belongs to the critical region is known as the **level of significance.**

$$P(t \in w/H_0) = \alpha$$

i.e., the level of significance is the size of the type I error (refer art. 9.30) or the maximum producer's risk.

We select the appropriate level of significance in advance depending on the reliability of the estimates.

Step 4. Test statistic (or test criterion): We compute the test statistic z under the null hypothesis. For larger samples corresponding to the statistic t, the variable $z = \dfrac{t - E(t)}{S.E.(t)}$ is normally distributed with mean 0 and variance 1. The value of z given above under the null hypothesis is known as **test statistic.**

Step 5. Conclusion: We compare the computed value of z with the critical value z_α at level of significance (α). The critical value of z_α of the test statistic at level of significance α for a two tailed test is given by

$$p(|z| > z_\alpha) = \alpha \qquad ...(1)$$

i.e., z_α is the value of z so that the total area of the critical region on both tails is α. Since the normal curve is symmetrical, from equation (1), we get

$$p(z > z_\alpha) + p(z < -z_\alpha) = \alpha; \text{ i.e. } 2p(z > z_\alpha) = \alpha; \text{ i.e., } p(z > z_\alpha) = \alpha/2$$

i.e., the area of each tail is $\alpha/2$.

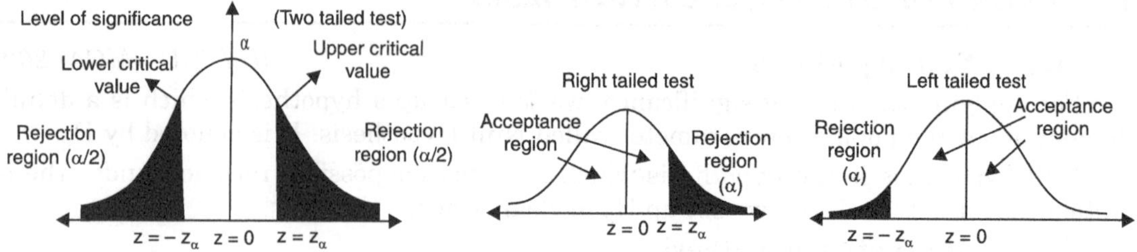

The critical value z_α is that value such that the area to the right of z_α is $\alpha/2$ and the area to the left of $-z_\alpha$ is $\alpha/2$.

In the case of one tailed test,

$p(z > z_\alpha) = \alpha$ if it is right tailed; $p(z < -z_\alpha) = \alpha$ if it is left tailed.

The critical value of z for a single tailed test (right or left) at level of significance α is same as the critical value of z for two tailed test at level of significance 2α.

Using the equation, also using the normal tables, the critical value of z at different levels of significance (α) for both single tailed and two tailed test are calculated and listed below. The equations are

$$p(|z| > z_\alpha) = \alpha;\ p(z > z_\alpha) = \alpha;\ p(z < -z_\alpha) = \alpha$$

	Level of significance		
	1% (0.01)	5% (0.05)	10% (0.1)
Two tailed test	$\lvert z_\alpha \rvert = 2.58$	$\lvert z_\alpha \rvert = 1.96$	$\lvert z_\alpha \rvert = 1.645$
Right tailed test	$z_\alpha = 2.33$	$z_\alpha = 1.645$	$z_\alpha = 1.28$
Left tailed test	$z_\alpha = -2.33$	$z_\alpha = -1.645$	$z_\alpha = -1.28$

If $|z| > z_\alpha$, we reject H_0 and conclude that there is significant difference. If $|z| < z_\alpha$, we accept H_0 and conclude that there is no significant difference.

9.33. ERRORS IN SAMPLING

The main aim of the sampling theory is to draw a valid conclusion about the population parameters on the basis of the sample results. In doing this we may commit the following two types of errors:

Type I Error *[U.P.T.U. (MCA) 2008, 2007]*

When H_0 is true, we may reject it. P(Reject H_0 when it is true) = P(Reject H_0/H_0) = α. α is called the size of the type I error, also referred to as **producer's risk.**

Type II Error: When H_0 is wrong, we may accept it. P(Accept H_0 when it is wrong) = P(Accept H_0/H_1) = β. β is called the size of the type II error, also referred to as **consumer's risk.**

Note. The values of the test statistic which separates the critical region and acceptance region are called the **critical values** or **significant values.** This value is dependent on (*i*) the level of significance used and (*ii*) the alternative hypothesis, whether it is one tailed or two tailed.

9.34. TEST OF SIGNIFICANCE FOR LARGE SAMPLES

If the sample size $n > 30$, the sample is taken as large sample. For such sample we apply distributions, as Binomial, Poisson, which are closely approximated by normal distributions assuming the population as normal.

Under large sample test, the following are the important tests to test the significance:

1. *Testing of significance for single proportion.*
2. *Testing of significance for difference of proportions.*
3. *Testing of significance for single mean.*
4. *Testing of significance for difference of means.*
5. *Testing of significance for difference of standard deviations.*

9.34.1. Testing of Significance for Single Proportion

This test is used to find the significant difference between proportion of the sample and the population. Let X be the number of successes in n independent trials with constant probability P of success for each trial.

$$E(X) = nP;\ V(X) = nPQ;\ Q = 1 - P = \text{Probability of failure.}$$

Let $\quad p = X/n$ called the observed proportion of success.

$$E(p) = E(X/n) = \frac{1}{n}E(X) = \frac{nP}{n} = P$$

$$V(p) = V(X/n) = \frac{1}{n^2}V(X) = \frac{nPQ}{n^2} = PQ/n$$

$$\text{S.E.}(p) = \sqrt{\frac{PQ}{n}}\ ;\ z = \frac{p - E(p)}{\text{S.E.}(p)} = \frac{p - P}{\sqrt{PQ/n}} \sim N(0, 1)$$

This z is called test statistic which is used to test the significant difference of sample and population proportion.

Note. 1. The probable limits for the observed proportion of successes are $P \pm 3\sqrt{PQ/n}$.

2. If p is not known, the probable limits for the proportion in the population are $p \pm z_\alpha\sqrt{pq/n}$, $q = 1 - p$, where sample proportion, p is taken as an estimate of p and z_α is the significant value of z at level of significance α.

EXAMPLES

Example 1. *A coin was tossed 400 times and the head turned up 216 times. Test the hypothesis that the coin is unbiased.*

Sol. Null hypothesis:

H_0: The coin is unbiased *i.e.*, P = 0.5

Alternative hypothesis:

H_1: The coin is biased *i.e.*, $P \neq 0.5$

Hence we use **two tailed test.**

Here, $n = 400$, X = no. of success = 216

$\therefore \quad p$ = proportion of success in the sample $= \frac{X}{n} = \frac{216}{400} = 0.54$

P = population proportion = 0.5, Q = 1 – P = 0.5

Test Statistic:

Under H_0, test statistic $z = \dfrac{p - P}{\sqrt{PQ/n}}$

$$|z| = \left| \frac{0.54 - 0.5}{\sqrt{\dfrac{0.5 \times 0.5}{400}}} \right| = 1.6$$

Conclusion:

Since $|z| = 1.6 < 1.96$ *i.e.*, $|z| < z_\alpha$ where z_α is the significant value of z at 5% level of significance.

Hence we accept H_0 and conclude that the coin is unbiased.

Example 2. *A machine is producing bolts of which a certain fraction is defective. A random sample of 400 is taken from a large batch and is found to contain 30 defective bolts. Does this indicate that the proportion of defectives is larger than that claimed by the manufacturer where the manufacturer claims that only 5% of his product are defective. Find 95% confidence limits of the proportion of defective bolts in batch.*

Sol. Null hypothesis H_0: The manufacturer claim is accepted *i.e.*, $P = \dfrac{5}{100} = 0.05$

$$Q = 1 - P = 1 - 0.05 = 0.95$$

Alternative hypothesis: $P > 0.05$

Hence we use **Right tailed test.**

p = observed proportion of sample $= \dfrac{30}{400} = 0.075$

Test statistic

Under H_0, the test statistic $z = \dfrac{p - P}{\sqrt{PQ/n}}$ $\therefore$ $z = \dfrac{0.075 - 0.05}{\sqrt{\dfrac{0.05 \times 0.95}{400}}} = 2.2941.$

Conclusion: The tabulated value of z at 5% level of significance for right tailed test is

$z_\alpha = 1.645$. Since $|z| = 2.2941 > 1.645$, H_0 is rejected at 5% level of significance. *i.e.*, the proportion of defective is larger than the manufacturer claim.

To find 95% confidence limits of the proportion.

It is given by $P \pm z_\alpha \sqrt{PQ/n}$

i.e., $$0.05 \pm 1.96 \sqrt{\frac{0.05 \times 0.95}{400}} = 0.05 \pm 0.02135 = 0.07136,\ 0.02865$$

Hence 95% confidence limits for the proportion of defective bolts are (0.07136, 0.02865).

ASSIGNMENT

1. In a hospital 475 female and 525 male babies were born in a week. Do these figures confirm the hypothesis that males and females are born in equal number?
2. In a city a sample of 1000 people were taken and out of them 540 are vegetarian and the rest are non-vegetarian. Can we say that the both habits of eating (vegetarian or non-vegetarian) are equally popular in the city at (*i*) 1% level of significance (*ii*) 5% level of significance?
3. 325 men out of 600 men chosen from a big city were found to be smokers. Does this information support the conclusion that the majority of men in the city are smokers?

Answers

1. H_0 accepted at 5% level **2.** H_0 rejected at 5% level, accepted at 1% level
3. H_0 rejected at 5% level.

9.34.2. Testing of Significance for Difference of Proportions

Consider two samples X_1 and X_2 of sizes n_1 and n_2 respectively taken from two different populations. To test the significance of the difference between the sample proportions p_1 and p_2, the test statistic under the null hypothesis H_0, that there is no significant difference between the two sample proportion, is

$$z = \frac{p_1 - p_2}{\sqrt{PQ\left(\frac{1}{n_1} + \frac{1}{n_2}\right)}}, \quad \text{where} \quad P = \frac{n_1 p_1 + n_2 p_2}{n_1 + n_2} \quad \text{and} \quad Q = 1 - P.$$

EXAMPLES

Example 1. *Before an increase in excise duty on tea, 800 people out of a sample of 1000 persons were found to be tea drinkers. After an increase in the duty, 800 persons were known to be tea drinkers in a sample of 1200 people. Do you think that there has been a significant decrease in the consumption of tea after the increase in the excise duty?*

Sol. Here $n_1 = 800, n_2 = 1200$

$$p_1 = \frac{X_1}{n_1} = \frac{800}{1000} = \frac{4}{5}; \; p_2 = \frac{X_2}{n_2} = \frac{800}{1200} = \frac{2}{3}$$

$$P = \frac{p_1 n_1 + p_2 n_2}{n_1 + n_2} = \frac{X_1 + X_2}{n_1 + n_2} = \frac{800 + 800}{1000 + 1200} = \frac{8}{11}; \; Q = \frac{3}{11}$$

Null hypothesis H_0: $p_1 = p_2$ *i.e.*, there is no significant difference in the consumption of tea before and after increase of excise duty.

Alternative hypothesis $H_1 : p_1 > p_2$

Hence we use **right tailed test.**

Test statistic:

The test statistic is
$$z = \frac{p_1 - p_2}{\sqrt{PQ\left(\frac{1}{n_1} + \frac{1}{n_2}\right)}} = \frac{0.8 - 0.6666}{\sqrt{\frac{8}{11} \times \frac{3}{11}\left(\frac{1}{1000} + \frac{1}{1200}\right)}} = 6.842.$$

Conclusion: Since the calculated value of $| z | > 1.645$ and also $| z | > 2.33$, both the significant values of z at 5% and 1% level of significance, hence H_0 is rejected *i.e.*, there is a significant decrease in the consumption of tea due to increase in excise duty.

Example 2. *A machine produced 16 defective articles in a batch of 500. After overhauling it produced 3 defectives in a batch of 100. Has the machine improved?*

Sol. $p_1 = \frac{16}{500} = 0.032, \quad n_1 = 500$

$p_2 = \frac{3}{100} = 0.03, \quad n_2 = 100$

Null hypothesis:

H_0: The machine has not improved due to overhauling *i.e.*, $p_1 = p_2$.

Alternative hypothesis:

$H_1: p_1 > p_2$

Hence we use **right tailed test.**

$$\therefore \quad P = \frac{p_1 n_1 + p_2 n_2}{n_1 + n_2} = \frac{19}{600} \cong 0.032$$

Test Statistic:

Under H_0, the test statistic

$$z = \frac{p_1 - p_2}{\sqrt{PQ\left(\frac{1}{n_1} + \frac{1}{n_2}\right)}} = 0.104$$

Conclusion: The calculated value of $|z| < 1.645$ which is the significant value of z at 5% level of significance, H_0 is accepted *i.e.*, the machine has not improved due to overhauling.

ASSIGNMENT

1. Random sample of 400 men and 600 women were asked whether they would like to have a school near their residence. 200 men and 325 women were in favour of proposal. Test the hypothesis that the proportion of men and women in favour of the proposal are same at 5% level of significance.
2. In a town A, there were 956 births of which 52.5% were males while in towns A and B combined, this proportion in total of 1406 births was 0.496. Is there any significant difference in the proportion of male births in the two towns ?

Answers

1. H_0 : Accepted **2.** H_0 : Rejected.

9.34.3. Testing of Significance for Single Mean

To test whether the difference between sample mean and population mean is significant or not.

Let $X_1, X_2, ..., X_n$ be a random sample of size n from a large population $X_1, X_2, ..., X_N$ of size N with mean μ and variance σ^2. $\therefore$ the standard error of mean of a random sample of size n from a population with variance σ^2 is $\sigma/\sqrt{n}$.

To test whether the given sample of size n has been drawn from a population with mean μ *i.e.*, to test whether the difference between the sample mean and population mean is significant or not under the null hypothesis that there is no difference between the sample mean and population mean.

The test statistic is $z = \dfrac{\bar{x} - \mu}{\sigma/\sqrt{n}}$, where σ is the standard deviation of the population.

If σ is not known, we use the test statistic $z = \dfrac{\bar{x} - \mu}{s/\sqrt{n}}$, where s is the standard deviation of the sample.

Note. If the level of significance is α and z_α is the critical value $-z_\alpha < |z| = \left|\dfrac{\bar{x} - \mu}{\sigma/\sqrt{n}}\right| < z_\alpha$.

The limits of the population mean μ are given by $\bar{x} - z_\alpha \dfrac{\sigma}{\sqrt{n}} < \mu < \bar{x} + z_\alpha \dfrac{\sigma}{\sqrt{n}}$.

At 5% level of significance, 95% confidence limits are $\bar{x} - 1.96 \dfrac{\sigma}{\sqrt{n}} < \mu < \bar{x} + 1.96 \dfrac{\sigma}{\sqrt{n}}$

At 1% level of significance, 99% confidence limits are $\bar{x} - 2.58 \dfrac{\sigma}{\sqrt{n}} < \mu < \bar{x} + 2.58 \dfrac{\sigma}{\sqrt{n}}$.

These limits are called **confidence limits** or **fiducial limits.**

EXAMPLES

Example 1. *A random sample of 900 members has a mean 3.4 cms. Can it be reasonably regarded as a sample from a large population of mean 3.2 cms and S.D. 2.3 cms?*

Sol. Here $n = 900$, $\bar{x} = 3.4$, $\mu = 3.2$, $\sigma = 2.3$

Null hypothesis:

H_0 : Assume that the sample is drawn from a large population with mean 3.2 and S.D. 2.3

Alternative hypothesis:

$H_1 : \mu \neq 3.2$ (**two tailed test**)

Test statistic:

Under H_0 ; $z = \dfrac{\bar{x} - \mu}{\sigma/\sqrt{n}} = \dfrac{3.4 - 3.2}{2.3/\sqrt{900}} = 0.261.$

Conclusion: As the calculated value of $|z| = 0.261 < 1.96$, the significant value of z at 5% level of significance, H_0 is accepted *i.e.*, the sample is drawn from the population with mean 3.2 and S.D. 2.3.

Example 2. *The mean weight obtained from a random sample of size 100 is 64 gms. The S.D. of the weight distribution of the population is 3 gms. Test the statement that the mean weight of the population is 67 gms at 5% level of significance. Also set up 99% confidence limits of the mean weight of the population.*

Sol. Here $n = 100$, $\mu = 67$, $\bar{x} = 64$, $\sigma = 3$

Null hypothesis:

H_0: There is no significant difference between sample and population mean.

i.e., $\mu = 67$, the sample is drawn from the population with $\mu = 67$.

Alternative hypothesis:

H_1: $\mu \neq 67$ **(Two tailed test).**

Test statistic:

Under H_0, $z = \dfrac{\overline{x} - \mu}{\sigma/\sqrt{n}} = \dfrac{64 - 67}{3/\sqrt{100}} = -10 \quad \therefore \quad |z| = 10.$

Conclusion: Since the calculated value of $|z| > 1.96$, the significant value of z at 5% level of significance, H_0 is rejected *i.e.,* the sample is not drawn from the population with mean 67.

To find 99% confidence limits. It is given by $\overline{x} \pm 2.58\,\sigma/\sqrt{n} = 64 \pm 2.58(3/\sqrt{100}) = 64.774$, 63.226.

ASSIGNMENT

1. A sample of 1000 students from a university was taken and their average weight was found to be 112 pounds with a S.D. of 20 pounds. Could the mean weight of students in the population be 120 pounds?
2. A sample of 400 male students is found to have a mean height of 160 cms. Can it be reasonably regarded as a sample from a large population with mean height 162.5 cms and standard deviation 4.5 cms?
3. A random sample of 200 measurements from a large population gave a mean value of 50 and a S.D. of 9. Determine 95% confidence interval for the mean of population.

Answers

1. H_0 is rejected **2.** H_0 accepted **3.** 48.8 and 51.2.

9.34.4. Test of Significance for Difference of Means of Two Large Samples

Let $\overline{x}_1$ be the mean of a sample of size n_1 from a population with mean μ_1, and variance σ_1^2. Let $\overline{x}_2$ be the mean of an independent sample of size n_2 from another population with mean μ_2 and variance σ_2^2. The test statistic is given by $z = \dfrac{\overline{x}_1 - \overline{x}_2}{\sqrt{\dfrac{\sigma_1^2}{n_1} + \dfrac{\sigma_2^2}{n_2}}}$.

Under the null hypothesis that the samples are drawn from the same population where $\sigma_1 = \sigma_2 = \sigma$ *i.e.,* $\mu_1 = \mu_2$ the test statistic is given by $z = \dfrac{\overline{x}_1 - \overline{x}_2}{\sigma\sqrt{\dfrac{1}{n_1} + \dfrac{1}{n_2}}}$.

Note 1. If σ_1, σ_2 are not known and $\sigma_1 \neq \sigma_2$ the test statistic in this case is $z = \dfrac{\overline{x}_1 - \overline{x}_2}{\sqrt{\dfrac{s_1^2 + s_2^2}{n_1 + n_2}}}$.

Note 2. If σ is not known and $\sigma_1 = \sigma_2$. We use $\sigma^2 = \dfrac{n_1 s_1^2 + n_2 s_2^2}{n_1 + n_2}$ to calculate σ.

EXAMPLES

Example 1. *The average income of persons was ₹210 with a S.D. of ₹10 in sample of 100 people of a city. For another sample of 150 persons, the average income was ₹220 with S.D. of ₹12. The S.D. of incomes of the people of the city was ₹11. Test whether there is any significant difference between the average incomes of the localities.*

Sol. Here $n_1 = 100$, $n_2 = 150$, $\bar{x}_1 = 210$, $\bar{x}_2 = 220$, $s_1 = 10$, $s_2 = 12$.

Null hypothesis: The difference is not significant. *i.e.,* there is no difference between the incomes of the localities. H_0: $\bar{x}_1 = \bar{x}_2$

Alternative hypothesis

$H_1 : \bar{x}_1 \neq \bar{x}_2$ **(two tailed test)**

Test statistic:

Under H_0, $z = \dfrac{\bar{x}_1 - \bar{x}_2}{\sqrt{\dfrac{s_1^2}{n_1} + \dfrac{s_2^2}{n_2}}} = \dfrac{210 - 220}{\sqrt{\dfrac{10^2}{100} + \dfrac{12^2}{150}}} = -7.1428 \quad \therefore \quad |z| = 7.1428.$

Conclusion: As the calculated value of $|z| > 1.96$, the significant value of z at 5% level of significance, H_0 is rejected *i.e.,* there is significant difference between the average incomes of the localities.

Example 2. *Intelligence tests were given to two groups of boys and girls.*

	Mean	*S.D.*	*Size*
Girls	*75*	*8*	*60*
Boys	*73*	*10*	*100*

Examine if the difference between mean scores is significant.

Sol. Null hypothesis H_0: There is no significant difference between mean scores *i.e.,* $\bar{x}_1 = \bar{x}_2$.

Alternative hypothesis H_1: $\bar{x}_1 \neq \bar{x}_2$ **(two tailed test)**

Test statistic: Under the null hypothesis, $z = \dfrac{\bar{x}_1 - \bar{x}_2}{\sqrt{\dfrac{s_1^2}{n_1} + \dfrac{s_2^2}{n_2}}} = \dfrac{75 - 73}{\sqrt{\dfrac{8^2}{60} + \dfrac{10^2}{100}}} = 1.3912.$

Conclusion: As the calculated value of $|z| < 1.96$, the significant value of z at 5% level of significance, H_0 is accepted *i.e.,* there is no significant difference between mean scores.

ASSIGNMENT

1. Two random samples of sizes 1000 and 2000 farms gave an average yield of 2000 kg and 2050 kg respectively. The variance of wheat farms in the country may be taken as 100 kg. Examine whether the two samples differ significantly in yield.
2. The means of two large samples of 1000 and 2000 members are 168.75 cms and 170 cms respectively. Can the samples be regarded as drawn from the same population of standard deviation 6.25 cms?

3. In a survey of buying habits, 400 women shoppers are chosen at random in supermarket A. Their average weekly food expenditure is ₹ 250 with a S.D. of ₹ 40. For 500 women shoppers chosen at supermarket B, the average weekly food expenditure is ₹ 220 with a S.D. of ₹ 45. Test at 1% level of significance whether the average food expenditures of the two groups are equal.

Answers

1. Highly significant **2.** Not significant **3.** Highly significant.

9.34.5. Test of Significance for the Difference of Standard Deviations

If s_1 and s_2 are the standard deviations of two independent samples, then under the null hypothesis $H_0 : \sigma_1 = \sigma_2$, *i.e.*, the sample standard deviations don't differ significantly, the statistic

$$z = \frac{s_1 - s_2}{\sqrt{\dfrac{\sigma_1^2}{2n_1} + \dfrac{\sigma_2^2}{2n_2}}}, \text{ where } \sigma_1 \text{ and } \sigma_2 \text{ are population standard deviations.}$$

When population standard deviations are not known, then $z = \dfrac{s_1 - s_2}{\sqrt{\dfrac{s_1^2}{2n_1} + \dfrac{s_2^2}{2n_2}}}$.

Example. *Random samples drawn from two countries gave the following data relating to the heights of adult males:*

	Country A	*Country B*
Mean height (in inches)	*67.42*	*67.25*
Standard deviation	*2.58*	*2.50*
Number in samples	*1000*	*1200*

(i) Is the difference between the means significant?
(ii) Is the difference between the standard deviations significant?

Sol. Given: $n_1 = 1000$, $n_2 = 1200$, $\bar{x}_1 = 67.42$; $\bar{x}_2 = 67.25$, $s_1 = 2.58$, $s_2 = 2.50$
Since the samples size are large we can take $\sigma_1 = s_1 = 2.58$; $\sigma_2 = s_2 = 2.50$.
(*i*) **Null hypothesis** $H_0 : \mu_1 = \mu_2$ *i.e.*, sample means do not differ significantly.
Alternative hypothesis $H_1 : \mu_1 \neq \mu_2$ **(two tailed test)**

Test statistic:
$$z = \frac{\bar{x}_1 - \bar{x}_2}{\sqrt{\dfrac{s_1^2}{n_1} + \dfrac{s_2^2}{n_2}}} = \frac{67.42 - 67.25}{\sqrt{\dfrac{(2.58)^2}{1000} + \dfrac{(2.50)^2}{1200}}} = 1.56.$$

Conclusion:
Since $|z| < 1.96$ we accept the null hypothesis at 5% level of significance.
(*ii*) **Null hypothesis:**
$H_0: \sigma_1 = \sigma_2$ *i.e.*, the sample S.D.'s do not differ significantly.

Alternative hypothesis H_1: $\sigma_1 \neq \sigma_2$ (two tailed test)
Test statistic:

$$z = \frac{s_1 - s_2}{\sqrt{\frac{{\sigma_1}^2}{2n_1} + \frac{{\sigma_2}^2}{2n_2}}} = \frac{s_1 - s_2}{\sqrt{\frac{{s_1}^2}{2n_1} + \frac{{s_2}^2}{2n_2}}} = 1.0387.$$

Since $| z | < 1.96$ we accept the null hypothesis at 5% level of significance.

ASSIGNMENT

1. The mean yield of two sets of plots and their variability are as given. Examine
(*i*) whether the difference in the mean yield of the two sets of plots is significant.
(*ii*) whether the difference in the variability in yields is significant.

	Set of 40 plots	*Set of 60 plots*
Mean yield per plot	1258 lb	1243 lb
S.D. per plot	34	28

2. The yield of wheat in a random sample of 1000 farms in a certain area has a S.D. of 192 kg. Another random sample of 1000 farms gives a S.D. of 224 kg. Are the S.D's significantly different?

Answers

1. $z = 2.315$, Difference significant at 5% level ; $z = 1.31$, Difference not significant at 5% level
2. $z = 4.851$. The S.D's are significantly different.

9.35. TEST OF SIGNIFICANCE OF SMALL SAMPLES

When the size of the sample is less than 30, then the sample is called small sample. For such sample it will not be possible for us to assume that the random sampling distribution of a statistic is approximately normal and the values given by the sample data are sufficiently close to the population values and can be used in their place for the calculation of the standard error of the estimate.

9.36. STUDENT'S t-DISTRIBUTION (t-Test)

[*G.B.T.U. (MBA) 2011 ; G.B.T.U. (MCA) 2010*]

This t-distribution is used when sample size is ≤ 30 and the population standard deviation is unknown.

t-statistic is defined as

$$t = \frac{\bar{x} - \mu}{S/\sqrt{n}} \qquad \text{where,} \qquad S = \sqrt{\frac{\Sigma(x - \bar{x})^2}{n - 1}}$$

$\bar{x}$ is the mean of sample, μ is population mean. S is the standard deviation of population and n is sample size.

If the standard deviation of the sample 's' is given then t-statistic is defined as

$$t = \frac{\bar{x} - \mu}{s/\sqrt{n-1}}$$

Note. The relation between s and S is $ns^2 = (n - 1)S^2$.

9.36.1. The t-Table

The t-table given at the end is the probability integral of t-distribution. The t-distribution has different values for each degrees of freedom and when the degrees of freedom are infinitely large, the t-distribution is equivalent to normal distribution and the probabilities shown in the normal distribution tables are applicable.

9.36.2. Applications of t-Distribution [*G.B.T.U. (MBA) 2011*]

Some of the applications of t-distribution are given below:

1. *To test if the sample mean* ($\bar{x}$) *differs significantly from the hypothetical value* μ *of the population mean.*
2. *To test the significance between two sample means.*
3. *To test the significance of observed partial and multiple correlation coefficients.*

9.36.3. Critical Value of t

The critical value or significant value of t at level of significance α, degrees of freedom γ for two tailed test is given by

$$P[\,|\,t\,| > t_\gamma(\alpha)] = \alpha$$

$$P[\,|\,t\,| \le t_\gamma(\alpha)] = 1 - \alpha$$

The significant value of t at level of significance α, for a single tailed test can be got from those of two tailed test by referring to the values at 2α.

9.37. TEST I: t-TEST OF SIGNIFICANCE OF THE MEAN OF A RANDOM SAMPLE

To test whether the mean of a sample drawn from a normal population deviates significantly from a stated value when variance of the population is unknown.

H_0: There is no significant difference between the sample mean $\bar{x}$ and the population mean μ *i.e.,* we use the statistic

$$t = \frac{\bar{x} - \mu}{S/\sqrt{n}} \qquad \text{where} \quad S = \sqrt{\frac{\Sigma(x - \bar{x})^2}{n - 1}}$$

with degree of freedom $n - 1$.

At given level of significance α and degrees of freedom $(n - 1)$, we refer to t-table t_α (two tailed or one tailed). If calculated t value is such that $|\,t\,| < t_\alpha$, the null hypothesis is accepted. If $|\,t\,| > t_\alpha$, H_0 is rejected.

9.37.1. Fiducial Limits of Population Mean

If t_α is the value of t at level of significance α at $(n - 1)$ degrees of freedom then,

$$\left|\frac{\bar{x} - \mu}{S/\sqrt{n}}\right| < t_\alpha \text{ for acceptance of } H_0.$$

$$\bar{x} - t_\alpha S/\sqrt{n} < \mu < \bar{x} + t_\alpha S/\sqrt{n}$$

95% confidence limits (level of significance 5%) are $\bar{x} \pm t_{0.05}\text{S}/\sqrt{n}$.

99% confidence limits (level of significance 1%) are $\bar{x} \pm t_{0.01}\text{S}/\sqrt{n}$.

EXAMPLES

Example 1. *A random sample of size 16 has 53 as mean. The sum of squares of the deviation from mean is 135. Can this sample be regarded as taken from the population having 56 as mean? Obtain 95% and 99% confidence limits of the mean of the population.*

Sol. Null hypothesis H_0: There is no significant difference between the sample mean and hypothetical population mean *i.e.*, $\mu = 56$.

Alternative hypothesis H_1: $\mu \neq 56$ **(Two tailed test)**

Test statistic: Under H_0, test statistic is $t = \dfrac{\bar{x} - \mu}{\text{S}/\sqrt{n}}$

Given : $\bar{x} = 53$, $\mu = 56$, $n = 16$, $\Sigma(x - \bar{x})^2 = 135$

$$\text{S} = \sqrt{\frac{\Sigma(x - \bar{x})^2}{n - 1}} = \sqrt{\frac{135}{15}} = 3$$

$$t = \frac{\bar{x} - \mu}{\text{S}/\sqrt{n}} = \frac{53 - 56}{3/\sqrt{16}} = -4$$

$$|\,t\,| = 4$$

$$d.f\!v. = 16 - 1 = 15.$$

Conclusion: Since $|\,t\,| = 4 > t_{0.05} = 2.13$ *i.e.*, the calculated value of t is more than the tabulated value, the null hypothesis is rejected. Hence, the sample mean has not come from a population having 56 as mean.

95% confidence limits of the population mean

$$= \bar{x} \pm \frac{\text{S}}{\sqrt{n}}\, t_{0.05} = 53 \pm \frac{3}{\sqrt{16}}\,(2.13) = 51.4025,\ 54.5975$$

99% confidence limits of the population mean

$$= \bar{x} \pm \frac{\text{S}}{\sqrt{n}}\, t_{0.01}, = 53 \pm \frac{3}{\sqrt{16}}\,(2.95) = 50.7875,\ 55.2125.$$

Example 2. *The lifetime of electric bulbs for a random sample of 10 from a large consignment gave the following data:*

Item	*1*	*2*	*3*	*4*	*5*	*6*	*7*	*8*	*9*	*10*
Life in '000 hrs.	*4.2*	*4.6*	*3.9*	*4.1*	*5.2*	*3.8*	*3.9*	*4.3*	*4.4*	*5.6*

Can we accept the hypothesis that the average lifetime of bulb is 4000 hrs?

Sol. Null hypothesis H_0 : There is no significant difference in the sample mean and population mean. *i.e.*, $\mu = 4000$ hrs.

Alternative hypothesis: $\mu \neq 4000$ hrs **(Two tailed test)**

Test statistic: Under H_0, the test statistic is $t = \dfrac{\bar{x} - \mu}{\text{S}/\sqrt{n}}$

x	4.2	4.6	3.9	4.1	5.2	3.8	3.9	4.3	4.4	5.6
$x-\bar{x}$	– 0.2	0.2	– 0.5	– 0.3	0.8	– 0.6	– 0.5	– 0.1	0	1.2
$(x-\bar{x})^2$	0.04	0.04	0.25	0.09	0.64	0.36	0.25	0.01	0	1.44

$$\bar{x} = \frac{\Sigma x}{n} = \frac{44}{10} = 4.4, \qquad \Sigma(x-\bar{x})^2 = 3.12$$

$$S = \sqrt{\frac{\Sigma(x-\bar{x})^2}{n-1}} = 0.589$$

$$t = \frac{\bar{x}-\mu}{S/\sqrt{n}} = \frac{4.4-4}{\left(\frac{0.589}{\sqrt{10}}\right)} = 2.123$$

For $\gamma = 9$, $t_{0.05} = 2.26$.

Conclusion: Since the calculated value of t is less than the tabulated value of t at 5% level of significance. ∴ The null hypothesis $\mu = 4000$ hrs is accepted *i.e.*, the average lifetime of bulbs could be 4000 hrs.

Example 3. *A sample of 20 items has mean 42 units and S.D. 5 units. Test the hypothesis that it is a random sample from a normal population with mean 45 units.*

Sol. Null hypothesis H_0: There is no significant difference between the sample mean and the population mean. *i.e.*, $\mu = 45$ units

Alternative hypothesis H_1: $\mu \neq 45$ **(Two tailed test)**

Given: $n = 20$, $\bar{x} = 42$, $s = 5$; $\gamma = 19$ d.f.

Test statistic: Under H_0, the test statistic is

$$t = \frac{\bar{x}-\mu}{s/\sqrt{n-1}} = \frac{42-45}{5/\sqrt{19}} = -2.615$$

$$\therefore \qquad |t| = 2.615$$

The tabulated value of t at 5% level for 19 d.f. is $t_{0.05} = 2.09$.

Conclusion: Since the calculated value $|t|$ is greater than the tabulated value of t at 5% level of significance, the null hypothesis H_0 is rejected. *i.e.*, there is significant difference between the sample mean and population mean.

i.e., the sample could not have come from this population.

Example 4. *The 9 items of a sample have the following values*

45, 47, 50, 52, 48, 47, 49, 53, 51.

Does the mean of these values differ significantly from the assumed mean 47.5?

Sol. Here, $n = 9$, $\mu = 47.5$, $\bar{x} = \frac{\Sigma x}{n} = 49.1$

x	45	47	50	52	48	47	49	53	51
$x-\bar{x}$	– 4.1	– 2.1	0.9	2.9	– 1.1	– 2.1	– 0.1	3.9	1.9
$(x-\bar{x})^2$	16.81	4.41	0.81	8.41	1.21	4.41	0.01	15.21	3.61

$$\Sigma(x - \bar{x})^2 = 54.89,$$

$$S^2 = \frac{\Sigma(x-\bar{x})^2}{n-1} = 6.86$$

$$\therefore \qquad S = 2.619$$

Null hypothesis:

$$H_0: \mu = 47.5$$

i.e., there is no significant difference between the sample and population means.

Alternative hypothesis:

$$H_1: \mu \neq 47.5$$

Hence we apply **two-tailed test.**

Test statistic: Under H_0, the test statistic is

$$t = \frac{\bar{x} - \mu}{S/\sqrt{n}} = \frac{49.1 - 47.5}{(2.619/\sqrt{9})} = 1.8327$$

$$t_{0.05} = 2.31 \text{ for } \gamma = 8$$

Conclusion: Since $|t|_{\text{calculated}} < t_{\text{tabulated}}$ at 5% level of significance, the null hypothesis H_0 is accepted *i.e.,* there is no significant difference between their means.

ASSIGNMENT

1. Ten individuals are chosen at random from a normal population of students and their marks are found to be 63, 63, 66, 67, 68, 69, 70, 70, 71, 71. In the light of these data, discuss the suggestion that mean mark of the population of students is 66.
2. The following values gives the lengths of 12 samples of Egyptian cotton taken from a consignment: 48, 46, 49, 46, 52, 45, 43, 47, 47, 46, 45, 50. Test if the mean length of the consignment can be taken as 46.
3. A sample of 18 items has a mean 24 units and standard deviation 3 units. Test the hypothesis that it is a random sample from a normal population with mean 27 units.
4. A random sample of 10 boys had the I.Q.'s 70, 120, 110, 101, 88, 83, 95, 98, 107 and 100. Do these data support the assumption of a population mean I.Q. of 160?

9.38. TEST II: t-TEST FOR DIFFERENCE OF MEANS OF TWO SMALL SAMPLES (from a Normal Population)

This test is used to test whether the two samples $x_1, x_2, \ldots\ldots, x_{n_1}, y_1, y_2, \ldots\ldots, y_{n_2}$ of sizes n_1, n_2 have been drawn from two normal populations with mean μ_1 and μ_2 respectively under the assumption that the population variance are equal. $(\sigma_1 = \sigma_2 = \sigma)$.

H_0: The samples have been drawn from the normal population with means μ_1 and μ_2 *i.e.,* $H_0: \mu_1 \neq \mu_2$.

Let $\bar{x}$, $\bar{y}$ be their means of the two samples.

Under this H_0 the test statistic t is given by $t = \dfrac{(\overline{x} - \overline{y})}{S\sqrt{\dfrac{1}{n_1} + \dfrac{1}{n_2}}}$

Degree of freedom is $n_1 + n_2 - 2$.

Note 1. If the two sample's standard deviations s_1, s_2 are given then we have $S^2 = \dfrac{n_1 s_1^2 + n_2 s_2^2}{n_1 + n_2 - 2}$.

Note 2. If s_1, s_2 are not given then $S^2 = \dfrac{\Sigma(x_1 - \overline{x}_1)^2 + \Sigma(x_2 - \overline{x}_2)^2}{n_1 + n_2 - 2}$.

EXAMPLES

Example 1. *Two samples of sodium vapour bulbs were tested for length of life and the following results were got:*

	Size	*Sample mean*	*Sample S.D.*
Type I	*8*	*1234 hrs*	*36 hrs*
Type II	*7*	*1036 hrs*	*40 hrs*

Is the difference in the means significant to generalise that Type I is superior to Type II regarding length of life?

Sol. Null hypothesis:

$H_0 : \mu_1 = \mu_2$ *i.e.,* two types of bulbs have same lifetime.

Alternative hypothesis:

$H_1 : \mu_1 > \mu_2$ *i.e.,* type I is superior to Type II.

Hence we use **right tailed test.**

$$S^2 = \frac{n_1 s_1^2 + n_2 s_2^2}{n_1 + n_2 - 2} = \frac{8(36)^2 + 7(40)^2}{8 + 7 - 2} = 1659.076$$

$\therefore$ $S = 40.7317$

Test statistic: Under H_0, the test statistic t is given by

$$t = \frac{\overline{x}_1 - \overline{x}_2}{S\sqrt{\dfrac{1}{n_1} + \dfrac{1}{n_2}}} = \frac{1234 - 1036}{40.7317\sqrt{\dfrac{1}{8} + \dfrac{1}{7}}} = 18.1480$$

$t_{0.05}$ at d.f. $\gamma = n_1 + n_2 - 2 = 13$ is 1.77.

Conclusion: Since calculated $| t | > t_{\text{tabulated}}$ at 5% level of significance, H_0 is rejected.

$\therefore$ Type I is definitely superior to Type II.

Example 2. *Samples of sizes 10 and 14 were taken from two normal populations with S.D. 3.5 and 5.2. The sample means were found to be 20.3 and 18.6. Test whether the means of the two populations are the same at 5% level.*

Sol. We have, $\overline{x}_1 = 20.3$, $\overline{x}_2 = 18.6$, $n_1 = 10$, $n_2 = 14$, $s_1 = 3.5$, $s_2 = 5.2$

$$S^2 = \frac{n_1 s_1^2 + n_2 s_2^2}{n_1 + n_2 - 2} = 22.775$$

$$\therefore \quad S = 4.772$$

Null hypothesis:

$H_0 : \mu_1 = \mu_2$ *i.e.*, the means of the two populations are the same.

Alternative hypothesis:

$H_1 : \mu_1 \neq \mu_2$

Test statistic: Under H_0, the test statistic is

$$t = \frac{\bar{x}_1 - \bar{x}_2}{S\sqrt{\frac{1}{n_1} + \frac{1}{n_2}}} = \frac{20.3 - 18.6}{4.772\sqrt{\frac{1}{10} + \frac{1}{14}}} = 0.8604$$

The tabulated value of t at 5% level of significance for 22 *d.f.* is $t_{0.05} = 2.0739$

Conclusion:

Since $t = 0.8604 < t_{0.05}$, the null hypothesis H_0 is accepted; *i.e.*, there is no significant difference between their means.

Example 3. *The height of 6 randomly chosen sailors in inches are 63, 65, 68, 69, 71 and 72. Those of 9 randomly chosen soldiers are 61, 62, 65, 66, 69, 70, 71, 72 and 73. Test whether the sailors are on the average taller than soldiers.*

Sol. Let X_1 and X_2 be the two samples denoting the heights of sailors and soldiers.

$$n_1 = 6,\ n_2 = 9$$

Null hypothesis H_0: $\mu_1 = \mu_2$.

i.e., the mean of both the population are the same.

Alternative hypothesis H_1: $\mu_1 > \mu_2$ **(one tailed test)**

Calculation of two sample means :

X_1	63	65	68	69	71	72
$X_1 - \bar{X}_1$	– 5	– 3	0	1	3	4
$(X_1 - \bar{X}_1)^2$	25	9	0	1	9	16

$$\bar{X}_1 = \frac{\Sigma X_1}{n_1} = 68;\ \Sigma(X_1 - \bar{X}_1)^2 = 60$$

X_2	61	62	65	66	69	70	71	72	73
$X_2 - \bar{X}_2$	– 6.66	– 5.66	– 2.66	1.66	1.34	2.34	3.34	4.34	5.34
$(X_2 - \bar{X}_2)^2$	44.36	32.035	7.0756	2.7556	1.7956	5.4756	11.1556	18.8356	28.5156

$$\bar{X}_2 = \frac{\Sigma X_2}{n_2} = 67.66;\ \Sigma(X_2 - \bar{X}_2)^2 = 152.0002$$

$$S^2 = \frac{1}{n_1 + n_2 - 2}[\Sigma(X_1 - \overline{X}_1)^2 + \Sigma(X_2 - \overline{X}_2)^2] = 16.3077$$

$\therefore$ $S = 4.038$

Test statistic:

Under H_0, $$t = \frac{\overline{X}_1 - \overline{X}_2}{S\sqrt{\frac{1}{n_1} + \frac{1}{n_2}}} = \frac{68 - 67.666}{4.038\sqrt{\frac{1}{6} + \frac{1}{9}}} = 0.1569$$

The value of t at 5% level of significance for 13 d.f. is 1.77. (d.f. $= n_1 + n_2 - 2$)

Conclusion: Since $t_{\text{calculated}} < t_{0.05} = 1.77$, the null hypothesis H_0 is accepted.

i.e., there is no significant difference between their average.

i.e., the sailors are not on the average taller than the soldiers.

ASSIGNMENT

1. The mean life of 10 electric motors was found to be 1450 hrs with S.D. of 423 hrs. A second sample of 17 motors chosen from a different batch showed a mean life of 1280 hrs with a S.D. of 398 hrs. Is there a significant difference between means of the two samples?
2. The marks obtained by a group of 9 regular course students and another group of 11 part time course students in a test are given below:

Regular :	56	62	63	54	60	51	67	69	58		
Part time :	62	70	71	62	60	56	75	64	72	68	66

   Examine whether the marks obtained by regular students and part time students differ significantly at 5% and 1% level of significance.
3. A group of 5 patients treated with the medicine A weigh 42, 39, 48, 60 and 41 kgs. A second group of 7 patients from the same hospital treated with medicine B weigh 38, 42, 56, 64, 68, 69 and 62 kg. Do you agree with the claim that medicine B increases the weight significantly? It is given that the value of t at 10% level of significance for 10 degree of freedom is 1.81.

   [*G.B.T.U. (B. Pharm.) 2010*]
4. Two independent samples of sizes 7 and 9 have the following values:

Sample A :	10	12	10	13	14	11	10		
Sample B :	10	13	15	12	10	14	11	12	11

   Test whether the difference between the mean is significant.
5. The average number of articles produced by two machines per day are 200 and 250 with standard deviation 20 and 25 respectively on the basis of records of 25 days production. Can you regard both the machines equally efficient at 5% level of significance?

9.39. SNEDECOR'S VARIANCE RATIO TEST OR F-TEST

In testing the significance of the difference of two means of two samples, we assumed that the two samples came from the same population or population with equal variance. The object of the F-test is to discover whether two independent estimates of population variance differ significantly or whether the two samples may be regarded as drawn from the normal populations having the same variance. Hence before applying the t-test for the significance of the difference of two means, we have to test for the equality of population variance by using F-test.

Let n_1 and n_2 be the sizes of two samples with variance s_1^2 and s_2^2. The estimate of the population variance based on these samples are $s_1^2 = \frac{n_1 s_1^2}{n_1 - 1}$ and $s_2^2 = \frac{n_2 s_2^2}{n_2 - 1}$. The degrees of freedom of these estimates are $\nu_1 = n_1 - 1$, $\nu_2 = n_2 - 1$.

To test whether these estimates s_1^2 and s_2^2 are significantly different or if the samples may be regarded as drawn from the same population or from two populations with same variance σ^2, we set-up the null hypothesis $H_0 : \sigma_1^2 = \sigma_2^2 = \sigma^2$.

i.e., the independent estimates of the common population do not differ significantly.

To carry out the test of significance of the difference of the variances we calculate the test statistic $F = \frac{s_1^2}{s_2^2}$, the Numerator is greater than the Denominator. *i.e.,* $s_1^2 > s_2^2$.

Conclusion: If the calculated value of F exceeds $F_{0.05}$ for $(n_1 - 1)$, $(n_2 - 1)$ degrees of freedom given in table we conclude that the ratio is significant at 5% level.

i.e., we conclude that the sample could have come from two normal population with same variance.

The assumptions on which F-test is based are:

1. *The populations for each sample must be normally distributed.*
2. *The samples must be random and independent.*
3. *The ratio of* σ_1^2 to σ_2^2 *should be equal to 1 or greater than 1. That is why we take the larger variance in the Numerator of the ratio.*

Applications: *F-test is used to test*

(i) whether two independent samples have been drawn from the normal populations with the same variance σ^2.

(ii) Whether the two independent estimates of the population variance are homogeneous or not.

EXAMPLES

Example 1. *Two random samples drawn from 2 normal populations are as follows:*

A	*17*	*27*	*18*	*25*	*27*	*29*	*13*	*17*
B	*16*	*16*	*20*	*27*	*26*	*25*	*21*	

Test whether the samples are drawn from the same normal population.

Sol. To test if two independent samples have been drawn from the same population we have to test (*i*) equality of the means by applying the *t*-test and (*ii*) equality of population variance by applying F-test.

Since the *t*-test assumes that the sample variances are equal, we shall first apply the F-test.

F-test: 1. **Null hypothesis H_0:** $\sigma_1^2 = \sigma_2^2$ *i.e.*, the population variance do not differ significantly.

Alternative hypothesis H_1: $\sigma_1^2 \neq \sigma_2^2$

Test statistic: $F = \frac{s_1^2}{s_2^2}$, (if $s_1^2 > s_2^2$)

Computations for s_1^2 and s_2^2

X_1	$X_1 - \bar{X}_1$	$(X_1 - \bar{X}_1)^2$	X_2	$X_2 - \bar{X}_2$	$(X_2 - \bar{X}_2)^2$
17	– 4.625	21.39	16	– 2.714	7.365
27	5.735	28.89	16	– 2.714	7.365
18	– 3.625	13.14	20	1.286	1.653
25	3.375	11.39	27	8.286	68.657
27	5.735	28.89	26	7.286	53.085
29	7.735	54.39	25	6.286	39.513
13	– 8.625	74.39	21	2.286	5.226
17	– 4.625	21.39			

$$\bar{X}_1 = 21.625;\ n_1 = 8;\ \Sigma(\bar{X}_1 - \bar{X}_1)^2 = 253.87$$

$$\bar{X}_2 = 18.714;\ n_2 = 7;\ \Sigma(X_2 - \bar{X}_2)^2 = 182.859$$

$$s_1^2 = \frac{\Sigma(X_1 - \bar{X}_1)^2}{n_1 - 1} = \frac{253.87}{7} = 36.267;\ s_2^2 = \frac{\Sigma(X_2 - \bar{X}_2)^2}{n_2 - 1} = \frac{182.859}{6} = 30.47$$

$$F = \frac{s_1^2}{s_2^2} = \frac{36.267}{30.47} = 1.190.$$

Conclusion: The table value of F for $v_1 = 7$ and $v_2 = 6$ degrees of freedom at 5% level is 4.21. The calculated value of F is less than the tabulated value of F. $\therefore$ H_0 is accepted. Hence we conclude that the variability in two populations is same.

t-test: Null hypothesis H_0: $\mu_1 = \mu_2$ *i.e.,* the population means are equal.

Alternative hypothesis H_1: $\mu_1 \neq \mu_2$

Test of statistic

$$s^2 = \frac{\Sigma(X_1 - \bar{X}_1)^2 + \Sigma(X_2 - \bar{X}_2)^2}{n_1 + n_2 - 2} = \frac{253.87 + 182.859}{8 + 7 - 2} = 33.594 \quad \therefore \quad s = 5.796$$

$$t = \frac{\bar{X}_1 - \bar{X}_2}{s\sqrt{\frac{1}{n_1} + \frac{1}{n_2}}} = \frac{21.625 - 18.714}{5.796\sqrt{\frac{1}{8} + \frac{1}{7}}} = 0.9704 \sim t(n_1 + n_2 - 2) \text{ d.f.}$$

Conclusion: The tabulated value of t at 5% level of significance for 13 d.f. is 2.16.

The calculated value of t is less than the tabulated value. H_0 is accepted *i.e.*, there is no significant difference between the population mean. *i.e.*, $\mu_1 = \mu_2$. $\therefore$ We conclude that the two samples have been drawn from the same normal population.

Example 2. *Two independent sample of sizes 7 and 6 had the following values:*

Sample A	*28*	*30*	*32*	*33*	*31*	*29*	*34*
Sample B	*29*	*30*	*30*	*24*	*27*	*28*	

Examine whether the samples have been drawn from normal populations having the same variance.

Sol. H_0: The variance are equal. *i.e.*, $\sigma_1^2 = \sigma_2^2$

i.e., the samples have been drawn from normal populations with same variance.

$$H_1: \sigma_1^2 \neq \sigma_2^2$$

Under null hypothesis, the test statistic $F = \frac{s_1^2}{s_2^2} \; (s_1^2 > s_2^2)$

Computations for s_1^2 and s_2^2

X_1	$X_1 - \bar{X}_1$	$(X_1 - \bar{X}_1)^2$	X_2	$X_2 - \bar{X}_2$	$(X_2 - \bar{X}_2)^2$
28	– 3	9	29	1	1
30	– 1	1	30	2	4
32	1	1	30	2	4
33	2	4	24	– 4	16
31	0	0	27	– 1	1
29	– 2	4	28	0	0
34	3	9			
		28			26

$$\bar{X}_1 = 31, \quad n_1 = 7; \quad \Sigma(X_1 - \bar{X}_1)^2 = 28$$

$$\bar{X}_2 = 28, \quad n_2 = 6; \quad \Sigma(X_2 - \bar{X}_2)^2 = 26$$

$$s_1^2 = \frac{\Sigma(X_1 - \bar{X}_1)^2}{n_1 - 1} = \frac{28}{6} = 4.666; \quad s_2^2 = \frac{\Sigma(X_2 - \bar{X}_2)^2}{n_2 - 1} = \frac{26}{5} = 5.2$$

$$F = \frac{s_2^2}{s_1^2} = \frac{5.2}{4.666} = 1.1158. \qquad (\because \; s_2^2 > s_1^2)$$

Conclusion: The tabulated value of F at $\upsilon_1 = 6 - 1$ and $\upsilon_2 = 7 - 1$ d.f. for 5% level of significance is 4.39. Since the tabulated value of F is less than the calculated value, H_0 is accepted *i.e.*, there is no significant difference between the variance. *i.e.*, the samples have been drawn from the normal population with same variance.

Example 3. *The two random samples reveal the following data:*

Sample no.	*Size*	*Mean*	*Variance*
I	*16*	*440*	*40*
II	*25*	*460*	*42*

Test whether the samples come from the same normal population.

Sol. A normal population has two parameters namely the mean μ and the variance σ^2. To test whether the two independent samples have been drawn from the same normal population, we have to test

(*i*) the equality of means (*ii*) the equality of variance.

Since the *t*-test assumes that the sample variance are equal, we first apply F-test.

F-test: Null hypothesis: $\sigma_1^2 = \sigma_2^2$

The population variance do not differ significantly.

Alternative hypothesis: $\sigma_1^2 \neq \sigma_2^2$

Under the null hypothesis the test statistic is given by $F = \dfrac{s_1^2}{s_2^2}$, $(s_1^2 > s_2^2)$

Given: $n_1 = 16, n_2 = 25; s_1^2 = 40, s_2^2 = 42$

$$\therefore \qquad F = \frac{s_1^2}{s_2^2} = \frac{\dfrac{n_1 s_1^2}{n_1 - 1}}{\dfrac{n_2 s_2^2}{n_2 - 1}} = \frac{16 \times 40}{15} \times \frac{24}{25 \times 42} = 0.9752.$$

Conclusion: The calculated value of F is 0.9752. The tabulated value of F at 16 – 1, 25 – 1 d.f. for 5% level of significance is 2.11.

Since the calculated value is less than that of the tabulated value, H_0 is accepted. *i.e.,* the population variance are equal.

t-test: Null hypothesis $\mathbf{H_0}$ **:** $\mu_1 = \mu_2$ *i.e.,* the population means are equal.

Alternative hypothesis $\mathbf{H_1}$ **:** $\mu_1 \neq \mu_2$

Given: $n_1 = 16, n_2 = 25, \overline{X}_1 = 440, \overline{X}_2 = 460$

$$s^2 = \frac{n_1 s_1^2 + n_2 s_2^2}{n_1 + n_2 - 2} = \frac{16 \times 40 + 25 \times 42}{16 + 25 - 2} = 43.333 \quad \therefore \quad s = 6.582$$

$$t = \frac{\overline{X}_1 - \overline{X}_2}{s\sqrt{\dfrac{1}{n_1} + \dfrac{1}{n_2}}} = \frac{440 - 460}{6.582\sqrt{\dfrac{1}{16} + \dfrac{1}{25}}} = -9.490 \text{ for } (n_1 + n_2 - 2) \text{ d.f.}$$

Conclusion: The calculated value of $|\ t\ |$ is 9.490. The tabulated value of t at 39 d.f. for 5% level of significance is 1.96.

Since the calculated value is greater than the tabulated value, H_0 is rejected. *i.e.,* there is significant difference between means. *i.e.,* $\mu_1 \neq \mu_2$.

Since there is significant difference between means, and no significant difference between variance, we conclude that the samples do not come from the same normal population.

ASSIGNMENT

1. From the following two sample values, find out whether they have come from the same population:

Sample 1	17	27	18	25	27	29	27	23	17
Sample 2	16	16	20	16	20	17	15	21	

2. The daily wages in Rupees of skilled workers in two cities are as follows:

	Size of sample of workers	*S.D. of wages in the sample*
City A	16	25
City B	13	32

3. The standard deviation calculated from two random samples of sizes 9 and 13 are 2.1 and 1.8 respectively. Can the samples be regarded as drawn from normal populations with the same standard deviation?
4. Two independent samples of size 8 and 9 had the following values of the variables:

Sample I	20	30	23	25	21	22	23	24	
Sample II	30	31	32	34	35	29	28	27	26

Do the estimates of the population variance differ significantly?

Answers

1. rejected **2.** accepted **3.** accepted **4.** accepted.

9.40. CHI-SQUARE (χ^2) TEST [*G.B.T.U. 2010 ; G.B.T.U. MCA (SUM) 2010*]

When a coin is tossed 200 times, the theoretical considerations lead us to expect 100 heads and 100 tails. But in practice, these results are rarely achieved. The quantity χ^2 (a Greek letter, pronounced as chi-square) describes the magnitude of discrepancy between theory and observation. If $\chi^2 = 0$, the observed and expected frequencies completely coincide. The greater the discrepancy between the observed and expected frequencies, the greater is the value of χ^2. Thus χ^2 **affords a measure of the correspondence between theory and observation.**

If O_i $(i = 1, 2, ..., n)$ is a set of observed (experimental) frequencies and E_i $(i = 1, 2, ..., n)$ is the corresponding set of expected (theoretical or hypothetical) frequencies, then, χ^2 **is defined as**

$$\chi^2 = \sum_{i=1}^{n} \left[\frac{(O_i - E_i)^2}{E_i} \right]$$

where $\Sigma O_i = \Sigma E_i = N$ (total frequency) and degrees of freedom (d.f.) $= (n - 1)$.

Note. (*i*) If $\chi^2 = 0$, the observed and theoretical frequencies agree exactly.

(*ii*) If $\chi^2 > 0$ they do not agree exactly.

9.41. DEGREES OF FREEDOM

While comparing the calculated value of χ^2 with the tabular value, we have to determine the degrees of freedom.

If we have to choose any four numbers whose sum is 50, we can exercise our independent choice for any three numbers only, the fourth being 50 minus the total of the three numbers selected. Thus, though we were to choose any four numbers, our choice was reduced to three because of one condition imposed. There was only one restraint on our freedom and our degrees of freedom were $4 - 1 = 3$. If two restrictions are imposed, our freedom to choose will be further curtailed and degrees of freedom will be $4 - 2 = 2$.

In general, the number of degrees of freedom is the total number of observations less the number of independent constraints imposed on the observations. Degrees of freedom (d.f.) are usually denoted by ν.

Thus, $\nu = n - k$, where k is the number of independent constraints in a set of data of n observations.

Note. (*i*) For a $p \times q$ contingency table (p columns and q rows), $\nu = (p - 1)(q - 1)$

(*ii*) In the case of a contingency table, the expected frequency of any class

$$= \frac{\text{Total of rows in which it occurs} \times \text{Total of columns in which it occurs}}{\text{Total number of observations}}$$

9.42. APPLICATIONS OF CHI-SQUARE TEST

χ^2 test is one of the simplest and the most general test known. It is applicable to a very large number of problems in practice which can be summed up under the following heads:

(*i*) as a test of goodness of fit.

(*ii*) as a test of independence of attributes.

(*iii*) as a test of homogeneity of independent estimates of the population variance.

(*iv*) as a test of the hypothetical value of the population variance σ^2.

(*v*) as a list to the homogeneity of independent estimates of the population correlation coefficient.

9.43. CONDITIONS FOR APPLYING χ^2 TEST

χ^2 test is an approximate test for large values of n. For the validity of chi-square test of goodness of fit between theory and experiment, the following conditions must be satisfied.

(*a*) The sample observations should be independent.

(*b*) The constraints on the cell frequencies, if any, should be linear *e.g.*, $\Sigma n_i = \Sigma \lambda_i$ or $\Sigma O_i = \Sigma E_i$.

(*c*) N, the total number of frequencies should be reasonably large. It is difficult to say what constitutes largeness, but as an arbitrary figure, we may say that **N should be at least 50,** however, few the cells.

(*d*) No theoretical cell-frequency should be small. Here again, it is difficult to say what constitutes smallness, but 5 should be regarded as the very minimum and **10 is better.** If small theoretical frequencies occur (*i.e.*, < 10), the difficulty is overcome by grouping two or more classes together before calculating (O – E). **It is important to remember that the number of degrees of freedom is determined with the number of classes after regrouping.**

Note 1. If any one of the theoretical frequency is less than 5, then we apply a corrected given by F Yates, which is usually known as 'Yates correction for continuity', we add 0.5 to the cell frequency which is less than 5 and adjust the remaining cell frequency suitably so that the marginal total is not changed.

Note 2. It may be noted that the χ^2 test depends only on the set of observed and expected frequencies and on degrees of freedom (d.f.). It does not make any assumption regarding the parent population from which the observations are taken. Since χ^2 does not involve any population parameters, it is termed as a statistic and the test is known as Non-parametric test or Distribution-free test.

9.44. THE χ^2 DISTRIBUTION

For large sample sizes, the sampling distribution of χ^2 can be closely approximated by a continuous curve known as the chi-square distribution. The probability function of χ^2 distribution is given by

$$f(\chi^2) = c(\chi^2)^{(\nu/2-1)}\, e^{-x^2/2}$$

where $e = 2.71828$, ν = number of degrees of freedom; c = a constant depending only on ν.

Symbolically, the degrees of freedom are denoted by the symbol ν or by d.f. and are obtained by the rule $\nu = n - k$, where k refers to the number of independent constraints.

In general, when we fit a binomial distribution the number of degrees of freedom is one less than the number of classes; when we fit a Poisson distribution the degrees of freedom are 2 less than the number of classes, because we use the total frequency and the arithmetic mean to get the parameter of the Poisson distribution. When we fit a normal curve the number of degrees of freedom are 3 less than the number of classes, because in this fitting we use the total frequency, mean and standard deviation.

If the data is given in a series of "n" numbers then degrees of freedom = $n - 1$.

In the case of Binomial distribution d.f. = $n - 1$

In the case of Poisson distribution d.f. = $n - 2$

In the case of Normal distribution d.f. = $n - 3$.

9.45. χ^2 TEST AS A TEST OF GOODNESS OF FIT

χ^2 test enables us to ascertain how well the theoretical distributions such as Binomial, Poisson or Normal etc., fit empirical distributions, *i.e.*, distributions obtained from sample data. If the **calculated value of χ^2 is less than the tabular value** at a specified level (generally 5%) of significance, the **fit is considered to be good** *i.e.*, the divergence between actual and expected frequencies is attributed to fluctuations of simple sampling. If the calculated value of χ^2 is greater than the tabular value, the fit is considered to be poor.

EXAMPLES

Example 1. *In experiments on pea breeding, the following frequencies of seeds were obtained:*

Round and yellow	*Wrinkled and yellow*	*Round and green*	*Wrinkled and green*	*Total*
315	*101*	*108*	*32*	*556*

Theory predicts that the frequencies should be in proportions 9 : 3 : 3 : 1. Examine the correspondence between theory and experiment.

Sol. Null hypothesis

H_0 : The experimental result support the theory *i.e.,* there is no significant difference between the observed and theoretical frequency.

Under H_0, The theoretical (expected) frequencies can be calculated as follows:

$$E_1 = \frac{556 \times 9}{16} = 312.75$$

$$E_2 = \frac{556 \times 3}{16} = 104.25$$

$$E_3 = \frac{556 \times 3}{16} = 104.25$$

$$E_4 = \frac{556 \times 1}{16} = 34.75$$

To calculate the value of χ^2:

Observed frequency O_i	315	101	108	32
Expected Frequency E_i	312.75	104.25	104.25	34.75
$\frac{(O_i - E_i)^2}{E_i}$	0.016187	0.101319	0.134892	0.217626

$$\chi^2 = \sum \left[\frac{(O_i - E_i)^2}{E_i}\right] = 0.470024$$

Tabular value of χ^2 at 5% level of significance for $n - 1 = 3$ *d.f.* is 7.815 *i.e.,* $\chi^2_{0.05} = 7.815$.

Conclusion: Since the calculated value of χ^2 is less than that of the tabulated value, hence H_0 is accepted. Therefore, the experimental results support the theory.

Example 2. *The following table gives the number of accidents that took place in an industry during various days of the week. Test if accidents are uniformly distributed over the week.*

Day	*Mon*	*Tue*	*Wed*	*Thu*	*Fri*	*Sat*
No. of accidents	*14*	*18*	*12*	*11*	*15*	*14*

Sol. Null hypothesis H_0 : The accidents are uniformly distributed over the week.

Under this H_0, the expected frequencies of the accidents on each of these days $= \frac{84}{6} = 14$

Observed frequency O_i	14	18	12	11	15	14
Expected frequency E_i	14	14	14	14	14	14
$(O_i - E_i)^2$	0	16	4	9	1	0

$$\chi^2 = \sum \left[\frac{(O_i - E_i)^2}{E_i} \right] = \frac{\Sigma(O_i - E_i)^2}{E_i} = \frac{30}{14} = 2.1428.$$

Tabular value of χ^2 at 5% level for (6 – 1 = 5 d.f.) is 11.09.

Conclusion: Since the calculated value of χ^2 is less than the tabulated value, H_0 is accepted *i.e.*, the accidents are uniformly distributed over the week.

Example 3. *A die is thrown 276 times and the results of these throws are given below:*

No. appeared on the die	*1*	*2*	*3*	*4*	*5*	*6*
Frequency	*40*	*32*	*29*	*59*	*57*	*59*

Test whether the die is biased or not.

Sol. Null hypothesis H_0: Die is unbiased.

Under this H_0, the expected frequencies for each digit is $\frac{276}{6} = 46$.

To find the value of χ^2

O_i	40	32	29	59	57	59
E_i	46	46	46	46	46	46
$(O_i - E_i)^2$	36	196	289	169	121	169

$$\chi^2 = \sum \left[\frac{(O_i - E_i)^2}{E_i} \right] = \frac{\Sigma(O_i - E_i)^2}{E_i} = \frac{980}{46} = 21.30.$$

Tabulated value of χ^2 at 5% level of significance for (6 – 1 = 5) d.f. is 11.09.

Conclusion: Since the calculated value of $\chi^2 = 21.30 > 11.07$ the tabulated value, H_0 is rejected. *i.e.*, die is not unbiased or die is biased.

Example 4. *Records taken of the number of male and female births in 800 families having four children are as follows:* [U.P.T.U. (MCA) 2009]

No. of male births	*0*	*1*	*2*	*3*	*4*
No. of female births	*4*	*3*	*2*	*1*	*0*
No. of families	*32*	*178*	*290*	*236*	*64*

Test whether the data are consistent with the hypothesis that the Binomial law holds and the chance of male birth is equal to that of female birth, namely $p = q = 1/2$.

Sol. Null hypothesis H_0: The data are consistent with the hypothesis of equal probability for male and female births. *i.e.*, $p = q = 1/2$.

We use Binomial distribution to calculate theoretical frequency given by:

$$N(r) = N \times P(X = r) = N \times {}^nC_r \, p^r q^{n-r}$$

where N is the total frequency, $N(r)$ is the number of families with r male children.

p and q are probabilities of male and female births respectively, n is the number of children.

$$N(0) = 800 \times {}^4C_0 \left(\frac{1}{2}\right)^4 = 50,$$

$N(1) = 200$, $N(2) = 300$, $N(3) = 200$ and $N(4) = 50$

Observed frequency O_i	32	178	290	236	64
Expected frequency E_i	50	200	300	200	50
$(O_i - E_i)^2$	324	484	100	1296	196
$\dfrac{(O_i - E_i)^2}{E_i}$	6.48	2.42	0.333	6.48	3.92

$$\chi^2 = \sum \left[\frac{(O_i - E_i)^2}{E_i}\right] = 19.633.$$

Tabular value of χ^2 at 5% level of significance for 5 – 1 = 4 d.f. is 9.49.

Conclusion: Since the calculated value of χ^2 is greater than the tabulated value, H_0 is rejected. *i.e.,* the data are not consistent with the hypothesis that the Binomial law holds and that the chance of a male birth is not equal to that of a female birth.

Example 5. *The theory predicts the proportion of beans in the four groups, G_1, G_2, G_3, G_4 should be in the ratio 9 : 3 : 3 : 1. In an experiment with 1600 beans the numbers in the four groups were 882, 313, 287 and 118. Does the experimental result support the theory?*

Sol. Null hypothesis H_0 : The experimental result support the theory. *i.e.,* there is no significant difference between the observed and theoretical frequency.

Under H_0, the theoretical frequency can be calculated as follows:

$$E(G_1) = \frac{1600 \times 9}{16} = 900; \quad E(G_2) = \frac{1600 \times 3}{16} = 300;$$

$$E(G_3) = \frac{1600 \times 3}{16} = 300; \quad E(G_4) = \frac{1600 \times 1}{16} = 100$$

To calculate the value of χ^2.

Observed frequency O_i	882	313	287	118
Expected frequency E_i	900	300	300	100
$\dfrac{(O_i - E_i)^2}{E_i}$	0.36	0.5633	0.5633	3.24

$$\chi^2 = \sum \left[\frac{(O_i - E_i)^2}{E_i}\right] = 4.7266.$$

Tablular value of χ^2 at 5% level of significance for 3 d.f. is 7.815.

Conclusion. Since the calculated value of χ^2 is less than that of the tabulated value, hence H_0 is accepted. *i.e.,* the experimental results support the theory.

Example 6. *The following table shows the distribution of digits in numbers chosen at random from a telephone directory:*

Digits	*0*	*1*	*2*	*3*	*4*	*5*	*6*	*7*	*8*	*9*
Frequency	*1026*	*1107*	*997*	*966*	*1075*	*933*	*1107*	*972*	*964*	*853*

Test whether the digits may be taken to occur equally frequently in the directory.

[G.B.T.U. (MCA) 2011]

Sol. Null hypothesis H_0 : The digits taken in the directory occur equally frequently *i.e.*, there is no significant difference between the observed and expected frequency.

Under H_0, the expected frequency $= \dfrac{10000}{10} = 1000$

Calculation of χ^2

O_i	1026	1107	997	966	1075	933	1107	972	964	853
E_i	1000	1000	1000	1000	1000	1000	1000	1000	1000	1000
$(O_i - E_i)^2$	676	11449	9	1156	5625	4489	11449	784	1296	21609

$$\chi^2 = \sum \left[\frac{(O_i - E_i)^2}{E_i}\right] = \frac{58542}{1000} = 58.542$$

The tabulated value of χ^2 at 5% level of significance for 9 d.f. is 16.919.

Conclusion: Since $\chi^2_{\text{calculated}} > \chi^2_{\text{tabulated}}$, H_0 is rejected *i.e.*, there is significant difference between the observed and theoretical frequencies. Therefore, the digits taken in the directory donot occur equally frequently.

Example 7. *When the first proof of 392 pages of a book of 1200 pages were read, the distribution of printing mistakes were found to be as follows:*

No. of mistakes in a page (x) :	0	1	2	3	4	5	6
No. of pages (f) :	275	72	30	7	5	2	1

Fit a poisson distribution to the above data and test the goodness of fit.

Sol. Null Hypothesis H_0: Poisson distribution is a good fit to the data.

$$\text{Mean } (\lambda) = \frac{\sum fx}{\sum f} = \frac{189}{392} = 0.4821$$

The frequency of x mistakes per page is given by the poisson law as follows:

$$N(x) = N \cdot P(x)$$

$$= 392\left[\frac{e^{-0.4821}(0.4821)^x}{x!}\right] = \frac{242.05(0.4821)^x}{x!} \;;\; 0 \le x \le 6$$

Under H_0, expected frequencies are,

N(0) = 242.05, N(1) = 116.69, N(2) = 28.13, N(3) = 4.52

N(4) = 0.54, N(5) = 0.052, N(6) = 0.0042

The χ^2-table is as follows:

Mistakes per page (x)	*Observed frequency (O_i)*	*Expected frequency (E_i) (correct to one place of decimal)*	$(O_i - E_i)^2$	$\frac{(O_i - E_i)^2}{E_i}$
0	275	242.1	1082.41	4.471
1	72	116.7	1998.09	17.121
2	30	28.1	3.61	0.128
3	7 }	4.5 }		
4	5 } 15	0.5 } 5.1		
5	2 }	0.1 }	98.01	19.217
6	1 }	0 }		
Total	392	392		40.937

$$\chi^2_{\text{cal.}} = \sum \left[\frac{(O_i - E_i)^2}{E_i}\right] = 40.937$$

$$\text{d.f.} = 7 - 1 - 1 - 3 = 2$$

One d.f. is lost because of linear constraint $\Sigma O_i = \Sigma E_i$. One d.f. is lost because the parameter λ has been estimated from the given data and is then used for computing the expected frequencies. 3 d.f. are lost because of grouping the last four expected cell frequencies which were less than 5.

Tabulated value of χ^2 for 2 d.f. at 5% level of significance is 5.991.

Conclusion: Since $\chi^2_{\text{cal.}} > \chi^2_{\text{tab.}}$, the null hypothesis is rejected at 5% level of significance. Hence, we conclude that poisson distribution is not a good fit to the given data.

Example 8. *Fit a Poisson distribution to the following data and best the goodness of fit:*

x :	0	1	2	3	4
f :	109	65	22	3	1

Sol. Null hypothesis H_0 : Poisson distribution is a good fit to the data.

$$\text{Mean } (\lambda) = \frac{\Sigma fx}{\Sigma f} = \frac{122}{200} = 0.61$$

$$N(x) = N \cdot P(x)$$

$$= (200) \frac{e^{-0.61}(0.61)^x}{x!} = \frac{(108.67)(0.61)^x}{x!}$$

Under H_0, expected frequencies are

N(0) = 108.67 ≈ 109, N(1) = 66.29 ≈ 66, N(2) = 20.22 ≈ 20

N(3) = 4.11 ≈ 4, N(4) = 0.63 ≈ 1

The χ^2-table is as follows :

x	O_i	E_i	$(O_i - E_i)^2$	$\frac{(O_i - E_i)^2}{E_i}$
0	109	109	0	0
1	65	66	1	0.01515
2	22	20	4	0.2
3	3 } 4	4 } 5	1	0.2
4	1	1		
Total	200	200		0.41515

$$\chi^2_{\text{cal.}} = \sum \left[\frac{(O_i - E_i)^2}{E_i}\right] = 0.41515$$

$$\text{d.f.} = 5 - 1 - 1 - 1 = 2$$

Tabulated value of χ^2 for 2 d.f. at 5% level of significance is 5.991.

Conclusion: Since $\chi^2_{\text{cal.}} < \chi^2_{\text{tab.}}$, the null hypothesis H_0 is accepted at 5% level of significance. Hence we conclude that Poisson distribution is a good fit to the given data.

ASSIGNMENT

1. A sample analysis of examination results of 500 students, it was found that 220 students have failed, 170 have secured a third class, 90 have secured a second class and the rest, a first class. Do these figures support the general belief that above categories are in the ratio 4 : 3 : 2 : 1 respectively? (The tabular value of χ^2 for d.f. 3 at 5% level of significance is 7.81)

[U.P.T.U. (MBA) 2009]

2. What is χ^2–test? *[G.B.T.U. 2010 ; G.B.T.U. MCA (C.O.) 2010]*

A die is thrown 90 times with the following results:

Face :	1	2	3	4	5	6	Total
Frequency :	10	12	16	14	18	20	90

Use χ^2-test to test whether these data are consistent with the hypothesis that die is unbiased.

Given $\chi^2_{0.05} = 11.07$ for 5 degrees of freedom. *[U.P.T.U. (MCA) 2007]*

3. A survey of 320 families with 5 children shows the following distribution:

No. of boys & girls :	5 boys & 0 girl	4 boys & 1 girl	3 boys & 2 girls	2 boys & 3 girls	1 boy & 4 girls	0 boy & 5 girls	Total
No. of families :	18	56	110	88	40	8	320

Given that values of χ^2 for 5 degrees of freedom are 11.1 and 15.1 at 0.05 and 0.01 significance level respectively, test the hypothesis that male and female births are equally probable.

(G.B.T.U. 2010)

4. A chemical extraction plant processes sea water to collect sodium chloride and magnesium. It is known that sea water contains sodium chloride, magnesium and other elements in the ratio 62 : 4 : 34. A sample of 200 tonnes of sea water has resulted in 130 tonnes of sodium chloride and

6 tonnes of magnesium. Are these data consistent with the known composition of sea water at 5% level of significance? (Given that the tabular value of χ^2 is 5.991 for 2 degree of freedom).

[*U.P.T.U. MCA (C.O.) 2008*]

5. The demand for a particular spare part in a factory was found to vary from day-to-day. In a sample study, the following information was obtained :

Days :	Mon	Tue	Wed	Thurs	Fri	Sat
No. of parts demanded :	1124	1125	1110	1120	1126	1115

Test the hypothesis that the number of parts demanded does not depend on the day of the week.

[**Given.** The values of chi-square significance at 5, 6, 7 d.f. are respectively 11.07, 12.59, 14.07 at 5% level of significance] (*G.B.T.U. 2011*)

6. The sales in a supermarket during a week are given below. Test the hypothesis that the sales donot depend on the day of the week using a significant level of 0.05.

Days	*Mon*	*Tue*	*Wed*	*Thurs*	*Fri*	*Sat*
Sales (in 1000 ₹)	65	54	60	56	71	84

7. 4 coins were tossed at a time and this operation is repeated 160 times. It is found that 4 heads occur 6 times, 3 heads occur 43 times, 2 heads occur 69 times, one head occur 34 times. Discuss whether the coin may be regarded as unbiased?

8. 200 digits are chosen at random from a set of tables. The frequencies of the digits were:

Digits :	0	1	2	3	4	5	6	7	8	9
Frequency :	18	19	23	21	16	25	22	20	21	15

Use χ^2-test to assess the correctness of the hypothesis that the digits were distributed in equal numbers in the table, given that the value of χ^2 are respectively 16.9, 18.3 and 19.7 for 9, 10 and 11 degrees of freedom at 5% level of significance.

9. A genetical law says that children having one parent of blood group M and the other parent of blood group N will always be one of the three blood groups M, MN, N and that the average no. of children in these groups will be in the ratio 1 : 2 : 1. The report on an experiment states as follows:

"Of 162 children having one M parent and one N parent, 28.4% were found to be of group M, 42% of group MN and the rest of the group N." Do the data in the report conform to the expected genetic ratio 1 : 2 : 1?

10. Every clinical thermometer is classified into one of the four categories A, B, C and D on the basis of inspection and test. From past experience, it is knwon that thermometers produced by a certain manufacturer are distributed among the four categories in the following proportions:

Category :	A	B	C	D
Proportion :	0.87	0.09	0.03	0.01

A new lot of 1336 thermometers is submitted by the manufacturer for inspection and test and the following distribution into four categories results:

Category :	A	B	C	D
No. of thermometers reported :	1188	91	47	10

Does this new lot of thermometers differ from the previous experience with regards to proportion of thermometers in each category?

11. Test for goodness of fit of a poisson distribution at 5% level of significance to the following frequency distribution :

(*i*)

x	0	1	2	3	4	5	6	7	8
f	52	151	130	102	45	12	5	1	2

[**Hint.** Group the last three frequencies]

(*ii*)

x	0	1	2	3	4	5	6	7	8	9	10	11	12	13
f	3	15	47	76	68	74	46	39	15	9	5	2	0	1

[**Hint.** Group the first two and last four frequencies]

(*iii*)

x	0	1	2	3	4	5
f	275	138	75	7	4	1

[**Hint.** Club the last three frequencies]

(*iv*)

x	0	1	2	3	4
f	419	352	154	56	19

12. (*i*) Fit a binomial distribution to the data and test for goodness of fit at 5% level of significance.

x	0	1	2	3	4	5
y	38	144	342	287	164	25

(*ii*) A random number table of 250 digits showed the following distribution of digits 0, 1, 2, ..., 9.

Digit	0	1	2	3	4	5	6	7	8	9
Observed Frequency	17	31	29	18	14	20	35	30	20	36
Expected Frequency	25	25	25	25	25	25	25	25	25	25

Does the observed distribution differ significantly from expected distributions using a significance level of 0.01? Given that $\chi^2_{0.99}$ for 9 degrees of freedom is 21.7 [*G.B.T.U. MCA (SUM) 2010*]

Answers

1. No **2.** Yes

3. H_0 accepted at 1% level of significance and rejected at 5% level of significance

4. $\chi^2 = 1.025$, Yes **5.** H_0 accepted at 5% level **6.** H_0 accepted

7. Coin is unbiased **8.** H_0 accepted at 5% level **9.** H_0 accepted at 5% level

10. H_0 rejected at 5% level

11. (*i*) H_0 accepted at 5% level, (*ii*) H_0 accepted at 5% level, (*iii*) H_0 rejected at 5% level, not a good fit. (*iv*) H_0 accepted at 5% level

12. (*i*) H_0 accepted at 5% level, provides a good fit. (*ii*) Yes.

9.46. χ^2 TEST AS A TEST OF INDEPENDENCE

With the help of χ^2 test, we can find whether or not, two attributes are associated. We take the null hypothesis that there is no association between the attributes under study, *i.e.*, **we assume that the two attributes are independent. If the calculated value of χ^2 is less than the table value** at a specified level (generally 5%) of significance, the hypothesis holds good, *i.e.*, **the attributes are independent** and do not bear any association. On the other hand, if the calculated value of χ^2 is greater than the table value at a specified level of significance, we say that the results of the experiment do not support the hypothesis. In other words, the attributes are associated. Thus a very useful application of χ^2 test is to investigate the relationship between trials or attributes which can be classified into two or more categories.

The sample data set out into two-way table, called **contingency table.**

Let us consider two attributes A and B divided into r classes $A_1, A_2, A_3, \ldots\ldots, A_r$ and B divided into s classes $B_1, B_2, B_3, \ldots\ldots, B_s$. If (A_i), (B_j) represents the number of persons possessing the attributes A_i, B_j respectively, ($i = 1, 2, \ldots\ldots, r, j = 1, 2, \ldots\ldots, s$) and $(A_i B_j)$ represent the number of persons possessing attributes A_i and B_j. Also we have $\sum_{i=1}^{r} A_i = \sum_{j=1}^{s} B_j = N$, where N is the total frequency. The contingency table for $r \times s$ is given as follows :

A / *B*	A_1	A_2	A_3	$\ldots A_r$	*Total*
B_1	(A_1B_1)	(A_2B_1)	(A_3B_1)	$\ldots\ldots(A_rB_1)$	B_1
B_2	(A_1B_2)	(A_2B_2)	(A_3B_2)	$\ldots\ldots(A_rB_2)$	B_2
B_3	(A_1B_3)	(A_2B_3)	(A_3B_3)	$\ldots\ldots(A_rB_3)$	B_3
......	......	......	......	......	......
......	......	......	......	......	......
B_s	(A_1B_s)	(A_2B_s)	(A_3B_s)	$\ldots\ldots(A_rB_s)$	(B_s)
Total	(A_1)	(A_2)	(A_3)	$\ldots\ldots(A_r)$	N

H_0 : Both the attributes are independent. *i.e.*, A and B are independent under the null hypothesis, we calculate the expected frequency as follows:

$$P(A_i) = \text{Probability that a person possesses the attribute } A_i = \frac{(A_i)}{N} \quad i = 1, 2, \ldots\ldots, r$$

$$P(B_j) = \text{Probability that a person possesses the attribute } B_j = \frac{(B_j)}{N}$$

$$P(A_iB_j) = \text{Probability that a person possesses both attributes } A_i \text{ and } B_j = \frac{(A_iB_j)}{N}$$

If $(A_iB_j)_0$ is the expected number of persons possessing both the attributes A_i and B_j

$$(A_iB_j)_0 = NP(A_iB_j) = NP(A_i)(B_j)$$

$$= N\frac{(A_i)}{N}\frac{(B_j)}{N} = \frac{(A_i)(B_j)}{N} \qquad (\because \text{ A and B are independent})$$

Hence
$$\chi^2 = \sum_{i=1}^{r}\sum_{j=1}^{s}\left[\frac{[(A_iB_j) - (A_iB_j)_0]^2}{(A_iB_j)_0}\right]$$

which is distributed as a χ^2 variate with $(r - 1)(s - 1)$ degrees of freedom.

Note 1. For a 2 × 2 contingency table where the frequencies are $\frac{a/b}{c/d}$, χ^2 can be calculated from independent frequencies as $\chi^2 = \frac{(a+b+c+d)(ad-bc)^2}{(a+b)(c+d)(b+d)(a+c)}$.

Note 2. If the contingency table is not 2 × 2, then the above formula for calculating χ^2 can't be used. Hence, we have another formula for calculating the expected frequency $(A_iB_j)_0 = \frac{(A_i)(B_j)}{N}$

i.e., expected frequency in each cell is $= \frac{\text{Product of column total and row total}}{\text{whole total}}$.

Note 3. If $\frac{a|b}{c|d}$ is the 2 × 2 contingency table with two attributes, $Q = \frac{ad-bc}{ad+bc}$ is called the coefficient of association. If the attributes are independent then $\frac{a}{b} = \frac{c}{d}$.

Note 4. Yates's Correction. In a 2 × 2 table, if the frequencies of a cell is small, we make Yates's correction to make χ^2 continuous. Decrease by $\frac{1}{2}$ those cell frequencies which are greater than expected frequencies, and increase by $\frac{1}{2}$ those which are less than expectation. This will not affect the marginal columns. This correction is known as Yates's correction to continuity. After Yates's correction

$$\chi^2 = \frac{N\left(bc - ad - \frac{1}{2}N\right)^2}{(a+c)(b+d)(c+d)(a+b)} \quad \text{when} \quad ad - bc < 0$$

and

$$\chi^2 = \frac{N\left(ad - bc - \frac{1}{2}N\right)^2}{(a+c)(b+d)(c+d)(a+b)} \quad \text{when} \quad ad - bc > 0.$$

EXAMPLES

Example 1. *What are the expected frequencies of 2 × 2 contingency tables given below:*

(*i*)

a	*b*
c	*d*

(*ii*)

2	10
6	6

Sol. Observed frequencies → Expected frequencies

(*i*)

a	*b*	*a* + *b*
c	*d*	*c* + *d*
a + *c*	*b* + *d*	*a* + *b* + *c* + *d* = N

→

$\frac{(a+c)(a+b)}{a+b+c+d}$	$\frac{(b+d)(a+b)}{a+b+c+d}$
$\frac{(a+c)(c+d)}{a+b+c+d}$	$\frac{(b+d)(c+d)}{a+b+c+d}$

(ii) Observed frequencies

2	10	12
6	6	12
8	16	24

→ Expected frequencies

$\frac{8 \times 12}{24} = 4$	$\frac{16 \times 12}{24} = 8$
$\frac{8 \times 12}{24} = 4$	$\frac{16 \times 12}{24} = 8$

Example 2. *From the following table regarding the colour of eyes of father and son, test if the colour of son's eye is associated with that of the father.*

		Eye colour of son	
		Light	*Not light*
Eye colour of father	*Light*	*471*	*51*
	Not light	*148*	*230*

Sol. Null hypothesis H_0: The colour of son's eye is not associated with that of the father, *i.e.,* they are independent.

Under H_0, we calculate

$$\text{the expected frequency in each cell} = \frac{\text{Product of column total and row total}}{\text{whole total}}$$

Expected frequencies are:

Eye colour of son / *Eye colour of father*	*Light*	*Not light*	*Total*
Light	$\frac{619 \times 522}{900} = 359.02$	$\frac{289 \times 522}{900} = 167.62$	522
Not light	$\frac{619 \times 378}{900} = 259.98$	$\frac{289 \times 378}{900} = 121.38$	378
Total	619	289	900

$$\chi^2 = \frac{(471 - 359.02)^2}{359.02} + \frac{(51 - 167.62)^2}{167.62} + \frac{(148 - 259.98)^2}{259.98} + \frac{(230 - 121.38)^2}{121.38} = 261.498.$$

Tabulated value of χ^2 at 5% level for 1 d.f. is 3.841.

Conclusion. Since the calculated value of χ^2 > tabulated value of χ^2, H_0 is rejected. They are dependent *i.e.,* the colour of son's eye is associated with that of the father.

Example 3. *The following table gives the number of good and bad parts produced by each of the three shifts in a factory:*

	Good parts	*Bad parts*	*Total*
Day shift	*960*	*40*	*1000*
Evening shift	*940*	*50*	*990*
Night shift	*950*	*45*	*995*
Total	*2850*	*135*	*2985*

Test whether or not the production of bad parts is independent of the shift on which they were produced.

Sol. Null hypothesis H_0: The production of bad parts is independent of the shift on which they were produced. *i.e.,* the two attributes, production and shifts are independent.

Under H_0,
$$\chi^2 = \sum_{i=1}^{2} \sum_{j=1}^{3} \left[\frac{[(A_iB_j)_0 - (A_iB_j)]^2}{(A_iB_j)_0} \right]$$

Calculation of expected frequencies

Let A and B be the two attributes namely production and shifts. A is divided into two classes A_1, A_2 and B is divided into three classes B_1, B_2, B_3.

$$(A_1B_1)_0 = \frac{(A_1)(B_1)}{N} = \frac{(2850) \times (1000)}{2985} = 954.77$$

$$(A_1B_2)_0 = \frac{(A_1)(B_2)}{N} = \frac{(2850) \times (990)}{2985} = 945.226$$

$$(A_1B_3)_0 = \frac{(A_1)(B_3)}{N} = \frac{(2850) \times (995)}{2985} = 950$$

$$(A_2B_1)_0 = \frac{(A_2)(B_1)}{N} = \frac{(135) \times (1000)}{2985} = 45.27$$

$$(A_2B_2)_0 = \frac{(A_2)(B_2)}{N} = \frac{(135) \times (990)}{2985} = 44.773$$

$$(A_2B_3)_0 = \frac{(A_2)(B_3)}{N} = \frac{(135) \times (995)}{2985} = 45.$$

To calculate the value of χ^2

Class	O_i	E_i	$(O_i - E_i)^2$	$(O_i - E_i)^2/E_i$
(A_1B_1)	960	954.77	27.3529	0.02864
(A_1B_2)	940	945.226	27.3110	0.02889
(A_1B_3)	950	950	0	0
(A_2B_1)	40	45.27	27.7729	0.61349
(A_2B_2)	50	44.773	27.3215	0.61022
(A_2B_3)	45	45	0	0
				1.28126

The tabulated value of χ^2 at 5% level of significance for 2 degrees of freedom $(r-1)(s-1)$ is 5.991.

Conclusion: Since the calculated value of χ^2 is less than the tabulated value, we accept H_0. *i.e.*, the production of bad parts is independent of the shift on which they were produced.

Example 4. *From the following data, find whether hair colour and sex are associated.*

Sex \ *Colour*	*Fair*	*Red*	*Medium*	*Dark*	*Black*	*Total*
Boys	*592*	*849*	*504*	*119*	*36*	*2100*
Girls	*544*	*677*	*451*	*97*	*14*	*1783*
Total	*1136*	*1526*	*955*	*216*	*50*	*3883*

Sol. Null hypothesis H_0: The two attributes hair colour and sex are not associated.

i.e., they are independent.

Let A and B be the attributes hair colour and sex respectively. A is divides into 5 classes $(r = 5)$. B is divided into 2 classes $(s = 2)$.

$\therefore$ Degrees of freedom $= (r-1)(s-1) = (5-1)(2-1) = 4$

Under H_0, we calculate $\chi^2 = \sum_{i=1}^{5} \sum_{j=1}^{2} \frac{[(A_iB_j)_0 - (A_iB_j)]^2}{(A_iB_j)_0}$

To calculate the expected frequency $(A_i B_j)_0$ as follows:

$$(A_1B_1)_0 = \frac{(A_1)(B_1)}{N} = \frac{1136 \times 2100}{3883} = 614.37$$

$$(A_1B_2)_0 = \frac{(A_1)(B_2)}{N} = \frac{1136 \times 1783}{3883} = 521.629$$

$$(A_2B_1)_0 = \frac{(A_2)(B_1)}{N} = \frac{1526 \times 2100}{3883} = 852.289$$

$$(A_2B_2)_0 = \frac{(A_2)(B_2)}{N} = \frac{1526 \times 1783}{3883} = 700.71$$

$$(A_3B_1)_0 = \frac{(A_3)(B_1)}{N} = \frac{955 \times 2100}{3883} = 516.482$$

$$(A_3B_2)_0 = \frac{(A_3)(B_2)}{N} = \frac{955 \times 1783}{3883} = 483.517$$

$$(A_4B_1)_0 = \frac{(A_4)(B_1)}{N} = \frac{216 \times 2100}{3883} = 116.816$$

$$(A_4B_2)_0 = \frac{(A_4)(B_2)}{N} = \frac{216 \times 1783}{3883} = 99.183$$

$$(A_5B_1)_0 = \frac{(A_5)(B_1)}{N} = \frac{50 \times 2100}{3883} = 27.04$$

$$(A_5B_2)_0 = \frac{(A_5)(B_2)}{N} = \frac{50 \times 1783}{3883} = 22.959$$

Calculation of χ^2

Class	O_i	E_i	$(O_i - E_i)^2$	$\frac{(O_i - E_i)^2}{E_i}$
A_1B_1	592	614.37	500.416	0.8145
A_1B_2	544	521.629	500.462	0.959
A_2B_1	849	852.289	10.8175	0.0127
A_2B_2	677	700.71	562.1641	0.8023
A_3B_1	504	516.482	155.800	0.3016
A_3B_2	451	438.517	155.825	0.3553
A_4B_1	119	116.816	4.7698	0.0408
A_4B_2	97	99.183	4.7654	0.0480
A_5B_1	36	27.04	80.2816	2.9689
A_5B_2	14	22.959	80.2636	3.495
				9.79975

$$\chi^2_{cal.} = 9.799.$$

Tabular value of χ^2 at 5% level of significance for 4 d.f. is 9.488.

Conclusion. Since the calculated value of $\chi^2 <$ tabulated value, H_0 is rejected. *i.e.,* the two attributes are not independent. *i.e.,* the hair colour and sex are associated.

Example 5. *Can vaccination be regarded as preventive measure of smallpox as evidenced by the following data of 1482 persons exposed to smallpox in a locality. 368 in all were attacked of these 1482 persons and 343 were vaccinated and of these only 35 were attacked.*

Sol. For the given data we form the contingency table. Let the two attributes be vaccination and exposed to smallpox. Each attributes is divided into two classes.

Vaccination A / *Disease small-pox B*	*Vaccinated*	*Not*	*Total*
Attacked	35	333	368
Not	308	806	1114
Total	343	1139	1482

Null hypothesis H_0: The two attributes are independent *i.e.,* vaccination can't be regarded as preventive measure of smallpox.

Degrees of freedom $\nu = (r - 1)(s - 1) = (2 - 1)(2 - 1) = 1$

Under H_0, $\chi^2 = \sum_{i=1}^{2} \sum_{j=1}^{2} \frac{[(A_iB_j)_0 - (A_iB_j)]^2}{(A_iB_j)_0}$

Calculation of expected frequency

$$(A_1B_1)_0 = \frac{(A_1)(B_1)}{N} = \frac{343 \times 368}{1482} = 85.1713$$

$$(A_1B_2)_0 = \frac{(A_1)(B_2)}{N} = \frac{343 \times 1114}{1482} = 257.828$$

$$(A_2B_1)_0 = \frac{(A_2)(B_1)}{N} = \frac{1139 \times 368}{1482} = 282.828$$

$$(A_2B_2)_0 = \frac{(A_2)(B_2)}{N} = \frac{1139 \times 1114}{1482} = 856.171$$

Calculation of χ^2

Class	O_i	E_i	$(O_i - E_i)^2$	$\frac{(O_i - E_i)^2}{E_i}$
(A_1B_1)	35	85.1713	2517.159	29.554
(A_1B_2)	308	257.828	2517.229	8.1728
(A_2B_1)	333	282.828	2517.2295	7.5592
(A_2B_2)	806	856.171	2517.1292	2.9399
				48.2261

Calculated value of $\chi^2 = 48.2261$.

Tabulated value of χ^2 at 5% level of significance for 1 d.f. is 3.841.

Conclusion: Since the calculated value of $\chi^2 >$ tabulated value, H_0 is rejected.

i.e., the two attributes are not independent. *i.e.,* the vaccination can be regarded as preventive measure of smallpox.

Example 6. *To test the effectiveness of inoculation against cholera, the following table was obtained:*

	Attacked	*Not attacked*	*Total*
Inoculated	*30*	*160*	*190*
Not inoculated	*140*	*460*	*600*
Total	*170*	*620*	*790*

(The figures represent the number of persons.)

Use χ^2-test to defend or refute the statement that the inoculation prevents attack from cholera. (U.P.T.U. 2009)

Sol. Null hypothesis H_0: The inoculation does not prevent attack from cholera.

Under H_0, we calculate the expected frequencies as:

	Attacked	*Not attacked*
Inoculated	$\frac{190 \times 170}{790} = 40.886$	$\frac{190 \times 620}{790} = 149.11$
Not inoculated	$\frac{600 \times 170}{790} = 129.11$	$\frac{600 \times 620}{790} = 470.89$

Calculation of χ^2

O_i	30	160	140	460
E_i	40.886	149.11	129.11	470.89
$\frac{(O_i - E_i)^2}{E_i}$	2.898	0.795	0.918	0.252

$$\chi^2_{\text{cal.}} = \sum \frac{(O_i - E_i)^2}{E_i} = 4.863$$

Tabulated value of χ^2 at 5% level of significance for 1 d.f. is 3.841.

Conclusion: Since $\chi^2_{\text{cal.}} > \chi^2_{\text{tab.}}$ at 5% level of significance, null hypothesis H_0 is rejected. Hence we defend the statement that inoculation prevents attack from cholera.

ASSIGNMENT

1. In a locality 100 persons were randomly selected and asked about their educational achievements. The results are given below:

		Education		
		Middle	*High school*	*College*
Sex	Male	10	15	25
	Female	25	10	15

Based on this information can you say that the education depends on sex.

2. The following data is collected on two characters:

	Smokers	*Non smokers*
Literate	83	57
Illiterate	45	68

Based on this information can you say that there is no relation between habit of smoking and literacy.

3. 500 students at school were graded according to their intelligences and economic conditions of their homes. Examine whether there is any association between economic condition and intelligence, from the following data:

Economic conditions	*Intelligence*	
	Good	*Bad*
Rich	85	75
Poor	165	175

4. In an experiment on the immunisation of goats from anthrox, the following results were obtained. Derive your inferences on the efficiency of the vaccine.

	Died anthrox	*Survived*
Inoculated with vaccine	2	10
Not inoculated	6	6

5. By using χ^2-test, find out whether there is any association between income level and type of schooling:

Income	*Public School*	*Govt. School*
Low	200	400
High	1000	400

(Given for degree of freedom 1, $\chi^2_{0.05} = 3.84$) *[U.P.T.U. 2008, G.B.T.U. (MBA) 2011)*

6. Examine by any suitable method, whether the nature of area is related to voting preference in the election for which the data are tabulated below:

Votes for Area	*A*	*B*	*Total*
Rural	620	480	1100
Urban	380	520	900
Total	1000	1000	2000

(U.P.T.U. 2006)

Answers

1. Yes 2. No 3. No 4. Not effective
5. Yes 6. Yes

9.47. ANALYSIS OF VARIANCE (ANOVA) *[G.B.T.U. (MCA) 2011, 2008, 2007, 2006]*

ANOVA is a statistical technique which can be used to make comparisons among more than two groups. For example, suppose we want to see the effects of three different fertilisers on the yield of a crop. We select 100 identical plots of which 25 are control plots and 75 are experimental plots. Plants are grown in all the 100 plots in the same manner except that no fertiliser is applied in the control plots, while the three fertilisers are applied in the 75 experimental plots. The 75 experimental plots are divided into 3 groups of 25 plots each. Each of these groups is treated with different kinds of fertiliser. When the crop is harvested, the yield of each individual plot is recorded in four groups. We calculate the mean yield of all the

100 plots. Then we apply the technique (analysis of variance) to find out if there is any significant difference between the overall mean yield and the mean yields of the individual groups.

Similarly, suppose we want to test the effectiveness of various doses of a drug on blood pressure. We take a large number of individuals and divide them into several groups depending on the number of doses. For example, if we want to test four different doses, we make five groups (one control group and four experimental groups). Each experimental group is meant for a given dose of the drug.

One way ANOVA is used to see the effects of an independent variable on a given dependent variable. Two way ANOVA is used to see the effects of two independent variables on a given dependent variable.

In ANOVA, we compare the variations existing in the observed values of the dependent variable in the classified groups. We calculate the variance of the total population, variance between the groups and the variance within the groups. Then we examine whether there is any significant difference between the calculated variances. If we find, by ANOVA, that the variance between the groups is not significantly different from the variance within the groups, we conclude that there is no significant difference between the means of the groups, and hence the independent variable (factor) has no effect on the dependent variable.

9.47.1. ANOVA Table

The technique of analysis of variance is referred to as ANOVA. A table showing the source of variation, the sum of squares, degrees of freedom, mean square (variance) and the formula for the F-ratio is known as ANOVA table.

9.47.2. Computation of Test Statistic

The actual analysis of variance is carried out on the basis of ratio between the variances. This ratio forms the test statistic known as *F-statistic, given by*

$$\text{F-statistic} = \frac{\text{Variance between the samples}}{\text{Variance within the samples}}$$

9.47.3. Assumptions

Following are the assumptions for the study of analysis of variance:

(*i*) Each of the samples is a simple random sample.

(*ii*) Population, from which the samples are selected, are normally distributed.

(*iii*) Each of the samples is independent of the other samples.

(*iv*) Each of the population has the same variations and identical means.

(*v*) The effects of various components are additive.

9.48. ONE WAY CLASSIFICATION

(*a*) **Null hypothesis H_0:** $\mu_1 = \mu_2 = \ldots = \mu_p$, *i.e.*, the means of the populations from which p samples are drawn are equal to one another.

(*b*) **Alternative Hypothesis H_1:** At least two of the means of the populations are unequal, or *all the* μ_i's *are not equal*.

(*c*) **Computation of test statistic:** To obtain the test statistic known as F-value, we define certain terms as follows:

Sample observation x_{ij} : A sample observation x_{ij} has two subscripts. The subscript i denotes the row or *sample observation*, while the subscript j denotes the column or *population from which the observation came*. Thus x_{ij} is the ith observation from the jth population.

The total observations in the above matrix A is $m \times n$.

The various sums of squares involved in the computation of F-statistics are:

(*i*) **Sum of the squares of Variations Amongst the Columns (SSC):** It is the sum of the squares of deviation between the column or group means and the grand mean, *i.e.*,

$$\text{SSC} = r\,\Sigma(\bar{x}_j - \bar{x})^2,$$

where $\bar{x}_j$ = mean of the jth sample, $\bar{x}$ = mean of the sample (column) means, r = number of rows or size of each sample.

Variance amongst columns = $\boxed{\text{MSC} = \dfrac{\text{SSC}}{c-1}}$, where c is number of columns.

It indicates the degree of explained variance due to sampling variations.

(*ii*) **Sum of the Squares of Variations within Columns (SSE):** It is the sum of the squares of variations between individual items and the column means, *i.e.*,

$$\text{SSE} = \sum_i \sum_j (x_{ij} - \bar{x}_j)^2$$

where x_{ij} = i^{th} observation in j^{th} column, $\bar{x}_j$ = mean of jth column

Mean of the square of Column Errors = $\boxed{\text{MSE} = \dfrac{\text{SSE}}{c(r-1)}}$

where c is number of columns and r is number of rows.

This is called *Unexplained Variance* as it indicates only the chance variation which cannot be explained in terms of variation in population.

(*iii*) **Total Sum of Squares of Variation (SST).**

$$\text{SST} = \sum_j \sum_i x_{ij}^2 - \text{C},$$

where C = Correction factor = $\dfrac{\text{T}^2}{rc}$, T = grand total of the values in all samples,

r = number of rows, c = number of columns.

It is the sum of squares of observations between the individual values and the grand mean $\bar{x}$.

Also, **SST = SSC + SSE.**

$$\text{Total Variance} = \frac{\text{SST}}{n-1},$$

where $n = r \times c$ = total number of observations in all the samples and $(n - 1)$ is the degree of freedom.

Test Statistic: The test statistic is the **F-value** or **F-statistic** and is given by

$$\textbf{F-statistic or F-value} = \frac{\textbf{Explained variance}}{\textbf{Unexplained variance}} = \frac{\textbf{MSC}}{\textbf{MSE}}.$$

$$\Rightarrow \qquad \textbf{F} = \frac{\textbf{MSC}}{\textbf{MSE}} \text{ with } (c-1) \text{ and } c\,(r-1) \text{ degrees of freedom.}$$

Thus we have

ANOVA Table for one-way classification for equal sample

Source of variation	*Sum of squares*	*Degree of freedom*	*Mean square*	*F*
Between samples (Column Means)	SSC	$c-1$	$\text{MSC} = \dfrac{\text{SSC}}{c-1}$	
Within Samples	SSE	$c(r-1)$	$\text{MSE} = \dfrac{\text{SSE}}{c(r-1)}$	$\text{F} = \dfrac{\text{MSC}}{\text{MSE}}$
Total	SST	$cr-1$		

(*d*) **Level of significance:** It is denoted by α and the value is taken generally as $\alpha = 0.05$.

(*e*) **Conclusion:** If $F_{computed} < F_{tabular}$ at α level of significance then the null hypothesis H_0 is accepted and if $F_{computed} > F_{tabular}$ at α level of significance then the null hypothesis H_0 is rejected and H_1 is accepted.

9.49. PROCEDURE TO PREPARE ANOVA TABLE

The basic structure of ANOVA table is

Source of variation	*Sum of squares*	*Degree of freedom*	*Mean sum of squares*	*Variance ratio or F-statistic*
Between samples				
Within samples				
Total				

(*i*) Find the sum of the values of all the items of all the samples. We call it **Grand Total (G.T.).**

$$\text{G.T.} = \Sigma A + \Sigma B + \Sigma C + \ldots..$$

(*ii*) Calculate the correction factor (C.F.)

$$\text{C.F.} = \frac{(\text{G.T.})^2}{n}$$

where n is the total number of items in all the samples.

(*iii*) Find the total sum of squares. It is obtained as $(\Sigma A^2 + \Sigma B^2 + \Sigma C^2 + \ldots...) - \text{C.F.}$

(*iv*) Find the sum of squares between samples.

It is obtained as

$$\left[\frac{(\Sigma A)^2}{n_1} + \frac{(\Sigma B)^2}{n_2} + \frac{(\Sigma C)^2}{n_3} + \ldots..\right] - \text{C.F.}$$

(*v*) Calculate the sum of squares within samples.

Sum of squares within samples = (Total sum of squares) – (Sum of squares between samples)

(*vi*) Find total degree of freedom and degree of freedom between samples. Degree of freedom within samples is obtained by subtraction.

(*vii*) Mean sum of squares is obtained by dividing sum of squares by degree of freedom.

(*viii*) Variance ratio is obtained by dividing the corresponding mean sum of squares.

This completes the preparation of ANOVA table.

9.50. CHANGE OF ORIGIN METHOD (Coding Method)

F remains unchanged if all the figures are multiplied or divided by a common factor or if a common factor is added to or subtracted from each figure. This property helps in calculating F-ratio when the figures are large. When such simplifications are done, it is said that data have been coded to simplify calculations.

EXAMPLES

Example 1. *It is desired to compare three hospitals with regards to the number of deaths per month. A sample of death records were selected from the records of each hospital and the number of deaths was as given below. From these data, suggest a difference in the no. of the deaths per months among three hospitals:*

Hospitals

A	B	C
3	6	7
4	3	3
3	3	4
5	4	6
0	4	5

Sol. Null hypothesis H_0: There is no difference in the no. of deaths per months among three hospitals.

Alternate hypothesis H_1: There is a significant difference in the no. of deaths per months among three hospitals.

Level of significance: We use 5% level of significance.

Test statistic: To find the variance ratio, F, we set up an ANOVA table as follows:

Sample totals:

$$\Sigma y_A = 3 + 4 + 3 + 5 + 0 = 15$$

$$\Sigma y_B = 6 + 3 + 3 + 4 + 4 = 20$$

$$\Sigma y_C = 7 + 3 + 4 + 6 + 5 = 25$$

$$\text{Grand total (G.T.)} = \Sigma y_A + \Sigma y_B + \Sigma y_C = 60$$

$$\text{Correction factor (C.F.)} = \frac{(\text{G.T})^2}{n} = \frac{(60)^2}{15} = 240$$

Sum of squares of samples:

$$\Sigma y_A^2 = 3^2 + 4^2 + 3^2 + 5^2 + 0^2 = 59$$

$$\Sigma y_B^2 = 6^2 + 3^2 + 3^2 + 4^2 + 4^2 = 86$$

$$\Sigma y_C^2 = 7^2 + 3^2 + 4^2 + 6^2 + 5^2 = 135$$

Total sum of squares $= \Sigma y_A^2 + \Sigma y_B^2 + \Sigma y_C^2 - \text{C.F.}$

$= 59 + 86 + 135 - 240 = 40$

Sum of squares between samples

$$= \frac{(\Sigma y_A)^2}{n_1} + \frac{(\Sigma y_B)^2}{n_2} + \frac{(\Sigma y_C)^2}{n_3} - \text{C.F.}$$

$$= \frac{(15)^2}{5} + \frac{(20)^2}{5} + \frac{(25)^2}{5} - 240 = 10$$

Sum of squares within samples

= Total sum of squares – sum of squares between samples

= 40 – 10 = 30

Degrees of freedom for total sum of squares $= n - 1 = 15 - 1 = 14$

Degrees of freedom for Hospitals $= k - 1 = 3 - 1 = 2$

Degrees of freedom for error $= n - k = 15 - 3 = 12$

ANOVA TABLE

Source of variation	*Sum of squares*	*Degree of freedom*	*Mean sum of squares*	*Variance ratio or F*
Between samples	10	2	5	$F_{2,12} = \frac{5}{2.5} = 2$
Within samples	30	12	2.5	
Total	40	14	—	—

The tabular value of F at 5% level of significance with $\nu_1 = 2$, $\nu_2 = 12$ is 3.89

Conclusion: Since $F_{cal.} < F_{tab.}$, the difference is insignificant and we conclude that data donot suggest a difference in the number of deaths per month among the three hospitals.

Example 2. *A manufacturing company purchased three new machines of different makes and wishes to determine whether one of them is faster than the others in producing a certain output. Five hourly production figures are observed at random from each machine and results are given below:*

Observations	A_1	A_2	A_3
1	*25*	*31*	*24*
2	*30*	*39*	*30*
3	*36*	*38*	*28*
4	*38*	*42*	*25*
5	*31*	*35*	*28*

Use ANOVA and determine whether the machines are significantly different in their mean speed. (Given: at 5% level, $F_{2,\,12} = 3.89$) (U.P.T.U. 2007)

Sol. Null hypothesis H_0: Machines are not significantly different in their mean speeds *i.e.,* $\mu_1 = \mu_2 = \mu_3$

Alternate hypothesis H_1: Machines are significantly different in their mean speed.

Level of significance: We use 5% level of significance.

Test statistic: To find the variance ratio F, we set up an ANOVA table as follows: let us shift the origin at 30 *i.e.,* reduce each observation by 30.

Now,

Observations	A_1	A_2	A_3
1	– 5	1	– 6
2	0	9	0
3	6	8	– 2
4	8	12	– 5
5	1	5	– 2

Machine totals:

$$\Sigma A_1 = -5 + 0 + 6 + 8 + 1 = 10$$

$$\Sigma A_2 = 1 + 9 + 8 + 12 + 5 = 35$$

$$\Sigma A_3 = -6 + 0 - 2 - 5 - 2 = -15$$

$$\text{Grand total (G.T.)} = \Sigma A_1 + \Sigma A_2 + \Sigma A_3 = 30$$

$$\text{Correction factor (C.F)} = \frac{(30)^2}{15} = 60$$

Sum of squares of samples

$$\Sigma A_1^2 = (-5)^2 + 0^2 + 6^2 + 8^2 + 1^2 = 126$$

Similarly, $\Sigma A_2^2 = 315, \Sigma A_3^2 = 69$

Total sum of squares $= 126 + 315 + 69 - (\text{C.F.}) = 510 - 60 = 450$

$$\text{Machine sum of squares (between samples)} = \frac{(10)^2}{5} + \frac{(35)^2}{5} + \frac{(-15)^2}{5} - \text{C.F.}$$

$$= 310 - 60 = 250$$

Error sum of squares (within samples)

$$= \text{Total sum of squares} - \text{Machine sum of squares}$$

$$= 450 - 250 = 200$$

Degrees of freedom for total sum of squares $= n - 1 = 15 - 1 = 14$

Degrees of freedom for Machines $= k - 1 = 3 - 1 = 2$

Degrees of freedom for Error $= n - k = 15 - 3 = 12$

ANOVA TABLE

Source of variation	*Sum of squares*	*Degrees of freedom*	*Mean sum of squares*	*Variance ratio of F*
Machine (between samples)	250	2	$\frac{250}{2} = 125$	$F_{2, 12} = \frac{125}{16.67}$
Error (within samples)	200	12	$\frac{200}{12} = 16.67$	$= 7.498$
Total	450	14	—	—

The tabular value of F at 5% level of significance with $\nu_1 = 2$, $\nu_2 = 12$ is 3.89 (given).

Conclusion: Since $F_{calculated} > F_{tabulated}$, the null hypothesis is rejected and the difference is significant and we conclude that there is a significant difference in the mean speed of machines.

ASSIGNMENT

1. To test the significance of the variations of the retail prices in the commodity in three principal cities : Mumbai, Bangalore and Chennai, the four shops were chosen at random in each city and prices observed in rupees were as follows:

Mumbai	16	8	12	14
Bangalore	14	10	10	6
Chennai	4	10	8	8

Do the data indicate that the prices in the three cities are significantly different?

2. Below are given the yield kg for four varieties of tablets. Prepare ANOVA table and test that varieties differ significantly.

A	*B*	*C*	*D*
20	25	24	23
19	23	20	20
21	21	22	20

[*U.P.T.U. (B.Pharm.) 2008*]

[**Hint.** Shift the origin at 20]

3. The following table gives the yields on 15 sample plots under three varieties of seeds:

Variety I:	20	21	23	16	20
Variety II:	18	20	17	15	25
Variety III:	25	28	22	28	32

Show that the seed varieties show variations more than could be covered by sampling variations. Given the tabulated value of F for $v_1 = 2$ and $v_2 = 12$ at 5% level of significance is 3.88.

4. The following figures relate to the production in kg of three varieties of wheat A, B and C used on 15 plots.

Wheat Variety			*Yields (kg)*			
RR 21–A	14	17	16	16		
K.68–B	15	11	13	15	13	14
Sonalika–C	18	16	18	19	15	

Test whether there is any significant difference in the production of three varieties.
[**Hint.** Shift the origin at 16]

5. The following figures relate to the production in kg of three varieties I, II, III of wheat shown in 12 plots:

Variety I:	14	16	18		
Variety II:	14	13	15	22	
Variety III:	18	16	19	19	20

Is there any significant difference in the production of three varieties? Given the tabulated value of F for $\nu_1 = 2$ and $\nu_2 = 9$ at 5% level of significance is 4.26.

6. A trucking company wishes to test the average life of each of the four brands of tyres. The company uses all brands on randomly selected trucks. The records showing the lives (thousands of miles) of tyres are as given in the table given below:

Brand I:	20	23	18	17	
Brand II:	19	15	17	20	16
Brand III:	21	19	20	17	16
Brand IV:	15	17	16	18	

Test the hypothesis that the average life for each brand of tyres is the same. Assume $\alpha = 0.01$.

7. What is analysis of variance? Mention its importance and uses.

8. Write short notes on:
   (*i*) ANOVA [*U.P.T.U. (MCA) 2006, 2007, 2008; G.B.T.U. 2011*]
   (*ii*) One-way classification.

9. Under what conditions do we require to use one way Analysis of Variance ? Give examples and explain the method involved by taking a hypothetical example. [*U.P.T.U. (MBA) 2009*]

Answers

1. No **2.** Varieties donot differ significantly.
4. The difference is significant. **5.** No
6. No significant difference between the average lives.

9.51. TIME-SERIES [*U.P.T.U. (MBA) 2006*]

A time series is a set of numerical values of a given variable listed at successive intervals of time. That is, the data regarding the variable is listed in chronological order. Usually the interval of time is taken as uniform. For example:

Yearly production of wheat in the country, hourly temperature of a city, bimonthly electricity bills etc.

Now, we will study the components and analysis time series along with its importance. We will discuss the behaviour of a time-series over periods of time.

9.52. COMPONENTS OF TIME-SERIES [*U.P.T.U. (MBA) 2008*]

The presence of certain characteristic movements or fluctuations are normally seen in a time-series. These characteristic movements of time-series over a period of time can be classified into different categories called **components of a time-series.** There are four basic components of a time-series which are:

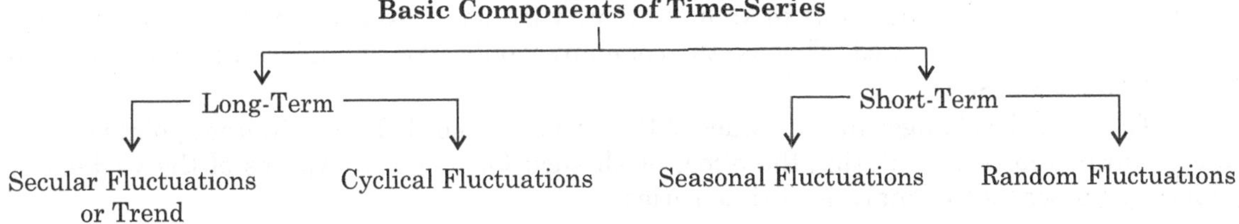

(*a*) **Secular fluctuations or trend:** [*U.P.T.U. (MCA) 2006*]

The component responsible for the general behaviour of the time-series is called the trend. In fact, secular is that characteristic of a time-series which extends consistently throughout the entire period of time under consideration. This gives a long-term tendency of a particular activity to grow or to decline. The trend may be upwards as well as downwards. The factors which are constant over a long period (or even if they vary) produce the trend. Prices of books since 1980 which are constantly increasing is an example of upward trends. On the other hand, the infant mortality rate since 1950 which is constantly decreasing every year, is an example of downward trend.

(*b*) **Seasonal fluctuations** [*U.P.T.U. (MCA) 2006*]

The component responsible for the regular rise and fall in the magnitude of the time-series is called seasonal fluctuation. These fluctuations occur in regular sequence at specific intervals of time and thus are strictly periodical. Their period may be one year, a quarter year, a month, a week, a day or even fraction of a day etc. But in no case, this period is to exceed one year. This component is definite and precise and can be foreseen; for example, the price of wheat or an agricultural commodities falls during the harvest period every year, the sale of gold and clothes goes up in marriage period.

(*c*) **Cyclical fluctuations** [*U.P.T.U. (MCA) 2006*]

The oscillatory fluctuation of the time-series having the period of oscillation as more than a year is known as cyclical fluctuation. Cyclical fluctuations are not necessarily periodic but they reveal the influence of good and bad times on the series. The causes of cyclical fluctuations, its nature, its phases and its duration are more or less guesses but based on the factual evidence of the past.

(*d*) **Random fluctuations:**

Random fluctuations are the fluctuations caused by sudden and unexpected happenings such as floods, wars, strikes, earthquakes, etc. The fluctuations produced by these causes are random or irregular and so the word random is used to specify the fluctuations.

9.53. ANALYSIS OF TIME-SERIES [*U.P.T.U. MCA (C.O.) 2008*]

Given a time series, we wish to

(*i*) Study the forces that influence the variations in time series, and

(*ii*) Study the behaviours of phenomenon over the given period of time.

For example, consider the sale of TV sets (in thousands) by a producing company

Years	1995	1996	1997	1998	1999	2000
Number sold (in thousands)	12	14	16	12	10	18

We would like to analyse the above data and give some trends about the sales. For example, the company would like to know as to why the sales dropped in 1998 and 1999, and then why the sales increased. That is, the company would like to analyse the various forces that effect the sales.

There can be changes in the values of the variable recorded over different points of time due to various forces. Analysing the effect of all such forces on the values of the variable is generally known as the analysis of time series.

Broadly there can be four types of changes in the values of the variable as discussed below:

(*i*) Changes which generally occur due to general tendency of the data to increase or decrease.

(*ii*) Changes which occur due to change in climate, weather conditions, festivals etc.

(*iii*) Changes which occur due to booms and depressions.

(*iv*) Changes which occur due to some unpredictable forces like floods, famines, earthquakes etc.

9.54. IMPORTANCE OF TIME-SERIES

[U.P.T.U. MCA (C.O.) 2008]

1. Comparative study of the behaviour of the variable over different periods of time can be done. The variable may be export figures, quantity of industrial production etc.
2. Forecasting can be done using the time series. By studying the variations and other behaviour of the variables over a sufficiently long period of time, it may be possible to forecast the future behaviour of the variables. However, such a forecast has meaning only if the period of forecast is a normal period. For example, various five-year plans by the Government of India are formulated by studying the time series and forecasting.
3. Study of the time series helps in analysing the post behaviour of the variables. This helps in identifying the various forces that effect its behaviour.

9.55. TIME-SERIES GRAPH

To analyse the time-series, a time-series graph is drawn frequently. It brings out the pattern of fluctuations in time-series data and facilitates drawing meaningful results about its likely future behaviour. In drawing a time-series graph, time is measured along the horizontal axis and the observed data along the vertical axis. Points are then plotted against the magnitudes corresponding to each successive time period and joined by means of line segments. The resulting zig-zag curve is called the time-series graph. A time-series graph is shown in the figure for the sale of a commodity during the period 1991–1999 given as:

Years	1991	1992	1993	1994	1995	1996	1997	1998	1999
Sales	30	25	35	40	20	25	30	40	45

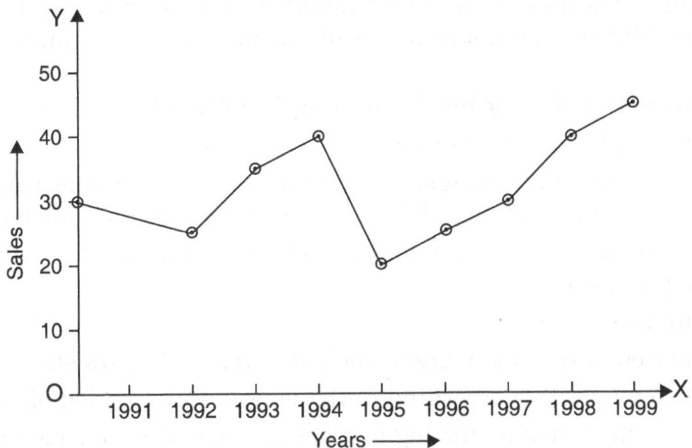

Time-Series Graph

9.56. MEASUREMENT OF TREND

Following are the methods of measuring the trend of a time-series:

(*i*) Free hand or graphic method (*ii*) Method of semi-averages

(*iii*) Method of curve fitting by principle of least squares

(*iv*) Method of moving-averages.

1. Free hand method: In this method, we plot the values of the variable against time on a graph paper and join these points. The trend line is then fitted by inspecting the graph of the time series. Fitting a trend line by this method is arbitrary. The trend line is usually drawn such that the number of fluctuations on either side are approximately the same. The trend line should be a smooth curve. The free hand method has some disadvantages. They are:

(*i*) It depends on individual judgement,

(*ii*) It cannot be used for any predictions of trends, as drawing the trend curve is arbitrary.

2. Method of semi-averages: In this method, the whole data is divided into two parts with respect to time *e.g.*, if we are given y_t for t from 2001–2012 *i.e.*, over a period of 12 years, the two equal parts will be the data from 2001 to 2006 and 2007 to 2012. In case of odd number of years, the two parts are obtained by omitting the value corresponding to the middle year *e.g.*, for the data from 2001 to 2011, the value corresponding to middle year 2006 being omitted. Next we compute the arithmetic mean for each part and plot these two averages (means) against the mid-values of the respective time periods covered by each part.

The line obtained on joining these two points is the required trend line and may be extended both ways to estimate intermediate or future values.

Merits: (*i*) As compared with graphic method, the obvious advantage is its objectivity in the sense that everyone who applies it would get the same results. Moreover, we can also estimate the trend values.

(*ii*) It is readily comprehensible as compared to the method of least squares or the moving averages method.

Limitations: This method assumes linear relationship between the plotted points which may not exist. Moreover, the limitations of arithmetic mean as an average also stand in its way.

3. Method of curve-fitting by the principle of least squares

We have already discussed it before.

4. Method of moving averages: This method is used for smoothing the time-series. That is, it smoothens the fluctuations of the data by the method of moving averages.

(*a*) **When period of moving average is odd:** To determine the trend by this method, we use the following method:

(*i*) Obtain the time-series.

(*ii*) Select a period of moving average such as 3 years, 5 years etc.

(*iii*) Compute moving totals according to the length of the period of moving average.

If the length of the period of moving average is 3, *i.e.,* 3-yearly moving average is to be calculated, compute moving totals as follows:

$$a + b + c, b + c + d, c + d + e, d + e + f, \ldots$$

For 5-yearly moving average, moving totals are computed as follows:

$$a + b + c + d + e, b + c + d + e + f, c + d + e + f + g, \ldots\ldots$$

Place the moving totals at the centre of the time span from which they are computed.

(*iv*) Compute moving averages by moving totals in step (*iii*) by the length of the period of moving average and place them at the centre of the time span from which the moving totals are computed. These moving averages are also called the trend values.

By plotting these trend values (if desired) one can obtain the trend curve with the help of which we can determine the trend whether it is increasing or decreasing.

If needed, one can also compute short-term fluctuations by subtracting the trend values from the actual values.

(*b*) **When period of moving averages is even:** When period of moving average is even (4-years, 6-years etc.), we compute the moving averages by using the following steps:

(*i*) Obtain the time-series.

(*ii*) Obtain the length of the period of moving average. Let the length of the moving averages period be 4-years.

(*iii*) Compute 4-yearly moving totals and place them at the centre of time span.

The four-yearly moving totals are computed as follows:

$$a + b + c + d, b + c + d + e, c + d + e + f, \ldots$$

(*iv*) Compute 4-yearly moving average and place them at the centre of the time span. Note that this placement is inconvenient, because the moving average so placed would not coincide with original time period.

(*v*) Take two-period moving average of moving averages and place them at the middle of the periods. This process is called centering of moving averages.

EXAMPLES

Example 1. *Fit a trend line to the following data by the free hand graphical method:*

Years	*1980*	*1981*	*1982*	*1983*	*1984*	*1985*	*1986*
Sales	*35*	*60*	*45*	*70*	*65*	*62*	*80*

Sol. Plot the points (1980, 35), (1981, 60), (1982, 45), (1983, 70), (1984, 65), (1985, 62) and (1986, 80) as shown in figure below. Join these points to get the actual data lines. Now, the trend line can be drawn (as shown in the figure) by free hand in such a way that the sum of the vertical deviations from the trend of observations above the trend is equal to the sum of the vertical deviations from the trend of observations below the trend.

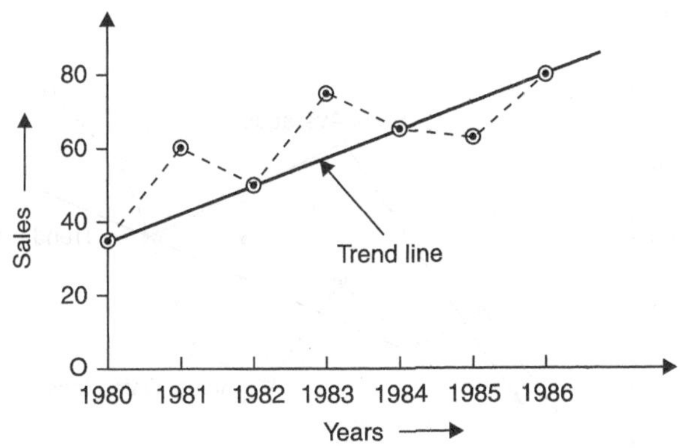

Trend Line by Free Hand (Graphical) Method

The trend line can be extended to predict future values or to determine intermediate values.

Example 2. *Draw a trend line by the method of semi-averages to the following data:*

Years	*1991*	*1992*	*1993*	*1994*	*1995*	*1996*	*1997*	*1998*	*1999*
Sales	*32*	*38*	*50*	*48*	*54*	*42*	*48*	*72*	*82*

Sol. Divide the data into two equal parts. Then find the average of each part called the semi-average. Since there are nine years, the middle year 1995 shall be left out. The average of sales of first four years and the average of sales of last four years are found as per table given as:

Years	*Sales*	*Semi-Total of sales*	*Semi-Averages*
1991	32		
1992	38		
1993	50	32 + 38 + 50 + 48 = 168	$\frac{168}{4} = 42$
1994	48		
1995	54		
1996	42		
1997	48	42 + 48 + 72 + 82 = 244	$\frac{244}{4} = 61$
1998	72		
1999	82		

Now, the two semi-averages 42 and 61 are plotted against the middle of their respective periods, the night between 31st December 1992 and 1st January 1993' and 'the night between 31st December 1997 and 1st January 1998' respectively. Join these points to get the desired trend line which is shown in the figure below:

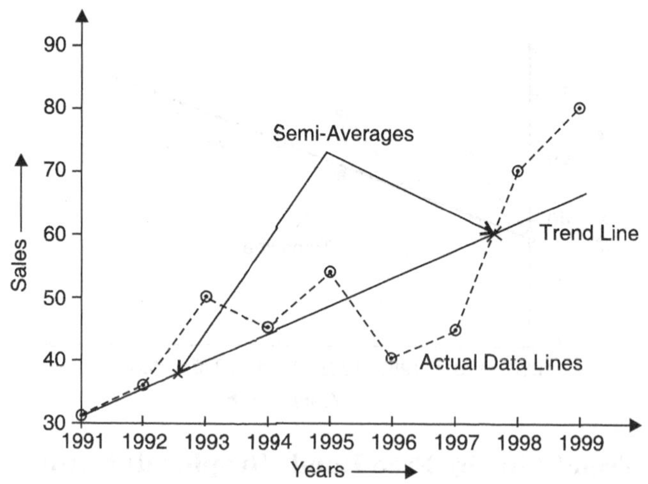

Trend Line by Semi-Averages Method

Example 3. *Work out the centered 4-yearly moving average for the following data:*

Year	*Tonnage of goods carried*
1990	*2204*
1991	*2500*
1992	*2360*
1993	*2680*
1994	*2424*
1995	*2634*
1996	*2904*
1997	*3098*
1998	*3172*
1999	*2952*
2000	*3248*
2001	*3172*

Sol. We calculate the four yearly moving average in the following table:

Year	*Tonnage of goods carried*	*Column of differences*	*Four yearly moving totals (not centered)*	*2-period moving totals of col. (4) (centered)*	*4-yearly moving averages (centered) trend values*
(1)	(2)	(3)	(4)	(5)	(6) [col (5)/8]
1990	2204				
1991	2500				
		2424 – 2204 = 220	9744		
1992	2360			19708	2463.5
		2634 – 2500 = 134	9964		
1993	2680			20062	2507.75
		2904 – 2360 = 544	10098		
1994	2424			20740	2592.5
		3098 – 2680 = 418	10642		
1995	2634			21702	2712.75
		3172 – 2424 = 748	11060		
1996	2904			22868	2858.5
		2952 – 2634 = 318	11808		
1997	3098			23934	2991.75
		3248 – 2904 = 344	12126		
1998	3172			24596	3074.5
		3172 – 3098 = 74	12470		
1999	2952			25014	3126.75
			12544		
2000	3248				
2001	3172				

9.57. LIMITATIONS OF THE METHOD OF MOVING AVERAGES

(1) Some trend values at the beginning and some at the end remains unestimated (undetermined). Their number increases with an increase in time period of the moving averages.

(2) The choice of the period of moving average is sometimes subjective. Actually there is no hard and fast rule for the choice of the period and things depends mostly on personal judgement.

(3) The method gives good results if the trend is linear or at least approximately so. If trend is non-linear, say concave upward then a moving average will over-estimate the trend values, and if it is convex upward, it will under estimate.

(4) Moving averages cannot be represented readily by a mathematical formula. Thus, the method is not useful for comparison of the trends.

(5) Cyclical fluctuations affecting the data must be regular in their duration and their amplitude. If the data contains the cyclical influences which are irregular in their periodicity and amplitude, the moving average method will not completely remove the cyclical influences and hence it cannot display a good picture of the general long-run-movement (*i.e.*, of forecasting).

9.58. MEASUREMENT OF SEASONAL FLUCTUATIONS

To discuss various methods of isolating seasonal variation, it must be clearly understood that the effect of the seasons on a variable is present only when we have six-monthly, quarterly, monthly, weekly, daily time-series data. Since seasonal variations recur during the course of a year, we cannot see the effects of seasons if the data is lumped (thrown into a mass) together by years or by longer time periods. This is so because if the values of a variable for any twelve consecutive months or fifty-two consecutive weeks or 365 consecutive days is totalled up, the effects of the seasons disappear automatically. From this, it follows that the problem of isolating the effects of the seasons arises only when the data is given by parts of years.

Seasonal variations are measured through their indices called the seasonal indices. The measurement of seasonal variations requires determining the seasonal component S_t, which indicates how a time-series varies from month-to-month or week-to-week or day-to-day or even to quarterly (3 months)-to-quarterly (3 months) or half year-to-half year in a given year. A set of data showing the relative values of a variable for each of the 12 months of a year is known as **'seasonal index'.** This is expressed in percentage. Average seasonal index for the whole year should be 100% or in other words, the sum of the seasonal indices for the 12 months should be 1200%.

The following are the different methods of measuring the seasonal variations:

(*i*) simple averaging method (*ii*) modified averaging method

(*iii*) percentage trend method (*iv*) link relative method.

(*i*) **Simple averaging method:** It employs the following computational steps:

(*a*) First of all, the month-wise arithmetic mean of all yearly figures are calculated. Thus, the simple monthly averages over the given years are obtained. These monthly averages are called the seasonal variations.

(*b*) Then express these monthly averages as the percentage ratio of the averages of all monthly averages. These figures are called the seasonal indices. Mathematically, seasonal indices are found by using the following formula:

$$\text{Seasonal Index for any month} = \frac{(\text{Average of the month over the given years}) \times 1200}{\text{Total of the monthly averages}}$$

The following table explains how to compute the seasonal indices:

Table 1: Calculation of Seasonal Indices by Simple Averaging Method

Years	*Jan.*	*Feb.*	*March*	*April*	*May*	*June*	*July*	*Aug.*	*Sept.*	*Oct.*	*Nov.*	*Dec.*	*Total*	*Yearly Average*
1991	18	17	15	13	10	9	10	11	14	18	20	22	177	177/12 = 14.75
1992	20	17	14	14	12	11	12	13	16	19	21	23	192	192/12 = 16.00
1993	22	20	19	17	15	13	10	14	17	20	22	24	213	213/12 = 17.75
1994	24	22	20	18	16	14	9	15	18	18	24	25	223	223/12 = 18.58
1995	25	23	20	19	18	15	10	16	20	20	26	27	239	239/12 = 19.92
Total	109	99	88	81	71	62	51	69	85	95	113	121	1044	1044/12 = 87.00
Monthly Average	21.8	19.8	17.6	16.2	14.2	12.4	10.2	13.8	17.0	19.0	22.6	24.2	208.8	208.8/12 = 17.4
Seasonal Index	125.3	113.8	101.1	93.1	81.6	71.3	58.6	79.3	97.7	109.2	129.9	139.1	1200	1200/12 = 100

The seasonal indices shown in the last row of the Table 1 do not represent the seasonal variations truely, since the long time trends are also involved in them. This method, therefore, be usefully employed only if, the original data has no long-term tendencies. However, a modified formula is available to give seasonal indices.

Remark: The values for the months over all the years as given in Table 1 are called 'specific seasonals'. Specific seasonals of any period divided by their number in that period are called typical seasonals, *i.e.*, mathematically, we have:

$$\text{Typical seasonals} = \frac{\text{Specific seasonals for any period}}{\text{The number of years}}$$

(*ii*) **Modified averaging method:** It employs the following computational steps:

(*a*) First of all, calculate the monthly totals for each year, obtain the monthly averages by dividing the monthly totals by the number of months.

(*b*) Then calculate yearly averages for all the years.

(*c*) Fit a straight line between the years (x) and the yearly-averages (y) by using the method of least squares.

(*d*) Shift annual straight line trend equation to a monthly basis. The trend value of 1st July is equal to the grand average, *i.e.*, average of all monthly averages. To compute the centred trend for 15th July add 1/12 of the value of the slope of trend line (*i.e.*, b if the line of annual trend is $y = a + bx$). Then with the increment b, the other trend values are obtained.

(*e*) The seasonal indices are now computed by expressing the monthly average as percentage of the trends.

This method is illustrated below:

Let the trend line be $y = a + bx$

Using the method of least squares, we have following two normal equations to obtain the values of 'a' and 'b'.

$$\Sigma y = na + b\ \Sigma x$$

$$\Sigma xy = a\ \Sigma x + b\Sigma x^2$$

The following Table 2 explains how to compute the seasonal indices:

Table 2: Calculation of Trend by Least Square Method and Seasonal Indices by Modified Averaging Method

Years	*Jan.*	*Feb.*	*March*	*April*	*May*	*June*	*July*	*Aug.*	*Sept.*	*Oct.*	*Nov.*	*Dec.*	*Total*	*Yearly Avg.* (*y*)	*x*	x^2	*2xy*
1991	18	17	15	13	10	9	10	11	14	18	20	22	177	14.75	– 2	4	– 29.50
1992	20	17	14	14	12	11	12	13	16	19	21	23	192	16.00	– 1	1	– 16.00
1993	22	20	19	17	15	13	10	14	17	20	22	24	213	17.75	0	0	00.00
1994	24	22	20	18	16	14	9	15	18	18	24	25	223	18.58	+ 1	1	18.58
1995	25	23	20	19	18	15	10	16	20	20	26	27	239	19.92	+ 2	4	39.84
Total	109	99	88	81	71	62	51	69	85	95	113	121	1044	87.00	0	10	12.92
Mont. Avg.	21.8	19.8	17.6	16.2	14.2	12.4	10.2	13.8	17.0	19.0	22.6	24.2	208.8	17.4			
Trend	16.795	16.905	17.015	17.125	17.235	17.345	17.455	17.565	17.675	17.785	17.895	18.005	—	—			
Seas. Index	129.8	117.2	103.4	94.6	82.4	71.5	58.6	78.6	96.2	106.8	126.3	134.4	—	—			

Here, $n = 5$, $\Sigma x = 0$, $\Sigma x^2 = 10$, $\Sigma xy = 12.92$ and $\Sigma y = 87.00$.

Thus, normal equations provide us $a = \frac{87.00}{5} = 17.4$ and $b = \frac{12.92}{10} = 1.292$.

Here, we note that the grand mean coincides with 'a' as was expected because 'a' gives the trend value at the middle. Now, we have twelve months (even number), therefore, 'a' will be the trend value for 1st July and $b = 1.292$ is the rate of yearly changes. Therefore, rate of monthly change is 1.292/12 = 0.1077 = 0.11 (approx.)

To find the trend value in the centre of the month of July, we add 0.11/2 to 17.4. Thus 17.455 will be the trend value for 15th July. The trend value for 15th June will be 17.455 – 0.11 = 17.345 and so on.

Lastly, we calculate seasonal indices as below:

The seasonal index for January $= \frac{21.8}{16.795} \times 100 = 129.8$

The seasonal index for February $= \frac{19.8}{16.905} \times 100 = 117.2$

The seasonal index for March $= \frac{17.6}{17.015} \times 100 = 103.4$

and so on.

The seasonal indices shown in the last row of the Table 2 are free from trend and give a fair idea about the seasonal variations.

(*iii*) **Percentage trend (or ratio to trend) method:** In this method, the data for each month are expressed as percentage of the monthly trend values. An appropriate average of these percentage over the years for different months is obtained to construct the required index.

This method is also known as ratio to moving averages method if trend is computed by the method of moving averages.

The following steps are involved in the computation of seasonal indices:

(*a*) Compute twelve-monthly moving averages and the centre at the middle, *i.e.*, the 7th month (if the data is month-wise). These are the trend values (T_t).

(*b*) Divide each given entry by these trend values and multiply by 100, *i.e.*, obtain $\frac{u_t}{T_t} \times 100$.

(*c*) Sort out these percentages month-wise and find the median or mean percentages for each month.

(*d*) Express each of these medians or means as the percentage of the average of all twelve-monthly averages or medians. These are the seasonal indices.

The assumption in this method is that if a monthly time-series is affected by the seasonal variations due to the 12 months of the year, then a moving average of period 12 will remove these variations.

(*iv*) **Link relative method:** This method is also known as Pearson's method and expresses each monthly figure as a relative of the immediately preceding month. The seasonal pattern is found by averaging all the link relatives for the same month and taking residual trend out of the chain relatives computed from these average link relatives. It involves the following steps:

(*a*) Compute link relatives by dividing each entry by the previous entry and multiplying this quotient by 100. Thus, there will be no link relative against the first entry.

(*b*) Then sort out these link relatives by the months if data is month-wise, and obtain mean or median link relative for each month. It is mentioned here, that median will be easier to locate in comparison to mean.

(*c*) Now compute the chain relatives by fixing the chain relative of the 1st month as 100 and compute the chain relatives of other months as below:

Chain relative of any month

$$= \frac{\text{(Average link relative of that month)} \times \text{(Chain relative of previous month)}}{100}.$$

Carry on this process to include the first month again in the last.

(*d*) If this last chain relative is 100, then the column of these chain relatives will give seasonal indices (unadjusted) and are to be adjusted to give a total of 1200. If, however, this last chain relative is not 100, subtract if from 100. This is called discrepancy. It may be both negative and positive.

(*e*) Now add algebraically 1/12 of this discrepancy in the chain relative of second month; 2/12 of this discrepancy in the chain relative of third month and so on till 11/12 of the same is added in the last 12th month. These give the unadjusted seasonal indices corrected for discrepancy.

(*f*) Lastly, bring the total of these unadjusted seasonal indices to 1200. These will then, be the seasonal indices.

The method is explained by taking the data given in Table 1 and the calculations in the Table 3 given below are according to the steps given above. For example, 94.4 is the link relative of the month February which is obtained as: (17/18) × 100 = 94.4. Similarly, 88.2 is the link relative of the month March and other values of link relatives are given in the table.

After calculating these link relatives, the medians are calculated merely by inspection. To calculate the chain relatives, the figure for January is set at 100 and for February, the figure is obtained by multiplying the February link relative by the January chain relative and dividing by 100. This is carried up to December and then January again which is obtained by multiplying the chain relative of December with the link relative of January and divided by 100, *i.e.*, (96.7 × 97.85)/100 = 94.6.

Thus, the discrepancy is 100 – 94.6 = 5.4, and $\frac{1}{12} \times 5.4, \frac{2}{12} \times 5.4, \frac{3}{12} \times 5.4, ..., \frac{11}{12} \times 5.4$ are added to the chain relatives of February, March, April, ..., December respectively. After this adjustment, these values are expressed as a percentage of their average. These are the seasonal indices. For example, the seasonal index for the month of January is obtained as:

$$\left(\frac{100}{906.5/12}\right) \times 100 = 132.4.$$

Since 906.5/12 is the average of adjusted trend values and the figure for January, *i.e.*, 100 is expressed as a percentage of this average.

Similarly, the seasonal index for the month of February is obtained as:

$$\left(\frac{92.15}{906.5/12}\right) \times 100 = 122.0 \text{ and so on.}$$

Table 3: Calculation of Link Relatives of the Data given in Table 1 and Calculation of the Seasonal Indices

Years	*Jan.*	*Feb.*	*March*	*April*	*May*	*June*	*July*	*Aug.*	*Sept.*	*Oct.*	*Nov.*	*Dec.*	*Jan.*	*Total*
1991	–	94.4	88.2	86.7	76.9	90.0	111.1	110.0	127.3	128.6	111.1	110.0		
1992	90.9	85.0	82.4	100.0	85.7	91.7	109.1	108.3	123.1	118.8	110.5	109.5	–	
1993	95.7	90.9	95.0	89.5	88.2	86.7	76.9	140.0	121.4	117.6	110.0	109.1	–	
1994	100.0	91.7	90.9	90.0	88.9	87.5	64.3	166.7	120.0	100.0	133.3	104.2	–	
1995	100.0	92.0	87.0	95.0	94.7	83.3	66.7	160.0	125.0	100.0	130.0	103.8	–	
Median	97.85	91.7	82.4	90.0	88.2	87.5	76.9	140.0	123.1	117.6	111.1	109.1	–	
Chain relative	100	91.7	75.6	68.0	60.0	52.5	40.4	56.5	67.8	79.8	88.6	96.7	94.6	
Adj. for Trend	100	92.15	76.5	69.35	61.8	54.75	43.10	59.65	71.4	83.05	93.1	101.65	–	906.5
Seas. Index	132.4	122.0	101.3	91.8	81.8	72.5	57.1	79.0	94.5	110.0	123.3	134.3	–	1200

9.59. MEASUREMENT OF CYCLICAL VARIATION

Cyclical component has a period of more than a year. If the period of the cycle is known, then the cyclical variations can very easily be removed from the time series by taking the moving averages with that time period. However, the cyclical period can be estimated by plotting the time series on a graph paper. Suppose that the series has been plotted on the graph paper and a 'best fit' to the data is made merely by inspection. Then we shall note that the fitted straight line will cut the original series at several points. We may assume the lower portion of the series as negative part and the upper portion as positive part, then a point where series changes its sign, according to our assumption, from negative to positive, is called an 'upcross'. The distances between all the upcrosses of the series are noted. The mean distance of all these distances is called the expected mean period of the cycle. If moving averages are calculated with this mean period, then the cyclical component C_t are removed from the series.

When time series assumes a multiplicative model, then cyclical and random components are obtained in combined form by dividing the original series by trend and seasonal component and when time-series assumes an additive model, then cyclical and random components are obtained by subtracting trend and seasonal component from the data. Cyclical variations are obtained by removing the random variations from these residuals which were obtained by eliminating trend and seasonal variations from the given data. This is done by averaging these residuals directly or through moving averages.

ASSIGNMENT

1. What is the method of moving averages and what are its limitations?
   Calculate the three-yearly moving average of profits of a commercial concern from the following data: *[U.P.T.U. MCA (C.O.) 2008]*

Years	1991	1992	1993	1994	1995	1996	1997	1998
Profits	42	47	52	45	14	64	36	59

2. What is time-series analysis? Explain the objectives of this analysis. Why is the time series analysis important in social sciences? Also discuss the characteristic movements in a time series. *[U.P.T.U. MCA (C.O.) 2008]*
3. Explain the following terms:
   (*i*) Moving average (*ii*) Smoothening of curves
4. Define the following terms in time series. *[U.P.T.U. (MCA) 2006]*
   (*i*) Secular trend (*ii*) Seasonal variations (*iii*) Cyclical variations
5. Fit a straight line trend by the method of least squares to the following data:

Years	1951	1952	1953	1954	1955	1956
Price index	107	110	114	112	115	113

6. Assuming 5 yearly moving averages, calculate trend values from the data given below and draw approximately on answer sheet:

Year	1971	1972	1973	1974	1975	1976	1977	1978	1979	1980	1981	1982	1983
Production (1000 tons)	105	107	109	112	114	116	118	121	123	124	125	127	129

[*U.P.T.U. (MCA) 2009*]

7. Explain the various components of a time-series.

8. Discuss advantages and disadvantages of moving average method used for estimation of trend values.

9. From the following series of annual data, find the trend line of semi-averages.

Year	2000	2001	2002	2003	2004	2005	2006	2007	2008
Actual value	170	231	261	267	278	302	299	298	340

[*G.B.T.U. 2011*]

Answers

1.

Years	*Profits*	*Three-yearly moving total*	*Three-yearly moving averages*
1991	42		
1992	47	42 + 47 + 52 = 141	141/3 = 47
1993	52	47 + 52 + 45 = 144	144/3 = 48
1994	45	52 + 45 + 14 = 111	111/3 = 37
1995	14	45 + 14 + 64 = 123	123/3 = 41
1996	64	14 + 64 + 36 = 114	114/3 = 38
1997	36	64 + 36 + 59 = 159	159/3 = 53
1998	59		

5. $T_t = 111.83 + 1.23\left(\frac{t - 1953.50}{0.5}\right)$.

9.60. FORECASTING

Forecasting is the process of estimation in unknown situations. Prediction is a similar, but more general term. Both can refer to estimation of time series, cross-sectional or longitudinal data. Usage can differ between areas of application: for example, in hydrology, the terms "forecast" and "forecasting" are sometimes reserved for estimates of values at certain specific future times, while the term "prediction" is used for more general estimates, such as the number of times floods will occur over a long period. Risk and uncertainty are central to forecasting and prediction. Forecasting is used in the practice of Customer Demand Planning in every day business forecasting for manufacturing companies. The discipline of demand planning, also sometimes referred to as supply chain forecasting, embraces both statistical forecasting and a consensus process. Forecasting is commonly used in discussion of time-series data.

Table I : SIGNIFICANT VALUES $t_v(\alpha)$ OF t-DISTRIBUTION (TWO-TAIL AREAS) $P[|t| > t_v(\alpha)] = \alpha$

d.f.	*Probability (Level of Significance)*					
(v)	*0.50*	*0.10*	*0.05*	*0.02*	*0.01*	*0.001*
1	1.00	6.31	12.71	31.82	63.66	636.62
2	0.82	2.92	4.30	6.97	6.93	31.60
3	0.77	2.35	3.18	4.54	5.84	12.94
4	0.74	2.13	2.78	3.75	4.60	8.61
5	0.73	2.02	2.57	3.37	4.03	6.86
6	0.72	1.94	2.45	3.14	3.71	5.96
7	0.71	1.90	2.37	3.00	3.50	5.41
8	0.71	1.86	2.31	2.90	3.36	5.04
9	0.70	1.83	2.26	2.82	3.25	4.78
10	0.70	1.81	2.23	2.76	3.17	4.59
11	0.70	1.80	2.20	2.72	3.11	4.44
12	0.70	1.78	2.18	2.68	3.06	4.32
13	0.69	1.77	2.16	2.65	3.01	4.22
14	0.69	1.76	2.15	2.62	2.98	4.14
15	0.69	1.75	2.13	2.60	2.95	4.07
16	0.69	1.75	2.12	2.58	2.92	4.02
17	0.69	1.74	2.11	2.57	2.90	3.97
18	0.69	1.73	2.10	2.55	2.88	3.92
19	0.69	1.73	2.09	2.54	2.86	3.88
20	0.69	1.73	2.09	2.53	2.85	3.85
21	0.69	1.72	2.08	2.52	2.83	3.83
22	0.69	1.72	2.07	2.51	2.82	3.79
23	0.69	1.71	2.07	2.50	2.81	3.77
24	0.69	1.71	2.06	5.49	2.80	3.75
25	0.68	1.71	2.06	2.49	2.79	3.73
26	0.68	1.71	2.06	2.48	2.78	3.71
27	0.68	1.70	2.05	2.47	2.77	3.69
28	0.68	1.70	2.05	2.47	2.76	3.67
29	0.68	1.70	2.05	2.46	2.76	3.66
30	0.68	1.70	2.04	2.46	2.75	3.65
∞	0.67	1.65	1.96	2.33	2.58	3.29

Table II-A
SIGNIFICANT VALUES OF THE VARIANCE RATIO F-DISTRIBUTION (RIGHT TAIL AREAS) 5 PER CENT POINTS

v_1 / v_2	1	2	3	4	5	6	8	12	24	∞
1	161.40	199.50	215.70	224.60	230.20	234.00	238.90	243.90	249.00	254.30
2	18.51	19.00	19.16	19.25	19.30	19.35	19.37	19.41	19.45	19.50
3	10.13	9.55	9.28	9.12	9.01	8.94	8.84	8.74	8.64	8.55
4	7.71	6.94	6.59	6.39	6.26	6.16	6.04	5.91	5.77	5.65
5	6.61	5.79	5.41	5.19	5.05	4.95	4.82	4.68	4.53	4.96
6	5.99	5.14	4.76	4.53	4.39	4.28	4.15	4.00	3.84	3.67
7	5.59	4.74	4.35	4.12	3.97	3.87	3.73	3.57	3.41	3.23
8	5.32	4.46	4.07	3.84	3.69	3.58	3.44	3.28	3.12	2.93
9	5.12	4.26	3.865	3.63	3.48	3.37	3.23	3.07	2.90	2.71
10	4.96	4.10	3.71	3.48	3.33	3.22	3.07	2.91	2.74	2.54
11	4.84	3.98	3.59	3.365	3.20	3.09	2.95	2.79	2.61	2.40
12	4.75	3.88	4.49	3.26	3.11	3.00	2.85	2.69	2.50	2.30
13	4.67	3.80	3.41	3.18	3.02	2.92	2.77	2.60	2.42	2.21
14	4.60	3.74	3.34	3.11	2.96	2.85	2.70	2.53	2.35	2.13
15	4.54	3.68	3.29	3.06	2.90	2.79	2.64	2.48	2.29	2.07
16	4.49	3.63	3.24	3.01	2.85	2.74	2.59	2.42	2.24	2.01
17	4.45	3.59	3.20	2.96	2.81	2.70	2.55	2.38	2.19	1.96
18	4.41	3.55	3.16	2.93	2.77	2.66	2.51	2.34	2.15	1.92
19	4.38	3.52	3.13	2.90	2.74	2.63	2.48	2.31	2.11	1.88
20	4.35	3.49	3.10	2.87	2.71	2.60	2.45	2.28	2.08	1.84
21	4.32	3.47	3.07	2.84	2.68	2.57	2.42	2.25	2.05	1.81
22	4.30	3.44	3.05	2.82	2.66	2.55	2.40	2.23	2.03	1.76
23	4.28	3.42	3.03	2.80	2.64	2.53	2.38	2.20	2.00	1.76
24	4.26	3.40	3.01	2.78	2.62	2.51	2.36	2.18	1.98	1.73
25	4.24	3.38	2.99	2.76	2.60	2.49	2.34	2.16	1.96	1.71
26	4.22	3.37	2.98	2.74	2.59	2.47	2.32	2.15	1.95	1.60
27	4.21	3.35	2.96	2.73	2.57	2.46	2.30	2.13	1.93	1.67
28	4.20	3.34	2.95	2.71	2.56	2.44	2.29	2.12	1.91	1.65
29	4.18	3.33	2.93	2.70	2.54	2.43	2.28	2.10	1.90	1.64
30	4.17	3.32	2.92	2.69	2.53	2.42	2.27	2.09	1.89	1.62
40	4.08	3.23	2.84	2.61	2.45	2.34	2.18	2.00	1.79	1.51
60	4.00	3.15	2.76	2.53	2.37	2.25	2.10	1.92	1.70	1.30
120	3.92	3.87	2.68	2.45	2.29	2.17	2.02	1.83	1.62	1.25
240	3.84	2.99	2.60	2.37	2.21	2.09	1.94	1.75	1.52	1.00

Table II-B
SIGNIFICANT VALUES OF THE VARIANCE RATIO
F-DISTRIBUTION (RIGHT TAIL AREAS)—1 PER CENT POINTS

v_1 / v_2	1	2	3	4	5	6	8	12	24	∞
1	4052	4999.5	5403	5625	5764	5859	5982	6106	6235	6366
2	98.50	99.00	99.17	99.25	99.30	99.33	99.37	99.42	99.46	99.50
3	34.12	30.82	29.46	28.71	28.24	27.91	27.49	27.05	26.60	26.13
4	21.20	18.00	16.69	15.98	15.52	15.21	14.80	14.37	13.93	13.46
5	16.26	13.27	12.06	11.39	10.97	10.67	10.29	9.89	9.47	9.02
6	13.75	10.92	9.78	9.15	8.75	8.47	8.10	7.72	7.31	6.88
7	12.25	9.95	8.45	7.85	7.46	7.19	6.84	6.47	6.07	5.65
8	11.26	8.65	7.59	7.01	6.63	6.37	6.03	5.67	5.28	4.86
9	10.56	8.02	6.99	6.42	6.06	5.80	5.47	5.11	4.73	4.31
10	10.04	7.56	6.55	5.99	5.64	5.39	5.06	4.71	4.33	3.91
11	9.65	7.21	6.22	5.67	5.32	5.07	4.74	4.40	4.02	3.60
12	9.33	6.93	5.95	5.41	5.06	4.82	4.50	4.16	3.78	3.36
13	9.07	6.70	5.74	5.21	4.86	4.62	4.30	3.96	3.59	3.17
14	8.86	6.51	5.56	5.04	4.69	4.46	4.14	3.80	3.43	3.00
15	8.68	6.36	5.42	4.89	4.56	4.32	4.00	3.67	3.29	2.87
16	8.53	6.23	5.29	4.77	4.44	4.20	3.89	3.55	3.18	2.75
17	8.40	6.11	5.18	4.67	4.34	4.10	3.79	3.46	3.08	2.65
18	8.29	6.01	5.09	4.58	4.25	4.01	3.71	3.37	3.00	2.57
19	8.18	5.93	5.01	4.50	4.17	3.94	3.63	3.30	2.92	2.49
20	8.10	5.85	4.94	4.43	4.10	3.87	3.56	3.23	2.86	2.42
21	8.02	5.78	4.87	4.37	4.04	3.81	3.51	3.17	2.80	2.36
22	7.95	5.72	4.82	4.31	3.99	3.76	3.45	3.12	2.75	2.31
23	7.88	5.66	4.76	4.26	3.94	3.71	3.41	3.07	2.70	2.26
24	7.82	5.61	4.72	4.22	3.90	3.67	3.36	3.03	2.66	2.21
25	7.77	5.57	4.68	4.18	3.85	3.63	3.32	2.99	2.62	2.17
26	7.72	5.53	4.64	4.14	3.82	3.59	3.29	2.96	2.58	2.13
27	7.68	5.49	4.60	4.11	3.78	3.56	3.26	2.93	2.55	2.10
28	7.64	5.45	4.57	4.07	3.75	3.53	3.23	2.90	2.52	2.06
29	7.60	5.42	4.54	4.04	3.73	3.50	3.20	2.87	2.49	2.03
30	7.56	5.39	4.51	4.02	3.70	3.47	3.17	2.84	2.47	2.01
40	7.31	5.18	4.31	3.83	3.51	3.29	2.99	2.66	2.29	1.80
60	7.08	4.98	4.13	3.65	3.34	3.12	2.82	2.50	2.12	1.60
120	6.85	4.79	3.95	3.48	3.17	2.96	2.66	2.34	1.95	1.38
∞	6.63	4.61	3.78	3.32	3.02	2.80	2.51	2.18	1.79	1.00

Table III—TRANSFORMATION FROM r TO $Z = \frac{1}{2}\log_e\left(\frac{1+r}{1-r}\right)$

r	0.00	0.01	0.02	0.03	0.04	0.05	0.06	0.07	0.08	0.09
0	0.0000	0.0100	0.0200	0.0300	0.0400	0.0500	0.0601	0.0701	0.0802	0.0902
.1	0.1003	0.1104	0.1206	0.1307	0.1409	0.1511	0.1614	0.7117	0.1820	0.1923
.2	0.2027	0.2132	0.2237	0.2342	0.2448	0.2554	0.2661	0.2769	0.2877	0.2986
.3	0.3005	0.3205	0.3316	0.3428	0.3541	0.3654	0.3769	0.3884	0.4001	0.4118
.4	0.4236	0.4356	0.4477	0.4599	0.4722	0.4847	0.4973	0.5101	0.5230	0.5361
.5	0.5493	0.5627	0.5763	0.5901	0.6042	0.6184	0.6328	0.6475	0.6625	0.6777
.6	0.6931	0.7089	0.7250	0.7414	0.7582	0.7753	0.7928	0.8107	0.8291	0.8480
.7	0.8673	0.8872	0.9076	0.9287	0.9505	0.9730	0.9962	1.0203	1.0454	1.0714
.8	1.0996	1.1270	1.1568	1.1881	1.2212	1.2562	1.2933	1.3331	1.3758	1.4219
.9	1.4722	1.5275	1.5890	1.6584	1.7380	1.8318	1.9459	2.0923	2.2976	2.6467

Table 4 : CHI-SQUARE

Significant Values χ^2 (α) of Chi-Square Distribution Right Tail Areas for Given Probability α,

$P = P_r (\chi^2 > \chi^2 (\alpha)) = \alpha$

And v is Degrees of Freedom (d.f.)

Degree of freedom (v)	*Probability (Level of Significance)*						
	0 = .99	*0.95*	*0.50*	*0.10*	*0.05*	*0.02*	*0.01*
1	.000157	.00393	.455	2.706	3.841	5.214	6.635
2	.0201	.103	1.386	4.605	5.991	7.824	9.210
3	.115	.352	2.366	6.251	7.815	9.837	11.341
4	.297	.711	3.357	7.779	9.488	11.668	13.277
5	.554	1.145	4.351	9.236	11.070	13.388	15.086
6	.872	2.635	5.348	10.645	12.592	15.033	16.812
7	1.239	2.167	6.346	12.017	14.067	16.622	18.475
8	1.646	2.733	7.344	13.362	15.507	18.168	20.090
9	2.088	3.325	8.343	14.684	16.919	19.679	21.669
10	2.558	3.940	9.340	15.987	18.307	21.161	23.209
11	3.053	4.575	10.341	17.275	19.675	22.618	24.725
12	3.571	5.226	11.340	18.549	21.026	24.054	26.217
13	4.107	5.892	12.340	19.812	22.362	25.472	27.688
14	4.660	6.571	13.339	21.064	23.685	26.873	29.141
15	4.229	7.261	14.339	22.307	24.996	28.259	30.578
16	5.812	7.962	15.338	23.542	26.296	29.633	32.000
17	6.408	8.672	15.338	24.769	27.587	30.995	33.409
18	7.015	9.390	17.338	25.989	28.869	32.346	34.805
19	7.633	10.117	18.338	27.204	30.144	33.687	36.191
20	8.260	10.851	19.337	28.412	31.410	35.020	37.566
21	8.897	11.591	20.337	29.615	32.671	36.343	38.932
22	9.542	12.338	21.337	30.813	33.924	37.659	40.289
23	10.196	13.091	22.337	32.007	35.172	38.968	41.638
24	10.856	13.848	23.337	32.196	36.415	40.270	42.980
25	11.524	14.611	24.337	34.382	37.65	41.566	44.314
26	12.198	15.379	25.336	35.363	38.885	41.856	45.642
27	12.879	16.151	26.336	36.741	40.113	41.140	46.963
28	13.565	16.928	27.336	37.916	41.337	45.419	48.278
29	14.256	17.708	28.336	39.087	42.557	46.693	49.588
30	14.933	18.493	29.336	40.256	43.773	47.962	50.892

Note. For degrees of freedom (v) greater than 30, the quantity $\sqrt{2\chi^2} - \sqrt{2v-1}$ may be used as a normal variate with unit variance.

Table 5 : NORMAL TABLE
AREAS UNDER THE STANDARD NORMAL

$$\text{CURVE} = \frac{1}{\sqrt{2\pi}} \int_0^z e^{-\frac{z^2}{2}} dz$$

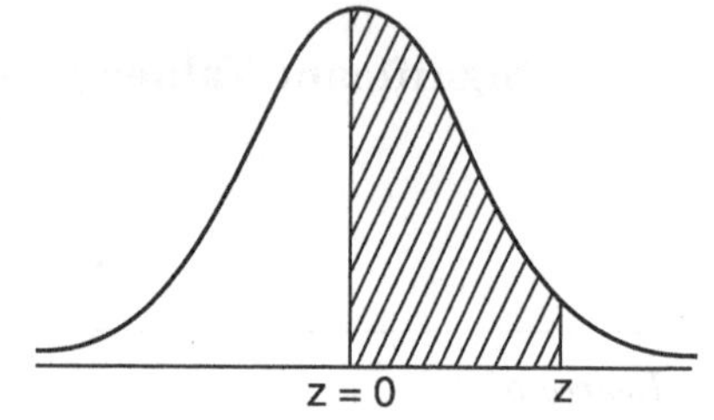

z	.00	.01	.02	.03	.04	.05	.06	.07	.08	.09
0.0	.0000	.0040	.0080	.0120	.0160	.0199	.0239	.0279	.0319	.0359
0.1	.0398	.0438	.0478	.0517	.0557	.0596	.0636	.0675	.0714	.0754
0.2	.0793	.0832	.0871	.0910	.0948	.0987	.1026	.1064	.1103	.1141
0.3	.1179	.1217	.1255	.1293	.1331	.1368	.1406	.1443	.1480	.1517
0.4	.1554	.1591	.1628	.1664	.1700	.1736	.1772	.1808	.1844	.1879
0.5	.1915	.1950	.1985	.2019	.2054	.2088	.2123	.2157	.2190	.2224
0.6	.2257	.2291	.2324	.2357	.2389	.2422	.2454	.2485	.2517	.2549
0.7	.2580	.2611	.2642	.2673	.2704	.2734	.2764	.2794	.2823	.2852
0.8	.2881	.2910	.2939	.2967	.2995	.3023	.3051	.3078	.3106	.3133
0.9	.3159	.3186	.3212	.3238	.3264	.3289	.3315	.3340	.3365	.3389
1.0	.3413	.3438	.3461	.3485	.3508	.3531	.3554	.3577	.3599	.3621
1.1	.3643	.3665	.3686	.3708	.3729	.3749	.3770	.3790	.3810	.3830
1.2	.3849	.3869	.3888	.3907	.3925	.3944	.3962	.3980	.3997	.4015
1.3	.4032	.4049	.4066	.4082	.4099	.4115	.4131	.4147	.4162	.4177
1.4	.4192	.4207	.4222	.4236	.4251	.4255	.4279	.4292	.4306	.4319
1.5	.4332	.4345	.4357	.4370	.4382	.4394	.4406	.4418	.4429	.4441
1.6	.4452	.4463	.4474	.4484	.4495	.4505	.4515	.4525	.4535	.4545
1.7	.4554	.4564	.4573	.4582	.4591	.4599	.4608	.4616	.4625	.4633
1.8	.4641	.4649	.4656	.4664	.4671	.4678	.4686	.4693	.4699	.4706
1.9	.4713	.4719	.4726	.4732	.4738	.4744	.4750	.4756	.4761	.4767
2.0	.4772	.4778	.4783	.4788	.4793	.4798	.4803	.4808	.4812	.4817
2.1	.4821	.4826	.4830	.4834	.4838	.4842	.4846	.4850	.4854	.4857
2.2	.4861	.4864	.4868	.4871	.4875	.4878	.4881	.4884	.4887	.4890
2.3	.4893	.4896	.4898	.4901	.4904	.4906	.4909	.4911	.4913	.4916
2.4	.4918	.4920	.4922	.4925	.4927	.4929	.4931	.4932	.4934	.4936
2.5	.4938	.4940	.4941	.4943	.4945	.4946	.4948	.4949	.4951	.4952
2.6	.4953	.4955	.4956	.4957	.4959	.4930	.4961	.4962	.4963	.4964
2.7	.4965	.4966	.4967	.4968	.4969	.4970	.4971	.4972	.4973	.4974
2.8	.4974	.4975	.4976	.4977	.4977	.4978	.4979	.4979	.4980	.4981
2.9	.4981	.4982	.4982	.4983	.4984	.4984	.4985	.4985	.4986	.4986
3.0	.4987	.4987	.4987	.4988	.4988	.4989	.4999	.4989	.4990	.4990
3.1	.4990	.4991	.4991	.4991	.4992	.4992	.4992	.4992	.4993	.4993
3.2	.4993	.4993	.4994	.4994	.4994	.4994	.4994	.4995	.4995	.4995
3.3	.4995	.4995	.4995	.4996	.4996	.4996	.4996	.4996	.4996	.4997
3.4	.4997	.4997	.4997	.4997	.4997	.4997	.4997	.4997	.4997	.4998
3.5	.4998	.4998	.4998	.4998	.4998	.4998	.4998	.4998	.4998	.4998